THE COLLECTED WORKS OF
SAMUEL TAYLOR COLERIDGE · 2

THE WATCHMAN

General Editor: KATHLEEN COBURN

Associate Editor: BART WINER

THE COLLECTED WORKS

SAMUEL TAYLOR COLERIDGE
from a crayon portrait executed by Robert Hancock
for Joseph Cottle in 1796.
London: The National Portrait Gallery.

THE COLLECTED WORKS OF

Samuel Taylor Coleridge

The Watchman

EDITED BY

Lewis Patton

ROUTLEDGE & KEGAN PAUL

BOLLINGEN SERIES LXXV
PRINCETON UNIVERSITY PRESS

The Collected Works, sponsored by Bollingen Foundation,
is published in Great Britain
by Routledge & Kegan Paul Ltd
Broadway House, 68–74 Carter Lane, London EC4
and in the United States of America
by Princeton University Press, Princeton, New Jersey
The Collected Works constitutes
the seventy-fifth publication in Bollingen Series

The present work is number 2 of the Collected Works

Designed by Richard Garnett
Printed in Great Britain by
Butler and Tanner Ltd, Frome and London

THIS EDITION
OF THE WORKS OF
SAMUEL TAYLOR COLERIDGE
IS DEDICATED
IN GRATITUDE TO
THE FAMILY EDITORS
IN EACH GENERATION

CONTENTS

LIST OF ILLUSTRATIONS

ACKNOWLEDGMENTS

MANY scholarly works of recent years have laid the groundwork for an edition of *The Watchman*: of particular value are Miss Kathleen Coburn's edition of the Coleridge notebooks and Earl Leslie Griggs's edition of the letters; and also the publications of Mr John Colmer, Professor George Whalley, and Professor Carl Woodring. Much additional aid has come from private communications of persons too numerous to specify here, as well as from other published works; but I will mention Mr George Watson, Mr J. B. Beer, Sir Rupert Hart-Davis, Professor David Erdman, Mr Edmund Blunden, and Mr Richard Garnett. I am indebted to the late C. B. Tinker for aid when portions of this work were presented as a Yale dissertation and to Professor Frederick A. Pottle for advice.

My grateful acknowledgments also go to the staffs of several libraries—most of all to the Duke University Library, especially to Miss Florence Blakeley, Miss Mary Cannada, Miss Isabel Masterson, Miss Mary Frances Morris, and Mr Emerson Ford. I have been long indebted to the Yale University Library, particularly to Miss Marjorie Gray Wynne; and also to the Harvard College Library. To the late John D. Gordan and the Berg Collection of the New York Public Library, the Pierpont Morgan Library, the Henry E. Huntington Library, the Victoria College Library, the Library of the University of North Carolina, and the Houghton Library and Miss Jakeman; and also to the British Museum and its staff, to the Cambridge University Library, and to Mr Peter Heaton and the Bristol Central Library: to all these I wish to return my sincere thanks. In addition, the librarians or staff members of many other libraries have patiently and often in considerable detail answered my questions about their Coleridge holdings. The list includes the Boston Athenaeum, the Boston Public Library, the William L. Clements Library, the Free Library of Philadelphia, and the Carl Pforzheimer Library; also the libraries of the following universities: Brown, University of California at Los Angeles, Chicago, Columbia, Dartmouth, Johns Hopkins, Illinois, Indiana, Michigan, Minnesota,

Northwestern, Pennsylvania, Princeton, Texas, Virginia, Washington, and Wisconsin.

The Bollingen Foundation has been most generous, and I wish to express my appreciation to Mr John D. Barrett and Miss Vaun Gillmor. Miss Dorothy Roberts, Mrs Mary Muller, and Mrs Grace Hawke have cheerfully come to my aid in the typing. At various times my friends William Blackburn, John Cunningham, and George Walton Williams have lent assistance. To my close associates in this edition I am especially indebted: to Kathleen Coburn, for her great knowledge always willingly shared, and to Bart Winer, whose vigilance, skill, and scholarship have immeasurably improved every part of this work; to both of these, many thanks for many kindnesses. I am grateful to my wife for coming to my aid on numerous occasions.

LEWIS PATTON

Duke University
1 September 1968

EDITORIAL PRACTICE
SYMBOLS, AND ABBREVIATIONS

THE text of the present edition follows Coleridge's 1796 edition, except for the correction of obvious printer's errors. The corrections listed at the end of No 9 of the original edition have been incorporated into the text. The second printing of No 1 is used as text, with the variants of the first printing given in textual notes at the foot of the page. The two corrections made in the later run of No 5 are also given as text, with the earlier variants printed as textual notes. "Corrections" in Coleridge's annotated copies are given in the footnotes. Passages in Greek are given as printed in 1796 except for accents. Because Coleridge took his items from a variety of sources, the spellings of names and places are not always his; conventional or corrected forms are given in the footnotes or in the index.

A manuscript source for *The Watchman* is found only in the fragmentary PML manuscript MA 1916, from which variants are indicated in the footnotes. Pointed brackets enclose Coleridge's manuscript insertions, and square brackets the editor's insertions.

Coleridge's footnotes are indicated by symbols (*, †, etc) and are printed full measure. Editor's footnotes are numbered and (when not too brief) printed in double columns. The order of the editor's footnotes follows (perhaps Coleridgean) logic; i.e. it is assumed that when the text contains an asterisk or a dagger the reader then turns from text to note and then goes back again. The editor's footnotes, which are sometimes notes on Coleridge's footnotes, follow that order. Thus the footnote indicators within the text may leap from 1 to 5, notes 2–4 being notes on Coleridge's footnotes. Textual notes ([a–b], etc) at the foot of the page, preceding the editor's notes, give the earlier wording of Nos 1 and 5.

The editions referred to in the editor's footnotes are, when they are known, those Coleridge used; "see" before the edition indicates that it is not necessarily the edition Coleridge cites or quotes (though it may be an edition he is known to have used).

ABBREVIATIONS

AR	S. T. Coleridge *Aids to Reflection in the Formation of a Manly Character* (1825).
B Critic	*The British Critic* (1793–1826).

BE	*Biographia Epistolaris* ed A. Turnbull (2 vols 1811).
BL (1907)	S. T. Coleridge *Biographia Literaria* ed John Shawcross (2 vols Oxford 1907).
Bl M	*Blackwood's Edinburgh Magazine* (1817–).
BM	British Museum
B Poets	*The Works of the British Poets* ed Robert Anderson (13 vols Edinburgh 1792–5; vol XIV 1807).
Bristol LB	George Whalley "The Bristol Library Borrowings of Southey and Coleridge" *Library* IV (Sept 1949) 114–31.
C	Samuel Taylor Coleridge
C Bibl (Wise *TLP*)	Thomas J. Wise *Two Lake Poets* (1927).
CC	*The Collected Works of Samuel Taylor Coleridge* (London and New York 1969–).
CI	*The Cambridge Intelligencer* (1793–1800).
CL	*Collected Letters of Samuel Taylor Coleridge* ed Earl Leslie Griggs (Oxford and New York 1956–69).
C Life (EKC)	Sir E. K. Chambers *Samuel Taylor Coleridge* (1938).
C Life (JDC)	James Dykes Campbell *Samuel Taylor Coleridge* (1894).
CN	*The Notebooks of Samuel Taylor Coleridge* ed Kathleen Coburn (New York and London 1957–).
Conciones	S. T. Coleridge *Conciones ad Populum. Or Addresses to the People* (1795).
Cottle *E Rec*	Joseph Cottle *Early Recollections, Chiefly Relating to the Late Samuel Taylor Coleridge During His Long Residence in Bristol* (2 vols 1837).
Cottle *Rem*	Joseph Cottle *Reminiscences of Samuel Taylor Coleridge and Robert Southey* (1847).
C Rev	*The Critical Review; or, Annals of Literature* (1756–1817).
DC	Derwent Coleridge
DNB	*Dictionary of National Biography* (1885–).
DW	Dorothy Wordsworth
EHC	Ernest Hartley Coleridge
Eng R	*The English Review* (1783–96).
EOT	S. T. Coleridge *Essays on His Own Times, Forming a Second Series of "The Friend"* ed Sara Coleridge (3 vols 1850).
Friend (*CC*)	S. T. Coleridge *The Friend* ed Barbara E. Rooke (2 vols London and New York 1969). *The Collected Works of Samuel Taylor Coleridge* IV.
G Mag	*The Gentleman's Magazine* (1731–1907).

H Works	*The Complete Works of William Hazlitt* ed P. P. Howe (21 vols 1930–4).
JDC	James Dykes Campbell
LCL	Loeb Classical Library
Lects 1795	S. T. Coleridge *Lectures 1795: On Politics and Religion* ed Lewis Patton and Peter Mann (*CC* I).
LL	*The Letters of Charles Lamb to Which Are Added Those of His Sister Mary Lamb* ed E. V. Lucas (3 vols 1935).
M Chron	*The Morning Chronicle* (1769–1862).
M Herald	*The Morning Herald* (1780–1869).
Misc C	*Coleridge's Miscellaneous Criticism* ed T. M. Raysor (Cambridge, Mass. 1936).
M Mag	*The Monthly Magazine* (1796–1843).
MPL	S. T. Coleridge *A Moral and Political Lecture* (Bristol [1795]).
M Post	*The Morning Post* (1772–1937).
M Review	*The Monthly Review* (1749–1845).
Mrs C	Sara (Fricker) Coleridge
N&Q	*Notes and Queries* (1849–).
OED	*Oxford English Dictionary* (13 vols Oxford 1933).
Parl Reg	*The Parliamentary Register* [ed John Almon] (1774–1813).
PD	S. T. Coleridge *The Plot Discovered; or, An Address to the People Against Ministerial Treason* (Bristol 1795).
P Lects (1949)	*The Philosophical Lectures of Samuel Taylor Coleridge* ed Kathleen Coburn (London and New York 1949).
PML	Pierpont Morgan Library
Poems (1796)	S. T. Coleridge *Poems on Various Subjects* (Bristol 1796).
Poems (1797)	S. T. Coleridge *Poems . . . To Which Are Now Added, Poems by Charles Lamb and Charles Lloyd* (Bristol and London 1797).
Poems (1803)	S. T. Coleridge *Poems* (1803).
Poole	M. E. Sandford *Thomas Poole and His Friends* (2 vols 1888).
PW (1828)	*The Poetical Works of Samuel Taylor Coleridge* (3 vols 1828).
PW (1829)	*The Poetical Works of Samuel Taylor Coleridge* (3 vols 1829).
PW (1834)	*The Poetical Works of Samuel Taylor Coleridge* [ed H. N. Coleridge] (3 vols 1834).

PW (EHC)	*The Complete Poetical Works of Samuel Taylor Coleridge* ed E. H. Coleridge (2 vols Oxford 1912).
PW (JDC)	*The Poetical Works of Samuel Taylor Coleridge* ed J. D. Campbell (1893).
RES	*Review of English Studies* (1925–).
RS	Robert Southey
RX	John Livingston Lowes *The Road to Xanadu* (rev ed 1930).
SC	Sara Coleridge
SH	Sara Hutchinson
SL	S. T. Coleridge *Sibylline Leaves* (1817).
S Letters (Curry)	*New Letters of Robert Southey* ed Kenneth Curry (2 vols New York and London 1965).
SM (1816)	S. T. Coleridge *The Stateman's Manual; or, the Bible, the Best Guide to Political Skill and Foresight. A Lay-Sermon Addressed to the Higher Classes of Society* (1816).
Studies	*Coleridge: Studies by Several Hands on the Hundredth Anniversary of His Death* ed Edmund Blunden and Earl Leslie Griggs (1934).
TLS	*The Times Literary Supplement* (1902–).
TT (1923)	S. T. Coleridge *The Table Talk and Omniana* ed T. Ashe (1923).
VCL	Victoria College Library
WL (*E*)	*The Letters of William and Dorothy Wordsworth: the Early Years 1787–1805* ed Ernest de Selincourt revised Chester L. Shaver (Oxford 1967).
WW	William Wordsworth

CHRONOLOGICAL TABLE
1772–1834

(public events to the publication of *The Watchman*)

1772	(21 Oct) C b at Ottery St Mary, Devonshire to Rev John and Ann (Bowden) Coleridge, youngest of their 10 children	George III king Wordsworth 2 years old Scott 1 year old *M Post* began
1774		Southey b
1775		American War of Independence C. Lamb b
1776		Adam Smith *Wealth of Nations*
1778		Hazlitt b Rousseau and Voltaire d
1781	(Oct) Death of C's father	Kant *Kritik der reinen Vernunft* Schiller *Die Räuber*
1782	(Jul) Enrolled at Christ's Hospital preparatory school for girls and boys, Hertford (Sept) Christ's Hospital School, London, with C. Lamb, G. Dyer, T. F. Middleton, Robert Allen, J. M. Gutch, Le Grice brothers; met Evans family	Priestley *Corruptions of Christianity* Rousseau *Confessions*
1783		Pitt's first ministry (–1801)
1784		Samuel Johnson d
1785		De Quincey b Paley *Principles of Moral and Political Philosophy*
1789		(14 Jul) French Revolution Blake *Songs of Innocence* Bowles *Sonnets*
1790		Burke *Reflections on the Revolution in France*
1791	(Sept) Jesus College, Cambridge, Exhibitioner, Sizar, Rustat Scholar; met S. Butler, Frend, Porson, C. Wordsworth, Wrangham	(Mar) John Wesley d Paine *Rights of Man* pt I (pt II 1792) Boswell *Life of Johnson* Anti-Jacobin riots at Birmingham
1792	(3 Jul) Encaenia, C's prize-winning Greek Sapphic *Ode on the Slave Trade*	Pitt's attack on the slave-trade Fox's Libel Bill

1793	(May) Attended Cambridge trial of Frend (8 Nov) first poem in *Morning Chronicle* (2 Dec) enlisted in 15th Light Dragoons as Silas Tomkyn Comberbache	(21 Jan) Louis XVI executed (1 Feb) France declared war on England and Holland (Mar–Dec) Revolt of La Vendée (16 Oct) Marie Antoinette executed Godwin *Political Justice* Wordsworth *An Evening Walk* and *Descriptive Sketches*
1794	(7–10 Apr) Back at Cambridge (Jun) poems in *Cambridge Intelligencer*; set out with Joseph Hucks to Oxford (met Southey), pantisocracy planned; Welsh tour (Aug–Sept) met Thomas Poole, engaged to Sara Fricker (Sept) with RS published *The Fall of Robespierre* (Cambridge); *Monody on Chatterton* published with *Rowley Poems* (Cambridge) (Dec) left Cambridge; sonnet in *M Chron* (24 Dec) began *Religious Musings*	(17 May) Suspension of Habeas Corpus Robespierre executed, end of the Terror (Oct–Dec) State Trials: Tooke, Hardy, and Thelwall acquitted of charge of treason Paine *Age of Reason* (–1795) Paley *Evidences of Christianity*
1795	(Jan) Bristol lodgings with George Burnett and RS (Jan–Feb) Political lectures (Mar–Apr) RS's historical lectures (May–Jun) Lectures on Revealed Religion (16 June) Lecture on the Slave Trade (summer) quarrel with RS, pantisocracy abandoned (4 Oct) married Sara Fricker (26 Nov) Lecture against the Two Bills (3 Dec) *Conciones* published (Dec) *Answer to "A Letter to Edward Long Fox"* and *Plot Discovered* published; planning *The Watchman*	(Jun–Jul) Quiberon expedition (26 Sept) WW and DW at Racedown (Nov) Directory begins (6 Nov) Treason and Sedition Bills introduced (18 Dec) Two Acts put into effect Lewis *Ambrosio, or the Monk*
1796	(9 Jan–13 Feb) Tour to Midlands to sell *The Watchman*; met Erasmus Darwin and Joseph Wright (painter) (1 Mar) *The Watchman* No 1 published (9 Mar) *Watchman* No 2 (17 Mar) *Watchman* No 3 (25 Mar) *Watchman* No 4 (2 Apr) *Watchman* No 5 (11 Apr) *Watchman* No 6 (16 Apr) *Poems on Various Subjects* (19 Apr) *Watchman* No 7 (27 Apr) *Watchman* No 8 (5 May) *Watchman* No 9 (13 May) *Watchman* No 10 (19 Sept) Hartley b; reconciliation with RS	England treating for peace with France (Apr) Napoleon Bonaparte's successful Italian campaign

	(31 Dec) *Ode to the Departing Year* in *Cambridge Intelligencer*; move to Nether Stowey
1797	(Mar) WW at Stowey
	(5 Jun) at Racedown
	(Jul) DW, WW, and Lamb at Stowey; DW and WW in Alfoxden House
	(16 Oct) *Osorio* finished; *Poems, to Which Are Now Added, Poems by Charles Lamb and Charles Lloyd*
	(13–16 Nov) C and WW's walk to Lynton and *Ancient Mariner* begun
1798	(Jan) C's Unitarian sermons at Shrewsbury; Wedgwood annuity £150 accepted
	(Mar) *Ancient Mariner* completed
	(Apr) *Fears in Solitude*
	(18 Sept) *Lyrical Ballads* published; WW, DW, and C to Hamburg; met Klopstock
	(Oct) C to Ratzeburg
1799	(Apr) C had news of death of Berkeley; C at University of Göttingen
	(May) ascent of Brocken
	(29 Jul) in Stowey again
	(Sept–Oct) Devon walking tour with RS; met Humphry Davy in Bristol; experiments with nitrous oxide
	(27 Oct) first Lakes tour, with WW
	(27 Nov) arrived in London to accept *M Post* offer
	(Dec) DW and WW at Town End (later Dove Cottage)
1800	(Jan–27 Mar) *M Post* reporter and leader-writer; translating *Wallenstein* at Lamb's
	(Apr) to Grasmere and WW
	(May–Jun) in Stowey and Bristol
	(24 Jul) move to Greta Hall, Keswick
	(Sept–Oct) superintends printing of *Lyrical Ballads* (2nd ed)
1801	(Jan) *Lyrical Ballads* (1800) published; prolonged illness
	(Jul–Aug) with SH at Stockton
	(15 Nov) in London writing for *M Post*
	Christmas at Stowey
1802	(Jan) In London; attends Davy's lectures at Royal Institution; writing for *M Post*
	(Mar–Nov) in Lakes, severe domestic discord
	(Apr) *Dejection*
	(Aug) Scafell climb; visit of the Lambs
	(Sept–Oct) writing for *M Post*
	(Nov) tour of S Wales with Tom and Sally Wedgwood
	(23 Dec) Sara C b
1803	(Jan–Feb) In Somerset with Wedgwoods, Poole; with Lamb in London; made his will
	(Jun) *Poems* (1803)
	(summer) visits by Hazlitt, Beaumonts, and S. Rogers to Lakes; Hazlitt's portrait of C
	(15–29 Aug) Scottish tour with DW and WW
	(30 Aug–15 Sept) alone
1804	(Jan) Ill at Grasmere, then to London; portrait by Northcote
	(9 Apr) in convoy to Malta
	(Aug–Nov) Sicily, two ascents of Etna; stayed with J. F. Leckie; private secretary to Alexander Ball, British High Commissioner at Malta

1805 (Jan) Appointed Acting Public Secretary in Malta; news of loss of John Wordsworth on *Abergavenny*
(Sept–Dec) in Sicily
(Dec) to Naples and Rome

1806 (Jan) In Rome, met Washington Allston, the Humboldts, L. Tieck; to Florence, Pisa
(23 Jun) sailed from Leghorn
(17 Aug) landed in England; London, job-hunting, Parndon with the Clarksons and to Cambridge
(26 Oct) in Kendal
(Nov) Keswick, determined on separation from Mrs C
(Dec) at Coleorton with WW and SH, crisis of jealous disillusionment with them

1807 Coleorton; heard WW read *Prelude* and wrote *Lines to William Wordsworth*
(Jun) with C family at Stowey
(Aug) met De Quincey; in Bristol
(Nov) in London

1808 (15 Jan–Jun) In rooms at *Courier* office, Strand; lectures at Royal Institution on Poetry and Principles of Taste; illnesses, Bury St Edmunds
(Jun–Aug) Bristol, Leeds, Keswick
(Jul) review of Clarkson's *History of the Abolition of the Slave-Trade*
(1 Sept) arrived Allan Bank, Grasmere
(Nov) first prospectus of *The Friend*; Kendal

1809 (1 Jun–15 Mar 1810) *The Friend*, 27 numbers plus supernumerary
(7 Dec–20 Jan 1810) "Letters on the Spaniards" in *Courier*

1810 (Mar) SH left for Wales; last number of *Friend*
(Oct) to London; Montagu precipitates WW–C quarrel; with Morgans in Hammersmith
(Nov) personal association with H. Crabb Robinson begins

1811 (Mar–Apr) Miniature painted by M. Betham; met Gratton (20 Apr); first table-talk recorded by John Taylor Coleridge
(Apr–Sept) contributions to *Courier*; J. Payne Collier met C
(18 Nov–27 Jan 1811) lectures on Shakespeare and Milton at Scot's Corporation Hall, Collier, Byron, Rogers, Robinson attending; George Dawe's bust of C

1812 (Feb–Mar) Last journey to Lakes to collect copies of *Friend*
(Apr) with Morgans, Berners St
(May–Aug) lectures on drama in Willis's Rooms; portrait by Dawe
(May) Lamb and Crabb Robinson patch WW quarrel
(Jun) Catherine Wordsworth d; *The Friend* reissued
(3 Nov–26 Jan 1813) Shakespeare lectures in Surrey Institution
(Nov) half Wedgwood annuity withdrawn; RS and C *Omniana*
(Dec) Thomas Wordsworth (WW's son) d

1813 (23 Jan) *Remorse* opened at Drury Lane
(2 Sept) met Mme de Staël
(Oct–Nov) Bristol lectures on Shakespeare and education; with Morgans at Ashley

1814 (5 Apr) Lectures at Bristol on Milton, Cervantes, Taste; lecture on French Revolution and Napoleon; under medical care of Dr Daniel for opium addiction and suicidal depression

	(1 Aug) *Remorse* performed in Bristol
	(Aug–Sept) Allston portrait of C; Allston's exhibition of paintings; essays "On the Principles of Genial Criticism" in *Felix Farley's Bristol Journal*
	(Sept) at Ashley with the Morgans
	(20 Sept–10 Dec) "Letters to Mr. Justice Fletcher" in *Courier*
1815	(Mar) At Calne with the Morgans
	(Jun) *Remorse* performed at Calne
	(Jul–Sept) dictating *Biographia Literaria*
	(Aug–Sept) *Sibylline Leaves* and *Biographia* sent for publication in Bristol
1816	(Feb) Grant from Literary Fund, also from Byron
	(Mar) London: illness
	(10 Apr) sent *Zapolya* to Byron
	(15 Apr) accepted as patient and housemate by Dr Gillman, Moreton House, Highgate
	(May–Jun) *Christabel* published (three editions); renews acquaintance with Hookham Frere
	(Dec) *Statesman's Manual* published
	Hazlitt's antagonistic reviews in *Examiner* (Jun, Sept, Dec) and *Edinburgh Review* (Dec)
1817	(Apr) Second *Lay Sermon* published
	(14 Apr) *Remorse* revived
	(Jul) *Biographia Literaria*, *Sibylline Leaves* published
	(summer) met J. H. Green
	(Sept) met Henry Cary
	(Nov) *Zapolya* published; C's tr of Hurwitz's *Hebrew Dirge* for Princess Charlotte; Tieck visited C
1818	(Jan) "Treatise on Method" for *Encyclopaedia Metropolitana* published
	(Jan–Mar) lectures on poetry and drama
	(Jan) met T. Allsop
	(Apr) two pamphlets supporting Peel's Bill against exploitation of child-labour
	(Nov) *The Friend* (3-vol edition)
	(Dec) Lectures on the History of Philosophy (Dec–Mar 1819); literary lectures (Dec–Mar 1819)
1819	(Mar) Financial losses in bankruptcy of publisher Rest Fenner
	(29 Mar) lectures end
	(11 Apr) met Keats in Millfield Lane; Hartley Coleridge elected Fellow of Oriel; revived interest in chemistry; occasional contributions to *Blackwood's* (to 1822)
1820	(May) Hartley Coleridge deprived of Oriel Fellowship (Oct) Derwent Coleridge to St John's, Cambridge
1821	(Jul) Reunion with brother, the Rev George Coleridge (autumn) invitation to lecture in Dublin refused
1822	(spring) C's "Thursday-evening class" began; SC's tr of Martin Dobrizhoffer *An Account of the Abipones, an Equestrian People of Paraguay*
	(Nov–Feb 1823) wife and daughter visit C at Highgate
	(29 Dec) Henry Nelson Coleridge began recording his *Table Talk*
	Edward Irving's first visit
	Derwent Coleridge left Cambridge prematurely
1823	(Sept) *Youth and Age* begun
	(Dec) Gillmans and C move to 3, The Grove

1824 (Mar) Elected FRSL, annuity of £100
(Jun) Carlyle and Gabriele Rossetti called at Highgate
Derwent Coleridge B.A. Cambridge

1825 (May) *Aids to Reflection* published
(18 May) Royal Society of Literature essay on the *Prometheus* of Aeschylus
proposed three lectures on projected London University
Derwent Coleridge ordained

1827 (May) Thomas Chalmers called at Highgate; C's serious illness; his first communion since Cambridge; visit from Poole
Derwent Coleridge married Mary Pridham
Sir George Beaumont d, leaving £100 to Mrs C

1828 (22 Apr) Fenimore Cooper met C
(21 Jun–7 Aug) Netherlands and Rhine tour with Dora and WW
(Aug) *Poetical Works* (3 vols); John Sterling called at Highgate

1829 *Poetical Works* (2nd ed)
Poetical Works of Coleridge, Shelley, and Keats (Galignani, Paris)
(Sept) SC married cousin Henry Nelson Coleridge; Lady Beaumont left C £50; Poole visited Highgate
(Dec) *On the Constitution of the Church and State*

1830 *On the Constitution of the Church and State* (2nd ed)
(Jun) Henry Nelson Coleridge and SC settled in Hampstead
(Jul) C makes his will
republication of *The Devil's Walk* "by Professor Porson"

1831 Last meetings with WW
Aids to Reflection (2nd ed)
(Sept) attended British Association, first meetings

1832 Legacy of £300 from Steinmetz

1833 Hartley Coleridge's *Poems* dedicated to C
(24–9 Jun) to Cambridge for meetings of British Association
(5 Aug) Emerson called at Highgate
Hartley Coleridge's *Biographia Borealis*

1834 (Jul) proofs of *Poetical Works* (3rd ed)
(25 Jul) death at Highgate

EDITOR'S INTRODUCTION

IN the spring of 1796 Samuel Taylor Coleridge, then aged twenty-three, published at eight-day intervals a miscellany that he called *The Watchman*. Each number consisted of thirty-two pages and bore on its masthead the motto: "THAT ALL MAY KNOW THE TRUTH; AND THAT THE TRUTH MAY MAKE US FREE!" It ran for ten issues, the first dated 1 March and the last 13 May, which closed with the words: "O Watchman! thou has watched in vain!"

Young as he was, Coleridge had already attained a reputation for brilliance and had lived for several years in a milieu in which journalism seemed a natural and inevitable means of expressing one's views, marketing one's verse, and making one's living. At Cambridge he had known and admired the *Cambridge Intelligencer* and its proprietor, Benjamin Flower, who had published some of his poems and printed *The Fall of Robespierre*. The London *Morning Chronicle* had paid money for, and flattering attention to, a series of his sonnets. As his self-confidence fed on success, he grew increasingly charmed by the possibility of starting a journal of his own, but by temperament he needed some idealistic motive to inspire his energies. For a time he thought he had such a motive when, with Robert Southey, he evolved a somewhat utopian scheme called *pantisocracy* and planned to finance it with the proceeds of a "Provincial Magazine".[1] Pantisocracy was to be a polity based on the theory that the ownership of property was the chief evil of mankind; the two young poets planned to emigrate, with two Fricker sisters (after properly marrying them) and a few congenial friends, to the banks of the Susquehanna River in Pennsylvania, and there establish, in the uncorrupted wilderness, an uncorrupted society. All land was to be owned in common, and because everybody would work it was hoped that nobody would have to work very much. Though often dismissed as a callow whim, the plan, as the long-unpublished Lectures on Revealed Religion help to show, was based on a profound awareness of the defects of established, so-called Christian society. But Coleridge and Southey quarrelled, and the whole scheme

[1] C to Thomas Poole [7 Oct 1795]: *CL* I 161 and n.

collapsed, both journal and utopia. Coleridge had to content himself with the doubtful blessing of his marriage to Sara Fricker.

On 29 October 1795, less than a month after Coleridge was married, an extraordinary event occurred. George III on his way to open Parliament was hissed and hooted by a mob, and a pebble or a bullet shattered the window of the state carriage. On the King's return journey there were cries of "Bread! Peace! No Pitt!" and after he alighted the carriage was almost destroyed. The ministry seized this attack on the King as a pretext for introducing two bills—the Seditious Meetings Bill and the Treasonable Practices Bill—in an attempt to contain and suppress the voices of progress and reform. And Coleridge, a Unitarian and an advocate of wide political freedom, discovered within himself powers that enabled him to become a public spokesman for those voices of change. At last he had found a cause in whose service he hoped to focus the previously unconcerted elements of his nature. In this way, perhaps, he could play a part in the world suitable to his talents and promise.[1]

AGAINST THE TWO BILLS

Several weeks after the attack on the King the citizens of Bristol met in the Guildhall to congratulate the King on his "providential escape" and show their abhorrence of the act. At the meeting of 17 November it developed that a large and articulate group wished also to implore him to remove the distresses of the people by restoring peace (the war with France had officially begun 1 February 1793). The London *Star*, reporting the meeting at length in its issue of 23 November, noted: "After a considerable time spent in fruitlessly calling '*Mr. Mayor! Mr. Mayor!*' in a tone of voice, and with that sweetness of emphasis which would have fascinated the attention even of a Robespierre; Mr. Coleridge began the most elegant, the most pathetic, and the most sublime Address that was ever heard, perhaps, within the walls of that building." After saying, "Though the war may take much from the property of the rich, it left them much; but a PENNY taken from the pocket of a poor man might

[1] The only person in the mob arrested and singled out for prosecution in connexion with the attack was Kyd Wake, a journeyman printer accused of hissing the King and shouting, "No George, no War!" It is an irony of *The Watchman*, which had its inception in this reaction against the King and the war-party, that one of the last items in the final number was a report of Kyd Wake's conviction and sentence —the pillory, five years' imprisonment at hard labour followed by sureties of £1000 for good behaviour for ten years (and imprisonment till those sureties were found). See below, p 369.

deprive him of a dinner", Coleridge was "authoritatively stopped" by the horrified Tory mayor. Three days later the anti-war group who had asserted themselves at the previous meeting again met, this time to send a petition to Parliament against the Two Bills, agreed unanimously, and signed the petition.[1]

Less than a month later, the so called "Two Bills" were passed and became law, but the agitation against them had produced so great a volume of protest that the Opposition forces, though disappointed, imagined that by further effort they could turn the political tide. They could not doubt that the nation shared their views and that the voice of the people would prevail. The ministry was certainly in trouble: the war with France was unpopular and costly—though occasionally successful at sea, it had been marked by almost uninterrupted disasters on land; the triumphs in the West Indies had been vitiated by the ravages of yellow fever; and even the weather had proved adverse, for in 1795 severe cold, with attendant miseries, had so damaged the crops that famine seemed imminent. Everything, in short, encouraged the hope of a change in public affairs that would lead to a more liberal administration.

Possibly it was the eloquent advocate and Whig orator, Thomas Erskine, who supplied Coleridge with the animating spark and the title for his periodical. Deploring the government's encroachment upon traditional rights, Erskine, in an address to the Whig Club on 20 December, called for a mighty effort to undo the mischief of the Two Acts. Every friend of freedom, he said, should accept the responsibility of acting as "a species of watchman on the outworks of the Constitution".[2] "Watchman" was a favourite word of Coleridge's favourite prophets, Ezekiel and Isaiah—a word that bound together his deepest convictions, religious and political, in a union that reveals itself in all his thinking. Now, used in the cause of freedom, it must have resounded in Coleridge's mind, to awake familiar and thrilling echoes.[3]

COLERIDGE AND COTTLE

About this time—late December 1795—Coleridge attended a meeting at the Rummer Tavern in Bristol, where, as he puts it, he was

[1] The meetings of 17 and 20 November were reported in full in the *Star* 23 Nov 1795.

[2] *M Chron* 21 Dec 1795.

[3] J. B. Beer, in *N&Q* CCVI (1961) 217, suggests as a possible source of C's title a pamphlet by N. Hill, *The Watchman's Report and Advice*, a sermon preached 25 Feb 1795, which was reviewed in a periodical C read, the *C Rev* for Nov 1795.

"persuaded by sundry Philanthropists and Anti-polemists to set on foot a periodical work".[1] Perhaps the meeting was called by some of the Bristolians who had petitioned Parliament, or perhaps Coleridge himself called the meeting. The first mention of *The Watchman* is found in a note first published in Joseph Cottle's *Early Recollections* (1837):

My dear friend,
I am fearful that you felt hurt at my not mentioning to you the proposed "Watchman," and from my not requesting you to attend the meeting. My dear friend, my reasons were these. All who met were expected to become subscribers to a fund; I knew there would be enough without you, and I knew, and felt, how much money had been drawn away from you lately.

God Almighty love you!
S. T. C.[2]

According to Cottle, Coleridge "convened his chief friends, with dexterous secrecy . . . to determine on the size, price, and time of publishing, with all other preliminaries . . .".[3]

In tracing the history of *The Watchman* one is hampered by the fact that its two principal witnesses—Coleridge himself and Joseph Cottle—were too partial, each in his particular way, to leave entirely unprejudiced accounts of the endeavour. Writing after a lapse of some two decades, of himself in the middle 1790's, Coleridge was moved by a wish to minimise the radicalism of his earlier years and dealt cautiously with that little chapter of his life; in the *Biographia Literaria*, published in 1817, his account of *The Watchman* treats it in a tone of indulgent jocosity, as a freak of youth—and includes no mention of Cottle. Cottle, when he wrote about Coleridge in his *Early Recollections*, published three years after Coleridge's death, was smarting under a series of disappointments and apparent affronts. His own career was a failure both in business and in authorship. Recognition of his rôle as a patron of Wordsworth and Coleridge might have given him a degree of worldly dignity, but though generous with private encomiums, both of them—especially Coleridge, whose obligation was the greater—had been stingy with public praise. When Coleridge's silence in the *Biographia* threatened him with an immortality of insignificance, Cottle saw his *Early Recollections* as a chance for self-restitution and, what is more, revenge. In his preface he complains of the way in which Coleridge ignores

[1] *BL* ch 10 (1907) I 114.
[2] Cottle *E Rec* I 150–1; reprinted *CL* 174 (dated "late December 1795"). No holograph or ms copy exists.
[3] Cottle *E Rec* I 150.

Bristol—a city so important in his life—and does not disguise the heart-burning resentment occasioned by Coleridge's neglect to make any reference to his own assistance.

Cottle's resentment is easy to understand when one considers how deeply he was involved in Coleridge's affairs and how kindly, if often officious, were his efforts on Coleridge's behalf. He published the first issue of *Lyrical Ballads*, the *Poems* of 1796 and of 1797, and, when *The Watchman* was embarked upon, placed himself much at Coleridge's disposal. True, Coleridge did exclude Cottle from the meeting at the Rummer Tavern, probably to avoid falling uncomfortably into Cottle's further debt; but he did not exclude him from performances of essential services without which *The Watchman*—brief as its life was to be—could never have existed at all. Cottle engaged in a campaign to enlist subscribers in Bristol; he sold *The Watchman* at his shop—a service for which, he says, he refused payment; he advised Coleridge on matters of printing and publishing; he bought paper for at least six issues.[1] But this was not all. "On the publication of the first Number, besides my trouble in sending round to so many subscribers . . . it occupied Mr. Coleridge and myself four full hours to arrange, reckon, (each pile being counted by Mr. C. after myself, to be quite satisfied that there was no extra 3 1/2 d. one slipped in unawares,) pack up, and write invoices and letters, for the London and country customers", Cottle writes, and adds: "This routine was repeated with every fresh number".[2] Besides undertaking such chores, Cottle shared in—if, indeed, he did not actually carry out—the distribution of *The Watchman*. And he stood ready frequently to supply money on no security beyond the prospects and genius of its recipient.

Cottle was not ungenerous; a few grateful words from Coleridge, uttered freely for the world to hear, would have discharged all debts. But the words never came,[3] and, in their absence, certain actions of Coleridge seemed instances of contempt. For example, in *The Watchman* and generally elsewhere Coleridge ignored Cottle's poetry; later, in 1800, he handled Cottle's epic, *Alfred*, rather roughly, arousing "wounded & angry" feelings;[4] and later still, in preparing

[1] Cottle *E Rec* I 162; C to Poole 5 May 1796: *CL* I 208. The paper was not an outright gift, as C at the time supposed, but Cottle was apparently not fully recompensed; see below, p lvii.

[2] Cottle *E Rec* I 155–6.

[3] An ambiguously complimentary poem addressed to Cottle, *To the Author of Poems* (*PW*—EHC—I 102–4), was included in early editions of C's poems but was not reprinted after 1803.

[4] C to Josiah Wedgwood 21 Apr 1800: *CL* I 586.

to write *Early Recollections*, Cottle borrowed some private letters of Coleridge that contained unflattering references to himself. Hence Cottle, stung to the quick and eager to even the account, was led into distortions and suppressions of the truth that render all his Coleridgiana unreliable except when sifted of error and pieced together with the evidence of contemporaneous letters.

PROSPECTUS AND SUBSCRIBERS

After the meeting at the Rummer Tavern, subscribers to *The Watchman* were solicited in Bristol—Cottle collecting 250 and another Bristol bookseller, Reed, 120.[1] These, however, were not enough to pay for the work, and Coleridge determined to try his luck in the Midland towns. In preparation for this tour to the north, he drew up a "flaming prospectus",[2] announcing as the chief objects of his miscellany co-operation with the Whig Club in procuring the repeal of the Two Acts and with "the PATRIOTIC SOCIETIES, for obtaining a Right of Suffrage general and frequent".[3] *The Watchman* would contain domestic and foreign news, parliamentary reports, essays, and poetry "chiefly or altogether political".[4] Rather than the normal practice in the provinces of publishing weekly, it would be published every eighth day "to exempt it from the stamp-tax, and likewise to contribute as little as possible to the supposed guilt of a war against freedom",[5] would contain no advertisements, and for thirty-two pages would cost only fourpence. (The London newspapers then charged fourpence halfpenny an issue, which consisted of four pages, the front one of which was usually filled with income-producing advertisements.) Because of its octavo form *The Watchman* might be bound at the end of the year "and become an Annual Register".[6] (The London handbills announcing No I proclaimed the uniqueness of *The Watchman*: "To supply at once the places of a Review, Newspaper, and Annual Register!!!" and added another item to the contents: reviews of interesting and important publications.)[7]

The Prospectus promised that the work would be "a faithful WATCHMAN, to proclaim the State of the Political Atmosphere, and preserve Freedom and her Friends from the attacks of Robbers and Assassins!!"[8] More soberly Coleridge indicated the special function he had in mind for his miscellany, namely, to remedy the dearth of

[1] Cottle *E Rec* I 152–3.
[2] *BL* ch 10 (1907) I 114.
[3] See below, p 5.
[4] Ibid.
[5] *BL* ch 10 (1907) I 114.
[6] See below, p 5.
[7] See below, App A, p 380.
[8] See below, p 6.

That All may know the TRUTH;
And that the TRUTH may make us FREE!!

On Friday, the 5th Day of February, 1796,

WILL BE PUBLISHED,

N°. I.

(PRICE FOUR PENCE)

OF A

MISCELLANY, TO BE PUBLISHED EVERY EIGHTH DAY,

UNDER THE NAME OF

THE WATCHMAN.

BY S. T. COLERIDGE,

AUTHOR OF

ADDRESSES TO THE PEOPLE,
A PLOT DISCOVERED, &c. &c.

The Publiſhers in the different Towns and Cities will be ſpecified in future Advertiſements.

2. The Prospectus of *The Watchman* p 1.
From a copy in the British Museum, Ashley 406. See p 3.

good provincial journals, for most of the newspapers outside London were, he said, dependent on the Treasury, which sent them papers with particular paragraphs marked for reprinting; thus only the government point of view was disseminated. It was certainly true that the opposition point of view found few spokesmen in the provinces.[1] The centres of liberal thought outside London, chiefly clusters of Unitarians and other "rational Dissenters", had little chance to spread their views or expand their influence. To a limited degree Coleridge's friend Benjamin Flower and his *Cambridge Intelligencer* served this purpose. Coleridge evidently saw the opportunity of operating from Bristol and drawing support from the wealthy Midland towns, where Dissenters and liberals were most numerous and powerful. Such persons were the intended, and became in fact the principal, readers of *The Watchman*.

The Prospectus had announced No 1 to appear on Friday, 5 February. Armed with his prospectuses and, probably, supplied with a bit of money from the subscribers' loan,[2] Coleridge set out from Bristol on 9 January on a journey of which he has left a detailed record in a series of letters mainly to Josiah Wade, a merchant friend in Bristol.[3] Because of the length of his absence from Bristol in recruiting subscribers, by 29 January he had moved the date of publication forward to Tuesday, 1 March.[4] Coleridge's letters show that he was well supplied with letters of introduction, for many of his Bristol friends had connexions, mercantile and religious, in the Midlands. His first stop was Worcester, where the "aristocrats" were so numerous that no bookseller would venture to publish a radical journal.[5] His failure there was more than compensated for by his success in Birmingham, his next stop. In Birmingham, though handicapped by a cold, he preached two sermons "*preciously peppered with Politics*",[6] secured a hundred subscribers, and made the acquaintance of the pastor of the New Meeting chapel, the Rev John Edwards, who was to become a contributor to *The Watchman*. Derby likewise

[1] In Bristol, for example, four of the five newspapers were pro-ministerial.

[2] See C's letters to Cottle [late Dec 1795] and to Josiah Wade [2 Feb 1796]: *CL* I 174, 181.

[3] An unpublished letter to Wade, stamped Worcester, 10 Jan 1796, shows that the latter supplied some funds for the trips. C said: "The five pound is perfectly adequate to all my expenses, both here and at Birmingham . . .". I am indebted to the James Marshall and Marie-Louise Osborn Collection in the Yale University Library for the use of this letter.

[4] C to the Rev John Edwards [29 Jan 1796]: *CL* I 179.

[5] C to Wade [10 Jan 1796]: *CL* I 175. In the political sense an "aristocrat" meant a defender of the established order. See below, pp xxxix, 30 n 2.

[6] C to Wade [18] Jan 1796: *CL* I 176.

treated him well and gave him forty or fifty subscribers; there he had the interesting experience of meeting a celebrity, Dr Erasmus Darwin, who "bantered me on the subject of religion".[1] At Nottingham, his next stop, he happened in on a birthday dinner to Charles James Fox, which, by collecting together the Whigs, gave him access to a group of natural supporters of his liberal periodical.[2] Here another chance to preach was favourable for *Watchman* purposes, and this time he gained a point of principle: in Birmingham he had been "overpersuaded" to preach in the hated priestly colour of black; now he appeared in the meeting-house "in a blue coat and white waistcoat, that not a rag of the woman of Babylon might be seen on me".[3] Preaching, in addition to promoting business, "spread a sort of sanctity over my *Sedition*".[4] At Nottingham an aristocrat, given a prospectus, glanced at the motto—"That all may know the truth; and that the truth may make us free":

A *Seditious* beginning! quoth he—. Sir! said Mr Fellowes [who had given him the Prospectus]—the motto is quoted from another Author—Poo! quoth the Aristocrat—what Odds is it whether he wrote it himself or quoted it from any *other seditious Dog*? Please (replied Mr F.) to look into the 32nd [Verse of the 8th] Chapter of John, and you will find, Sir! that that *seditious Dog* was—JESUS CHRIST![5]

Coleridge was well received at Sheffield, but met with a difficulty: James Montgomery, the poet, who was editor and proprietor of the Sheffield *Iris*, one of the rare liberal papers in the provinces, was in prison, serving a sentence for libel. His friends felt that to promote *The Watchman* would injure the *Iris*, a sentiment in which Coleridge heartily concurred. Nevertheless, Smith the bookseller promised to dispose of twenty or thirty copies among friends.[6] Coleridge visited Manchester but tells nothing of his fortunes there;[7] at Lichfield he fared well,[8] and he intended to canvass both Liverpool and London, but the illness of his wife Sara brought him home.

It was the zealous Wade who, with the help of Robert Allen, Coleridge's schoolfellow, took over the London arrangements for advertisements and for finding a publisher. Coleridge had wanted Ridgway, but in the end Parsons was engaged.[9] Advertisements

[1] C to Wade 27 Jan 1796: *CL* I 177.

[2] Ibid 178.

[3] C to Wade [2 Feb 1796]: *CL* I 180; *BL* ch 10 (1907) I 114.

[4] C to Edwards [29 Jan 1796]: *CL* I 179.

[5] Ibid.

[6] C to Edwards 4 Feb [1796]: *CL* I 183. John Pye Smith (1774–1851)—later to be ordained, and well known as a Biblical exegete—edited the *Iris* during Montgomery's imprisonment.

[7] C to Wade [6 Feb 1796]: *CL* I 184.

[8] C to Wade [c 10 Feb 1796]: *CL* I 184.

[9] C to Wade [2 Feb 1796]: *CL* I 181; see also Allen to Wade 25 Feb: ibid 181n. James Ridgway was still in

were placed in the Whig journals, the *Morning Chronicle* and the *Star*, and broadsides were circulated.[1] No precise gauge of the success of these efforts remains. Coleridge later stated that he gathered a thousand subscriptions on his tour, but some such figure could easily represent the total subscription list of *The Watchman*.[2] Then and afterwards he expressed satisfaction with the numbers secured, but as the time for publication approached he sank into a state of melancholy.

COLERIDGE BEFORE PUBLICATION

Coleridge's anxious mood was probably induced by the self-examination and the self-doubts that the prospect of action and responsibility had forced him to take. He was becoming disenchanted with his marriage; his past seemed a "gloomy huddle of strange actions",[3] and his future was shrouded in "cloud & thick darkness".[4] In his letters he freely revealed the degree of his distress and catalogued his domestic difficulties. He had no proper domicile. During the late winter he lived with his mother-in-law in a household that combined tediousness, confusion, and lack of privacy. For the peace and quiet necessary for composition he was obliged to take to the fields. Sara's pregnancy went hard with her, and she did not suffer in silence. "I am in a quickset hedge of embarrassments, and whichever way I turn, a thorn runs into me", Coleridge wrote to Cottle.[5] Though he did, towards the end of March, move into a house of his own, his family troubles went with him. Sara was still ailing, at one time close to miscarriage, and her relatives were not, themselves, in any condition to sustain and comfort her distraught young husband. In early May, Coleridge surveyed the scene: "My wife's Mother has *lived dying* these last six weeks, and she is not yet dead—& the Husband of my Wife's Sister, Robert Lovell . . . died . . . of a putrid fever".[6] All one night Coleridge sat up with Mrs Lovell to the accompaniment of the dying man's groans. In the previous weeks

Newgate Prison, serving a four-year sentence (he had been convicted 1794) for having published an edition of Paine's *Rights of Man* and Charles Pigott's *History of the Jockey Club*, an exposé of high society.

[1] *BL* ch 10 (1907) I 119. See also below, App A, pp 379–81.

[2] *BL* (1907) I 119. See also Cottle *E Rec* I 155, 162, where Cottle says that a thousand subscriptions poured in and that Biggs the printer printed a thousand sheets per issue. But this would make *five hundred* copies, for each number was printed on two sheets.

[3] C to Wade [c 10 Feb 1796]: *CL* I 184.

[4] C to Cottle 22 Feb 1796: *CL* I 185.

[5] Ibid.

[6] C to Poole 5 May 1796: *CL* I 207. Mrs Fricker survived as late as 1809, when C was still paying her annuity; see his letter to George Coleridge 9 Oct 1809: *CL* III 238. She died at the end of Oct 1809; see *The Friend* (*CC*) II 497.

Coleridge had spent much time with his brother-in-law, and having helped convert him to Christianity seemed only an isolated consolation for the nerve-racking experience.

Amidst these painful distractions, Coleridge was finishing a volume of poems contracted for before his marriage—indeed, as a means of supporting that marriage—and still, despite many promises to Cottle, his publisher, incomplete. Obviously, conditions were unfavourable for composition, and not until early March, after *The Watchman* had already begun, could he complete *Religious Musings*, the crowning poem of the collection. Small wonder that the project of the periodical, embraced early with optimism, now seemed an incubus on the present and the future! He expected only modest profits—possibly two pounds a week—but even a larger sum could not pay, he felt, for the harassment of weekly slavery. Interestingly enough, the very real danger of prosecution that menaced the reformist country editor, so sharply outlined during his subscription tour by James Montgomery's plight, does not appear to have borne much weight in his thinking. Later, in the *Biographia Literaria*, Coleridge analysed his attitudes of 1796 and explained why he went ahead with a repellent and apparently hopeless task. The reason was that compulsion toward duty led him to take a course opposite to that of self-interest; he was "so compleatly hag-ridden by the fear of being influenced by selfish motives, that to know a mode of conduct to be the dictate of *prudence* was a sort of presumptive proof to my feelings, that the contrary was the dictate of *duty*".[1] This explanation serves to illuminate the complicated Coleridgean psychology in which "head and heart" were inextricably yoked together. At any rate—whether to avoid the sting of a sensitive conscience or simply the chagrin of abandoning a scheme in which he had involved many friends and acquaintances—Coleridge persisted in his venture. It was perhaps, too, an alternative pulpit to the one he rejected when he refused to take orders, and to the Unitarian one, yet it could be a vehicle for discharging some responsibilities toward society. So ruing the day he had promised to do so, he managed to bring the first issue of *The Watchman* into the world.

CHANGE IN POLITICAL ATMOSPHERE BEFORE PUBLICATION

The interval between the planning and the issuance of *The Watchman* was a little more than two months. During this time the complexion

[1] *BL* ch 10 (1907) I 119.

of public affairs and the Whig cause changed in such a way as to affect Coleridge's intentions for *The Watchman*. On 8 December 1795 Pitt announced in Parliament that the King was ready to negotiate with France for peace. The following day the Whig Club met to pass resolutions on how to save the Constitution and free speech (the Two Bills had not yet been passed),[1] and held further meetings on 12 and 23 January 1796 to perfect plans for seeking the repeal of the Two Acts. In the *Morning Chronicle* of 27 January an advertisement indicated places where signatures were being collected for an association "to regain their lost rights and recover their abrogated constitution". Similar advertisements in the daily press were repeated frequently until the middle of February.[2] When Parliament reconvened on 2 February, the Whigs, taking their cue from Charles Grey, were silent upon the Two Acts but attacked the policies of the government on the war with France and the allied matter of the military establishment. On 15 February Grey called attention to the failure of the ministry to show any results from their declared intention of welcoming negotiations with the enemy. To this query Pitt gave one of his splendidly indefinite replies. About this time Fox, who was loyally supporting his young friend Grey, wrote to his nephew Lord Holland, then living abroad: "I do not know what to write to you about our politics here, the whole country seems dead, and yet they certainly showed some spirit while the Bills were pending; and I cannot help flattering myself that the great coldness at present is owing to people being in expectation and doubt with respect to what Pitt means to do in regard to peace".[3]

So the effervescence of December had subsided; the "association to regain lost rights" was abandoned—it was not even mentioned in the *Morning Chronicle*'s report of the 8 March meeting of the Whig Club; and Coleridge, like the Whigs, dropped agitation against the Two Acts. He consoled himself in the first number of *The Watchman* by saying that "the friends of rational and progressive Liberty may view with diminished indignation two recent acts of Parliament, which, though breaches of the Constitution . . . yet will not have been useless if they should render the language of political publications more cool and guarded, or even confine us for a while to the teaching of first principles, or the diffusion of that general knowledge which

[1] See below, App B, pp 385–90.

[2] The last advertisement appeared 20 Feb.

[3] Letter dated 18 Feb 1796: *Memorials and Correspondence of Charles James Fox* ed Lord John Russell (4 vols 1853–7) III 129–30.

should be the basis or substratum of politics".[1] The other "chief object" of *The Watchman*, as stated in the Prospectus—parliamentary reform—this, too, he passed over with only the barest mention, though this was a small sacrifice, since the *forms* of government were of little moment to him. The plans for the "association" had been predicated on a ground-swell of popular feeling against the Two Acts. This feeling had not materialised, as Fox dejectedly admitted, and the war, naturally enough, obscured all other issues. The public seemed to hold itself aloof, suspended between contrary forces, waiting to see what Pitt would do and what the French would do.

POLITICS AND *THE WATCHMAN*

Though the spring of 1796 offered no public events to match the magnitude of those which distinguished 1789 and 1815 (i.e. the shock of the French Revolution and the triumph of Waterloo), that, in its way, was a blessing to Coleridge the journalist, for such happenings, by their very weight and reverberation, can be repressive to thoughtful journalism, interdicting the free play of the mind. In the spring of 1796, Coleridge was afforded the opportunity to comment on most of the major concerns and controversies of his day. The long and historic sixth session of the seventeenth Parliament was drawing to a close: earlier it had supported the declaration of war against France, passed and renewed the suspension of habeas corpus, and passed Pitt's and Grenville's bills—the Two Acts—to restrict the right of assembly and the free discussion of constitutional questions. *The Watchman*'s account of the Binns-Jones case records what was probably the first of the few applications of those acts. Now Parliament was debating the permanent barracking of troops—a step leading to the establishment of a standing army; it was considering the game-laws, a bastion of feudal privilege; a crisis was arising over the government's obligation to relieve the wants of the poor; there was much wrangling over the then novel matter of a large public debt; the Irish question was approaching yet another crisis; and soon—during the lifetime of *The Watchman*—Wilberforce's bill for the abolition of the slave-trade would be narrowly defeated. Above everything rode the transcendent issue of war and peace.

In 1796 England looked across the water to unfriendly shores. Spain, once her ally, was now preparing to become France's. To the east she faced a Belgium absorbed by France, and a Holland,

[1] See below, pp 13–14.

now the Batavian Republic, a subsidiary of France, and her stadtholder a refugee in England. The nearest friendly port was Hamburg, and beyond Hamburg lay the way to the great states of Prussia, Austria, and Russia, which, though enemies to France, were friends of no one else. Too jealous of one another to agree except in pillage, they had recently concluded the partitioning of Poland. *The Watchman* records the final obsequies of that hapless kingdom, exterminated just as she began to adopt a popular form of government. Russia, at the expense of the Ottoman Empire, had established dominion over the Crimea and had placed a fleet on the Black Sea; she threatened to take Georgia, upon which Turkey, as well as Persia, had designs. *The Watchman* relates with gory detail an incident of this struggle. Russia's historic ambitions focussed on Constantinople, and Turkey's survival in Europe depended upon the neutralising effect of the conflicting greeds of the European powers. All these international affairs, and others, find their way, in some fashion, into *The Watchman*. Even the Indian problem touches its pages through some echoes of the trial of Warren Hastings. But the chief attention of Coleridge, as of all England, was fixed on France.

Those parts of *The Watchman* which bear directly upon France comprise little more than a quarter of its contents, but most of its remaining material is coloured by the controversy over the French war or French principles. The fact that England was at war with France roused in Coleridge not anti-French but anti-Pitt sentiments. Among the "Friends of Freedom", the word *patriotism* took on a novel meaning. In *The Watchman*, patriotism, used in this special sense, implied a wider allegiance and a higher loyalty than that owed to one's own country—a loyalty to the welfare of mankind. It was a word to couple with *philanthropy*, and its antonyms were *despotism*, *aristocracy*, and *priesthood*. Thus, it was natural for Coleridge to accuse Pitt, as Pitt had in effect accused Lord North, of being "at war with a nation of patriots",[1] for to Coleridge, as to many liberals of the day, France symbolised an aspiration toward human liberty. It was assumed that the worst excesses of the Revolution were past, that the Directory, though scarcely exemplifying the purest strain of republicanism, at least showed progress by putting aside the guillotine, and that even the "Giant Frenzy"[2] of the Revolution's early days was, seen in a larger context, a part of divine justice as set forth in the Apocalypse. Moreover, that "frenzy" had been an

[1] See below, p 241.

[2] *Religious Musings* line 317: see below, p 66.

inevitable reflex released by the actions of neighbouring tyrants. In short, the virtues of France were her own; her faults were traceable to William Pitt and his Continental allies.

The Watchman reflects the orthodox Whig line, and Coleridge quotes with approval the parliamentary speeches of Fox, Grey, and Sheridan. His commitment to the "nation of patriots" is shown also in the relish with which he points out the rising strength of the French. Pitt, a student of finance, had confidently awaited the depletion of French economic power. Certainly the finances of France were in disorder—her printing-house currency, called *assignats*, having sunk to worthlessness, were succeeded by a dubious issue called *mandats*—but perversely the French economy refused to collapse. Indeed, it showed positive signs of improvement. The Opposition insisted that it was England whose financial prospects were gloomy; she had squandered much money in subsidies to allies who had disappointed her. The coin that would buy their loyalty had not been discovered. All too often the Continental allies would take the money, exert themselves but little, and go their own selfish way. And the sound fiscal responsibility of England had resulted only in the accumulation of a large national debt.

The high hopes of the English ministry for fomenting internal rebellion in France had for some time been encouraged by the actions of the peasantry and their leaders in western France, but *The Watchman* tells the story of Charette's capture and the final collapse of the revolt in La Vendée. Other British hopes centred in the Navy, whose greatest triumphs still lay in the future and whose principal task, at the time, was the blockading of French ports. Though the capture of Toulon had been a naval feat, holding it proved impossible, and its loss suspended the English hold on the Mediterranean. *The Watchman* carries a report of French prowess in seizing British prizes in the Atlantic.

But *The Watchman* does more than retail the discomfiture of Pitt; it shows, as well, the embarrassments of the Opposition. Political commitment has its uneasy moments: one's friends sometimes behave worse than one's enemies. The French war was particularly tormenting to the English admirers of France. To the natural trauma of favouring the enemy of one's country, though really the enemy of one's *government*, and the inevitable nausea incurred by the Jacobin massacres, was added another perplexity. This was the outward expansion of French hegemony. Try as one might to see the foreign acquisitions of France as a sort of sharing of the word and spreading of the gospel, one saw them, at times, only as the re-enactment of the old conquests of kings.

A poignant instance of this kind of dilemma occurred during the lifetime of *The Watchman*. On this occasion the English ministry, as it had before promised to do, made overtures of negotiation to France, and its overtures were rebuffed. The papers involved in this exchange, the Wickham-Barthélemy correspondence, were printed in No 7 of *The Watchman* and commented upon in No 8. It is clear that this event had a powerful effect upon Coleridge—not upon his political principles but upon his view of France. Another sad turn of affairs in France was the adoption, after a period of relaxation, of restrictions on the right of assembly and of printing political news—decrees that bore a family resemblance to the despised Two Acts of England. Coleridge reminded his readers that the French had a greater power of redress than England through their broader electoral base; but despite such attempts at exculpation he had moved, at the end of *The Watchman*, to a posture toward French affairs that was very different from the one he had held at the beginning. Later in the year he wrote to Benjamin Flower of the *Cambridge Intelligencer*: "Indeed, I am out of heart with the French. In one of the numbers of my Watchman I wrote 'a remonstrance to the French Legislators': it contain'd *my* politics, & the splendid Victories of the French since that time have produced no alterations in them. I am tired of reading butcheries and altho' I should be unworthy of the name of Man, if I did not feel my Head & Heart awefully interested in the final Event, yet, I confess, my Curiosity is worn out with regard to the particulars of this process."[1] Of the nature of this "final Event" there can be little doubt. The real war was not the mistaken one against the French, but one against poverty, slavery, and repression, and had as its aim to convert "the present state of society" into the "blest Future".[2]

"FACTS" AND NEWS

Coleridge drew nearly all the news for *The Watchman* from the London newspapers, which apparently arrived in Bristol on the day after publication.[3] He relied most heavily upon the *Morning Chronicle*

[1] C to Flower [11 Dec 1796]: *CL* I 268–9. The "Remonstrance" had appeared in No 8; see below, pp 269–73.

[2] See below, pp 64–7, *The Present State of Society*, an excerpt from *Religious Musings*, printed in No 2.

[3] Writing on a Sunday morning, he refers to an article in Friday's London *Star*; to Edwards 20 Mar 1796: *CL* I 191.

and the *Star* because he found their politics congenial and admired their parliamentary reporting,[1] but he also used material from two other Whig papers, the *Gazetteer* and the *Morning Post*, and from the *Sun*, the *Oracle*, and *The Times*, which were pro-government in sympathy.

In his statement of policy in No 1 Coleridge declared his intention of "relating facts simply and nakedly, without epithets or comments".[2] This self-denying ordinance proved too stringent and really pointless, for *The Watchman* was in large degree a personal organ of S. T. Coleridge. At any rate, editorial intervention, so confidently forsworn, soon became a regular practice. Two pages after his promise of neutrality Coleridge in a news article drops a footnote denouncing a ministerial fallacy.[3] His most usual mode of intervening, however, is the use of mechanical indicators—italics, capitals, exclamation points. This last device, which had its heyday in the eighteenth and nineteenth centuries, Coleridge employed with great frequency. A notable example is a footnote consisting simply of five exclamation points.[4] Likewise, he was a heavy user of italics. Almost every reprint of debates produced a number of them, very often pointing up the absurdity, perfidy, or enormity of the statement thus emphasised. Degrees of emphasis are typographically indicated in the debate on the loan, where the contractor's profit of £900,000 is set in italics, while the later and larger figure for such profits of £2,160,000 is set in large type.[5] Though italics generally denote irony or some other form of censure they sometimes express ordinary emphasis,[6] or favourable attention.[7]

The news matter, though covering the broad fields of domestic and foreign events, was necessarily condensed, for Coleridge could not hope in his few pages to provide detailed reporting. This summarisation was no great disadvantage since he was in competition primarily with provincial weeklies, not metropolitan dailies.[8] In

[1] Cf *The New Morality* lines 328–32:
Couriers and *Stars*, Sedition's Evening Host,
Thou *Morning Chronicle*, and *Morning Post*,
Whether you make the Rights of Man your theme,
Your Country libel, and your God blaspheme,
Or dirt on private worth and virtue throw . . .
Anti-Jacobin No 36 (9 Jul 1798) II 635.

[2] See below, p 14.

[3] See below, p 17n.

[4] See below, p 125n.

[5] See below, p 58.

[6] See e.g. below, p 13.

[7] See e.g. below, p 86.

[8] *The Watchman* was unusual in the quality of its digest of London news. Most provincial weeklies were government papers, many actually in the pay of the Treasury. Others were mainly excuses for agricultural advertisements

general news reporting *The Watchman* considerably exceeds most provincial papers, but in its coverage of local matters falls behind them. Coleridge in serving the needs of the Midland towns obviously could not supply local news for each community. He made no attempt to do so. It was not until the fourth number, for example, that a Birmingham dateline appeared, and then only because the Binns-Jones case, to which the dateline applied, involved the application of the Two Acts and so was worthy of national attention.

This absence of local news in *The Watchman*, so clearly based on common sense and necessity,[1] caused dissatisfaction in the Midlands. "In London, & Bristol", Coleridge said, "the Watchman is read for it's original matter, & the News & Debates barely tolerated: the people [at] Liverpool, Manchester, Birmingham &c take [it only] as a Newspaper, & regard the Essays and Poems [as in]truders unwished for & unwelcome. In short, a Subscriber instead of regarding himself as a point in the circumference entitled to some one diverging ray, considers me as the circumference & himself as the Centre to which *all* the rays ought to converge."[2] That being the nature of subscribers in all ages, the problem was vexatious—perhaps in the case of *The Watchman* insoluble, but certainly unsolved.

THE "ESSAY ON FASTS"

The education of Coleridge in the peculiarities of subscribers was accelerated by a contretemps over the "Essay on Fasts" in No 2, dated 9 March, a special national fast-day.[3] The subject seemed safe enough: the setting of fast-days by the Church, an old practice, was uniformly deplored by all Dissenting sects, which formed the great bulk of *Watchman* readers. It was a custom redolent of formalism, if not of popery. Here was a congenial subject, but Coleridge erupted in a flow of high spirits and raucous humour that startled his sober readers. The incident discloses an aspect of Coleridge's nature usually hidden; we see a bold, gay, satirical person who must have been well known to his friends, but whom we as his readers seldom meet. Granted that the essay is unsuitable and wrong in tone; yet

—for the sale of land, horses, seed, etc —with occasional reports of livestock auctions and such matters.

[1] And perhaps caution. From gaol Montgomery wrote to warn the editor of the *Iris* "to be particularly careful in the Sheffield news not to insert any *home occurrence* without the most indubitable authority". To J. P. Smith 1 May 1796: John Holland and James Everett *Memoirs of James Montgomery* (7 vols 1854–6) I 264.

[2] C to Poole 11 Apr 1796: *CL* I 202. Cf Cottle *E Rec* I 156–7.

[3] See below, pp 51–5.

it is rather refreshing and briskly conveys a serious point, namely, that the national fasts were imposed by an upper class, whose fast-day meals would be feasts to the lower classes.

Coleridge's facetious sally produced frowns among his pious friends, and he was at once, and repeatedly, repentant. "What so many men wiser and better than myself think a solemn subject ought not to have been treated ludicrously".[1] In the *Biographia* he said that the fast-day essay, "with a most censurable application of a text from Isaiah for its motto, lost me near five hundred of my subscribers at one blow".[2] At the time the damage was expressed in more moderate terms: "The Essay on Fasting has not promoted my work".[3] It may have been to counteract the effects of his unseasonable humour that in the next issue he attacked the "modern patriots".[4] Where he had in the fast-day article come close to the freethinker's scoffing at miracles, in "Modern Patriotism" he insisted on the necessity of a belief in God and immortality. His insistence was quite sincere, for he held a settled conviction that only faith in a future state could sustain in this life the practice of altruism.

POETRY IN *THE WATCHMAN*

As would be expected of an eighteenth-century miscellany, *The Watchman* is well stocked with verse—some written by other poets. An examination of the purposes of this verse will shed light upon what Coleridge regarded as the function of *The Watchman*. The use there of his own verse was restricted by the fact that *The Watchman*, as a literary vehicle, was in competition with *Poems on Various Subjects*, the publication of which impended.[5] The readers of *The Watchman* and of the *Poems* were likely to be the same persons and unlikely to tolerate unlimited duplication of material. Since Coleridge had made his selections for the 1796 *Poems* before he began *The Watchman*, we may reasonably suppose that they represented his best work and that he used in his miscellany such culls as had, from want of quality or harmony of tone, been deemed unfit for his volume. Undoubtedly, he wished to maintain in both works a high standard of excellence, for he valued his name as a poet—but the need to fill *The Watchman* was a pressing one, and he could not afford to be too nice.

[1] C to Edwards 20 Mar 1796: *CL* I 191.

[2] *BL* ch 10 (1907) I 119–20. For the motto, see below, p 51.

[3] C to Edwards 20 Mar 1796: *CL* I 191.

[4] See below, pp 98–100.

[5] The volume of poems actually appeared on 16 Apr, between Nos 6 and 7 of *The Watchman*.

In No 1 Coleridge used a part of his own contribution to Southey's *Joan of Arc*; in No 2, a translation from the Latinist Casimir Sarbiewski, intended for his book of translations from the modern Latin poets; in No 3 his *Elegy Imitated from Akenside*, previously published in the *Morning Chronicle* and not to reappear until *Sibylline Leaves* (1817), *The Hour When We Shall Meet Again*, which later was published in the *Poems* of 1797 and 1803, and another poem, *Lines on the Portrait of a Lady*, which I suppose to be Coleridge's, though neither before nor after included in his work. Nor did he claim elsewhere, either, *The Early Year's Fast-flying Vapours Stray* and *A Morning Effusion* in No 4, the latter almost certainly his, though signed "G.A.U.N.T.".

The Watchman poetry pleased readers, as witness Coleridge's comment on 30 March:

> I have received two or three letters from different Anonymi requesting me to give more Poetry—. One of them writes—"Sir! I detest your principles, your prose I think so so—; but your poetry is so exquisitely beautiful, so gorgeously sublime, that I take in your *Watchman* solely on account of it—In Justice therefore to me & some others of my stamp I intreat you to give us more Verse & less democratic scurrility—
>
> Your admirer not
> Esteemer."[1]

In No 5 *Recollection* is a curiosity; it consists of passages drawn together from various poems in such a fashion that James Dykes Campbell treats it in his edition of Coleridge's *Poetical Works* (1893), as Coleridge does here, as a separate poem, yet it contains no original lines. To No 6 Coleridge contributed his *Lines on Observing a Blossom*, which is dated 1 February 1796 and so was too late to be included in *Poems on Various Subjects*, but was in all subsequent editions.

More significant are the poems that Coleridge included in both the 1796 volume and the miscellany, showing by this deliberate duplication, that he considered them indispensable to a proper representation of his views. The first of these, which appears in No 1, is entitled *To a Young Lady, with a Poem on the French Revolution.* Though the poem is here addressed to Sara, Coleridge had sent it, in 1794, with a copy of his and Southey's play, *The Fall of Robespierre*, to Ann Brunton, an actress with whom he was engaged in a mild flirtation.[2] It may have existed even before 1794 in a different version, apostrophising a different lady, but in its present form the poem

[1] To Poole: *CL* I 195.

[2] Then, in line 41 the words "Nor, Sara" had read "Nor, Brunton". See also below, p 27 and n 1.

unquestionably contains the views of Coleridge on a great and portentous subject. It traces a pattern of change: a state first of solitary sensibility and meditation, followed by involvement in political fever, succeeded by another withdrawal into the haunts of peaceful virtue, where he seeks the healing powers of love, goodness, and gladness. This was the sort of oscillation or rhythmical reaction that Coleridge had already experienced in the retreat to Clevedon Cottage and was to continue throughout his life until his final retirement to Highgate.[1] Each impulse, rather than negating, seemed to create the other. But the theme of *To a Young Lady*, though founded on biography, does not end there; it concerns itself primarily with the plight of the humanitarian consciousness. One whose sensibilities seemed charged to the point of distention by the fact of the death of a single person, and that person dead from natural causes, is confronted with the death of thousands who did not die in the course of nature but by the hand of fellow-men. And, paradoxically, the same feelings that led him to weep for one rouse him to exult over the death of myriads, because his eyes were fixed upon the ultimate good of all men. Yet the convictions of the mind, though valid, could not still the pangs of sympathy, and "my heart aches, tho' Mercy struck the blow". The theme of the poem, however personal, has a general application. In the first issue of *The Watchman* it serves to strengthen the effect of Coleridge's manifesto of his beliefs concerning France.

The planning of this first issue results in a cumulative and collaborative effect of considerable power. Though Coleridge moves from argument to argument, he moves as one in his native element, and he never forgets his essential purpose. He begins with a review of the motions for peace in Parliament, showing the shifting and shifty defences of the government's case for war; he then crosses the Channel for a sampling of French opinion and finds there a high state of morale, which confutes the ministry's prediction of the imminent fall of French power; home from that excursion, he reviews Burke's *Letter to a Noble Lord* and depicts Burke's views on France as the ravings of an overwrought mind; next, under the heading "Foreign Intelligence", he describes the timorous reluctance of Pitt's ally, Austria; he follows this with a letter from the venerable Washington rejoicing in the liberation of the French people, and concludes the issue with an account of a debate in the Commons in which the

[1] The alternation of "surge and recoil" is discussed in Woodring *Politics in the Poetry of Coleridge* 62–3.

Opposition exposed the carelessness and profusion of British war-finance. His strategy throughout is calculated less to defend the French than to attack the British ministry and, by insinuation or assertion, reveal its greed, love of power, insincerity, and ineffectiveness. As a part of this strategy, *To a Young Lady* recapitulates much of Coleridge's argument by showing us how Pity can exculpate France, since *her* bloody deeds were done for the sake of ultimate justice, but must incriminate the ministry whose war is only the defence of the indefensible.

Coleridge's principal poem in *The Watchman* is entitled *The Present State of Society*[1] and forms a part of a larger poem earlier called a "Nativity" poem and now *Religious Musings*. The poem, begun in December 1794, had by the autumn of 1795 grown to "not quite three hundred Lines".[2] Since the section in *The Watchman* makes up lines 279–378 in the poem, we may assume that it was written in late 1795 or early 1796; actually, the poem as a whole was not complete until after *The Watchman* was begun. Coleridge considered it, as his repeated assertions show, his most considerable poem and probably thought it to date his greatest achievement in any field.[3] Perhaps a variety of reasons impelled him toward philosophical verse. Earlier, he had appealed to his readers through sympathy, and he defended his poems against the charge of "querulous egotism" by saying: "The communicativeness of our nature leads us to describe our own sorrows; in the endeavor to describe them intellectual activity is exerted; and by a benevolent law of our nature from intellectual activity a pleasure results which is gradually associated and mingles as a corrective with the painful subject of the description."[4] This is David Hartley's associationism, and to Hartley's contemporary, Akenside, he was indebted for the motto to *Religious Musings*:

> What tho' first
> In years unseason'd, I attun'd the lay
> To idle Passion and unreal Woe?
> Yet serious Truth her empire o'er my song
> Hath now asserted; Falsehood's evil brood,
> Vice and deceitful Pleasure, she at once
> Excluded, and by Fancy's careless toil
> Drew to the better cause![5]

---

[1] In No 2; see below, pp 64–7.

[2] C to Cottle [Oct 1795]: *CL* I 162–3.

[3] See, among other references in his letters, *CL* I 197, 203, 205.

[4] Preface to *Poems* (1796): *PW* (EHC) II 1135–6.

[5] Mark Akenside *The Pleasures of the Imagination* [second version] bk I lines 49–59 (adapted): *Poems* (1772) 129.

Religious Musings occupies for a time a central position in Coleridge's thought in that it represents the sort of poetry he now intended to cultivate, as illustrated later in 1796 by *The Destiny of Nations* and to some extent by the *Ode to the Departing Year*; it is also the key to *The Watchman*. More deeply even than the introductory essay it lays bare Coleridge's core of belief, or the vantage-point from which he surveyed the events recorded in the pages of *The Watchman*. In brief, the poem states that the property of the nation has been usurped by the few, leaving the many in want, as they are also deprived of the blessings of knowledge; Scripture and the recent events in France combine to tell us that the day of tyranny is almost over, and oppressors, whether they wear the scarlet robes of rank or the black robes of priesthood, will suffer a well-merited but ghastly punishment; where now exists a "*blest* Society" in the present (Coleridge's ironical italics) there will be a "blest Future" in which man will be self-governing, living in love and equality. Coleridge is still a pantisocrat, still convinced that the source of social evil lay in the institution of property.[1] Faith and piety, by casting out fear and bringing in love, can create a society which commends itself to the heart and to the head. By placing the resource of poetry in the service of such a cause, one raised rather than lowered the dignity of art.

REVIEWS IN *THE WATCHMAN*

In his introductory essay to *The Watchman* Coleridge expresses dissatisfaction with the practices of reviewers writing for the London papers, specifically deploring back-scratching, the venting of spleen, and the settling of personal quarrels. He promises that his remoteness from the metropolis will confer upon him detachment and purer criteria. He adds that higher standards will result from the necessity of reviewing fewer, and therefore better, books, and here, by his mention of Combe's edition of Horace, he leads one to suppose that he will review belles-lettres.[2] In fact, his reviews, which, indeed, were few enough—only four in the ten numbers—were subordinated to the purposes of politics and humane legislation. In No 1 he reviews Burke's latest pamphlet, *A Letter to a Noble Lord*, commending Burke's eloquence and condemning, as I have previously noted, his opinions on revolutionary France. In No 3 he comments upon Dr Beddoes's *Letter to Pitt on . . . the Present Scarcity*, a short piece

[1] Cf *CN* I 81, 103, 161 [f], and 174 [21a].

[2] See below, p 15 and n 2.

in which Beddoes sketched briefly some practical measures for the relief of the needy, censured Pitt, and warned the rich not to oppress the poor to the point of revolt. In No 5 the review consists largely of quotations illustrating the means by which the ingenious and benevolent Count Rumford improved the lot of the poor in Munich and introduced measures to render the Bavarian army useful in peacetime as well as more effective in military science. In No 9 he returns to the work of Dr Beddoes—this time *An Essay on the Public Merits of Mr. Pitt*—and combines, with the function of the review, the function of the leading editorial; though the review contains extensive quotations, it is deserving of study because it results in a statement of Coleridge's own principles of government. Of the four reviews, only the first and the last reflect Coleridge's real powers. The other two are the products of hasty composition.

COLERIDGE'S ESSAYS

To most but not all numbers of *The Watchman* Coleridge contributed an essay of some length. A number of these are valuable in giving a picture of Coleridge's mind in the mid-90's. Both the editorial introduction in No 1 and the lamented "Essay on Fasts" in No 2 are fresh essays, written specifically for *The Watchman*, but the essay on the ancient Germans, in No 3, is a joint fashioning by Coleridge and Southey and dates, in part, from a lecture of 1795. In No 4 Coleridge relinquishes the first page to a dispatch from the Rev John Edwards—an urgent news article on the arrest of Binns and Jones; his own important essay on the slave-trade, later in this issue, is reworked from his lecture of 16 June 1795, in Bristol.[1] In the next three numbers Coleridge writes no essay, but in No 8 there appears his "Remonstrance to the French Legislators", in which, startled by the revelation of French nationalism, he meets the new state of things candidly and moves toward the renunciation that he was eventually to express in *France: an Ode*. This essay is a first-rate example of Coleridge's political eloquence, and one that, later, he would surely have reprinted had it not demonstrated, by the very shock of its disillusion, how deeply he had been committed to the principles of the French Revolution. In No 9 he editoralises, as we have seen, through the medium of a review, and in No 10 again borrows from himself in his essay on the surrender by the Danes of their liberty.

[1] The text of this lecture is reproduced in *Lects 1795*. The debate in the Commons on the abolition of the slave-trade is reported at length in the same No 4.

As badly as he needed good materials, Coleridge did not cannibalise from either *Conciones ad Populum* or *The Plot Discovered*, though they were works in which he justly took pride. Plainly the reason was that these works were still in print, and their sale was being actively promoted. They served as reinforcements to the message of *The Watchman*. In his Prospectus he had identified himself as the "author of *Addresses to the People, A Plot Discovered*".

Coleridge was quickly responsive to timely issues that lent themselves as a kind of provocation to the release of pent-up speech. When such an issue arose he showed great talent in mobilising his powers for an incisive comment that made his essay successful—full of fervour and light and confidence. For essays requiring meditation and study, and for elaborate literary efforts, he used previously composed pieces. *The Watchman* was very nearly a single-handed performance, and Coleridge simply lacked the time for leisurely composition.

CONTRIBUTIONS FROM OTHERS

The octavo form of *The Watchman*, permitting it to be bound at the end of the year as "an Annual Register", would have for writers, Coleridge expected, an advantage over "more perishable publications, as the vehicle of their effusions".[1] His appeal for contributions, to be sent post-paid, was repeated in the first issue and met with only moderate response. Some of his friends, however, exerted themselves on his behalf. Charles Lamb, his erstwhile schoolfellow at Christ's Hospital, sent in nothing of his own but may have sent *The Braes of Yarrow*, by John Logan, with which Coleridge was greatly pleased.[2] Of his Cambridge acquaintances, only William Frend, as far as we know, became a contributor. Robert Southey, away in Portugal, was no longer a friend—though he *was* a brother-in-law; in his absence Coleridge borrowed from his epic, *Joan of Arc*, on which he, Coleridge, felt he had acquired a lien by having composed some of its passages; he also used the essay on Germany that he and Southey had written together.

Newer friends were more helpful. John Edwards (1768–1808), the Unitarian divine whom he had met on his subscription tour, was so useful to Coleridge in the spring and summer of 1796 that his

[1] See below, p 5.

[2] Ms evidence in J. D. Campbell marginalia in Duke University Library. However, in the course of his mention and praise of the poem in his letter to C c 24–31 May 1796, Lamb betrays no sign of such participation; see *LL* I 9. But he quotes six lines from the poem in a later letter to C, 14 Jun 1796, and four lines from it in a letter to C in Feb 1797: see *LL* I 30, 94.

disappearance thereafter from Coleridge's life is surprising. At Coleridge's request he sent, under the name "Phocion", the instalments of the Binns-Jones affair and also the speech of Thomas Erskine; he may have been the channel of communicating a poem by his friend William Roscoe. Phocion's pieces are still of value, for they were not only timely but in some cases unique. A few strangers sent in contributions: a lively poem came from James Bisset, who, like Edwards, was from Birmingham, as was "E. N", who supplied a poem. ("The Birminghamites are my best Friends.")[1] We do not know the identity of "Patriot", "Henry", or "Bristoliensis", nor, except by easy conjecture in the last case, their places of origin. Nor have I even a guess as to the identity of "H. F. I.", who warned of the evils of dram-drinking. From neighbouring Stowey, Thomas Poole sent one item to *The Watchman.*

We can identify only two contributors from Bristol: one, the mad and brilliant William Gilbert, author of an economic essay in No 5 and a charming bit of verse; the other, Dr Thomas Beddoes, who was to remain Coleridge's staunch friend until his death in 1808. Beddoes sent several items, and Coleridge reviewed two of his timely pamphlets. All Beddoes's works, like the actions of his life, reveal a deep concern for humanity and considerable talents with which to serve it. To his merit as a translator of foreign scientific works, a leading experimental scientist, and a pioneer exponent of Kant's philosophy, he added daily toil as a practitioner of medicine. In his practice he learned much of the sufferings of the poor, whom he tried to aid in a number of publications dealing with preventive medicine and recommending radical solutions for the relief of their distress. "To announce a work from the pen of Dr. Beddoes", Coleridge said, "is to inform the benevolent in every city and parish, that they are appointed agents to some new and practicable scheme for increasing the comforts or alleviating the miseries of their fellow-creatures."[2]

EXCERPTS FROM THE PRESS AND BOOKS

Lacking an adequate flow of contributions, Coleridge had to go foraging.[3] He gathered materials from newspapers so extensively

[1] C to Edwards 20 Mar 1796: *CL* I 191–2.

[2] See below, p 100.

[3] It is disappointing that Wordsworth contributed nothing to *The Watchman*, as he was to do later to *The Friend*; but he was absorbed by *Salisbury Plain*, which, as the Pinney papers show, C was reading during *The Watchman* period. Pinney MSS,

that one anonymous correspondent, a "pseudo-Samaritan", as Coleridge called him, wrote: "Alas! alas! COLERIDGE, the digito-monstratus of Cambridge, commenced Polit[ical] Newsmonger, Newspaper-paragraph-thief, Re-retailer of retailed Scurrility, keeper of [an] Asylum for old, poor, and decayed Jokes"[1]—as if journalists could live without taking in each other's washing. Such materials were in the public domain; one helped oneself; and the quality of Coleridge's jokes was as high as that of newspapers generally, though a little less broad. A good deal of extracted material came from magazines, anthologies, and miscellanea; sometimes the sources of this material were named and sometimes not. No one accused Coleridge of dishonesty; even Pseudo-Samaritan's reproof implies not that he was doing wrong but that he was content to be a hack. Yet Coleridge nearly always uses his borrowed miscellanea toward the end of illumination. Even items that appear, at a glance, to be mere space-fillers may on inspection prove to be details in a significant pattern in which selection and juxtaposition are modes of commentary. For example, the Wickham-Barthélemy correspondence on the peace negotiations is followed by an article on the horrors of war, and the article demonstrating the civilised behaviour of the so-called uncivilised Russians sharpens the satire of the article on the uncivilised custom of duelling among the so-called civilised Britons.

Most of Coleridge's friends hoped devoutly that by sheer genius and the energy generated by the momentum of his project he would be able to keep *The Watchman* going, but some of them—often those who knew him best—were less than sanguine about his ability to sustain steady editorial burdens. The prophecy of his Cambridge friend, G. L. Tuckett, is classic: "You know how subject Coleridge is to fits of idleness. Now, I'll lay any wager . . . that after three or four numbers the sheets will contain nothing but Parliamentary Debates, and Coleridge will add a note at the bottom of the page: 'I should think myself deficient in my duty to the Public if I did not give these *interesting* Debates at *full* length.' "[2] S. F. Johnson suggests that, joking aside, something of this sort did happen: that during its course *The Watchman* suffered a progressive decline in original matter, and that its failure was due not, as Coleridge ex-

---

Bristol University Library. See Mary Moorman *William Wordsworth: The Early Years* (Oxford 1957) 291.

[1] C to Edwards 20 Mar 1796: *CL* I 191–2.

[2] *CL* I 192n.

plained, to the fact that "the Work does not pay its expences",[1] but to Coleridge's "indolence and loss of interest".[2] The Coleridge indolence—or is procrastination a better term?—is almost as famous as the Hapsburg jaw. In his letters Coleridge laments it in tones of bitter remorse—and we would be fatuous if we insisted that the failing did not exist and laid all Coleridge's troubles to the bitcheries of Fortune.[3] But in this instance—that is, as applied to his conduct of *The Watchman*—indolence is an inappropriate word. When we examine *The Watchman*, noting, with greater certainty than was formerly possible, the sources of its contents, we find in it evidence of much systematic labour and regard for excellence. And when we consider the odds against which Coleridge worked in the spring of '96—his youth and inexperience, his unequal marriage, his Fricker connexions, his financial difficulties, and his constant longing for free time in which to write poetry—we may marvel more that he brought out *The Watchman* at all than that he ceased to do so after its tenth issue.

The material in *The Watchman* can be divided into four categories: (1) original matter written by Coleridge especially for *The Watchman*; (2) matter by Coleridge already on hand; (3) matter written by contributors; (4) excerpts (not by Coleridge) taken from matter printed elsewhere and reprinted without change or with slight changes. In original matter No 1 of *The Watchman* is the richest (twelve pages, or more than a third of the issue), a fact that is not surprising since Coleridge, while accumulating material for this issue, had not been hampered by the "quotidian bustle" that began after the miscellany was launched; No 10 is poorest, which, likewise, is to be expected since Coleridge had decided by the time of its preparation to drop the work and his heart was not in it. In Nos 2 through 9 the amount of original matter fluctuates, but not in a downward curve: 5—5—10½—7½—6—3½—3½—7½ pages. The matter in the second category—drafts upon Coleridge's stock of mss—reaches a peak of six pages in the third issue and then levels off to a page or two in each subsequent issue. Matter in the third category—contributions—reaches its height in the fourth and fifth issues and then again in the tenth issue.

In Tuckett's joke parliamentary debates were to be the principal

[1] See below, p 374.

[2] S. F. Johnson "Coleridge's *The Watchman:* Decline and Fall" *RES* N.S. IV (1953), 147–8.

[3] See also the Prospectus to *The Friend*: ". . . this Want of Perseverance has been produced in the Main by an Over-activity of Thought, modified by a constitutional Indolence . . ." *Friend* (*CC*) II 16.

stuffing of *The Watchman*, but debates as Coleridge usually handled them—digesting them and adding his own comment—did not provide an easy way to fill space. None of the debates is reported exactly as it appeared in any of the London dailies. Cottle reminisced that this "profitless part of the work gave the most trouble to the compiler. Its dulness, I know, fretted Mr. Coleridge exceedingly. It was indeed the Hunter bearing the Pack Saddle."[1] The easy way to fill space was to use undigested and unrevised excerpts—the matter contained in our fourth category—and these bulk large in the later issues of *The Watchman*.[2] Their presence need not indicate that Coleridge was soldiering, however fagged he may have been. Unused as he was to editing a periodical, he seemed to have got the hang of it, and there is evidence that *The Watchman* not only came out on time, but also with No 3 was being sent by carriage to subscriber cities the very day it was published.[3] The large number of unrevised excerpts does indicate that Coleridge had used up his backlog of suitable matter; that he had not the leisure in which to compose much fresh material; and that contributions did not arrive in the quantity he hoped for. One reason for the failure of *The Watchman* to attract many contributors was its inability to pay anything for material accepted; another was its not being long enough in existence to engage the loyalty of a substantial body of subscribers, who might have formed the habit of sending in letters or other items for publication.

WATCHMAN WATCHED IN VAIN

The time came when Coleridge could no longer ignore the truth that his earlier doubts about the chances of *The Watchman* to succeed had been all too cogent. According to Cottle's later testimony, Coleridge's joys of editing decreased, perplexities multiplied, and

[1] Cottle *E Rec* I 156. However great the tedium, C well understood the necessity of including the debates. "The country was interested in the proceedings of Parliament to a degree almost inconceivable to-day, and the right to publish the parliamentary debates gave newspaper proprietors almost unrestricted access to their most important single source of news. When Parliament was in session, so enormous was the public appetite for reports of the debates, these, together with advertisements, practically monopolized the space." A. Aspinall *Politics and the Press c. 1780–1850* (1949 35.

[2] "Unrevised" is perhaps an unfair word. See, for example, what Coleridge has done with two excerpts printed in No 9, the anecdote about Boissy the poet and the prose renderings of Estonian poetry, below, pp 313–15, 316–19.

[3] C to Edwards 12 Mar [1796]: *CL* I 188.

subscribers rapidly fell off. "One pitiful subscriber of fourpence, every eighth day, thought his boy 'did not improve much under it' ".[1] On the day No 9 was published, 5 May, Coleridge wrote to Poole: "It is not pleasant, Thomas Poole! to have worked 14 weeks for nothing—*for nothing*—nay—to have given the Public in addition to that toil 5 & 40 pounds!—When I began the Watchman, I had forty pounds worth of paper *given me*—yet *with this* I shall not have received a farthing at the end of the Quarter of the Year.... In short, my tradesman's Bill[s] for the Watchman, including what Paper I have bought since the seventh number, the Printing, &c—amount to exactly five pounds more than the whole amount of my receipts".[2] Cottle, writing years later, concurs entirely: "It was a losing concern, altogether, and I was willing, and did bear, uncomplaining, my proportion of the loss."[3]

So, with its tenth number, *The Watchman* ceased publication. In an address to his readers, on the last page, Coleridge gave his reasons for dropping the work, complimented the *Cambridge Intelligencer* and the new *Monthly Magazine*, and wrote that "it must be attributed to defect of ability, not of inclination or effort, if the words of the Prophet be altogether applicable to me, '*O Watchman! thou hast watched in vain!*' "[4] "It was with much concern", wrote one of the subscribers, William Roscoe, author of the *Life of Lorenzo de' Medici*, "I found he had adopted the resolution of discontinuing his periodical paper of the 'Watchman.' . . . I have no doubt that the paper in question would, if continued, have been of very extensive utility . . .".[5]

Coleridge was left in debt to Biggs, his printer, and, otherwise, in unhappy financial circumstances; but Poole and some of his other friends subscribed to a fund for his benefit.[6] This fund, which was expected to continue annually to the amount of thirty-five or forty pounds, rescued Coleridge from a needy state that was bad enough, he said, to please even "the most Trinitarian Anathematizer, or rampant Philo-despot".[7]

Surprisingly, as a sequel to this story of calamity, *The Watchman* almost came to life again. The details are lost: did some patron

[1] Cottle *E Rec* I 157.

[2] *CL* I 208.

[3] Cottle *E Rec* I 162.

[4] See below, p 375.

[5] Roscoe to Edwards 20 Jul 1796: Henry Roscoe *The Life of William Roscoe* (2 vols 1833) I 232.

[6] See *CL* I 210, n to Letter 125. Poole, however, had drafted the plan of the fund as early as 28 Mar, three days after *Watchman* No 4 had appeared. See *Poole* I 142.

[7] To Poole 5 May 1796: *CL* I 208.

come forward, or was there a sufficiently lively chorus of regret from subscribers?[1] At any rate, Lamb wrote to Coleridge in late May: "I am glad you resume the Watchman—change the name, leave out all articles of News, and whatever things are peculiar to News Papers, and confine yourself to Ethics, verse, criticism, or, rather do not confine yourself. Let your plan be as diffuse as the Spectator, and I'll answer for it the work prospers."[2] But as obscurely as it arose, the plan vanished, and Coleridge waited more than a dozen years before he carried out Lamb's suggestion, including the suitable change of name, in *The Friend*.

COLERIDGE'S PRINTER

No printer's name appears on *The Watchman*, but it was Nathaniel Biggs.[3] Biggs was to serve as Coleridge's printer many times. He probably printed *Poems* (1796), certainly *Poems* (1797), and, as Biggs and Cottle, *Lyrical Ballads* (1798), and, having migrated to Crane-court, Fleet-street in London, *Poems* (1803). In the meantime he had printed Southey's *Annual Anthology* of 1800, in which Coleridge had many poems. If printers wrote books they could no doubt tell harrowing tales, but as it is, in the catalogue of Coleridge's miseries "the repeated and most injurious blunders of my Printer" form a prominent part.[4] Delay was another grievance; however, "My printing promises to go on with clock-work regularity—and you will have Thursday's 'Watchman' on Thursday" (i.e. No 3, dated 17 March).[5] We hear no more of a failure to meet schedule, if indeed it was a failure to meet the printing schedule. Coleridge's complaints seem to be centred on the *delivery* of the copies to the subscribers.[6] On 11 April it appears that the schedule was being

[1] Poole's younger brother, Richard, "having lately been at Stowey, and seeing my brother's several numbers of your *Watchman*, with which I was much delighted", wrote to C as late as 3 May to "trouble [him] to send me in future two of the numbers weekly, one for myself, the other for a friend here". *Poole* I 137.

[2] *LL* I 10. See also the report of subscribers to C's *Poems* to compensate him "for his disappointment in The Watchman": *CL* I 219 and n 1.

[3] *CL* I 202, 368, 387.

[4] To Poole 30 Mar 1796: *CL* I 194. Biggs's "blunders" were, however, no more serious than those of the typical printer of a provincial periodical. Though Southey, too, became vexed with Biggs, it was apparently because of his "slow pace"; see his letter to Charles Danvers 20 Jan 1801: *S Letters* (Curry) I 237.

[5] C to Edwards 12 Mar [1796]: *CL* I 188.

[6] See *CL* I 194, 196 (C sent twenty-five copies of No 5 to Smith of Sheffield a day earlier than the printed date of the issue), 210 as well as 188, the letter to Edwards, above. Unlike provincial newspapers, which were delivered to subscribers by the post (at

maintained, for he wrote to Poole: "I have sent the fifth, sixth [published that day], & *part* of the seventh number"—the last to be published eight days away.[1]

The end of *The Watchman* found Coleridge in debt to Biggs, apparently for the amount of five pounds, according to Coleridge's letters of May 1796 and early 1798.[2] In the light of these specific statements it is difficult to understand Coleridge's later assertion in the *Biographia Literaria* that at the time of the death of *The Watchman* "I should have been inevitably thrown into jail by my Bristol printer, who refused to wait even for a month for a sum between eighty and ninety pounds". From this situation he says he was rescued by a "dear friend", meaning Poole.[3] Cottle, in his *Early Recollections*, attributes the statement to a defect of memory. "The plain fact is, I purchased the whole of the paper for the 'Watchman', allowing Mr. C. to have it at prime cost, and receiving small sums from Mr. C. occasionally in liquidation." The entire printing cost, said Cottle, "came to only thirty-five pounds. The paper amounted to much more than the printing."[4] But Cottle's memory, too, was defective, for at the time of *The Watchman* Coleridge wrote that he had been given forty pounds' worth of paper and had bought paper since the seventh number.[5] Perhaps Coleridge, like Cottle, was including in his loss from *The Watchman* venture those sums owing from Parsons, the London bookseller, who never paid a farthing for 200 copies of each issue he sold and never paid as well for the many copies of *Poems* (1796) and *Joan of Arc* he also received and sold.[6] In fact, Cottle claimed that he had also never been paid for all the copies of *Poems* and *Joan* sent to the north, apparently to *Watchman* subscribers or booksellers.[7] Coleridge, too, may have been thinking of such matters when he arrived at the figure of eighty or ninety pounds. But there is no evidence that Biggs refused to wait for his money—in 1798 Coleridge still notes that he owes Biggs five pounds: "Parsons, the Bookseller, owes me more than this considerably; but he is a rogue, & will not pay me."[8]

no cost, for the wrapper of a newspaper was printed with the name of some MP as a frank), copies of *The Watchman* had to bear the carriage costs of delivery. Wilberforce, e.g., had been used on the *Sheffield Register* up to Jan 1794, and when he withdrew use of his name, that of Grey was substituted. See Holland and Everett *Memoirs of James Montgomery* I 163–4n.

[1] *CL* I 202.

[2] *CL* I 208, 368.

[3] *BL* ch 10 (1907) I 120–1.

[4] Cottle *E Rec* I 162–3.

[5] See above, C's letter to Poole, p lv.

[6] Cottle *E Rec* I 163.

[7] Ibid 163–4.

[8] C to John Prior Estlin [6 Jan 1798]:

COLERIDGE IN *THE WATCHMAN*

If we use the episode of *The Watchman* as a gauge of the firmness with which Coleridge propounded his true beliefs, we find, in general, frankness rather than evasion, and restraint rather than timidity. It is true that he withheld much of his fire on such specific issues as the iniquities of the Two Acts; but so did the whole reform-party. He was not too prudent to speak out on what he called "first principles", nor to challenge received opinion in every issue of *The Watchman*. He charged the Church of England with teaching hatred in the name of the God of love (p 11) and ridiculed the miracles of the New Testament (p 52); he called the Two Acts breaches of the Constitution (p 13); he declared that the possessions of the rich rightfully belonged to the poor (p 64); he predicted that by providential means kings and potentates would shortly be overthrown, and a good thing, too (pp 65–6); he quoted with approval a declaration in favour of the rights of man (p 372) and that nations other than France and the United States, which had been "too long the dupes of perfidious kings, nobles, and priests, will eventually recover their rights" (p 373); he urged the enlargement of the right of suffrage in England (p 209); he asserted that in the purer and more radical days of the French Revolution "the victories of Frenchmen" were "the victories of Human Nature" (p 270); and he likened Pitt to Judas Iscariot and hoped that he would be struck by a thunderbolt (p 167). But if these extracts, chosen as instances of candour, give an impression of rashness or bombast, as well they might, the impression is false. The tone of *The Watchman* was prevailingly temperate—kept so, I think, because Coleridge believed that the knowledge of truth was best disseminated in a climate of thoughtfulness and in "cool and guarded" language.

*

THE TEXT OF THIS EDITION

The Watchman consists of the ten numbers, each number containing thirty-two pages, printed on two sheets. All copies known to me are in a bound state. The pagination is continuous throughout the first six numbers, but between Nos 6 and 7 there is a gap of four pages:

CL I 368. In 1809 Biggs became a subscriber to C's later periodical, *The Friend*: see *Friend* (*CC*) II 415.

THE

WATCHMAN.

No. I.

TUESDAY, MARCH 1, 1796.

Published by the Author, S. T. COLERIDGE,

Bristol:

And fold by the Bookfellers and Newfcarriers in Town and Country.

THAT ALL MAY KNOW THE TRUTH;

AND THAT THE TRUTH MAY MAKE US FREE!

AMONG the calamities which eventually have produced the moft important bleffings, we may particularize the capture of Conftantinople by the Turks in 1453. The number of learned Greeks, whom this event drove into the Weft, in conjunction with the recent difcovery of printing, kindled the love of knowledge in Europe, and fupplied opportunities for the attainment of it. Princes emulated each other in the patronage of men of ability, and endeavoured to excite a fpirit of literature among their fubjects, by every encouragement which their rude policy fuggefted, or the genius of the age would permit. The firft fcanty twilight of knowledge was fufficient to fhew what horrors had refulted from ignorance; and no experience had yet taught them that general illumination is incompatible with undelegated power. This incipient diffufion of truth was aided by the Lutheran fchifm, which roufed the Clergy of Europe from their long doze of fenfuality, and by the keen goading of religious controverfy forced each party into literary exertion. And after the Reformation it was fortunate for the interefts of Britain, that the Puritans, her firft partizans for civil and religious freedom, were greatly inferior to their antagonifts in acquired knowledge. The govern-

B ment

3. *The Watchman* (1796) No I.
The first page of the first printing. Cf p 9, the text of the second printing.

No 6 ends on p 192, and No 7 begins on [p 197]. Thereafter the pagination is again continuous to the end. *The Watchman* exists in but one edition,[1] and one printing, except for the first number, of which there are two issues. The second issue of No 1 (also dated 1 March) possibly came about as the result of a reorder from Parsons, the London agent for *The Watchman*. In a letter to Cottle, Coleridge quotes Parsons as conveying readers' compliments on the poetry in *The Watchman* and asking for "100 of the first number".[2] E. L. Griggs dates this letter "early April" because in it Coleridge also requests Cottle to send if possible some copies of *Poems* (1796) if he can get them ready "by to morrow", and the volume was not published until 16 April. But as the *Poems* was in type long before the preface and notes were added, Coleridge was probably willing to send it early in March in this form, as he did to Benjamin Flower on 1 April.[3] To accept the early April rather than an early March date for Coleridge's letter to Cottle, we should have to accept the improbability that Parsons passed over the intervening four issues or so (No 5 was published on 2 April), to reorder the first number of *The Watchman*. It seems more likely that he was reordering the then current issue, i.e. No 1, dated 1 March. The reorder would have coincided with Parsons's advertisement.[4]

This edition of *The Watchman* reproduces Coleridge's text, excluding palpable printer's errors. The misspellings of (usually foreign) names and places have been reproduced from Coleridge, as he reproduced them from the London newspapers. Conventional or corrected forms of these names and places are, however, given in footnotes and in the index. The reprinted No 1 has been used as the basic text, for Coleridge revised it both in substance and in punctuation. Except for differences in punctuation, readings from the first printing are recorded in textual notes. While No 5 was being printed, Coleridge made a stop-press emendation in the article on Colonel Cawthorne's trial, adding from the *Sun* a fact not given in the earlier *Times* account.[5] Here, too, the corrected version is given as text, with the original readings recorded in textual notes. At the end of

[1] C reprinted with some alterations an excerpt from his article on the slave-trade (below, pp 130–40) in Southey's *Omniana* (3 vols 1812) II 2–4. Sara Coleridge quoted extensively from *The Watchman* in her collection of her father's journalistic writings, *Essays on His Own Times* (3 vols 1850) I 99–178; but this work has no textual interest.

[2] *CL* I 201. Parsons probably originally ordered 100; see above, p xxxiv.

[3] See *CL* I 196–7 and Cottle *E Rec* II 52.

[4] See below, p 380.

[5] See below, p 187 and n 1.

No 9 Coleridge listed errata within the issue; the corrections have been incorporated into the text.

Two copies of *The Watchman* annotated by Coleridge have come to light: Ashley 2842 in the British Museum and a copy at one time in the possession of the bookseller A. E. Dobell. The corrections and alterations in these copies are recorded in the notes. The only traceable manuscript of *The Watchman* consists of some fragments in the Pierpont Morgan Library (MA 1916). Besides non-*Watchman* matter, these fragments are Patrick O'Fleherty's letter (below, p 203), a part of "An Interesting Narration" (p 238), Thomas Dermody's *An Irregular Ode to the Moon* (p 249), a version of *To a Young Lady* (p 27), and *An Epitaph on an Infant* (p 316). Three of the pieces were copied from the *Anthologia Hibernica* I (Dublin 1793): O'Fleherty's letter, *An Irregular Ode*, and a Latin poem called *Verses Written on the Gate of Bologna* (I 221). The last did not appear in *The Watchman* but was probably copied for use if needed.[1] Significant variants are recorded in the notes. This manuscript is the one EHC calls "MS 4°", describing it as "A collection of early poems in the handwriting of S. T. Coleridge (*circ.* 1796)."[2] It is only partly in his hand; some of the material is written in another hand, possibly Sara's. The manuscript is also referred to in Campbell's edition of the *Poetical Works*.[3]

In an attempt to separate Coleridge's contributions from those of others, a strenuous effort has been made—unfortunately, not always with results—to identify in the footnotes not only the long or self-contained excerpts but even the slightest newspaper report or squib. Sometimes, what sounded authentically like Coleridge's voice turned out to be that of the leader-writer of the *Star*. Except in the sections of each issue devoted to domestic and foreign news, where unidentified items are not likely to be of Coleridge's composition but rather from untraced newspapers, articles not identified as by someone else are presumably his. However, to assign an item to another source is not necessarily to rob it of its significance in the study of Coleridge. That he chose it from among copious, competing materials attached to it some flavour of his own preferences or reactions. And if it contained an idea, or the germ of an idea, it almost certainly became embedded in his capacious and retentive memory.

[1] The presence of non-*Watchman* material, and the relatively clean condition of the mss, seem to show that they were not used as printer's copy, and thus help to explain their preservation.

[2] *PW* (EHC) I xxv.

[3] *PW* (JDC) 562.

PROSPECTUS OF
THE WATCHMAN

That All may know the TRUTH;
And that the TRUTH may make us FREE!![1]

On Friday, the 5th Day of February, 1796,

WILL BE PUBLISHED,

No. I

(PRICE FOUR PENCE)

OF A MISCELLANY

TO BE PUBLISHED EVERY EIGHTH DAY

UNDER THE NAME OF

THE WATCHMAN[2]

BY S. T. COLERIDGE,

AUTHOR OF

ADDRESSES TO THE PEOPLE, A PLOT DISCOVERED,
&c. &c.

The Publishers in the different Towns and Cities
will be specified in future Advertisements.

[1] The motto, adapted from John 8.32, appeared in each issue.

[2] For the title and other details regarding the Prospectus, see above, Introduction, pp xxxii–xxxiii, xxxviii.

PROSPECTUS

IN an enslaved State the Rulers form and supply the opinions of the People. This is the mark by which Despotism is distinguished: for it is the power, by which Despotism is begun and continued.—"*The abuses, that are rooted in all the old Governments of Europe, give such numbers of men such a direct interest in supporting, cherishing, and defending abuses, that no wonder advocates for tyranny of every species are found in every country and almost in every company. What a mass of People in every part of England are some way or other interested in the present representation of the people, in tythes, charters, corporations, monopolies, and taxation! and not merely in the things themselves, but in all the abuses attending them; and how many are there who derive their profit or their consideration in life, not merely from such institutions, but from the evils they engender!*"

ARTHUR YOUNG'S TRAVELS.[1]

Among the most powerful advocates and auxiliaries of abuses we must class (with a few honorable exceptions) the weekly provincial Newspapers, the Editors of which receive the Treasury Prints gratis, and in some instances *with particular paragraphs marked out for their insertion.*—These Papers form the chief, and sometimes the only, reading of that large and important body of men, who living out of towns and cities have no opportunity of hearing calumnies exposed and false statements detected. Thus are Administrations enabled to steal away their Rights and Liberties, either so gradually as to undermine their Freedom without alarming them; or if it be necessary to carry any great point suddenly, to overthrow their Freedom by alarming them against themselves.

A PEOPLE ARE FREE IN PROPORTION AS THEY FORM THEIR OWN OPINIONS. In the strictest sense of the word KNOWLEDGE IS POWER.[2] Without previous illumination a change in the *forms*

[1] Arthur Young *Travels, during the Years 1787, 1788, 1789 . . .* [*in*] *France* (Bury St Edmunds 1792) 540n (slightly altered). Young (1741–1820), in his *Travels*, had shown the pressing need for reform in France. When Pitt in 1793 created the board of agriculture and gave Young the lucrative post of secretary, critics traced a connexion between the post and the change of view reflected in *The Example of France, a Warning to Britain* (1793), in which Young took a strongly pro-government stand. See *Conciones* (1795) 8 and below, pp 11, 38 n 2.

[2] From Francis Bacon "De haeresibus", in his *Meditationes sacrae*. The phrase is quoted by Joseph Priestley in *An Essay on the First Principles of Government* (1768) 7, and contemporaneously with C by "The Enquirer" in *M Mag* I (Feb 1796) 5.

of Government will be of no avail. These are but the shadows, the virtue and rationality of the People at large are the substance, of Freedom: and where Corruption and Ignorance are prevalent, the best *forms* of Government are but the "Shadows of a Shade!"[1] We actually transfer the Sovereignty to the People, when we make them susceptible of it. In the present perilous state of our Constitution the Friends of Freedom, of Reason, and of Human Nature, must feel it their duty by every mean in their power to supply or circulate political information. We ask not their patronage: It will be obtained in proportion as we shall be found to deserve it.—Our Miscellany will be comprized in two sheets, or thirty-two pages, closely printed, the size and type the same as of this PROSPECTUS.—The contents will be

I.—An History of the domestic and foreign Occurrences of the preceding days.

II.—The Speeches in both Houses of Parliament: and during the Recess, select Parliamentary Speeches, from the commencement of the reign of Charles the First to the present æra, with Notes historical and biographical.

III.—Original Essays and Poetry, chiefly or altogether political.

It's chief objects are to co-operate (1) with the WHIG CLUB[2] in procuring a repeal of Lord Grenville's and Mr. Pitt's bills, now passed into laws,[3] and (2) with the PATRIOTIC SOCIETIES, for obtaining a Right of Suffrage general and frequent.

In the cities of London, Bristol, , , and , it will appear as regularly as a Newspaper, over which it will have these advantages:

I.—There being no advertisement, a greater quantity of original matter must be given.

II.—From its form, it may be bound up at the end of the year, and become an Annual Register.

III.—This last circumstance may induce Men of Letters to prefer this Miscellany to more perishable publications, as the vehicle of their effusions.

It remains to say, that whatever powers or acquirements the

[1] Edward Young *A Paraphrase on Part of the Book of Job* line 187 (var).

[2] See above, Introduction, p xxxvii.

[3] The Two Acts, passed into law 18 Dec 1795, were (1) the Treasonable Practices (or Treason) Bill, which made treasonable the stirring-up by speech or writing of hatred of king or constitution, and (2) the Seditious Meetings (or Convention) Bill, which empowered magistrates to disperse political meetings of fifty persons or more. C's *Plot Discovered* (1795) was written in opposition to these acts.

Editor possesses, he will dedicate *entirely* to this work; and (which is of more importance to the Public) he has received promises of occasional assistance from literary men of eminence and established reputation. With such encouragement he offers himself to the Public as a faithful

WATCHMAN,

to proclaim the State of the Political Atmosphere, and preserve Freedom and her Friends from the attacks of Robbers and Assassins!!

THE WATCHMAN

THE WATCHMAN

No. I. TUESDAY, MARCH 1, 1796

Published by the Author, S. T. COLERIDGE, Bristol;
And sold by the Booksellers and Newscarriers in Town & Country

THAT ALL MAY KNOW THE TRUTH;
AND THAT THE TRUTH MAY MAKE US FREE!

AMONG the calamities, which eventually have produced the most important blessings, we may particularize the capture of Constantinople by the Turks in 1453. The number of learned Greeks, whom this event drove into the West, in conjunction with the recent discovery of printing, kindled the love of knowledge in Europe, and supplied opportunities for the attainment of it.[1] Princes emulated each other in the patronage of men of ability, and endeavoured to excite a spirit of literature among their subjects by every encouragement which their rude policy suggested, or the genius of the age would permit. The first scanty twilight of knowledge was sufficient to shew what horrors had resulted from ignorance; and no experience had yet taught them that general illumination is incompatible with undelegated power.[2] This incipient diffusion of truth was aided by the Lutheran schism, which roused the Clergy of Europe from their long doze of sensuality, and by the keen goading of religious controversy forced each party into literary exertion. And after the Reformation it [a]was again[b] fortunate for the interests of Britain,

[a–b] was

[1] A historical assumption frequently made; cf William Godwin *An Enquiry Concerning Political Justice* (2 vols 2nd ed 1796) I 450–1: "The taking of Constantinople by the Turks (1453) dispersed among European nations the small fragment of learning which was at that time shut up within the walls of this metropolis. The discovery of printing was nearly contemporary with that event. These two circumstances greatly favoured the reformation of religion, which gave an irrecoverable shock to the empire of superstition and implicit obedience". Cf also David Hume *History of England* ch 26 (8 vols 1778) III 406–7. Cf *CN* I 128: "Art of printing diffused greater knowledge than Christianity—??—" See *CN* I 128n.

[2] Godwin *Political Justice* (2 vols 1st ed 1793) I 249 quotes Condorcet's life of Voltaire: "It is true, the more men are enlightened, the more they will be free; but let us not put despots on their guard, and incite them to form a league against the progress of reason. Let us conceal from them the strict and eternal union that subsists between knowledge and liberty."

that the Puritans, her first partizans for civil and religious freedom, were greatly inferior to their antagonists in acquired knowledge. The government would otherwise have been alarmed, while yet alarm could have led to prevention; and [a]Despotism, Aristocracy, and Priesthood[b] might have strangled the infant[c] whom this dark tri-unity unconsciously benefited human nature by nursing and protecting.[1] The mistake was discovered too late; but the struggle was violent, nor has it been discontinued. From the reign of Elizabeth to the present hour, the propagation of civil and religious wisdom has never been altogether free from danger; and the diffusion of general information has been impeded by accumulated taxes on paper, by stamp duties, and by every mode, direct and indirect, of preventing knowledge from coming within the circle of a poor man's expences. In the debate concerning an additional duty on newspapers, Mr. Pitt asserted that they were fit objects of taxation, as being *mere luxuries*.[2] A *mere luxury* for the proprietors to be informed concerning the measures of the directors![3] a *mere luxury* for the principals to know what their agents are doing. But the children of this world are wiser

[a–b] the triple-giant (Despotism, Aristocracy, and Priesthood)
[c] infant Hercules

[1] C in revising this passage saw that he had run the risk of confusing the reader by an echo of the myth of Hercules strangling the serpent: the triple-giant Geryon did not threaten the infant Hercules; the man Hercules in his tenth labour killed the triple-giant. In Horne Tooke's trial on a charge of high treason in 1794 Chief Justice Eyre, in his charge to the jury, quoted from the London Corresponding Society's papers the statement that " Freedom, though an infant, makes Herculean efforts, and the vipers Monarchy and Aristocracy are panting and writhing under its grasp", commenting on the fact that " Monarchy and Aristocracy are treated of . . . as vipers writhing and panting under the Herculean efforts of freedom". *The Trial of John Horne Tooke, for High Treason* taken in shorthand by Joseph Gurney (2 vols 1795) II 352. Cf Wordsworth's more conventional Hercules image in *The Prelude* x 391–3:

> The Herculean Commonwealth
> [France] had put forth her arms,
> And throttled with an infant godhead's might
> The snakes about her cradle.

[2] The tax on newspapers published at intervals of a week or less was raised in 1789 from three halfpence per half-sheet to twopence. For Pitt's speech of 3 Jul 1789 see *Parl Reg* XXVI 343–4. William Pitt (1759–1806), made prime minister in 1783 at the age of twenty-four, with much aid from George III and later the "Old Whigs", commanded an overwhelming majority in Parliament; though formerly a spokesman for peace and reform, he was now regarded by those of C's way of thinking as a renegade and a bulwark of special privilege. See *Conciones* (1795) 53: "I think of Edmund Burke's declamatory Invectives with emotion; yet while I shudder at the excesses, I must admire the strength, of this Hercules Furens of Oratory. But our Premier's Harangues!—Mystery concealing Meanness, as steam-clouds invelope a dunghill".

[3] Cf James Burgh *Political Disquisi-*

in their generation than the children of light.[1] The poor man's curiosity remains unabated with respect to events in which, above all others, he is most deeply interested; and, as by the enormous expence he is precluded from having a weekly newspaper at his home, he flies to the Ale-house for the perusal. There he contracts habits of drunkenness and sloth; [a]and then[b] the depravity of his mind is urged as an argument against the melioration of his condition: the dreadful nature of the *effects* the only plausible argument for the continuance of the *causes!* The revenue too is increased; and as the Publican depends for his license on the pleasure of the Justice of Peace, who depends for his commission on the pleasure of the Minister, the ministerial prints exclusively are forced upon him: and the poor man is not only prevented from hearing the truth, but inflamed to a kind of political suicide by the false statements and calumnies, with which the creativeness of ministerial genius is accustomed to adorn its weekly or diurnal productions.

At the alehouse likewise he meets the Exciseman: and hears his *impartial* invectives against reformers, with scarcely less deference, than when he listens to the equally *impartial* Orator of the Pulpit, who teaches him hatred in the name of the God of Love. Indeed (to use the expressive language of Arthur Young) "The abuses that are rooted in all the old governments of Europe, give such numbers of men such a direct interest in supporting, cherishing, and defending abuses, that advocates for Tyranny are found in every country and almost in every company. What a mass of people in all parts of England are some way or other interested in the present representation of the people, in tythes, charters, monopolies, and taxation! and not merely in the things themselves, but in all the abuses attending them."[2]—What a mass indeed! so large, as to form an establishment of political schoolmasters, and realize a national education! If we except honesty, sobriety, brotherly-kindness, and the art of reading and writing, what may not the poor man learn, who is employed,

[a-b] and

tions (3 vols 1774–5) I 260: " 'I think it not natural, nor rational, that the *people* who *sent* us hither, should not be *informed* of our actions' [Sir F. Winnington in Parliament in 1681]. Suppose the directors of the *East-India* company were to shut out the proprietors from their house, and then *dispose* of their *property* at their pleasure, defying all *responsibility*, how would this be taken by the *proprietors*?" For C's opinion of Burgh see *PD* 28n.

[1] Luke 16.8 (var).

[2] See above, Prospectus, p 4 n 1.

perhaps, by a Corporator,[1] whose Landlord is a Justice of the Peace, who swallows all the Priest teaches in the pulpit, and all the Exciseman pours forth in the alehouse!

Such are the impediments to the diffusion of Knowledge. The means by which Providence seems to be counteracting these impediments are—First and principally, the progress of the Methodists, and other disciples of Calvinism.[2] It has been a common remark, that implicit faith in mysteries prepares the mind for implicit obedience to tyranny.[3] But this is plausible rather than just. Facts are against it. The most thorough-paced Republicans in the days of Charles the First were religious Enthusiasts: and in the present day, a large majority among our sectaries are fervent in their zeal against political abuses. The truth seems to be, that Superstition is unfavorable to civil Freedom then only, when it teaches sensuality, as among Atheists and Pagans, and Mussulmen; or when it is in alliance with power and avarice, as in the religious establishments of Europe. In all other cases, to forego, even in solitude, the high pleasures which the human mind receives from the free exertion of its faculties, through the dread of an invisible spectator or the hope of a future reward, implies so great a conquest over the tyranny of the present impulse, and so large a power of self-government, that whoever is conscious of it, will be grateful for the existence of an external government [a]no farther than[b] as it protects him from the attacks of others; which when that government omits to do, or when by promoting ignorance and depravity it produces the contrary effects, he is prepared to declare hostilities against it, and by the warmth of his feelings and the gregariousness of his nature is enabled to prosecute them more effectually, than a myriad of detached metaphysical systematizers.[4] Besides, the very act of dissenting from

[a–b] only

1 A member of a municipal corporaation composed of the governing authorities of a town—hence a member of the "establishment".

2 C has in mind the "enthusiastic" sects, though it is not clear why he refers to them as Calvinists, for the most numerous branch of the Methodists, the Wesleyans, were Arminian.

3 C appears to be answering Godwin, who remarked that "superstitions" such as the belief in immortality were friendly to a stationary view of society, "persuading [men] passively to submit to despotism and injustice, that they may receive the recompense of their patience hereafter. . . . It is injustice that stands most in need of superstition and mystery, and will most frequently be a gainer by it". *Political Justice* (1793) II 502–7; (1796) II 124–9.

4 Evidently the Godwinians. William Godwin's rationalism and disbelief—his failure to unite "heart" and "head"—were to C's thinking not only invalid but also ineffectual. Cf *Conciones* (1795) 26: "In that barbarous tumult of inimical Interests, which

established opinions must generate habits precursive to the love of freedom. Man begins to be free when he begins to examine. To this we may add, that men can hardly apply themselves with such persevarant zeal to the instruction and comforting of the Poor, without feeling affection for them; and these feelings of love must necessarily lead to a blameless indignation against the authors of their complicated miseries. Nor should we forget, that however absurd their enthusiasm may be, yet if Methodism produce sobriety and domestic habits among the lower classes, it makes them susceptible of liberty; and this very enthusiasm does perhaps supersede the use of spiritous liquors, and bring on the same pleasing tumult of the brain without injuring the health or exhausting the wages. And although by the power of prejudice these Sectaries may deduce from the Gospel doctrines which it does not contain, yet it is impossible that they should peruse the New Testament so frequently and with such attention, without perceiving and remembering the precepts which it does contain. Yes! they shudder with pious horror at the idea of defending by famine, and fire, and blood,[1] that Religion which teaches its followers.—"If thine enemy hunger, feed him; if he thirst, give him drink: *for by so doing thou shalt melt him into repentance*."[2]

Secondly—The institution of large manufactories; in many of which it is the custom for a newspaper to be regularly read, and sometimes larger publications. Which party they adopt, is of little comparative consequence! Men always serve the cause of freedom by *thinking*, even though their first reflections may lead them to oppose it. And on account of these men, whose passions are frequently inflamed by drunkenness, the friends of rational and progressive Liberty may review with diminished indignation two recent acts of Parliament,[3] which, though breaches of the Constitution, and under pretence of protecting the *head* of the State, evidently passed to prevent our cutting off an enormous *wen*[a] [4] that grows upon it (I mean

[a] wen

the present state of Society exhibits, Religion appears to offer the only means universally *efficient*".

[1] Cf *Fire, Famine, and Slaughter*, C's "War Ecologue": *PW* (EHC) I 237. Like the poem, *The Watchman* has many references to bloodshed arising from the royalist rebellion in La Vendée and from the suppression of the Irish peasantry, both enormities being chargeable, directly or indirectly, C felt, to the English ministry. Cf below, pp 75–7 and 112.

[2] Rom 12.20 (altered).

[3] See above, p 5 n 3.

[4] Milton *Of Reformation* bk II: *A Complete Collection of the Historical, Political, and Miscellaneous Works* ed J. Toland (2 vols Amsterdam [London] 1694–8) I 266. See *CN* I 110 and n.

the system of secret influence,)[1] yet will not have been useless if they should render the language of political publications more cool and guarded, or even confine us for a while to the teaching of first principles, or the diffusion of that general knowledge which should be the basis or substratum of politics.

Thirdly, The number of Book-Societies established in almost every town and city of the kingdom;[2] and, Fourthly, the increasing experience of the dreadful effects of War and Corruption.[3]

I shall be happy if my exertions should ever form one link, however small, in this chain of causes.

It is usual, at the commencement of works resembling the present, to make some preliminary professions, which may serve as promissory notes to the public. In compliance with this custom, I declare my intention of relating facts simply and nakedly, without epithets or comments; and if at any time the opposition and ministerial prints differ from each other in their detail of events, faithfully to state such difference. It would be absurd to promise an equal neutrality in the political Essays. My bias, however, is in favor of principles, not men: and though I may be classed with a party, I scorn to be of a faction. I trust, however, that I shall write what I believe to be the Truth in the spirit of meekness.[4] It remains for me to speak concerning my proposed attempt to analyse important and interesting

[1] The phrase designates that power by which George III and his ministers controlled Parliament through pensions, places, and other rewards. A conspicuous example was the King's perusading the House of Lords to reject Fox's India Bill (Dec 1783) and thus bringing down the Fox–North ministry. This opened the way for the younger Pitt (whose father had opposed secret influence) to come to power. Secret influence and William Paley's attempt to justify it were satirised in C's verses sent to the *M Post* 10 Jan 1800, *Talleyrand to Lord Grenville* lines 14–20: *PW* (EHC) I 341. See also *Conciones* (1795) 60.

[2] C refers not to the circulating libraries, run by shopkeepers to dispense light reading-matter, but to those such as the Bristol Library, so valuable to him (see *Bristol LB*), and the one in Nether Stowey on which Thomas Poole lavished his attention. *Poole* I 44–5, 85–6. The book-societies, a growth of the eighteenth century, brought collections of serious books, old and new, within the reach of the, middle-class townsfolk. The Bristol Library, with its probably typical entrance fee of a guinea and an annual subscription of the same amount, was above the reach of the working-classes. The latter, however, were learning to read and were being brought into contact with books not so much by libraries as by both radical and evangelical societies with their cheap tracts. C passes over this interesting new development. See Richard D. Altick *The English Common Reader* (Chicago 1957) ch 3.

[3] A further consequence of the fourth providential intervention is suggested in *CN* I 103: "Continuance of the War likely to produce an abolition of Property".

[4] Cf 1 Cor 4.21 and Gal 6.1.

publications—a task which may seem to have been rendered unnecessary by the existing Reviews.[1] But, in the first place, I shall never review more than one work in each number; and none but works of apparent merit, whether such as teach true principles with energy, or recommend false principles by the decorations of genius. I shall not carry with me to the perusal of unexpected excellence the ill-humour or disgust occasioned by having previously toiled thro' pages of frippery or dullness. Secondly, although the existing Reviews are conducted with considerable ability, yet they appear to me valuable from their wide diffusion of general knowledge, rather than as the fair appreciators of literary merit. I may safely aver (and I believe I am not singular in the complaint) that I never purchased a book entirely on the credit of the reviews, in which I did not find myself disappointed. How, indeed, should it be otherwise? So many and so varying are the writers employed by the proprietary Booksellers, that it is hardly possible for an author, whose literary acquaintance is even moderately large, to publish a work which shall not be flattered in some one of the reviews by a personal friend, or calumniated by an enemy. As the last assertion ought not to be made without accompanying proofs, out of many instances in my memory, I select the review of Combe's Horace, in the British Critic, by Dr. Parr.[2] Far from the haunts of literary men, and personally acquainted with very few of them,[3] if I execute my criticisms with less ability, I will however pledge myself to perform the duty, which I have undertaken, without compliment and without resentment. This, then, is my plan—to contribute my small but assiduous labors to the cause of Piety and Justice.

That all may know the truth; and that the truth may make us free!

If any condescend to favor this work by their communications, they will be pleased to direct them (post paid) to S. T. Coleridge, Bristol.

[1] Cf *CN* I 131: "Reviews, a kind of establishment".

[2] See *B Critic* III (1794) 48–61, 121–39, 238, 302–30, 412–24. Dr Samuel Parr (1747–1825) censured Dr Charles Combe (1743–1817) for, among other things, not giving sufficient credit to his deceased co-editor, Henry Homer, a friend of Parr's, in the 2-vol edition of Horace *Opera* (1792–3). In his notebooks C ridiculed and parodied Parr's style; see *CN* I 101, 112, 278 and nn. But he sent Parr his *Poems* (1797); see *CL* I 331.

[3] In a notebook C congratulated himself on never having been "prematured by Intercourse with literary men". *CN* I 6 (1.9).

REVIEW OF THE MOTIONS IN THE LEGISLATURE FOR A PEACE WITH FRANCE

December 14, 1792.

MR. FOX,[1] at the conclusion of an eloquent and argumentative speech, moved the following amendment to the Address: "Trusting that your Majesty will employ every species of negociation to prevent the calamities of War, that may be deemed consistent with the honor and dignity of the French[2] Nation."

MR. BURKE[3] replied in a train of frenzied eloquence; and was followed by Mr. Dundas,[4] who assigned as a motive for entering into a war with France, the *probability that the French Republic meditated an attack on Holland.* The Amendment was negatived without a division.

December 15, 1792.

MR. FOX moved, that the House would address his Majesty and entreat that his Majesty would be graciously pleased to send a Minister to France, in order to negociate with the present existing Government of that country, relative to their dispute with Holland. He was answered by Lord Sheffield,[5] who averred *the impossibility of negociating with a gang of robbers and cut-throats, with a murderous and savage banditti*; and by Mr. Jenkinson,[6] who observed, that *as we had sent no Minister before France avowed her offensive intentions with respect to the Scheldt, we could not send one now, lest it should look like fear. Neither can we treat with France, because she is without a Constitution; nor could we treat, when she should have a Constitution. For if the French Government were improperly constituted, it would be*

[1] Charles James Fox (1749–1806), rejected by Burke and the majority of Whigs because of his conciliatory attitude toward France, became the leader of the Opposition party of "New Whigs", small but intensely loyal to him.

[2] An error for "British".

[3] Edmund Burke (1729–97), who by his *Reflections on the Revolution in France* (1790) and other writings and speeches crystallised English hostility to revolutionary France, in 1791 severed his old friendship with Fox over this issue.

[4] Henry Dundas (1742–1811), later 1st Viscount Melville, now secretary of state for war and president of the board of control, was Pitt's closest associate and political lieutenant.

[5] John Baker Holroyd (1735–1821), 1st Baron (later 1st Earl of) Sheffield in the Irish peerage, MP for Bristol, was Gibbon's friend and editor—his *Miscellaneous Works of Edward Gibbon, Esquire. With Memoirs of His Life and Writings; Composed by Himself; Illustrated from His Letters, with Occasional Notes and Narrative* (2 vols) appeared in Apr 1796.

[6] Robert Banks Jenkinson (1770–1828), MP for Rye, succeeded as 2nd Earl of Liverpool in 1808 and was Tory prime minister 1812–27.

*unworthy of us to treat with them; and if it were well constituted, we ought to engage in a war with her, because then there would be reason to dread her power.** The motion was negatived without a division.

February 1, 1793.

In the debate on his Majesty's Message, communicating certain papers received from M. Chauvelin,[1] and recommending a further augmentation of the forces by sea and land,—Lord Stanhope,[2] after having read extracts from a letter which he had received from Condorcet,[3] and which disavowed any intention on the part of the French Government to interfere in the government of England, moved an Amendment to the Address, "humbly entreating his Majesty to take such measures as might preserve the continuance of the Peace." He was seconded by Lord Lauderdale.[4]—They were answered by Lord Loughborough,[5] who stated the *Atheism* and *Ambition* of the French, as motives for the War against them. The Amendment was negatived without a division.

* Admirable reasoning! Suppose that some Family were agitated by internal quarrels, and that a neighbouring Family were heard to declare, "We must of necessity endeavour to destroy that Family: for it is impossible to live on a friendly footing with them, while they commit such excesses among themselves; and if they should make it up, and act well and wisely for the future, it will still be highly prudent for us to persevere in our first resolution, lest they should undersell us in the market, and grow richer than we!!"

[1] François-Bernard, Marquis de Chauvelin (1766–1832), a French politician associated with Talleyrand, was in 1792–3 French ambassador to England.

[2] Charles, 3rd Earl Stanhope (1753–1816), who, though Pitt's brother-in-law, was called "Citizen" Stanhope because of his ardent advocacy of the French Revolution. He was a scientist and an inventor as well as a politician. For his daughter's marriage, see below, p 46 and n 2.

[3] Jean-Antoine-Nicolas Caritat, Marquis de Condorcet (1743–94), mathematician and philosopher, then a member of the National Convention, whose championing of the Revolution did not save him from the Terror. While in hiding after being proscribed, he indulged his passion for human improvement and perfectibility by writing *Une Esquisse d'un tableau historique des progrès de l'esprit humain*, published posthumously in 1795 and translated the same year for English publication. (For a quotation from this work, see below, p 272.) Condorcet died in prison, possibly a suicide, the day after his arrest.

[4] James Maitland, 8th Earl of Lauderdale (1759–1839), representative peer of Scotland and Whig leader in the House of Lords. For a quotation from Lauderdale, see below, pp 253–4.

[5] Alexander Wedderburn, 1st Baron Loughborough, later 1st Earl of Rosslyn (1733–1805), was in 1793 made lord chancellor.

February 12, 1793.

In the debate on his Majesty's Message respecting the War with France,[1] instead of the Address proposed by Lord Grenville,[2] Lord Stanhope moved that the following be substituted: "That an humble Address be presented to his Majesty, to represent to his Majesty, that, by directing the French Ambassador to leave this kingdom, his Majesty's Ministers have (independently of repeated provocations) produced a rupture between this kingdom and France, in as much as by the second article of the Treaty of Navigation, &c. made in the year 1786, between Great-Britain and France, it is expressly declared,[3] that the sending away from either nation the Ambassador of the other nation, shall be deemed a rupture between the two countries.—And humbly to represent to his Majesty, that, before this House can encourage his Majesty to concur in measures for carrying on a War against France, this House humbly requests to be informed of the objects which his Majesty proposes to obtain thereby." Negatived.

February 18, 1793.

MR. FOX moved the following Resolutions:—"That none of the Causes assigned for making war on France are tenable, either in point, 1. of Policy; or 2. of Justice. 3. That the Measures of his Majesty's Ministers, in the late negociation between them and the French Government, were such as tend to exasperate, not remedy. 4. That the security of Europe, and the rights of independent nations, which have been stated as grounds of War against France, have never appeared to influence his Majesty's Ministers in the case of Poland.[4] 5. That it is the Duty of his Majesty's Ministers, in the present crisis,

[1] The execution of Louis XVI on 21 Jan 1793 was followed by the dismissal of the French ambassador to England. France responded by declaring war 1 Feb, and England retaliated on 11 Feb.

[2] William Wyndham Grenville, Baron Grenville (1759–1834), appointed secretary of state for foreign affairs in 1791, was, when in office under Pitt, a prime Whig target, but in 1806 he took office in coalition with Fox in the Ministry of All the Talents.

[3] See George Chalmers *A Collection of Treaties Between Great Britain and Other Powers* (2 vols 1790) I 519.

[4] Poland was an object of Whig sympathy because (1) after having suffered repeatedly from the rapacity of its powerful neighbours, Austria, Russia, and Prussia, it was totally dismembered in 1795; (2) the heroic Kosciusko served freedom first in the American cause and then in his own country (see below, pp 367–9); and (3) the Poles had made efforts to institute a more popular government, in contrast to the absolutism that surrounded and finally subjugated them. The Whig Opposition was anti-interventionist (as opposed to Burke's view), but felt that if intervention was to be the policy, it was better to rescue a brave nation from oblivion than to attempt the restoration of the traditionally tyrannical Bourbons.

to advise his Majesty against entering into engagements which may prevent Great-Britain from making separate Peace." Negatived by a Majority of 226—Those who voted in favor of the Resolutions being only 44.

February 21, 1793.

MR. GREY[1] made a number of connected motions, in which he reviewed in a masterly manner the causes, pretexts, and probable events of the War; and concluded with the following:—"We therefore, his Majesty's faithful Commons, humbly implore his Majesty to listen no longer to the Councils which have forced us into this unhappy war; but to embrace the earliest occasion which his wisdom may discover, of restoring to his People the blessings of Peace."

June 17, 1793.

MR. FOX moved, "That his Majesty be earnestly and solemnly requested to employ the earliest means for procuring an honorable Peace." He was answered by Mr. Pitt,[2] the force of whose argument was, that *there existed in France no one with whom Great-Britain could safely treat.* For the motion, 47—Against, 187.

January 21, 1794.

In the debate on the Address to his Majesty, on the Speech from the Throne, the Earl of Guildford[3] moved an amendment to the following effect:—"That the House hoped, his Majesty would seize the earliest opportunity to conclude a peace: and humbly requested that the form of Government established in France may not be considered as any impediment."—Opposed by the Duke of Portland,[4] who "considered the War to be merely grounded on one principle—the preservation of the CHRISTIAN RELIGION:" and by Earl Spencer,[5] who "conceived the vigorous prosecution of the War with France the only means of *preserving the British Constitution.*" The Amendment was negatived by a majority of 85 out of 109.

[1] Charles Grey (1764–1845), MP for Northumberland. Later, after he had succeeded as 2nd Earl Grey, he became prime minister and presided over the passage of the Reform Bill of 1832.

[2] See above, p 10 n 2.

[3] George Augustus North (1757–1802), who succeeded as 3rd Earl of Guilford in 1792, was son of Lord North, the prime minister (1770–82), later 2nd Earl of Guilford.

[4] William Henry Cavendish Bentinck (1738–1809), 3rd Duke of Portland; Whig leader who crossed over to Pitt in 1794 and was rewarded with the home secretaryship (1794–1801). C made a similar statement about him in *M Post* 25 Jan 1800: *EOT* I 255; and cf *PW* (EHC) I 115n.

[5] George John, 2nd Earl Spencer (1758–1834), a Whig who joined Pitt in 1794 and became first lord of the admiralty.

On the same day, in the House of Commons, Mr. Fox proposed an amendment to the address of the same nature with the Earl of Guildford's. Opposed by Mr. Pitt, who "*stated as motives for continuing the war, the necessity of security against future injuries from the French Government, and indemnity for the past; and thought the restoration of Monarchy the most probable means of procuring both.*"

January 23, 1794.

EARL STANHOPE moved that an Address be presented to his Majesty for the discontinuance of hostilities and the acknowledgement of the French Republic.—Negatived without a division.

February 17, 1794.

The MARQUIS of LANSDOWN[1] made a series of motions, addressing his Majesty for Peace. Negatived by 90 out of 106.

May 30, 1794.

The DUKE of BEDFORD[2] moved a number of resolutions, condemning the conduct of the Ministry, with a view to the establishment of a Peace with France.—Opposed (among others) by Lord Abingdon[3] in these remarkable words: "*The best road to Peace, my Lords! is* WAR: *and* WAR *carried on in the same manner in which we are taught to worship our* CREATOR, *namely, with all our souls, and with all our minds, and with all our hearts, and with all our strength.*"[4]—The Resolutions negatived.

On the same day, in the House of Commons, Mr. Fox moved 14 resolutions of the same import with the Duke of Bedford.—Negatived —the minority being 55.

January 26, 1795.

MR. GREY concluded an animated train of argument with moving, "That it is the opinion of this House, that the existence of the present

[1] William Petty, Earl of Shelburne, created (1784) Marquis of Lansdowne (1737–1805). Prime Minister in 1782–83, he was now active in opposition and was reconciled with Fox. Though unsuccessful in politics and the object of distrust, he was one of the most philosophic of public men and was given to entertaining men of letters and learning. Joseph Priestley was for several years his librarian. See a sonnet to him, below, p 371.

[2] Francis Russell, 5th Duke of Bedford (1765–1802), a friend of Lauderdale and Fox and one of the Whig grandees. He was attacked by Burke in *A Letter to a Noble Lord* (see below, pp 35–6).

[3] Willoughby Bertie, 4th Earl of Abingdon (1740–99), whose politics were not consistently Tory or Whig.

[4] Cf Book of Common Prayer: Catechism, and Mark 12.30.

Government of France ought not to be considered as precluding at this time a Negociation for Peace." Opposed by Mr. Pitt, on the grounds, that Security was not attainable from the present Governors of France; and that the ruined state of French Resources afforded us ample encouragement to proceed. Negatived—the Minority 86.

January 27, 1795.

The DUKE of BEDFORD made the same motion in the House of Lords.—Opposed by Lord Grenville, on the grounds, that it was impossible to treat with men who had changed the worship of God into Idolatry of personified Abstractions (*Freedom* &c.) and who appeared to have declined even to tolerate the Christian Religion.—Negatived—the Minority 15.

February 6, 1795.

MR. GREY moved, that "this House is of opinion that the French Government is competent to entertain and conclude a negociation for Peace with Great-Britain." Supported by Mr. Wilberforce.[1] Negatived—the Minority 60.

February 12, 1795.

The DUKE of BEDFORD made the same motion in the House of Lords. Minority 12. A protest against the war, signed Bedford, Guildford, Lauderdale, Buckingham.[2]

May 17, 1795.

MR. WILBERFORCE made a similar motion. Opposed by Mr. Pitt, who deemed it, "*premature, though he looked forward to negociation at no remote period.*"

June 5, 1795.

The EARL of LAUDERDALE moved an Address to his Majesty for a speedy negociation with France. Minority 8.

December 8, 1795.

MR. PITT brought up a Message from the King, acquainting the House, "that the crisis which was depending at the commencement of

[1] William Wilberforce (1759–1833), as leader of the parliamentary forces seeking the abolition of the slave-trade, was soon to suffer defeat. See below, pp 155–8. His joining the peace party is a rare instance of divergence from his close friend, Pitt.

[2] George Nugent-Temple-Grenville, 1st Marquis of Buckingham (1753–1813), brother of Lord Grenville above (p 18 and n 2).

the present session of France,[1] had led to such an order of things in France, as will induce his Majesty to meet any disposition for negociation on the part of the Enemy."[2]

February 15, 1796.

MR. GREY introduced a motion for Peace, seeing the hope created by his Majesty's Message had been disappointed. Answered by Mr. Pitt, "that measures had been taken; and were now actually in train, which must lead at no remote period to a negociation. Whether it would go farther, and lead to Peace, he could not pretend to state; that must depend on the state of the enemies' affairs, whether they were sufficiently distressed and exhausted to induce them to submit to terms very different from any which their Language and Professions for some time had pointed out."

Thus we have given a rapid review of the motions for Peace; regretting that in the fourth year of this bloody contest, we are exactly where we should have been at the beginning of any other war. Yet must not these motions be considered as having been altogether ineffectual: they have beyond all doubt removed the prejudices of many, and have inspired notions and feelings which will not die with the subject that caused them.

Still survives
Th' imperishable seed, soon to become
That Tree, beneath whose vast and mighty shade
The Sons of Men shall pitch their tents in peace,
And in the unity of Truth preserve
The bond of Peace. For by the Eye of God
Hath VIRTUE sworn, that never one good Deed
Was worked in vain![3]

What the language and professions of the French Legislature are, how little they consider themselves as distressed and exhausted, and how high the views which they entertain,[4] our readers will be enabled

[1] An error for "Parliament".

[2] France had passed under the rule of the Directory in October.

[3] Southey *Joan of Arc* (1796) III lines 74, 76–82 (var). This is part of C's contribution to the poem, later excised by mutual agreement of the authors. See *PW* (EHC) II 1029.

[4] In the French materials C's selections were determined by his policy of discouraging further participation in the war with France through revealing English weakness, due to a bad cause and a bad ministry, and French strength, resting on better principles and persisting despite the financial

to judge by the following extract[a] from a debate on the junction of the Netherlands which we do not recollect to have seen translated in any of our English Prints.[1] The idea of giving up the Netherlands to the Emperor[2] was repelled unanimously and with scorn: some proposed to establish them as an independent Republic: but the third opinion prevailed by a vast majority.

MERLIN, the Reporter,[3] says, that the partizans of Austria have done every thing to render the French name odious in Belgium, and that they have been ill used by some agents of the Convention; "but the mass of the people remain[b] nevertheless attached to the cause of liberty, and their hearts not less turned towards France: just as in France itself the patriots harrassed by a decemviral tyranny, in the name of a Republic which did not yet exist, remained nevertheless faithful to the principles of Republicans[c]." All the other Speakers, who have been in Belgium, make the body of the people attached to France. Merlin's chief reasons for the junction, are, to strip the House of Austria of a possession which supported its ambition, and enabled it incessantly to trouble the repose of Europe;—to enlarge the means of defence of France against governments which will remain her secret enemies after laying down their arms; to incline the balance of commerce in favour of France; to deprive the English of several branches of that commerce which they carry on with so much advantage.

[a] extracts [b] remains [c] a Republican. N.B.

muddle of the country. The clarity of the contrast between the two nations was clouded when the Directory in effect rejected an English overture to negotiate. Still another sort of crisis arose with the victories of Bonaparte in Italy (recorded in Nos 9 and 10), which C probably looked on with mixed emotions.

[1] C probably owed the translation of these passages from the French (of which he was ignorant; see his letter to John Thelwall 19 Nov [1796]: *CL* I 260) to some friend, who in this case was almost certainly Dr Beddoes. Thomas Beddoes, in his *Essay on the Public Merits of Mr. Pitt* (Bristol 1796), quoted (pp 134–5) from a speech by "Lefebure" (same misspelling in *The Watchman*) from which C also quotes on p 25, a speech delivered in the same debate as that below in which Merlin, Roberjot, and Carnot joined. For Beddoes's pamphlet, see below, pp 305–13.

[2] Francis II (1768–1835), known also as emperor of Germany, the last Holy Roman emperor; after the abolition of the empire by Napoleon in 1806, Francis I of Austria.

[3] Philippe-Antoine, Comte Merlin, called Merlin de Douai (1754–1838), author of the "Law of the Suspect", which established the Terror, issued the *Rapports* of the Corps Législatif. Minister of justice 1795–9, he was minister of police in the spring of 1796. The quoted passage is from the *Moniteur* 3 Oct 1795: see *La Gazette Nationale, ou Le Moniteur universel* (Paris 1854) XXVI 87b.

ROBERJOT (a Belgic Commissary)[1] gives a curious account of the disposition of the Belgians, but makes the great majority desire an union. Of the advantages for France, he says, "Calculate how highly useful the treaty of the Hague[2] is for you! and acknowledge that the clauses of this treaty are false, if the United Provinces do not become contiguous to the territory of the Republic. At present you are under the necessity of importing annually foreign grain, according to accurate calculation, to the amount of a twelfth part of your wants.

"In re-uniting the Austrian Low countries and Liege, you will no longer be tributary to other nations, you will always be secure from scarcity and want. Can any country be more fertile than Belgium? Do we know any country where the soil is so productive? In my opinion, upon the re-union of the conquered countries, which I am now going to enlarge upon, I observed to you, that till now, neither the political or commercial balance, which are the true power of a state, have ever been in your favour; I said that a re-union is the only means of obtaining this balance to the destruction of the power of England, your rival, and most ardent enemy.

"Not to extenuate any objections which may be made, some people say, if you do not render this country independent, you must be subject to great expences, you must be subject to pay the debts of the government, to support a great number of public establishments, to repair the fortifications, and to furnish the garrison that must defend them with soldiers.

"But will the resources which the Emperor found to supply all these expences, be only imaginary and of no avail to you? We know that all those charges were defrayed by ordinary means, and that the taxes paid by these rich countries, far exceeded the exaggerated expences which they incurred. The suppression of useless employments, the sale of buildings consecrated to establishments of little importance, order, and œconomy, would create resources, did not the country already promise all that we can hope.

"They can have but little knowledge of the nature and the extent of the commerce of these countries, to doubt of the advantages that would accrue to France from a nearer connection with a country which produces in abundance the chief and most necessary materials

[1] Claude Roberjot (1752–99) was by profession a diplomat. For the quotations from the *Moniteur* 6 Oct 1795, see ibid XXVI 108a, 108b.

[2] In the Treaty of the Hague, May 1795, between France and the newly created Batavian Republic, the latter agreed to an offensive-defensive policy with France and ceded territory and paid indemnities to France.

for industry; which employs a great number of hands in this same industry, and which contains a number of merchants zealously devoted to every species of commerce. Antwerp[a] has long been the first market in Europe: Bruges was the cradle of the herring fishery: these cities wait only for liberty to make new [b]exertions. Rising[c] out of that insignificance to which they have been reduced by other powers, these countries will have a distinct commerce of their own, the inhabitants will regain their former skill in navigation, ships will be substituted for boats, and the maritime commerce of France will acquire an activity which will restore abundance; considerable ports will be added to those you have already, and a coast of forty leagues to your coasts, having at its command the course of the Scheldt[d] and the Meuse, together with the mouths of those rivers and of the Rhine; France will on all sides be mistress of the commerce which England had engrossed, she will share with Holland every branch of commerce which the northern seas afford, together with the Rhine and the German rivers which flow into them. Such are the advantages of commerce which will accrue to France from the union of the Low Countries and of Liege."

LEFEBURE (a Belgic Commissary.)[1] "None of you can be ignorant that the country proposed to be united, produces, of grain on an average, three times as much as its consumption. I can add, that according to a sure calculation the harvest of this year, which in truth has been uncommonly abundant, will be sufficient for the support of one third of the inhabitants of France, leaving an ample supply for the Belgians. It will therefore secure you against the most pressing of wants,* the supply of which has been ever attended with a great efflux of specie, and great disadvantage to your trade. Under this interesting point of view, the interest of France requires that the richest and best cultivated country in Europe should be inseparably[e] confounded with the Republic.

* A Spanish gentleman, just arrived in London from Paris, who has traversed the whole Republic, asserts, that agriculture is every where flourishing, bread plentiful, and that the institutions for public education are perfectly on foot and well attended.

[a] Anvers [b-c] exertions; and rising [d]Escaut [e]inevitably

[1] Julien Lefebvre de la Chauvière (1757–1816). An advocate of union with Belgium, he was sent by the National Convention as an envoy to that country, where he proclaimed the freedom of the navigation of the Scheldt. Quotations from the *Moniteur* 6 Oct 1795: see *La Gazette nationale* XXVI 109a, 109b, 110a.

"Belgium is invited by the opening of the Scheldt, to the highest commercial prosperity. Antwerp may and ought to become one of the first commercial powers of Europe. Her prosperity will be considered with an evil eye by the commercial powers, and especially by England—frequent disputes may arise—the Belgic flag, if the country be independent, may be insulted, and France, her protectress, may see herself obliged to plunge into a naval war, of which Belgium would never be able to reimburse the expences."

CARNOT (the celebrated military Member).[1]—"In keeping Luxembourg, you not only deprive the enemy of the strongest fortress in Europe, next to Gibraltar, and the most dangerous for yourselves, but you take possession of this impregnable fortress to guard your frontier, which was very strong; it gives, moreover, a facility in carrying forward the war, without being stopped by any thing, and thus becomes the sure token of a solid and durable peace; for the enemy will cease to attack you, when they see that the immediate and inevitable result of their aggression, would be an invasion of their own country then deprived of every means of resistance.

"They say we must terminate the War. Yes, without doubt it must terminate, and quickly; but for this very reason, we must keep Belgium: for the war will not be over, if we must begin it again next year; but this will certainly happen, if you do not prevent the enemy whilst it is in your power from the possibility of [a]attacking you[b] again. A foundation must be laid upon the nature of things, and not upon [c]confidence in[d] the good faith of a cunning enemy, whose constant interest, and consequently whose eternal efforts, will be to annihilate you.—Cut the talons[e] of the leopard, [f]beat down[g] at least one of the heads of the eagle, if you would have the cock sleep in quiet!"*[h]

* The Leopard, we believe, is the Arms of Bohemia, the Eagle of Germany, and Gallus, the Latin word for the Cock, signifies likewise a Gaul or Frenchman.

[a-b] attacking [c-d] the fidelity of [e] talons or nails
[f-g] lower [h] [No footnote]

[1] Lazare-Nicolas-Marguerite Carnot (1753–1823), French general and one of the five Directors. Quotations from the *Moniteur* 8 Oct 1795: see *La Gazette nationale* XXVI 121–2.

TO A YOUNG LADY,

WITH A POEM ON THE FRENCH REVOLUTION[1]

MUCH on my early youth I love to dwell,
Ere yet I bade that friendly dome[2] farewell,
Where first, beneath the echoing cloisters pale,
I heard of guilt, and wonder'd at the tale!
Yet, tho' the hours flew[a] on careless wing,
Full heavily of Sorrow would I sing.
Aye, as the star of evening flung its beam
In broken radiance on the wavy stream,
My soul, amid the pensive twilight gloom,
Mourn'd with the breeze, O LEE BOO!* o'er thy tomb.

* LEE BOO, son of ABBA THULE, chief of the Pelew Islands. He came over to England with Captain Wilson, died of the small pox, and is buried in Greenwich Church-yard.[3]

[a] flew by

[1] Cf *PW* (EHC) I 64–6. These verses, now addressed to Sara Coleridge, his wife, had formerly, in a slightly different form, been inscribed in a copy of his and Southey's play, *The Fall of Robespierre*, a gift to the actress Ann Brunton (letter to RS 21 Oct [1794]: *CL* I 117–18). C in *Poems* (1797) and *Poems* (1803) gives as the date Sept 1794; in *PW* (1828) and *PW* (1834), it is Sept 1792. JDC accepts the latter date and supposes the poem to have been originally addressed to Miss Fanny Nesbitt (*PW*—JDC—562), but Carl R. Woodring points out that the Nesbitt episode took place in 1793 and, on other evidence as well, shows that the poem in its present form could not have existed before 1794. *Politics in the Poetry of Coleridge* (Madison 1961) 255. What particular event of the French Revolution is described here is not clear, though lines 17–18 were taken from C's youthful poem, *Destruction of the Bastille*: cf lines 7–8: *PW* (EHC) I 10. When inscribed in *The Fall of Robespierre* they came perilously close to justifying the Reign of Terror, but in *The Watchman* the reference is vague. By "Tyrants" (line 25) C may refer to the royalists or to the would-be foreign invaders of France, who were halted at Valmy (20 Sept 1792) and defeated at Jemappes (6 Nov 1792). But cf *PW* (EHC) I 65 and *The Fall of Robespierre* I lines 3, 27, 49: *PW* (EHC) II 496–7, where the word is singular, meaning Robespierre.

[2] C's school, Christ's Hospital. See below, end of following note.

[3] The history of the young Melanesian, Lee Boo, is given in George Keate *An Account of the Pelew Islands . . . Composed from the Journals of Captain Henry Wilson* (1788). Keate quotes (2nd ed 1788 p 361) the inscription on his tomb in Rotherhithe (not Greenwich) churchyard: "To the memory of Prince LEE BOO, A native of the Pelew . . . Islands; and son to ABBA THULLE, Rupack or king of the Island COOROORAA; who departed this Life on the 27th of December 1784, aged 20 years; This Stone is inscribed by the Honourable United EAST INDIA COMPANY, as a Testimony of Esteem for the humane and kind Treatment afforded by HIS FATHER to the Crew of their Ship the ANTELOPE, Captain

Where'er I wandered, PITY still was near,
Breath'd from the heart and glisten'd in the tear:
No knell that toll'd, but fill'd my anxious eye,
And suff'ring Nature wept that *one* should die![1]

Thus, to sad sympathies I sooth'd my breast
Calm as the rainbow in the weeping West:
When slum'bring FREEDOM rous'd by high DISDAIN
With giant fury burst her triple chain![2]

WILSON, which was wrecked off that Island in the Night of the 9th of August 1783.

" 'Stop, Reader, Stop!—Let NATURE claim a Tear—
A Prince of *Mine*, LEE BOO, lies bury'd here.' "

When Lee Boo with the *Antelope*'s company left for England, one of the crew elected to remain in the Pelews and died a century or so too early to receive an inquisitive "Letter to Madan Blanchard" from E. M. Forster (*Hogarth Letters* 1931). Woodring (*Politics in the Poetry of Coleridge* 255) makes the probable suggestion that C was reminded of Lee Boo by Bowles's poems of 1794, though the name had been rather widely known; Lord Derby's horse, Lee Boo, won at Newmarket in 1790! There may have been a more personal connexion: John Wedgebrough and Robert White, "Two youths from Christ's Hospital, apprentices, and acting as midshipmen", sailed among the crew of the *Antelope*, which brought Lee Boo to England in Jul 1784. Keate p 3.

[1] In PML MS MA 1916 (f 19) C drops a note and instructs the printer: "Put as a note [to] the fourteenth Line of this Poem these Lines

When eager patriots fly the news to spread
Of glorious conquest and of thousands dead;
All feel the mighty glow of victor Joy:
. . . .
But if extended on the gory plain
And snatch'd in conquest some lov'd friend be dead—
Affection's tears will dim the sorrowing Eye
And suff'ring Nature grieve that one should die.
From The Retrospect by Robert Southey—published by Dilly."

Robert Lovell and RS *Poems Containing The Retrospect, Odes, Elegies, Sonnets, &c* (Bath 1794) 9–10 (C has written "dead" for "slain"). Though the note did not appear in *The Watchman*, C acknowledged the indebtedness in *Poems* (1796) 177. Cf *PW* (EHC) I 65n.

[2] From C's *Destruction of the Bastille* (see above, p 27 n 1), written c 1789 but unpublished until 1834. The ms source is MS Ottery, dated "cir. 1793": *PW* (EHC) I xxv. The lines bear a resemblance to a passage from Erasmus Darwin *Botanic Garden* (1791) pt I canto II lines 377–8, 381–2, 385–6:

Long had the Giant-form on Gallia's plains
Inglorious slept, unconscious of his chains;
. . . .
O'er his closed eyes a triple veil was bound,
And steely rivets lock'd him to the ground;
. . . .
Touch'd by the patriot-flame, he rent amazed
The flimsy bonds . . .

Than the love-wilder'd Maniac's Brain hath seen
Shaping celestial forms in vacant air;
If these demand th'empassion'd Poet's care—
If Mirth, and soften'd Sense, and Wit refin'd,
The blameless features of a lovely mind;
Then haply shall my trembling hand assign
No fading wreath to Beauty's saintly shrine.

Nor, Sara! thou these ~~simple~~ early flowers refuse:
No serpent lurks beneath their simple hues.
No purple blooms from
~~From~~ Flatt'ry's Night-shade ~~to such bloom I bring~~ bring
~~A~~ The Child of Nature as ~~I~~ he feels, ~~I~~ he sings.

Nor, Sara! thou these early flowers refuse
Ne'er lurk'd the Snake beneath their simple hues.
Nature's pure Child from Flatt'ry's night-shade brings
No blooms rich-purpling: as he feels, he sings.

*. Put as a note the fourteenth line of this Poem these Lines.

~~But~~ When eager patriots fly the news to spread
Of glorious conquest and of thousands dead;
All feel the mighty glow of victor joy—

But if extended on the gory plain
And snatch'd in conquest some lov'd friend be ~~dead~~ slain
Affection's tears will dim the sorrowing Eye
And suff'ring Nature ~~[illegible]~~ grieve that one should die.
From the Retrospect by Robert Southey published by Dilly.

4. A leaf from a manuscript of *To a Young Lady, with a Poem on the French Revolution*. The Pierpont Morgan Library manuscript MA 1916 f 19, reproduced by permission. See pp 28 n 1, 29.

Fierce on her front the blasting Dog-star glow'd;
Her Banners, like a midnight Meteor,[1] flow'd;
Amid the yelling of the storm-rent skies
She came, and scatter'd battles from her eyes!
Then EXULTATION waked the patriot fire
And swept with wilder hand th' Alcæan lyre:
Red from the Tyrants' wound I shook the lance,
And strode in joy the reeking plains of France![2]

In ghastly horror lie th' Oppressors low,
And my heart aches, tho' MERCY struck the blow.
With wearied thought once more I seek the shade,
Where peaceful Virtue weaves the Myrtle braid.
And oh! if EYES, whose holy glances roll,
The eloquent messengers of the pure soul;
If SMILES more winning, and a gentler MIEN,
Than the love-wilder'd Maniac's brain hath seen,
Shaping celestial forms in vacant air;
If these demand th' empassion'd Poet's care—
If MIRTH, and soften'd SENSE, and WIT refin'd,
The blameless features of a lovely mind;
Then haply shall my trembling hand assign
No fading wreath to BEAUTY'S saintly shrine.
Nor, SARA! thou these early flowers refuse—
Ne'er lurked the snake beneath their simple hues:
No purple bloom the Child of Nature brings
From Flatt'ry's night-shade: as he feels, he sings.

REVIEW OF BURKE'S LETTER TO A NOBLE LORD[3]

But what is Man at enmity with truth?
What were the fruits of Wentworth's copious mind,

[1] Cf *The Fall of Robespierre* I line 6: "In splendor gloomy, as the midnight meteor". *PW* (EHC) II 496.

[2] Cf ibid II lines 127–8: *PW* (EHC) II 506.

[3] *A Letter from the Right Honourable Edmund Burke to a Noble Lord, on the Attacks Made upon Him and His Pension . . .* (1796) was addressed to William Wentworth Fitzwilliam, 2nd Earl Fitzwilliam (1748–1833), Burke's patron, nephew and heir of his previous patron, the Marquis of Rockingham. Charles Lamb, c 31 May 1796, wrote to C: "Of your *Watchmen* the Review of Burke was the best prose". *LL* I 8.

When (blighted all the promise of his youth)
The patriot in a tyrant's league had joined?

* * * * * *

And sure, when Nature kind
Hath deck'd some favor'd breast above the throng,
That Man with grievous wrong
Affronts and wounds his genius, if he bends
To Guilt's ignoble ends
The functions of his ill-submitting mind.

AKENSIDE.[1]

WHEN men of low and creeping faculties wish to depreciate works of genius, it is their fashion to sneer at them as "*mere declamation.*" However accurate the facts, however just the inferences, yet if to these be added the tones of feeling, and the decorations of fancy, "*it is all mere declamation.*" Whatever is dull and frigid is extolled as *cool reasoning*; and where, confessedly, nothing else is possessed, sound judgment is charitably attributed. This mode of evading an adversary's argument is fashionable among the aristocratic faction,[2] when they speak of the French writers;[3] and has been applied with nauseous frequency to the writings of EDMUND BURKE by some low-minded sophisters who disgrace the cause of freedom. Mr. Burke always appeared to me to have displayed great vigor of intellect, and an almost prophetic keenness of penetration; nor can I think his merit diminished, because he has secured the aids of sympathy to his cause by the warmth of his own emotions, and delighted the imagination of his readers by a multitude and rapid

[1] The first passage is extracted from Mark Akenside *Odes* bk II Ode IV (*To the Hon. Charles Townshend, in the Country*, 1750) st iv 3 lines 1–4. The second passage is from the same poem, st v 1 lines 5–10. See Akenside *Poems* (1772) 304, 305, a volume C had borrowed from the Bristol Library 24 Dec 1795–8 Jan 1796: *Bristol LB* 122. For further evidence of C's interest in Akenside see *CN* I 123n; see also below, p 44 n 1, p 104 n 1.

[2] The special political use of "aristocrat" or "aristocratic" is shown in the practice of Lord Stanhope, an aristocrat by birth but a democrat in politics, in customarily referring to Burke, middle class in origin, as an "aristocrat". See Ghita Stanhope and G. P. Gooch *The Life of Charles, Third Earl Stanhope* (London & New York 1914) 147 and passim. See also Woodring *Politics in the Poetry of Coleridge* 86–91.

[3] Cf the dedication to *The Fall of Robespierre*: ". . . it has been my sole aim to imitate the empassioned and highly figurative language of the French orators . . .". *PW* (EHC) II 495.

succession of remote analogies.[1] It seems characteristic of true eloquence, to reason *in* metaphors; of declamation, to argue *by* metaphors.

With such notions of the matter and manner of Mr. Burke's former publication, I ought not to be suspected of party prejudice, when I declare the woeful inferiority of the present work—Alas! we fear that this Sun of Genius[2] is well nigh extinguished: a few bright spots linger on its orb, but scarcely larger or more numerous than the dark *maculæ* visible on it in the hour of its strength and effulgence. A tender and pleasing melancholy pervades those passages in which he alludes to his Son;[3] and renders the fierceness and vulgarity of the rest more wonderful. It might have been expected, that domestic calamity would have softened his heart, and by occupying it with private and lonely feelings, have precluded the throb and tempest of political fanaticism. But ere I begin the task of blame, I shall seize the opportunity of illuminating my pages by the following exquisitely beautiful and pathetic tribute to the memory of a departed great man:

"No man lives too long, who lives to do with spirit, and suffer with resignation, what Providence pleases to command or inflict: but indeed they are sharp incommodities which beset old age. It was but the other day, that on putting in order some things which had been brought here on my taking leave of London for ever, I looked over a number of fine portraits, most of them of persons now dead, but whose society, in my better days, made this a proud and happy place. Amongst these was the picture of Lord Keppel.[4] It was painted by an artist worthy of the subject, the excellent friend of that excellent man from their earliest youth, and a common friend of us both, with whom

[1] Hazlitt, in "My First Acquaintance with Poets", quoted C as saying in 1798: "Burke was an orator (almost a poet) who reasoned in figures, because he had an eye for nature . . .". *H Works* XVII 111.

[2] The original phrase is "Great Son of Genius", line 5 of the sonnet to Burke, first published in the *M Chron* 9 Dec 1794: *PW* (EHC) I 80. But C made a pun and found a metaphor (Woodring p 96), though when he came to reprint the sonnet in *Poems* (1796) he eschewed the pun. He called WW a "great son of genius! full of light and love" in an early version of *Dejection: an Ode*: see *PW* (EHC) I 366 (n to line 75).

[3] In June 1794 Burke finished his labours as one of the managers of the impeachment of Warren Hastings, in July he retired from Parliament, and in August he suffered the loss of his only son, Richard.

[4] When Admiral Augustus Keppel (1725–86), later Viscount Keppel, was court-martialled and acquitted in 1779, Burke as one of his counsel received a present of Keppel's portrait painted by Sir Joshua Reynolds; it is now in the Tate Gallery in London.

we lived for many years without a moment of coldness, of peevishness, of jealousy, or of jar, to the day of our final separation.

"I ever looked on Lord Keppel as one of the greatest and best men of his age; and I loved, and cultivated him accordingly. He was much in my heart, and I believe I was in his to the very last beat. It was after his trial at Portsmouth that he gave me this picture. With what zeal and anxious affection I attended him through that his agony of glory; what part my son took in the early flush and enthusiasm of his virtue, and the pious passion with which he attached himself to all my connexions,[a] with what prodigality we both squandered ourselves in courting almost every sort of enmity for his sake, I believe he felt, just as I should have felt such friendship on such an occasion. I partook indeed of this honour, with several of the first, and best, and ablest in the kingdom, but I was behind hand with none of them; and I am sure, that if to the eternal disgrace of this nation, and to the total annihilation of every trace of honour and virtue in it, things had taken a different turn from what they did, I should have attended him to the quarter-deck with no less good will and more pride, though with far other feelings, than I partook of the general flow of national joy that attended the justice that was done to his virtue.

"Pardon, my Lord, the feeble garrulity of age, which loves to diffuse itself in discourse of the departed great.—At my years we live in retrospect alone: and, wholly unfitted for the society of vigorous life, we enjoy, the best balm to all wounds, the consolation of friendship, in those only whom we have lost for ever."[1]

The remaining parts of the letter consist of attacks, first on Frenchmen and French principles; secondly, on geometry, chemistry, and metaphysics; thirdly, on the Duke of Bedford,[b] and lastly, of a defence of the pension.

First, therefore, of the attack on Frenchmen and French principles. David Hartley enumerates among the causes of Madness, an intense and long-continued attention to some one particular subject, falling in with an original bodily predisposition.[2] The too frequent recurrency of one particular set of ideas makes the vibrations belonging thereto

[a] connections [b] Bedford's ancestor, in the reign of Henry VIIIth;

[1] *Letter . . . to a Noble Lord* (1st ed 1796) 69–71.

[2] David Hartley *Observations on Man* (3 vols 1791) I 165, 400–3 (C's annotated copy is in the BM). The primacy of Hartley (1705–57) in C's thinking was shown when C named his eldest child (born Sept 1796) for "that great master of *Christian* Philosophy". Letter to Thomas Poole 24 Sept 1796: *CL* I 236. See also *Religious Musings* lines 391–4: ". . . and he of mortal kind | Wisest, he first who mark'd the ideal tribes | Down the fine

more than ordinarily vivid, and occasions that particular train to be associated with every common circumstance of life; till at length every common circumstance re-calls that particular train, and makes the recurrency perpetual: which is a species of madness.—If this be a just theory, the following is an alarming passage:

"The French Revolutionists complained of every thing; they refused to reform any thing; and they left nothing, no, nothing at all *unchanged.*—The consequences are *before* us,—not in remote history; not in future prognostication: they are about us; they are upon us. They shake the public security; they menace private enjoyment. They dwarf the growth of the young; they break the quiet of the old. *If we travel, they stop our way. They infest us in town; they pursue us to the country. Our business is interrupted; our repose is troubled; our pleasures are saddened; our very studies are poisoned and perverted, and knowledge is rendered worse than ignorance, by the enormous evils of this dreadful innovation.*"[1]

Indeed the phrenetic extravagance of the whole of this part of the Letter, "must make every reflecting mind, and every feeling heart, perfectly thought-sick."[2] In descanting on the excesses of the French, Mr. Burke has never chosen to examine what portion of them may be fairly attributed to the indignation and terror excited by the Combined Forces,[3] and what portion ought to be considered as the natural effects of Despotism and Superstition, so malignant and so long-continued.

> Warm'd with new influence the unwholesome plain
> Sent up its foulest fogs to meet the morn:
> The Sun, that rose on FREEDOM, rose in blood!
>
> JOAN OF ARC.[4]

Secondly—on Geometry, Chemistry, and Metaphysics. "Nothing can be conceived more hard than the heart of a thorough-bred Meta-

---

fibres from the sentient brain | Roll subtly-surging". *Poems* (1796) 164–5. Cf *PW* (EHC) I 123 (lines 368–71). For an exposition of Hartley's thought and its significance to C see Basil Willey *The Eighteenth Century Background* (1940) ch 8.

[1] *Letter . . . to a Noble Lord* 20–1 (except the first italicised word, C's italics).

[2] Ibid 22 (var).

[3] It was a commonplace among Friends of Freedom, such as C, that the excesses of the French Revolution sprang from the terror inspired by the coalition of foreign powers arrayed against France, principally Austria, Prussia, Russia, and England.

[4] *Joan of Arc* (1796) II 431–3. These are C's lines, and he later made them a part of *The Destiny of Nations* (lines 448–50). *PW* (EHC) I 146.

physician. It comes nearer to the cold malignity of a wicked spirit than to the frailty and passion of a man. It is like that of the principle of Evil* himself, incorporeal, pure unmixed, dephlegmated, defecated evil!"[2]—"The Geometricians and the Chemists bring, the one from the dry bones of their diagrams, and the other from the soot of their furnaces, dispositions that make them worse than indifferent about those feelings and habitudes, which are the supports of the moral world."[3]

Alas! how vile must that system be, which can reckon by anticipation among its certain enemies, the Metaphysician who employs the strength and subtlety of reason to investigate, by what causes being acted on, the human mind acts most worthily; the Geometrician, who tames into living and embodied uses the proud possibilities of Truth, and who has leavened the whole mass of his thoughts and feelings with the love of proportion; and the Chemist, whose faculties are swallowed up in the great task of discovering those perfect laws by which the Supreme Wisdom governs the Universe! Plato, with whom, as the dazzling Mystic of ancient days, it might have been expected that Mr. Burke would have fraternized, placed over the entrance of Academus, ουδεις αγεωμετρετος εισιτω.[4]—But I recollect, that Plato was the first Manufacturer of Utopian Commonwealths: a crime, for which even the Universals and intelligential worlds of the divine Anti-experimentalist will make an insufficient atonement. But the sciences suffer for their professors; and Geometry, Metaphysics, and Chemistry, are Condorcet, Abbe Sieyes,[5] and Priestley,[6] generalized.

* Quere.—Is Edmund Burke a Manichæan?[1]

[1] Cf below, p 92: "The Oriental system of Two Principles".

[2] *Letter . . . to a Noble Lord* 61 (var). See *CN* I 1623, II 2503 and n.

[3] *Letter . . . to a Noble Lord* 61.

[4] C may have remembered these words because he saw them in William Enfield *The History of Philosophy* (2 vols 1791) I 206. He borrowed vol I from the Bristol Library 27 Mar–6 Apr 1795: *Bristol LB* 119. Tr by Enfield: "Let no one, who is unacquainted with geometry, enter here". For a later use of the quotation, in a slightly different form, see *CN* II 2894n.

[5] Emmanuel-Joseph, Abbé Sieyès (1748–1836), a cleric who sided with the revolutionists; deputy to the Convention 1792–5. Burke (*Letter* 63) had ridiculed Sieyès's facility in the making of constitutions.

[6] Joseph Priestley (1733–1804), scientist, Unitarian theologian, and social reformer, whose house and laboratory in 1791 had been burned by the "Church and King" mobs. In 1794 he had settled in Pennsylvania. Cf *Religious Musings* lines 395–402:

> Lo! Priestley there, Patriot, and Saint, and Sage,
> Whom that my fleshly eye hath never seen
> A childish pang of impotent regret
> Hath thrill'd my heart. Him from his native land

It is lucky for Poetry, that Milton did not live in our days: and I suppose, that Sir Joshua Reynolds only could have made a vicarious satisfaction for the crimes of David,[1] and protected Painting.—But Mr. Burke is not the only writer who has lampooned God Almighty for having made men rational! I cannot conclude this part of my analysis in more appropriate words than these of Toland: "Such men seem perfectly distracted at the just disappointment they have met with in the loss of their interest and reputation among their friends; and to revenge themselves, having prepared a composition of Rage, Malice, and Uncharitableness, and lighted it with a blind and burning zeal, they draw clouds of darkness all around them, put themselves into[a] a wild confusion, and scatter their indignation (the overflowings of a disturbed fancy) at random."—(Nature and Consequences of Enthusiasm, p. 38.)[2]

Thirdly—the attack on the Duke of Bedford, for enjoying the senatorial office by hereditary right,[b] or (to use Mr. Burke's own words) for being "nursed, and swaddled, and dandled into a legislator;" for his immense property, which overshadows and "oppresses the industry of humble men;" and for his ingratitude to him (Mr. Burke) "the defender of his order,"[3] *i.e.* of the two former charges.

[a] with [b] rights

Statesmen blood-stain'd and Priests idolatrous
By dark lies mad'ning the blind multitude
Drove with vain hate: calm, pitying, he retir'd,
And mus'd expectant on these promis'd years.

Poems (1796) 165. Cf *PW* (EHC) I 123 (lines 371–6).

[1] Jacques-Louis David (1748–1825), whose paintings record the faces and attitudes of revolutionary and Napoleonic France.

[2] By Thomas Morgan (d 1743), not Toland. The passage occurs in a "Postscript: Occasion'd by Mr. Bradbury's Discourse" to *The Nature and Consequence of Enthusiasm Consider'd* (2nd ed 1720), "by a Protestant Dissenter"; see Morgan *A Collection of Tracts, Relating to the Right of Private Judgement*... (1726) 44. In his quotation C has changed the third person singular (referring to Bradbury) throughout to the plural. Toland may have come into C's mind about this time because he was reading in the latter's edition of Milton; see above, p 13 n 4, and cf *CN* I 39n. John Toland (1670–1722)—like Morgan, a deist—author of *Christianity Not Mysterious* (1696), also wrote a life of Milton, which he prefixed to his edition of Milton's prose works (1694–8). But Morgan and Toland may have been confused in C's mind because he was making a sly answer to a query by Burke: "Who, born within the last forty years, has read one word of Collins, and Toland, and Tindal, and Chubb, and Morgan, and that whole race who called themselves Freethinkers? Who now reads Bolingbroke?" *Reflections on the Revolution in France* (1790) 133. For C's interest in the deists see *CL* I 33.

[3] *Letter... to a Noble Lord* 28–9, 33, 52 (altered).

In other words, the Duke is sneered at for not being a Republican and an Agrarian; and reviled for his unthankfulness to the man who struggles to prevent him from being either. This is not the only instance to be met with in the course of Mr. Burke's writings, in which he lays down propositions, from which his adversaries are entitled to draw strange corollaries. The egg is his: Paine[1] and Barlow[2] *hatch* it.

Fourthly—a defence of his Pension; which is conducted on the following pleas: That Mr. Russell,[3] the founder of the Duke of Bedford's family, received a much larger grant from the Crown, without having deserved any thing; that Henry VIII, from whom Mr. Russell received his grants, was by no means so good a man as King George the Third, from whom he (Mr. Burke) received his pension: that it was received unsolicited, and "when he was entirely out of the way of serving or hurting any statesman or any party:"[4] and that it had been merited by his former services.—The two first grounds of defence are pitiably ridiculous; the third is a falsehood; the last we should be unwilling not to concede.

"When I could no longer serve them, the Ministers have considered my situation. When I could no longer hurt them, the Revolutionists have trampled on my infirmity."[5]

By what means did Mr. Burke serve the Ministers? By the effect which his speeches produced on the House of Commons? Or by his publications? Assuredly, by the latter! And is he not then serving and about to serve them? But did[a] Mr. Burke receive no gratuity anterior to his retirement from public life? In the *Cambridge*

[a] did not

[1] Thomas Paine (1737–1809). Following the publication of Burke's *Reflections*, Paine made his reply in *Rights of Man* (2 pts 1791–2) and was convicted in an English court on the charge of sedition. He had, however, previously withdrawn to France, where he earned the hostility of the Jacobins by his attempt to save the life of the King, and his own life was saved first by chance and ultimately by the claim that he was an American citizen.

[2] Joel Barlow (1754–1812) was an American poet and political theorist who went to Europe to sell land but remained to purvey revolutionary doctrines. Associated in London 1790–2 with Priestley, Paine, and other reformers, he wrote his *Advice to the Privileged Orders* (1792), which was suppressed by the government, and, like Paine, took refuge in France. In this present reference C seems to be trying to cap Burke, who had said in his *Letter* (p 11): "The revolution harpies of France . . . cuckoo-like, adulterously lay their eggs, and brood over and hatch them in the nest of every neighbouring State".

[3] John Russell (c 1486–1555), 1st Earl of Bedford.

[4] *Letter . . . to a Noble Lord* 5 (var).

[5] Ibid 6.

Intelligencer of Saturday, November 21, 1795, we find the following paragraph:[1]

"*When Mr. Burke first crossed over the House of Commons, from the Opposition to the Ministry, he received a pension of* 1200*l. a-year charged on the King's Privy Purse!* When he had completed his labours, it was then a question what recompence his services deserved. Mr. Burke wanting a present supply of money, it was thought that a pension of 2000l. per annum *for forty years certain*, would sell for eighteen years purchase, and bring him of course 36,000l. But this pension must, by the very unfortunate act, of which Mr. Burke was himself the author, have come before Parliament. Instead of this Mr. Pitt suggested the idea of a pension of 2000l. a-year *for three lives*, to be charged on the King's Revenue of the West India 4⅛ per cents. This was tried at the market, but it was found that it would not produce the 36,000l. which were wanted. In consequence of this a pension of 2,500l. per annum, *for three lives*, on the 4½ West India Fund, the lives to be nominated by Mr. Burke, that he may accommodate the purchasers, is *finally* granted to this disinterested patriot! He has thus retired from the trade of politics, with pensions to the amount of 3,700l. a-year."

If Mr. Burke's past services have merited* the pension, yet he himself confesses that money is not their proper recompence. At this time especially, when the cry against corruption is so loud and general, a good man sincerely zealous for the preservation of the present system, would have been delicate even to anxiety, and jealously disinterested. He would have remembered the words, which the eloquent Sheridan[3] put into the mouth of the Chancellor of the Exchequer.

* Mr. Burke's Reform Bills, in 1782, effected an annual saving to the public of eighty thousand pounds—not the fiftieth part of the interest to be paid for the millions spent in this HIS war.[2]

[1] C used this same quotation from *CI* as a note to line 9 of his sonnet to Burke—"Yet never, BURKE! drank'st Corruption's bowl!"—in *Poems* (1796) 177–9, prefaced by : "When I composed this line, I had not read the following paragraph . . ."; see *PW* (EHC) I 80–1.

[2] C ignores Burke's explanation in his *Letter* that the Economic Reform Bills were designed not merely for saving money but even more for the purification and curbing of the executive branch of government.

[3] Richard Brinsley Sheridan (1751–1816), who after writing the best comedies of the age, had become, as the pages of *The Watchman* show, an eloquent spokesman in Parliament for the Whigs. C here paraphrases portions of Sheridan's reply to Lord Mornington's speech on 21 Jan 1794. *Parl Reg* XXXVII 135–40. William Hazlitt recorded with approval an opinion that Sheridan's speech was "the most brilliant reply that perhaps was ever made in the House of Commons". *H Works* I 174.

"All the gentlemen, who will come forward in support of this great and glorious war, are to share in the taxes that are to be laid on the people; and accordingly look round me, and see how I have fattened and aggrandized all the persons who have come forward to my aid. No man now can make a boast of the sacrifices he has made, in order the better to oppose the friends of Brissot[1] in England. Not merely themselves, but their nephews and cousins, to the third and fourth remove, have been loaded with spoils, and have been appointed paymasters, agents, commissaries with pensions, entailed upon the country, whatever might be their services, merely for coming over to the support of the war. Good God, Sir, what a contrast do we exhibit, that, in such a moment as this, in times so big with national fate, the money squeezed from the pockets of an impoverished people, from the toils, the labours, and the sweat of their brows, should thus be squandered as the price of political apostacy! it misbecomes the honour of a gentleman to give, it misbecomes the honour of a gentleman to take, in such a moment. This is not a day for jobs, and the little dirty traffic of lucre and emolument, unless it is meant to promulgate it as a doctrine, that all public men are impostors, that every libel of the French is founded in truth."

We feel not, however, for the Public in the present instance: we feel for the honor of Genius; and mourn to find one of her most richly-gifted Children associated with the Youngs, Wyndhams, and Reeveses of the day;[2] "matched in mouth"[3] with

> "Mastiff, bloodhound, mungril grim,
> Cur, and spaniel, brache, and lym,
> Bobtail tike and trundle-tail;"[4]

[1] See below, p 39 n 4.

[2] Brought together by C for purposes of damnation, these Tory apologists are Arthur Young (see above, p 4 and n 1); William Windham (1750–1810), admirer of Burke and once a Whig, who on his conversion in 1794 became secretary at war; and John Reeves (c 1752–1829), who as chairman of the Association for Preserving Liberty and Property against Republicans and Levellers, was a leading anti-Jacobin, the "captain commandant of the spy-gang" to C: *PD* (1795) 30n.

[3] *A Midsummer Night's Dream* IV i 126.

[4] *King Lear* III vi 71–3 (var). C regularly modifies his quotations, Shakespeare and the Bible not excepted. See JDC "Coleridge's Quotations" *Athenaeum* No 3382 (20 Aug 1892) 259–60. Here he has replaced "grey-hound" with "bloodhound" and "hound" with "Cur". He is quoting five lines after the passage: "The little dogs and all, Tray, Blanch, and Sweetheart, see, they bark at me", which Burke had discharged at his foes of the Opposition on a famous occasion in 1791, when he finally broke with Fox. See Sir James Prior *Life of Edmund Burke* (1891) 340. C probably remembered, and expected his readers to remember, the scene of several years before.

and the rest of that motley pack, that open in most hideous concert, whenever our State-Nimrod[1] provokes the scent by a trail of rancid plots and false insurrections! For of the *rationality* of these animals I am inclined to entertain a doubt, a *charitable* doubt! since such is the system which they support, that we add to their integrity whatever we detract from their understanding:

—Fibris increvit opimum
Pingue: carent culpa.[2]

It is consoling to the lovers of human nature, to reflect that Edmund Burke, the only writer of that Faction "whose name would not sully the page of an opponent,"[3] learnt the discipline of genius in a different corps. At the flames which rise from the altar of Freedom, he kindled that torch with which he since endeavoured to set fire to her temple. Peace be to his spirit, when it departs from us: this is the severest punishment I wish him—that he may be appointed under-porter to St. Peter, and be obliged to open the gate of Heaven to Brissot, Roland, Condorcet, Fayette,[4] and Priestley![5]

FOREIGN INTELLIGENCE

THE hope, that the armistice[6] would lead to a peace, has vanished. The French Government demand that Belgium and Liege shall be

[1] Pitt.

[2] Persius *Satires* 3.32–3 (altered). Quoted also in *An Answer to "A Letter to Edward Long Fox, M.D."* 8 (see below, n 5). Tr: "Comfortable fat has grown round the liver [i.e. heart]: they are not to blame".

[3] Quotation not traced.

[4] Jean-Pierre (or Jacques-Pierre) Brissot (1754–93), who had previously written under the name of Brissot de Warville, became after the Revolution a republican pamphleteer, allied with the Girondists. A member of the Assembly and the Convention, he was guillotined in Oct 1793. He, like other persons here listed, was of the moderate party. (For an "anecdote" about him, see below, pp 356–7; see also *Conciones*—1795—10, 31). Jean-Marie Roland de la Platière (1734–93), a Girondist leader, whose wife was also a noted figure. It was she who was reported to exclaim: "O Liberty! what crimes are committed in thy name!" when led to the guillotine. Roland, who had fled from Paris, killed himself when he learned of her execution. Marie-Roch-Gilbert Motier, Marquis de la Fayette (1757–1834), a major-general in the American Revolution at the age of twenty, commander-in-chief of the National Guard after the fall of the Bastille (1789–91). For his later career see below, p 183 and n 1.

[5] The two concluding paragraphs are almost identical with the conclusion of C. T. S. *An Answer to "A Letter to Edward Long Fox, M.D."* (Bristol [1795]). For a discussion of this pamphlet, attributed to C, see R. A. Potts *Athenaeum* No 4201 (2 May 1908) 543 and n.

[6] France and Austria arranged an armistice in the Rhineland in Dec 1795. Fighting was resumed there in the summer of 1796. Most of this paragraph is condensed from the *Sun* or the *Gazetteer, and New Daily Advertiser*, 25 Feb, from two mails from Hamburg that arrived the day before.

formally ceded to France, and the Constitution, which Holland proposes to establish for itself, be acknowledged by the Allied Powers. Austria and England will not listen to these pretensions. The French Army on the Rhine will be augmented to 300,000 men. The Emperor will re-inforce his army on the Rhine with 30,000 men, most of whom have indeed already joined. *It is said*, that the Empress of Russia[1] has at length determined to send 40,000 men to the assistance of the Emperor; and that 30,000 Prussians are on their march to the Circle of Franconia. The Austrian armies on the Rhine will early in this month consist of 200,000 men. Field-Marshal de Clerfaye[2] was to have taken upon him the command of the Imperial army, and that of the Empire, with unlimited powers; but after repeated solicitations, his Imperial Majesty has permitted him to resign the honor; and his Royal Highness the Arch-duke Charles[3] has been appointed in his stead. The forces of the Allied powers in Italy are to consist of 50,000 men, exclusive of the Italian troops; and will be commanded by General Wurmser.[4] The letters from Germany speak of the preparations of the French, as being infinitely beyond all their former exertions, great and wonderful as they were: and such was Marshal Clerfaye's account of them to the Emperor, who in consequence of it, is said to have leaned to peace, and was by no means willing to enter into fresh engagements with England. But the influence of the English Minister prevailed over every consideration, and at length brought over the Emperor to the desperate attempt of a fresh campaign.

"New years of havock urge their destin'd course."[5]

In Paris a national bank has been established, the shares 600

[1] Catherine II (1729–96), nearing the end of her remarkable career, was at sixty-seven still living with a lover, whom she spoiled as Byron has her spoiling Don Juan. She, as *The Watchman* shows, had recently with Prussia and Austria completed the process of partitioning Poland. She died before the year was out, and Coleridge devotes a number of lines to her in *Ode to the Departing Year*, and a note, part of which reads: "Why should I recal the poisoning of her husband, her iniquities in Poland, or her late unmotived attack on Persia, the desolating ambition of her public life, or the libidinous excesses of her private hours! I have no wish to qualify myself for the office of Historiographer to the King of Hell—!" *PW* (EHC) I 162–3n.

[2] François-Sébastien-Charles-Joseph de Croix de Drumez, Comte de Clerfayt (or Clairfayt, 1733–98), was a Belgian commander of the Austrian forces who thwarted French designs upon the Rhineland in 1795.

[3] Archduke Charles Louis (1771–1847), son of Leopold II and field-marshal.

[4] Count Dagobert Siegmund von Wurmser (1724–97), Austrian field-marshal.

[5] Thomas Gray *The Bard* II 3 line 9 (var).

livres. It is to be directed by a Council of ten Administrators and a Director-general. The Subscribers delegate to the Council the power of treating with the Government in such a way, as that in no case the Bank engagements shall exceed the half of the real value of the assets lodged in the Bank itself. To be entitled to vote in the general meetings of the Bank, it is necessary to hold twenty shares; on the demand of fifty Subscribers having votes, the Council shall be obliged to call a general meeting within ten days; and the accounts of the establishments are to be balanced daily.—All the forms, plates, matrices, and punches employed in the manufacture of assignats, were broken up, and afterwards melted on the 1st Ventose (Feb. 20.)[1]

We feel a deep concern that a law for limiting the liberty of the press will probably be soon in the French Legislature.

Charette[2] is in great force; but the Royalists are formidable in no other light than as[a] sanguinary banditti. They are said to consist of eighty divisions of 4,000 men each; and to possess so large an extent of territory, that Emigrants, who avoid towns and municipalities, may ride many hundred miles without meeting an enemy. For the truth of this information, we rely on the report of *The Star*.[3]

Unless Mr. Pitt's *epileptic* memory[4] be a contagious distemper, Mr. Burke will not have forgotten his magnificent panegyric on General Washington.[5] What, then, must be his feelings when he reads the American President's answer on receiving the standard of the French regicides, sent from the Committee of Public Safety, by order of the National Convention, as a token of friendship to the United States.

[a] as a

[1] Actually 19 Feb. This paragraph condensed from the *Star* 26 Feb 1796. See below, n 3.

[2] François-Athanase Charette de la Contrie (1763–96), royalist general in the Vendéan insurrection. For his capture and execution, see below, pp 212–13, 245–6, 285–7. The pages of *The Watchman* record the extinction of foreign hopes that the Revolution would be conquered from within.

[3] From the *Star* 26 Feb 1796. The *Star* was an Opposition evening newspaper conducted by John Mayne. See Lucyle Werkmeister *The London Daily Press 1772–1792* (Lincoln, Nebraska 1963) 366.

[4] When the Rev John Horne Tooke was tried for high treason in 1794, he called Pitt to the stand as a witness. As he was being questioned, Pitt could not at first recollect having attended a meeting of delegates for parliamentary reform at the Thatched-House Tavern in 1782. Opposition orators and writers did not allow him to forget this lapse of memory. C had alluded to Pitt's epileptic memory in *An Answer to "A Letter to Edward Long Fox, M.D."* [1795] 7. *OED* lists an obsolete figurative use of "epileptical" meaning "spasmodic", "inconstant".

[5] Source not traced.

The Answer of the President of the United States to the Address of the Minister Plenipotentiary of the French Republic, on his presenting the Colours of France to the United States.[1]

"BORN, Sir, in a land of Liberty; having early learned its value; having engaged in a perilous conflict to defend it; having, in a word, devoted the best years of my life to secure its permanent establishment in my own country, my anxious recollection, my sympathetic feelings, and my best wishes, are irresistibly excited, whensoever in any country, I see an oppressed nation unfurl the banners of freedom. But above all, the events of the French Revolution have produced the deepest solicitude, as well as the highest admiration. To call your nation brave, were to pronounce but common praise. Wonderful people! Ages to come will read with astonishment the history of your brilliant exploits! I rejoice that the period of your toils and of your immense sacrifices is approaching. I rejoice that the interesting revolutionary movements of so many years have issued in the formation of a constitution designed to give permanency to the great object for which you have contended. I rejoice that liberty, which you have so long embraced with enthusiasm—liberty, of which you have been the invincible defenders, now finds an asylum in the bosom of a regularly organized Government; a Government, which, being formed to secure the happiness of the French People, corresponds with the ardent wishes of my heart, while it gratifies the pride of every citizen of the United States by its resemblance to their own. On these glorious events, accept, Sir, my sincere congratulations.

"In delivering to you these sentiments, I express not my own feelings only, but those of my fellow citizens, in relation to the commencement, the progress, and the issue of the French Revolution; and they will cordially join with me [a]in the[b] purest wishes to the Supreme Being, that the citizens of our sister Republic, our magnanimous allies, may soon enjoy in peace, that liberty, which they have purchased at so great a price, and all the happiness which liberty can bestow.

"I receive, Sir, with lively sensibility, the symbol of the triumphs and of the enfranchisement of your nation, the colours of France, which you have now presented to the United States. The transaction

[a–b] in

[1] From the *Star* or *M Chron* 25 Feb or *M Post* 26 Feb 1796. For the French minister's speech, see below, pp 372–3.

will be announced to Congress; and the colours will be deposited with those archives of the United States, which are at once the evidences and the memorials of their Freedom and independence. May these be perpetual! and may the friendship of the two Republics be commensurate with their existence.

GEO. WASHINGTON."

United States, Jan. 1, 1796.

True Copy.

GEO. TAYLOR, Jun.

Chief Clerk in the Dep. of State.

The flag is to be deposited in the archives of the United States.

DOMESTIC INTELLIGENCE

BARRACKS are fitting up in the town of Southampton, for the reception of ten thousand Emigrant and other foreign troops: accounts have been already received of their embarkation from the Continent.[1]

SALISBURY, *Feb.* 22. "The remnant of the 88th regiment arrived in this city on Saturday se'nnight, from Bristol, and marched on Monday last for Portsmouth.

"This regiment, when embarked for the Continent about two years ago, was 1100 strong: in the course of service, but principally by the severe winter of 1794–5, and the consequent hardships they encountered in evacuating Holland, their number was reduced when landed in England to about 250 men.

"They lately embarked for the West Indies, in the Jamaica transport, one of Admiral Christian's[2] convoy, and sickness again followed this ill-fated corps, a raging fever carrying off about five a day: in consequence, though far on their voyage, they were ordered to return, and endeavour to make the first port. At the chops of the Channel, when looking out for land, they descried a frigate under English colours, from which they hoped to receive protection, but the frigate, on approaching nearer, hoisted the French national flag, and proving to be an enemy, ransacked the transport of arms and other valuables, took out the Officers (Captain Silver, of Winchester, another Captain, and 6 Lieutenants), and put a prize-master on

[1] From the *Star* 25 Feb 1796.

[2] Sir Hugh Cloberry Christian (1747–98), rear-admiral; commander-in-chief in the West Indies in 1796. See below, p 220.

board, with orders to follow the frigate into Brest; nearly at the entrance of which port, the Trusty English man of war, of 50 guns, came up between the transport and frigate, and putting an officer on board the former, to supersede the French prize-master, went in chase of the frigate, though with little prospect of success. Once again the transport made for an English port, but carrying too great a press of sail, her masts fell by the board, and she continued in this helpless and almost hopeless state for many days, when she was providentially fallen in with by an American brig bound[a] for Bristol; by this vessel's great and timely assistance, the transport was enabled to follow her into port. The corps, now reduced to about 100, marched under the command of an officer of the 80th, for Portsmouth, where they will probably be drafted into some other corps."

[b]After the perusal of the preceding account, my[c] readers will thank me for selecting the following [d]appropriate and[e] beautiful passages from the *Joan of Arc*, by Robert Southey; a poem which exhibits fresh proof that great poetical talents and high sentiments of liberty do reciprocally produce and assist each other.[1]

Thus the King exclaim'd:
O chosen by Heaven! defer awhile thy march,
That o'er the land my Heralds may proclaim
A general Fast.
Severe the Maid replied:
Monarch of France! and canst thou think that God
Beholds well-pleas'd the mockery of a Fast![2]

[a] found [b–c] My [d–e] appropriate

[1] Akenside *Poems* (1772) 344 (Notes on the Two Books of Odes): ". . . great poetical talents, and high sentiments of liberty, do reciprocally produce and assist each other".Cf *BL* ch 10 (1907) I 140: "In Pindar, Chaucer, Dante, Milton, &c., &c., we have instances of the close connection of poetic genius with the love of liberty and of genuine reformation." Later C commented sarcastically on "the transmogrification of the fanatic Virago into a modern novel-pawing Proselyte of the age of Reason, a Tom Paine in Petticoats, but *so* lovely!—& in love, moreover!" and was "astonished" at "the utter want of all rhythm in the verse, the monotony & dead *plumb down* of the Pauses—& the absence of all Bone, Muscle, & Sinew in the single Lines". To J. J. Morgan [16 Jun 1814]: *CL* III 510.

[2] See *Joan of Arc* (1796) p 115n, a note to this line quoting a long passage from *Conciones* (1795) 55-6 that includes a passage from William Crowe's *Verses Intended to Have Been Spoken . . . to the Duke of Portland*, which is more extensively excerpted in *The Watchman*, below, pp 179–80. See also below, C's "Essay on Fasts", pp 51–5.

Luxurious lordly Riot is content,
And willingly obedient to command,
Feasts on some sainted dainty. The poor man,
From the hard labour of the day debarred,
Loses his hard meal too. It were to waste
The hour in impious folly, so to bribe
The all-creating Parent to destroy
The works he made. Proud tyranny to man,
To God foul insult! Mortify your pride;
Be clad in sackcloth when the Conqueror's car
Rolls o'er the field of blood!—Believe me, King!
If thou didst know the untold misery
When from the bosom of domestic love
But one—one victim goes! if that thine heart
Be human, it would bleed!

Book the Fourth, l. 484.[1]

The death of a common Soldier from *Book the Seventh, l.* 320.[2]

Of unrecorded name
Died the mean man, yet did he leave behind,
One who did never say her daily prayers
Of him forgetful; who to every tale
Of the distant war lending an eager ear,
Grew pale and trembled. At her cottage door
The wretched one shall sit, and with dim eye
Gaze o'er the plain, where, on his parting steps,
Her last look hung. Nor ever shall she know
Her husband dead, but tortured with vain hope
Gaze on—then heartsick turn to her poor babe,
And weep it fatherless!

A squadron has been ordered to put immediately to sea from Spithead; its destination is to go in quest of a Dutch Squadron of considerable force now at sea. The same orders have been sent to the fleet in the Downs. The Dutch Fleet consists of fourteen sail. It left the Texel on Tuesday morning, and was seen to steer northward.[3]

The Officers on board the Transport lately put into the port of

[1] *Joan of Arc* (1796) IV 484–504 (var: "luxurious" for "luxuriant"; C's italics).

[2] Ibid VII 320–31.

[3] Above item condensed from the *Star* 26 Feb 1796.

Bristol, displayed an heroic energy, which will not be forgotten by future historians. The troops on board this transport were four companies of Lowestein's Chasseurs. They had been separated from Admiral Christian's fleet, and driven westward; when the common soldiers formed the resolution of murdering their officers, and carrying the ship into Algiers. A very few minutes before the proposed execution of this detestable scheme, an individual concerned, betrayed it to the officers—a moment only for consultation was their's, nor did they lose that moment. They first fastened down the hatches on the men, long enough to be able to get at three barrels of gunpowder; the heads of which they beat out, and standing over them with lighted matches, told the Mutineers, that if the vessel were prevented from being steered into an English port, their determination was to blow her up, and that all should perish together. For several days the officers remained at their perilous post, relieving one another by turns in this desperate service, till the vessel cast anchor at Bristol.[1]

Earl Stanhope does not *talk* only: he feels, and acts in contempt of aristocratic prejudices. Mr. Taylor, the son of an Apothecary at Seven Oaks, in Kent, had gained the affections of his daughter. The young Lady, truly noble from the advantages of her education, did not disguise the state of her feelings, but made her father her confidant. "Is he not honest and intelligent?" replied the Earl.—"Assuredly, I approve of your choice." The match was accordingly made; and from the idea that there is a want of ingenuous publicity in a licence, the banns were called last Sunday, and the young couple will be shortly married according to the old and regular forms of the church.[2]

[1] Above item from the *Star* 26 Feb 1796; the first sentence, however, is C's.

[2] Reported in the *Star* 26 Feb 1796. James Gillray commemorated this wedding of Lady Lucy Stanhope to Thomas Taylor, apothecary and Stanhope family doctor, in a cartoon entitled *Democratic Leveling;—Alliance a la Françoise; or—The Union of the Coronet & Clyster-pipe*, showing Fox, the officiating Clergyman, reading the service from Paine's *Rights of Man*, while Lord Stanhope pushes his daughter toward the groom. That the radical Stanhope took such a view of the marriage was generally assumed at the time, but his biographers tell another story. According to them, the father reacted more conventionally to the misalliance by disowning his daughter. Ironically enough, it was the bride's uncle, Pitt himself, who befriended the couple by giving the husband a government post. See Stanhope and Gooch *The Life of Charles, Third Earl Stanhope* 238. C had addressed a laudatory sonnet to Stanhope in 1795 (*PW*—EHC—I 89–90) and wrote but discarded a dedication to Stanhope of his *Poems* (1796). See *PW* (EHC) II 1137.

COURT NEWS....On Thursday the Queen had a drawing-room at St James's Palace, *and all that*—[1]

COPY OF A HAND-BILL[2]

WHEREAS the Right Honourable WILLIAM PITT, Chancellor of his Majesty's Exchequer, did, on the night of Monday last, and on or about the hour of six o'clock, utter, in his place in the House of Commons, certain sentences, or phrases,[3] containing several assurances, denials, promises, retractions, persuasions, explanations, hints, insinuations, and intimations, and expressing much hope, fear, joy, sorrow, confidence, and doubt, upon the subject of Peace, then and there recommended by CHARLES GREY, Esq. Member of the aforesaid House of Commons for the county of

[1] Cf *The Times* 4 Mar 1796, a typical item in the London dailies: "Yesterday the Queen held a Drawing Room at St. James's Palace; which began at two o'clock, and was over at half past four". C, in addition to warning his readers not to expect fashionable chit-chat, half discloses his antimonarchical sentiments. The mocking phrase recalls the lines (III 17–18) in *The Rape of the Lock*:

> *Snuff*, or the *Fan*, supply each Pause of Chat,
> With singing, laughing, ogling, and all that.

[2] Cf *M Post* 18 Feb 1796:

ONE THOUSAND POUNDS REWARD!!!

Whereas on the night of the 15th instant the Right Honourable W. PITT made a Speech in the House of Commons on the Question of *Peace* or *War*; and whereas divers, different, and very contrary opinions have arisen respecting the meaning and tenor of the same; now we thinking it of the highest importance that its true intent and meaning should be well understood, do hereby offer a REWARD of *One Thousand Pounds* to any person or persons who shall within the space of one week from the date hereof make FULL DISCOVERY whether the said WILLIAM PITT gave most reason to hope for Peace, or to dread the Continuance of the War; or whether he had any meaning in said Speech, other than to conceal his intentions.

THE BULLS AND BEARS
Stock Exchange, Feb. 17, 1796.

[3] For Pitt's speech of 15 Feb see *Parl Reg* XLIV 41–54. In elaborating this *jeu d'esprit* C is traversing familiar ground for antiministerialist spokesmen. Fox had said of Pitt: "He employed the gift of words not like other men for the sake of being distinct but for the purpose of being misunderstood". *M Chron* 25 Mar 1795. Pitt's followers recognised—perhaps took a certain pride in—the talent of their chief. George Canning, one of Pitt's promising young recruits, pictures in a letter (8 Feb 1804) an imaginary scene in which a disciple of Pitt is seeking the master's views. Satisfied, he takes his leave. "Just when he is picking his way across the street . . . on his return home to repeat what he has heard, it will dart across his mind that he has, in fact, heard *nothing*". *Lord Granville Leveson Gower: Private Correspondence* ed Castalia, Countess Granville (2 vols 1916) I 445–6.

Northumberland; and whereas the entire, effectual, and certain meaning of the whole of the said sentences, phrases, denials, promises, retractions, persuasions, explanations, hints, insinuations, and intimations, has escaped and fled, so that what remains is to plain understandings[a] incomprehensible, and to many good men is matter of painful contemplation: now this is to promise, to any person who shall restore the said lost meaning, or shall illustrate, simplify, and explain, the said meaning, the sum of FIVE THOUSAND POUNDS, to be paid on the first day of *April* next, at the office of JOHN BULL, Esq. PAY-ALL and FIGHT-ALL to the several High contracting Powers engaged in the present *just* and *necessary* War![1]

Done at the Office of Mr JOHN BULL'S Chief Decypherer, Turnagain-lane, Circumbendibus-street, Obscurity-square, February 18, 1796.

PROCEEDINGS OF THE BRITISH LEGISLATURE

HOUSE OF COMMONS

MONDAY, *Feb.* 22.

MR. WHITBREAD[2] was happy to find that his speech on Tuesday last, on an intended Bill for the Relief of the LABOURING POOR, had induced the Chancellor of the Exchequer to take up a measure of such great internal policy. He chearfully relinquished the business in favour of the Right Honorable Gentleman, promising him his cordial assistance to procure it expedition in the adoption, and to render it effectual in its operation.

The Order of the Day was then read for the third reading of the Vote of Credit Bill.

Mr. GREY renewed his animadversions on the irregularity of introducing a vote of credit at so early a period of the sessions. He stated, that, in the first place, a vote of credit was usually passed to

[a] understanding

[1] Burke had echoed this phrase in a Latin form, "Justa bella quibus *necessaria*", in his *Reflections* (1790) 43—a misquotation from Livy. But "just and necessary war" was a commonplace; Dryden uses it, for instance, in the preface to *Annus Mirabilis*. As with the Opposition in the American war, the opponents of the French war in the 1790's used the phrase ironically, as here, or contrarily, in the phrase "unjust and unnecessary war". Cf below, p 310. Cf article 37 of the Thirty-nine Articles of 1563: "Christianis licet . . . iusta bella administrare".

[2] Samuel Whitbread (c 1758–1815), MP for Bedford and rich brewer, was a leading Whig. Sydney Smith nicknamed him "the great fermentator".

provide for some extraordinary or unforeseen expence which had been incurred when Parliament was not sitting, and which in such case would be specifically stated: or for some expences likely to be incurred when parliament is not sitting, which were not foreseen when the estimates were made and laid before the House; and in such cases that it was the uniform practice to make it the last business of the Sessions. In the war of 1756, and during the American war, no vote of credit was ever introduced till a few days before the end of the Session. From this irregularity, therefore, and from the honorable gentleman's (Mr. Rose)[1] declaration on Friday last, that delay would be attended with inconvenience, he strongly suspected that in the present vote of credit bill the house was not called upon to provide for any prospective events, but for past occurrences. Nor was the magnitude less unprecedented than the time of the demand. In the two former wars, no greater demand was ever made than for one million of money as a vote of credit: but of late it had been the practice to increase that demand to the extravagant demand of 2,500,000l. By this careless mode of granting money for unknown purposes, the House ceased to be the guardians of the public purse; and by diminishing the necessity of accuracy in the accounts of Ministers, increased the temptations to[a] fraudulence. He moved that the third reading of the bill be postponed till that day three weeks.

The CHANCELLOR of the EXCHEQUER agreed with Mr. Grey, that a vote of credit was not usually applied for till the end of the sessions. He conceived, however, that when the extraordinary expences were foreseen, the most regular way was to apply for it when the Committees of Supply, and Ways and Means were open. In pursuance of this idea, the vote of credit this year was stated as an article of supply, and might be applicable or not, as the exigencies of the case required. Since Ministers would be accountable at all times for the expenditure, he did not perceive the necessity of the distinct appropriation of each sum to some separate purpose: but thought that to defray all demands on the public from one common purse not only more suited to sudden emergencies, but also a more œconomic plan, than such distinct appropriation: since in the [b]latter case[c] sums must be reserved for a long time without any use whatever, and lie dead, until the period, the remote perhaps and distant period, arrived, for their specification.

[a] of [b-c] latter

[1] George Rose (1744–1818), MP for Christchurch, rendered much political assistance to his friend Pitt.

MR. FOX supported Mr. Grey's motion. He professed himself not perfectly satisfied with the Right Honorable Gentleman's explanation. The Right Honorable Gentleman appeared to allow, that the present was an unusual mode of application; but he had contended, that it was more likely to effect a system of rigid regularity in the payment of the different departments of Government. Who would not collect from this, that such promptness of payment was the constant practice of the Ministry? but he seemed to have forgotten, that the ordnance is in arrear, that the navy is in arrear, that the civil list is in arrear, and in short, that arrears were never so much complained of as at present. Excepting a few particular arrangements under Lord Moira,[1] there are arrears due to every officer in the army. The staff had been provided for upon the estimates; yet there are staff officers returned from abroad who since the year 1793 have not received one shilling. These were not facts favorable to the Right Honorable Gentleman's reasonings; and if such a system were pursued, a system in which persons do not receive money which is due and has been voted to them, we might expect to be always in our present situation of multiplied arrears.

MR. SHERIDAN remarked, that even if the Right Honorable Gentleman's explanation had been more plausible than it appeared to him to be, yet no reasonings could justify an unconstitutional mode of application. By the laws of his country the Right Honorable Gentleman (and every other Minister) was bound to apply all money to the purposes for which it had been specifically voted. But by this plan of a common purse the Right Honorable Gentleman destroyed all distinction between the money granted by a vote of credit, and that granted upon the estimates; and of course rendered the estimates presented to Parliament an unmeaning ceremony. He confessed, that the delay of the Bill might create much inconvenience; but [a]he deemed[b] the general consequences of allowing unconstitutional practices more alarming than any particular embarrassments.

The House then divided—for Mr. Grey's motion 25—against it 102. The Bill was then read a third time and passed.

[a-b] be

[1] Francis Rawdon-Hastings, 2nd Earl of Moira, later 1st Marquis of Hastings (1754–1826). As Lord Rawdon he had fought at Bunker Hill and later commanded troops in South Carolina during the American Revolution; promoted to major-general 1793. He was an intimate friend of the Prince of Wales.

THE WATCHMAN

No. II. WEDNESDAY, MARCH 9, 1796

Published by the Author, S. T. COLERIDGE, Bristol;
And by PARSONS, Paternoster-Row, London.[1]

THAT ALL MAY KNOW THE TRUTH;
AND THAT THE TRUTH MAY MAKE US FREE!

ESSAY ON FASTS[2]

Wherefore my Bowels shall sound like an Harp.
ISAIAH, xvi. 11.

FASTING has been commanded by every religion except the Christian.—It was practised with extreme rigour by the ancient Priests; a fact which disproves the common opinion, that Priests are the same in all ages.—We collect from Herodotus and Porphyry, that before their annual sacrifice of a cow to Isis, the Ægyptians fasted forty days: and Pythagoras, in addition to the perpetual and fishless Lent which he observed, is reported to have abstained from

[1] See above, Introduction, pp xxxiv, lvii, lix.

[2] Fasting, the subject of much contention throughout the eighteenth century, was timely because of the conjunction of Lent and a special fast-day set for 9 Mar, the date of this *Watchman*; see *A Form of Prayer, to Be Used in All Churches and Chapels Throughout . . . England, Wales, and the Town of Berwick upon Tweed, upon Wednesday the Ninth of March Next . . . by His Majesty's Special Command* (1796). Fasting was repellent to C on several counts: (1) as a Dissenter he viewed it as one of many impurities introduced into Christianity by prelacy. Cf also Johann Lorenz von Mosheim *An Ecclesiastical History, Ancient and Modern* tr A. Maclaine (1782) I 130–1; Priestley *An History of the Corruptions of Christianity* (1782) pt 8 § 4: *Theological and Miscellaneous Works* ed J. T. Rutt (25 vols 1817–32) V 306–11; Hartley *Observations on Man* (1791) III 636–7, 644–50 (additions by Pistorius). (2) As an eighteenth-century classical student he condemned it as gothic. Conyers Middleton (see below), Gibbon, and Porson were influential figures in this tradition. (3) As a Friend of Freedom he resented the use government was making of the Church as a channel of political propaganda. Relevant references to C's history of fasting are Herodotus 2.40, Diogenes Laërtius 8.40, Porphyry *Life of Pythagoras* 34, Iamblichus *Of the Pythagorean Life* 27; but he might have collected his data from any one of the evangelical histories of the Christian Church. Note Southey's condemnation of fasting, above, pp 44–5. Cf also *Conciones* 55–9.

all food whatsoever, forty days: and so did Elijah,[1] but with this advantage over Pythagoras, that he had double-dined on viands angelically prepared. This coincidence of number in the days seems to cast a shade of doubt on the genuineness of the beginning of the fourth chapter of Matthew and of Luke: in which the same miraculous circumstance is related of our Saviour. It was the policy of the early Christians to assimilate their religion to that of the Heathens in all possible respects. The ceremonies of the Romish church have been traced to this source by Middleton;[2] the miraculous conception is a palpable imitation of the story of Romulus, the son of a vestal virgin, by the descent of a Deity; and so, I suppose, because Pythagoras fasted forty days, the Interpolators of the Gospels must needs palm the same useless prodigy on Jesus. Indeed the conversion of the Heathens to Christianity, after the first century, does very much resemble Mahomet's miracle: as the mountain would not come over to him, he went over to the mountain. I recollect to have read of two rational fasts, and two only; and both on the same occasion. The Lacedemonians ordained a fast throughout the whole of their dominions without excepting even the domestic animals, in order that they might be enabled to spare provisions from[3] an allied city then suffering siege.—When Tarentum was besieged by the Romans, their neighbours, the inhabitants of Rhegium, proclaimed a General Fast throughout their whole territories: and threw the provisions, so nobly obtained, into the besieged town.—The Romans decamped, and the Tarentines, in memory of this deliverance, instituted an annual Fast: which, in my humble opinion, was not a very wise action, as an annual *Feast* in the nature of things would have stimulated the gratitude of their posterity much more effectually. I have omitted to mention that some Divines assert, that Fasting was the first command given by God, when he forbad our first parents to eat of the *Tree of Knowledge*: they disobeyed, and were severely punished; and our Divines seem to have been effectually warned by their example.

It seems the Devil which possesses the French, is of that kind "which goeth not out but by prayer and fasting."[4] The devotional compositions appointed for all churches and chapels, contain each year an abridgement of the Minister's latest harangues against the

[1] 1 Kings 17.16, 19.8.

[2] See Conyers Middleton *A Letter from Rome, Shewing an Exact Conformity between Popery and Paganism* (4th ed 1741). For C's later reading of Middleton see *CN* II 2664, 2729, and nn.

[3] An error for "for".

[4] Matt 17.21.

French: and the good people of this country, "in the most devout and solemn manner," tell God Almighty all that the Minister has told *them*.[1] In the new Form of Prayer (or, as the women bawl it about the streets, the *new former* prayer—bye the bye, no *unmeaning* blunder), we are humbly to acknowledge the sins of our enemies; making "earnest prayer and supplication in behalf of ourselves and other Christian nations exposed at this time to violence, or groaning under the oppression of apostates from the truth, who threaten desolation to every country where they can erect their standard! And we confess that their horrible crimes and astonishing impieties," are designed by God as the punishment of our own *foibles*. For, to be sure, we ought to acknowledge with penitent hearts that we (the church-people) have been blessed beyond other nations in the knowledge of the truth (i.e. the Athanasian Creed and the Thirty-nine Articles), and the undisturbed profession of it (no Test-acts[2] and Birmingham Mobs[3] against *us*), and in the long possession of abundant temporal prosperity! (*This last clause of the acknowledgment, we suppose, is confined to the mahogany pews lined with green baize, the possessors of which ought indeed to have known better manners than to "have turned their backs on the Lord"*).[4] Then follows the portion from scripture selected with great care, and the significant words of which are usually marked by the Priest with an emphasis, which answers all the purposes of a running commentary. The pleasure which a pious Churchman receives from these appropriate chapters, is precisely the same with that which a coffee-house politician experiences when reading over a state-libel full of Mr. —— and my Lord, and the ***** of ——, he applauds himself for his sagacity in being able to substitute the intended names. For instance, in the Epistle selected for this day from the Second Peter, chapter ii. 'But there were false prophets also among the people (*just such ones, I suppose, as Richard Brothers and William Bryant*),[5] even as there

[1] WW speaks of his "conflict of sensations" when similar prayers were offered up in church. *Prelude* x 288–99.

[2] The Test and Corporation Acts of Charles II barred Dissenters and Roman Catholics from holding municipal and national offices. Though suspended in the late eighteenth century, the laws remained on the books until 1828.

[3] The "Church and King" mobs that in 1791 attacked the houses of prominent Dissenters, with the magistrates, it is said, looking on with indifference or acquiescence.

[4] Cf Neh 9.26.

[5] Richard Brothers (1757–1824), once a lieutenant in the Royal Navy, was discharged as insane when he joined political reform with religious prophecy, insisted on the sharing of wealth, and fancied himself the nephew of the Almighty. He was the author of *A Revealed Knowledge of the Prophecies & Times . . . Wrote under the Direction of the Lord God, and*

shall be false teachers among you; who shall bring in damnable heresies (*Priestley and his Set—damnable indeed!*) and bring upon themselves swift destruction."[1]—(*God be praised!*).

The general confession, beginning with "Almighty and most merciful Father, we have erred and strayed, &c." is, we believe, omitted, and not without good reason: for as on these annual Fast Days our Legislators are expected to renew civilities with their old acquaintance the Church, it might yield an unholy pleasure to disaffected and seditious persons to hear from their own mouths: "We have left undone what we ought to have done, and we have done those things which we ought not to have done."

There are many difficulties that attend the subject of a GENERAL FAST. For, first of all, it is ridiculous to enjoin fasting on the poor (they are Pythagoreans,[2] and already eat neither fish, flesh, or fowl at any time), and it is the crimes of the poor and labouring classes that have brought down the Judgement of Heaven on the nation. This is *probable* a priori from their being incalculably the larger number, and it is *proved* by the absurd and dangerous consequences of the contrary supposition: for if our public calamities were to be attributed to the wickedness of the rich and powerful, it would more than insinuate doubts of the incorruptness of our House of Commons, and the justice and the necessity of the present war—for by the rich and powerful chiefly was the present war begun and supported, and in every country, directly or indirectly, the rich and powerful hold the reins of Government. I can scarcely venture to add a suggestion of a Punster of my acquaintance, "that by two recent Acts of Parliament the mouths of the poor have been *made fast* already."[3]

Secondly, Altho' the higher classes of society were inclined to make atonement for the vices of their ragged relations in the family of human nature, and fast in their behalf—yet as it were foolish to expect total abstinence the poor would prove ungrateful, and forsooth because *they* can afford to eat nothing but bread and cheese on Christmas days, will pretend not to be able to conceive, how an

---

Published by His Sacred Command . . . (1794). William Bryan, a Bristol druggist and Brothers's disciple, wrote *A Testimony of the Spirit of Truth, Concerning Richard Brothers . . . with Some account of the Manner of the Lord's Gracious Dealing with His Servant* (1795).

[1] 2 Pet 2.1 (var).

[2] For Pythagoras's diet see Diogenes Laërtius 8.19.

[3] Silenced, that is, by the Two Acts of Dec 1795 (see above, p 5 n 3). The punster could have been C himself.

hearty dinner on salt fish, egg sauce, and parsnips, can be *fasting* on any day.—Thirdly, the precepts of Scripture seem to oppose this custom as superstitious or hypocritical—Jesus Christ forbad his Disciples to fast while he remained with them, although he prophesied "The days will come when the Bridegroom shall be taken away from them, and then shall they fast in those days;"[1] in other words—"while I am alive, they are joyful; but after my death, they who act up to my precepts, will by these very precepts be precluded from all the customary means of getting forward in the world. A true Disciple of mine can neither lie, over reach, give votes against conscience, steal, pimp, or flatter—and he who possesses none of these accomplishments, must fast at least one day in the week, if he would have a mouthful the other six." But the Prophet Isaiah is terrible in his eloquent irony on this *constitutional* practice, and with his words I shall conclude this desultory Essay—

"When ye spread forth your hands, I will hide mine eyes from you: yea, when ye make many prayers, I will not hear: *your hands are full of blood!*

"Behold, ye fast for strife and debate, and to smite with the hand of wickedness. Ye shall not fast as ye do this day. Is it such a fast that I have chosen? a day for a man to afflict his soul? Is it to bow down his head as a bullrush, and to spread sackcloth and ashes under him? Wilt thou call this a fast and an acceptable day to the Lord? This is the Fast that I have chosen, *to loose the bands of wickedness, to undo the heavy burthens, and to let the oppressed go free, and that ye break every yoke:* to deal thy bread to the hungry, to bring the unhoused poor to thy table, and when thou seest the naked that thou cover him." Isaiah ch. lviii.[2]

THE LOAN

In the present state of our nature we do not expect, or indeed wish, that the whole of each parliamentary harangue should consist of pure and defecated reasoning. But in obscure or involved points (such as deliberations on the expenditure of public money, &c.) it would greatly facilitate a right understanding of the subject in debate, if it were fashionable to observe the following or some similar arrangement. I. A statement of the case. II. Deductions from it. III. Reply to objections. IV. Personalities, allusions, witticisms, appeals to our common feelings, &c. These might be placed at the

[1] Luke 5.35.

[2] Isa 1.15 and 58.4–7 (altered).

beginning or the conclusion, or both at the beginning and the conclusion, at the discretion of the orator; or they might even be confounded with the department of replication: but the statement and the deductions from it should be holy ground, and no sentence or syllable admitted not immediately and necessarily connected with the subject. Thus each part reflecting its appropriate rays, the eye would be enabled to catch it readily, to look on it attentively, and to trace its boundaries with precision. But now all are jumbled in each, and the result is a fatiguing and colourless confusion. That much of this perplexity is to be attributed to the legal disadvantages which attend the task of *reporting* the speeches[1] we are willing to acknowledge; but, wherever the fault *originates*, the effect is the same. The only mode of remedy that has suggested itself we have adopted. In all *intricate* debates we shall carefully read over the different speeches, and omitting the long preambles in excuse of length, apologies for differing from Right Honourable Friends—remarks on the disingenuous conduct of Honourable or Right Honourable Antagonists; and the whole parade of egotisms and *tuisms*:[2] we shall select from each speech whatever lines contain a fact or argument not before urged in the debate, scummed and clarified in the following manner.

On Monday, February 22, Mr. Smith[3] introduced the business of the late Loan. The subject was renewed on Friday, February 26.

THE OPPOSITION

Stated, That in the month of September, 1795, Walter Boyd, Esq.[4] did, at the request of the Chancellor of the Exchequer, undertake to advance money for the use of Government, to the amount of

[1] The press still had no legal right to report debates but exercised in varying degrees a *de facto* privilege. The *Morning Chronicle*, noted for its parliamentary reporting, had established a firm friendship with the doorkeeper of the House of Commons. See H. R. Fox Bourne *English Newspapers* (2 vols 1887) I 265.

[2] In a notebook C explains that *tuism* is a disguised egotism, e.g. praising in another a quality one admires in oneself: *CN* I 74. In *MPL* (1795) [5] he speaks of "the disgusting Egotisms of an affected Humility". Cf also "modest egotisms, and flattering illeisms": *BL* ch I (1907) I 5.

[3] William Smith (1756–1835), MP, a Whig who perhaps transmitted his reforming instincts to his granddaughter, Florence Nightingale. C admired him in 1796 but denounced him in 1817 after Smith had called attention in Parliament to Southey's radical play *Wat Tyler* (written in 1794), recently pirated to embarrass him, the new poet laureate. See *EOT* III 939–62.

[4] Walter Boyd (c 1754–1837), a banker in Paris before the Revolution, was a member of the firm of Boyd, Benfield and Co, merchants.

1,000,000l. for which he was to reimburse himself by bills to be drawn upon the Lords Commissioners of the Treasury, in the name of Walter Boyd, Jun. and bearing a fictitious date at Hamburgh, several weeks preceding the time at which with the privity of the Chancellor of the Exchequer they were really drawn in London; and that the said Walter Boyd, Jun. is a gentleman not engaged in any house of business in Hamburgh.—That the said bills, though drawn in London, yet professing to be foreign and not written on stamped paper, were of such a nature and description, as the bank of England would have refused to discount for any Commercial House whatever, and such as it would have been injurious to the credit of any private House to have negociated.

That on the 25th of November, 1795, the day appointed by the Chancellor of the Exchequer, for a meeting of the several competitors for the Loan, to settle the preliminaries thereof; and when they were all assembled, the Chancellor of the Exchequer, after a separate conference with Boyd and his Party, did propose to the other competitors, viz. Mellish and Morgan,[1] to bid for the Loan, on condition, "that an option should be reserved to the party of Boyd, of taking the Loan at such a price as should be equal in value to one half per cent. on the whole sum borrowed, above the highest offer of the competitors." That the said Mellish and Morgan refused to become competitors, deeming this a departure from the principle of free and open competition, to which they had been invited: That immediately after, without proposing any other terms, the Chancellor of the Exchequer did agree with Boyd and his Party: That Mr. James Morgan, one of the persons intending to be competitors for the late Loan, has given in evidence, that he would have offered on the 25th of Nov. terms 499,500l, more advantageous to the Public, than the terms made to the Chancellor of the Exchequer by the party of Boyd and Co. And that his Majesty's gracious Message, containing a communication that his Majesty would be induced to meet any disposition for negociation on the part of the enemy, with the earnest desire to give it the fullest and speediest effect, was not delivered to the House of Commons till Tuesday the eighth of December, although it is notorious that long before this it had been in the intentions of Ministry: That in consequence of the intimation contained in the Message, the value of the Loan suddenly rose above

[1] James Morgan (with John Julius Angerstein) was the contractor of a loan of exchequer bills in 1793. Mellish, of Messrs Mellish, is William Mellish (1764–1838), merchant and a director of the Bank of England.

five per cent. creating by that operation only, an additional profit on the whole Loan of more than *nine hundred thousand pounds* sterling; which sum might have been saved to the Public, if his Majesty's Message had been communicated to the House prior to the settlement of the competition.

The Opposition therefore deduced, that in every part of the transaction of the late Loan, the public interest has been sacrificed by the Chancellor of the Exchequer; and that through his departure from the principle of free and open competition, which he had uniformly professed till the very day of the final and abrupt settlement of the Loan; and through his delay in communicating his Majesty's Message; the profits of the Contractors, at the expence of the nation, have been so exorbitably swelled, as to have risen even before the deposit was made thereon, to an amount greatly exceeding the deposit itself, viz. on a Loan of EIGHTEEN MILLIONS, to the enormous sum of TWO MILLIONS, ONE HUNDRED and SIXTY THOUSAND POUNDS sterling.

And that this bargain was not improvident only, but made under very suspicious circumstances: namely, the obligations to which the Chancellor of the Exchequer had subjected himself, by the fraudulent transaction of the Hamburgh Bills; and the biass in favor of administration, which the enormous profits of the Loan appeared to have produced in the minds of many of the Citizens of London: a deduction incapable of absolute proof, but rendered highly probable by the circumstance, that those persons, who signed the requisition for the meeting at Grocer's Hall,[1] and addressed the House in favor of the two Bills, are all Subscribers to the Loan.

The speakers in defence of the transaction stated, that the Hamburgh Bills were to be the subject of a separate deliberation on a future day: that the only charge which could be fairly brought against the Chancellor of the Exchequer, in the transaction of the Loan, was, that through his disinclination to depart from the principle of a free and open competition, he had not attended to Boyd's claim so soon as perhaps he ought to have done. That Boyd had justly represented in behalf of himself and the other contractors for the Loan of last year, that the contract was entered into under the condition that no other public loan for this country should be made, until the period fixed for the last payment of the Loan, then contracted for, should have elapsed. And that this condition and the claim founded thereon is founded in justice and the nature of things,

[1] On 2 Dec 1795.

is proved by the circumstance, that on the 24th of Nov. (*i.e.* the day before the final settlement of the new Loan), there was floating in the market, and unconverted into stock, the value of five millions, according to Boyd's statement, but certainly three millions of money in scrip: and that several of the Contractors for the last Loan were holders of this scrip, and they would have inevitably suffered by the introduction of 18 millions more into the market, while so large a portion of last year's scrip was still on hand: that it was therefore incumbent on the Minister of a great country to compensate them by the chance of the advantage to rise from the new Loan: that a strict adherence to an engagement and a liberality beyond the reach of little motives, must produce a more powerful confidence and more permanent advantages to the country than the saving of two and a half per cent.

In reply to his delay in the communication of the intentions of Government respecting the possibility of a negociation with France, the Chancellor of the Exchequer *asserted*, "that the King's Message was not in his mind, when the bargain was made."

The Opposition replied to this contra-statement:

1. That the condition assumed by Mr. Boyd, if it had been entered into, ought to have existed in writing. It is the duty of the House of Commons not to lean securely on the veracity of an interested Contractor, nor to consider the vague promises of a Minister as a sufficient reason for the unnecessary expenditure of more than two millions sterling. 2. That such a condition ought not to have been entered into, as it might preclude sudden energies,[1] and prove highly detrimental to the public service. 3. That no injury would have arisen to Mr. Boyd from the introduction of a new Loan. (N.B. *This was attempted to be proved by calculations, which do not appear in the printed Reports.*) 4. That if this *were* the case, yet it equally applied to any other contributor who was possessed of scrip, as well as to Mr. Boyd; whereas the other contributors do not presume to say, that they have any right whatever to a preference in the English Loan. 5. That therefore the right which Boyd claims, "as founded in justice and recognized by constant practice," is not founded in justice; and so far is it from being recognized by constant practice, *that before all the payments due for the Loan of* 1794 *were completed, the Chancellor of the Exchequer did negociate a new Loan with Boyd and his Party for the service of the year* 1795, *and that the contributors to the Loan of* 1794 *did not make any objection to such negociation,*

[1] An error for "emergencies".

though it affected all the funds, and though it was expected that the deposit was to be made at a very early period.

MONDAY, *February* 29.

MR. JEKYLL[1] introduced the discussion of the Hamburgh Bills; in the course of which he stated, 1. That in September 1795, the Chancellor of the Exchequer wanted a million of money; which supply, from some unknown cause, he was unable to obtain from the Directors of the Bank by way of anticipation. 2. That at the request of the Chancellor of the Exchequer, Walter Boyd did cause Bills, to the amount of 700,000l. to be drawn on the Commissioners of the Treasury, in the name of Walter Boyd, jun. bearing a fictitious date at Hamburgh, of several weeks preceding the time at which, with the privity of the Chancellor of the Exchequer, they were really drawn in London; and that the said Walter Boyd, jun. is not engaged in any House of Business in Hamburgh. 3. That these Bills being therefore inland Bills, were yet without stamps; so that if any cause had come into a Court of Law respecting these Bills, the moment it was discovered they were inland Bills, and drawn on unstamped paper, the parties would have been nonsuited, and the Bills, together with the right of action, would have fallen to the ground. 4. That the sum of 700,000l. (the amount of these Bills) was paid to the Paymaster-General of his Majesty's Forces, by order of the Lords Commissioners of his Majesty's Treasury, in direct breach of an act of Parliament passed in the twenty-third year of his present Majesty.

Mr. Jekyll deduced, therefore, that the Minister, in connivance with Mr. Boyd, had acted illegally and unconstitutionally.

Mr. CHARLES LONG,[2] on the part of the Ministers, stated, 1. That early in the month of August, 1795, it was found necessary to raise money for the public service in anticipation of certain portions of the payments on the Loan and Lottery, which remained unpaid up to, and became due in the months of November, December, and January. 2. That Mr. Boyd was in consequence applied to, who through the means of a relation at Hamburgh, his agent there, agreed to accommodate Government. 3. That before this business actually took place, Mr. Boyd, Jun. arrived in London, and the exigency of public affairs would not permit them to send to

[1] Joseph Jekyll (1754–1837), MP for Calne, Whig politician and notable wit.

[2] Charles Long, later Baron Farnborough (1760–1838), MP for Rye and joint secretary to the treasury.

Hamburgh for a remittance of such bills as they wanted. 4. That on the 10th of December, 1795, there was money in the Exchequer, paid in upon the old Loan and Lottery, more than sufficient to discharge the 700,000l. raised by the negociation of these bills, without any anticipation of the new Loan: That therefore the transaction, if deceptious at all, was deceptious in *forms* only; and carried on without any view to defraud, or chance of defrauding.

Respecting the payment of the 700,000l. to the Paymaster-General of his Majesty's forces, Mr. Long asserted, that it offended against the letter, not against the spirit of the act of Parliament. He knew that balances were not left in the Paymaster-General's hands; but he did not understand that money was not to be paid in his name (for that had always been the regular mode), although the money did not remain at his office, but was carried immediately to the bank, and there placed in his name. By carrying it to the Accomptant of the Post-Office, notice was thereby given him of the transaction.

The Opposition regarded Mr. Long's statement as an *history* of the Trick, not a *defence* of it. That the exigency of the public affairs demanded it, is saying little more than that the Minister had not been guilty of the fraud without some temptation.—Mr. Grey deemed the distinction between the spirit and the letter of the law, a dangerous doctrine. But even with the spirit of the act, it was irregular; for he found by a paper on the table, that a sum of two millions had been paid to the Bank for the purpose of the Paymaster-General's Department, and by no means sent to the Accomptant-General's Office, which had been said to have been always their regular mode.

Such is the substance of the debates on these two mysterious transactions. We agree with Mr. Grey, that the distinction between the spirit and the letter of the LAW is a dangerous doctrine; though admirably adapted for those who wish to practise a "*vigor* beyond LAW."[1] As for instance, if the Minister had caused to be apprehended one of the late "Acquitted Felons,"[2] and *killed* him *off*[3]

[1] A phrase used by William Windham in the House of Commons 23 Nov 1795 in response to Fox's claim of the subject's right of resistance. *Parl Reg* XLIII 323. (For another use of the phrase see below, p 259.) Windham, though a great orator, made vehement and unguarded statements, which the Opposition quoted as indications of the government's intention—in this case, to enforce stringently the Two Acts.

[2] Attributed to Windham also—*Parl Reg* XXXIX (30 Dec 1794) 1029. The "acquitted felons" were the acquitted defendants in the State Trials of 1794—John Thelwall, Horne Tooke, Thomas Hardy, and the others.

[3] Windham again—*Parl Reg* XLIII (2 Dec 1795) 499. This commonplace

without the form of a trial, he might come forward and confess that he had offended against the *letter* of the laws which forbade such energetic proceedings, but by no means against the *spirit* of them. For the *spirit* of these laws (he might say) is evidently to preserve the Constitution; and if at any pressing exigency the *letter* of them tend to preclude the means necessary to such prevention, it may allowably be disregarded—since nothing can be more irrational than that the law should itself be the means of frustrating its own intentions. But that the present exigency is pressing beyond all experience of former ages, that a new and unheard of danger besets the Constitution, and that no measures, but the vigorous ones actually taken, could have preserved it, are facts for which the Gentlemen on the Treasury side of the House will ask no proofs. They must be indignant at the blindness of the Gentlemen opposite. Need I appeal to the Plots and Insurrections in every part of the kingdom? Plots so boldly carried on, that the Papers proving their existence, are transcribed from the public News-Journals; and Insurrections so artfully conducted, as to be absolutely invisible, &c. &c. &c.

As to the former part of the transaction, the *Knowing-Ones*, who are the best-qualified judges in such a cause, speak of it as a *sharp thing*: which, to say the truth, it certainly was, though less suited to the genius of the antient than of the modern Greeks. The School-boy recorded in the Joke-Journal of Mr. Joseph Millar,[1] for having translated *Necessitas non habet lex*, i.e. *legem*, by "Necessity has no legs;" if he had lived in our days, might have been apprized of his mistake in matter of *fact* as well as of interpretation.—Necessity has *black legs* upon occasion.

The real cause of the preference given to Boyd was suffered to

expression, used with reference to troops, was supposed to show Windham's indifference to human life. The *M Post* 4 Mar 1796 commented: "The Company of *Apothecaries* have it in agitation to present the Freedom of their Guild to Secretary WINDHAM in a *Pill Box*. The *humane* phraze of 'killed off', they conceive peculiarly applicable to their Fraternity!"

[1] *Joe Miller's Jests: or, The Wits Vade-mecum. Being a collection of the Most Brilliant Jests; the Politest Repartees; the Most Elegant Bons Mots, and the Most Pleasant Short Stories in the English Language. First Carefully Collected in the Company, and Many of Them Transcribed from the Mouth of the Facetious Gentleman, Whose Name They Bear; and Now Set Forth and Published by His Lamentable Friend and Former Companion, Elijah Jenkins, Esq.* (1739). The lamentable Jenkins was not responsible for C's joke, which may have come from one of the numerous later editions. Elijah Jenkins was a pseudonym for the dramatist John Mottley (1692–1750), who compiled the book of jests the year after the death of Joe Miller, a well-known comic actor.

escape by Mr. Douglas[1] in his answer to Mr. Smith's motions. "At the first interview which Mr. Boyd had with the Chancellor, he spoke of his claim to a preference, but had not stated it with that *precision* and *force* as to induce the Chancellor of the Exchequer to depart from his principle of competition." Mr. Boyd, in his letter, states, that the negociation of a new Loan before the period fixed for the last payment of the old, was contrary to the condition under which he and his party had contracted for the old Loan, and that they would be greatly injured by such negociation, which would introduce eighteen millions more into the market, while so large a part of last year's scrip was yet unconverted into stock. Here is a plain statement, that contains the whole of his claim; and that Mr. Boyd should have neglected to make it in his first interview, or that, if he had made it, it should not be understood by Mr. Pitt, are improbabilities absolutely indigestible. But (*inter nos*) those two *just* and *necessary* Bills did excite a strange and alarming opposition: the Treasury benches trembled through the agitations of them who sate thereon. Mr. Pitt saw the necessity of a respectable support from the wealthier Citizens of London, with a "*force* and *precision*," which left him no doubt of the justice of the claim of Messrs. Boyd and Party. It was "*founded in the nature* of things!*"

Mr. Pitt "felt a confiderable degree of satisfaction from the Report of the Committee, because it established, beyond a doubt of contradiction, that no person connected with Government had interfered at all in the distribution of the Loan." Is not Mr. Boyd *connected with Government?* Had he not been "palpably preferred and immoderately benefited" by Government? Can we doubt but that persons favourable to Government were selected by him to participate in his good fortune? What a fine thing it is to be a CONTRACTOR?[2] Nothing but Calms ruffle,—nothing but Peace disquiets him! The slaughter of thousands makes *him* all alive; and Famine herself shakes the horn of Plenty over his head!

* It is a right which is founded in Justice and the nature of things.—
BOYD'S LETTER.

[1] Sylvester Douglas, later Baron Glenbervie (1743–1823), MP for Fowey.

[2] Used here in the special sense of one who contracts with government to furnish services or materials. Cf *PD* (1795) 40.

THE PRESENT STATE OF SOCIETY

AH! far remov'd all that glads the sense,
From all that softens or ennobles man,
The wretched Many! Bent beneath their loads
They gape at PAGEANT POWER, nor recognize
Their Cot's transmuted plunder! From the tree
Of Knowlege, ere the vernal sap had risen,
Rudely disbranch'd. O *blest* Society!
Fitliest depictur'd by some sun-scorch'd waste,
Where oft majestic thro' the tainted noon
The SIMOOM* sails, before whose purple pomp[2]
Who falls not prostrate dies: and where, at night,
Fast by each precious fountain on green herbs
The LION couches; or HYÆNA dips
Deep in the lucid stream his bloody jaws;
Or SERPENT plants his vast moon-glittering bulk,
Caught in whose monstrous twine BEHEMOTH† yells,
His bones loud-crashing.
O ye numberless
Whom foul OPPRESSION'S ruffian gluttony
Drives from Life's plenteous feast! O thou poor Wretch,
Who nurs'd in darkness and made wild by want
Roamest for prey, yea thy unnatural hand
Dar'st lift to deeds of blood! O pale-eyed Form!

* "At eleven o'clock, while we contemplated with great pleasure the rugged top of Chiggre, to which we were fast approaching, and where we were to solace ourselves with plenty of good water, Idris cried out, with a loud voice, 'Fall upon your faces, for here is the Simoom.' I saw from the S. E. an haze come on, in colour like the purple part of the rainbow, but not so compressed or thick. It did not occupy twenty yards in breadth, and was about twelve feet high from the ground. We all lay flat on the ground, as if dead, till Idris told us it was blown over. The meteor, or purple haze, which I saw, was indeed passed; but the light air that still blew was of heat to threaten suffocation."

(BRUCE'S Travels, Vol. 4, page 557.)[1]

† Used poetically for a very large quadruped; but in general it designates the Elephant.

[1] James Bruce *Travels to Discover the Source of the Nile* (5 vols London & Edinburgh 1790) IV 557 (one sentence omitted). The same passage occurs as a footnote, in less accurate form, in Erasmus Darwin *Botanic Garden* pt I (3rd ed 1795) 166–7n.

[2] This line is a refashioning of Erasmus Darwin *Botanic Garden* pt I canto IV line 65: see *RX* 495 n 31.

The Victim of Seduction, doom'd to know
Polluted nights and days of blasphemy;
Who in loath'd orgies with lewd Wassailers
Must gaily laugh, while thy remember'd home
Gnaws, like a Viper, at thy secret heart.
O aged Women! ye who weekly catch
The morsel tost by law-forc'd Charity,
And die so slowly, that none call it murder!
O loathly-visag'd Supplicants! that oft
Rack'd with disease from the unopen'd gate
Of the full lazar-house heart-broken crawl!
O ye that streaming to the silent Noon
People with Death red-eyed Ambition's plains!
O wretched Widow who in dreams dost view
Thy Husband's mangled corse—and from short doze
Start'st with a shriek! or in thy half thatch'd cot,
Wak'd by the wintry night-storm, wet and cold,
Cow'rst o'er thy screaming baby! Rest awhile,
Children of Wretchedness! More groans must rise,
More blood must stream, or ere your wrongs be full.
Yet is the day of Retribution nigh:
The Lamb of God* hath open'd the fifth seal,
And upwards spring on swiftest plume of fire
The innumerable multitude of wrongs
By man on man inflicted! Rest awhile,
Children of Wretchedness! the hour is nigh:
And lo! the Great, the Rich, the Mighty men,

* See the sixth Chapter of the Revelation of St. John the Divine. "And I looked and beheld a pale Horse; and his name that sat on him was Death, and Hell followed with him. And power was given unto them over the FOURTH part of the Earth, to kill with sword, and with hunger, and with pestilence, and with the beasts of the Earth.—And when he had opened the fifth seal, I saw under the altar the souls of them that were slain for the word of God, and for the testimony which they held: and white robes were given unto every one of them; and it was said unto them, that they should rest yet for a little season, until their fellow-servants also, and their brethren, that should be killed as they were, should be fulfilled. And I beheld, when he had opened the sixth seal, the stars of Heaven fell unto the Earth, even as a fig-tree casteth her untimely figs, when she is shaken of a mighty wind: And the Kings of the Earth, and the great men, and the rich men, and the chief captains," &c.[1]

[1] Rev 6.8–9 (var), 11–13 (with an omission).

The Kings and the Chief Captains of the World,
With all, that fix'd on high, like stars of Heaven,
Shot baleful influence, shall be cast to earth
Vile and down-trodden, as the untimely fruit
Shook from the fig-tree by a sudden storm.
Ev'n now the storm begins![1] Each gentle name,
Faith and meek Piety, with fearful Joy,
Tremble far-off. For lo! the GIANT FRENZY,
Uprooting Empires with his whirlwind arm,
Mocketh high Heaven; burst hideous from the cell,
Where the Old Hag, unconquerable, huge,
Creation's eyeless Drudge, black RUIN sits
Nursing th'impatient Earthquake.
O return!
Pure FAITH! meek PIETY! The abhorred Form,*[2]
Whose scarlet robe was stiff with earthly pomp;
Who drank iniquity in cups of gold;
Whose names were many and all blasphemous;
Hath met the horrible judgment! Whence that cry?
The mighty army of foul spirits shriek'd,
Disherited of earth! For She hath fallen,
On whose black front was written MYSTERY;
She that reel'd heavily, whose wine was blood;
She that work'd whoredom with the DÆMON POWER,
And from the dark embrace all evil things
Brought forth and nurtur'd: mitred ATHEISM;[3]
And patient FOLLY, who on bended knee
Gives back the steel that stabb'd him; and pale FEAR
Hunted by ghastlier Terrors, than surround
Moon-blasted Madness when he yells at midnight!
Return, pure FAITH! return, meek PIETY!
The kingdoms of the World are your's: each heart

[1] See C's note to this line in *Poems* (1797) 141, on "the union of Religion with Power and Wealth": *PW* (EHC) I 121n.

[2] C or his printer omitted the note that was to appear in *Poems* (1796) 175: "And there came one of the seven Angels which had the seven vials and talked with me, saying unto me, come hither! I will shew unto thee the judgment of the great Whore, that sitteth upon many waters: with whom the Kings of the earth have committed fornication, &c. Revelation of St. John the Divine, chapter the seventeenth."

[3] Cf a letter to RS [11 Sept 1794]: "Horsley, the Bishop, is believed . . . to be—a determined *Deist*—What a villain, if it is true!" *CL* I 102. See below, p 68 and n 1.

Self-govern'd, the vast Family of Love,
Rais'd from the common earth by common toil,
Enjoy the equal produce. Such delights
As float to earth, permitted visitants!
When on some solemn Jubilee of Saints
The sapphire-blazing gates of Paradise
Are thrown wide open, and thence voyage forth
Detachments wild of seraph-warbled airs,
And odors snatch'd from beds of amaranth,
And they, that from the chrystal river of life
Spring up on freshen'd wing, ambrosial gales!
The favour'd good Man, in his lonely walk,
Perceives them, and his silent spirit drinks
Strange bliss, which he shall recognize in Heaven.[1]
And such delights, such strange beatitude,
Have seiz'd my young anticipating heart,
When that blest Future rushes on my view!

(Extract from "Religious Musings," one of the "Poems by S. T. Coleridge.")[2]

A Defence of the Church Establishment from its similitude to the grand and simple Laws of the Planetary System.

THE fifth definition of the first book of Sir Isaac Newton's Principia is as follows: "The centripetal force is that force by which bodies are from all parts drawn, driven, or do any how tend to a certain point as to a centre."[3] Now as the Sun of the planetary, so is the Court, the centre of the ecclesiastical system; and its centripetal force is its power of conferring good livings and lucrative dignities. The Bishops are the larger bodies in this system, some at greater, some at lesser distances, but all revolving round their Sun, and rejoicing in the heat and radiance of ministerial favour. The Moons are their Lordship's Chaplains.

[1] The preceding twelve lines were, according to C, one of the two passages of *Religious Musings* chosen for praise by WW. Letter to Thelwall 13 May 1796: *CL* I 216.

[2] *Religious Musings* lines 279–378 (var), published in full in C's *Poems* (1796), which did not appear until 16 Apr, more than five weeks later. It would seem that he had not yet chosen a title for his volume of poems, for when published it was called *Poems on Various Subjects*. Cf *Religious Musings* lines 260–357: *PW* (EHC) I 118–20.

[3] Newton *Principia mathematica* bk I Definitio 5: *Opera quae exstant omnia* (5 vols 1779–85) II 3.

Of the planets, or larger bodies, Bishop Horsley may be Venus;[1] and Bishop Prettyman,[2] from his personal charms, Venus, unless Mercury be thought a more proper emblem for one who lacqueys so closely the great Bestower of splendour. The words of the definition "by which bodies are from all parts drawn," imply that atheists, papists, jacobites, and jacobines are lured to the church by hopes of livings and stalls: and the words "are driven" import, that by force of parental authority or apprehensions of starving, many are compelled to subscribe what they cannot but disbelieve. The last sentence "or do *any how* tend to the centre," signifies, that in this universal gravitation towards the Sun of Royal Patronage, it is of comparatively little consequence what measures a man takes to arrive at preferment provided he get there at last.

CASIMIR

IF we except Lucretius and Statius,[3] I know not of any Latin Poet, ancient or modern, who has equalled Casimir in boldness of conception, opulence of fancy, or beauty of versification.[4] The ODES of

[1] Samuel Horsley, bp of Rochester, later of St Asaph (1733–1806), the editor of the above edition of Newton, won renown in the Church by his attacks on Priestley's theology. He was a staunch defender of the establishment and an opponent of France. C had previously attacked Horsley in *PD* (1795) 3. "Venus" is corrected to "Mars" by C in a copy of *The Watchman* now in the BM (Ashley 2842 p 48). It is also so corrected in the *CI*, where the item was reprinted 2 Apr 1796.

[2] George Pretyman, bp of Lincoln (1750–1827), Pitt's college tutor and inseparably connected with him thereafter as secretary, adviser, and beneficiary of patronage. C's remark is an anticipation of Porson's quip when told that Pretyman had been left a large estate by a person who had seen him only once: "It would not have happened if the person had seen him twice". Alexander Dyce *Recollections of the Table-talk of Samuel Rogers, to Which Is Added Porsoniana* (1856) 319. Pretyman changed his name to Tomline in 1803, on inheriting the estate of Marmaduke Tomline, whom he had seen perhaps five times.

[3] Perhaps the earliest reference to Lucretius in C's writings (cf his reference to "the atheistic Poem of Lucretius" the following month when sending John Thelwall his *Poems*: *CL* I 205), but he quoted Statius in *Conciones* (1795) 36.

[4] When C was in college, one of his most prized possessions was a copy of the Barbou edition of Casimir (letter to his brother George [26 Mar 1794]: *CL* I 76–7), whose writings he hoped to include in his "Imitations from the Modern Latin Poets". This was Maciej Kazimierz Sarbiewski (or Sarbievius) *Carmina* ed J. Barbou (Paris 1791). JDC believed that the present poem, and perhaps one or two more, are all that remain of the projected volume of "Imitations" advertised in Jun and Jul 1794 in the *CI* and the end of *The Fall of Robespierre* (1794). *C Life* (JDC) 30. C still admired Casimir, "the Polish Horace", in 1817; see *BL* ch 24 (1907) II 209 and n for a quotation from Casimir and remarks on his "classicism".

this illustrious Jesuit were translated into English about one hundred and fifty years ago, by a Thomas Hill,[1] I think. I never saw the translation. A few of the ODES have been translated in a very animated manner by Watts.[2] I have subjoined the third Ode of the second book, which, with the exception of the first line, is an effusion of exquisite elegance. In the imitation attempted, I am sensible that I have destroyed *the effect of suddenness*, by translating into two stanzas what is one in the original.

AD LYRAM[3]

Sonora buxi Filia sutilis,
Pendebis alta, Barbite, populo,
Dum ridet aer, et supinas
Solicitat levis aura frondes:

Te sibilantis lenior halitus
Perflabit Euri: me juvet interim
Collum reclinasse, et virenti
Sic temere jacuisse ripa.

Eheu! serenum quæ nebulæ tegunt,
Repente cælum! quis sonus imbrium!
Surgamus! heu semper fugaci
Gaudia præteritura passu!

IMITATION

The solemn-breathing air is ended—
Cease, O Lyre! thy kindred lay!
From the Poplar branch suspended,
Glitter to the eye of Day!

[1] G. H[ils or Hills] *The Odes of Casimire* appeared in London in 1646.

[2] For C's reading of Isaac Watts's imitations, see *CN* I 161[a]n; for a quotation from one, see below, p 287. Watts wrote in the preface to *Horae Lyricae* (5th ed 1727) xxix: "The *Imitations* [i.e. free translations] of that noblest *Latin* Poet of modern Ages, *Casimire Sarbiewski* of *Poland*, would need no Excuse, did they but arise to the Beauty of the Original. . . . I wish some *English* Pen would import more of his Treasures, and bless our Nation".

[3] *Odes* 2.3 (entitled *Ad suam testudinem*): *Carmina* (Paris 1791) 58. C's imitation, which first appeared here, has been dated 1794: *PW* (EHC) I 59–60.

On thy wires hov'ring, dying,
Softly sighs the summer wind:
I will slumber, careless lying,
By yon *waterfall* reclin'd.

In the forest hollow-roaring,
Hark! I hear a deep'ning sound—
Clouds rise thick with heavy louring!
See! th' horizon blackens round!

Parent of the soothing measure,
Let me seize thy wetted string!
Swiftly flies the flatterer, Pleasure,
Headlong, ever on the wing.

We should be happy if any Friend would enable us to give our English Readers a more perfect idea of the inimitable Original, or of the following sublime—Epigram shall I call it? of the same Author:

Mater Neronis ad Neronem.[1]
Quo gladium vibras? Utero, mammisne minaris?
Ah reprimat cæcus barbara tela furor!
Lactabam mammis, utero te, Nate, ferebam:
Dignus erit venia forsan uterque locus.
Erramus—Qui te miseras male fudit in auras,
Dignus uterque mori: Cæsar, utrumque feri.

FOREIGN INTELLIGENCE

VIENNA, *Feb.* 12.[2] A misunderstanding supposed to exist between the Courts of St. James's and Berlin, engrosses the attention of our Cabinet. The French would consent to the restoration of the Stadtholderate,[3] but on conditions and under restrictions which

[1] *Epigrammata* LVII: *Carmina* 415. Tr Lorna Arnold: "*Nero's Mother to Nero.* At what do you brandish your sword? | Do you threaten my womb, my breasts? | Ah, let your blind rage hold back its barbarous weapons! | With my breasts I fed you, son; in my womb I bore you: | Both parts perchance shall merit clemency. | I err—Both parts which sent you forth into the unhappy air, | Both deserve death: Caesar, strike both."

[2] The first paragraph from *M Chron* 1 Mar 1796, the second from ibid 2 Mar or the *Star* 1 Mar.

[3] William V (1748–1806) was stadtholder of Holland from 1751 to 1795 (but affairs of state were conducted by the queen mother and the regents until 1766), when on the revolutionary uprising he sought refuge in England. The Batavian Republic lasted till his death. See also below, p 216.

would prevent Great Britain from regaining her former influence in the Republic of the United Netherlands. The King of Prussia,[1] it seems, had favoured this plan of restoration, at which the British Cabinet has taken offence; and his Prussian Majesty, on the other hand, accuses the former of keeping the Stadtholderian Family, like hostages, in Great Britain; and of preventing it from withdrawing to Berlin, where it would be more easy to obtain their consent to measures calculated to procure them an easy and speedy return to their country and dignities.

By another letter from Vienna, we learn that a marriage was expected to be solemnized between the daughter of Lewis XVI. and the Arch-Duke Charles. But when the proposal was made to the Princess, she replied, that she was precluded from accepting it by an act of her Father. Prior to his death, he had disposed of her hand: she had promised to comply with his will, and would keep her engagement.[2]

FRANCFORT, *Feb.* 12.[3] The accounts of what have passed in Persia and Georgia have heretofore been much confused. Our last accounts seem to throw some light on the parts which Russia and the Porte mean to take. The Usurper Aaga Mahmet (an Eunuch), after having dethroned and conquered, in two battles, the young Prince Lolf Alikan, and made himself master of Shiras, with the Imperial Treasury and the property to[4] all the great Persian families there, has invaded Georgia.

Prince Heraclius of Georgia (who for some years past has put himself under the protection of Russia), and the young dethroned Prince of Persia, have implored assistance of the Empress.—The latter has offered to give up to her any of his provinces which she may choose, if she will aid him against the Usurper.

Lolf Ali is returned with the wreck of his army to Kerman; from whence he has sent to the Kan of Mazandarn, ordering him to collect some troops, and march against Ghilan, and attack the Usurper before the promised reinforcements from Russia are received.

Fifteen hundred Russians having set out from Astracan, are already arrived at Recht, the capital of Ghilan, by way of the Caspian Sea. Some Russian regiments have also joined the Georgian troops

1 Frederick William II (1744–97), nephew of and successor to Frederick the Great.

2 Marie-Thérèse-Charlotte (1778–1851) married her cousin Louis, Duc d'Angoulême in 1799; he was the last dauphin of France.

3 From *M Chron* 1 Mar 1796.

4 An error for "of".

of Prince Heraclius; who are to attack the Usurper at Shirvan, at the same time that the Kan of Mazandarn attacks him by Aderbigian. If the success is equal to what might be expected from the superiority of the Russian troops to those of Persia, there is reason to believe that the Usurper will not long enjoy his triumph, and that the Persian Provinces to the west of the Caspian Sea will be a recompence for the assistance of Russia to the dethroned Prince.[1]

We have not yet heard of the Porte having taken part in the dispute; but we may presume that it will not be very well pleased to find the Russian sceptre extended to the provinces of Asia, by the cessions which will be made to it on the northern part of Persia.[2]

The Russian General de Derfelden, who left Warsaw in the middle of January, has been assassinated at a few days journey from that place.—He is said to be mortally wounded.[3]

CONSTANTINOPLE, *Jan.* 9.[4] Our Court appears more than ever intent on the introduction of European tactics. Our squares are full of soldiers, exercising in the military revolutions, under French, English, and Swedish officers; but whatever efforts are made, or whatever sums expended to obtain this end, our most intelligent friends are of opinion it will never succeed, the natural aversion of the Turks for every thing foreign, and their dislike to discipline, are obstacles which it will be impossible to entirely surmount.—Mr. d'Ash, Swedish Minister here,[5] has notified to the Porte the marriage of his King to the Princess Mecklenberg Schwerin, and that he was come out of his minority[6]—he then presented M. de Mouradjea

[1] The above account is still "confused". Aga Muhammad Khan (1720–97) had captured Kerman from the young shah of Persia, Lutf Ali Khan, who was shortly afterward captured and killed (1795). See C's later report of this, below, p 114. The usurper then crossed into Georgia with his army of 60,000 and captured Tiflis. Heraclius —Irakli II, king of Georgia (1716–98) —had signed a treaty (1783) with Catherine the Great whereby Russia was to protect the integrity of Georgia, but Russian troops were not sent to her Georgian ally until the spring of 1796.

[2] Rumours of war between Russia and Turkey grew louder (see below, pp 149, 296–7), but Turkey did not enter the dispute. The Russian armies won victories in northern Persia, but with death of the empress (Nov 1796) they were withdrawn, and Russia kept only Derbent and Baku.

[3] The report was untrue; General Wilhelm Christoforovich von Derfelden (1735–1819) lived on.

[4] From *M Chron* 1 Mar 1796 (C has omitted the first part of the report).

[5] The name is d'Asp in *M Chron.* Pehr Olof von Asp (1745–1808), the Swedish minister at Constantinople, was then dispatched to London.

[6] Gustavus IV (1778–1837) reigned (under the regency of his uncle) from 1792 to 1800, when crowned. He did not marry the princess, or the granddaughter of Catherine the Great, to whom he was betrothed later that year (1796), but the daughter of the grand duke of Baden (1797). He was deposed in 1809 in favour of his uncle and died in exile, poor and unknown.

d'Ossoun[1] as his successor here. This nomination is regarded as an event which may have the happiest effects for the Ottoman Empire: his attachments to its interests are well known; and if, as there is all appearance, an alliance is formed between Turkey, France, Sweden, and Denmark, it will be to his cares we shall be indebted for it. A Maltese corsair had been taken by the Captain Pacha's Kirlaughis, but rather than be brought here, the crew set fire to the powder-room, and blew themselves and the ship up together.

HAGUE, *Feb.* 18.[2] Zealand and Friezland have at length formally acceded to the calling of a National Convention. Friezland unconditionally, but Zealand with the reserve of the sovereignty of the people of Zealand. Reports of a speedy peace are renewed at Vienna; but we fear on no sufficient foundation. It is certain that the illustrious Clairfayt does not retire from indisposition so much as in disgust at the Court Cabal, which has so malignantly assailed him on every side. Among the many vain attempts to injure him in the breast of his gracious Master, we may mention the following lampoon (originally in French Verse) which was dropped at the Emperor's feet. The Emperor read it with evident displeasure.

"He who abandoned without fight the Meuse,
Who Rouen deserted, Juliers evacuated,
Who staid not at the Rhine his shameful flight,
And ran even to the Meine to seek his laurels:
Holland and Maestricht he permitted both
And Luxembourg without an effort—all
With Manheim, Dusseldorff, to fall to France:
This Hero bids our troops a last farewell!
He at the last obeyed, advanced one step,
Though Cæsar oft in vain commanded it.
For this cheap Victory they stile him Hero,
Though it but justifies his pardon; while
The feeble Germans in his praise forget
The names of TRAUN and EUGENE and LAUDOHN."[3]

[1] Ignatius Mouradgea d'Ohsson (1740–1807), an Armenian in the service of Sweden; Swedish minister to Turkey, 1795–9.

[2] From the *Star* 3 Mar 1796. Beginning with the fourth sentence C has tacked on to this report a separate report from Vienna.

[3] Otto Ferdinand, Count von Abensperg und Traun (1677 1748). Prince Eugene of Savoy (1663–1736), and Gideon Ernst, Freiherr von Laudon or Loudon (1717–90) were Austrian field-marshals.

Dispatches were received Wednesday last[1] by our Government, brought over land from India, and forwarded from Vienna by Sir Martin Eden.[2] They contain the intelligence that Rear-Admiral RAINIER,[3] in his Majesty's Ship the Suffolk of 74 Guns, and the rest of the Squadron under his command, have captured the Dutch Settlement of Malacca, the southern part of the Peninsula of India; Cochin on the coast of Ceylon. They also brought accounts of the death of NABOB of ARCOT.[4] He was succeeded without any difficulty by his eldest son.

POLITICS WITH NAPLES[5]

(*Extracted from the French Journal l'Ami des Lois*)

"The King of Naples[6] is so influenced by his wife, sister to Marie Antoinette and Joseph the Second, that he knows no other interests than those of Austria. He would never accede to the Family Compact; and he prefers incurring the displeasure of the King of Spain, his father,[7] by preserving his Prime Minister, ACTON,[8] the sworn enemy of France and Spain, and so attached to the Imperial and British Courts, that he has induced the King to grant them free admission into all his ports, and to furnish them daily with all possible assistance, in troops, money, and provisions. He is one of our most bitter enemies.

"In this state of things what ought France to do?

"She ought to unite with the King of Spain, now become her

[1] That is, 2 Mar: this paragraph slightly condensed from the *Star* 3 Mar 1796.

[2] Sir Morton Eden, later Baron Henley (1752–1830), envoy extraordinary to Vienna (1794–9).

[3] Peter Rainier (c 1741–1808), commander-in-chief of the East Indian station till 1804.

[4] Muhammad Ali (1717–95), nawob of Arcot, was a man whose debts conferred immortality upon him, for it was their enormous extent and the usurious payments on them that convinced Burke that the nawob was a tool of the East India Company and led to Burke's great speech of Feb 1785 on "a coalition between the men of intrigue in India and the ministry of intrigue in England". On the death of Muhammad Ali he was succeeded by his son, Umdat'l Umara.

[5] From the *Gazetteer* 7 Mar 1796 (C omits the first four paragraphs).

[6] Ferdinand IV (1751–1825), king of Naples (1759–1806, 1815–25) and the Two Sicilies (1816–25), was dominated by his wife, Maria Carolina (1752–1814), daughter of the Empress Maria Theresa. He had joined the coalition against France.

[7] Charles III of Spain, who had signed the Family Compact (1761) with France against England, had died 1788; it was Ferdinand's brother, Charles IV (1748–1819), who was then king of Spain (1788–1808).

[8] Sir John Francis Edward Acton, 6th Bt (1736–1811), the queen's favourite.

friend and ally,[1] to force the King of Naples to throw off the Austrian yoke; to engage the Queen to confine herself to the care and education of her children; to dismiss the Minister, ACTON; to replace him by a Spanish Minister; and finally, to make a common cause with the French Republic, Spain, and Sardinia. These four Powers, actuated by the same spirit and will, would acquire that consequence, credit, and pre-eminence that are due to them."

A fishing smack arrived Friday morning (March 4), at Harwich,[2] which fell in with the Dutch fleet on the 25th of last month, steering a northerly course, about fifty-three leagues from Yarmouth. The smack was boarded at one o'clock in the morning, and the Captain was carried on board a Dutch sixty-four gun-ship, where he remained till nine o'clock. The Dutch Captain, after putting several questions to him, suffered him to depart, and wished him a good voyage. From the Dutch sailors the crew of the smack learned, that the fleet was bound not to Brest, but to the Cape of Good Hope.—There were six sail of the line, nine frigates, and two brigs.

IRELAND

Mr. GRATTAN[3] described the outrages in Armagh, in the debate of the 25th February, in a way that must petrify every heart.[4]

Mr. Grattan said, of those outrages he had received the most dreadful accounts; that their object was the extermination of all the Catholics of that country; it was a persecution conceived in the bitterness of bigotry, carried on with the most ferocious barbarity, by a banditti, who being of the religion of the State, had committed with the greater audacity and confidence the most horrid murders, and had proceeded from robbery and massacre to extermination: that they had repealed by their own authority all the laws lately passed in favour of the Catholics, had established in the place of those laws the inquisition of a mob resembling Lord George Gordon's fanatics,[5]

[1] France and Spain had signed a peace treaty in July 1795.

[2] Condensed from the *Gazetteer* 7 Mar 1796.

[3] Henry Grattan (1746–1820). First active in the Irish Parliament (1775–97, 1800) in seeking Catholic emancipation and Irish welfare generally, after the Union he was a distinguished member of the British Parliament (1805–20). C met Grattan, whom he greatly admired, in the spring of 1811. *CL* III 312–13, 335–6.

[4] The passage on the outrages is verbatim from *M Chron* 4 Mar 1796, but C omits the end of the final paragraph.

[5] Gordon (1751–93), the Protestant fanatic who precipitated the anti-Catholic riots that in 1780 placed London for several days under mob rule.

equalling them in outrage, and surpassing far in perseverance and success.

That their modes of outrage were as various as they were atrocious; they sometimes forced by terror the masters of families to dismiss their Catholic servants; they sometimes forced landlords by terror to dismiss their Catholic tenantry; they seized as deserters numbers of Catholic weavers; sent them to the County gaol, transmitted them to Dublin, where they remained in close prison until some Lawyers from compassion pleaded their cause and procured their enlargement, nothing appearing against them of any kind whatsoever; those insurgents, who called themselves Orange Boys,[1] or Protestant Boys, that is, a banditti of murderers, committing massacre in the name of God, and exercising despotic power in the name of Liberty; those insurgents have organized their rebellion, and have formed themselves into a committee, who sit and try the Catholic weavers and inhabitants when apprehended falsely and illegally as deserters; this rebellious committee they call the Committee of Elders, who when the unfortunate Catholic is torn from his family and his loom, and brought before them, sit in judgment upon his case; if he gives them liquor or money they sometimes discharge him; otherwise they send him to a recruiting office as a deserter; they had very generally given the Catholics notice to quit their farms and dwellings, which notice is plaistered on his house, and conceived in these short but plain words—"Go to Hell, Connaught won't receive you—fire and faggot. —Will. Thresham and John Thrustout." That they followed these notices by a faithful and punctual execution of the horrid threat, soon after visited the house, robbed the family, and destroyed what they did not take, and finally completed the atrocious persecutions by forcing the unfortunate inhabitants to leave their land, their dwellings, and their trade, and to travel with their miserable family, and with whatever their miserable family could save from the wreck of their houses and tenements, and take refuge in villages as fortifications against invaders, where they described themselves, as I have seen in their affidavits, in the following manner—"We (mentioning their names) formerly of Armagh, weavers, now of no fixed place of abode, or means of living, &c." In many instances this banditti of persecution threw down the houses of the tenantry, or what they call rack'd the house, so that the family must fly or be buried in the grave of their own cabin.

[1] The Orange-men, a Protestant society founded in Ulster in 1795, took their name from William of Orange (William III).

I have heard, but have not heard them so ascertained as to state them to this House, but from all the enquiries I could make, I collect that the Catholic inhabitants of Armagh, have been actually *put out of the protection of the law*—that the magistrates have been supine or partial, and that the horrid banditti has met with complete success, and from the magistracy with very little discouragement.

DOMESTIC INTELLIGENCE

THE following paragraph is extracted from the Sun[1] of Monday February 29. "We have great pleasure in assuring the public, and the friends of humanity in particular, that the dogs made use of lately in Jamaica are merely for the purpose of tracing through the pathless woods to their lurking places those deluded wretches, the Maroon negroes, and of preventing our brave troops from falling into their ambuscades; and not for the cruel uses assigned to them by Lord Balcarres's *Friend*[2] in the House of Commons on Friday night. It is to be hoped such pure friendship will meet with its desert when his Lordship returns to this country."—The eagerness, with which this ministerial paper has embraced Mr. York's[3] *conjecture*, reminds us of that part in the Rehearsal, in which Mr. Smith having enquired how ten thousand men could lie hid in Brentford, Bayes is startled and remains silent, till Mr. Johnson helps him out by observing—"Yes they might, if only the innkeepers were the Prince's friends."—"Friends? (replies the delighted Bayes), his most intimate acquaintance, egad!"[4] We profess not to understand Mr. York's solution of this matter. General Macleod never supposed that the bloodhounds (having been previously instructed whom they were to consider as enemies) were sent out with unlimited powers to hunt by themselves! Beyond all doubt, the sportsmen will accompany their dogs—but will these dogs when they discover a maroon keep at an harmless distance and *point* at him? Mr. Yorke should have shown how and in what respect the British commander's conduct differed from that of the old Spanish exterminators in this particular charge.

[1] A London newspaper supporting the ministry, founded (1792) under government sponsorship by James Bland Burges, then undersecretary of state for foreign affairs, and Charles Long.

[2] Alexander Lindsay, 6th Earl of Balcarres (1752–1825), governor of Jamaica, had recently suppressed a rebellion there. His "friend" was General Norman Macleod (1754–1801), MP for Inverness-shire. For a full report, see below, p 81.

[3] Charles Philip Yorke (1764–1834), MP for Cambridgeshire.

[4] George Villiers, Duke of Buckingham (and others) *The Rehearsal* III v.

That blood hounds have been employed in our own country, is too true: they were employed against the friends of the Pretender, both in the reign of William the Third, and by the Duke of Cumberland. The inhabitants of Scotland remember it and may be excused for occasionally bringing it to our recollection.

Nos certe taceamus, et obruta multa
Nocte tegi nostræ patiamur crimina gentis![1]

The conclusion of the paragraph is, we hope, unintelligible. It is impossible the editors of the *Sun* should anticipate with pleasure any act of *fashionable* revenge.[2] No! they could not mean *this*! *They* are zealous admirers of the laws of their country! *They* are struck with horror at the impiety of the French in contemning the religion of the *meek* and *forgiving* Jesus.

Statement of the distribution of the British naval force at the present time, exclusive of the hired armed vessels which are chiefly employed in protecting the coasting trade of Great Britain.[3]

	Line.	50'*s.*	*Frig.*	*Sps.*	*Tot.*
In port and fitting -	32	7	46	52	137
Guard-ships, hospital-ships, and prison-ships, at the several ports - - - -	10	2	1	0	13
In the English and Irish Channels	16	2	23	33	74
In the Downs and North Seas	9	3	15	13	40
At the West-India Islands, and on the passage - - -	7	4	19	15	45
At Jamaica - - - - -	6	0	6	9	21
America and Newfoundland -	3	0	7	6	16
East Indies, and on the passage	7	1	5	8	21
Coast of Africa - - -	0	1	3	3	7
Gibraltar and Mediterranean	24	0	25	10	59
Total in commission	114	20	150	149	433

1 Statius *Silvae* 5.2.89–90 (var: *nostrae* for *propriae*). Tr J. H. Mozley (LCL 1928) I 295: "Let us at least keep silence, and suffer the crimes of our own house to be buried deep in whelming darkness".

2 All aristocratic vice was to C of a darker hue, but he had a special reason for detesting duelling because during his first year at Cambridge an undergraduate was killed in a duel. See *CL* I 19 and Bruce Dickins "The Pembroke Hall Duel of 1791" *Cambridge Review* LXXXIV (9 Feb 1963) 255. Cf below, pp 251–2 and 337–40; also *CN* II 1971 and n.

3 From the *Star* 1 Mar 1796.

	[*Line*.	50's.	*Frig*.	*Sps*.	*Tot*.
Total in commission -	114	20	150	149	433]
Receiving ships - - - -	9	2	2	1	14
Serviceable and repairing for service - - - - -	8	1	4	3	16
In ordinary - - -	15	3	15	52	85
Building - - - - -	24	4	10	11	49
Total	170	30	181	216	597

On Tuesday March 1 (being St. Davids day), the annual meeting of the Society of Ancient Britons[1] was held at the Crown and Anchor, and honoured, for the first time, with the presence of his Royal Highness the Prince of Wales, who prefaced his congratulary toast by a short address, well-conceived and gracefully delivered. The Duke of Norfolk[2] gave the health of the infant Princess;[3] observing, that she might have been born on Taffy's Day, if the Prince's Welch blood could have endured any specific delay—*Ha! ha! ha! a very good joke, your Grace!*

Mr. SHERIDAN, on Friday night, styled the business of the Hamburgh Bills[4] a transaction not honourable, scarcely honest, and certainly illegal. When a second resolution of Jekyll's was about to be negatived without a division, Sir W. Young[5] insisted on a division, with a view of exposing the weakness of the minority, many of whom had left the House. This conduct was deemed so unworthy a senator, that, on re-entering the House, Mr. Grey moved a vote of censure against Sir W. Young. The Speaker[6] declared the Baronet's conduct unusual, and that it might be considered as unbecoming. After much asperity Mr. Grey's motion was withdrawn. Sir W. Young, we

1 A charitable and social society devoting itself to the care of poor children of Welsh parentage. C condenses the report in the *Sun* 7 Mar 1796 and adds his own conclusion.

2 Charles Howard, 11th Duke of Norfolk (1746–1815), was one of the nobles who by their riches and prestige helped to offset the slender numbers of the Opposition. Others included the Dukes of Bedford, Devonshire, Grafton, and Northumberland and the Earl of Derby. For a report of a duel fought by Norfolk, see below, pp 337–40.

3 Princess Charlotte, daughter of George, Prince of Wales, and his consort, the Princess Caroline of Brunswick, was born 7 Jan 1796. She was heir-presumptive to the throne until her death in 1817.

4 See above, pp 56–63. "Friday night" was 26 Feb, a session that lasted until 4 AM: *M Post* 27 Feb 1796.

5 Sir William Young, 2nd Bt (1749–1815), MP for St Mawes.

6 Henry Addington, later Viscount Sidmouth (1757–1844), MP for Devizes and speaker of the Commons (from 1789). Prime Minister 1801–3.

suppose, apprehended that people might conclude, there must be a large number on that side, on which they perceived all the wit, eloquence, and argument to lie: and wished to shew us, that something more than demonstration is requisite to produce *practical* conviction.

It would surely be more congruous with the sadness of this Day, if fewer *powdered heads* were seen in our churches and other places of worship. All the eloquence of Burke, and all the *palaver* of Pitt, are unable to ward off that one remark of the poor man's, "I am hungry! that, which you waste on your hair, might yield me a morsel of bread." I would that the Friends of Freedom, at least, were more consistent in their conduct. At this season of national distress it ill beseems the Patriot to excite the envy of the Poor by unmanly ostentation and expensive frivolity. These odious and absurd superfluities, contrasted with his own want of necessaries, and increasing that want, may tend to make fierce the hearts of the lower classes, and excite them to deeds of revenge.[1]

Go, struggle with thy fate! pursue thy way—
Though thou art poor, the world around is gay.
Thou hast no bread; but on thy aching sight
Proud Luxury's pavillions glitter bright;
The Croud prolong their hollow revelry,
Nor one relenting bosom thinks of thee!
Ah will not then despite or bitter need
Urge on thy temper to some fearful deed?
Pale Fraud shall call thee to her timid band,
Or Murder beckon thee with reeking hand.[2]

[1] Powdering one's hair not only was wasteful, but from C's point of view helped, by the new tax, to support an unjust war. Pitt, in introducing the measure, said: "The last article to which he should resort would . . . probably excite a smile. It was a tax upon the wearers of hair powder". The tax, passed in May 1795, required users of hair powder (made of flour, then in scarcity) to take out a licence costing one guinea. As the names of licence-holders were posted on the doors of parish-churches, the reference above to powdered heads in church was especially fitting. The Opposition press, in retaliation for Burke's unfortunate phrase "the swinish multitude" in his *Reflections*, called those who paid the tax "guinea pigs". C had lectured on the hair-powder tax, keeping his audience "in good feeling, by the happy union of wit, humour and argument". Cottle *E Rec* I 20. He also used the lecture for a sermon at Bath. Ibid I 182.

[2] William Lisle Bowles *The Philanthropic Society* lines 71–4, 77–8 (var), 81–4 (var). Line 83 in Bowles reads: "Pale Guilt shall call thee to her ghastly band".

PROCEEDINGS OF THE BRITISH LEGISLATURE

HOUSE OF COMMONS

FRIDAY, *Feb.* 26

GENERAL MACLEOD called the attention of the House to a circumstance which deeply involved not only the reputation of a Nobleman, whom as friend and fellow-soldier he highly respected, but the character of the country and of Mankind. He had read in a daily paper (the Morning Post)[1] a communication from Jamaica purporting that ONE HUNDRED BLOOD HOUNDS and 20 Spanish Chasseurs had arrived from the Island of Cuba to be employed in hunting out the Maroons. "The conduct of the French (General Macleod observed) had never reached such enormity. I have seen war in all its Shapes and Horrors, but I never saw such barbarity as this. At present I shall only ask the Right Honourable Gentleman (Mr. Pitt) if he could inform the House on the subject. I hope, the communication is founded in falsehood; but if it be true, much as I respect the Noble Lord, I pledge myself to bring him to the Bar of the House of Peers to answer for so horrible a measure."

The Chancellor of the Exchequer found himself unable to make any particular answer to so important a charge. But this he would say, that it never had been the intention of Government to employ such means of Warfare. Mr. Yorke described the atrocious conduct of the Maroons. Dogs had been employed in this country to trace out thieves, and they might have been used to trace the haunts of the Maroons, though not as means of Warfare.

The adjourned Debate on the resolutions moved by Mr. Smith respecting the Loan, were resumed: the Speakers on the ministerial side were Mr. Douglas, Mr Steel,[2] and the Chancellor of the Exchequer; on the part of opposition Mr. Francis,[3] Mr. Fox, Mr. Sheridan, and Mr. W. Smith.—The first Resolution moved by Mr. Smith was amended—For the Amendment, 171: for the original

[1] Lucyle Werkmeister informs me that Daniel Stuart had already assumed control of the *M Post*. Under his management it rose "to a power and prestige not hitherto attained by any English newspaper". Wilfrid Hindle *The Morning Post 1772–1937* (1937) 65. C had in later years something to do with this prosperity.

[2] Thomas Steele (1753–1823), MP for Chichester.

[3] Philip Francis, later Sir Philip (1740–1818), MP for Bletchingley, the reputed author of the *Letters of Junius*, was an associate of Burke in the trial of Warren Hastings.

Resolution, 23. All the other Resolutions of Mr. W. Smith except the two last, were got rid of by moving the previous question. The two last were directly negatived, and then two Resolutions passed expressing the House's approbation of Mr. Pitt's conduct through the whole of the Business.—The particulars of this intricate Subject with the arguments for and against the transaction have been given page 56 of this Number.

House of Commons, Monday, *Feb.* 29.

Sir George Shuckburgh Evelyn[1] obtained leave to present a petition from the Executors of the late Dr. John Hunter,[2] who in his will had directed the Trustees therein appointed to offer to the British Government that invaluable Museum or collection of Subjects in natural History, which he had made with vast scientific knowledge, unceasing perseverance and an expenditure of 20,000l. at least. If this Government rejected it, it was then to be offered to any foreign Government and afterward to private Individuals. Mr. Curwen[3] opposed it on the principle that we are already overburthened and distressed, and that we ought to be just before we pretend to be generous. He was ably answered by Mr. Hawkins Browne,[4] Sir William Young, and Mr. Courtenay.[5] The Petition was referred to a select Committee, after which the order of the Day was read for the House to resolve itself into a Committee upon a Bill proposing to grant a bounty for the cultivation of Potatoes. Mr. Powys[6] expected that some reasons would have been stated for the necessity of this Bill. Sir John Sinclair[7] replied that the Reasons for the Bill had been stated in the Report of the Board of Agriculture; but (after a conversation between Mr. Duncombe, Mr. Sumner, and Mr. Buxton;[8] wherein they all agreed that the bounty on the importation

[1] Sir George Augustus William Shuckburgh-Evelyn, 6th Bt (1751–1804), MP for Warwickshire and a noted scientist.

[2] Dr John Hunter (1728–93), the surgeon-general. His collection was later bought by Parliament for £15,000 and in 1800 was given to the Royal College of Surgeons.

[3] John Christian Curwen (c 1756–1828), MP for Carlisle, later franked the numbers of C's *The Friend.*

[4] Isaac Hawkins Browne, the younger (1745–1818), MP for Bridgnorth.

[5] John Courtenay (1738–1816), MP for Tamworth; friend of Boswell.

[6] Thomas Powys, later 1st Baron Lilford (1743–1800), MP for Northamptonshire.

[7] Sir John Sinclair, Bt (1754–1835), MP for Caithness and president of the board of agriculture on its creation in 1793.

[8] Charles Duncombe, later 1st Baron Feversham (1764–1841), MP for Shaftesbury; George Holme Sumner (1760–1838), MP for Guildford; Robert John Buxton, 1st Bt (1753–1839), MP for Thetford.

of Corn rendered all other bounties needless and inexpedient) he said, he had no desire to press the Bill against the general opinion: and the motion for the commitment was negatived. Mr. Jekyll moved two Resolutions respecting the Hamburgh Bills. After a long and warm Debate the House divided—for the previous Question 109—for the original Resolution 24. The House divided on the second Resolution—For it 8—Against it 108. For the facts and arguments adduced by the different Speakers on this transaction, see page 58 of the present Number.

HOUSE OF COMMONS, TUESDAY, *March* 1.

The Chancellor of the Exchequer moved for leave to bring in a bill to amend and enforce the existing Laws for the more effectual relief and employment of the Poor. He meant the Bill to be discussed before Easter in a committee, and then printed to give time and opportunity during the recess for further improvements. Leave granted. The House having resolved itself into a committee on the high price of Corn, Mr. Lechmere[1] professed his intention of submitting to the House a Motion for more effectually preventing Exportation of Corn. The distresses of the Poor, occasioned by the enormous price of Corn and Flour, and aggravated by the present severity of the weather, demanded an immediate remedy. The consolidation of small farms into large ones he considered as the root of the mischief. It facilitates monopoly, and it tends to make the large farmer careless, or at least it obliges him to depend too much on the fidelity of hired labourers—one consequence of which he would state to the House in the business of threshing. On Saturday last the coachman of a Mrs. Harrison in Grosvenor Square came to him with a quarter-peck of as good coloured wheat as he had ever seen, and a small bunch of unpounded wheat: this the man said he had from one truss of straw. If this fact be general, it follows that there is a quantity of wheat equivalent to thirty quartern loaves in every load of straw brought* to market. He thought that the labourer should be compelled to thresh his Corn by the day: as whether he is paid by truss or bushel, equal temptations arise to

* In consequence of Mr. Lechmere's information, the Duke of Portland ordered his coachman, on Wednesday, to purchase a load of straw: when it was carried home, it was immediately threshed, and to the surprise of the Duke, it yielded a bushel and an half of Corn.

[1] Edmund Lechmere (c 1748–98), MP for Worcester City.

leaving the wheat imperfectly threshed. He likewise wished that there should be a handmill in every parish for the convenience of the Poor, that they might grind their small quantities without expence, and that there should be likewise an oven for baking it when ground. He concluded a speech, which evinced great benevolence and extensive observation on this important subject with moving "That the chairman be directed to move the House for leave to bring in a Bill for preventing the Exportation of Corn; and also one to prevent the selling of Corn by the sample:" a practice which Mr. Lechmere reprobated in the course of his remarks as favouring monopolizers. Mr. Francis seconded the Motion. He thought the clamour against large farms and great corn-dealers injudicious. The granaries of opulent farmers ought to be considered in the light of state-magazines. As to grinding and baking he entirely agreed with Mr. Lechmere. The miller's profit was wonderful: out of 62lb of wheat he returned only 54lb; and the best remedy for this was to pay the miller in money not in kind. In India the inhabitants universally ground with handmills—at every door men, women and children were seen grinding. He had used this *handmill (which he minutely described) in his own house, and recommended the general adoption of it; observing that the expence of it would not exceed fifteen shillings. Mr. Rose informed the House, that the Exportation of Corn is already forbidden by law, and that this law is strictly and rigorously executed. The Chancellor of the Exchequer thought there was a real scarcity in the article of wheat; but that no evil would be felt from it, if people accustomed themselves to use mixed bread. He lamented that there was such difficulty in prevailing on the poor to adopt the substitute; but he could not consent to enforcing it by law. *The prejudices and enjoyments of the Poor were sacred with him.* General Smith[2] thought otherwise, and contended, that as the public interests absolutely required it, one stated mixture of bread should be appointed for rich and poor, and the use of it enforced directly.—Mr.

* We have heard that a gentleman of Bristol, well known for his great mechanic genius and his benevolent application of it, has recently invented a portable corn-mill, a communication from which may be fastened to the wheel of a coach, cart, or waggon—thus grinding the corn while the farmer is carrying out or bringing home his loads.[1]

[1] The Bristol inventor has not been traced.

[2] Richard Smith (1734–1803), MP for Wareham, had made a fortune by lending money to the nawob of Arcot; Samuel Foote had satirised him in *The Nabob* (1772).

Buxton moved for the chairman to leave the chair, which was carried unanimously. After which the Legacy Bill went through the committee, in which several amendments were proposed by the Solicitor-General. It was ordered to be reprinted with the amendments.

HOUSE OF LORDS

THURSDAY, *March* 3

LORD LAUDERDALE, after an invective against the unconstitutional and disgraceful practices of ministers with respect to the Hamburgh Bills, moved "that the order of the day for the reading of the vote of credit Bill be postponed to this day three weeks." This debate was extremely desultory, and travelled through a wild[1] field of extraneous matter. Lord Lauderdale avowed his friendship for Brissot, whom he deemed an honest man. Lord Grenville could not acknowledge honesty in that man who deposed his Sovereign two months after he had sworn allegiance to him; particularly as there is reason to believe, that he meditated his deposition at the time of taking the oath. The most remarkable passage in this debate is the following from Lord Lauderdale's reply to the Earl of Mansfield[2] and Lord Hawkesbury.[3] "I have heard often and much of the influence which rich individuals possessed; but what was their power of resistance compared with the immense power and influence of the executive Government at this moment, who had the expenditure of twenty-five Millions per annum in their hands, and the influence and patronage annexed to the mode of raising that enormous sum—a circumstance that of itself made ministers absolute. Rome in its most convulsed state exhibited no such extensive power and influence in any set of men: the wealth of Crœsus, when it was the dread of Cæsar and of Pompey, was nothing equal to it: he never was worth more than three millions."

The Question was negatived without a division, and the Bill went through the Committee and was reported.

In the House of Commons on the same day the Bill for the Abolition of the Slave Trade was read a second time in a very thin House, and was then ordered to be laid before a Committee of the whole House on Monday next.

[1] Probably an error for "wide".

[2] David Murray, 2nd Earl of Mansfield (1727–96), diplomat and lord president of the council (1794–6).

[3] Charles Jenkinson, Baron Hawkesbury and, after May 1796, 1st Earl of Liverpool (1729–1808), president of the board of trade 1791–1801.

HOUSE OF LORDS,

FRIDAY, *March* 4

The Vote of Credit Bill was read a third time. Lord Thurlow,[1] the Duke of Grafton,[2] and the Earl of Lauderdale opposed the passing of this Bill at so early a period: but at length it passed without a division. After which the Earl of Lauderdale introduced the subject of Mr. Burke's pension by moving that the Clerk should read the Act of the 10th of King William. chap. 3. relative to the four per cents, by which that fund was appropriated to the Civil List. There was read also various parts of the Journals of the House relative to this subject, and Act of Queen Anne, chap. 7. Lord Lauderdale then said, that he was about to open a subject of the utmost importance. It regarded the application of a fund which their ancestors had dedicated to appropriate purposes: and such was its importance that Lord Clarendon,[3] of the articles against whom the misapplication of this fund formed one, declared, the restored prosperity of the country to have been owing in great measure to the operation of this fund. He was sensible that he laboured under many disadvantages in bringing this subject before the House. Such was the profusion to which their Lordships were now accustomed, such were the immense sums now voted away without consideration, that a misapplication of smaller sums would attract but little regard. But he was emboldened by the reflection, that *Reform could only be effected by the frequent and solicitous display of existing grievances and abuses.* He felt likewise that the provision of a certain individual was connected with the discussion of the present subject—that a recent publication[4] must have roused the curiosity of the Public and of their Lordships, to hear him canvass the merit of that character and of that provision. From this however he was resolved carefully to abstain: and no ability however distinguished, no genius however brilliant should seduce him into it. That talents so transcendent should be employed in such a manner he might lament. He might admire the genius, and drop a tear over it fallen and degraded. The

[1] Edward Thurlow, 1st Baron Thurlow (1731–1806), lord chancellor until succeeded by Lord Loughborough in 1792.

[2] Augustus Henry Fitzroy, 3rd Duke of Grafton (1735–1811), earlier the target of "Junius"; at this time he voted with the Opposition.

[3] Edward Hyde, 1st Earl of Clarendon (1609–74), lord chancellor and author of the *History of the Rebellion* (published posthumously 1702–4), the proceeds of which were used to endow the Clarendon Press. He had been tried for high treason 1667.

[4] Burke's *Letter . . . to a Noble Lord.*

question to which he called the attention of the House was of an interesting public nature.

To be continued.[1]

TO CORRESPONDENTS.

We are obliged to G. N. for his friendly caution to the *Watchman*, "*not to get into the wrong box.*"

We have received J. B. * * * * 's[2] communication, " Knight of *no* barren Muse." It will appear in our next number.

[1] See below, p 119.

[2] "J. B." 's *Supposition* appeared in No 3; see below, pp 110–11. C's quoted remark is possibly a play on Martial 5.14, "a knight of no ill-repute".

THE WATCHMAN

No. III. THURSDAY, MARCH 17, 1796

Published by the Author, S. T. COLERIDGE, Bristol;
And by PARSONS, Paternoster-Row, London.

THAT ALL MAY KNOW THE TRUTH;
AND THAT THE TRUTH MAY MAKE US FREE!

HISTORICAL SKETCH[1]

OF THE

Manners and Religion of the ancient Germans, introductory to a Sketch of the Manners, Religion, and Politics of present Germany.

THE dark forests of Germany were inhabited by a race of men against whom the Romans, in the time of their Republic, maintained a doubtful contest; the contest could not long be doubtful between a free nation, fierce in the enthusiasm of a warlike superstition, and the timid slaves of Rome, accustomed to crouch beneath every libertine or tyrant that oppressed them.

The manners of the Germans have been delineated by Tacitus, the most philosophic of historians. They elected their Kings on account of their noble birth; their leaders for their personal valour. The table of their chief was rudely furnished, but it was furnished with abundance: and the warriors who shared his feast, and received sometimes

[1] This essay had its beginning in the Historical Lectures of the spring of 1795, delivered by Southey but discussed and probably jointly composed with C. Southey's part in it is confirmed by information kindly sent me by Messrs Charles J. Sawyer, Ltd, booksellers, of Grafton Street, London, from Southey's own copy of *The Watchman*. At the conclusion of the "Historical Sketch" Southey appended his initials, "R. S.". His sixth Historical Lecture was on the "Manners and Irruptions of the Northern Nations" (Cottle *E Rec* I 37). C claimed the larger intellectual share in these lectures (to RS [13] Nov 1795: *CL* I 172), and he was on such strained relations with Southey at this time that he would hardly have included the "Sketch" here unless he had felt an assurance of ownership. A paragraph of the Green report of C's 1818 lectures is very close to *The Watchman* article. *Misc C* 6–7. For his Northern lore C relied, as was then commonly done, upon Bishop Percy's translation of Paul-Henri Mallet's *Introduction à l'histoire de Dannemarc* (1755–6), *Northern Antiquities* (2 vols 1770).

of him a horse trained for war, sometimes a victorious and bloody lance, gratified their own favourite passion in the return they made of military service. Matters of small importance were decided by their chiefs, but all things of moment were determined by the General Assembly; here, too, they elected their leaders. The field of battle was the only road to preferment, and the only method to obtain the favour of the Gods, was valour.

The education of the Germans gave them strength and stature, and their strength was preserved by the remarkable continence that so peculiarly and honorably distinguished them; "but there," says Tacitus, "no one laughs at vice, nor is it called the fashion to corrupt and be corrupted."[1] They looked upon women as their equals and companions, and whoever wished for the love of a woman, first made himself worthy of her esteem. They deemed them favoured by the Gods, and we find frequent mention of Prophetesses attending upon their armies. Nor is this wonderful, for they constantly employed themselves either in war or hunting. They left the study of simples and the heart[2] of healing to the women; and the art was as mysterious as the occasion was frequent. The women were respected, and therefore they became respectable.

It has been observed, "that the refinements of life corrupt while they polish the intercourse of the sexes;"[3] and the rude poverty of Germany has been assigned as one cause of the German continence. If refinement consist in "luxurious entertainments, midnight dances, and licentious spectacles," we may agree with Gibbon,[4] that they at once present temptation and opportunity to frailty, but that only can with propriety be stiled refinement, which, by strengthening the intellect, purifies the manners. All else enervates and depraves. If a mind skilled in the routine of etiquette, and the nothingness of *politesse*, and a body enfeebled by the delicate languor of fashion, constitute refinement, I must turn to contemplate the dignity of woman in the tent of a barbarian.

"But (says the historian) heroines of such a cast may claim our admiration; but they were most assuredly neither lovely, nor very susceptible of love. Whilst they affected to emulate the stern virtues of *man*, they must have resigned that attractive softness in which principally consists the charm and weakness of *woman*."[5] Of this

[1] Tacitus *Germania* § 19.
[2] An error for "art".
[3] Edward Gibbon *The History of the Decline and Fall of the Roman Empire* (6 vols 1776–88) I 232.
[4] Ibid.
[5] Ibid I 233.

I must say with Mary Woolstonecraft, "that it is the philosophy of sensuality."[1] The women of Germany were the free and equal companions of their husbands: they were treated by them with esteem and confidence, and consulted on every occasion of importance. What then, is this love which woman loses by becoming respectable?

The religion of the earlier inhabitants of Germany taught the being of a supreme God, master of the universe, to whom all things were submissive and obedient: he is called in the Edda, "The Author of every[thing] that existeth; the Eternal Being; the Searcher into concealed things; the Being that never changeth; infinite power, boundless knowledge and justice, were attributed to him."[2] To erect statues to this Deity, or to think of confining him within the inclosure of walls, was held absurd and impious: "it was only within woods and consecrated forests that they could serve him properly. There he seemed to reign in silence, and to make himself felt by the respect which he inspired."[3] An infinite number of inferior deities and genii, residing in every part of nature and directing its operations, were emanations of this divinity. This Supreme Being, though irritated by the sins of mankind, was merciful, and capable of being appeased by prayer and repentance: to serve him with sacrifices and prayers, to do no wrong to others, and to be brave and intrepid in themselves, constituted all the morality they derived from religion. The breach of these was to be punished by a future state of torment, and the observance rewarded by joys without number and without end.

Such was the religion of the more antient Scandinavians; but, about seventy years before the birth of Christ, this degenerate Sabeism[4] yielded to the institutions of Odin.

Sigge, the son of Fridulf, commanded the Ases, a Scythian people situated between the Euxine and Caspian seas, when Pompey conducted the Mithridatic war. As the priest of Odin, he assumed the name of that Deity. Sharing in the defeat of Mithridates, Odin collected together all who preferred danger and freedom to subjection, and led them towards the north of Europe, subduing the nations in his way, and giving them to one or other of his sons or companions.

[1] For the idea, not precisely in these words, see Mary Wollstonecraft *A Vindication of the Rights of Woman* (1792) ch 4, "Observations on the State of Degradation to which Woman is Reduced by Various Causes".

[2] Mallet *Northern Antiquities* (1770) I 78 (var).

[3] Ibid I 79.

[4] "Sabeism" (star-worship), not in Mallet, here used satirically, in that Scandinavian religion was corrupted by Odin's imposture just as Christianity was corrupted by priestly imposture. For another use of the word by C see *CN* II 2453.

This extraordinary man was the inventor of the Runic characters; and by his persuasive eloquence, his skill in extempore poetry, and his impostures, made himself respected as a deity. The Runic Chapter, or the Magic of Odin, is still preserved as his composition: he enumerates in it the wonders he could perform by his songs, mingling the operations of magic with those powerful effects which poetry has been known to produce. The death of Odin was conformable to his life: perceiving that his end drew near, he called together his friends and companions, and giving himself nine wounds in the form of a circle, told them, whilst dying, that he went to take his seat among the other gods, where he would receive those who exposed themselves fearlessly in battle and died in arms.

The religion of Scandinavia was entirely changed—Odin was worshipped as the Supreme Being, and the Father and Creator of mankind represented as delighting in the blood of men. He was stiled, "the Terrible and Severe God—the God that carrieth desolation and fire—the Father of Slaughter."[1] The Oriental system of Two Principles[2] (an error absurd in itself, and dangerous in its consequences, which has infected every superstition, and even crept into Christianity) formed part of the Scandinavian mythology. Valhalla, the shield-roofed hall, was the palace of Odin, where he received those who fell in fight. The joys of heaven consisted in cutting each other to pieces, and drinking ale out of the skulls of their enemies. Niflheim was the place reserved for the feeble; it was the abode of Hela or Death, the daughter of the Scandinavian Satan: Anguish was her palace—the threshold of her door was Precipice—her table Famine—her waiters were Expectation and Delay—her bed Sickness and Pain.

SHAKSPEARE MSS.[3]

CRITICISM and illustration have been so long and variously exercised on Shakspeare, by the labours of the most learned and penetrating writers of the British nation, that it seemed as if little

[1] Mallet *Northern Antiquities* I 86–7.

[2] See the reference to Manichaeanism above, p 34n.

[3] From *M Mag* I (Feb 1796) 42–3, with concluding paragraphs by C (see below, p 96 n 4). This is C's first of several borrowings from the *Monthly Magazine*, a new periodical backed by Richard Phillips and published by Joseph Johnson, the bookseller and printer who issued works by Price, Priestley, and other Dissenters. Before Phillips assumed the editorship, Dr Aikin, assisted by his sister Mrs Barbauld and William Enfield, edited the magazine, with contributions from

more could be gathered on the subject, even in the way of explanation. Much less did any prospect remain, after such enquiries, that new matter would be found to throw additional light upon his character, or that unheard-of productions from his pen should be suddenly brought to view. And yet such is really the case, if credit is to be given to the authority of Mr. Ireland, the editor of a splendid volume,[1] and to the papers which he has brought forward, as well as to those which remain in his possession. On a subject of this magnitude, it is natural for opinion to be suspended, and even for credulity itself to receive these pieces with double caution. Mr. Ireland ought certainly not to be offended at the jealousy with which critics behold these productions, at the inquisitiveness with which they conceive it right to examine them, and the enquiries which from thence they hold themselves authorised to put, concerning the means of their discovery, and the cause of their mysterious concealment. All this is natural, as it comes within the exact limits of critical justice. At the same time, it is but fair to let Mr. Ireland speak for himself. In his preface, he observes, that " from the first moment of this discovery to the present hour, he has incessantly laboured, by every means in his power, to inform himself with respect to the validity of these interesting papers. Throughout this period, there has not been an ingenuous character, or disinterested individual in the circle of literature, to whose critical eye he has not been earnest

Godwin, Holcroft, and others. It aimed at being "both amusing and instructive", to lend aid "to the propagation of those liberal principles . . . which have been either deserted or virulently opposed by other Periodical Miscellanies . . .": *M Mag* I (Feb 1796) iii. See also C's concluding address to his readers, below, pp 374–375.

[1] In Dec 1795 Samuel Ireland, writer and engraver, published *Miscellaneous Papers and Legal Instruments under the Hand and Seal of William Shakspeare: Including the Tragedy of King Lear and a Small Fragment of Hamlet, from the Original MSS. in the Possession of Samuel Ireland, of Norfolk Street.* The "original" mss and papers had been given to him by his nineteen-year-old son, William (or Samuel) Henry Ireland (1777–1835). In an age predisposed to accept antiquarian forgeries (as Chatterton and *Ossian* had already shown), young Ireland was clever enough to fool not merely his father, but also Joseph Warton, George Chalmers, and Boswell. Besides the documents and fragments, he also fabricated two plays, *Henry II* and *Vortigern and Rowena.* Sheridan had taken *Vortigern* for production at Drury Lane, where it would shortly have its *première.* (See below, p 218, for a notice of the opening.) James Boaden and Edmund Malone soon exposed the fraud, and young Ireland confessed to it before the end of the year, swearing that his father had been an innocent victim. "I should never have gone so far", he wrote, "but that the world praised the papers so much, and thereby flattered my vanity". W. H. Ireland *An Authentic Account of the Shaksperian Manuscripts &c* (1796) 42.

that the whole should be subjected. He has courted, he has even challenged the critical judgment of those who are best skilled in the poetry and phraseology of the times in which Shakspeare lived, as well as those whose profession or course of study has made them conversant in ancient deeds, writings, seals, and autographs. Wide and extensive as this range may appear, and it includes the scholar, the man of taste, the antiquarian, and the herald, his inquiries have not rested in the closet of the speculatist; he has been equally anxious that the whole should be submitted to the practical experience of the mechanic, and be pronounced upon by the paper-maker, &c. as well as by the author. He has ever been desirous of placing them in any view, and under any light that could be thrown upon them; and he has, in consequence, the satisfaction of announcing to the public, that, as far as he has been able to collect the sentiments of the several classes of people above referred to, they have unanimously testified in favour of their authenticity; and declared that, where there was such a mass of evidences, internal and external, it was impossible, amidst such various sources of detection, for the art of imitation to have hazarded so much without betraying itself; and, consequently, that *these papers can be no other than the production of Shakspeare himself*."[1]

To the question of discovery, Mr. Ireland replies, that "he received them from his son, Samuel Henry Ireland, a young man then under 19 years of age, by whom the discovery was accidentally made, at the house of a gentleman of considerable property. Amongst a mass of family papers, the contracts between Shakspeare, Lowine, Condelle, and the lease granted by him and Hemynge to Michael Fraser,[2] which was first found, were discovered; and, soon afterwards, the deed of gift to William Henry Ireland (described as the friend of Shakspeare, in consequence of his having saved his life on the river Thames, when in extreme danger of being drowned) and also the deed of trust to John Hemynge, were discovered. In pursuing this search, he was so fortunate as to meet with some deeds very material to the interests of this gentleman, and such as established, beyond all doubt, his title to a considerable property; deeds of which this gentleman was as ignorant, as he was of his having in his possession any of the MSS. of Shakspeare. In return for this service, added to

1 *Miscellaneous Papers* (Preface) 1–2.

2 John Lowin or Lowine (1576–c 1659), John Heming or Hemminge (d 1630), and Henry Condell or Cundell (d 1627) were among the principal actors in Shakespeare's plays; the last two were also the editors of the First Folio. Fraser was an invention.

the consideration that the young man bore the same name and arms with the person who saved the life of Shakspeare, this gentleman promised him every thing relative to the present subject, that had been, or should be, found, either in town, or at his house in the country. At his house, the principal part of the papers, together with a great variety of books, containing his MS. notes, and three MS. plays, with part of another, were discovered."[1]

Here follows the enquiry, "Who the gentleman is from whom these papers have been obtained?" To this Mr. Ireland answers, that "when he applied to the original possessor of the papers for permission to print them, it was not obtained but under the strongest injunction that his name should not appear. This injunction has, throughout all the stages of this business, been uniformly declared; and as this gentleman has dealt most liberally with the editor, he can confidently say, that in turn, he has, with equal openness and candour, conducted himself towards the public, to whom, immediately upon every communication made, every thing has been submitted, without reserve."[2]

Mr. Ireland further informs the public, that (besides the play of Vortigern now preparing for representation at Drury-lane Theatre) another and more interesting historical play has been discovered amongst the other papers, in the hand-writing of Shakspeare; and that this will, in due time, be laid before the public.

He likewise acquaints them, that "he is in possession of a great part of Shakspeare's library, in which are many books, with notes in his own hand, and those of a very curious nature. Some of these he most probably will reprint."[3]

The following are the contents of this volume:

Fac-simile of Shakspeare's Autograph.

Fac-simile of Queen Elizabeth's Letter to him.

Fac-simile of four Miscellaneous papers.

Fac-simile of a Letter to Anne Hatheway (whom Shakspeare after married), inclosing a lock of his hair.

Fac-simile of a copy of verse to the same.[4]

[1] *Miscellaneous Papers* 2.

[2] Ibid 3 (altered).

[3] Ibid 9.

[4] As a sample of Ireland's style as imitator of Shakespeare, here is a stanza from *Verses to Anna Hatherrewaye:*

Is there inne heavenne aught more rare
Thanne thou sweete Nymphe of Avon fayre
Is there onne Earthe a Manne more trewe
Thanne Willy Shakspeare is toe you

Miscellaneous Papers [37].

[Fac-simile of Shakespeare's Letter to the Earl of Southampton.][1]

Fac-simile of the Earl's Answer.

Fac-simile of Shakspear's profession of his Faith.

Fac-simile of a Letter to Richard Cowley.[2]

Fac-simile of a pen-drawing or sketch of Shakspeare by himself, with his arms and crest, with two signatures of his name.

Fac-simile of the Reverse, with his initials, &c.

A deed of gift to William Henry Ireland, with fac-similes of his signature and seal.

Fac-simile of tributary lines to Ireland, with the arms of Ireland and Shakspeare linked together by a chain, sketched by himself.

Fac-simile, a pen-sketch of Ireland's house in Blackfriars.

Fac-simile of the arms of Shakspeare and Ireland.

Fac-simile of Shakspeare in the characters of Bassanio and Shylock, whole length tinted drawings.

Agreement with Lowine.

Agreement with Condelle.

Lease to Michael Fraser and his wife.

Deed of trust to John Hemynge.

Tragedy of King Lear, with fac-similes.

Fac-simile of the first-page of Hamlet.

Several controversial pamphlets have already appeared, in which the affirmative and negative side of the question relative to the authenticity of these remains, are maintained; but the public expectation is particularly excited by an announced work of Mr. Malone,[3] which he entitles a Detection of the Forgery, and the appearance of which is only delayed by the time requisite for finishing certain engravings.[4]

Meantime the play of *Vortigern* is preparing for exhibition at the Theatre-Royal, of Drury-lane; and it cannot be doubted, that attack on one side will be forcibly repelled by defence on the other.

[1] Henry Wriothesley, 3rd Earl of Southampton (1573–1624), Shakespeare's patron.

[2] Richard Cowley (d 1619) was included in the Folio list of principal actors in Shakespeare's plays.

[3] Edmund (or Edmond) Malone (1741–1812), who in 1790 had published his 10-vol Shakespeare, issued his pamphlet under the title, *An Inquiry into the Authenticity of Certain Miscellaneous and Legal Instruments Published Dec. 24, 1795, and Attributed to Shakspeare, Queen Elizabeth, and Henry, Earl of Southampton . . .* (1796).

[4] The article from the *M Mag* concludes here. The remainder is by C, with help from the *Eng R* XXVII (Feb 1796) 175–8, a review of Boaden's pamphlet (see next note). This is the first of many borrowings from this review, which was edited and published by John Murray II. In this year it was merged with the *Analytical Review*.

The arguments adduced against the authenticity of these papers by Mr. Boaden, in his letter to George Steevens, Esq.[1] are such, as we fear Mr. Ireland will find it difficult to invalidate.[2] Mr. Boaden has delicately declined to press Mr. Ireland on the mysterious concealment of the Gentleman's name[3] (a concealment imperfectly accounted for by the Gentleman's disinclination to meet the doubts and cavils of critics and witlings), he has confined himself to the internal evidence; and contends, that the various readings may be in general found in the older editions of Shakspeare; that it cuts the knot of difficulties which a legitimate copy would untie, by omitting scenes and passages in which readings occur that have baffled the sagacity of conjectural criticism; and that its mode of spelling is unlike that of any period of English literature, in the multitude and awkwardness of the superfluous Letters introduced. Mr. Boaden shrewdly adds, Mr. Ireland is a complete Antiquarian;—he can himself design and engrave:—he must know how easily the graphic art can produce such titles as seals and autographs. With regard to the paper, Mr. Boaden pledges himself to produce more in one week, by pulling blank leaves, &c. from manuscripts in Elizabeth's reign, than Mr. Ireland's whole stock amounts to.

Mr. Boaden has subjoined Extracts from Vortigern—lines written by himself, and intended to shew that the manner of Shakspeare may easily be imitated.[4] Mr. Boaden has to a certain degree imitated the phraseology of the bard of Avon, or, as Mr. Ireland profanely stiles him—of "the Author of Nature:"[5] but the uncommonness and rapid succession of his images are not attainable by the Writer of Fontainville Forest.[6] If this rapidity and opulence of imagination shall be found to characterize the Vortigern and Rowena, we certainly should vote in favour of its authenticity; unless there should

[1] James Boaden *A Letter to George Steevens, Esq., Containing a Critical Examination of the Papers of Shakspeare; Published by Mr. Samuel Ireland. To Which Are Added, Extracts from Vortigern* (1796).

[2] Cf *Eng R* XXVII (Feb 1796) 177: "Upon the whole, we doubt very much whether Mr. Ireland will be able to invalidate the objections brought in this pamphlet to the authenticity of his manuscripts."

[3] Young Ireland told his father that a rich gentleman who wished to be known only by his initials, M. H., had given him the documents. The elder Ireland wrote to M. H. via the son.

[4] Cf *Eng R* XXVII (1796) 177–8.

[5] Boaden *Letter* 6, 11, and 53. Ireland's Preface ran in part: "That spontaneous flow of soul and simple diction, which so eminently distinguish this great Author of Nature". *Miscellaneous Papers* 4.

[6] Boaden's play *Fontainville Forest* (1794) was based on Mrs Radcliffe's *A Romance of the Forest*.

be any reason to suspect *Edmund Burke* of having been an accomplice in the Forgery.[1]

MODERN PATRIOTISM[2]

IT is advisable that men should not deceive themselves, or their neighbours, by assuming titles which do not belong to them. Good Citizen ——?[3] why do you call yourself a PATRIOT?[4] You talk loudly[5] and rapidly; but powers of vociferation do not constitute a PATRIOT. You wish to be distinguished from the herd; you like victory in an argument; you are the tongue-major of every company: therefore you love a Tavern better than your own fire-side. Alas! you hate power in others, because you love power[6] yourself! You are not a PATRIOT! You have studied Mr. Godwin's Essay on

[1] In a note to his poem *The Raven* in *M Post* (10 Mar 1798) C pretends that he in the manner of Ireland found the ms; "it resembles SPENSER's minor Poems as nearly as Vortigern and Rowena the Tragedies of WILLIAM SHAKESPEARE": *PW* (EHC) I 169n. In 1800 C told Southey that he had "ample materials" for a history of literary forgery concluding with Ireland (*CL* I 585). Lamb (in a letter to Thomas Manning 17 Mar 1800) said that C "has suggested . . . the forgery of a supposed manuscript of Burton the anatomist". *LL* I 178. For a modern account of the Ireland forgeries, see Derk Bodde *Shakspere and the Ireland Forgeries* (Cambridge, Mass. 1930). See below, pp 278–80, for "S. England's" discovery of "lost Tragedies of Sophocles".

[2] For purposes of this satire on Godwinian and many other misguided "patriots" C has slightly modified the language of Bishop Berkeley's "Maxims Concerning Patriotism". The attack was foreshadowed by an entry in the Gutch Memorandum Book: "Berkley's Maxims—Vol. II, 345". *CN* I 174 (21). C had borrowed the second volume of George Berkeley's *Works* (2 vols 1784) from the Bristol Library 10–28 Mar 1796: *Bristol LB* 122. C's title comes from Berkeley's Maxim 21: "I have no opinion of your bumper patriots. Some eat, some drink, some quarrel for their country. MODERN PATRIOTISM!" *Works* II 346. See below, pp 194–5, for a reader's attack on C for his remarks on Godwin.

[3] The use of "citizen" as a title calls to mind the London Corresponding Society, among whose members John Thelwall (1764–1834) stood out. See below, p 267 n 3. Some parts of the satire fit him but others do not, and C clearly means to include not only the Godwinians (like Thelwall) but also the whole range of worldly reformers, not leaving out the parliamentary Opposition.

[4] *OED* on "patriot": "The name has been at various times borne or assumed by persons or parties whose claim to it has been disputed, denied, or ridiculed by others. Hence the name itself fell into discredit in the earlier half of the 18th c., being used, according to Dr. Johnson, 'ironically for a factious disturber of the government' ". William Cowper used the word satirically in his *The Modern Patriot* (1780). But the "patriotic societies" bore the name proudly (see above, Prospectus, p 5), and the reformers in general applied it to themselves.

[5] Cf Berkeley Maxim 23: "We are not to think every clamorous haranguer, or every splenetic repiner against a court, is therefore a patriot". *Works* II 346. See also Maxim 2. Ibid II 345.

[6] Cf Maxim 3: he is no patriot "whose appetite is keen for power". Ibid.

Political Justice;[1] but to think filial affection folly, gratitude a crime, marriage injustice, and the promiscuous intercourse of the sexes right and wise, may class you among the despisers of vulgar prejudices,[2] but cannot increase the probability that you are a PATRIOT. But you act up to your principles.—So much the worse! Your principles are villainous ones! I would not entrust my wife or sister to you—[3] Think you, I would entrust my country? The PATRIOT indulges himself in no comfort, which, if society were properly constituted, all men might not enjoy; but you get drunk on claret,[4] and you frequent public dinners, where whole joints are stewed down into essences—and all for your country! You are a Gamester—*you* a Patriot!—A very poor man was lately hovering round a Butcher's shop—he wanted to buy a sheep's liver; but your footman in livery outbid him, and your spaniel had it![5] I doubt your Patriotism. You harangue against the Slave-Trade; you attribute the present scarcity to the war—yet you wear powder, and eat pies and sugar! Your patriotism and philanthrophy cost you very little. If I might presume so far, I would inform *how* you might become a Patriot. Your *heart* must believe,[6] that the good of the whole is the greatest possible good of each individual:[7] that *therefore* it is your *duty* to be just, because it is your *interest*. In the present state of society,[8] taking away Hope and Fear, you cannot believe this—for it is not true;

[1] *Enquiry Concerning Political Justice, and its Influence on General Virtue and Happiness* (2 vols 1793). The 2nd ed (1796) is subtitled . . . *and Its Influence on Morals and Happiness.*

[2] In several maxims Berkeley asserts the incompatibility of corrupt morals and pure patriotism, e.g. Maxim 25: "Gamesters, fops, rakes, bullies, stockjobbers: alas! what patriots?" *Works* II 347.

[3] Cf Maxim 9: "A man who hath no sense of God or conscience: would you make such a one guardian to your child? if not, why guardian to the state?" Ibid II 345. See also Maxim 7.

[4] Cf Maxim 5: "It is impossible an epicure should be a patriot". Ibid. See also Maxims 11 and 21. Ibid II 346.

[5] Cf *CN* I 67: "Reason for a Tax upon Dogs—Poor man—sheepsheads &c"; see also *CN* I 67n and below, p 189.

[6] Cf Maxim 32: "Where the heart is right, there is true patriotism". *Works* II 347. Cf also Maxim 27 (below).

[7] Cf Maxim 27: "The patriot aims at his private good in the public" and "considers himself as part of a whole". Ibid. Possibly Hartley is also relevant here: "The hopes and fears relating to a future state . . . may be considered as proceeding from rational self-interest. . . . These hopes and fears are also the strongest of our selfish affections, and yet at the same time the chief foundation of the pure disinterested love of God, and of our neighbour, and the principal means of transferring our associations . . . in the manner the best suited to our attainment of our greatest possible happiness". *Observations on Man* I 465.

[8] C used this phrase to label the fragment of *Religious Musings* in No 2 above (p 64).

yet you cannot be a Patriot unless you do believe it. How shall we reconcile this apparent contradiction? You must give up your sensuality and your philosophy, the pimp of your sensuality; you must condescend to believe in a God,[1] and in the existence of a Future State![2]

Review of "A Letter to the Right Hon. WILLIAM PITT, on the Means of relieving the present Scarcity and preventing the Diseases that arise from meagre Food". By THOMAS BEDDOES, M.D.[3]

TO announce a work from the pen of Dr. Beddoes is to inform the benevolent in every city and parish, that they are appointed agents to some new and practicable scheme for increasing the comforts or alleviating the miseries of their fellow-creatures. The present Letter is introduced by an attack on our Minister for his criminal improvidence in not having guarded against the contingency of unproductive years; and contrasts his supineness with the successful activity of the enemy. In a strain of keenest irony the Doctor notices the singular fact, that, while the French have pressed into their service all the inventive powers of the chemist and mechanic, the sons of science in Britain (almost without an exception) are known to regard the system and measures of the Minister with contempt or abhorrence: nor does he omit to glance on the recent practice of electing Members of the Royal Society from the colour of their political opinions. He then proceeds to unfold the various means by which the stock of provisions may be increased. The first mean recommended is, the conversion of roots eatable by men into fodder for cattle. If, instead of grass or clover, our pasture-lands were planted with potatoes, we could never suffer from famine. The diet allowed to the inferior ranks of Being in seasons of plenty might, "without any change of his habits,"[4] be resumed by man in a year of scarcity. The practicability of feeding horses on potatoes, the Doctor

[1] Cf Maxim 4: ". . . a believer [rather] than an infidel [has] a better chance for being [a] patriot". *Works* II 345. Cf also Maxims 9, 15, and 16. Ibid II 345–6.

[2] With the subtitle "Addressed to all whom it may concern", this essay was reprinted in the *CI* 2 Apr 1796 and the *Manchester Gazette and Weekly Advertiser* 16 Apr with minor changes and the following conclusion: "You must feel the important truth, that unless you can sacrifice your inclinations, and in certain cases, your dearest earthly interests, your virtue, your patriotism, and your religion are in the sight of *God*, of no more worth than *sounding brass or a tinkling cymbal.*" Possibly an addition by Benjamin Flower.

[3] London 1796. For C and Thomas Beddoes (1760–1808), see above, Introduction, p li.

[4] Beddoes *Letter . . . on . . . Scarcity* 16.

affirms from his own experience. The second mode, and that most "commensurate with private means and ordinary talents,"[1] is the dissolving of mere bones into a palatable and nutritious soup by a *broth machine*: for a particular description of which, as communicated to Dr. Beddoes by a scientific friend, we refer our readers to the pamphlet. Two hundred quarts of soup may be made for half-a crown, exclusive of the expence of fire and labour. The original expence of the *broth-machine* is not mentioned; but it should appear to be somewhat above a poor man's* opportunities; and from the necessity of regulating the pressure on the steam-valve by a mercurial guage, to require more management than can reasonably be expected from the ignorant. Such a machine might indeed be a fit companion to the public hand-mill and oven, which it has been recommended to erect in every parish; but then there must be a man paid to superintend it; and if the poor were fed daily in this manner, they would rely less and less on their own industry, and sink at last into a class resembling the Neapolitan Lazaroni.

These objections probably possess very little strength; or at least the urgency of the distress may demand such a palliative, even though, like other medicines of temporary efficacy, it should tend to render permanent the disease which it alleviates.

This broth must be thickened with barley; and the Doctor proposes to prohibit by law, or to try by influence of example to prevent, the manufacture of any beer, the strength of which exceeds six bushels of malt to the hogshead. The last proposal, and apparently the least practicable, is couched in the modest form of a quere.—"Can any stimulating substances be added to poor aliment without detriment to health in the long run, so as to give it the greater power of nourishment? If opium could be used without danger of inducing bad habits, could it be used to advantage?"[2] We may venture to answer, that in the first [place], the poor and ignorant could never be prevailed upon to use it at all, or any other stimulant which they had been accustomed to consider as medicine: and secondly, that although their prejudices were removable, yet opium could *not* be used without danger of inducing bad habits. Misery would not refrain from the intemperate use of a drug, the properties of which so nearly resemble those of wine.[3]†

* Exclusive of the expence of fire from twelve to eighteen hours.

† There are plants which may indirectly contribute to our nourishment

[1] Ibid 17.

[2] Ibid 27–8 (C has omitted seven sentences between the two he quotes).

[3] Five days before this number of

Dr. Beddoes concludes his letter, by expressing his apprehensions that the majority of our wealthy men, labouring beneath "the feverish fullness" of daily feasting may rather envy than hasten to relieve "the cool and relaxed condition of hungry poverty."[2] To counteract this slowness to good works, which may arise from total inexperience of the miseries of a scanty meal, we would address a few questions[3] to the two accessible parts of a rich man's heart—his avarice and his fears. 1. Whether the wealth of the higher classes does not ultimately depend on the labour of the lower classes?[4] 2. Whether the man, who has been accustomed to love beef and clean linen, will not have stronger motives to labour, as well as greater ability, than the man who has used himself to exist without either? and whether extreme poverty does not necessarily produce laziness?[5] 3. Whether therefore to provide plentifully for the poor be not feeding the root, the juices from which will shoot upwards into the branches, and cause the top to flourish.[6] 4. When the root yieldeth insufficient nourishment, whether wise men would not wish to top the tree in order to make the lower branches thrive?[7] 5. Whether hungry cattle do not leap over bounds?[8] And lastly, whether it would not have been a wise law, which should have appropriated one week at least

---

by becoming substitutes of wheat or potatoes in articles of luxury. A pure and excellent starch may be made from the Maranta, or Indian Arrow-root, in Jamaica. This plant, which has already obtained the name of the Starch-plant, may be raised in that island to any extent. Some families have made biscuits from it remarkable for their lightness and flavour. For a more particular account of this plant see a pamphlet written by Mr. Ryder, and published by Bell, Oxford-street.[1]

The Watchman was printed, 12 Mar 1796, C had written the Rev J. Edwards that, "tottering on the edge of madness", he had "been obliged to take Laudanum almost every night": *CL* I 188.

[1] Thomas Ryder *Some Account of the Maranta, or Indian Arrow Root: in Which It Is Considered and Recommended as a Substitute for Starch Prepared from Corn* (1796). C's descriptive phrases occur on pp 16 and 18, but C's note (except the first sentence) is taken from *Eng R* XXVII (Feb 1796) 196.

[2] Beddoes *Letter . . . on . . . Scarcity* 31–2.

[3] C is again drawing upon Berkeley, here from *The Querist*, which follows "Maxims Concerning Modern Patriotism" in the *Works* (1784) C borrowed from the Bristol Library: II 349–417.

[4] Cf *The Querist* Nos 4 and 487: *Works* II 351, 405.

[5] Cf ibid Nos 20, 61, 107, 353, and 355: II 353, 358, 363, 390.

[6] Ibid No 59: II 357.

[7] Cf ibid No 158: II 369.

[8] Cf ibid No 178: II 371.

of every month in each session of Parliament to the discussion of schemes for the national benefit? And whether Dr. Beddoes, Dr. Priestley, Dr. Kirwan, Mr. Keir, and the Earl of Dundonald,[1] might not have suggested modes of employing two hundred millions of money to more beneficial purposes than the murder of two millions of their fellow-creatures? And whether to produce and make happy be not to imitate God; and to slaugher and desolate, and to take pleasure therein, be not practices very nearly resembling those of the Devil?[2]

ORIGIN OF THE MAYPOLE[3]

THE leisure days after seed-time had been chosen by our Saxon ancestors for folk motes, or conventions of the people. Not till after the Norman conquest, the Pagan festival of Whitsuntide fully melted into the Christian holiday of Pentecost. Its original name is Wittentide, the time of choosing the *wits* or *wise men* to *the Wittenagemotte*. It was consecrated to Hertha, the Goddess of Peace and Fertility; and no quarrels might be maintained, no blood shed, during this truce of the Goddess. Each village, in the absence of the Baron at the assembly of the nation, enjoyed a kind of Saturnalia. The vassals met upon the common green around the May-pole, where they elected a village lord, or king, as he was called, who chose his queen. He wore an oaken, and she a hawthorn wreath, and together they gave laws to the rustic sports during these sweet days of freedom. The MAY-POLE, then, is the *English Tree of Liberty!*[4] Are there many yet standing!

[1] Richard Kirwan (1733–1812), a chemist, as were also James Keir (1735–1820) and Archibald Cochrane, 9th Earl of Dundonald (1749–1831). Kirwan had recently published *Manures . . . Applicable . . . to Soil* (1795), Dundonald *Connexion . . . Between Agriculture and Chemistry* (1795).

[2] The last query seems indebted to *The Querist* Nos 13, 346, and 499: *Works* II 352, 389–90, 406.

[3] From *M Mag* I (Feb 1796) 29 (also in *M Chron* 4 Mar 1796). SC included this as C's in *EOT* I 137.

[4] The Tree of Liberty, a symbol used by the Americans in their War of Independence and adopted in France by the Jacobins in 1790. In England at this time, singing a republican song "Plant, plant the Tree of Liberty" was sufficient to cause arrest on the charge of sedition.

ELEGY[1]

NEAR the lone Pile with ivy overspread,
Fast by the riv'let's sleep-persuading sound,
Where "sleeps the moonlight,"[2] on yon verdant bed—
O humbly press *that* consecrated ground!

For there does Edmund rest, the learned swain!
And there his spirit most delights to rove.
Young Edmund! fam'd for each harmonious strain,
And the sore wounds of ill-requited Love.

Like some tall tree that spreads it's branches wide,
And loads the West-wind with its soft perfume,
His manhood blossom'd; till the faithless pride
Of fair Matilda sank him to the tomb.

But soon did righteous Heaven her guilt pursue!
Wheree'er with 'wilder'd steps she wandered pale,
Still Edmund's image rose to blast her view,
Still Edmund's voice accus'd her in each gale.

With keen regret, and conscious guilt's alarms,
Amid the pomp of affluence she pin'd:
Nor all that lur'd her faith from Edmund's arms,
Could lull the wakeful horrors of her mind.

Go, Trav'ller! tell the tale with sorrow fraught:
Some tearful Maid perchance, or blooming Youth
May hold it in remembrance; and be taught
That Riches cannot pay for Love or Truth.

T.

[1] First published in *M Chron* 23 Sept 1794. Included in *PW* (EHC) I 69–70 with the reminder that the poem was omitted from the 1852 edition as "of doubtful origin" (C, however, had included it in *SL* and *Poems* 1828, 1829, 1834). In a BM copy of *The Watchman* (Ashley 2842) there is at this point (p 77) a marginal note by C: "Rhymified by me, S. T. C., from the much nobler blank Verse Poem of Akenside". Akenside's poem is *Inscriptions* III: *Poems* (1772) 373–4.

[2] Shakespeare *Merchant of Venice* v i 54.

THE HOUR WHEN WE SHALL MEET AGAIN[1]

(*Composed during Illness, and in Absence.*)

DIM Hour! that sleep'st on pillowing clouds afar,
O rise and yoke the Turtles to thy car!
Bend o'er the traces, blame each lingering Dove,
And give me to the bosom of my Love!
My gentle Love, caressing and carest,
With heaving heart shall cradle me to rest;
Shed the warm tear-drop from her smiling eyes,
Lull with fond woe, and med'cine me with sighs:
While finely-flushing float her kisses meek,
Like melted rubies, o'er my pallid cheek.
Chill'd by the night, the drooping Rose of May
Mourns the long absence of the lovely Day:
Young Day returning at her promis'd hour
Weeps o'er the sorrows of her fav'rite flower;
Weeps the soft dew, the balmy gale she sighs,
And darts a trembling lustre from her eyes.
New life and joy th' expanding flow'ret feels:
His pitying Mistress mourns, and mourning heals!

C.

LINES ON THE PORTRAIT OF A LADY[2]

TENDER as the sweets of Spring
Wafted on the Western gale,
When the breeze with dewy wing
Wanders thro' the Primrose vale;

Tranquil as the hush of night
To the Hermit's holy dream;

[1] *PW* (EHC) I 96. This poem first appeared here and was included in *Poems* (1797). C drew Poole's attention to it (30 Mar 1796: *CL* I 195) and hoped that he would like it. Poole did (11 Apr 1796: *CL* I 203). Line 17, originally "Now life . . .", was corrected to "New life . . .": see C to J. Edwards 20 Mar 1796: *CL* I 203. It is also corrected in the BM copy of *The Watchman* (see above, p 104 n 1) p 78.

[2] C did not acknowledge this poem, but it must be his, for notice the signatures of this and the two preceding poems—"T. C. S.". C was notoriously fond of his initials in their normal order or scrambled. He signed *An Answer to "A Letter to Edward Long Fox, M.D."* with "C. T. S.".

While the Moon with lovely light,
Quivers on the rippling stream;

Cheerful as the Beams of Morn,
Laughing on the Mountain's side;
Spotless as the Cygnet's form,
Heaving on the silver'd Tide.

Who can paint this varied grace,
Charms that mock the mimic art?
Yet, my Laura! these I trace,
With the pencil of the Heart.

S.

Simple, deeply pathetic, and even sublime, the following Song may, without exaggerated praise, be pronounced the most exquisite performance in our language. It was written by Mr. LOGAN,[1] a Scotch Divine and Historian, who died in London, the 28th of December 1788, in the 40th year of his age. As its popularity is by no means equal to its merits, we have reprinted it in THE WATCHMAN, confident that to be admired universally and with enthusiasm, it needs only be known.

SONG.

THE BRAES OF YARROW

THY braes were bonny, Yarrow stream!
When first on them I met my lover:
Thy braes how dreary, Yarrow stream!
When now thy waves his body cover!
For ever now, O Yarrow stream!
Thou art to me a stream of sorrow;
For never on thy banks shall I
Behold my love, the flower of Yarrow!

He promised me a milk-white steed
To bear me to his father's bowers;
He promised me a little page
To squire me to his father's towers;

[1] John Logan (1748–88), Scottish divine and poet, better known for his *Ode to the Cuckoo*. Possibly C saw this in *B Poets* XI 1035 or *Eng R* XXV (Apr 1795) 306–7 (Lovell's and Southey's *Poems* was reviewed in the Mar and May numbers). C omits the last stanza. See Introduction, above, p l and n 2.

He promised me a wedding-ring—
  The wedding-day was fix'd to-morrow!
Now he is wedded to his grave—
  Alas! his watery grave in Yarrow.

Sweet were his words when last we met;
  My passion I as freely told him!
Clasp'd in his arms, I little thought
  That I should never more behold him!
Scarce was he gone, I saw his ghost!
  It vanish'd with a shriek of sorrow—
Thrice did the water-wraith* ascend,
  And gave a doleful groan thro' Yarrow!

His mother from the window look'd
  With all the longings of a mother;
His little sister weeping walk'd
  The green-wood path to meet her brother.
They sought him East, they sought him West,
  They sought him all the forest thorough;
They only saw the cloud of night,
  They only heard the roar of Yarrow!

No longer from the window look,
  Thou hast no son, thou tender mother!
No longer walk, thou lovely maid!
  Alas! thou hast no more a brother.
No longer seek him East or West,
  And search no more the forest thorough;
For wandering in the night so dark,
  He fell a lifeless corse in Yarrow!

* The Water-fiend: sometimes called the Kelpie.

THE WAR[1]

ITS OBJECTS	OBTAINED
	December 1792
To prevent the Opening of the Scheldt,	By its being solemnly opened.
To save Holland,	By its being conquered.
To prevent the aggrandizement of France,	By France conquering territories almost equal in extent to her own.
	June 1793
Indemnity for the past,	Martinico, Pondicherry, and Corsica, gained at an expence of Sixty Millions sterling, being more than twenty times their value.
Security for the future,	In making France an armed nation, and the greatest military power in Europe.
Gratitude to our Allies.	Most of whom have taken our money and left us in the lurch, and the others only fight with us as long as we can pay them.
	October 1793
The Restoration of Monarchy in France,	By establishing a Republic, and seeing those who voted the death of Louis the XVIth appointed to the supreme Government of France.
The Renunciation of the system of Fraternity,	By the French consolidating the Netherlands, Savoy, &c. and even wishing to consolidate a great part of Germany with their Republic.
The destruction of Jacobin principles,	By the appointment of Jacobins to fill the Offices of Government.

[1] From *M Post* 9 Mar 1796, signed "A. Fogg".

ITS OBJECTS	OBTAINED
February 1795	
That France should have a Government capable of maintaining the accustomed Relations of Peace and Amity with other Powers.	France never was without such a Government. She observed the Relations of Peace and Amity with Sweden, Denmark, Switzerland, America, &c.
29 *October* 1795	
Till the stability of the New Constitution is proved,	And it was *fully* proved in less than six weeks, namely, on the 8th of December, 1795.[1]
March 1796	
God knows the object of the War!	God knows whether it is obtained.

EFFECTS OF THE WAR[2]

In 1690, the number of Houses in England and Wales was — — 1,319,215
In 1759, the number was reduced to — 986,482
In 1777, the number did not exceed — 952,734

And it is extremely probable that the American war and the present has still further reduced them. The above are the reports made by the Collectors of the House and Window Taxes; so that allowing five persons to each house, the number of inhabitants has decreased two millions, or almost one-third of what it was at the time of the Revolution.

This decrease also is most felt in that class of the community who are the most useful.

In 1689, the number of Cottages was — 554,631
In 1777, the number was reduced to — 251,261

So that between these two periods the decrease was more than one half, that is above 300,000 Cottages, which, at five to a Cottage, make 1,500,000 labourers less than a century ago. What can this be ascribed to, but the difficulty of procuring subsistence by labour?

[1] On this date, the English ministry reversed its stand, and, through the King's message to Parliament, announced its willingness to open negotiations for peace with France.

[2] From *M Chron* 8 Mar 1796, including italics; there *labour* in the last sentence is also italicised.

These calculations have been ably made by a writer in the new Monthly Magazine,[1] who fairly states that as all duties necessarily fall on the head of a family, our taxes *amount to 25l. per annum on every house in the kingdom.*

Can we go on this way? Is it in the nature of things that a society so constituted should continue?—No industry, no labour can support themselves under such burthens; and the rapid and sure consequence must be the extinction of all the active class of society, and that we shall soon have but two orders, the rich few, into whose hands all the opulence of the kingdom will devolve, and the poor, dependant on their benevolence; for it is always to be remembered, that taxation does not carry treasure out of a country. It only takes it from the many, and gives it to the few; but this in truth impoverishes the whole, since all the active powers of a nation are paralyzed, and the bulk of the people become dependant on *bounty* instead of labour for their daily bread.

SUPPOSITION—A NEW SONG[2]

Tune—SHELAH NEGARI

I

YE Friends give attention awhile to my lay,
'Tis what you can't meet with (at least ev'ry day),
'Tis all Supposition, of this and of that,
For the Devil himself cannot tell what I am at.
Some Wiseacres doubtless to puzzle their brains,
May try to find out, Sir—"my Ways and my Means."
Tho' my Budget is ope—till I give 'em the cue,
They'll ne'er find me out—I'll be d—d if they do.
Fol de ral, &c.

[1] *M Mag* I (Feb 1796) 7–8, "Hints on the Population of Great-Britain", which the *Star* 12 Mar 1796 attributed to William Morgan, author of *Facts ... Respecting the Expence of the War*; see below, p 220 n 3.

[2] "J. B.", whom C above, p 87, thanked for this contribution, is James Bisset (c 1762–1832), artist, publisher, and poet (*CL* I 188 and 193n), who set up "a museum and shop for the sale of curiosities" (*DNB*). Bisset again advertises his "museum" on the title-page of his *The Converts. A Moral Tale* (n.d.). A Dissenter, he may have heard C when the latter held two religious services in Birmingham during his January visit (*CL* I 176). Bisset had suffered for his opinions at the time of the Birmingham riots in 1791, having been dragged down the stone steps of a public-house because he would not drink to the toast: "Damn all Presbyterians". John Binns *Recollections* (Philadelphia 1854) 68–9.

II

Supposition's my motto—then let me *suppose*
A parcel of Asses, who're led by the nose;
Suppose then again that their Masters are such,
They'd load the poor Devils a little too much;
Suppose from the top of the head to the toe,
They're burthen'd so heavy they cannot well go:
Yet forc'd to jog on, Sir, their *strength* to evince,
Now supposing all this—don't you think they might
wince? *Fal de ral, &c.*

III

Suppose then again, for the sake of the joke,
(As Asses of old, we are told once have spoke:)
These Asses complain'd of this heart-rending grief,
And beg'd their Taskmasters to give some relief.
"Oh no!" says their Leaders, "find fault to our face?
But now, my dear Creatures, we'll alter the case.
Mum Chance you shall live—not a Word shall you
say,
For we'll MUZZLE you so, that you never shall bray."
Fal de ral, &c.

IV

Some Asses I'm told—but *suppose* it a hum,
Rejoic'd when they found that the "Order was Mum!"
And said they would go if their Leaders thought fit,
Blindfold down the gulph—of the bottomless Pitt.
The muzzles were made, and it then came to pass,
They stop'd up the mouth of John Bull's simple Ass,
Who then sunk, alas! in a woeful condition;
But remember, my friends—This is all *Supposition!*
Fal de ral, &c. &c.

J. B——.

MUSEUM, *Birmingham, March* 3.

FOREIGN INTELLIGENCE[1]

A TREATY of Commerce, it is said, is being negociated between Denmark, Sweden, France, and Spain. A great number of transports with ammunition, &c. are on their road to Luxembourg and Friesland; as the former is to be made a place of arms for the French army on the Upper Rhine, and the latter for that on the Lower. From Munich we learn that the States of Bavaria have voted the ELECTOR[2] three millions and a half of Florins for the organization of an army of 30,000 men, of which, in case of the continuance of the war, 18,000 men will be sent to the Austrian army. It is reported that the operations of the Imperial army, in the ensuing campaign, will be made dependant on a Military Council at Vienna: an additional instance of the proneness of the Combined Powers to imitate the policy and measures of the French. STOFFLET[3] and five of his accomplices were tried at Angers, on the 6th Ventose, and were shot the next day.—A letter from Angers says, that CHARETTE is dead of his wounds.[4]

In General Hoche's admirable Memoir* on the War in La Vendee,[6] and on the accusations against him, he asserts that SIX HUNDRED THOUSAND FRENCHMEN HAVE PERISHED IN LA VENDEE! —The French Legislature is still employed on the Finances. The Council of 500, on March 1, received a message from the Executive Directory, respecting the necessity of enforcing the law for the suppression of Clubs. It is an animated and judicious composition: and in a country where the power frequently returns to the people at large, the measure ought not to be deemed an oppressive one, in the present dangerous and unsettled situation of the country. Five

* It is the intention of the Editor to publish, every half year, an APPENDIX (price six-pence), containing the State papers of the preceding months.[5]

[1] Following two paragraphs condensed from reports in the *Gazetteer* 8–9 Mar 1796.

[2] Charles Theodore (1724–99), the Elector Palatine of Bavaria, succeeded in 1777.

[3] Jean-Nicolas Stofflet (1741–96), co-leader with Charette of the royalist forces in La Vendée, was captured early in 1796.

[4] An unfounded rumour; see below, pp 212–13.

[5] Coleridge's publication would have enjoyed considerable priority in time over the usual sources of such documents, the *Annual Register*, which had fallen years behind, and the *New Annual Register*, which appeared but once a year and usually six months or more after the end of the year. Debrett's *State Papers* may have given C his idea.

[6] Quoted from *M Chron* 9 Mar 1796; the *Star* 8 Mar 1796 published the "Memoir".

Societies, one Theatre, and the Edifice called the Church of St. Andre des Arts, have been shut up by an Arret of the Directory.

MANHEIM, *Feb.* 18.[1] The French, contrary to every expectation, have just proposed a prolongation of the Armistice. We do not know whether this proposition will be acceded to by the Austrians. A convention of the Empire, to be holden here, is talked of.

POLAND[2]

(*Extract of a Letter from Grodno, inserted in a Paris Paper.*)

"ALTHOUGH the abdication of the King of Poland[3] is already known, the particulars attending that event cannot fail to be interesting; this new example of the vicissitude of fortune may afford useful lessons, even to Republicans. It is of consequence to know how a certain Court, *the friend of justice*, behaves to a deposed King.

"On St. Catherine's day, Repnin[4] went to the King, and laid before him several papers that had been sent from Petersburgh, as the act of his abdication, a resignation of his pretensions to the Crown, &c. which Stanislaus signed in the morning, and which Repnin immediately made public through the city. The King of Poland, afterwards, at dinner, introduced his former mistress Gradbowka,[5] declared that she had been married to him seven years, and legitimatizing all the children he had had by her, made over to them the remainder of his fortune—then, bursting into tears, his usual relief in misery, he dismissed his faithful servants. There was in the evening a ball, at which Repnin, aggravating his shame, presented himself the dethroned King to the Company. Such was the end of Stanislaus's reign. Let us now cast our eyes upon the martyrs of Polish liberty. At Minster, on the day when the new Governor made his entrance, the prisoners of war were assembled, and the Empress's edict, ordering them to be dispersed into the Russian regiments, was read to them.

"One of the Poles, as soon as he had heard the Edict, advanced from the ranks, and addressing himself to General Chrouchef,[6] de-

[1] From the *Star* 9 Mar (one sentence omitted).

[2] From the *Gazetteer* 11 Mar 1796.

[3] Stanislas Poniatowski (1732–98), who became in 1764 (as Stanislas II) last king of Poland, abdicated 25 Nov 1795 at the completion of the Third Partition.

[4] Prince Nikolai Vasilievich Repnin (1734–1801), Russian statesman, diplomat, and general, was Catherine's minister to Poland in 1795.

[5] Countess Elzbieta Gradbowska (1748/9–1810).

[6] Andrei Ivanovich Khrushchov (d 1805), an infantry general who served under Suvorov. Either the general was merely wounded or the story is apocryphal.

claimed, with the greatest energy, against the want of faith, and the tyranny of his Sovereign; in the midst of his speech the General approached him to make him feel the weight of his cane—that wonderful stimulus, that makes the Russian march, and the German move; but the freeman, indignant at being treated like a slave, drew a dagger from his pocket, killed the General, wounded a Major, who ran to the General's assistance, and then stabbing himself, said to the Russians that surrounded him, 'Tell the Czarina, before whom you only crawl and cringe, that Poland still contains Republicans.' "

By the last news which have reached Bombay from Persia,[1] we learn that LUFTY ALLY KHAN,[2] after experiencing the caprice of fortune, and being betrayed by the treachery of his adherents, fled, with a few partizans, to the city of Kerman, which was immediately surrounded by MAHOMED ALLY KHAN. After a blockade of eight or nine months, the citizens, urged by famine and despair, opened their gates to the merciless victor. For seven days was the town delivered to the pillage of a rapacious cruel soldiery. To add to the horrors of this work of rapine, the tyrant, in order to execute his vengeance upon the most obnoxious, directed the *extraction of their eyes*; and so many are said to be the victims, that it is calculated two maunds of *human eyes* were the fruits of this diabolical command. This tragic scene was closed by totally annihilating the city of Kerman, and passing the plough over its foundation. To return to LUFTY ALLY KHAN, he is said to have escaped, in the confusion of the surrender, to Bamm a small town to the southward of Kerman, where he was speedily overtaken. Being brought into the presence of MAHOMED ALLY, his conduct discovered the magnanimity of his spirit. He replied to the charges of disloyalty with reproaches of contempt and defiance; and, in the end, *was condemned to the loss of his eyes.* This he suffered; and shortly, by means not accurately ascertained, put a period to his existence.

THE NATIONAL CONVENTION OF THE UNITED PROVINCES MET AT THE HAGUE ON THE FIRST OF THIS MONTH. The ceremony of the opening of the Convention was splendid. The Deputies

[1] This report verbatim (including italics) from the *M Herald* 11 Mar 1796, or the *Star* 12 Mar, or the *M Post* 14 Mar.

[2] See above, pp 71–2. To his catalogue of tyrants (see Catherine above) and their repulsive habits C is able to add Muhammad Ali Khan and his maunds of eyes, which for once surpass the iniquities of the "insatiate Hag". See *Ode to the Departing Year* line 45: *PW* (EHC) I 162.

were escorted by the National Guards to the Hall of the Convention, where the Commission was opened. The Assembly of the States General then declared, that its functions were at an end, and dissolved itself. The ships displayed the National Flag.[1]

DOMESTIC INTELLIGENCE

We are happy to announce among the Candidates for the Borough of Leominster, at the ensuing general Election, GEORGE AUGUSTUS POLLEN, Esq. a man who will be long remembered by the University of Cambridge, for his various erudition, for his splendid natural talents, and above all, for that, compared with which these are but the pomp and pageantry of Intellect, for his ardent and active Benevolence.[2] He was introduced by Lord Viscount Malden.[3]

On Sunday, (*Feb.* 29),[4] as the ferry-boat was crossing the river from Common-Straith Quay to Old Lynn, at seven in the evening, with about thirty persons on board, it ran foul of the cable of a barge, and was overset, by which accident upwards of twenty persons have lost their lives: four more must inevitably have perished, but for the active and vigorous exertions of one of the passengers (John Price, a sailor), who, at the hazard of his own life, and with that intrepid humanity which characterizes an English Tar, rescued them: he had seized a fifth (a woman), but the rapidity of the tide tore her from him, and he himself was nearly lost in this last attempt. It

[1] Above item condensed from the *Star* 14 Mar 1796.

[2] To Pollen (c 1775–1807), his junior by a year at Cambridge, C had asked Cottle to send a copy of his poems (*CL* I 201). This gesture and the present reference to "Benevolence" were made before C had read the sarcastic announcement in the *M Post* (30 Mar) that "Mr. POLLIN . . . once a firm advocate for the Rights of the People, is to come into Parliament next Session for a Ministerial Borough. . . . Mr. P. . . . relinquishes all his absurd notions of Liberty, to join the persevering *howlings* of the Alarmists". (On the dating of C's letter to Cottle see above, Introduction, p lix. Cf *CL* I 201n.) Pollen was successful in his candidacy for Leominster. For another mention of him I quote Lady Holland (1799): "Ld. H. met at Sheridan's one day lately, Mr. Pollen, the man who dreaded invasion for the sake of the chastity of the ladies". Holland learned that he was called "Prodigy" Pollen, for whenever anything extraordinary was mentioned, Pollen would cite a similar occurrence in his experience. *The Journal of Elizabeth Lady Holland (1791–1811)* ed Earl of Ilchester (2 vols 1908) I 222–3.

[3] George Capel-Coningsby (1757–1839), MP for New Radnor, held the courtesy title of Viscount Malden until 1799, when he succeeded as 5th Earl of Essex. For the account of a duel arising from this election, see below pp 337–40.

[4] From the *CI* 5 Mar 1796 (with slight omissions). Sunday was 28 Feb.

is just 166 years since a similar accident happened at the same ferry, when eighteen persons were unfortunately drowned.

CAMBRIDGE, *March* 5.[1] Of the two gold Medals (value 15 guineas each, annually given by his Grace the Duke of Grafton to those Bachelors of Arts who shall excel in classical learning) the first is adjudged to Mr. Samuel Butler, of St. John's College,[2] and the second to Mr. John D'Oyley, of Bennet College.[3] Mr. Samuel Butler, while he was yet in his Non-ens, won Sir W. Brown's Gold Medal for a Latin Ode on the subject of the Slave Trade, at the same time that the Editor of the WATCHMAN was honoured with the prize for a Greek Ode on the same subject.[4] Since that time Mr. Butler, with a

[1] Sentence immediately following from the *CI* 5 Mar 1796; the rest is C's.

[2] Samuel Butler (1774–1839), later headmaster of Shrewsbury and bp of Lichfield, was eighteen when he won the Sir William Browne Medal for the Latin ode on the slave-trade (Jul 1792) and the University Scholarship (Nov 1792). C's good-will toward Butler appears in *CL* I 47 and 82 (letters of 5 Feb [1793] and c 14 Jun 1794). After C's death Butler published a letter testifying to his admiration for C. See Samuel Butler *The Life and Letters of Dr. Samuel Butler* (2 vols 1896) II 94. Richard Porson, one of the examiners, must have been in C's mind when he said that "the most elegant Scholar among the examiners gave a decided Vote in my Favor": to his brother George 13 [Jan 1793]: *CL* I 46. See *CL* I 45–7 and *PW* (JDC) 476–7, 654n. In a review of *BL* in Oct 1817 C's Cambridge record was attacked by a writer in *Bl M* who quoted Porson's offering to show one hundred and thirty-four examples of bad Greek in C's prize ode. *Bl M* II (1818) 12n. If we may believe this statement, I suspect it was made after Porson had learned of C's change in politics, for Porson was a staunch Whig. C himself spoke disparagingly of the Greek in the prize ode (see *PW*—EHC—I 146–147n) and to Cottle he wrote (*CL* I 330, c 3 Jul 1797) that the "finest poem, I ever wrote, lost the prize—& that which gained it, was contemptible". The ode that lost in the contest for the Browne medal in 1793 was on astronomy (see *CL* I 56 and n), when C was second to John Keate. Cottle said: "Mr. Coleridge used to speak in high terms of Porson . . . and regretted that when his unsuccessful Ode was delivered in, Porson happened not to be one of the examiners; which circumstance, Mr. C. thought, lost him the prize." *E Rec* I 253n. However that may be, there is no doubt of C's admiration for Porson, from whom he may, by the way, have acquired some prejudices, such as a low opinion of Godwin, Holcroft, and Dr Parr. See *CL* I 138–9 and M. L. Clarke *Richard Porson. A Biographical Essay* (Cambridge 1937) 20. Perhaps the scoffing tone of the "Essay on Fasts" owes something to Porson's *The Orgies of Bacchus* (1793–4), especially as regards miracles. For the *Orgies* see *The Spirit of the Public Journals for 1797* (3rd ed 1802) I 261–84. Interestingly enough, Porson had a passion for making marginalia in books. See Samuel Rogers *Table Talk* (1953) 171.

[3] John D'Oyly (1774–1824) was created baronet in 1821 for his services in the government of Ceylon. Bennet was the name then used for Corpus Christi College.

[4] Writing c 3 Mar 1808 to Thomas Clarkson, C reviewed his efforts in behalf of Abolition: ". . . my first public Effort was a Greek Ode against the Slave Trade, for which I had a Gold Medal, & which I spoke publickly in the Senate House, and . . . at Bristol I

success unknown since the time of Mr. Tweddel,[1] has swept almost all the Prizes of each year θαητὸς μεθ' ἑτάροισιν στεφάνων ἑκάτι.[2] For the University Scholarship he proved the successful Candidate.—We shall be pardoned, I trust, for having indulged a retrospective glance on events,

> "Now past, and but remembered like sweet sounds
> Of yesterday!
> Hours of delight and hope, in the gay tide
> Of Youth, and *many friends now scattered wide*
> *By many fates*."[3]

The hand of the *Princess Royal* is solicited by the Hereditary *Prince of Wirtemberg*.[4] M. Zipillen is the love-maker,[5] but he has not yet obtained the King and Queen's consent. The Prince is forty years of age; our Princess is thirty.

Among the curiosities of a venerable Antiquary, lately brought under the hammer, were a Sculpture of the Venus de Medicis in BLACK marble, and a Blackmoor's head in ALABASTER! This is much in the same spirit with Sam. Foot's revival of *The Fair Penitent*, at the Haymarket Theatre; the part of Calissa, for one night only, [was played] *by a young Negro from the coast of Guinea*.[6]

The importance of Bills which entrench on the liberty of the Irish People, will always be felt by Englishmen with a lively interest, not merely from the generous sentiment of regard for the rights of their

---

gave an especial Lecture against the falling off zeal in the friends of Abolition, combating the various arguments, exposing the true causes, and re-awakening the fervor & the horror, and published a long Essay in the Watchman on the Trade in general, in confutation of all the arguments, *all* of which I there stated, besides a Poem, & several Parts of Poems". *CL* III 78.

[1] John Tweddell (1769–99), Fellow of Trinity College, Cambridge, was a classical and archaeological scholar of great promise.

[2] Pindar *Pythians* 10.58 (var). Tr: "Distinguished among his companions for his prizes".

[3] By William Lisle Bowles. Lines 1–2 are from *Associations* lines 4–5; lines 3–5 from *Oxford Revisited* lines 8–10 (var).

[4] Charlotte Augusta Matilda (1766–1828), eldest daughter of George III, married 18 May 1797 Frederick William Charles (1754–1816), Prince (later Duke Frederick II, subsequently King Frederick I) of Württemberg. Her parents' hesitation resulted from rumours about the part the Prince may have played in the death of his first wife. *The Times* 15 Mar 1796 branded this item, which appeared in the London papers 11 Mar, "among the lies of the day".

[5] Johann Karl, Count von Zeppelin (1767–1801), German general and diplomat, had been sent to England as a special envoy.

[6] Samuel Foote (1720–77), actor and dramatist; Nicholas Rowe's play was first produced in 1703. Calista was one of Mrs Siddons's famous rôles. This item is from *M Chron* 14 Mar 1796.

fellow subjects but also from the more personal motive of his own safety; since he knows that Ireland is considered as a favourable soil for political experiments; and that a slip of every new restraint on the subject is regularly transplanted into England.[1]

We copy therefore from the Dublin Evening Post, a short abstract of the new Bill against Insurrections, that our readers may see the provisions of this intended Law. It is a melancholy truth that the spirit of insurrection, in the Sister Kingdom, requires a strong remedy, but we prophecy, that it will not be found in statutes that entrench on Constitutional Liberty. The curse of a bad system is come upon the country. The debasement of a whole class of men by laws abhorrent to reason, together with the state of misery in which they are held, has made them desperate. In such a state of society, it is not laws of coercion, but the laws of amelioration that will be efficacious. Their condition must be coerced, for it is in vain to hope that ignorant men, starving, oppressed, and degraded, will feel that obedience is a duty. If a man who labours from morning till night cannot *earn* bread to eat for himself and family, the bond of protection and obedience, the very end of society is broken, and we seriously put it to our own Legislators, if this is not hastening to be the case in England as well as in Ireland.

Outlines of the Enactments of the Bill for more effectually suppressing Insurrections in Ireland.

It first makes the administration of any unlawful oath or *engagement* felony of death; those who take it, if not by force, to be deemed felons and transported. Force to be no plea, unless a discovery is made before a Magistrate of all the circumstances attending the transaction. And unless such discovery be made before the 1st of June next, the plea of force or necessity to be no plea for any oath taken within the last five years.

It obliges all persons to register their arms by the first of May next, and to swear to the truth of their registry, under penalty of 10l. for the first, 20l. for the second, and four months imprisonment for the third. It also authorizes Magistrates to grant warrants to break into houses, and every part of them in search of unregistered arms.

It makes the written information of any witness who shall be

[1] This and the following paragraph as well as the "Outlines" from *M Chron* 9 Mar 1796, including italics and exclamation points. The *Star* 10 Mar also printed the "Outlines".

murdered, evidence, and gives a power to the Grand Jury to present for such a sum as they may think proper to the personal representative of such murdered or maimed witness.

It enables Magistrates to send for strangers and commit them to gaol, if they do not find bail for their good behaviour—to hold a Special Session of the Peace, and signify to the Lord Lieutenant that the county is in a disturbed state, or in immediate danger of becoming so, who may thereupon proclaim it, when the Magistrates are to hold Petty Sessions, and warn the inhabitants to keep within their dwellings between sun set and sun rise on pain of being *sent on board his Majesty's fleet!!!* no trial by Jury!

If persons coming within these clauses *give bail*, they may appeal from the single Magistrate, to the Magistrates of Session, *one* of whom is to be of the *quorum!*

If any persons shall assemble tumultuously in the *day time*, the Magistrate is enabled to send them *on board the fleet*—no trial by Jury!

Any person obstructing or opposing Magistrates in searching at night for inhabitants, lodgers, or arms, to be *sent on board the fleet!* no trial by Jury!

Any person vending or selling any seditious paper, or paper unstamped which is required by law to be stamped, to be taken up as a vagabond, and by two Magistrates to be *sent on board the fleet*—no trial by Jury!

Any woman vending or selling such seditious or unstamped paper, to be committed to gaol, *there to remain* until she shall discover the person from whom she received such paper!

Should an action be brought against any Magistrate for acting under this Bill, and *damages given by a Jury* to any amount, the plaintiff shall be entitled to no more than *sixpence*, and no costs, if it shall appear to the Judge that there was *probable* cause for the Magistrate acting as he did!!!

HOUSE OF LORDS

March, 4

(*Concluded from page* 87).

So early as the year 1663, certain duties of $4\frac{1}{2}$ per cent. were granted by the Assembly of Inhabitants for the defence and fortifications of the Leeward Islands. In the reign of Queen Anne, in consequence of a petition from the planters, an act was passed, appropriating these funds to their original purposes, her Majesty's word was pledged, that the fund should be employed to its proper objects. The point thus solemnly established was confirmed by the practice of many years: and if any deviations took place, at least no pension was settled on this fund, till that of Lord Chatham. It had begun with the example of a very great man; and he hoped, that with the present distinguished character[1] it would be concluded. The remaining funds were not sufficient for the defence of the Islands. He reminded the House, that in 1785 a message had been carried down to the House of Commons, representing that this fund was greatly burdened. It was stated by the Minister upon that occasion, that there was a debt upon this fund of 53,000l. And he likewise proposed to Parliament to pay off this debt, and to transfer the allowance of the Duke of Gloucester[2] from this fund to the public expences: both which proposals were complied with. The fund being thus relieved, soon improved from 28,000l. to upwards of 40,000l. By an unexpected incident it had come to his knowledge, that at different times 23,000l. and 25,000l. had been taken from this fund for the relief of the Civil List, in direct violation of the spirit of the act of the twenty-third of his present Majesty. It was worthy of remark, that whenever this fund was burthened, the public were called upon to discharge the arrear. On the other hand, when there was an overflowing, it was made the pretence for filling the pockets of the Sovereign without the knowledge or the consent of Parliament. He concluded with moving, "That an Address be presented to his Majesty, praying, that he would be graciously pleased to give orders, that the Funds arising from the grants of money in the Leeward Islands, called the $4\frac{1}{2}$ per cent. be applied to the fortification and defence of the Islands themselves."— Opposed by Lord Grenville, who gave a very long but not very interesting history of these funds; and produced a variety of facts to evince, that Parliament had tacitly approved grants on these funds. Lord Lauderdale replied, and endeavoured to detect the misstatements of Lord Grenville. The House then divided on Lord Lauderdale's motion.

Not Contents	42	Contents	6
Proxies	31	Proxies	4
	—		—
	73		10

[1] Edmund Burke.
[2] Prince William Henry (1743–1805), brother of George III, created duke 1764.

Lord Lauderdale, towards the close of his reply to Lord Grenville, digressed, upon observing some noble Lords enter the House. He said, he discovered some noble Lords who had just come down to swell the ministerial side of the question, though they had not heard one word of the argument. He asked them, whether it was proper in regard to their own dignity or the duty they owed the public to come down to a debate so constantly as they were in the habit of doing, to give their votes at random. He left them to excriminate themselves in the opinion of the public, with what decency they might, and to pursue their favourite system as long as they pleased. He did not wish to spoil their moments of revelry, or break in on amusements more congenial to their tempers and talents than senatorial deliberations*.

IN the House of Commons, on the same evening, Mr. Curwen called the attention of the House to the subject of the Game Laws —the injustice of which could only be equalled by their impolicy. He detailed the history of these laws, and the tyrannical and absurd acts that had been passed from the reign of Charles II. to the present day; and contended that they counteracted their own intentions, and tended to destroy the game. For farmers, who were debarred from all the benefits, yet were subject to all depredations of these birds (and the worse injuries of the eager sportsman) were naturally led to destroy the eggs wherever they met with them. It was singular enough (Mr. Curwen observed), that England, which boasted of its freedom, was, in respect of its Game Laws, in a more despotic condition than the most despotic State in Europe; and that it required fifty times as much money to kill a partridge legally as to vote for a representative in Parliament. He then moved that the different acts of James I. Charles II. of William and Mary, and of Anne, be read *pro forma*; which having been done, he moved, "That leave be given to bring in a Bill to repeal the said acts, or such parts thereof as may be particularly specified; and also to substitute other provisions in lieu thereof." Mr. Buxton said, that these laws ought no longer to disgrace our statute-book—he wished to make game private property; yet he did not wish to make the plunder of that property felony. Mr. Francis said, that in the present state of society, every thing was beneficial which might operate as an allurement to the wealthy to spend some part of their time in the country. If game were made private property hare-hunting will be at an end. The Secretary of

* The public will honour Lord Lauderdale for this spirited rebuke. Surely the Earl should not have left untouched the 31 proxies!

War considered these laws as objectionable chiefly, because the breach of them was not considered by the mass of the public as a breach of a morality; of which however a breach of these laws was too generally the fore-runner. He deprecated these arguments in favour of the repeal of these laws which had been founded on abstract notions of natural rights; all which he deemed in the highest degree chimerical*. Mr. Fox would not offend the gentleman who spoke last by saying any thing on the natural rights of man. But although on the principles of property it might not be absolutely unjust to make a distinction between the qualification to kill game and any other qualification, yet on the principle of congruity and policy the Game Laws were certainly indefensible; for it appeared that a great number of the most opulent part of the people of this country were not permitted to enjoy the luxury of sporting with game. But was it not true that these laws were ineffectual? Is it not true that there is no place whatever where game is not or may not be purchased, contrary to these laws? As long as rich men want game, poor men will procure game. He would not say, he should never accede to a proposition which made that criminal by law, which was not morally considered as criminal; but it was certain that those laws were most generally obeyed, which in their declarations of criminality, coincide with the general feelings of mankind, and the moral sense. Mr. Fox deemed it advisable to make game private property. But if he were compelled to choose between the two questions, whether these laws should remain as they are, or be totally repealed, he should say, without hesitation, that they ought to be totally repealed, even though nothing were substituted in their stead. They were a mass of in-

* This sentiment is so lugged into every debate, that it has degenerated into mere parrotry. Those duties are called DUTIES which we exercise towards others; those duties are called RIGHTS which we exercise in favour of ourselves.[1] It is the DUTY of each individual to aim at producing the greatest possible happiness to the whole: and as the happiness of the whole is made up of the happiness of its parts, it is the RIGHT of each individual to enjoy every pleasure which does not injure himself, nor lessen or render insecure the enjoyments of others. This Wyndham[2] is a professed imitator of Mr. Burke, whom he resembles as nearly as a stream of melted lead resembles the lava from Mount Vesuvius.

[1] An early and often repeated distinction; cf *SM* (1816) App C viii, *Friend* (*CC*) I 166.

[2] On William Windham cf *CN* I 1428: "Goose—would be a noble Bird if it did not remind us of the Swan = Wyndham :: Burke". Cf *An Answer to "A Letter to Edward Long Fox, M.D."* p 7 for a similar comparison.

sufferable tyranny. They were disgraceful to a free state from their oppressiveness; and would be absurd in any state from their inefficacy. They do not protect the game; for they make it the farmer's interest to destroy it in the egg. The penalties were most commonly solicited by the parties in consequence of some quarrel, and were levied by Magistrates who were themselves interested in the conviction of the offender; and, lastly, by introducing a necessity of fraud and secresy in an action of no moral guilt, they tended to deprave the minds of the peasantry, and prepare them for the commission of actual crimes.

MR. JENKINSON would not vote for the motion in its present state; he allowed the laws to be tyrannical; but thought they had been exercised with great lenity. He moved that the House do adjourn.

MR. CURWEN made a short and energetic reply.—These (he observed) were not the times to attempt the justification of harsh laws. Government could now command the opinions of the people, only by adhering to the principles of justice and humanity.—The House divided.—For the adjournment 27.—Against it 50.

MR. CURWEN then moved, "That this House do resolve itself into a Committee of the whole House to consider of the Game Laws this day se'nnight." Carried without a division.

HOUSE OF COMMONS, *March* 7.

The House resolved itself into a Committee of the whole House, on the Bill for abolishing the Slave-Trade.

MR. WILBERFORCE proposed, that the trade should be finally abolished on the first of March, 1797.

MR. DENT[1] opposed the Bill. So long as Magna Charta remained it would be a disgrace to the country. It was the express declaration of Magna Charta, "That Right shall be neither sold, delayed, or denied." What were the Committee now doing? Evidently selling, delaying, and denying the Right of the West India Merchants and Planters.

MR. SERJEANT ADAIR[2] turned the declaration in favour of the Bill. He agreed, that Right had been sold, delayed, and denied. Right was sold when the Africans were sold; Right was delayed,

[1] John Dent (c 1760–1826), MP for Lancaster Borough, nicknamed later this year "Dog" Dent for his tax on dogs. See below, p 255.

[2] James Adair (c 1743–98), MP for Higham Ferrers and king's sergeant.

when the Abolition of the Slave-Trade was delayed; Right will be denied, when the Legislature of this country shall refuse to put an end to that traffick which creates misery and promotes murder. The question for the commencement of the Bill on the first of March was put and carried, as was a Clause proposed by Mr. Wilberforce, subjecting those who shall be convicted of carrying on this trade against this act, to transportation to Botany Bay, or elsewhere, for fourteen years.

THE SECRETARY AT WAR brought up an estimate of Barracks intended to be built, and of the probable expence.—Adjourned.

HOUSE OF COMMONS, *March* 10.

MR. GREY called the attention of the House to the State of the Nation; and in an eloquent and argumentative speech established the following points:

That above seventy-seven millions eight hundred thousand pounds debt, incurred by the present war, had been already funded.

That twenty-two millions remained floating and unfunded; and that this sum of an hundred millions had been squandered in the three first years of this war.

That this was more than *double* the expence of *any* three years of *any* war in which this country was ever engaged.

That of this sum, almost as much had been spent without estimate, and consequently without the authority of Parliament, as with it.

That barracks were built for an army of *forty thousand men*, to be kept up in time of peace. Since the year 1790 *one million one hundred thousand pounds* had been expended in the erection of barracks.

That by the new system, the peace establishment, could not be less than twenty-two millions per annum.

That the permanent revenue was not likely to be more than 19,500,000l.

That consequently if peace were made to-morrow, independent of the winding up of the war expences, there must be additional taxes to the amount of 2,500,000l. *to carry on the peace*.

That, in direct violation of the provision of the Act of Queen Anne, which declares, that if the Bank should advance money to Government, without grants from Parliament, they should forfeit treble the sums advanced—Ministers had procured large sums of money in advance from the Bank.

That they had artfully smuggled into an Act a clause repealing the wholesome provision in the Act of Queen Anne; and that now the Bank was in advance the enormous sum of 11,800,000l.!

He therefore moved, "That the House do now resolve itself in a Committee of the whole House on the State of the Nation."

Mr. Grey was answered by Mr. Jenkinson, who attributed the greater expensiveness of the present than the preceding wars to the increased wealth and prosperity of the nation; and the unheard-of and fanatical exertions of the enemy. He dwelt on our acquisitions in the East-Indies; on the Cape of Good Hope; the Dutch Settlements; the port at St. Domingo; and the Islands of Martinique and Corsica. *He insisted that there never had been a more successful and glorious war**. After various other assertions he moved for the order of the day, which, after some observations on the same side of the argument by Mr. Steel, and an animated and indignant reply by Mr. Grey, was carried by 207 against 45. The Chancellor of the Exchequer did not speak.

TO CORRESPONDENTS

I am obliged to PATRIOT for his Anecdotes,[1] and I have received HENRY,[2] and BRISTOLIENSIS.[3]

I thank "a Well-wisher and old School-fellow,"[4] for his friendly, though severe, admonition; and request him to reflect, whether it be not *possible* that *my* prejudices may appear to him gigantic through the mist[5] occasioned by *his own*.

* *!!!!!*

[1] Items specifically called "Anecdotes" appear below, pp 189, 242–3, and 355–7, though the term could be applied to many others.

[2] No contributions identified.

[3] See below, p 145.

[4] One anonymous letter read "Alas! alas! COLERIDGE, the digito-monstratus of Cambridge, commenced Polit[ical] Newsmonger, Newspaper-paragraph-thief, Re-retailer of retailed Scurrility, keeper of [an] Asylum for old, poor, and decayed Jokes" (to J. Edwards 20 Mar 1796: *CL* I 191–2). Although Chambers (*C Life*—EKC—20) reads *digito-monstratus* as a term of scorn, it is clearly meant in its usual classical sense as the finger of fame; the writer is saying that C has declined from a Cambridge celebrity to a mere hack.

[5] An expression, possibly proverbial, also used in *Conciones* 39 and *TT* (1923) 326–7 ("Additional Table Talk"). Cf Robert Hall *An Apology for the Freedom of the Press, and for General Liberty* (1793) ii: "It seems a favourite point with a certain description of men, to stop the progress of enquiry, and throw mankind back into the darkness of the middle ages, from a persuasion, that ignorance will augment their power, as objects look largest in a mist."

THE WATCHMAN

No. IV. FRIDAY, MARCH 25, 1796
Published by the Author, S. T. COLERIDGE, Bristol:
And by PARSONS, Paternoster-Row, London

THAT ALL MAY KNOW THE TRUTH;
AND THAT THE TRUTH MAY MAKE US FREE!

TO THE EDITOR OF THE WATCHMAN

SIR,

IN the Birmingham Paper of Monday March 14th 1796, I perused the following article.

"On Friday night last Binns and Jones, two delegates from the London Corresponding Society,[1] *regardless of the laws and peace of the country*, delivered (the one at the Swan in Swallow Street, and the other at the Bell public house in Suffolk Street in this town) their *inflammatory lectures*; information of which being given to William Hicks, Esq. one of our Magistrates, he immediately repaired with the peace-officers to the *illegal assemblings*. The meeting at the Swan had broken up, but at the Bell they found Jones in a room haranguing about 70 people. *As soon as he saw the Magistrate he was silent*; but Mr. Hicks being made acquainted by several who were present of the seditious language he had held, immediately ordered the proclamation against disorderly meetings to be read, and the people in a few minutes dispersed. *Jones was admonished by the Magistrate* who warned him to beware of his conduct in future, as a strict watch should be kept over him, and all his associates."

[1] John Binns (1772–1860), an Irishman who came to London in 1794 and joined the London Corresponding Society and was chairman of the mammoth meeting of 26 Oct 1795 in the field behind Copenhagen House. Twice tried for sedition or treason and acquitted, he ultimately emigrated to America. See his *Recollections: Twenty-nine Years in Europe and Fifty-three Years in the United States* (Philadelphia 1854). John Gale Jones (1769–1838), a surgeon and political orator, was less fortunate than Binns, for he served two terms in prison for radical utterances. The purpose of Binns's and Jones's visit is indicated by an advertisement in *M Chron* 25 Mar, in which contributions are solicited for sending deputies into the country to agitate against the Two Bills.

I do not mean, Sir, to accuse the respectable editor of Aris's Gazette,[1] with any desire to misrepresent, or calumniate. But in the hurry which often necessarily attends the composition and printing, of a Newspaper, it is very possible, and very pardonable, to commit some slight inaccuracies. Perhaps, Sir, in the haste of insertion, that gentleman, might not perceive, that, this account, contains within itself, strong proof, of its not being absolutely, and totally authentic.

If the delegates had been "*regardless of the laws and peace of the country*," if they had "*delivered inflammatory Lectures*," and if they had actually "*held seditious language*," what would have been the catastrophe of the play?—Why, Sir, Mr. Jones and Mr. Binns would have been either bound over to their good behaviour, or sent to prison. As this was not the event we must conclude that no charge of this nature could be fixed upon them.

The person or persons who sent this article to the editor, either sent an exact account, or an inaccurate one. If the account be true and exact, they could as easily have informed Mr. Hicks, as Mr. Pearson—and then Mr. Hicks, must of necessity have done his duty as a Magistrate by sending the illegal disturbers of the public peace, to the dungeon. But as the event was, that Jones was only "*admonished by the Magistrate*," we necessarily suspect the accuracy, and authenticity, of that part of the paragraph, which informs us, "Mr. Hicks was made acquainted by several who were present of the seditious language Jones had held."

The candour and impartiality of the publisher and proprietor of Aris's Gazette, will lead him to rejoice in an opportunity, of doing justice to any character, he may have inadvertently misrepresented. This opportunity, I hope will be afforded him by an insertion of the truth, in your next Watchman. The fact seems to have been as follows. It appears that the Magistrate (who acted quite unexceptionably on the occasion) immediately upon being applied to, respecting these lecturers, went first of all to the Swan, but found Binns had finished. Thence he repaired to the Bell, where he found Jones haranguing. Jones, not knowing Mr. Hicks to be a Magistrate, went on. Mr. Hicks asked him, who he was, where he came from, what he was doing &c. all in a breath; upon which Jones asked if he were a Magistrate. Mr. Hicks replying in the affirmative, Jones threw him the paper of instructions from the Corresponding Society to him, as

[1] Pearson (see below). Thomas Pearson also printed and published William Hutton's *History of Birmingham* (see below, p 146).

their delegate. Mr. Hicks looked round, and said, you are more than 50.[1] Jones said, that had happened, not from any intention of disobeying the law, for that the company he met was under 50; but other persons, out of curiosity, forced themselves in. The magistrate then pulled out the proclamation, and dispersed the assembly by reading it. He admonished Mr. Jones, and told him, that he would attend him at every lecture—Jones replied, Sir, I shall be always very glad of your company.

I ought to have said, that Mr. Hicks in the course of this time of which I have been speaking, asked, if any person could inform him, whether any sedition had been uttered. A man, who appeared to have come in with the disposition of a spy, and who of course was very forward to become an informer, said he could give evidence. Well, said Mr. Hicks, what did he say? Why that the people had a right to be their own law-makers or words to that purpose. Q. Will you swear that? Ans. Yes I will. The Bible was sent for; when the man had got it in his hand, just about to take the oath, Mr. Jones, humanely interposed, to prevent the poor man from perjuring himself.—And then it came out upon the testimony of this very man that Mr. Jones had said no such thing, but only affirmed, that the people had a right, to chuse their own representatives. And it further appears, that the delegate recommended moderation, and pointed out the folly of resorting to violence or illegal modes of redressing grievances, in the strongest manner.

I would not Sir, have troubled you with this, had it not been one of the first, if not the very first instance, of the interference of a Magistrate,[2] under the late bills, of Pitt, and Grenville. If it be the first, it is a little[3] remarkable that it was a BIRMINGHAM JUSTICE. It has been said that in 1791 no intreaties could prevail on BIRMINGHAM JUSTICES so much as to read the Riot act, when the houses of the most respectable inhabitants of the town were devoted to destruction by a furious rabble.

The Supreme being, Sir, knows how to bring good out of evil. The flames which were then kindled in this town, have enlightened with unquenchable radiance, the lower classes of the inhabitants. No encouragement from power, or money, no *inaccurate* paragraphs

[1] Under the provisions of the Seditious Meetings Act no meeting of fifty persons or more could be held without previous notice to a magistrate.

[2] In refutation of the not-uncommon opinion that the Two Acts were never invoked (e.g. William Hunt *Political History of England*—1905—x 380), note that Jones was convicted at the assizes in Warwick in Apr 1797.

[3] Correctly "is little".

in a provincial or London paper, can now stimulate them, to burn, or destroy the houses, or persons, of good men.

Your's,

PHOCION.[1]

INVOCATION TO LIBERTY

OH Liberty, cœlestial power,
With thy electric influence blest,
Tho' clouds of darkness round us lour
Eternal sunshine cheers the breast.
Scar'd at thy frown, (with human Victims fed)
Oppression shrinks aghast, and hides his blood-stain'd head.

Thy Suppliant hear; and o'er the Land,
Evanid, shed thy vital ray,
Invigorate the suffering Band
Who long through many a dang'rous way
Have sought thee, fearless of the Tyrant's frown
"Opprest but not destroy'd, perplexed but not cast down."

Descend not, as the vile admire
In loose and wanton vesture clad,
But arm'd, with all thy genuine fire
To bless the good, and awe the bad;
Through the wide World, in awful splendour roll
And free from servile Bonds, the enervated Soul.

E. N.[2]

ON THE SLAVE TRADE[3]

WHENCE arise our Miseries? Whence arise our Vices? From *imaginary* Wants. No man is wicked without temptation, no

[1] "Phocion" is the Rev John Edwards, Unitarian minister and successor to Joseph Priestley at the New Meeting in Birmingham. C had solicited this communication (to Edwards 20 Mar 1796: *CL* I 191). "Phocion" continues the story of Binns and Jones below, p 160.

[2] A poem "far above mediocrity; but I do not understand the word 'Evanid': as there used . . . do you know who E. N. is?" So C wrote in a letter to Edwards (*CL* I 191–3). "E. N." 's identity is still a secret; his use of "evanid" for "transient" seems to be the same as Joseph Glanvill's in comparing the sun with an "evanid Meteor" in *The Vanity of Dogmatizing*.

[3] This essay, as EHC noted, is a reworking of C's lecture on the slave-trade given in Bristol 16 Jun 1795.

man is wretched without a cause. But if each among us confined his wishes to the actual necessaries and real comforts of Life, we should preclude all the causes of Complaint and all the motives to Iniquity. What Nature demands, she will supply, asking for it that portion only of *Toil*, which would otherwise have been necessary as *Exercise*. But Providence, which has distinguished Man from the lower orders of Being by the progressiveness of his nature, forbids him to be contented. It has given us the restless faculty of *Imagination*.[1]

Hence the soft Couch and many-colour'd Robe,
The Timbrel and arch'd Dome and costly Feast
With all th' inventive Arts that nurse the Soul
To forms of Beauty; and by sensual wants
Unsensualize the mind, which in the *Means*
Learns to forget the grossness of the *End*,
Best-pleasur'd with its own activity.
And *hence* DISEASE that withers manhood's arm,
The dagger'd ENVY, spirit-quenching WANT,
WARRIORS, and LORDS, and PRIESTS—all the sore ills
That vex and desolate our mortal life.
Wide-wasting ills! yet each th' immediate source
Of mightier good! Their keen necessities
To ceaseless action, goading human thought
Have made Earth's reasoning Animal her Lord,
And the pale-featur'd SAGE'S trembling hand
Strong as an Host of armed Deities!
From Avarice thus, from Luxury, and War
Sprang heavenly SCIENCE, and from SCIENCE FREEDOM!

RELIGIOUS MUSINGS.[2]

See *Studies* 20; also Cottle *E Rec* I 20. EHC's transcript "from M.S. of Lecture on the Slave Trade, partly in handwriting of S. T. C. & partly in that of R. S[outhey]", now in VCL, appears in *Lectures 1795* (*CC* I) with a more detailed study of sources. C's annotated copy of *The Watchman*, now in the BM, contains minor changes in punctuation and emphasis (e.g. small capitals for "in favour of the slave trade!" with an extra exclamation-point added) in this essay (pp 102–8). These changes have been incorporated into the text; word changes, however, are given in the notes below.

[1] *Imagination* as a servant of a necessitarian optimism appears to be Hartleian. Hartley devotes some chapters to an enquiry into "the rise and gradual increase of the pleasures . . . of imagination, ambition, self-interest, sympathy, theopathy, and the moral sense" (*Observations on Man* I 416), which are stages in man's growth. The present remarks on imagination appear to assign to it a larger rôle than does Hartley; cf also *The Destiny of Nations* lines 80–8: *PW* (EHC) I 134.

[2] Lines 226–44 (var) in *Poems* (1796); cf lines 206–25: *PW* (EHC) I 117.

I have the firmest Faith, that the final cause of all evils in the moral and natural world is to awaken intellectual activity. Man, a vicious and discontented *Animal*, by his vices and his discontent is urged to develop the powers of the Creator, and by new combinations of those powers to imitate his creativeness. And from such enlargement of mind Benevolence will necessarily follow; Benevolence which may be defined "Natural Sympathy made permanent by an acquired Conviction, that the Interests of each and of all are one and the same," or in fewer words, "Natural Sympathy made permanent by enlightened Selfishness." In my calmer moments I have the firmest Faith that all things work together for Good. But alas! it seems a long and a dark Process.

> The early Year's fast-flying Vapours stray
> In shadowing Trains across the orb of Day:
> And we, poor Insects of a few short Hours,
> Deem it a world of Gloom.
> Were it not better hope a nobler doom
> Proud to believe, that with more active powers
> On rapid many-coloured Wing
> We thro' one bright perpetual Spring
> Shall hover round the Fruits and Flowers
> Screen'd by those Clouds & cherish'd by those Showers!
>
> *From an unpublished Poem.*[1]

I have dwelt anxiously on this subject, with a particular view, to the Slave-trade, which, I knew, has insinuated in the minds of many, uneasy doubts respecting the existence of a beneficent Deity. And indeed the evils arising from the formation of *imaginary* Wants, have in no instance been so dreadfully exemplified, as in this inhuman Traffic. We receive from the West-India Islands Sugars, Rum, Cotton, Logwood,[2] Cocoa, Coffee, Pimento, Ginger, Indigo, Mahogany, and Conserves. Not one of these articles are necessary; indeed with the exception of Cotton and Mahogany we cannot truly call them even useful: and not one of them is at present attainable by the poor and labouring part of Society. In return we export vast quantities of necessary Tools, Raiment, and defensive Weapons, with great stores of Provision. So that in this Trade as in most others the

[1] This poem appeared here for the first and only time during C's life: *PW* (EHC) I 148, under the title *Ver Perpetuum*.

[2] The heart of *Haematoxylon campechianum*, used for making dyes for fabrics; hence not "necessary".

Poor are employed with unceasing toil first to raise, and then to send away the Comforts, which they themselves absolutely want, in order to procure idle superfluities for their Masters. If this Trade had never existed, no one human being would have been less comfortably cloathed, housed, or nourished. Such is its value—they who would estimate the price which we pay for it, may consult the evidence delivered before the House of Commons. I will not mangle the feelings of my readers by detailing enormities, which the gloomy Imagination of Dante would scarcely have dared attribute to the Inhabitants of Hell.[1] For the honour of our common nature, I would fain hope that these accounts have been exaggerated. But, by the confession of all, these enormities might have been perpetrated and with impunity: and when was power possessed and not exercised? By the confession of all parties great cruelties have been inflicted: and therefore before I can suspect exaggeration, I must disbelieve the oaths of the humane and disinterested in compliment to the assertions of men from whose shoulders though I should take mountains of guilt, enough would remain to sink them to perdition.—These Facts have been pressed on the Public even to satiety. It is my present purpose to consider the objections to the Abolition of this Commerce —which may be reduced to the five following—First, that the Abolition would be useless, since though we should not carry it on, other nations would. II. That the Africans are better treated and more happy in the Plantations than in their native Country. III. That the Revenue would be greatly injured. IV. That the Right of Property would be invaded. V. That this is not a fit opportunity.

I. That if England abolish the Slave-trade, other nations will carry it on. The same argument has been adduced by the *French Planters: a sufficient proof of its fallacy.[3] Somebody must *begin*; and there is

* "Very soon this society of Friends to the Negroes require an abolition of the slave-trade: that is to say, that the profits which may result from it to the French commerce should be transferred to foreigners. For never will their romantic philosophy persuade the other European Powers &c." See the address of the Planters of St. Domingo to the French Legislature.[2]

[1] C, who did not know Italian at this time, probably was acquainted with the *Inferno* in Henry Boyd's translation (2 vols 1785). See *CN* I 170 and n. Southey had borrowed the volumes from the Bristol Library in Sept and Oct 1794; see *Bristol LB* 118.

[2] The "Address" is quoted in *A Particular Account of the Commencement and Progress of the Insurrection of the Negroes in St. Domingo* . . . (2nd ed 1792) 18.

[3] Cf Bryan Edwards *The History, Civil and Commercial, of the British Colonies in the West Indies* (2 vols 1793) II 106–9. See *Bristol LB* 121.

little reason to fear, that a wise and politic example will not be followed. As Society is constituted, there will be always highway robberies: it is useless therefore to prevent any *one* man from committing them. Fortunately for Travellers this logic will not hold good in law. But although it cannot operate in favour of little Rogues, it appears to possess wonderful power in the higher circles of Villany. Assuming the universal depravity of Mankind as an axiom, a corrupt member of Parliament lulls his Conscience to sleep with "to be sure these bills are subversive of the Constitution; but with such immense treasures to bestow, Ministry *will* secure a majority in the House: my opposition will therefore be useless to my Country; and if I vote for them, I shall only assist to do what would be otherwise done without me—and why should I not have this contract, or this sinecure, as well as another man, who perhaps would make a worse use of it?" &c.

II. That the Slaves are more humanely treated and live more happily in the Plantations than in their native Country.—If any incredulous person should entertain a doubt of this, the slave-merchants, slave-holders, and slave-drivers together with the manufacturers of neck-collars and thumb-screws, are ready and willing to take their bible oaths of it!!—When treated with tolerable humanity the human race as well as other animals, multiply.—The Negroes multiply in their native country:—They do *not* multiply in the West-India Islands; for if they did, the slave-trade would have been abolished long ago by its inutility.—This is a fact which no perjury can overwhelm, which no sophistry can undermine.

The tyranny of the African Chiefs is in a great measure owing to the agency of Europeans, who flock to their Courts, and seduce them by bribery, and madden them by intoxication. The Africans are not slaves in their native Country; Slavery is their highest punishment for the greatest crimes, which their Chiefs now wantonly impute to the innocent for the sole purpose of making them slaves in order to sell them to the European Merchants: and with the same views the Chiefs make war with each other. Wadestrom,[1] a disinterested and religious man, who has travelled into the interior parts of Africa, informs us, that the Africans who are situated beyond the contagion of European Vice, are innocent and happy. The peaceful Inhabitants of a fertile soil, they cultivate their fields in common, and reap the crop as the common property of all. Each Family, like the Peasants in some parts of Europe, spins, weaves, sews, hunts, fishes, and makes

[1] Carl Bernhard Wadström *An Essay on Colonization* ... (2 pts 1794) I 12–17 and ch 2 passim. See *Bristol LB* 121.

baskets, fishing-tackle, and the implements of agriculture: and this variety of employment gives an acuteness of intellect to the Negro which the Mechanic whom the division of labor condemns to one simple operation is precluded from attaining.

III. That the Revenue would be injured.—To the friends of humanity this is indeed a cogent argument against the abolition. They will doubtless reflect, how worthily this Revenue has been employed for these last hundred years—they will review with delight waste-lands cultivated, sciences publickly protected and rewarded, population increased, and the peasantry of England and *Ireland* instructed in useful learning, and humanized. The universal plenty, which this Revenue has been applied to scatter and secure, they will recognize in every lane, hamlet, and cottage—REVENUE, the grand preventive against that fiendish composition of Murder and Suicide, called WAR-REVENUE! that so completely precludes Intoxication in the lower classes, Luxury in the higher ranks, and Bribery in all!—The friends of humanity may mourn that so excellent an end could not be effected by less calamitous means; but they will stifle their feelings, and lose the miseries of the West-Indies in the contemplation of that paradisiacal state of their native country—for which it is indebted to this well-raised, well-applied REVENUE, which while it remains in such *pure* hands, no friend of Freedom and Virtue can possibly wish diminished!!—If to start a doubt were practicable, it might perhaps be hinted, that the Revenue must be always in proportion to the wealth of the nation, and that it seems to have been proved, that the West-India trade is more often a losing than a winning trade—a Lottery with more blanks than prizes in it. It is likewise asserted to be the grave of our Seamen. This argument therefore, however cogent it would otherwise have been, ought not to have been adduced, till these doubts had been cleared up, and this assertion satisfactorily disproved.

IV. That the Right of Property would be injured.—Yes perhaps, if immediate emancipation had been the object of Mr. Wilberforce's bill.[1] But how would the right of property be invaded by a law which should leave the estate and every thing on it untouched, and only prevent the owner from *forcing* men to work for him? from *forcing* men to leave their friends and country, and live slaves in a climate so unwholesome or beneath a usage so unnatural, that contrary to the universal law of life they annually diminish? Can a man possess a right to commit actual and virtual murder? to shorten and

[1] For the fate of the bill see below, pp 155–8.

prevent existence? It is a well-known and incontrovertible fact, that in some few plantations in which tyranny has been instructed by an enlightened selfishness to relax and soften her features, there have been no slaves bought for a series of years. By whomever therefore they have been bought yearly, yearly murders must have been committed!

V. This is not the time.—This not the time? "The French (says Abbe Sieyes)[1] hear with delight of the numerous armaments which England sends to certain death in the West-India Islands. We make war there more effectually as well as economically by sending over a few adventurous officers to preach the rights of man to the negroes, and furnish them with weapons to assert those rights."—What can prevent the success of these intrigues among the slaves, but the most active humanity on the part of their present masters?

Such have been the cosmetics with which our parliamentary orators have endeavoured to conceal the deformities of a commerce, which is blotched all over with one leprosy of evil. In the year 1786 it's enormities became the subject of general conversation, and in the following years petitions poured into parliament from various parts of the kingdom, requesting it's abolition. The bill for that purpose passed the House of Commons mangled and mutilated by the *amendments* of Mr. Dundas, and it has been dying ever since of a slow decline in the House of Lords. The jealous spirit of liberty placed the Elector of Hanover on the throne of Great Britain: and the Duke of Clarence,[2] one of his illustrious descendants, made his maiden speech IN FAVOUR OF THE SLAVE TRADE!! For the last unsuccessful attempt to expedite the abolition in the House of Commons, see the proceedings in the British Legislature in this Number.[3] Gracious God! enormities, at which a Caligula might have turned pale, are authorised by our laws, and jocosely defended by our Princes; and yet we have the impudence to call the French a Nation of *Atheists!* They, who believe a God, believe him to be the loving Parent of all men—And is it possible that they who really believe and fear the Father, should fearlessly authorize the oppression of his Children? The Slavery and Tortures, and most horrible Murder of tens of thousands of his Children!

Yes! the wicked and malignant can believe a God—they need not the solutions, which the enlarged views of the Optimist prompt; their own hearts teach them, that an intelligent being may be malevolent;

[1] Quoted (var) *M Chron* 6 Jan 1796.

[2] The Duke of Clarence (1765–1837), the third son of George III; on the death of his brother George IV in 1830 he ascended the throne as William IV.

[3] Below, pp 155–8.

and what they themselves are, they impiously imagine of the Deity. These men are not Atheists: they are the causes of Atheism.—There are some who think Mr. Pitt sincere in his zeal for the abolition of this Trade; and I must certainly applaud their charity: but charity itself will allow that there are suspicious circumstances. Several violent and unpopular bills have lately been carried through both Houses—how came this bill, (certainly not an unpopular measure) to fail? It has been generally supposed, that a majority is always at the command of the existing minister; indeed that in the present state of the Constitution he could not guide the machine of government without an arranged majority. In answer to this objection, it has been confidently asserted by the advocates for Mr. Pitt, that the cabinet was divided on the subject; and at length agreed that the friends of the minister should be left, each individual to his own opinion. The cabinet therefore, we may suppose, were unanimous with regard to the late sedition and treason bills; and to this unanimity we may attribute the speed with which they were precipitated into laws. But it may be answered, that to unloose the fetters from the limbs of their brethren was a perfectly novel employment, and that therefore we ought not to wonder, if the minister and his friends are slow and aukward and finally unsuccessful. But to fasten them on is an old job, and difficult as it appears to the inexperienced, they executed it with an ease and rapidity which might have astonished the oldest turnkey in Newgate.

The Abbe Raynal computes that at the time of his writing,[1] nine millions of slaves had been consumed by the Europeans—add one million since, (for it is near thirty years since his book was first published) and recollect, that for one procured ten at least are slaughtered, that a fifth die in the passage, and a third in the seasoning; and the calculation will amount to ONE HUNDRED and EIGHTY MILLION! Ye who have joined in this confederacy, ask of yourselves this fearful question—"if the God of Justice inflict on us that mass only of anguish which we have wantonly heaped on our brethren, what must a state of retribution be?" But who are they who have joined in this tartarean confederacy? Who are these kidnappers, and assassins? In all reasonings neglecting the intermediate links we attribute the final effect to the first cause. And what is the first and constantly acting cause of the Slave-trade? That cause, by

[1] Guillaume-Thomas-François Raynal *A Philosophical and Political History of the Settlement and Trade of the Europeans in the East and West Indies* tr J. O. Justamond (8 vols 1783) v 274. It was originally published in 1770.

which it exists and deprived of which it would immediately cease? Is it not self-evidently the consumption of it's products? And does not then the guilt rest on the consumers? And is it not an allowed axiom in morality, that wickedness may be multiplied, but cannot be divided; and that the guilt of all, attaches to each one who is knowingly an accomplice? Think not of the slave-captains and slave-holders! these very men, their darkened minds, and brutalized hearts, will prove one part of the dreadful charge against you! They are more to be pitied than the slaves; because more depraved. I address myself to you who independently of all political distinctions, profess yourself Christians! As you hope to live with Christ hereafter, you are commanded to do unto others as ye would that others should do unto you. Would *you* choose, that a slave merchant should incite an intoxicated Chieftain to make war on your Country, and murder your Wife and Children before your face, or drag them with yourself to the Market? Would you choose to be sold? to have the hot iron hiss upon your breasts, after having been crammed into the hold of a Ship with so many fellow-victims, that the heat and stench, arising from your diseased bodies, should rot the very planks? Would *you*, that others should do this unto *you*? and if you shudder with selfish horror at the bare idea, do you yet dare be the occasion of it to others?—The application to the Legislature was altogether wrong. I am not convinced that on any occasion a Christian is justified in calling for the interference of secular power;[1] but on the present occasion it was superfluous. If only one tenth part among you who profess yourselves Christians; if one half only of the Petitioners; instead of bustling about with ostentatious sensibility, were to leave off—not *all* the West-India commodities—but only Sugar and Rum, the one useless and the other pernicious—all this misery might be stopped.[2] Gracious Heaven! At your meals you rise up, and pressing your hands to your bosoms, you lift up your eyes to God, and say, "O Lord! bless the food which thou hast given us!" A part of that

[1] Their religion, C explained to Thelwall in Dec 1796, commands Christians "never to use the arm of flesh, to be perfectly non-resistant". *CL* I 282.

[2] Changed to "ended" by C in the BM copy (Ashley 2842) of *The Watchman* p 108. Cf "A family that uses 5 lb. of sugar per week, with the proportion of rum, will, by abstaining from the consumption 21 months, prevent the slavery or murder of one fellow creature; eight such families in 19½ years prevent the slavery or murder of 100, and 38,000 would totally prevent the Slave Trade to supply our islands." William Fox *An Address to the People of Great Britain, on the Propriety of Abstaining from West India Sugar and Rum* (10th ed Birmingham 1791) 2–3 (the pamphlet reached its 26th ed in 1793). Fox, an attorney, published a periodical in 1796 called *The Friend.*

food among most of you, is sweetened with Brother's Blood. "Lord! bless the food which thou hast given us?" O Blasphemy! Did God give food mingled with the blood of the Murdered? Will God bless the food which is polluted with the Blood of his own innocent children? Surely if the inspired Philanthropist[1] of Galilee were to revisit Earth, and be among the Feasters as at Cana, he would not now change water into wine, but convert the produce into the things producing, the occasion into the things occasioned. Then with our fleshly eye should we behold what even now Imagination ought to paint to us; instead of conserves, tears and blood, and for music, groanings and the loud peals of the lash!

There is observable among the Many a false and bastard sensibility[2] that prompts them to remove those evils and those evils alone, which by hideous spectacle or clamorous outcry are present to their senses, and disturb their selfish enjoyments. Other miseries, though equally certain and far more horrible, they not only do not endeavour to remedy—they support, they fatten on them. Provided the dunghill[3] be not before their parlour window, they are well content to know that it exists, and that it is the hot-bed of their pestilent luxuries.—To this grievous failing we must attribute the frequency of wars, and the continuance of the Slave-trade. The merchant finds no argument against it in his ledger: the citizen at the crouded feast is not nauseated by the stench and filth of the slave-vessel—the fine lady's nerves are not shattered by the shrieks! She sips a beverage sweetened with human blood, even while she is weeping over the refined sorrows of Werter[4] or of Clementina.[5] Sensibility is not Benevolence. Nay, by making us tremblingly alive to trifling misfortunes, it frequently prevents it, and induces effeminate and cowardly selfishness. Our own sorrows, like the Princes of Hell in Milton's Pandemonium, sit enthroned "bulky and vast:"[6] while the miseries of our fellow-creatures dwindle into pigmy forms, and are crouded, an innumerable

[1] Changed by C to "redeeming Theanthropist" in the BM copy (Ashley 2842) p 108.

[2] This passage was reprinted (with alterations) in *Omniana* II 2–4, prefaced by the explanation that it derived from "an obscure and short-lived periodical publication, which has long since been *used off* as 'winding sheets for herrings and pilchards' ". Cf *AR* (1825) 51–4 (Reflections Respecting Morality).

[3] See *CN* I 223 and n.

[4] Translations of Goethe's *Sorrows of Werther* were numerous in England from 1779 onward.

[5] The lady Clementina, who went temporarily mad, in Richardson's *History of Sir Charles Grandison*.

[6] A misremembering of Samson's "Though in these chains, bulk without spirit vast" (*Samson Agonistes* line 1238)? Satan in hell, not Pandemonium, lay floating ". . . in bulk as huge | As whom the Fables name of monstrous size" (*Paradise Lost* I 196–7).

multitude, into some dark corner of the heart. There is one criterion by which we may always distinguish benevolence from mere sensibility —Benevolence impels to action, and is accompanied by self-denial.

P.S.[1] It has been objected, that if we leave off sugar and rum, why not the other West-India commodities, as cotton and mahogany? To this we answer, First, that if the reasons adduced against the use of sugar and rum be valid and irresistible, and the same reasons apply to cotton and mahogany, why should we not disuse them? Surely no impossibility, no insurmountable inconvenience is implied. The whole objection resolves itself into this—If sugar and rum were the only West-India commodities, I could be honest and act like a Christian; but because I like cotton better than linen, and think mahogany genteeler furniture than oak, it is impossible. Secondly, the disuse of sugar and rum only would in a certain number of years prove the adequate means of abolishing the whole of the trade. And there is reason to believe that the additional disuse of cotton, mahogany, &c. would not accelerate the time; for when we might proselyte fifty to the disuse of sugar, we could not perhaps make five persons converts to the disuse of *all* the West-India commodities. So that what we should gain in point of time by the greater quantity of commodities disused, we should more than lose by the smaller number of persons disusing them. This the very objection makes probable. For they, who start it, do not start it in favour of a severe consistency, but in the hope of keeping themselves in countenance by the multitude of their accomplices. But thirdly, the other West-India commodities do not require such intense labor in their growth and preparation, as the Sugar and Rum. They might be raised by European Labourers. The Sugar plantations make Africans necessary, and their slavery intolerable.

I have read and heard one argument in favour of the slave-trade, which I mention chiefly on account of its seditious and treasonable tendency. It has been asserted by more than one Writer on the subject, that the plantation slaves are at least as well off as the peasantry in England. Now I appeal to common sense, whether to affirm that the slaves are as well off as our peasantry, be not the same as to assert that our peasantry are as bad off as negro-slaves? And whether if our peasantry believed it, they would not be inclined to rebel?[2]

[1] In the BM copy of *The Watchman* (pp 108–9) C has marked this entire postscript for deletion, probably with a view to republication.

[2] The conclusion seems to echo Bishop Berkeley's use of the query (see above, p 102 and nn 3–8, 103 and n 2).

A MORNING EFFUSION[1]

YE Gales, that of the Lark's repose
  Th' impatient silence break,
To yon poor pilgrim's wearying woes
  Your gentle solace speak.
He heard the midnight whirlwind die,
He saw the sun-awakened sky
  Resume its slowly-purpling blue:
And ah! (he sigh'd) that I might find
The cloudless azure of the mind,
  And fortune's brightening hue.

Where-e'er in waving foliage hid
  The bird's gay charm ascends,
Or by the fretting current chid
  Some giant rock impends;
There let the lonely cares respire,
As small airs thrill the lonely lyre,
  And teach the soul its native calm;
While *Passion* with a waning eye
Bends o'er the fall of harmony,
  And drinks the sacred balm.

As slow the whispered measure creeps
  Along the steaming vale,
The alter'd eye of CONQUEST weeps,
  And ruthless WAR turns pale;
Relenting that his heart forsook
Soft concord of auspicious look,
  And love, and social poverty.
The family of tender fears,

[1] "These lines, first published in the *Watchman* . . . were included in the volume of MS Poems presented to Mrs. Estlin in April, 1795. They were never claimed by Coleridge or assigned to him, and are now collected for the first time". *PW* (EHC) I 35. If the lines are not C's, perhaps the signature G.A.U.N.T. stands for "MR. GAUNT, of Clare-hall" who in Feb 1795 was "preparing a translation of the poetry of Lucretius; omitting entirely the metaphysical parts", as announced in the second and last number of Benjamin Flower's *University Magazine* (Feb 1795) 133, immediately after an announcement that C would "shortly publish some Sonnets". The Lucretius was to appear in the spring, but no trace of this or any other work of C's contemporary at Cambridge, John Gaunt (BA 1795, MA 1800), has been discovered.

The sigh that saddens and endears,
And cares that sweeten joy.

Then cease, thy frantic outrage cease,
Thou scepter'd Demon, WAR!
Nor o'er the mangled corse of Peace
Urge on thy scythed car.
And ah! that Reason's voice might swell
With whisper'd airs and holy spell
To rouse thy gentler sense;
As bending o'er the flowret's bloom
The morning wakes its soft perfume
With breezy influence.

G. A. U. N. T.

The following Trial has been noticed in the Newspapers, but Mr. Erskine's speech has not been given in any of them.[1] We print it in the words in which it was communicated to us by a literary friend who was present at the trial.[2]

STAFFORD ASSIZES (LAW)
DOCKSEY against PANTING

ON Friday March 11th 1796 about eight in the morning, came on to be tried in the Great Church at Stafford a cause of considerable importance.

Mr. Erskine, counsel for the Plaintiff, began a speech of two hours, with observing to the Jury, that they were then in a place usually dedicated to very different purposes; but he hoped the verdict they would that day give, would come in aid to enforce those precepts of morality and religion, which it was the peculiar business of the pulpit to inculcate.

He said, in the whole course of his professional life, he had never

[1] Thomas Erskine (1750–1823), 1st Baron (1806), lord chancellor in 1806; a barrister who procured acquittal for most of those prosecuted by the Crown for treason and conspiracy. Percy Fitzgerald *The Life of David Garrick* (rev ed 1899) takes his account of the trial from *The Watchman* (p 433n).

[2] The Rev John Edwards sent this report, and in thanking him C said: "Erskine's speech was excellent—the quotation happy beyond any thing I ever read". *CL* I 191 (20 Mar 1796). The suit was brought by Merial Docksey, sister of Peter Garrick and wife of Thomas Docksey, against Stephen Panting, apothecary.

met with a cause which exhibited an instance of greater depravity, than that which would appear on the part of the Defendant.

The professions in this Kingdom, said Mr. Erskine, which are properly termed learned, because a man cannot well enter upon the discharge of them without having previously received a learned education, may be considered as confidential friends of the public, and guardians of the young, of the weak, of the disordered, and of the aged.

The Defendant was an Apothecary, and in that character had been introduced to the late Mr. Peter Garrick of Litchfield.[1] He stated, that Mr. Garrick from a temperate and regular life had reached to a period advanced in length beyond that which falls to the lot of the majority of the human race.—He had been remarkable for wit, vivacity, and quick intelligence—But *that* had happened to Mr. Garrick which happens to most men in the decline, and towards the conclusion of a life stretched to its utmost limits, not only his bodily strength and soundness forsook him, the faculties of his mind decayed, his memory was lost, even his character changed; from having been very frugal and careful of his property, he became profuse and lavish in his offers of it; and repeatedly pressed upon his friends the acceptance of large portions of it.

No man, said Mr. Erskine, could plead the cause of a brother of David Garrick,[2] without remembering that great man, who exalted into honour and respectability, a character which in this country it had been the custom to consider as low and disgraceful—that of a player.

He had himself often witnessed with delight, the exertion of Mr. Garrick's theatrical talents;—he considered himself individually and personally indebted to him: and was proud of an opportunity of doing in return any thing which might contribute to the happiness of the family of that justly celebrated actor. When called to consider over the case of his brother Mr. Peter Garrick, he could not help being struck with its resemblance to what had been so frequently and so exquisitely personated by Mr. David Garrick on the stage.

When he was told what one of the witnesses would tell the Jury, that Mr. Peter Garrick had been lost in one of the streets of a town in which he had lived so many years, at a few yards distance from his own door, as much lost as if he had been in the midst of the wildest desart; that he called out for assistance; that he had totally forgotten

[1] Peter Garrick (1710–95), older brother of David.

[2] It will be recalled that David Garrick (1717–79) left Lichfield in company with his former teacher and fellow-townsman, Samuel Johnson, and proceeded to London, where for a time David and Peter were in the wine trade. The latter was distressed by his brother's becoming a player.

the man whom in better times he well knew, and who had led him to his own door; that when got into his own hall he knew not where he was, had even lost all recollection of the house in which he lived, he thought he saw the melancholy reality of that admirable piece of acting of Mr. David Garrick in the character of King Lear, where the poet makes him say

> "Pray do not mock me:
> I am a very foolish fond old man
> Four-score and upward;
> Not an hour more or less: and to deal plainly,
> I fear I am not in my perfect mind.
> Methinks I should know you, and know this man;
> Yet I am doubtful: for I am mainly ignorant
> What place this is; and all the skill I have
> Remembers not these garments; nor I know not
> Where I did lodge last night"—[1]

It was in this state of mind, accompanied by a disease of body which required the application of opium, that Mr. Panting attended him as his apothecary;—And in this state did *that man* (for so we must call him) prevail upon Mr. Peter Garrick, to give him a title, not to a 1000 or 2000l. but to *the whole of his property*—he swept into his own lap the whole of a fortune amounting to 20 or 30,000l. without leaving a shilling for the legal heirs—all this did Mr. Panting get secured to *himself* by the strongest and most binding instruments, the laws of the land could be made to furnish by those professionally acquainted with them*.

This most iniquitous conduct, the indignant genius of the learned counsel, rebuked and stigmatized with all that energy of language, that pointed emphasis, that strength even to enthusiasm of feeling, which form the distinguishing characteristics of his eloquence—he warned the Defendant's counsel for the sake of his client, not to provoke him by following up with too much zeal and perseverance, so bad a cause; for that in case of such proceeding, he Mr. Erskine, would do all in his power to fasten upon the defendant, and his abettors in mischief, conviction; under an indictment for a conspiracy.

* Mrs. Docksey sister of Mr. Garrick claimed under a will dated 1791. Mr. Panting claimed under a deed of gift, a codicil, and subsequent will dated 1793; obtained in the 86th year of the deceased testator.

[1] *King Lear* IV vii 59–67.

He begged the Jury would by their verdict, prove to the Defendant, who was a young man; that honesty is the best policy, and that the prying eye of a court of Judicature, could penetrate thicker veils than *his* cunning had been able to draw over his wicked and nefarious actions.

Mr. Erskine having established every material assertion of his opening speech, by most undeniable and respectable testimony: the testimony of eleven witnesses—Mr. Plomer, the counsel for the Defendant,[1] informed the Jury that he thought it most respectful to his Lordship and to them, to call no evidence, although the catalogue of his witnesses was long: as though he was convinced he could by that means clear the character of his client, he could not establish for him any legal title to the property. Thus, to the satisfaction of almost every person present, the heirs of the late Peter Garrick were reinstated in their rights.

EPIGRAM[2]

SAID William to Edmund I can't guess the reason
Why Spencers abound in this bleak wintry season.
Quoth Edmund to William, I perceive you're no Solon—
Men may purchase a half-coat when they cannot a whole-one.

March 21, 1796. BRISTOLIENSIS.

WE SEE THINGS WITH DIFFERENT EYES![3]

HE who in company with a fine woman digests an excellent dinner at two guineas a head, perceives *that every thing goes well.* "Thank Heaven, the Jacobins are suppressed, the mouth of Sedition is shut. We have men and money in abundance; we shall force the

[1] Thomas Plumer (1753–1824), one of Hastings's defence counsel, later knighted (1807), vice-chancellor, and master of the rolls (1818).

[2] C acknowledged receipt of the epigram above, p 125. The joke may be diagrammed thus: (1) the spencer was a short coat, fashionable but economical; (2) its namesake, Earl Spencer, was a Whig who defected to Pitt in 1794; (3) "Pitt's war" had caused or accentuated the scarcity; (4) William is Pitt and Edmund is Burke, who, though favouring the war, was concerned with *Thoughts and Details on Scarcity* (1795), a pamphlet addressed to Pitt; (5) Pitt, it is implied here, had not waked up to the plight of the poor. A similar epigram on the spencer is quoted by Lamb in a letter to Sara Hutchinson 20 Jan 1825: *LL* II 453.

[3] Adapted from *M Chron* 18 Mar 1796. The idea may be traceable to Godwin, who condemns the insensibility of "persons, sitting at their ease and surrounded with the conveniences of life, who are apt to exclaim, 'We find things very well as they are' ". See *Enquiry Concerning Political Justice* (2 vols 1793) II 487 or (2nd ed 1796) II 109.

French to make Peace on our own terms: *shall we not, my Love?*" While this Sybarite is yawning and stretching himself in voluptuous indolence, let us turn to the man who has but one penny loaf of mixed bread, and a pound of boiled Potatoes to satisfy himself, his Wife, and three Children, and every instant dreads the entry of his Landlord demanding the long delayed payment of his Rent.—"Ah! (he exclaims with a groan of anguish), formerly I could buy my loaf for eightpence—my Wife had the pot upon the fire every day, and we had a joint of roast meat on Sundays.—Now I have scarcely victuals or clothes; and my neighbours are as bad off as myself. We have neither men nor money left, and *God knows when we shall have a Peace!*"

Come, come, John! (says his Wife) you know, you have partly yourself to blame for this: you was for the War like all the rest: you would vote at the Vestry because the Church-Wardens asked you. What business had *we* with the French?—But come, let us eat our potatoes before they are quite cold.—I wish we had a morsel of butter to them!

Extract from Hutton's History of Birmingham. 1795[1]

FOR the Barracks at Birmingham Government took a lease of five acres of land at a penny a yard, and in 1793 erected the Barracks, at 13,000l. cost. They will accommodate 162 men.—As the man who loves his country will rejoice at every saving system to lighten the load of three hundred millions, I shall state the account with precision.

			l.	*s.*
Annual Rent,	——	—	100	0
Interest on 13,000l.		—	650	0
Average loss of principal per annum during the term of 80 years, for which the Loan is granted,	——	—	162	10

Perhaps there will not, at a medium, be more than two-thirds of 162 men, or 108 accommodated.

We may reasonably suppose 6000l. will be expended in furniture, repairs, &c. during the term. This principal and half the interest,

[1] William Hutton *A History of Birmingham* (Birmingham 1795) 472 (slightly altered; C's small capitals). For C's scheme to use this book in applying Count Rumford's plan to Bristol, see his letter to Cottle 30 Apr 1796: *CL* I 206.

which is 150l. per annum must be sunk. When all these sums are added together, every man's lodging will be found to stand the country in about ELEVEN PENCE a night, or SIX SHILLINGS AND FIVE PENCE the week.

FOREIGN INTELLIGENCE

The Speech delivered by M. D'ORSINI,[1] the new Tuscan Minister at Paris, on presenting his credentials to the Executive Directory:

"Citizen President,

"ALL I bring with me is the frankness of *youth*, and the most distinguished respect and esteem for the *Government* of the French Republic, and *individuals* invested with those powers which the nation itself has granted. I feel happy in representing here a Prince,[2] who, since the very beginning of the war armed himself with the shield of *reason* and *philosophy*, in order to subdue every prejudice; who formally acknowledged the Republican Government *as soon* as he was acquainted with the sacred wish of the French people, and who, forced by *violent means*, known to all Europe, for a short time to renounce his political system, was but one month *in appearance* an enemy of France, and then, overcoming every obstacle, *sought* again her friendship.

"As to the conduct of my predecessor, my Government, by disavowing it in the most formal manner, and hastening to send me to you, has given a striking proof of its *regard* for the French Republic. I expect from you a full return of the same sentiments.—This expectation is founded on the *sacred maxims* of the public law which you have proclaimed, and on the line of conduct you have constantly observed, by placing your true glory *in respecting*, without distinction, all such Governments and nations as have remained sincerely attached to you."

CONSTANTINOPLE, *Feb.* 1.[3] A squadron of six or eight ships is ready to sail to bring home the Asiatic tributes, and protect the Turkish merchantmen from any accidents, in consequence of the appearance of English and French squadrons in the Archipelago.

All the palaces of the Foreign Ministers, the houses of the principal

[1] From the *London Packet* 11–14 Mar 1796, *The Times* 14 Mar, or the *Gazetteer* 15 Mar, including italics (also in the *Star* 14 Mar, but without the italics).

[2] Ferdinand III (1769–1824), Grand Duke of Tuscany, the first ruler to recognise the French Republic (1792), had been forced into the first coalition against France.

[3] From the *Star* 15 Mar 1796 or the *Gazetteer* 14 Mar.

Franks, &c. still remain shut in consequence of the plague, the symptoms of which still appear; between 20 and 30 bodies have been carried through Pera and the Port of Adrianople, in the course of several days. French Officers, Engineers, &c. arrive here almost every day.

PETERSBURGH, *Feb.* 16.[1] Sunday last, the 14th instant, his Imperial Highness, CONSTANTINE PAWLOWITSCH,[2] our Grand Duke, was betrothed with the most Serene Princess of SAXE-COBOURG, who on the day previous thereto, took upon her the name of ANNE FOEODOROWNA, on being received into the Greek church.—The said betrothing was celebrated at Court with the greatest magnificence. Her Imperial Majesty, seated under the canopy of the Throne, dined with all the Imperial Family. There was another numerous table, at which the five first classes had the honour of dining. In the evening there was a Ball at the Hermitage. The following morning every one, as low as the rank of Major, was admitted to kiss the Grand Duchess's hand. The Ladies had the same honour in the evening, and the day concluded with a Grand Ball at Court.

FLORENCE, *Feb.* 16.[3] It was in the night of the 1st instant, that the first symptoms of an earthquake were observed at Arezza, when, to invoke the divine assistance, a procession with the relicts of St. Donatius was set on foot, the Theatre ordered to be shut, &c. but at midnight the shocks became much more violent than before, several houses were damaged, and the roof of the Carthusian cloister fell entirely in. New shocks occurred on the following day, when most of the inhabitants fled to the churches, where they passed the greatest part of the night. For two days after, a penitentiary procession paraded the town, with the Magistrates at their head.—Nothing further has since happened.

VIENNA, *Feb.* 24.[4] Marquis DELLE TORRE, and Count MARSAN, Generals sent by his SARDINIAN MAJESTY[5] from the army, are expected here to-day or to-morrow. The object is said to be to concert a scheme of co-operation in the ensuing campaign; but letters from

[1] From the *Star* or the *M Post* 15 Mar 1796.

[2] Konstantin Pavlovich (1779–1831), Grand Duke, grandson of the Empress Catherine and second son of the heir-apparent, Paul. He later divorced Anna Feodorovna (the former Princess Juliana) and renounced his rights to the throne (1822).

[3] From the *Star* or *M Post* 15 Mar 1796.

[4] From ibid. Also in *Oracle* 15 Mar.

[5] Victor Amadeus III (1726–96), king of Sardinia (1773–96), joined the first coalition against France, 1792–3. His only claims to fame were that he received a subsidy from the British government and that he was at this time the oldest monarch in Europe.

Turin represent them as charged with an urgent expostulation from his SARDINIAN MAJESTY, who avows himself to be utterly unable to continue the war; and states, that as the French themselves offer advantageous propositions for Peace, the Cabinet of Vienna should either allow him to accept them, or by very powerful efforts indemnify him from the loss to which otherwise he must be inevitably subject.

WARSAW. *Feb.* 17.[1] It is positively asserted, that War is immediately to be declared between Russia and the Ottoman Porte. Field Marshall SUWARROW[2] has accepted the Command of the Troops on the Dniester, and is to have four Generals under him. Field Marshall Romanzow[3] will command a corps near Oczakow.

OFFICIAL NOTE OF COUNT BERNSTORF, DANISH MINISTER OF STATE.[4]

THE system of his Danish Majesty,[5] uninfluenced by passions and prejudices, is merely governed by Reason and Truth, and constantly assumes such modifications as are rendered both just and unavoidable by the obvious change in the posture of public affairs. So long as no other than a Revolutionary Government existed in France, his Majesty could not acknowledge the Minister of that Government; but now that the French Constitution is completely organized, and a regular Government established in France, his Majesty's obligation ceases in that respect, and M. Grouvelle[6] will, therefore, be acknowledged in the usual form. For the rest, this step remains an insulated measure, being neither more nor less than the natural consequence of circumstances, and an additional proof of the complete and truly impartial neutrality of the King.

On the day of opening their National Assembly, the Dutch exhibited

[1] From the *Sun* 21 Mar 1796 or the *Star* 22 Mar.

[2] Count Aleksandr Vasilievich Suvorov (1729–1800), Russian field-marshal, commanded the Russians at the siege of Ismail (1790) and later subdued Poland with much severity.

[3] Count Piotr Aleksandrovich Rumiantsev (1725–96), Russian hero of the Seven Years' War and a veteran of the Turkish campaigns.

[4] Andreas Peter, Count von Bernstorff (1735–97), the Danish prime minister, in this document notified all the foreign ministers that the French minister would be acknowledged. From *The Times* or the *Star* 15 Mar 1796 or *M Chron* 17 Mar.

[5] Christian VII (1749–1808), king of Denmark and Norway (1766–1808), became hopelessly insane in 1784 and relinquished control to Crown Prince Frederick, who ruled as regent (1774–1808). By reprinting this note, C is pointing a moral for the English to follow.

[6] Philippe-Antoine Grouvelle (1758–1806), French minister to Denmark.

a clumsy imitation of the French Revolutionary puppet-shows.—P. PAULUS[1] is elected President.

Preparations for the commencement of the Campaign are going on with unwonted vigour. The French Loan (like all the other measures of that Republic) has been surpassed in point of compulsory taxation by the Imperial Court; which has exacted one fourth of the Revenue of the Monks and Nuns of Lombardy.[2]

The troops of General Jourdan[3] are thus distributed for the opening of the campaign:—80,000 men are to act offensively in the Hundsruck, whilst a body of 12 or 15,000, entrenched on the Chartreuse, and in the environs of Coblentz, are to prevent the Austrians from passing the Rhine on that side. A line is also to be formed on the left side, as far as Crevelt: but this, it is intended, shall be merely sufficient to defend the principal posts.[4]

On the right bank of the Rhine the General Le Febvre[5] is to make a diversion at the head of 30,000 men, which cannot fail of being useful to the main army. In this arrangement, the garrison of Luxembourg, amounting to 12,000 men, is not included.—It is in this way that the Republic is determined to push the war; and, according to every probability, it cannot but be fatal to the remainder of the coalition.

DOMESTIC INTELLIGENCE

ADMIRAL DUNCAN[6] sailed with the squadron from the Downs on Saturday the 12th of March, and on Sunday he arrived off Yarmouth Roads, and Admiral Pringle's[7] squadron immediately weighed from the Roads, and three ships got out: the rest could not get out till the night flood, and they sailed together on Monday March 14th.[8]

It is with the greatest concern we state, that on the same morning

1 Pieter Paulus (1754–96), elected president of the National Assembly 1 Mar 1796, died a fortnight later, 17 Mar. See below, pp 225–6.

2 Above paragraph condensed from the *Star* 21 Mar 1796.

3 Jean-Baptiste (later Comte de) Jourdan (1762–1833), general of the French armies of the north, had concluded an armistice with the Austrians the previous Dec.

4 This paragraph and the following from the *Star* 17 Mar 1796.

5 Pierre-François-Joseph Lefebvre (1755–1820), later marshal of France and Duke of Danzig.

6 Adam Duncan (1731–1804), commander-in-chief of the North Sea fleet (1795–1801); for his victory over the Dutch fleet in 1797 he was created Viscount Duncan of Camperdown.

7 Thomas Pringle (d 1803), promoted to rear-admiral 1795.

8 From the *Star* 15 Mar 1796.

the Royal Sovereign, of 110 guns, Admiral Cornwallis,[1] who sailed from Portsmouth the 1st instant with a squadron, and large convoy for the West-Indies, returned to Spithead, owing to one of the transports, the Bellisarius, Captain Barge, running on board her, by which she received such considerable damage as to prevent her going on, and the wind at that time blew so exceedingly hard as to prevent the Admiral from shifting his flag to some other ship. The transport had near three hundred of the York Riflemen on board: She sunk immediately, and not more than a hundred and forty men were saved![2]

On Monday March 14th arrived three mails from Corunna, which brought dispatches to Government from the Marquis of Bute.[3] The Court of Madrid, it is said, has yielded to the remonstrances made by the Noble Lord, and has removed the suspicions entertained of its political conduct.—The Spanish Ministry have sent orders to Cadiz to dismantle twenty sail of the line, lying in that port: and a French privateer which was at Alicant, and had taken some of our vessels, has been ordered from thence to Toulon.[4]

DUBLIN, *March* 10.[5] Yesterday the soldiers convicted of Manslaughter for firing into St. Mary's Watchhouse, by which a Watchman was killed, were brought into Court, and discharged on account of their being PARDONED!!!

Mr. HASTINGS'S[6] pension is 4000l. a year, for twenty-seven years, from August 1795, to which the India Company have added the loan of 50,000l. for seventeen years, without interest, which is therefore an annuity for that term of all that it will bring of interest on a substantial security.

Mr. BURKE'S pensions are three in number:—[7]

[1] William Cornwallis (1744–1819), brother of Marquis Cornwallis, commander-in-chief in the West Indies at this time. When he refused to continue in a frigate, he was court-martialled. See below, p 190.

[2] From the *Star* 15 Mar 1796 or *M Chron* or *The Times* 16 Mar.

[3] John Stuart (1744–1814), 4th Earl and 1st Marquis of Bute; sent by Pitt as chargé-d'affaires to Madrid 1795.

[4] From the *M Chron* or *The Times* 16 Mar 1796 or the *Star* 17 Mar.

[5] From the *Star* 19 Mar 1796, dated 12 Mar (C's small capitals and exclamation points).

[6] Warren Hastings (1732–1818), governor-general of India; his impeachment trial (1788–95) reputedly cost him £70,000 and left him destitute. This item appeared in *M Chron* 12 Mar 1796, but C probably took it from the *Star* 15 Mar, where it was followed by the list of Burke's pensions.

[7] This list also appeared in the *M Chron* and *The Times* 15 Mar 1796, quoted from William Augustus Miles *Letter to H. Duncombe, Esq.* (2nd ed 1796), an answer to Burke's *Letter to a Noble Lord.*

1,200l. per annum, chargeable on the Civil List for the Lives of Mr. and Mrs. Burke, and the Survivor of them, to commence from January 5, 1793.
1,160l. per annum, chargeable on the 4½ per cent. fund for the lives of Edmund Burke, Esq. Lord Royston, and Anchitel Grey, Esq. and the survivor of them, to commence July 24, 1793.
1,340l. per annum, chargeable on the 4½ per cent. fund for the lives of the Princess Amelia, Lord Althorpe, and William Cavendish, Esq. and the survivor of them, to commence July 24, 1793.
______
3,700l. per annum.

Mr. Burke has been an Aristocrat from prejudice, as he is now a Royalist from gratitude. But can it be believed that this *Cameleon* of *hues*, as *brilliant* as they are *changing*, was once actually a Republican!—Take the proof from his speech in the House of Commons, on the 27th of January, 1789.

"If you are for a Republic, why do you not make it known in a direct and manly way? Why not openly declare your intentions? If you ask whether I hate a Republican Speculation, I will answer—No, I love, revere and adore the true principles of a Republic."[1]

The late Earl of Guildford[2] being told that his large pair of *gouty* shoes had been stolen "Well well, (said his Lordship, with his usual pleasantry), all the harm I wish the thief is, that they may *fit him.*"

Disinterested Piety.[3]—A gentleman of Macclesfield, who employs a great number of hands in both the silk and cotton manufactories, in order to encourage his work people in a due attendance at church, on the late Fast-day, told them, that, "if they went to church, they should receive their wages for that day, in the same manner as if they had been at work."—Upon which a deputation was appointed to acquaint their employer, that "if he would pay them for *over hours*, they would attend likewise at the Methodist chapel in the evening!"

[1] In repeating this gibe from the *M Chron* 10 Mar 1796 or the *CI* 19 Mar, C forgets that Burke reiterated his conditional approval of republics in his *Appeal from the New to the Old Whigs* (4th ed 1791) 10.

[2] Frederick, 2nd Earl of Guilford (1732–92), better known by his courtesy title Lord North, which he held while he was prime minister (1770–82). His opposition to Pitt accounts for the pleasant tone in which he is mentioned here. The item appeared in the *CI* 19 Mar 1796.

[3] From *CI* 19 Mar 1796; the *M Chron* 23 Mar 1796 has "Methodist Preaching-house" for "Methodist chapel" in its reprint of the item. The item also appeared in the *Star* 25 Mar, but without the title.

A man of the name of NATHANIEL SAUNDERS, lately died in Chelmsford Gaol, where he was six years a prisoner. The offence for which this punishment was inflicted was, that he had killed *a Hare!* [1]

THE HON. ADMIRAL JOHN FORBES,[2]

ADMIRAL OF THE FLEET, AND GENERAL OF MARINES.

IN the earlier part of his life, he was peculiarly noticed as an able, enterprising, and intrepid officer. He served with much reputation under Sir John Norris;[3] and was no less distinguished as Captain of the Norfolk, of eighty guns, in the action of Mathews and Lestock,[4] with the combined fleets of France and Spain, when his gallantry contributed in a high degree to save his brave friend Admiral Mathews, whose second he was in that engagement.—So bright was his honour, and so clear his reputation, in those turbulent days, that though his evidence on the trial of the Admirals went wholly against Admiral Lestock, yet that officer was often heard to declare, "that Mr. Forbes's testimony was given like an officer and a gentleman."

In Lord Chatham's glorious war, Admiral Forbes was selected as the ablest assistant the First Lord could have in the management of the Admiralty, and conducted himself in a manner highly creditable to his abilities, and eminently serviceable to his country.

When the warrant for executing the unfortunate Admiral Byng[5] was offered for signature at the Admiralty Board, Admiral Forbes refused to sign it, at the same time humbly laying at his late Majesty's feet his objections.

To detail the meritorious deeds of the venerable character before

[1] From the *Star* or *Oracle* 15 Mar 1796 or *M Chron* 16 Mar, including italics.

[2] John Forbes (1714–96), admiral of the fleet, died 10 Mar 1796. This obituary, with two additional opening paragraphs and a conclusion, appeared in the *M Herald* 14 Mar and *The Times* and *M Post* 15 Mar, but C probably took it from the *Oracle* 15 Mar or the *Star* 17 Mar, where it appeared as given here (except that C has omitted one sentence).

[3] Sir John Norris (c 1660–1749), admiral of the fleet.

[4] Admiral Thomas Mathews (1676–1751), commander-in-chief in the Mediterranean, was court-martialled on charges brought by Lestock (1746), and after a long trial was dismissed from the service (1747). Admiral Richard Lestock (c 1679–1746), who had a quarrel of long standing with Mathews, was tried by court-martial (1746), acquitted, and promoted.

[5] Admiral John Byng (1704–57) for neglect of duty was sentenced to death in 1757 by court-martial and executed. (The incident is alluded to and ridiculed by Voltaire in *Candide* as the method used by the English to keep their admirals alert.)

us would lead to a discussion too extensive, but the writer of this tribute to departed greatness cannot conclude it without inserting an anecdote, well known in the naval and political circles.

During a late Administration, it was thought expedient to offer Lord Howe[1] the office of General of Marines, held by Admiral Forbes, and spontaneously conferred upon him by his Majesty, as a reward for his many and long services. A Message was sent by the Ministers, to say it would forward the King's service if he would resign: and that he should be no loser by his accommodating the Government, as they proposed recommending it to the King to give him a pension in Ireland of 3000l. per annum, and a Peerage, to descend to his daughter. To this Admiral Forbes sent an immediate answer: he told the Ministers the Generalship of the Marines was a military employment, given him by his Majesty, as a reward for his services—that he thanked GOD he had never been a burthen to his country, which he had served during a long life to the best of his ability—and that he would not condescend to accept of a pension or bargain for a peerage. He concluded by laying his Generalship of the Marines, together with his rank in the navy, at the King's feet, entreating him to take both away, if they could forward his service; and, at the same time, assuring his Majesty, he would never prove himself unworthy of the former honours he had received, by ending the remnant of a long life as a pensioner, or accepting of a peerage, obtained by political arrangement.—His gracious Master applauded his manly spirit, ever after continued him in his high military honours, and, to the day of his death, condescended to shew him strong marks of his regard.

IT is with great pleasure we learn that on Tuesday[2] March 21st 1796, at a meeting for the choice of a Physician to attend the Hospital at BIRMINGHAM, Dr. Carmichael[3] was elected by a majority of thirteen. There were three candidates, and the numbers were for Dr. Salt 71, for Dr. Bree 74, and for Dr. Carmichael 87. The professional skill, the general science, and still more the long-tried humanity of the

[1] Richard, Earl Howe (1726–99), admiral of the fleet. *The Times* here reads: "... to offer a Noble Lord, very high in the naval profession, and very deservedly a favourite of his Sovereign and his country ...".

[2] An error for "Monday".

[3] C may have owed this item to Beddoes, for his *Considerations on the Medicinal Use and on the Production of Factitious Airs* (2nd ed Bristol 1795) included communications from Dr John Carmichael (pp 69–73, 83–91, 101–3).

successful candidate, authorize us to congratulate the charity upon the choice it has made.

PROCEEDINGS IN THE BRITISH LEGISLATURE

HOUSE OF COMMONS

TUESDAY, *March* 15

THE order of the day was read for the further consideration of the report of the Committee upon the bill for the abolition of the slave-trade.

SIR WILLIAM YOUNG opposed the bill on account of the injurious effects which he deemed it would have on property in the Mother-Country as well as in the West-Indies. The Bill might with propriety be called, a bill of General Foreclosure. Every Mortgagee in this Country upon West-India Estates would have the whole of his security withdrawn. Sir William dwelt likewise on the severity of the prosecutions, for they led to a sentence of fourteen years transportation, which would send *Gentlemen** of birth, temper, fortune, manners, and education, to mingle with the society of the lowest, meanest, and most abandoned of men: and this upon the information of an Overseer, who having been detected in importing slaves for his own advantage, might swear it was done with the connivance of his Master. Was this the return for the services of the West-India Planters in the present war? General SMITH defended the continuance of the Slave-trade on the plea, that, although confessedly most inhuman and unjust, it had been approved of, and even patronized by former Acts of Parliament: and that their policy and NECESSITY ought to justify these acts †equally as the acts for pressing seamen.

Mr. DUNDAS opposed the Bill on the grounds of its impolicy and impracticability. Its impolicy, as it would transfer the trade to

* In other words, those who contemning the laws of their country and of human nature, had been buying, (or kidnapping) *enslaving*, and (in the consequences) *murdering* some hundreds of their fellow-creatures, to mingle with the poor wretches, who, ignorant and half-famished had stolen a few paultry guineas!—*Gentlemen!!* "The Prince of Darkness is a *Gentleman!*" (Shakespear's Lear.) [1]

† *Equally*.

[1] *King Lear* III iv 148; see also *CN* I 121 and n. This equalitarian sentiment is of a piece with C's use of "aristocrat", e.g. p 152 above.

France and * America: its impracticability†, as without the co-operation of the colonial legislature, not all the naval and military force of the country could enforce the act, so as to prevent the ingress of Slaves. This assertion was founded on facts. In the course of the last Campaign in the West-Indies we had 28 ships of war wholly employed in watching the coasts of *two* French islands, in order to prevent communication between them and one or two of our own, but in vain. If then it was impracticable under the favourable circumstance of active and zealous co-operation on the part of the military and civil force of our own islands, joined to such a fleet—how much more impracticable must it prove, when the force by sea and land must be proportionably so much less, and when the civil interest of the island acts in an opposite direction. In the last Campaign a communication was effected openly and in defiance by large vessels, in the day—Can we expect, therefore, with a less force to prevent an intercourse, which would be conducted silently and cautiously by the rowing of canoes and barges off shore, and under cover of the night? As, therefore, it would be impossible to prevent the traffic, he deemed, that we should consult the interests of humanity as well as of the colonies by proposing gradual and conciliatory measures. Instead of representing the planters as savages exulting in every excess of barbarity and horror, he should deem it prudent to afford parliamentary protection not only to their property but to their characters.‡ Among the regulations which he thought advisable, he proposed to limit the power of sending slaves from one British island to another; and to prevent the importation of slaves above the age of twenty. The importation of aged negroes into the colonies was attended with danger. After they had grown bold in immorality and *irreligion* on the coast of Africa, it had been found difficult to make them tractable and obedient. He concluded by remonstrating against the

* Both of whom will in all human probability abolish it long before us. The only argument with them against the abolition is its impolicy, as it would transfer the whole trade to England!

† This argument depends for its validity on the strength of the former. If the other States of Europe abandoned the trade, the argument falls; and our perseverance in the trade is the chief objection urged against their abandonment. If, however, there be any force in the argument, if an effectual abolition of the trade be not within the power of the Legislature, this is an additional and coercive argument for the disuse of sugar and rum by the declaimers against the trade, which to a certainty would abolish it.

‡ We suppose, by a Bill to be entitled "An Act for the Abolition of PROPER NAMES."

intemperance of some of the speakers, who had spoken with undue levity of the West-India islands, and seemed disposed to threaten the planters with independence. By an account of the imports and exports of articles *imported from the West-India islands to Great Britain, he undertook to prove that the secession or independence of the colonies would be of material injury to the mother country.

Mr. Fox replied,—That as even the opposers of the present Bill allowed the inhumanity and injustice of the trade, the only difference that could remain was the policy or impolicy of this particular mode of abolishing it. On this part of the subject the Right Hon. Gentleman had endeavoured to prove, that we could not abolish the Slave-trade without the consent of the colonies; in other words, that the Slave-trade could never be abolished. But he himself had proposed two regulations to take place without their consent—and if these were practicable, the abolition was practicable. If it were possible to prevent any but negroes under twenty from being imported, it was possible to prevent any at all. If it were possible to prevent an intercourse between our own islands, it was possible to prevent an intercourse between those islands and foreign colonies.—The Right Honourable Gentleman had complained that the planters had been represented as men utterly destitute of humanity, &c. Now on this subject the House has heard evidence, and they found, what every man of sense expected to find, that where there is slavery there is cruelty. *Good God! while the House is hesitating, the West-India planters are tearing children from their mothers, and husbands from their wives, and hurrying them in chains and torment to slavery in a strange land.* Four years ago the House ordered this Trade to be abolished in February 1796;[1] that period had now elapsed, and the House were only called on to carry into effect its own resolution, and to keep its promise with the Public.

MR. ROSE made particular objections to several clauses of the Bill, which were explained by Sergeant ADAIR.

The SECRETARY at WAR professed himself faithful to his original sentiments in favour of the Abolition. All the havoc of the Rights of Man, had not blunted him to the Rights of Africans, nor had the

* That individuals are enriched by this trade may be true, but that the country at large can be benefited by a commerce, in which we give necessaries, which we ourselves want, for idle or pernicious superfluities, is a state-mystery, incomprehensible by ordinary understandings, and indigestible by unassisted faith.

[1] It was eventually abolished under the Fox–Grenville ministry in 1807.

example of French Liberty reconciled him to African Slavery. Disapproving the common arguments urged in favour of the abolition, he rested the propriety of such a measure on the effect which our example might probably produce on other nations. Still however from the insurrections and other unfavourable circumstances it was with great reluctance that he should vote for the Bill. A plan had been formed for the abolition of the slave-trade by a person (Mr. Burke) whose benevolence was commensurate with his genius. This plan he had viewed with that predilection which he entertained for every production of that excellent great man's wisdom. It meant to introduce such regulations into the treatment of negroes, as would secure their propagation, and make the trade gradually die away. Next to such a plan as this, he would have wished that at the present moment no plan at all had been adopted. As however he was certain of the iniquity of the Slave-Trade, and not certain of the validity of his objections to its immediate Abolition, he should vote in favor of the Bill.

The CHANCELLOR of the EXCHEQUER differed entirely from the last Speaker, and preferred the present plan. Mr. Burke's plan (he observed) postponed Abolition, which was not dangerous, in favor of a system of internal treatment, leading the Slaves to hopes of Emancipation that were full of dangers. As to any improvement in the disposition of the West-India Planters [that] was placed beyond the reach of expectation; for their own Petition contradicted the Resolution of the House and the Preamble of the Bill by denying the injustice and inhumanity of the Trade. Mr. Pitt objected to separate clauses of the Bill. That for permitting the Captors to sell for their own advantage the Slaves seized in vessels that were attempting to carry them after the passing of the Bill, should, he thought, be exchanged for one allowing head-money to the Officers who should take them; the Slaves being afterwards landed in one of the Establishments for Commerce and Civilization on the Coast of Africa.

GENERAL TARLETON[1] moved that the further consideration of the Report, be postponed to that day four months. Mr. Dent seconded the Motion.

The House divided on General Tarleton's amendment.—Ayes 74. Noes 70. Majority 4, AGAINST THE ABOLITION OF THE SLAVE-TRADE!

[1] Banastre Tarleton (1754–1833), MP for Liverpool, had distinguished himself as a cavalry leader of the British forces in the Carolinas during the American Revolution.

WEDNESDAY, *March* 16.

The order of the day for the second reading of the Wet-Dock Bill,[1] produced a desultory conversation, which issued in the postponement of the second reading of the Bill till Wednesday the 11th April next.

MONDAY, *March* 21*st*.

General MACLEOD moved that an humble address be presented to his Majesty, that he be graciously pleased to order such information to be laid on the table as his Majesty's Ministers have received respecting the mode of carrying on the War with the Maroons. The General prefaced his motion by reading an extract from Bartholomew de la Casas,[2] in proof of the ferocity of the Blood-hounds, and the manner in which they were applied by the old Spanish Exterminators. He then read an original letter from Jamaica, implying that they had been similarly applied by the British Planters, &c. The Maroons were Freemen who had never been slaves themselves, nor were their ancestors slaves. Mr. DUNDAS wished to wave the motion. He believed that these dogs were used merely to trace out the Negroes. Mr. SHERIDAN stated the origin of the War with these free natives. One of the Maroons was charged with stealing a pig: he was tried under our law and publickly whipped. Now by an express stipulation between us and the Maroons, they were to be tried by a tribunal of their own. The Chiefs of the Maroons remonstrated against this violation of treaty; and redress was refused them.

Mr. COURTENEY proved by facts, that it was the manner of Blood-hounds to fasten on human flesh, so as not to quit hold till they were pierced with bayonets. General Macleod said, he would never quit this subject, until he was satisfied that positive orders were sent from our Government not to use these Dogs. He withdrew his motion. The House adjourned.

[1] Because of the increase in commerce and the inadequacy of the wharfs and docks in London, a bill was introduced to build new wet docks at Wapping and Shadwell.

[2] Bartolomé de las Casas (1474–1566), Spanish Dominican missionary among the Indians. His work first appeared in English translation as *The Spanish Colonie* (1583).

POSTSCRIPT

To the Letter signed PHOCION,
in the beginning of this Number[1]

SINCE the above was written, the zeal of some spies, and informers, uniting with the industry of the Birmingham Justices, a Deposition was fabricated, and laid before his Majesty's Privy Council. *That loyal* and *patriotic* Nobleman, the Duke of Portland, is said to have replied to the Magistrates, that the information they had sent, was put into the hands of the Attorney-General,[2] who at present had not given his opinion, but that Binns was immediately to be apprehended, and confined.—In consequence of this Binns was taken into custody.

It does not appear that any deposition had been sent by the Justices to the Privy Council respecting Jones, or that the Justices had received any warrant from the Noble Duke to apprehend him. But men of such talent, station, and diligence, as the Justices of the town of Birmingham, are not fond of leaving "*rubs or botches in their work.*"[3]—Jones was still at large—and it is supposed they, upon their *own* authority issued a warrant for *his* apprehension.

The Prison-Keeper, and Constables, who appeared to have "acquainted themselves with the perfect spy o' the time,"[4] entered into a house, in a chamber of which, they found Jones sitting writing letters, and took him into custody.—These Gentlemen behaved with such insolence of office, as to pick the pockets of the master of the house in which Jones was apprehended, rifle his drawers, carry off his letters and papers, and seize his books and pamphlets, and when asked by what authority they thus acted, they refused to shew their warrant. When the Magistrates were applied to, for these books, and papers, by the owner of them, they refused to restore them. This took place on Thursday March 17th.

Upon the examination, it appeared that Mr. Jones is a surgeon—but I cannot learn, that any charge of Sedition, or of conduct contrary to any law of his country, has been fixed upon him. He received a letter from the society which delegated him, just after he was taken into custody; addressing himself to the constables and

[1] See above, pp 127–30.

[2] Sir John Scott (1751–1838), later lord chancellor, Earl of Eldon, and a pillar of orthodoxy, "the best hated man in England" (*DNB*). He incurred Shelley's wrath by denying him his children in 1817.

[3] *Macbeth* III i 134 (var).

[4] Ibid III i 130 (altered).

others who were with him, Jones said, "If there be any thing treasonable or seditious in the object of my mission, this letter, which I have just received from the Corresponding Society, and which I have not yet opened, will be likely to discover it:"—he opened the letter in the presence of them all, and begged the constable to read it aloud; the constable referred it back to him: Jones then read it to the company, and so convinced was the constable himself by the contents of the letter, that he congratulated Jones upon having so strong a testimony of his innocence.

Francis Bathurst,[1] who was president at the meeting in which Jones delivered his lecture, was so far warmed into the love of freedom by the eloquence of the delegate, as to make a speech of thanks to him when he had concluded, in which Bathurst was perhaps a little unguarded in his language; for it is reported that in the course of his speech he remarked that "Birmingham men knew how to make arms, and knew also how to use them when compelled by necessity, or when occasion called for it," or words to that purpose. The spies, and informers, have fully sworn to Bathurst's having made this sort of speech, and he is also under confinement.

I shall defer any remarks upon these circumstances till we see the conclusion; in the mean time we ask the minister of this country, O William Pitt, Son of the late Chatham, what wilt thou do in the end thereof?

When the worthy Magistrate of Birmingham, put a stop to the harangue of the Apostle of the Corresponding Society, a part of the audience was so unmannerly as to hiss. The chief Magistrate of the country, our present gracious Sovereign, it is well known, frequently receives this mark of British freedom, and bears it always with patience. Not so my little country Justice. Nemo me impune sibilat.[2] A constable seized one who was thought to be of the number of those who had presumed to attack the dignity of Mr. Hicks. He was a youth of sixteen or seventeen, and the constable swore that he hissed! However it appears it was but a constable's oath; for the youth had not hissed. If he had actually perpetrated this malicious and abominable deed, one would have thought a reprimand sufficient. But no, the profound sagacity of the Justices, saw this crime in a point of view in which ordinary understandings cannot place it, and

[1] Described by *M Post* (26 Mar 1796) as "a jobbing smith, of Deritend". Deritend is now a suburb of Birmingham.

[2] "No one may hiss at me with impunity"—a variation upon the motto of the Scottish Order of the Thistle: "Nemo me impune lacessit".

bound the youth over to his good behaviour for a twelve month in the sum of FORTY POUNDS!! N.B. "*Excessive bail* ought *not* to be required, nor *unusual* punishments inflicted;" Bill of Rights. That a man utterly ignorant of the principles of law and of the constitution of his country, and unblest with a liberal education, should act without attention to the habits, and feelings, of his fellow citizens is not at all extraordinary; we can expect nothing better; but, that a British House of Commons, should suffer such acts to pass, as must necessarily afford opportunities, to each petty Justice, of exercising a monstrous, and odious tyranny; *there lies the grief.*[1]

TO CORRESPONDENTS

If our anonymous *Friend* who has written so severely to the "Companion of his Youth," will favor the Editor with a few lines signifying *where*, and by what letters of the alphabet, he may be addressed, the Editor will answer him.

[1] Cf Shakespeare *Love's Labour's Lost* IV iii 171: "Where lies thy grief, O, tell me, good Dumain?"

THE WATCHMAN

No. V. SATURDAY, APRIL 2, 1796.

Published by the Author, S. T. COLERIDGE, Bristol;
And by PARSONS, Paternoster-Row, London.

THAT ALL MAY KNOW THE TRUTH;
AND THAT THE TRUTH MAY MAKE US FREE!

TO THE EDITOR OF THE WATCHMAN

SINCE I have been capable of reasoning, I have beheld with compassion and indignation the state of the Slaves in the West-Indies. —I have longed for the abolition of the slave-trade, as the abolition of the source of the evil, and for a system of laws which may finally lead to the emancipation of this oppressed race of Men—Latterly I have trembled on seeing intelligence from our Islands, lest I should read that the Negroes had at length by some horrid act of Justice avenged themselves on their oppressors—One night, after having mused long on this subject, I retired to rest, when I dreamt that, removed far from the din of modern politics, I had been travelling through distant countries, and had at last arrived at the West-Indies —My heart throbbed as it approached that land, which, since its acquaintance with Europeans, had witnessed every extravagance that Souls the most deeply polluted could suggest—I called up all my fortitude to bear with steadiness those scenes which I anticipated— abject and oppressed Slaves!—Masters in a state of disgusting luxury! —but how great was my amazement to find a People at once free and happy. On landing I was accosted with the utmost urbanity by a Negro, who with his Wife walking on the shore in a lovely evening, had been observing the approach of our vessel. I was delighted to see that some at least of these people were happy. He offered to conduct me to the neighbouring town; I thanked him, and on the way began to make those inquiries so natural, concerning the state of the slaves in that country—SLAVES! he cried, with a countenance of pity, indignation, and rapture,—we have no Slaves here,—The TIME IS PASSED—almost suffocated, but yet incredulous, I asked a hundred questions without waiting for a reply—He saw that I was unacquainted with the great revolution which had taken place during the few short years that I had been travelling among the isles of the southern ocean. He satisfied every interrogatory as quickly as I possibly could permit him. At length being in the town, he led me to a spacious square; in the midst of which, was placed on a magnificent pedestal, the statue of a Negroe. Behold said he our Hampden, our Tell, our Washington.[1] At the foot of this statue were engraved these words:—

TO THE AVENGER OF THE NEW WORLD

The head of the figure was naked, his arm stretched out, his eye sublime, the whole attitude noble, and commanding awe: the wrecks of twenty sceptres were scattered round him. I burst forth with renewed ecstacy. Yes, exclaimed my Conductor, with a warmth equal to my transports, Nature at length produced that astonishing man, who was destined to rid the world of the most atrocious, the most insulting and the longest tyranny;—his genius, his intrepidity, his patience and virtuous vengeance, were recompensed;—he broke the chains of his countrymen—*human beings* oppressed under the most odious slavery, who wanted only the opportunity to form as many heroes; the torrent which breaks its dams, the thunder which strikes, have an effect less instantaneous, less violent:—at the same moment of time we shed the blood of *all* our tyrants,—English, Spanish, Dutch, *all* were victims to fire, poison, and the sword—this earth drank greedily that blood after which it had long thirsted, and the bones of our ancestors, basely assassinated, seemed at that moment to rise anew and tremble with joy. The few remaining natives have reassumed the rights of man, for they are the rights of nature.—That heroic avenger, continued he, stretching forth his right arm, and pointing at the statue, that heroic avenger has given liberty to our hemisphere, and we almost worship him as a God. The inhabitants of Europe, now enlightened by pure Christianity and a liberal philosophy, emulate each other in paying homage to his memory. He came like a storm which broods over a guilty city ere it blasts it by its thunders. He was the exterminating angel whom the God of

[1] The choice of three national heroes from three freedom-loving countries gave to England as its representative John Hampden (1594–1643), the hero of the struggle for supremacy of Parliament over the Crown during the ship-money controversy of Charles I's time. A standing toast of the Whig Club was: "The cause for which Hampden bled in the field and Sidney on the scaffold". (For Algernon Sidney see below, p 176.)

justice armed with his sword. He has demonstrated, that sooner or later cruelty shall be punished; and that Providence has instruments in reserve, whom it lets loose on the earth to re-establish that equality which iniquity and ambition may destroy.—He ceased. A multitude who were by this time collected around, and who had sympathized with him as he spoke, after a few moments of dead silence, burst forth into a shout of such rapture, that it overcame the delusion of my mind and I awoke.

I must acknowledge that this dream made a strong impression on me, and I trust that now, when the public attention is recalled to the subject of the Slave-trade by the recent rejection of the Bill for its abolition, that every good man will by that easy self-denial so well recommended in your last Number, make at least a preliminary step towards a system which may avert the too probable horrors presented to me in a dream.

T. P.[1]
Stowey.

For the two following sublime and truly original Sonnets, the Watchman is indebted to Mr. ROBERT LOVELL,[2] Author of "Bristol, a Satire," and of some Poems published in conjunction with Mr. Southey.

SONNET

Stonehenge

WAS it a Spirit on yon shapeless pile?
It wore methought an hoary DRUID's form,

[1] Thomas Poole of Nether Stowey, to whom C wrote 30 Mar 1796, acknowledging "your communication" (*CL* I 194). D. V. Erdman points out that the source of the dream is Daniel Isaac Eaton *Politics for the People*; *or, Hog's Wash* No 10 [14 Dec 1793] I (1794) 137–41, where it is extracted from *Memoirs of the Year Two Thousand Five Hundred*, tr of Louis-Sébastien Mercier's *L'An 2440, rêve s'il en fut jamais* (London [Paris] 1772).

[2] Lovell (c 1770–96), a Pantisocrat, had married Mary Fricker, Mrs C's sister. In late May, Lamb asked in a letter to C: "What is become of Moschus? You sported some of his sublimities, I see, in your Watchman. Very decent things". *LL* I 8. In their joint volume of poems in 1794 Lovell was "Moschus" and Southey "Bion". To return to Lamb's query, Lovell had died on 3 May, a month after this number of *The Watchman* had appeared (C to Poole 5 May 1796: *CL* I 207). Lamb's tone seems to indicate his awareness of C's low opinion of Lovell's literary merits. See C to RS [11 Dec 1794]: *CL* I 134–5.

Musing on ancient days—the dying storm
Moans in his lifted locks;—thou, NIGHT! the while
Dost listen to his sad harp's wild complaint,
Mother of Shadows!—as to thee he pours
The broken strain, and plaintively deplores
The fall of Druid Fame—Hark Murmurs faint
Breathe on the wavy Air! and now more loud
Swells the deep dirge accustom'd to complain
Of holy Rites unpaid, and of the Crowd
Whose careless steps these sacred Haunts profane.
O'er the wild Plain the hurrying Tempest flies,
And 'mid the Storm unheard, the Song of Sorrow dies.

R. L.

SONNET

THE cloudy blackness gathers o'er the Sky
Shadowing these realms with that portentous storm
Ere long to burst, and haply to deform
Fair Nature's Face: for Indignation high
Might hurl promiscuous vengeance with wild hand,
And Fear, with fierce precipitation throw
Blind ruin wide: while Hate with scowling brow
Feigns patriot rage. O PRIESTLEY, for thy wand,
Or FRANKLIN! thine, with calm expectant joy
To tame the storm, and with mysterious force
In viewless channel shape the Light'ning's course
To purify Creation, not destroy.—
So should fair order from the Tempest rise
And Freedom's Sun-beams gild unclouded skies.

R. L.

TO MERCY[1]

Sonnet

NOT always should the Tear's ambrosial dew
Roll its soft anguish down thy furrow'd cheek;

[1] *To Mercy*, a denunciation of Pitt, when first published in *M Chron* 23 Dec 1794, was No 6 of a series of *Sonnets on Eminent Characters*. Later C disparaged it, saying to a friend: "I was glad to hear . . . that you abhor the morality of my Sonnet to Mercy—it is indeed detestable & the poetry is not above mediocrity". To Thelwall 13 Nov 1796: *CL* I 254. In *PW* (EHC) I 83–4 it appears (var) with the title *Pitt*, the title it had borne in *M Chron*.

Not always heaven-breath'd Tones of *Suppliance* meek
Beseem thee, MERCY! Yon dark Scowler view,
Who with proud words of dear-lov'd Freedom came,
More blasting than the mildew from the South!
And kiss'd his Country with *Iscariot* mouth
(Staining most foul a godlike Father's name)
Then fix'd her on the Cross of deep Distress,
And at safe distance marks the thirsty Lance
Pierce her big side! But O! if some strange Trance
The eye-lids of thy stern-brow'd * Sister press,
Seize, MERCY! thou more terrible the Brand,
And hurl her thunderbolts with fiercer hand.

S. T. C.

RECOLLECTION[1]

As the tir'd savage, who his drowsy frame
Had bask'd beneath the sun's unclouded flame,
Awakes amid the troubles of the air,
The skiey deluge and white lightning's glare,
Aghast he scours before the tempest's sweep,
And sad recalls the sunny hour of sleep!
So tost by storms along life's wild'ring way
Mine eye reverted views that cloudless day,
When by my native brook I wont to rove,
While HOPE with kisses nurs'd the infant LOVE.

Dear native brook! like peace so placidly
Smoothing thro' fertile fields thy current meek—
Dear native brook! where first young POESY
Star'd wildly eager in her noon-tide dream;
Where blameless Pleasures dimpled Quiet's cheek,
As water-lilies *ripple* thy slow stream!

* Justice.

[1] "Although a kind of cento put together by C from his own verses, *Recollection* is worth reprinting, for it is a coherent poem". *Poems* (JDC) 566. See *PW* (EHC) II 1023–4. It is made up of *Lines on an Autumnal Evening* lines 71–86 (var), *Sonnet to the River Otter* lines 2–11 (var), and *The Gentle Look* lines 13–14 or *Anna and Harland* lines 13–14. Cf *PW* (EHC) I 53–4, 48, 16.

How many various-fated years have past,
What blissful and what anguish'd hours, since last
I skimm'd the smooth thin stone along thy breast
Numb'ring its light leaps! Yet so deep imprest
Sink the sweet scenes of childhood, that mine eyes
I never shut amid the sunny blaze,
But strait, with all their tints, thy waters rise,
The crossing plank, and margin's willowy maze,
And bedded sand, that, vein'd with various dyes,
Gleam'd thro' thy bright transparence to the gaze,
Ah! fair tho' faint those forms of memory seem
Like Heaven's bright bow on thy smooth evening stream!

S. T. C.

The Editor returns his grateful acknowledgements to Mr. G—rt[1] for the following ESSAY, and will anxiously expect the remaining Numbers. The Editor is not perhaps equally convinced of the uses of Trade; but this small difference of opinion by no means lessens his admiration or gratitude. Mr. G. discovers much general knowledge, and when his reasonings are not perhaps unimpregnably solid, even then they are ingenious, and uniformly conveyed in a style luminous and elegant.

THE COMMERCIAL ACADEMIC
No. I

THE Academics were a sect of ancient Philosophers who rejected every *dogma* advanced by the other Schools; and pursued the middle path between the Stoic and the Pyrrhonist or Sceptic. As the Stoic affirmed, so the Pyrrhonist doubted every thing: one was as

[1] This is almost certainly William Gilbert (c 1760–1825), a fragment of whose *The Hurricane* appears in *The Watchman*, below, pp 350–1. (EHC *Studies* 20 "safely" assigned the essay to Davies Giddy, friend of Beddoes and early patron of Humphry Davy, but Giddy did not marry Miss Gilbert until 1808; he changed his name to Gilbert late in 1817.) Gilbert, a poet much admired by Coleridge, Southey, and Wordsworth, turned up in Bristol in 1796 (he had earlier spent a year in the Bristol Asylum). C describes him as one who "*was* a man of fine Genius, which, at intervals, he still discovers. But, ah me! Madness smote with her hand. . . . He is a man of fluent Eloquence & general knowlege, gentle in his manners, warm in his affections; but unfortunately he has received a few rays of supernatural Light thro' a crack in his upper story . . . indeed my heart achs when I think of him". To Thelwall 17 Dec [1796]: *CL* I 286. Gilbert, a barrister, left Bristol for America in 1796. See Cottle *E Rec* I 62–9, II 325–46.

fluctuating as the other was peremptory. The Pyrrhonist ended his life as he began it, in infantine hesitation, founded on no principle, aiming at no point. The Stoic, despising the volatility of Childhood, assumed the obstinacy of Age. The Academic tempered the principles of the two Sects. Doubt impelled to activity, not enfeebled—Confidence invigorated, not chained down his mind. He wandered, but it was for information, and he rested where the occasions of Life demanded a stand. He rested as long as was necessary for the purposes of practical benevolence, but without presuming to say—My resting-place has absolute certainty for its foundation, and I shall never be removed from it. In the spirit of an *Academic* I mean to investigate the system of Commerce.

The expectation that mankind will ever possess perfect wisdom, or virtue, is universally allowed to be Utopian. It runs counter to the leading principle of Society, which

On mutual wants builds mutual happiness.[1]

If every man were perfectly wise, strong and active, he would never have occasion for his neighbour. Each individual would be a kingdom within himself—a God. How does the case differ with respect to nations? If each nation could fully supply its own wants, or rather, if its desires were bounded by its absolute *wants*, there would be an end to commerce. From these premises I mean to draw the following theorems. First, HAPPINESS is the natural object of every communication between man and man, and between nation and nation. Secondly, Commerce is always opened for the attainment of luxuries, not necessaries. Thirdly, Luxuries are *necessaries*. Luxuries I mean as a general term for every thing beyond the rudest food and cloathing; for all those wants which originate in the necessity of our intellectual though not of our animal nature. If we confine the wants of man to the wants of the mere animal, we unravel the web of society and brutalize our nature; if we go farther and stamp every thing beyond with the harsh name of Vice, we arraign the Providence of Creation and cynically quarrel with our own bliss. What I affirm of an individual will apply to a nation, which is made up of individuals.

HAPPINESS is the cause and object of commerce, as every individual is the best judge of his own wants, or in other words of what will contribute to his own happiness,* and as national commerce can

* A point I will not give up to Statesmen or Divines.

[1] Is Gilbert thinking of Pope's "But mutual wants this happiness increase"? *Essay on Man* Epistle IV line 55. It is interesting that C later wrote: "As mutual Love seems like to Happiness". *To Asra* line 3: *PW* (EHC) I 361.

only be carried on to supply the wants and promote the happiness of individuals, it follows, that every restraint laid upon commerce is a restraint laid upon our happiness. As the NATIONS with whom we trade have precisely the same views in commerce as ourselves; as they cannot fully accomplish those ends if we derive from them a greater advantage than we impart, as EQUALITY IS EQUITY; and as human nature (in *nations* at least) will not, cannot, patiently endure inequality—it follows, that every unequal, unrepayed advantage gained by commerce is a step to war. I infer that, that idol, the BALANCE OF TRADE is a source of *War*.

War and Commerce are the points between which nations must constantly waver: as we recede from commerce we approach to war; and as we emerge from war we ascend to commerce. Again, the narrow and foolish attempts respectively to derive unequal advantages from commerce is a fountain of blood. One nation tricks another into a treaty of commerce, which the other finds by experience to be unfavourable to its interest. It of course breaks the treaty; and then the first nation declares war against the second—determined to murder, because it has been detected in swindling!

Equality is Policy as well as Equity. If the BALANCE of TRADE were universally in our favor, we should die from repletion. The Muscles, which give action to Commerce, would lose their tone, and the whole system would sink into languor and relaxation. Regular Industry would be destroyed by the influx of Riches: for the multitude and greatness of Capitals would introduce a rage of speculation among our rich men, which would gradually produce the oppression and dependence of the Poor. Regular Industry is necessarily attended with labor, which they will not submit to, who can obtain wealth by other means. A Nation's health consists in the free exercise of its functions, inspiration and respiration.—But in the nature of things it is impossible that the Balance should be universally in our favour. We might as well think of draining all the Seas in the world into the English Channel, as to draw all the advantages of Trade into England. That Equality is the only solid, lasting basis on which mankind as Individuals or as Nations can communicate: or in other words, that reciprocity of advantage is the essence of Commerce, is a proposition which I have appeared to myself to prove. But the ground that will be taken is this:

If Commerce be left unreservedly open, young manufactories will be stifled, and our bullion drawn off.—And first against free commerce with nations that draw off our bullion.

The following *wise* prophecy, is extracted from a Treatise on Trade, published in 1745, and addressed to the House of Commons, at the request of several Members of which it was compiled by an eminent Merchant of Bristol.[1] The author, after attacking our East-India Trade, root and branch, as defensible upon no one ground of argument, and destructive to the nation upon EVERY *principle*, goes on, and says. "The East-Indies is a bottomless pit for our bullion, which can never circulate hither again; whereas, if it was sent to any part of Europe, there might be some hopes, by the balance of our trade, to bring it back again; and WHEN *our bullion fails, that Trade must cease of* COURSE, *which it will* SOON *do, if the Company continue to carry out yearly as much as our other Trades bring in.*"

This being an hypothetical proposition, is not directly attackable; however, the East-Indian Trade still exists, and still exists in the same mode. This passage puts me in mind of one of Mr Boswell's anecdotes:[2]—a complaining Irishman, (who said England annually drew a large proportion of cash from Ireland; and yet, that the Irish were without Manufactures, and in short, without any way of making money) being hard pressed by Dr. Johnson, to know where they got it to export to England, answered in a passion, that *it came out their blood and guts.*

I have only one short remark to make on a Trade that exports money: If the returns it brings are more than we can consume, we sell them and get cash again; if it only brings as much as we want, we have our money's worth for our money, which I apprehend, is making full as good use of it, as if we were to keep it, in order to supply the place of brick and stone. It is strange to recommend to a nation a miserly spirit, which we should despise in a man.

I am apt to think the East-India Trade has not exported yearly as much bullion as our other Trades have brought in—or, in other words, that the total balance of Trade has, *unfortunately* been in our favour. I say *unfortunately*, because the only *proof* we have of it (for

[1] John Cary *A Discourse on Trade, and Other Matters Relative to It* (1745) 47 (Gilbert's italics and small capitals). The publisher's Advertisement [pp xxi–xxiv] notes that this is a reprint of an earlier second edition published just before Cary died. See Cary *An Essay Towards Regulating the Trade, and Employing the Poor of This Kingdom* (1719) esp 46.

[2] *The Journal of a Tour to the Hebrides with Samuel Johnson, LL.D.*, 16 Aug 1773; see *Boswell's Life of Johnson together with Boswell's Journal of a Tour to the Hebrides and Johnson's Diary of a Journey into North Wales* ed George Birkbeck Hill revised L. F. Powell (6 vols Oxford 1934–50) v 44. The remark was made by George Faulkner, Dublin printer and bookseller.

I defy *calculation*) is an existing EVIL—the subject of general complaint, and serious investigation, and a favourite argument to prove—that *we* must *suffer* in the proposed open Commerce with France—I mean the present high price of labour and provisions. We may beat about the bush for causes as long as we please, but if there were not plenty of money, plenty of money COULD NOT be paid. *Ex nihilo nihil fit.*[1] The use of paper currency will be recurred to, as affording some reason for this high price; it is supposed to be a sort of extraneous, unwholesome wealth, that incumbers without invigorating, and raises the price of our manufactures beyond the due ratio it should bear to our Commerce. I fancy I see something, which induces me to suspend my assent to this motion though apparently rational, till I have given it further examination. One thing is clear, that *a* BANK NOTE *has every essential property of* MONEY *as fully as* GOLD *and* SILVER *except* FOREIGN *circulation*; and that is an inconvenience we cannot feel, till we have exported *all* our manufactures, cash, and our bullion; and then—if ever *then* comes, it will very probably be remedied, by foreigners making it money also; and if foreigners put money in our funds, their taking our paper is only taking—*security*.

It is possible for a nation, as well as for a man, to be blind to those circumstances in itself, which it easily discerns in others. If the constant introduction of Gold and Silver makes a nation flourish, what do we say to Spain? Not the merest Tyro in Commerce, but can tell us, its riches are its bane[2]—that they depress the spirit of industry—that, without supplying the wants of the inhabitants, they blunt the edge of enterprize, which would stimulate them to labour—that they manure, without fertilizing—that they settle like a wen upon the body, and instead of circulating through, and nourishing the system, attract to one spot the juices—and attract to destroy.

TO THE EDITOR

SIR,

THE following very interesting extract from "MARSHALL'S account of the Norfolk Husbandry,"[3] will shew the propriety and

[1] "From nothing nothing can be made", a proverb originating with the pre-Socratics; cf *King Lear* I i 89.

[2] A reminiscence of Milton *Paradise Lost* I lines 690–2.

[3] William Marshall *The Rural Economy of Norfolk . . . and the Present Practice of Husbandry in That County* (2nd ed 2 vols 1795) I 177–83, with many alterations and omissions.

patriotism of Mr. CURWEN'S motion for the repeal of the Game Laws in the clearest manner; and therefore I hope you will please to give it a place in your Miscellany.

Your's, F—D.[1]

"From what I have seen myself, and from what I have learned of those whom woeful experience has taught, I am led to believe that there are not less that ONE THOUSAND ACRES OF TURNIPS; ONE THOUSAND ACRES OF CLOVER; ONE THOUSAND ACRES OF BARLEY, and ONE THOUSAND ACRES OF WHEAT, ANNUALLY DESTROYED, or materially injured, in the county of Norfolk, by HARES and PHEASANTS. That is, I am clearly of opinion, that a quantity equal to one acre in one hundred acres of wheat; to one acre in two hundred of barley; and to more than one acre in an hundred acres of turnips: as also one acre in an hundred acres of clover, is wholly destroyed or irreparably injured by HARES and PHEASANTS.—I do not mean that a thousand acres of any of these crops can be picked out; but that there is, upon the whole, a destruction adequate to the produce, on a *par*, of a thousand acres.

	l. s. d.
1000 acres of wheat, worth on an average of crop and price, - - - - - - - - - - -	6000 0 0
1000 acres of barley, worth 4l. 10s. - - - - -	4500 0 0
1000 acres of clover and the consequential damages, -	5000 0 0
750 acres of turnips, and ditto, at 10l - - -	7500 0 0
	£.23,000 0 0

"If we view this inordinate quantity of Game in a moral light, its evil consequences of a private and public nature, are yet greater. There are in this county an hundred, perhaps five hundred men whose principal dependance is on poaching. The coal-trade and fisheries are not more certain nurseries of seamen, than covers for game, are nurseries of poachers. An excessive quantity of game is

[1] EHC makes the very probable surmise that "F—d" is William Frend (1757–1841), who during C's time at Cambridge was deprived of his fellowship for holding heretical views in politics and religion, with some of which he had indoctrinated C (*Studies* 20). Frend had strongly condemned the game laws in his *Peace and Union Recommended to the Associated Bodies of Republicans and Anti-Republicans* (2nd ed Cambridge 1793) 27–8, a tract for which he had been banished from the university. The same excerpt, with a similar preface, also appeared in the *CI* 2 Apr 1796.

not more certainly destructive of the crops they have access to, than it is inevitably productive of idleness and dishonesty among the labourers in the neighbourhood.

"For a while the poacher may go on in security; but his ways and haunts being at length discovered, he is taken; and if not killed in the scuffle with the Keepers, sent to gaol. Having lain here his wonted time, he sallies forth again, not only a more desperate poacher, but an incorrigible rogue fit for any thing. Having been two or three times taken, and imprisoned perhaps twelve months, and so habituated to sloth and idleness, that he cannot reverse his way of life; yet being too notorious to carry on his poaching trade any longer, his case becomes desperate, and if he is not fortunate enough to get among a gang a smugglers, he, of course, takes to housebreaking or to the highways, and from thence to the gallows.

"Nor is this the sum of the mischief—A Gentleman who preserves an inordinate quantity of game, is, in the nature of things, perpetually in hot water with the Yeomanry and minor Gentlemen in his neighbourhood.

"To say that the Game Laws are disgraceful to this country, would be only repeating what has been said an hundred times by the first characters in it; nevertheless they still remain an absurdity, a disgrace to English jurisprudence.

"The Legislature having lately thought fit to make rural diversions an object of taxation; it strikes me that game might be rendered a public and private good.—Wherever personal property is ascertained, there also let a private property in game take place; and let every proprietor great or small have a full right to any he can find upon his estate. But the moment he steps off his own land, whether with, or without permission, let him become liable to a fine provided he do not pay the annual sum of five guineas, or a greater sum, towards the support of the State.—Let this pecuniary licence qualify him to sport on Forests, Wastes, and undivided property without leave: as also to sport, with permission, over any man's private estate. But notwithstanding his qualification, let him, for starting game without permission, upon private property, with an intent to kill, be guilty of an act of Larceny, or Felony, and subjected to the usual penalties of the law for such offences."

REVIEW OF COUNT RUMFORD's ESSAYS[1]

These, Virtue, are thy triumphs, that adorn
Fitliest our nature, and bespeak us born
For loftiest action; not to gaze and run
From clime to clime; or batten in the sun,
Dragging a drony flight from flow'r to flow'r,
Like summer insects in a gaudy hour;
Nor yet o'er love-sick tales with fancy range,
And cry " *'Tis pitiful, 'tis passing strange!*"
But on life's varied views to look around,
And raise expiring sorrow from the ground:—
And he—who thus hath borne his part assign'd,
In the sad fellowship of human kind,
Or for a moment sooth'd the bitter pain
Of a poor brother—has not lived in vain![2]

IF in some hour, when fancy had overruled our severer reason, we could prevail on ourselves to adopt the doctrine of the transmigration of souls, in COUNT RUMFORD we might hail the auspicious re-appearance of our great Howard, his zeal the same, his genius superior, his sphere of action more enlarged. I must confess, my heart is not so completely emancipated from the tyranny of vulgar prejudices,[3] but that it experienced a proud delight when I found that Count RUMFORD was an ENGLISHMAN. The recent rejection of the Bill for the abolition of the Slave-trade, had well nigh cured me of this fond partiality.—The Countryman of Alfred, of Milton, and of

[1] A native of Massachusetts, Sir Benjamin Thompson (1753–1814), in the service (1784–95) of the elector of Bavaria, who created him Count Rumford of the Holy Roman Empire (from Rumford, New Hampshire), began publishing his *Essays, Political, Economical, and Philosophical* in 1796. Among his many projects for the public good was building fireplaces that would not smoke (General Tilney in *Northanger Abbey* "Rumfordized" his chimneys, and C suggested "Rumfordizing" a chimney to Poole [18 Dec 1796]: *CL* I 288). For additional evidence of C's interest in Rumford see his letter to Cottle 30 Apr 1796: *CL* I 206.

[2] These verses, attributed to C by DC and JDC, were found by Thomas Hutchinson in William Lisle Bowles *On Mr. Howard's Account of Lazarettos* lines 93–106 (var). *Athenaeum* No 3888 (3 May 1902) 563. Note C's references to John Howard (c 1726–90), the prison reformer, in the first paragraph following. In line 4 above, for "batten" Bowles reads "flutter", and in line 6 for "summer" Bowles reads "sickly".

[3] An ironic phrase, glancing at Godwin's contempt for the private affections. See above, pp 98–100.

Sydney,[1] I blushed for my birth-place, and imagined a kind of contamination in the name of Briton. But no! the title shall still be high in honour among the nations of the world—HOWARD and RUMFORD were both BRITONS.

In the year 1784, with his Majesty's permission, Count Rumford engaged himself in the service of the Elector Palatine, reigning Duke of Bavaria.[2] His first employment and that which suggested his subsequent operations, was to introduce "a new system of order, discipline, and economy"[3] among the troops of his Electoral Highness; and to render the military force even in time of Peace, subservient to the Public Good. To facilitate these important objects he found it necessary to make Soldiers Citizens, and Citizens Soldiers. The pay of the army was increased, their exercises simplified, and all restrictions on their liberty not absolutely necessary were abolished. The soldiers were permitted and encouraged to work at their former occupations; and in addition to the wages they might obtain from their private labor they received their pay in general undiminished. Soldiers, who were natives of the country, and who had families or friends to go to, or private concerns to take care of were allowed "to go home on furlough, and to remain absent from the regiment from one annual exercise to the other, that is to say, ten months and a half each year."[4] Schools were established in all the regiments for instructing the soldiers in reading, writing and arithmetic; and into these schools the children likewise of the neighbouring citizens and peasants were admitted gratis, and school-books, paper, pens and ink were furnished for them at the expence of government. The paper in fact cost nothing, as it was afterwards used for making cartridges. But the most extraordinary of these military arrangements and that which evinces the greatest genius, is the formation of military gardens, by means of which the army became a society for the improvement of agriculture. Each private and non-commissioned officer had a piece of ground alloted to him; seeds of all kinds were given him, and the produce was sacred to his own use. By these means potatoes and some other vegetables till then almost unknown have been made common in Bavaria: as the soldiers on their furloughs always carry with them potatoes and garden seeds. Such were the interior arrangements of the army: which was afterwards em-

[1] Algernon Sidney (1622–83), the Puritan republican who, seeking the overthrow of Charles II, became implicated in the Rye House Plot and was put to death for treason; he was one of C's lifelong heroes.

[2] Charles Theodore; see above, p 112 n 2.

[3] Rumford *Essays* I (1796) 5.

[4] Ibid I 9.

ployed in clearing the country of beggars, whose numbers, indolence, and shameless debauchery were alike incredible: the restoration of whom to happiness and virtue posterity will reckon among the miracles of the 18th century. Every friend of human nature will of course be eager to peruse these valuable essays; to neglect it would be indeed an act of criminal self-denial.* The first essay contains the account of the establishment of the poor at Munwick; the following

* As the most convincing proof of the truth of this assertion, we add the contents of the first essay.

CONTENTS OF THE FIRST ESSAY[1]

INTRODUCTION.—Situation of the Author in the Service of his most Serene Highness the ELECTOR PALATINE, Reigning Duke of BAVARIA.—Reasons which induced him to undertake to form an Establishment for the Relief of the Poor.—CHAP. I. Of the Prevalence of Mendicity in Bavaria at the time when the measures for putting an end to it were adopted.—CHAP. II. Various Preparations made for putting an End to Mendicity in Bavaria.—Cantonment of the Cavalry in the Country Towns and Villages.—Formation of the Committee placed at the Head of the Institution for the Poor at Munich.—The Funds of that Institution.—CHAP. III. Preparations made for giving Employment to the Poor.—Difficulties attending that Undertaking.—The Measures adopted completely successful.—The Poor reclaimed to Habits of useful Industry.—Description of the House of Industry at Munich.—CHAP. IV. An account of the taking up of the Beggars at Munich.—The Inhabitants are called upon for their Assistance.—General Subscription for the Relief and Support of the Poor.—All other public and private Collections for the Poor abolished.—CHAP. V. The different Kinds of Employment given to the Beggars upon their being assembled in the House of Industry.—Their great Awkwardness at first.—Their Docility, and their Progress in useful Industry.—The Manner in which they were treated.—The Manner in which they were fed.—The Precautions used to prevent Abuses in the Public Kitchen from which they were fed.—CHAP. VI. Apology for the Want of Method in treating the Subject under Consideration.—Of the various Means used for encouraging Industry among the Poor.—Of the internal Arrangement and the Government of the House of Industry.—Why called the Military Work-house.—Of the Manner in which the Business is carried on there.—Of the various Means used for preventing Frauds in carrying on the Business in the different Manufactures.—Of the flourishing State of those Manufactures.—CHAP. VII. A farther Account of the Poor who were brought together in the House of Industry:—And of the interesting Change which was produced in their Manners and Dispositions.—Various Proofs that the Means used for making them industrious, comfortable, and happy, were successful.—CHAP. VIII. Of the Means used for the Relief of those poor Persons who were not Beggars.

[1] Ibid[vii–x].

essays, which we shall review in our next number,[3] treat of the principles on which similar establishments might be commenced in the different countries of Europe.

The style of these essays is unaffectedly elegant, and the observations interwoven with the narrative, evidence profound reflection as well as expansive benevolence: ex. gr. the following extract.[4]

"Many humane and well-disposed persons are often withheld from giving alms, on account of the bad character of beggars in general; but this circumstance, though it ought undoubtedly to be taken into consideration in determining the mode of administering our charitable assistance, should certainly not prevent our interesting ourselves in the fate of these unhappy beings. On the contrary, it ought to be an additional incitement to us to relieve them;—for nothing is more certain, than that their crimes are very often the *effects*, not the *causes* of their misery; and when this is the case, by removing the cause, the effects will cease.

"Those who take pleasure in depreciating all the social virtues, have represented pity as a mere selfish passion; and there are some circumstances which appear to justify this opinion. It is certain, that the misfortunes of others affect us, not in proportion to their greatness, but in proportion to their nearness to ourselves; or to the chances that they may reach us in our turns. A rich man is infinitely more affected at the misfortune of his neighbour, who, by the

—Of the large Sums of Money distributed to the Poor in Alms.—Of the Means used for rendering those who received Alms industrious.—Of the general Utility of the House of Industry to the Poor, and the distressed of all Denominations.—Of Public Kitchens for feeding the Poor,[1] united with Establishments for giving them Employment, and of the great Advantages which would be derived from forming them in every Parish.[2]—Of the Manner in which the Poor of Munich are lodged.—CHAP. IX. Of the Means used for extending the Influence of the Institution for the Poor at Munich, to other Parts of Bavaria.—Of the Progress which some of the Improvements introduced at Munich are making in other Countries.

[1] One of Lamb's "rejected mottoes", *Count Rumford*, may have been influenced by a recollection of *The Watchman*:

I deal in Aliments fictitious,
And teaze the Poor with soups nutritious;
Of bones and flint I make dilution,
And belong to the National Institution.

LL I 294. Rumford founded the National (later Royal) Institution in 1799.

[2] See C's letter to Cottle 30 Apr 1796 proposing a series of pamphlets addressed to the inhabitants of Bristol, Manchester, and Birmingham in application of Rumford's plan. *CL* I 205–6.

[3] Not reviewed in No 6.

[4] Rumford *Essays* I 90, 91–2.

failure of a banker, with whom he had trusted the greater part of his fortune;—by an unlucky run at play, or by other losses, is reduced from a state of affluence, to the necessity of laying down his carriage; leaving the town; and retiring into the country upon a few hundreds a-year;—than by the total ruin of the industrious tradesman over the way, who is dragged to prison, and his numerous family of young and helpless children left to starve.

"But however selfish pity may be, *benevolence* certainly springs from a more noble origin. It is a good-natured, generous sentiment, which does not require being put to the torture in order to be stimulated to action. And it is this sentiment, not pity, or compassion, which I would wish to excite. Pity is always attended with pain; and if our sufferings at being witnesses of the distresses of others, sometimes force us to relieve them, we can neither have much merit, nor any lasting satisfaction, from such involuntary acts of charity; but the enjoyments which result from acts of genuine benevolence are as lasting as they are exquisitely delightful."

We are happy in being able to present our readers with the following admirable lines, written by Mr. CROWE, the public Orator of the University of Oxford:[1] they were intended to have been spoken by an Under-Graduate at the Installation of the Duke of Portland; but were rejected by the Vice-Chancellor, on account of the *too free* sentiments which they conveyed. Mr. CROWE is the Author of LEWESDON-HILL, a Poem.—Quod qui non legit, legat, Qui legit, relegat.[2]

IN evil hour, and with unhallow'd voice
Profaning the pure gift of poesy
Did he begin to sing, he first who sung

[1] See William Crowe (1745–1829) *Verses Intended to Have Been Spoken in the Theatre to the Duke of Portland, at His Installation as Chancellor of the University of Oxford, in the Year 1793: Lewesdon Hill, considerably enlarged with Other Poems* (1804) 58–61 (where it continues with sixteen additional lines). The poem had appeared, without Crowe's name, in the *European Magazine* XXVII (Jun 1795) 418–19. C's admiration for Crowe's poetry persisted (*BL*—1907—I 11), and Crowe liked C's poetry (Joseph Farington *The Farington Diary* ed James Greig—8 vols 1922–8—II 217). C had borrowed *Lewesdon Hill* from the Bristol Library 2–10 Mar 1795 (*Bristol LB* 119). Azariah Pinney in the winter of 1795 lent *Lewesdon Hill* to WW, who afterwards praised it. Mary Moorman *William Wordsworth: The Early Years* (Oxford 1957) 290. *WL* (*E*) 166n.

[2] "Whoever has not read it should read it; who has read it should read it again". C's own words?

Of arms and combats, and the proud array
Of warriors on the embattled plain and raised
The aspiring spirit to hopes of fair renown
By deeds of violence. For since that time
The imperious victor, oft unsatisfied
With bloody spoil and tyrannous conquest, dares
To challenge fame and honour; and too oft
The poet, bending low to lawless power,
Hath paid unseemly reverence, yea, and brought
Streams clearest of the Aonian fount, to wash
Blood-stain'd ambition. If the stroke of war
Fell certain on the guilty head, none else;
If they who make the cause might taste the effect,
And drink themselves the bitter cup they mix,
Then might the bard (though child of peace) delight
To twine fresh wreaths around the conqueror's brow,
Or haply strike his high toned harp to swell
The trumpet's martial sound, and bid them on,
Whom justice arms for vengeance: but alas!
That undistinguishing and deathful storm
Beats heaviest on the exposed Innocent;
And they that stir its fury, while it raves
Stand at safe distance; send their mandate forth
Unto the mortal Ministers that wait
To do their bidding—Ah! who then regards
The Widow's tears, the friendless Orphan's cry,
And Famine, and the ghastly train of woes
That follow at the dogged heels of war?
They in the pomp and pride of victory,
Rejoicing o'er the desolated Earth,[1]
As at an altar wet with human blood,
And flaming with the fire of cities burnt,
Sing their mad hymns of triumph, hymns to God
O'er the destruction of his gracious works!—
Hymns to the Father o'er his slaughter'd Sons!
Detested be their sword, abhorred their name,
And scorn'd the tongues that praise them.

[1] C had quoted lines 33–8 in *Conciones* (1795) 56.

FOREIGN INTELLIGENCE

STATE PAPERS

WARSAW, *Feb.* 17.[1] It is now more than six weeks since the King of Poland wrote a very affecting letter to the Empress of Russia, relative to the fate he had just experienced, and to that which was destined for him in future.[2] The reply was impatiently expected; it was late in coming, but is at length arrived. It is as consolatory, as in the present state of things, now that he is stripped of his dignity, and his country divided between the neighbouring powers, his POLISH MAJESTY could have expected. It states in substance, "that his MAJESTY'S title to the property of all his possessions in Warsaw shall not be disputed. That the EMPRESS approves of his design of proceeding to Carlsbadt in Bohemia, and to Baden near Vienna, to drink the waters at those places.—And that she does not oppose his future residence in Italy, that of Rome having been chosen in preference by the KING, as the most conformable to his love of the arts." The EMPRESS adds "that his POLISH MAJESTY shall never be divested of the sacred character of Royalty, and that she will do every thing in her power to give to his establishment, wherever he may fix it, the lustre it ought to maintain." With respect to the other objects, his POLISH MAJESTY touches on in his last and preceding letters, she makes known to him that, to come to a determination on these points, it is necessary that she should concert in the first instance with her allies.

FRANCE

ARMY OF THE COASTS OF THE OCEAN

Head Quarters at St. Brieux, 7 Ventose,
March 27.[3]

Litaux, General of Brigade, to the Chief of the Etat-Major, General of the Grand Division of the Army of the West.

"I HASTEN, Citizen General, to communicate to you intelligence of the most agreeable nature. Puissaye,[4] the very soul of the

[1] From the *Star* 21 Mar 1796.

[2] See above, p 113 and n 3. Stanislas had formerly been Catherine's lover.

[3] From *M Chron* 28 Mar 1796. (The *Star* 28 Mar gives the date as 26 Feb and the general's name as Vallitaux, whereas *The Times* 28 Mar gives Vallitaux but the date as 17 Mar.) 7 Ventose was 25 Feb. The brigade general is Jean-André Valletaux (1755–1811).

[4] Joseph-Geneviève, Comte de Puisaye (1755–1827), royalist general who commanded the Quiberon expedition (see below, p 292). He later became a naturalised Briton.

Chouan war, has made his ignominious exit.—He was yesterday shot in the Commune of Mediac, by a party selected from the flying column under the command of Captain Bal.—Subjoined you have a letter that was found on him when he was taken. He had received a number of wounds which were not healed, and which apparently would have accelerated his death, even under the care of the most skilful surgeons. It should appear that he had received some of these wounds in the skirmish at the Chateau of Berquigny, near Rennes, where three Chiefs of the Chouans were taken, and shot after a trial before the Military Council, and others, in the memorable defeat of the enemy at Quiberon.

"One of his Aides-de-Camp was shot by his side, and fifteen officers and soldiers, who composed his body guard. Capt. Bal assures me, that he will transmit to you a detailed account of this transaction.

"On the same day, at seven in the morning, the flying column, which I have just formed, and put under the command of Capt. Dupin, of the 104th regiment, had fallen in with a horde of Brigands in the forest Lorge. Fifteen of them bit the dust, and nine of their horses have fallen into our hands. It is peculiarly gratifying to reflect, that the rebels were routed without losing a single drop of Republican blood. Since the 8th of this month, no less than 50 Brigands have been killed by my little reconnoitring party."

CALAMBOUR.[1] The meaning of the jest of *La Boutique d'un Savatier a vendre*,[2] was this. On the occasion of the *Forced Loan*, a cobler wrote upon his stall—

"This shop to let. The stock consists of[3]

500 *Savattes.*
250 *Sabots.*
5 *Tirants.*

He will give the whole for *one Louis.*"

[1] From *M Chron* 28 Mar 1796.

[2] "A cobbler's shop for sale"—i.e. a place for botching, referring to the work of the committee that drew up the new Constitution of the Year III (1795) establishing the Directory.

[3] The stock consisted of

	Literally	*Figuratively*	*Application*
500 *savates*	old shoes	incompetents	Council of 500
250 *sabots*	wooden shoes	knaves or saboteurs	Council of Elders
5 *tirants*	straps	homophone for *tyrans*	The Directors
He will give the whole for			
one Louis	20-franc gold-piece	The Bourbons	Louis XVIII

MADAME DE LA FAYETTE[1]

(From a German work entitled, Reflections on the French Fugitives).

THE Journey of Madame De [La] Fayette to Vienna was mentioned in the Journals in the month of October last—The Emperor gave her a kind reception and permitted her to go to Olmutz to attend her husband and to soften his doom. She flew thither, and arrived with her two daughters, the one eighteen, the other sixteen years of age. They were all searched with the most scrupulous care, and then thrown into the dungeon where M. De La Fayette has been immured—and from that moment to the present, the fate of that unhappy man has been theirs.

On Monday March 28th,[2] Letters were received in London, announcing the safe arrival in the West-Indies, of several of the Transports which sailed with Admiral CHRISTIAN'S Fleet. Three hundred of these Troops that were landed at St. Vincents, enabled Colonel Hunter[3] to attack the French on the 21st and 22d of January, over whom he obtained a complete victory.

On Tuesday night intelligence was received of the surrender of the Dutch Settlement of Bavaria[4] to the British.

Reports have been received of a general Insurrection in Sardinia, and of alarming conspiracies against the Court in the Kingdom of Naples. A conspiracy at Abruzza was discovered, and the inhabitants of the village suffered military execution.[5]

[1] From *M Chron* or *Star* 29 Mar 1796 or *Gazetteer* or *Oracle* 30 Mar. The work, according to the first two papers, was Joseph Marchena *Quelques Réflexions sur les fugitifs français*, published in Germany. Lafayette in 1792, to escape the wrath of the Executive Council, crossed the border into Austria. The Austrians, instead of treating him honourably, kept him prisoner until 1797. In reprinting this C is underlining the shabbiness of the Coalition. See also comment on Lameth below, pp 329–30.

[2] This item from the *Star* 29 Mar 1796.

[3] Martin Hunter, later General Hunter (1757–1846).

[4] An error for "Batavia". Condensed from a report in the *Star* 30 Mar 1796.

[5] The Abruzzo conspiracy was reported in the *Star* 31 May 1796.

DOMESTIC INTELLIGENCE[1]

THE great speculation in the funds is the topic of general animadversion, and the reports concerning it are as various as they are contradictory. It is certainly unexampled in its magnitude, and its consequences to the country are afflicting beyond calculation. The set of men to whom the public eye points as its authors, deny all connection with it, and it is therefore, involved in inscrutable mystery.—In the mean time the persons who so successfully accomplished the forgery of *L'Eclair*,[2] are its loudest supporters, and of course no expedient will be spared to facilitate its march, that cunning unrestrained by principle can devise.

Whether it be the foreign click to whom Mr. PITT has delivered himself up, that has set it on foot, we know not, but if the French Directory were the authors, there could not be a scheme better calculated to injure the country.

For let us enquire how it operates. The Bank, seriously alarmed at the operation, and observing that between forty and fifty per cent. for money is now paid to carry on these bargains, for a time have resolved to narrow their discounts so as to withhold from all adventurers the means of feeding this fire with fresh fuel. In doing this they cannot always distinguish between the paper of fair traders, and the bills of speculation; and to such a point of distress is all commerce brought to, by new and unheard-of projects of finance which Mr. PITT has so unwarily countenanced, that all credit, all confidence, all intercourse, and almost all trade are extinguished.

Persons at a distance will hardly believe the circumstances which daily present themselves in the city of London. The Bills of the most eminent commercial houses in England are thrown out at the Bank, without the slightest scruple, and no apparent distinction is made, as to the line of merchandize in which the houses are engaged.—

[1] Verbatim from *M Chron* 28 Mar 1796, a leading-article.

[2] On 12 Feb 1796 a forged edition of the Paris newspaper *L'Eclair* appeared in London containing a false account of peace negotiations between the emperor of Austria and the French. Some speculators made a profit in the ensuing rise in the funds. On 10 Feb 1796 a copy of the forged *L'Eclair*, accompanied by a confirmatory note supposedly in the hand of Daniel Stuart, had been delivered to the *Telegraph* office, and its contents were printed in good faith. The detection of the forgery damaged the reputation and circulation of the newspaper, and George Robinson and other proprietors of the *Telegraph* brought suit against Stuart and John Fuller, proprietors of the *M Post*, the alleged forgers. At the trial, held on 3 Jul (see *M Chron* 4 Jul), the plaintiffs were awarded £100 damages.

Whether Brokers or Bankers, Manufacturers or Merchants, the quantity discounted in proportion to the quantity sent in is trifling beyond measure; it is almost ridiculous to say that they discount at all. One great house, for instance, had 1400l. discounted out of 36,000l. sent in; another had 150l. taken out of 8000l.!

One would imagine that if all other bills, in such a moment of scarcity as the present, were rejected, *Corn Bills* would be favoured, no such thing!—Though to encourage importation, the nation is to give the unheard-of bounty of twenty shillings per quarter, the best bills by which the importation may be forwarded, are indiscriminately thrown out.

Nay, the prizes of the Lottery, though they are national security, and have only three months to run, are not discountable. One of the 20,000l. prizes was offered in vain at the Bank, and one of the 5000l. after being *hawked* about, was cashed at a discount of 7 per Cent. which was paying at the rate of 28 per Cent. per annum for the money!

And yet to this dreadful state of the country, the Parliament and the People shut their eyes! can we flatter ourselves that the French are ignorant of this distress, or that they are so little acquainted with figures, as not to be able to take their advantage of it? It is by no means impossible that while our Ministers are assisting all the manœuvres of ruinous *agiotage* in France, they are playing the same game upon us. Certain it is, we repeat, that the manœuvres, originate with whom they may, could not be more fatally directed, if they came from the avowed enemies of the land.

In the mean time we plume ourselves on the *comparative* state of the finances of the two countries, as if the cases could admit of comparison. As well might a woman of reputation find an excuse for levity of behaviour by reference to the conduct of a demirep! The finances of France! They make no secret of their embarrassments. They have no affectation on the subject. In the face of open day they propose a *forced Loan*. They violate the foundations of all credit, and they triumph by the very ruin of regular supply. But what they do with impunity we dare not even look at. A single *faux pas* with us is bankruptcy; and it is in vain to conceal from ourselves the dilemma into which we are brought—when we can no longer find ways and means consistent with national faith, nor fly to irregular practices consistent with national safety.

COLONEL CAWTHORNE[1]

(The following is a more particular account of the Sentence upon COLONEL CAWTHORNE than we have been able to collect before:)[2]

Horse Guards, March 21.

THE Court assembled this day at one o'clock, for the purpose of passing sentence on Colonel JOHN FENTON CAWTHORNE, of the Royal Westminster Regiment of Middlesex Militia.

A certificate from Dr. REYNOLDS was read, stating that the Colonel was so much indisposed as to be unable to attend the Court.

The DEPUTY JUDGE ADVOCATE then said, that his Majesty, having ratified the sentence of the Court, had directed that it should be conveyed to Colonel CAWTHORNE in person; but owing to his indisposition, and in consideration of the long attendance of the Members, his Majesty had since judged it expedient to dispense with that intention.

The opinion and sentence of the Court upon the different charges, fourteen in number, were then read.

The following is an accurate copy of the first:

That the said Colonel Cawthorne received from the Receiver-General of the Land-Tax for the County of Middlesex, in the year 1793, when the said Regiment was ordered into actual service, the Guineas, by an Act of Parliament, passed in the 26th year of his present Majesty, entitled, "An Act for amending and reducing into one Act of Parliament the laws relating to the Militia in that part of Great Britain called England," directed to be paid by the said Receiver-General to the Captain or other commanding officer, of every Company of Militia so ordered out, for the use of every private Militia-man belonging to his Company, and for the use of every Recruit, whilst in actual service aforesaid, commonly called marching Guineas, and did withhold the said several Guineas so by him

[1] The peculation and the dishonourable discharge of John Fenton Cawthorne (1753–1831), MP for Lincoln, are reported at length because, as the *M Chron* put it, 24 Mar 1796, he was "one of the warmest adherents of Mr. PITT in the present War in defence of *Honour* and *Property*; and no Gentleman was so *loud* at the Theatres in his cry for *God save the King*". Unlike *The Watchman*, the pro-government *Times* 22 Mar found the proceedings "so tedious, that it was . . . impossible to give the continuation of them in this Paper".

[2] C's account is made up of two reports from the *Sun*, the middle section quoting the first charge from the issue of 24 Mar, the remainder from that of 22 Mar (a similar but slightly different report appeared in the *Star* 22 Mar).

received, or some part thereof from the respective Captains or other Officers commanding companies in the said regiment, whereby the said Captains, or other Officers commanding companies were prevented from laying out such money for the advantage of such respective Militiamen, according to the direction of the said Act; and which receipt of the said money for Marching Guineas, by Colonel Cawthorne, and the withholding of the same from the Captains of the Regiment, are in direct violation of the 101st Section of the said Militia Act; and a misapplication of monies with which Colonel Cawthorne was entrusted, for the payment of the Soldiers under his command, against the 4th Article of the 13th Section of the Articles of War; and also against the second Article of the 23d Section of the said Articles of War.

The other charges were generally of a similar nature. Upon twelve of the fourteen the Colonel had been found guilty.

The sentence was then pronounced, in substance as follows:

"That the said JOHN FENTON CAWTHORNE, having acted in a scandalous and infamous manner, unbecoming the character of an Officer and a Gentleman, is ordered TO BE CASHIERED, AND RENDERED UNWORTHY AND INCAPABLE OF SERVING HIS MAJESTY IN ANY MILITARY CAPACITY WHATEVER. And, for the purpose of making the example more striking, his MAJESTY has given orders *that the adjudication of the Court shall be read at the head of every Militia Regiment in the Kingdom.*"

The Court, which was extremely crowded, was immediately dissolved on the sentence being pronounced. Col. CAWTHORNE is Member of Parliament for the City of Lincoln.

[a]COLONEL O' KELLY has likewise been[b] CASHIERED, but not with that ignominy attending Col. CAWTHORNE'S sentence.[1]

The Limerick Gazette[2] mentions that the coach called the Telegraph, in going from Kidorrery[c] to town, took fire in consequence

[a-b] We understand that another Militia Officer is also to be
[c] Kidostrery

[1] Lieut-Col Andrew Dennis O'Kelly of the Westminster Regiment of the Middlesex Militia at his court-martial (22 Mar) was acquitted of all charges but one—that of diverting the regiment's coal to his own home—was fined £100, and was dismissed from His Majesty's service. Whereas the King had refused to interfere in the Cawthorne case, though pressed by Cawthorne's family and government friends, he remitted O'Kelly's fine and merely changed the officer's rank and station. In its original form (see textual note above), this item appeared in *The Times* 22 Mar, following a report of Cawthorne's trial.

[2] This item from the *Star* 30 Mar (it also appeared in slightly shorter form in *The Times* and *Sun*).

of the great friction of the wheels. There were in the coach a young gentleman of the name of O'Bulkley, who was going with his father to get his marriage licence at Limerick, the Reverend Mr. Kelly, and a drunken soldier on the outside. The fire having communicated to a cask of gunpowder carrying to Mr. Flyn, the grocer, it blew up with a tremendous explosion. The parties in the carriage were blown to pieces, but the soldier, who fell off the carriage a short time before, escaped with only the fracture of an arm. The remainder of the coach, in flames, was carried by the terrified horses through the streets of Limerick to the stables of the owner, which were set on fire; but the flames were happily extinguished thro' the activity of the militia and others.

EPIGRAM

On a late Marriage between an OLD MAID and French PETIT MAITRE.[1]

THO' Miss ——'s match is a subject of mirth,
She considered the matter full well,
And wisely preferred leading one ape on earth
To perhaps a whole dozen in hell.

EPIGRAM

On an AMOROUS DOCTOR[2]

FROM Rufa's eye sly Cupid shot his dart
And left it sticking in Sangrado's heart.
No quiet from that moment has he known,
And peaceful sleep has from his eyelid's flown.
And opium's force, and what is more, alack!
His own orations cannot bring it back.
In short, unless she pities his afflictions,
Despair will make him take his *own prescriptions*.

[1] This epigram, attributed to C in *PW* (EHC) II 952, was actually reprinted by him from the *Anthologia Hibernica* I (Apr 1793) 307, with minor changes—C substituted a dash for "Phlogiston", thus eliminating the pun. The author was John Brenan. For "leading apes in hell" see *Much Ado about Nothing* II i 43, *Taming of the Shrew* II i 34. C borrowed the *Anthologia Hibernica* from the Bristol Library 28 Mar–25 Apr 1796: *Bristol LB* 122.

[2] Another epigram by John Brenan from the *Anthologia Hibernica* I 307, though assigned to C in *PW* (EHC) II 952. Line 3 reads: "Nor from that moment has he quiet known". Dr Sangrado is in Le Sage's *Gil Blas*.

ANECDOTE[1]

A RESPECTABLE character, after having long figured away in the gay world at Paris, was at length compelled to live in an obscure retreat in that city, the victim of severe and unforeseen misfortunes. He was so indigent that he subsisted only on an allowance from the parish. Every week a quantity of bread was sent to him sufficient for his support, and yet at length he demanded more. On this the Curate sent for him. He went. "Do you live alone?" said the Curate. "With whom, Sir!" answered the unfortunate man, "is it possible I should live? I am desolate and abandoned by all the world.—You see that I am, since I thus solicit such charity." "But Sir!" continued the Curate, "if you live alone, why do you ask for more bread than is sufficient for yourself?" The other was quite disconcerted, and at last, with much hesitation, confessed that he had a DOG. The Curate startled, observing that he was only the distributor of the bread that belonged to the poor, and that it was absolutely necessary that he should dispose of his dog. Ah Sir! exclaimed the poor man and burst into tears, *and if I should lose my dog, who is there then to love me?*

We address the preceding Anecdote to the Advocates for the Dog-Tax.

We are happy to announce that on Monday last,[2] Corn fell thirteen Shillings per quarter.

The collectors of the HAIR-POWDER Duty in Yorkshire are so numerous, that the whole produce of the tax does not more than pay their salaries! Mr. Wilberforce, however, assures the Minister that they are all necessary till after the *General Election.*[3]

Not only Theatricals, but Oratorios of Sacred Music were last week[4] prohibited; and the inhabitants of the Capital, for the sake of *morality* and *edifying example*, confined their pleasures to the *tavern*, the *brothel*, and the *gaming house*.

An estimate has been made on the number of days in each year that the establishment of *Telegraphs* may be expected to be useful

[1] Adapted from *M Chron* 1 Apr 1796, a part of a letter from "C. F.". For the dog tax see below, pp 255–8.

[2] I.e. 28 Mar.

[3] From *M Chron* 28 Mar 1796.

[4] Holy Week. With this exception *The Watchman* allows Lent and Easter to pass unnoticed. Item from *M Chron* 28 Mar 1796, including italics.

in the gloomy atmosphere of England. An accurate observer says, that he thinks the signals may be seen twenty-five days in each year, provided that the first station be out of the *smoke of London*.[1]

Marquis Cornwallis[2] has resigned his office of Master General of the Ordnance.

The Court-Martial against Admiral CORNWALLIS[3] is to be undertaken by the Admiralty itself; and the serious charge is, *disobedience of orders*, and his return to port without necessity. This is the first trial by the Executive Government, without the intervention of a private prosecutor, since the case of Admiral BYNG.[4]

There is said to be a design in contemplation, to form a Committee of Merchants, to inquire into the causes of the present alarming scarcity of money, and of the measure adopted by the Bank of limiting the discounts. It has been hinted, with what truth we know not, that this committee is only preparatory to a grand confederacy of opposition to the Bank of England; and that even plans have been circulated for establishing a rival bank.[5]

A Gentleman lately arrived from Paris gives the following description of the garden of the Thuilleries:—"This celebrated spot, which was once planted with potatoes to supply the wants of the people, forms now a curious and correct map of the eighty-eight departments of the Republic; and also of Savoy, Jemappes, and the other conquered places united to France. This idea, which is most artfully conceived to flatter the vanity of the Parisians, is as beautifully executed. Each path marks the boundary of a department; every mountain is represented by an hillock; every forest by a thicket; and every river has its corresponding streamlet: Thus every Parisian

[1] From *M Chron* 28 Mar 1796, including italics. The telegraph system—adapted from a French invention—had been built (Feb 1796) between the Admiralty in London and Deal. A series of shutters in frames, at stations along the way, opened and shut in various combinations to relay messages. Four persons at each station read the signals with telescopes, then operated the shutters to send on the message. News could be flashed from Deal to London—e.g. of the sailing of the Dutch fleet—in a little more than five minutes. The problem, however, as the *M Mag* wrote (I 70), was that the telegraph could "only be worked in very fine and clear weather, with any utility".

[2] Charles, 2nd Earl (1762) and 1st Marquis (1792) Cornwallis (1738–1805), surrendered the royal forces at Yorktown 1781; governor-general of Bengal 1786–93 and viceroy of Ireland 1798–1801. As master-general of the ordnance he held cabinet rank. From *M Chron* 28 Mar 1796. The *Star*, which reported the resignation 29 Mar, admitted two days later that it had made a mistake.

[3] Brother of the above; see above, p 151 n 1. This item from the *Star* 28 Mar 1796.

[4] See above, p 153 and n 5.

[5] Above item condensed from *M Chron* 29 Mar 1796.

in his morning's walk can now review the whole of the Republic, and of her conquests."[1]

BIRMINGHAM, March 27. Jones and Binns[2] are at length admitted to bail. The Birmingham magistrates, waiting for instructions, kept them confined till Thursday last, when the Solicitor of the Treasury[3] arrived in Birmingham, and Binns was liberated. Jones was not liberated till Saturday, his sureties having been objected to. All their papers are lodged in the hands of the Government. The Delegates mean to seek redress by legal process.

A List of Republican Men of War engaged by the Squadron under the Command of Sir J. B. Warren, Bt. K. B.[4] on the 20th of March, 1796.

La Proserpine, Captain Dogier, Commodore, 44 guns, 18 pounders, 500 men, escaped.

L'Unite, Captain Durand, 40 guns, 18 pounders, 400 men, escaped.

Le Coquille, 40 guns, 18 pounders, 400 men, escaped.

La Tamise, Captain Pradiee, 32 guns, 12 pounders, 300 men, escaped.

L'Etoile, Captain Bertheliee, 30 guns, 12 pounders, 160 men, taken.

Le Cygnone, Captain Pilet, 22 guns, twelve pounders, 150 men, escaped.

La Mouche, brig, 10 guns, six pounders, 80 men, went off with the convoy, at the commencement of the action.

A List of Vessels taken, by the Squadron under the Command of Sir John Borlase Warren, Bart. K. B. on the 20th of March, 1796, being part of a Convoy belonging to the French Republic.

Ship, name unknown, 500 tons burthen, from Brest, bound to Nantes.

Brig, name unknown, 300 tons burthen, from Brest, bound to Rochfort.

[1] Above item from the *Star* 21 Mar 1796.

[2] See above, pp 127–30, 160–2, and below, 199–201. This item from *M Chron* or *Star* 28 Mar (with omissions).

[3] Joseph White; see below, p 200.

[4] Sir John Borlase Warren (1753–1822), Bt; commodore 1794 and later admiral. These official lists, which appeared in the *London Gazette*, were reprinted in most of the London papers—the following three lists, e.g., in *M Chron*, *The Times*, *Sun*, and *Star* 28 Mar 1796.

Brig, name unknown, 200 tons burthen, from Brest, bound to L'Orient.

Brig, name unknown, 150 tons burthen, from Brest, bound to L'Orient.

La Pomone, Falmouth, March 24, 1796.

An Account of Officers and Men killed and wounded on board the Squadron under the command of Sir John Borlase Warren, Bart. K. B. on the 20th of March, 1796, in an Engagement with a Squadron belonging to the French Republic.

La Pomone, none killed or wounded.

Artois, no return made.

Galatea, Mr. Evans, Midshipman, and 1 seaman, killed; Mr. Burke, Acting Lieutenant, and 5 seamen, wounded.

Anson, none killed or wounded.

La Pomone, Falmouth, March 24, 1796.

PROCEEDINGS IN THE BRITISH LEGISLATURE

HOUSE OF COMMONS

TUESDAY, *March* 22

MR. LECHMERE moved "That there be laid before the House an account of the quantity of Corn exported from Great Britain in the years 1776 and 1777, and the years 1794 and 1795, distinguishing each year, and the ports from whence the same was exported, and the quantities exported from each port." The motion was put and carried.

The CHANCELLOR of the EXCHEQUER then moved the order of the day, to take into immediate consideration the report of the committee on the Bill for allowing certain additional Duty on Legacies. The motion was opposed by Alderman NEWMAN[1] on the grounds, that such a tax would give an inquisitorial power to Government to examine the whole of an executor's accounts—an hardship entirely new in this country. There might be many circumstances which a man might very fairly as well as prudently wish to conceal even from his partner in trade; but by this bill every thing belonging to a man's private concerns would be liable to public exposure. He objected to the tax, likewise, as it would severely affect illegitimate children; and moved that instead of the word *immediate* be substituted "this

[1] Nathaniel Newnham (c 1741–1809), MP for Ludgershall.

day four months." Mr. Fox opposed the motion on nearly the same grounds as Alderman Newman, particularizing several cases in which such a tax would be impracticable, and several in which it would be heavily unjust. It might, he thought, endanger the commerce of the country. He was confident, that from a sense of his duty he should vote for the total rejection of the bill. He should now, however, only desire that this bill be delayed until the other bill for taxing landed property should be laid before the House. Mr. GREY spoke in support and elucidation of Alderman Newman's and of Mr. Fox's arguments. The ATTORNEY GENERAL replied.—He deemed the present bill a parliamentary solution of the inexplicable difficulties and perplexities of the former acts respecting legacies. He reviewed these acts—those which were passed in 1780, 1783, and 1789, and found them all defective, yet every one of them permitting the inspection of private concerns. So far indeed was this from being an hardship entirely new in this country, that, supposing none of these acts had passed, he should be glad to know how many cases there were in which an individual was *not* compellable by law to make a full disclosure of the state of his affairs:—He replied to other objections, each of which he proved to have originated in misapprehension of this Bill, or applicable to a variety of other Laws against which such objections had never been adduced. The CHANCELLOR of the EXCHEQUER spoke in favour of an immediate consideration of the Report—after which the House divided, for the original motion 46, for Alderman Newman's Amendment 16. The report was then read and agreed to, and the bill ordered to be read a third time on the Thursday following.

WEDNESDAY, *March* 23. The third reading of the Legacy [Bill] which stood for Thursday, was on the motion of Mr. Pitt, discharged and fixed for Monday the 4th of April next.

THURSDAY, *March* 24. The Caldon Canal Bill was discussed[1]—For the Bill 51—Against 63. Lost.

The House adjourned till Monday, 4th of April.

[1] For canal-building see below, pp 221–4.

*TO CAIUS GRACCHUS**

YOU have attacked me because I ventured to disapprove of Mr. Godwin's Works: I notice your attack because it affords me an opportunity of expressing more fully my sentiments respecting those principles.—I must not however wholly pass over the former part of your letter. The sentence "implicating them with party and calumniating opinions," is so inaccurately worded, that I must *guess* at your meaning. In my first Essay I stated that literary works were generally reviewed by personal friends or private enemies of the Authors. This I *know* to be fact; and does the Spirit of Meekness forbid us to tell the Truth? The passage in my Review of Mr. Burke's late pamphlet, you have wilfully misquoted: "with respect

* CAIUS GRACCHUS's Letter is reprinted from the *Bristol Gazette* of Thursday, March 24. It was *paid* for as an Advertisement, which is the reason that it was not answered in the same Paper.

Messrs. PRINTERS.

THE "WATCHMAN" having within these few weeks attracted the Notice of the Citizens of Bristol, through the Channel of your Paper I presume to make a few Comments on the Execution of that Work. In the first Number we observe the *Debut* of this Publication upon the political Theatre made with "professions of Meekness." The Author's bias being towards principles not men, will lead him to write in the "Spirit of Meekness." The first effects of this Spirit, are, an abuse of every existing Review, implicating them with party and calumniating opinions—fully convinced of the little prejudice he possesses, he becomes Reviewer, declaring that he will execute the Trust "without Compliment or Resentment." The first specimen of his Critical Abilities is exhibited on the brilliant Pamphlet of *Mr. Burke*—His "Spirit of Meekness" is evident when he says "when men of low and creeping faculties wish to depreciate Works of Genius, it is their fashion to sneer at them as meer Declamation;—this mode has been practised by some low minded Sophisters with respect to the Work in Question," and passing immediately from these characters to himself and his opinions of Mr. Burke, he becomes the herald of his own fame; and with his "ere I begin the task of blame" adds to the many Trophies he already enjoys in his own ideas. In a few Numbers we shall it is probable, see his

"*Exegi monumentum œre perennius*"[1]—announced.

In the Court and Hand-bill news, he wished to have displayed his wit; but, as he soars above vulgar prejudices the Humour is hid from the profane Eye.

Odi profanum vulgus.[2]

[1] Horace *Odes* 3.30.1. Tr C. E. Bennett (LCL 1947) 279: "I have finished a monument more lasting than bronze".

[2] Ibid 3.1. Tr Bennett 169: "I hate the uninitiate crowd".

to the work in question," is an addition of your own. That work in question I myself considered as mere declamation; and *therefore* deemed it woefully inferior to the former production of the venerable Fanatic.—In what manner I could add to my numerous *ideal* trophies by quoting a beautiful passage from the pages which I was reviewing, I am ignorant. Perhaps the spirit of vanity lurked in the use of the word "*I*" "ere *I* begin the task of blame." It is pleasant to observe with what absurd anxiety this little monosyllable is

---

His "Spirit of Meekness" is visible in the Note under the Poem—had it been a Verse of the *Æneid* of *Virgil*, or the *Iliad* of *Homer*, less pomp could not have been used. I leave the Public to judge of the "Meekness of Spirit," so evident in this. Inconsistency in the character of this Philosopher, seems a prominent feature. Thus in p. 19. does he say "how vile must that system be, which can reckon by anticipation among its certain enemies the Metaphysician, who employs the strength and subtlety of his Reason to investigate by what causes being acted upon, the human mind acts most worthily." The "Enquiry concerning Political Justice" by *Mr. Godwin*, except by the prejudiced, will be allowed to be a deep Metaphysical Work though abstruse, yet to those who are earnest enquirers after Truth sufficiently clear in its deductions from every argument. It is a Work, which, if many of the ideas are not new has concentered the whole mass of argument in a manner unequalled in the English Language—Therefore, do we class it among those productions who seek by their discussions to meliorate the condition of Man. In p. 98, we find a chapter entitled "Modern Patriotism" "sententious and prejudiced";—in this *Mr. Godwin's* Enquiry is considered as vicious, and improper in its tendency. The Philosopher has mentioned the Arguments of *Mr. Godwin* without giving the Reasons of or the Deductions drawn from them by that acute writer;—should he find himself competent let him take up the Gauntlet and defend in a regular train of Argument supported by Reason, the system which he conceives to be injured by the Work.—But the Difference would be too great—the one a cool Reasoner supporting his Doctrine with propriety, and waiting for the human mind to be more enlightened to prepare it for his theory,*—the other an Enthusiast supporting his Arguments by lofty Metaphors and high-toned Declamation.

Wishing that the "WATCHMAN" in future, may be conducted with less prejudice and greater liberality.

I remain, your's &c.
CAIUS GRACCHUS.

---

* *Observations on the two late Bills*[1] *by* "a Lover of Order" *are attributed to Mr. G. a Publication well worthy the Attention of every Party.*

[1] Godwin's anonymous pamphlet was entitled *Considerations on Lord Grenville's and Mr. Pitt's Bills* (1795).

avoided.[1] Sometimes "the present Writer" appears as its substitute; sometimes the modest Author adopts the style of Royalty, swelling and multiplying himself into "We"; and sometimes to escape the egotistic phrases of "in my opinion," or, as I think, he utters dogmas, and positively asserts—exempli gratia. "*It is* a work, which, &c." You deem me inconsistent, because, having written in praise of the Metaphysician, I afterwards appear to condemn the Essay on political Justice. Would an eulogist of medical men be inconsistent if he should write against venders of (what he deemed) poisons? Without even the formality of a "since" or a "for" or a "because," you make an unqualified assertion, that this Essay will be allowed by all, except the prejudiced, to be a deep, metaphysical work, though abstruse, &c. &c. Caius Gracchus must have been little accustomed to abstruse disquisitions, if he deem Mr. Godwin's work abstruse:— A chief (and certainly not a small) merit is its perspicuous and *popular* language. My chapter on modern patriotism is that which has irritated you. You condemn me as prejudiced—O this enlightened age! when it can be seriously charged against an Essayist, that he is prejudiced in favour of gratitude, conjugal fidelity, filial affection, and the belief of God and a hereafter!!

Of smart pretty Fellows in Bristol are numbers, some
Who so modish are grown, that they think plain sense cumbersome;
And lest they should seem to be queer or ridiculous,
They affect to believe neither God or *old Nicholas!*[2]

I do consider Mr. Godwin's Principles as vicious; and his book as a Pandar to Sensuality. Once I thought otherwise—nay, even addressed a complimentary sonnet to the Author, in the Morning Chronicle, of which I confess with much moral and poetical contrition, that the lines and the subject were equally bad.[3] I have since *studied* his work; and long before you had sent me your contemptuous challenge, had been preparing an examination of it, which will shortly appear in "the

[1] In the preface to *Poems* (1796), published two weeks later, C says much the same thing: *PW* (EHC) II 1136. Cf also *CN* I 62: "Poetry without egotism comparatively uninteresting—Mem. Write an Ode to *Meat & Drink*". Possibly he originally reflected on the subject because of some remarks by his friend T. F. Middleton in his periodical the *Country Spectator* (Gainsborough 1793) 15 (No 2, 16 Oct 1792).

[2] Another borrowing from the *Anthologia Hibernica* (I—Feb 1793—142), attributed to C in *PW* (EHC) II 952. It is the second stanza of a song by a Dr M'Donnell, slightly altered ("Bristol" for "Limerick", "plain sense" for "good sense", and the last line for "They affect not to value either God . . .").

[3] *PW* (EHC) I 86. C did not include the sonnet in any edition of his poems.

Watchman" in a series of Essays.[1] You deem me an *Enthusiast*—an Enthusiast, I presume, because I am not quite convinced with yourself and Mr. Godwin that mind will be omnipotent over matter, that a plough will go into the field and perform its labour without the presence of the Agriculturist, that man will be immortal in this life, and that Death is an act of the Will!!!—You conclude with wishing that the Watchman "for the future may be conducted with less prejudice and greater liberality:"—I ought to be considered in two characters—as the Editor of the Miscellany, and as a frequent Contributor. In the latter I contribute what I believe to be truth; let him who thinks it error, contribute likewise, that where the poison is, there the antidote may be. In my former, that is, as the Editor, I leave to the Public the business of canvassing the nature of the principles, and assume to myself the power of admitting or rejecting any communications according to my best judgment of their style and ingenuity. The Miscellany is open to all *ingenious* men whatever their opinions may be, whether they be the Disciples of Filmer, of Locke,[2] of Paley,[3] or of Godwin. One word more of "the spirit of

[1] Having announced this intention, C referred to it during 1796 no fewer than five times in his letters (*CL* I 213, 247, 253, 267, and 293) and in his notebook (*CN* I 174 [16] and [17]), but the work did not appear. In a marginal note to Godwin *Thoughts Occasioned by the Perusal of Dr. Parr's Spital Sermon* (1801) 8, on Godwin's report of the attacks on his philosophy in *Political Justice*, C wrote: "I remember few passages in ancient or modern Authors that contained more just philosophy in appropriate, chaste, & beautiful diction than the five following pages. They reflect equal Honor on Godwin's Head & Heart. Tho' I did it only in the Zenith of his Reputation, yet I feel remorse *ever* to have spoken unkindly of such a Man. S. T. C.". (C's annotated copy is now in the BM.) To Godwin himself, whom he came to know, C wrote [29 Mar 1811]: "Ere I had yet read or seen your works, I at Southey's recommendation wrote a Sonnet in praise of the author. When I had read them, religious bigotry, the but half-understanding your principles, and the *not* half-understanding my own, combined to render me a warm & boisterous Anti-Godwinist". *CL* III 315. See also F. E. L. Priestley's remark in his edition of *Political Justice*: "Every objection raised in the *Watchman* and the *Conciones ad populum* is answered by a modification or clarification in later editions". *An Enquiry Concerning Political Justice* (3 vols Toronto 1946) III 106. Godwin read *Conciones* on 26 and 28 Mar 1796 (ms diary); he makes no mention of *The Watchman*, but ordinarily he does not record the reading of periodicals.

[2] Sir Robert Filmer (d 1653), whose writings were much esteemed by the Royalists during the Restoration period and whose *Patriarcha* (1680) was attacked in *Two Treatises of Government* (1690) by John Locke (1632–1704), who argued against the divine right of kings and attempted to justify the Revolution of 1688.

[3] William Paley (1743–1805), archdeacon of Carlisle, published in 1785 his *Principles of Moral and Political Philosophy*, a compendium of orthodox thinking, immensely influential for decades as a standard textbook.

meekness." I meant by this profession to declare my intention of attacking things without expressing malignity to persons. I am young; and may occasionally write with the intemperance of a young man's zeal. Let me borrow an apology from the great and excellent Dr. Hartley, who of all men least needed it. "I can truly say, that my free and unreserved manner of speaking, has flowed from the sincerity and earnestness of my heart."[1] But I will not undertake to justify all that I have said. Some things may be too hasty and censorious; or however, be unbecoming my age and station. I heartily wish that I could have observed the true medium. For want of candour is not less an offence against the Gospel of Christ, than false shame and want of courage in his Cause.

S. T. COLERIDGE.

[1] Hartley *Observations on Man* (1791) I v.

THE WATCHMAN

No. VI. MONDAY, APRIL 11, 1796

Published by the Author, S. T. COLERIDGE, Bristol;
And by PARSONS, Paternoster-Row, London

THAT ALL MAY KNOW THE TRUTH;
AND THAT THE TRUTH MAY MAKE US FREE!

TO THE EDITOR OF THE WATCHMAN

SIR,

WILL you permit me to prophecy, that those political dramas (whether farcical or tragic let time determine) the Treason and Sedition Bills, the first representation of which on a country stage, I announced to you in my last,[1] will not only immortalize the renown of ministerial audacity, but will ensure to the subtle and inventive genius of the present Chancellor of the Exchequer, the loud curses of the rising generation.

I considered the intelligence I sent you in my last, as generally interesting, because, though in itself local and individual, yet, as being a history of the first operation of those laws so new to Englishmen, and so hostile to the Constitution, it seemed calculated to arrest the attention, and excite the curiosity, not only of the lovers of freedom, but of the abettors of tyranny. The former would watch with jealousy, and indignation, each stride towards despotism, and the latter, must feel some little anxiety to learn, how readily, or how reluctantly, the shoulders of free-*born* men, would stoop to the iron yoke of bondage, which their brave fathers, instead of wearing, would instantly have dashed in pieces.

To the sequel of the story, your readers are entitled, which I will comprize in as few words as possible.

The Birmingham Justices, liable, like Justices of other places, and of other times, to be lost in the confusion incident to narrow faculties, and profound ignorance, when taken out of the horse-mill round they had been accustomed to tread, were charitably assisted by the

[1] Above, pp 160–2; see also below, pp 266–8.

Cabinet, with the skill, and presence, of the Solicitor of the Treasury, Mr. White.

On Tuesday, March 22d, Binns and Jones were brought before their Worships and the Treasury Solicitor. It may not be amiss to observe, that with a prudence by no means common, the prisoners were conveyed in a coach with as much privacy as possible, and introduced by a back-way into the public-office. The front-door of the public-office was shut, and a gentleman who wished admittance,[1] was told by the constable, that the Magistrates had with them a gentleman from London, and had given positive orders to let nobody come in. After a negociation, during which the constable twice consulted his superiors, the spirited and persevering remonstrances of the gentleman, procured him admittance.

The prisoners, after some examination were informed, that their offence was bailable, and the bail required was, that each prisoner should himself be bound in the sum of 500l. and should find two persons to be bound in the sum of 100l. each. The Justices gave them from that day, Tuesday, till Thursday, to procure this bail.

On Thursday, Binns and Jones came at the appointed time provided as they thought with sufficient bail. Binns gave bail, such as was accepted, and thought the business concluded and himself at liberty.—But mark the tenderness and sagacity of the successors to SHALLOW and SILENCE.[2]—"Mr. Binns (said they) are you prepared to give bail for your other offence?" They seem with the aid of Mr. White's ingenuity, to have contrived to split the indictment in two, and by thus surprizing the delegates, obtain a pretence from the want of bail, to protract their confinement. Binns gave bail for the second indictment, and was set free. Jones was not so fortunate, and had to return to his prison till Saturday, when he gave bail for both offences, and regained his liberty.

You may judge how intimately conversant we in this town are, with the laws of our country, and how careful to administer justice in mercy, from this circumstance—When Bathurst was brought up, it appeared that the thief-taker at whose house he was confined, had made him sleep every night in fetters. Mr. White very properly expressed his surprise at this treatment, and said that it ought not to

[1] Possibly Francis Place (1771–1854), who was sent by the London Corresponding Society to conduct the defence of Binns and Jones. Graham Wallas *The Life of Francis Place* (1925) 26n.

[2] The justices of Birmingham appear perhaps to bear a little resemblance to those of Gloucestershire in the "vice of lying" (*2 Henry IV* III ii 326) and in disregarding the rights of those who come before them.

have been done. But Bathurst, though released from his chains, has not as yet been able to give bail, and therefore is still imprisoned.

The intellect, and science, of Justices of the Peace, have long been proverbial. Knowledge is necessary to the practice of virtue, as well as good intention. Had wisdom, and virtue, been the characteristics of magistrates, it might produce some good effect to remark, that the Justice who said to Mr. Binns after *that* gentleman had given bail, "take care how you come before us again, for when you do, we shall not behave to you so gently as we have done this time," did no honour to his benevolence: and he who called out to the same gentleman to take care how he *offended* a second time, would have confirmed (had the previous proof admitted confirmation) our belief concerning his knowledge of the rights of Englishmen, and the most common maxims of the law.

This cause, in the usual course, will come on to be tried at Warwick, the next assize. It will naturally excite general attention. And its trial will instruct us, how far twelve honest men will coincide in opinion with a corrupt cabinet, and inform us more distinctly than the parliamentary debates, how much of our long boasted liberty is gone.[1] Perhaps the symptoms, which will then discover themselves, will indicate the time when we must neither speak nor hear nor read nor publish about what has hitherto been conceived of importance for all to understand; or encourage us with the hope, that remembering our fathers and our children, Britons will rouse from their lethargy, and with united and irresistible voice demand of a feeble tottering administration the restitution of their rights, and the impeachment of those who have dared to violate them.

PHOCION

SONNET[2]

As when the huge Leviathan is seen
Torpid and slumb'ring 'midst his native ice,
The Seamen ply the oar with anxious mien,
Quick every eye, and noiseless every voice—

[1] On 9 Apr 1797 John Gale Jones was found guilty of making seditious utterances, and John Binns was acquitted 18 Aug 1797. In 1810 Jones was again imprisoned, this time for a libel on Lord Castlereagh. C, disturbed by the rumour that Jones was being maltreated, visited him, accompanied by Daniel Stuart, but found the rumour untrue. See *G Mag* NS 3 x (Aug 1838) 127.

[2] Authorship unknown.

And now the keen harpoon its entrance makes,
At first unfelt; till deeper grows the wound,
When lo! th' enormous animal awakes
And his broad tail spreads death and terror round.—
So when a Nation, cold and sluggish, lies,
Silent and slow, th' oppressor drives his steel,
At first the wound's unfelt; again he tries,
Deep sinks the shaft, and now the people feel;
Pierc'd to the quick, the TAIL soon mounts on high,
And Despots, Priests and Peers, in one proud ruin lie.

LIVERPOOL, *March* 30, 1796.

LINES

On Observing a Blossom on the First of February, 1796.[1]
Written near Sheffield

SWEET Flower! that peeping from thy russet stem,
Unfoldest timidly—for in strange sort
This dark, freeze-coated, hoarse, teeth-chattering Month
Hath borrow'd Zephyr's voice, and gaz'd upon thee
With blue voluptuous eye—alas poor Flower!
These are but flatteries of the faithless Year.
Perchance escap'd its unknown polar cave
Ev'n now the keen North-East is on its way.
Flower, that must perish! shall I liken thee
To some sweet girl of too, too rapid growth
Nipp'd by Consumption mid untimely charms?
Or to Bristowa's * Bard, the wond'rous boy!
An Amaranth, which Earth scarce seem'd to own,

* Chatterton.[2]

[1] *PW* (EHC) I 148–9 (var). This poem, first published here, was a product of the trip to secure subscribers to *The Watchman*; hence his presence "near Sheffield". It was reprinted in the Sheffield *Iris* 20 May. According to James Montgomery's note in his file copy of the paper, he mistakenly thought it originally appeared in the *Iris* (he was then imprisoned in Castle York). See John Holland and James Everett *Memoirs of the Life and Writings of James Montgomery* (7 vols 1854–6) I 261. Lamb wrote to C (c 31 May 1796): "That is a capital line in your 6th no.: 'This dark, frieze-coated, hoarse, teeth-chattering Month'—they are exactly such epithets as Burns would have stumbled on, whose poem on the ploughed up daisy you seem to have had in mind". *LL* I 9. (Line 3 is "freeze-coated" in *Watchman*, a variant not noted in *PW*—EHC—I 148.)

[2] C had already lamented the suicide of the poet Thomas Chatterton in 1770 at the age of seventeen, in his *Monody on the Death of Chatterton*, first written at school in 1790 and revised for publication in 1794. *PW* (EHC) I 13–15 and 125–31.

Blooming mid poverty's drear wintry waste,
Till Disappointment came and pelting Wrong
Beat it to earth? Or with indignant grief
Shall I compare thee to poor POLAND's hopes,
Bright flower of hope kill'd in the opening bud!
Farewell, sweet blossom! better fate be thine
And mock my boding! Dim similitudes
Weaving in moral strains, I've stolen one hour
From black anxiety that gnaws my heart
For her who droops far off on a sick bed:[1]
And the warm wooings of this sunny day
Tremble along my frame, and harmonize
Th' attemper'd brain, that ev'n the saddest thoughts
Mix with some sweet sensations, like harsh tunes
Play'd deftly on a soft-ton'd instrument.

S. T. C.

MR. EDITOR,

NINE out of ten read those publications alone which favor their own opinions; they read not to discover truth, but to flatter their sagacity for having discovered it, or to indulge their malignant feelings against those who differ from them. I was pleased therefore when I observed in your last Number a promise that your Miscellany should be open to all *ingenious* productions,[2] however opposite their tendency might be to your own private opinions. In confidence of your sincerity I transmit you the following Letter which was lately handed about in *Ireland*; but the advice, which it contains, is equally applicable to your democratic Readers in this country. I remain, Sir, your personal Well-wisher, although an admirer of Mr. Pitt and (what is vulgarly called) AN ARISTOCRAT.[3]

April 3, 1796.

[1] See C's letter to J. Edwards 12 Mar [1796]: ". . . Mrs Coleridge dangerously ill, and expected hourly to miscarry. Such has been my situation for this last fortnight—I have been obliged to take Laudanum almost every night". *CL* I 188.

[2] See above, p 197.

[3] For the letter below, C has again dipped into the *Anthologia Hibernica* (I—Feb 1793—101–2, an anonymous contribution). The ruse is transparent: C, having invited communications from persons of opposite opinions and having received no suitable ones, makes good the deficiency himself. The stratagem of the editor addressing a letter to himself C used again in *Biographia Literaria* ch 13: *BL* (1907) I 198–201; see a letter to Thomas Curtis [29 Apr 1817]: *CL* IV 728. In PML MS MA 1916 (f 1) C has a note to the printer: "Leave few lines for a head-note—".

My dear Mister Printer

Ime a very plane man, I hav no Lattin, and very littel English, though I can tauk Irish as faste as any man in Munster, except my weif, who to be sure can tauk me def; and afterwards tauk onn till Ime tired of hearing hur. But though Ime not book larn'd, yet Father Tedy O'Borke, who is a deep skollard, offten tells when Ime giving him a jorum of whiskey punch, that tho' Ime ignorant, yet I have a goode understanding. But if this be aule Blarny, and if I have no understanding at aule, this need nat hindor me from riting abaute pollyticks, becaise this is a thing that every bodie understands. But it is time for me to be aftur telling you what it is I mane. The society of United Irishmen are sartingly mity fine people; they can't but noe every thing, for they hav among um aule profissions, atturnies, and bruers, and steymakurs, and docturs, and grand jontlemen, who ware formerly parliament men, and if they wer able to by burroes, wud be the seme agen; and they hav likeweys among um, preests and prospiterion ministers, and atheists, and all the otheer religions in the kingdom. Now this Society tells us that the French revolution is the most charmin, vartuous, nobel biznisse that the world ever sawe, and that we aut to immitete it as faste as we can. But, on the other hand, there ere topping makers who swere that is the most abominable hellish worke that ever was done sense adam was cristened, and that, if we attempt any such thing, we shall distroy all Ireland, and what is worser, destroy ourselves. Now, by the vessment, these great people bodder me so, by their palauvering on both sides, that I don't know what to think of it, at all at all; and therefore I send you my own thauts upon the subject.—I thinks then that tenn years is littel enuff for giving the French Revolution a fare triel. If we find in the year 1800 that it has brout to the Frenchmen, riches and honor, and happyness, and all that, then, in the name of the bless virgin, let us aule drawe our spedes, and flauns, and shilellies, and hav a grand bodderation of our one. But iff we see that it has maid the Frenchmen poor, and infimous, and wicked, then lett us remane snugg and pasible, and content ourselvs with wolunteering, and singing trezion, and rankeing rebellion, jist to sho that we are brave Irish boys, but not come the joak any farthur. In the mane time, until that hapy yeer shal come, in which we may posibly hav the pleesure of cutting one anoders troats, let us be indistrous, and ern a grete dele of money, and seve more. For tho' England, to be shure, is not match for us, yet in case of a war with hur, we shood want some mony.

War is like lawshute; and I know, to my grief, what a lawshute is, for I was almost ruineted by ganing a cauze against a gossup of mine, that cheted me; butt the divel shal hav all my gossups, men, wimen, and childrin, befoar I go to law with one of um agen.—War requiers money as bad as a lawshute: without mony our generals, and cornits, and grany deers wood'nt fire; without mony our preests wood'nt prey us out of purgaturry, when we were kilt; nay, our drummors wood no moar rattle their sticks without mony than Counsillor O'Currin,[1] or Counsillor Arskine[2] wood rattle their tongues, without their hire. When we hav got mony, then will be the time to invaid England, take Lonnon, bring it hoam with us, and build it in Belfast. My deer countrymen, every one of you noes parfitly, that you are a wize nashon; herfoar, my sweet duils, take a fools advice, and be quiet.

I am deer Printer, your sarvent, to command till death.

PATRICK O'FLEHERTY.

Ballybooby, near Tripperary.[3]

THE WAR[4]

The following Remonstrance from the City of London, to the Throne, in 1775, during Mr. WILKES'S[5] Mayoralty, is highly deserving the attention of our readers at this eventful epoch; how far the sentiments it contains apply to the present *just* and *necessary*, as well as to the American war, we leave the Citizens of London to determine.

TO THE KING'S MOST EXCELLENT MAJESTY.

The humble Address, Remonstrance, and Petition, of the Lord Mayor, Aldermen, and Livery of the City of London, in Common-hall assembled.

[1] John Philpot Curran (1750–1817), member of the Irish Parliament and at this time a famous Whig defence attorney.

[2] The *Anthologia Hibernica* has "O'Driscoll" here. C presumably is making a broad, though certainly not hostile, joke on the name of Thomas Erskine, the eminent liberal barrister.

[3] Where the source reads "Tipperary" C joins in the Irish fun and supplies "Tripperary" (PML MS MA 1916 f 4). "Oggus the first, 1792", the last line of the original, has been struck through.

[4] From the *CI* 2 Apr 1796; the introductory paragraph and the first remonstrance, but not the second remonstrance, had been reprinted in *M Chron* 8 Feb 1796.

[5] John Wilkes (1727–97) was Lord Mayor in 1774. His contest with the Crown ("Wilkes and Liberty!") and his friendship for the colonies are remembered in many American place-names.

Most Gracious Sovereign,

WE, your Majesty's most faithful subjects, the Lord Mayor, Aldermen, and Livery, of the City of London, in Common-hall assembled, are compelled again to disturb your Majesty's repose with our complaints.

We have already expressed to your Majesty our abhorrence of the tyrannical measures pursued against our fellow-subjects in America, as well as of the men who secretly advise, and of the ministers who execute these measures. We desire to repeat again, that the power contended for, over the Colonies, under the specious name of dignity, is to all intents and purposes *despotism.* That the exercise of despotic power in any part of the empire, is inconsistent with the character and safety of this country. *As we would not suffer any man or body of men, to establish arbitrary power over us*, we cannot acquiesce in an attempt to force it upon any part of our fellow-subjects. We are persuaded that by the sacred unalterable rights of human nature, as well as by every principle of the Constitution, the *Americans* ought to enjoy peace, liberty and safety; that whatever power invades these rights, ought to be resisted: we hold such resistance, in vindication of their constitutional rights, to be their indispensible duty to God (from whom those rights are derived) to themselves, who cannot be safe and happy without them; to their posterity, who have a right to claim this inheritance at their hands, unviolated and unimpaired.

We have already remonstrated to your Majesty, that these measures were big with all the consequences which could alarm a free and commercial people; *a deep, and perhaps fatal wound to commerce, the ruin of manufactures, the diminution of the revenue, and consequent increase of taxes*; the alienation of the colonies; and the blood of your Majesty's subjects. Unhappily, Sire, the worst of these apprehensions is now realized in all its horror. We have seen, with equal dread and concern, a civil war commenced in America, by your Majesty's commander in chief. Will your Majesty be pleased to consider, what must be the situation of your people here, who, having nothing now to expect from *America*, but gazettes of blood, and mutual lists of their slaughtered fellow-subjects? Every moment's prosecution of this fatal war, may loosen irreparably the bonds of that connexion, on which the glory and safety of the *British* empire depend. If any thing could add to the alarm of these events, it is your Majesty's having declared your confidence in the wisdom of men, *a majority of whom are notoriously bribed to betray their constituents, and their country.* It is the misfortune of your Majesty, it is the misfortune and grief of your people, to have a grand council and a representative, under an undue and dangerous influence; an influence, which though procured by your ministers, is dangerous to your Majesty, by deceiving you, and to your people by betraying them. In such a situation your petitioners are bound to declare to your Majesty, that they cannot and will not sit unconcerned, *that they will exert themselves at every hazard, to bring those who have advised these measures to the iustice of this country*, and of the much injured colonies.

We have already signified our persuasion, that these evils originate in the secret advice of those, who are equally enemies to your Majesty's title, and to the rights of your people. Your petitioners are now compelled to say, *that your throne is surrounded by men avowedly inimical to those principles on which your Majesty possessed the Crown, and this people their liberties.* At a time of such difficulty and danger, public confidence is essential to your Majesty's repose, and to the preservation of your people. *Such confidence cannot be obtained by ministers and advisers, who want wisdom, and hold principles incompatible with freedom*; nor can any hope of relief be expected from a parliament, chosen under a national delusion, insidiously raised by misrepresentations, touching the true state of *America.*

Your petitioners therefore again beseech your Majesty, to dismiss your present ministers and advisers, from your person and your councils for ever, to dissolve a parliament, who, by various acts of cruelty and injustice, have manifested a spirit of persecution against our brethren in *America*, and given their sanction to Popery and arbitrary power; *to put your future confidence in ministers, whose known and unshaken attachment to the Constitution, joined to their wisdom and integrity, may enable your Majesty to settle this alarming dispute, upon the sure, honourable and lasting foundation of general liberty.*

The following is an extract from another Remonstrance presented afterwards by the same Persons.

"The forms of the Constitution, like those of Religion, were not established for the form's sake, but for the substance; and we call God and men to witness, that as we do not owe our Liberty to those nice and subtle distinctions, which places and pensions and lucrative employments have invented; so neither will we be deprived of it by them; but as it was gained by the stern virtue of our ancestors, by the virtue of their descendants it shall be preserved."

Where has the spirit of the Citizens of London since fled, and why do they not NOW address the Throne in similar language?[1]

FOREIGN AND DOMESTIC INTELLIGENCE

FRANCE

MILITARY REGULATIONS.—In this Number we have given an account of the resignation of Pichegru.[2] Moreau,[3] a General of some reputation, is to be his successor.—According to the best accounts, the French have collected a force of near 500,000 effective men beyond the Weipper, and in the vicinity of Dusseldorf.[4]

FACTIONS.—The towns in the South of France (if we may believe Jourdan of the Bouches du Rhine[5]) are all Jacobinized: in Paris, it is said, there are seven Newspapers the avowed advocates of Royalty. The following paragraph we extract from the SUN,[6] which after announcing the capture and Execution of CHARETTE, proceeds,

"But whilst Republican perfidy is thus triumphant on the left banks of the *Loire*, the Royal Standard is yet floating with resplendent glory on the right banks of that river, and is daily joined by new adherents to the French Monarchy. *Brittany* is full of insurgents; SCEPAUX'S[7] Army covers *Anjou*; FROTE[8] organizes with success the insurrection of *La Mayenne*, the Royalist Party is daily increasing in *Lower Normandy*; and, if we may believe accounts, the authenticity of which we have no reason to doubt, M. PRECY,[9] the defender of

[1] Pitt had cemented strong ties with the City, and the radicals of Wilkes's and Alderman John Sawbridge's day (1775) were now in the minority. A speaker at Fox's birthday dinner had contrasted the Londoners of Lord Mayor Beckford's time (1760's) with the present "slaves and sycophants". *M Chron* 26 Jan 1796.

[2] Jean-Charles Pichegru (1761–1804), French general who commanded the armies of the Rhine and the Moselle (1793–4), and the army of the north (1794), had resigned after his implication in a conspiracy to restore the Bourbons. For the account, see below, pp 213–14.

[3] Jean-Victor Moreau (1763–1813), French soldier of revolutionary and Napoleonic armies; commanded the armies of the Rhine and the Moselle (1796) upon the resignation of Pichegru.

[4] This sentence, including the misspelling of Weisser, from the *Star* 1 Apr 1796.

[5] André-Joseph Jourdan (d 1831), deputy for the department of the Bouches-du-Rhône, spoke in favour of liberty of the press and of worship.

[6] *Sun* 2 Apr 1796.

[7] Marie-Paul-Alexandre-César de Boisguignon de Scépeaux (1769–1821), a leader of the royalist insurrection.

[8] Marie-Pierre-Louis, Comte de Frotté (1766–1800), royalist leader in Normandy.

[9] Louis-François Perrin, Comte de Précy (1742–1820), royalist general.

Lyons, is at the head of a considerable Corps of malcontents in the narrow passes of the *Jura* Country. All these partial insurrections stand only in need of a more regular organization, and more concert among the Leaders. They are now better provided with arms, ammunition, and money, than before. In order to prevent treasons, and avoid the fate of *La Vendee*, they must be able to act offensively."

INTERNAL REGULATIONS.—The Bank, on which the Directory founded such great hopes, has not been established. The attempt to stifle the freedom of the Press has failed. All clubs, associations, and assemblies of Petitioners are suppressed.—The friends of two recent Acts of Parliament triumph in this measure of which we allow the policy and even justice; but before this concession is transferable to the same measures in England, our rights of suffrage ought to be equally enlarged with that of France, and the recurrence of popular elections equally frequent. The National Convention in their establishments of Hospitals for the Infirm and Aged, profess to pay the most religious attention to the sensibilities as well as the wants of those who are to be benefited by them.

FINANCES.—The National Convention have issued Mandats to the amount of 2,400 millions of Livres, or one hundred millions Sterling. These differ from Assignats in the following particulars: I. The Assignats rested on the whole landed property of the Nation, or general security; the Mandats on specific security. They are bottomed on so much *specified* Domain as is equivalent in value to the mass issued. A printed list of the Lands set apart for the Mandats, is sent to every part of the Republic: and every holder of Mandats may apply to the administrators of the departments established near the national domain, he wishes to purchase; and the purchase being compleated, the Mandats which he pays for it, are burned in his presence. The Lands are to be sold for 22 times their net rent. II. There was no law fixing precisely the relative value of Assignats to specie: hence the enormous excesses of stock-jobbing. The Mandats are to be taken at par with specie. This financial measure seems founded in wisdom; and we have little doubt that it will succeed, for a time at least.

POLITICAL VIEWS.—If the resignation of Pichegru originated in his having advised *pacific* measures, and the cession of the Netherlands, this would seem to prove a spirit of aggrandizement in the Government of France which, we fear, will prove fatal to French Liberty. The establishment of the Batavian Convention gives a strong probability to the opinion that the French Directory are determined to bound their Empire in the East, by the Ocean only; while the devastation of the Netherlands by the excessive contributions under which they have laid the Inhabitants, seems to vindicate a despair of being able to confound them with the French Territories.[1] —The French are urging the junction of the Spanish Fleets with their own—They conjure Spain to feel that England is only attempting to destroy the French Marine, in order to deprive her of the mines of Peru and Mexico; that the capture of Trinquemale, Batavia, and the Cape of Good Hope, tend to nothing less than to render Great-Britain mistress of the Commerce of Asia; that therefore it behoves the Spanish Nation to recover Gibraltar and Jamaica, and to unite herself with France and the Porte, in order to resume that preponderance which she ought to have in the Mediterranean and in Africa.[2]—But Peace is, beyond all doubt, a far more certain means of giving to France a superiority over the World, than any territorial acquisition, however vast. Peace would heal up her wounds, revive agriculture, manufactures and commerce; consolidate the government, and give it security, by lessening the number of those whom Hunger or Hope long delayed have driven into Royalty or Jacobinism. The juvenile ardour of a nascent Republic would carry her on, by a rapid progression, in a splendid career of various improvement; and a large increase of wealth and knowledge would render her capable of the greatest atchievements of war: if indeed in that progress towards the perfection of human nature, which is her favourite philosophical tenet, she should not attain so much wisdom as to be persuaded that national glory as well as felicity may be increased in a far superior degree by Peace than by the deeds of Blood.—In the natural course of events, the Netherlands would be united in some way or other, and by some means or other, with France; and her Empire bounded only by the Alps, the Pyrenees, the Rhine, and the Ocean, might form and execute grander designs than ever were formed and executed, or ever conceived by the greatest Emperors; designs not of political Ambition and Conquest; not of stupendous Pyramids; or mountains hewed into gigantic Statues; but miracles of Philosophy for the amelioration of Nature, and the general comfort of all that live!!

[1] Above sentence from "National Affairs" in *Eng R* XXVII (Mar 1796) 298.

[2] C took this sentence from the *Star* 31 Mar 1796, quoting "The Official Journal of the Executive Directory of France". The rest of the paragraph comes from *Eng R* XXVII (Mar 1796) 293–4, with C's changes (e.g. "force of arms" becomes "deeds of Blood").

AMERICAN STATES

The seat of Government and the offices annexed thereto, are to be removed to the Borough of Lancaster, until the permanent seat is fixed by a future legislature. In the Morning Chronicle of Jan. 28th, 1796, is the following paragraph.—"The magnificent city of Washington, in America, has already seven thousand houses built in a very handsome style; and they continue building in a very rapid manner." And Mr. Winterbottam in his history of America, Vol. II. p. 72, says, "*The city now makes a noble appearance*."[1] In opposition to these statements we quote a paragraph from a pamphlet recently published, entitled "Look before you leap;"[2] but by no means making ourselves responsible for the truth of its information. "The city of Washington, which is to be the seat of the American Legislature in the year 1800, does not at present contain forty brick houses, and these not half finished: the remainder are wooden houses of a very bad kind; and the five streets so pompously laid out in the maps are *avenues cut through the woods* with not a solitary house standing in either of them. This place is the mere whim of the president of the United States, and lies contiguous to his own estate. During his life it may out of compliment to him be carried on in a slow manner; but I am apprehensive (and that not without reason) as soon as he is

[1] William Winterbotham *An Historical, Geographical, Commercial, and Philosophical View of the American United States, and of the European Settlements in America and the West-Indies* (4 vols 1795) III 72. Winterbotham (1763–1829), a dissenting minister, preached two sermons on Wat Tyler and the French Revolution, was tried and convicted for sedition, and spent four years (1793–7) in Newgate Prison (where the above book was written). Southey visited him there, and it was through Winterbotham that *Wat Tyler* was published. At the trial in 1817 whereby Southey sought to claim copyright and suppress further publication, Winterbotham swore that Southey had given him the ms after the publisher J. Ridgway had refused it. Southey claimed he had sent it to Ridgway (then in Newgate) by Lovell; that after promising to publish it Ridgway refused to do so, and Southey thought no more about it. Winterbotham claimed not to be responsible for the publication—that two visitors who read the ms at his house copied it surreptitiously and published it.

[2] *Look Before You Leap; Seriously Addressed to Artizans . . . and Others, Who Are Desirous of Emigrating to America* (3rd ed 1796) 54–7 (var). C's quotation from *M Chron* is on p 55n, from Winterbotham on p 57n (for C's source, however, see subsequent note). *Look Before You Leap*, which pretended to be a collection of letters from artisans, etc, was written to discredit Winterbotham's book and to discourage the emigration of skilled workers. See *M Review* NS XXI (1796) 343: "We *have looked*, and by looking we think that we have detected a counterfeit . . .". The *M Review* 343–4 then proceeded to point out discrepancies, contradictions, and the unsuitably literary style of "common mechanics".

defunct, the city will also be the same. *There are not above* 150 *mechanics of all descriptions employed there at present*."[1]

It has been ever our opinion, that in England the people are better than the government; in America that the government is better than the people. The Americans are lovers of freedom because their ledgers furnish irrefragable arguments in favour of it; but the vital spirit and high internal feelings of liberty[2] they appear not to possess. In looking over some printed accounts of the affairs of religious societies in America, we were particularly struck with the following paragraph:

Extract from minutes of the Baptist Association held at Philadelphia, Oct. 6, 7, 8, 1795.[3]

"On application for assistance to build a Meeting House in Savannah Georgia, large enough to admit some hundreds of blacks in the galleries, we recommend to the churches to make subscriptions or collections for the above purposes, and to forward the amount to Mr. Ustich, which Mr U. is requested to convey by the first opportunity, together with a letter of condolence to the above *mentioned blacks* and our ardent wishes that Providence may interfere in their favor, *at least so far* that their masters may be moved to allow them the free enjoyment of public and private worship."

CHARETTE[4]

To have waged a War for three years, in the heart of a potent Military Nation, with resources almost *self-derived*; to have mocked

[1] Except the first sentence, this item comes from a review of the pamphlet in *Eng R* XXVII (Mar 1796) 235–6.

[2] Ratification of the Jay–Grenville Treaty in 1794 substituted for a previous alignment between the United States and France an Anglo-American one. From pro-French sources in England came censures such as this from the *New Annual Register* for 1796 (p 193): " . . . the negotiation [by the U.S.] for a treaty of commerce with England soon taught the French what . . . confidence was to be reposed in the benevolence of a government, the standard of whose attachment . . . was to be known only by that of its avarice".

[3] *Minutes of the Philadelphia Baptist Association, from* A.D. *1707, to* A.D. *1807* ed A. D. Gillette (Philadelphia 1851) 307 (C's italics). Ustich is Thomas Ustick (c 1753–1803), Baptist minister of Philadelphia.

[4] The first two paragraphs from *M Chron* 2 Apr 1796, the third paragraph from ibid 1 Apr, the fourth and fifth paragraphs from the leading-article of the same day. (The third and fourth paragraphs also appeared in the *Star* 1 Apr.) For a fuller and personal report on Charette, see below, pp 245–6; also pp 285–7. C probably devotes so much space to Charette because, as the *M Mag* wrote in its obituary of him (I—Apr 1796—249), he "was the last and only resource of the Vendeans. The chiefs that remain have little knowledge, and no importance".

all the efforts for so long a period, which wisdom could devise, or terror employ, shewed a genius worthy of Hannibal, and which the pen of a Cæsar should convey to posterity. We speak not now of principle.—The man is dead, though the hero lives; and we pay a willing tribute to gallantry and enthusiasm.

This event is certainly decisive of the War in La Vendee—a War on which Mr. Pitt so confidently reckoned to increase the "pressure" on the French Republic; and which, we are also free to add, was dreaded even more by its successive Rulers than all the combined efforts of their external enemies! It was in this Country the boast and the *resource* of Ministers and their agents. Were our Allies defeated at Fleurus—there was Charette, at the head of 100,000 men, to avenge it in La Vendee! Were we compelled to retreat with loss in any engagement—40,000 Republicans bit the dust in La Vendee! Thus was the public mind, if not *consoled*, at least *diverted*, from its immediate object.—The consolation and the diversion are now no more.

Another important event, is the death of CHARETTE. Entirely defeated by the Republican army—his troops dispersed and incapable of being rallied—himself closely pursued, CHARETTE assumed the dress of a peasant, with a hope of eluding the strict search that was making after him. He wandered for some time among the fields alone, and was at length discovered and pursued by a Republican patrole. His strength being at last exhausted, he sunk upon the ground, and was taken by two Grenadiers, who carried him on their shoulders to the next post, from whence he was conveyed to Angers. At Angers he was tried and sentenced to be shot. The sentence was immediately carried into execution. Every idea of there being any powerful body of rebels in La Vendee must now be relinquished, for, as a French paper well observes, "if there be any such a body, would the most renowned Chiefs of the rebels have been forced to conceal themselves, and to fly in disguise from place to place unattended and alone?"

After the death of Charette, the most important intelligence is the resignation of General PICHEGRU: this event seems to have taken place in the interval of which we have not the papers, and we are therefore unacquainted with the cause. Whatever it may be, it is highly important to the war; for, if we may trust to the report of this great man, made by the English and Germans, to whom he was opposed, he was as exemplary in his conduct as a humane and generous enemy, as he was consummate in military genius, in gallantry and in skill. He was the author of a new scheme of tactics, the value of which he demonstrated by success. When called to the command of a multitude of undisciplined boys, he found no one principle of an army upon which to act, except enthusiasm in the cause in which they were engaged; he seized upon this great passion and made it equal to all the rest; discipline, science, maturity, fell before it.—With enthusiasm only as his support, he attacked the veteran armies of Germany *in mass*, and to the astonishment of a surrounding world, *for thirty-three successive days*, he brought this unorganized multitude to the charge, disciplined them in the midst of actual fire, and moulded them into a regular army upon heaps of slain. He exhibited a new scene in the history of arms. To be repulsed was not to him a defeat—to have his squadrons broken was not to be put into disorder—and he was the first General who could so rally his men, that though driven back to-day, he returned to the field with the same alacrity to-morrow, and as the incessant drop pierces the stone, converted his series of defeats into the most brilliant conquest. Such was the splendid opening of his military character towards the close of 1793, when he took the command of the motley host of requisition men, to resist the impetuous inroad of General WURMSER, who had cut through the lines of Weissembourg, and penetrated almost to the capital of Alsace. The whole of his military career since that time has been equal to the promise of his outset. He recovered all that the treachery of General DUMOURIER[1] had lost, and accomplished even more than his bombast had promised, and while he drove the veteran armies of Europe from the plains of Cambray to the Weser before him, his course of victory was stained by no acts of violence—his reports to his country by no vain exultation.

Such is the General, who has retired from the command of their army! It is not unbecoming in an enemy to do justice to such talents, and when the passions which now blind mankind shall subside, and the characters of the present day come to be fairly estimated, such, we prophecy, will be the tribute paid to his name! We may therefore be allowed to say, that his retirement, if true, is a most important thing to the cause of the French, and of course to the cause of the Allies. It is very material indeed to the Germans, when they have no longer a CLERFAYE to lead them on, that they have no longer a PICHEGRU to oppose.

[1] Charles-François Dumouriez (1739–1823), French general under Louis XVI who at the outbreak of the Revolution became a Jacobin. He was denounced by the National Assembly after his defeat at Neerwinden (1793) and went over to the Austrians. See an "anecdote" about him, below, pp 355–6.

The present Ministers[1] have the singular good fortune of discovering, not by the brilliancy of their success, but by the uniformity of their misconduct, to what point confidence may be carried, and how far a nation will bear to be ruined by their profusion, and disgraced by their incapacity. At any other period than this, with any other sentiments than the people of this country now display, the fate of the West-India expedition would have produced a torrent of just indignation and complaint, which no Minister could have withstood. He would have been arraigned by the public voice, he would have been tried at the bar of public opinion, and he would have been compelled to come fairly upon his defence, and to vindicate his innocence, or he would have fallen. But now every fresh disaster is added with careless indifference to the mass of misfortunes which in their turn have in vain demanded the public regard and indignation. The defeat of an enterprize creates as little emotion as the change of the wind, and the Minister may determine upon another campaign that will devote thousands of human beings to destruction, with as little opposition as would be given to a Canal or Inclosure Bill.

Of late[2] a practice is creeping into the House of Commons which entrenches on its established rules, and of which its independent Members ought to be jealous: it is an endeavour on the part of Ministers to consider every office which has any mixture of military duty in it, as an office purely military, and that therefore it does not vacate the seat in Parliament. This was attempted in the case of Sir GILBERT ELLIOT,[3] and no writ was issued until the question was agitated by the Opposition; and the same thing is now done on the appointment of Lord HOOD.[4] We are told that the Governorship of Greenwich Hospital is entirely military, though a very considerable civil trust belongs to the office; and certainly it was usual to vacate the seats of Members, as may be seen by the following precedents:

"Admiral Aylmer, Member for Dover, vacated his seat, being appointed Master of Greenwich Hospital, and a new writ issued on the 20th March, 1717.

"Sir John Jennings, Knight, Member for Rochester, vacated his seat on the same appointment, and a new writ issued the 8th December, 1720."[5]

[1] This paragraph from *M Chron* 1 Apr 1796.

[2] Another item from the same issue.

[3] Sir Gilbert Elliot (1751–1814), later 1st Earl of Minto. See also below, p 373.

[4] Samuel Hood, 1st Viscount (1724–1816), admiral; he held the post of governor of Greenwich Hospital till his death.

[5] Matthew, Lord Aylmer (d 1720), admiral, was succeeded as governor of

On Thursday[1] the STADTHOLDER and his suite, in ten heavy carriages, set off from this country for the Continent. His departure gives rise to a variety of speculations, which, as it is impossible for us to fathom, it is idle to state. It is not improbable that he considers the conduct of England in regard to the foreign Colonies of the United States, as at least suspicious, since instead of being taken, as the ships of the late King of France were at Toulon, *in trust* for his Serene Highness, the surrender has been made without qualification to his Majesty; and perhaps he may, therefore, consider himself as abandoned to his fate.[2]

On Thursday[3] Government began issuing their new Exchequer Bills, issued on the Vote of Credit lately passed, and with which they are to pay off a part of the Army Arrears. A small part of them was issued to the Army Clothiers; and yesterday, to the pretended surprise of Ministers, they bore a discount of 4l. 10s. per cent. What they will fall to, when the whole are issued, it is impossible to foresee. It is such a lesson to Government as, we trust, will be useful; for it is such a sign of an exhausted Country as England, never before exhibited.

Let it be considered, that this is a new order of Exchequer Bills, and that they bear 5 per cent; the ordinary Bills bear only 3d. per day, which is 4l. 11s. 3d. per cent. per annum: and yet, before 200,000l, of them are issued, they fall to this enormous discount.

Surely, it cannot be the design of Ministers to issue these Bills to the National Creditor at par, when they see that they bear this discount. It would be a kind of composition with our Creditors, inconsistent with National faith; for, in the first place, the services now to be discharged have been performed, and the money expended for the use of Government more than 18 months ago: and the Public Creditor has been in advance all that time. The fair interest of his money for that time is 7l. 10s. per cent; and, if he is to receive a Bill for every 100l. which is worth but 95l. 10s.—he is in truth paid 12l. per cent. short of his Debt.

A Correspondent[4] writes that at Birmingham, a man has just been

Greenwich Hospital by Sir John Jennings (1664–1743), also an admiral.

[1] This item from *M Chron* 2 Apr 1796.

[2] British commanders had captured the Dutch colonies of Ceylon, Malacca, the Moluccas, and the Cape of Good Hope in 1795, and in the spring of 1796 the West Indian colonies of Demerara, Essequibo, and Berbice. Except for Ceylon, the Dutch colonies were returned in 1802, under the Treaty of Amiens.

[3] This paragraph and the following two from *M Chron* 2 Apr 1796.

[4] The Rev J. Edwards?

taken up for Sedition: The charge against him is, that being at a public-house, he heard it said that the King had been shot at by some person, but that the man missed him—then said the fellow "he must have been a damn'd bad marksman." The Barrister who may chance to be employed in defence of this poor fellow, will surely find it easy to prove the speech a *libel* upon the man that *shot*; instead of *Sedition* against the great Personage *shot at*; and he may quote by way of precedent, Lonsdale versus Peter Pindar, for likening the Lord to the Devil.[1]—Mr. Erskine remarked that the action for libel should have come from another quarter—that the Poet had complimented his Lordship, but that the Devil might certainly bring his action for damages, could he but come into the Court with clean hands.

On Tuesday, April 5,[2] a Committee of Gentlemen met at the London Tavern, to consider the distressed state of public credit, (viz.)

Sir STEPHEN LUSHINGTON, Chairman.

Mr. Alderman Anderson,	Mr. Boyd,
Mr. Alderman Lushington,	Mr. Inglis, and
Sir James Saunderson,	Mr. Angerstein.[3]

The subject of the deliberations, and the report of the Committee not being yet in a state of maturity as to be fit for publication, we are only permitted at present to state the general result of the proposition

[1] Peter Pindar (John Wolcot) *A Commiserating Epistle to James Lowther, Earl of Lonsdale* (1791). Lord Lonsdale was the "bad Earl" who humiliated Boswell and wronged the Wordsworths. Wolcot had attacked Lonsdale for his tyranny over his Cumberland tenants and for closing his mines. See M. D. George *Catalogue of Political and Personal Satires . . . in the British Museum* VI (1938) 951–2. An application was made to the court of the king's bench for a criminal information against the printer of the *Oracle* for publishing an item: "The painters are much perplexed about the likeness of the Devil. To obviate this difficulty concerning His Infernal Majesty, PETER PINDAR has recommended to his friend OPIE the countenance of LORD LONSDALE". Erskine argued the case before Lord Kenyon. See Lord Campbell *Lives of the Chief Justices* (1873) IV 81–3.

[2] This report from the *Star* or *The Times* 6 Apr 1796.

[3] Sir Stephen Lushington, Bt (1744–1807), MP for Helston and a director of the East India Company. Sir John William Anderson (c 1736–1813), MP for London and alderman of the City of London. William Lushington (1747–1823), MP for London and alderman for Billingsgate. Sir James Sanderson, Bt (1741–98), MP for Malmesbury and alderman of the City of London. For Boyd, see above, p 56 n 4. Probably Sir Hugh Inglis, Bt (c 1744–1820), a director of the East India Company. John Julius Angerstein (1735–1823), financier and merchant and amateur of fine art, whose pictures formed the nucleus at its founding of the National Gallery.

which was yesterday submitted to Mr. Pitt on the part of the Committee, who were with the Minister near an hour and a half. In consequence of the extended trade of the country, and the narrowed circulation of the Bank paper, every mercantile man has lately felt the greatest inconvenience in carrying on his business, on account of the limitation which the Bank has prescribed to itself in discounting bills. To remedy this inconvenience, the Committee have generally proposed, that a paper currency should be issued for a limited time, not exceeding one year, under the sanction of Parliament, and under the controul of twenty-five Commissioners, towards the aid of public credit; and that this paper, so issued, should be either payable at sight (to do which a fund should be raised) or bear an interest, as suited to the holder.

This proposition produced a long conversation on the general state of public credit, which being confidential, it would be extremely indelicate even to hint at. We can therefore only say generally, that Mr. Pitt gave the Committee the most cordial reception, that he conducted himself with the greatest frankness, and promised to give the matter the most early consideration.

On Saturday, April 1st, the Play of Vortigern and Rowena, attributed to Shakespear, crouded Drury Lane.[1] The two first lines of the Prologue drew down a thunder of applause:—

> No common cause your verdict now demands,
> Before the court immortal Shakespear stands!

The two first Acts of the Play were heard with much patience and long-suffering; the three last Acts were received with loud laughter, intermingled with cries of indignation at the palpable and gross forgery. In theatrical phrase, it was completely DAMNED!!

Three Hamburgh Mails[2] arrived on Monday, April 4th. With respect to Peace or War, the Letters and Journals leave us in the same state of uncertainty as before. While we are assured by some that the Armistice between France and Austria had been prolonged by a formal Convention; others say, on the contrary, that Hostilities will re-commence in a few days. The Court of Berlin continues to exert all its influence in negociating a general Peace.

[1] See above, pp 93 n 1, 95, 96. The play was actually given Saturday 2 Apr, although originally scheduled for April Fool's Day. It was the first and only performance.

[2] With the French, Dutch, and Spanish ports closed to British ships, communication with the Continent was by way of Hamburg.

The Dutch Fleet are not destined for the Cape of Good Hope, as was surmised; but are about to join a Fleet in Brest.[1]

GREAT-BRITAIN

WAR REGULATIONS.—These are chiefly confined to our Naval power; which ought indeed to have been the plan of operation from the commencement of this disastrous contest. The number of three-decked vessels has been very much increased, and the new vessels of almost every rate, constructed on a much larger scale than formerly. Two new classes of Ships have been added to our Navy, that of eighty-gun ships on two decks, and that of large and powerful frigates carrying eighteen or twenty-four pounders upon their main decks. A number of fine ships have been transferred too from the Navy of our Enemies. We are sorry that truth obliges us to place in counter-balance to this statement of our Navy, the following interesting facts, quoted from "Letters written in France to a Friend in London, by Major Tench of the Marines," [2] and recently published.

"In the little time I have been in my new situation, nothing has surprized me more than in the quantity of English articles I every where observe. The Cheese, as I said before, was GLOUCESTER, the Plates it was served upon were STAFFORD, and the Knives it was cut by were SHEFFIELD; while the Coats, Hats, and Shoes of those that were eating it, were also chiefly of British Manufacture. To our enquiries where they obtained them, PRIZE, PRIZE, was the constant answer. Surely what one of their Officers told me cannot be true!!—Seeing me just now looking up one of the arms which help to form this capacious Port, (Brest) and which was crouded with shipping, he assured me that THEY WERE ALL ENGLISH, AND NOT LESS THAN FOUR HUNDRED IN NUMBER. It is too well ascertained that the French have been during the present War, wonderfully successful against our Trading Vessels. Their Frigates, I am informed, cruize in small detached squadrons to the Westward of Europe, while we confine ours almost totally to the Channels, which I presume to consider a very injudicious disposition of them, in a war where the Enemy have no privateers, and when consequently the little ports on the French Coast, within Ushant, should be less

[1] A Dutch fleet did sail to the Cape of Good Hope; it surrendered to Elphinstone at Saldanha Bay 16–17 Aug 1796. Item condensed from the *Star* 4 Apr 1796.

[2] [Watkin] Tench *Letters Written in France . . . 1794 . . . 1795* (1796) 22–3 (var). C may have found this extract in *Eng R* XXVII (Mar 1796) 248, a review of the work.

objects of our jealousy than heretofore. Provided our grand Fleet can, after a parade off Brest, return into Spithead or Torbay, we seem to be satisfied and conclude that all is going on well on the Waters."

COLONIES.—The Ships with troops on board, that parted from Admiral Christian's Fleet five weeks ago, have arrived safely and turned the tide of Fortune in St. Vincents.[1]—We however consider the fate of these guilty Islands, as extremely precarious; and the most watchful efforts are found necessary to prevent Tippoo Saib[2] from forming an immediate *Alliance* with the French in the East-Indies.

FINANCES.—On this intricate subject, Mr Morgan, the Nephew of Dr. Price,[3] has written a pamphlet, entitled FACTS—which, we presume, the larger number of our Readers have seen. An Answer has appeared on part of Government by Mr. Vansittart,[4] who appears to have detected some inaccuracies in Mr. Morgan's calculations; and to prove that the writer of the FACTS has totally overlooked *two* very important facts, namely, the prodigious increase of the price of provisions, and the vast disproportion of *effort* between this and the four last years of the American War. But however the dishonourable transaction of Hamburgh bills, the emission of assignats under the name of Exchequer bills, and the refusal on the part of the Bank of England to *discount*, are *proofs* of imprudent financiering too powerful to be *overturned* by calculations.

TRADE, COMMERCE.—Our commercial prosperity at present seems great. We enjoy the largest share by far of the European and

[1] In Nov 1795 Christian was appointed commander-in-chief of the West Indies and put to sea with a convoy of merchant ships and troop transports (see above, p 43); after shipwreck, storm, and three attempts, he finally sailed for the West Indies 20 Mar. Some of the ships survived the second attempt, however, and reached the West Indies. Item from the *Eng R* XXVII (Mar 1796) 299 (correctly reading "five months" for C's "five weeks").

[2] Tipu (or Tippoo) Sahib (1751–99), sultan of Mysore 1782–99, who had fought two wars against the British and was killed in a third while defending his capital. From a report in the *Star* 31 Mar 1796.

[3] Richard Price (1723–91), nonconformist minister and writer whose sermon at the Old Jewry in approbation of the French Revolution helped to provoke Burke's *Reflections*. His nephew was William Morgan (1750–1833), chief actuary to the Equitable Assurance Society, author of *Facts Addressed to the Serious Attention of the People of Great Britain, Respecting the Expence of the War and the State of the National Debt*, which went through four editions in 1796, and *Additional Facts . . .*, which also went through four editions that year.

[4] Nicholas Vansittart *An Inquiry into the State of the Finances of Great Britain; in Answer to Mr. Morgan's Facts . . .* (1796). Vansittart (1766–1851) was elected to Parliament that year, became chancellor of the exchequer 1812, and was created Baron Bexley 1823. See below, p 327 n 4.

American trade, and the whole of that of both the East and West-Indies.[1] Whether the influx of specie from this source is commensurate with the liberality of our minister, as grand subsidizer of beggarly potentates, we know not. But let us even suppose this immense influx undiminished by any foreign demands, is it favourable to general happiness? It diminishes the *value* of money, of itself: and the wages of the field-labourer do not rise in proportion. Journeymen manufacturers act in combination, and (although illegally) *can* and *do* force their masters to terms of composition: this is not practicable in the country. The consequence therefore is, that the poor in the country fly to towns whenever they can seize the opportunity! The most loathsome vices, and diseases are the natural consequences; and prepare the way for that greatest of evils, a revolution begotten by an unprincipled and extravagant government on a miserable, ignorant, and wicked people.

CANALS and WASTE-LANDS.— Among the more pleasing prospects, which the state of our country presents, we may mention the multiplying of CANALS.[2] The passion for Canals, which has lately risen to a degree of enthusiasm, appears by no means irrational. They may be considered as so many roads on which one horse will draw as much as thirty do on the ordinary turn-pike roads. They collect the dispersed materials for manufactures, and supply these, as well as all the necessaries of life at the cheapest rate. Canals are the great veins that carry on the circulation of internal trade, and replenish the reservoirs of external commerce.

Besides the canals already begun, others, of great magnitude as well as utility, are planned and agreed on, as the completion of the grand combination of canals, that shall unite the three great rivers of England, the Humber, the Severn, and the Thames; and others, both in England and Scotland, are in contemplation.

It is infinitely to be regretted, and it is undoubtedly a reproach to government, that a canal has not been made, long ago, between London and Portsmouth. Such a canal, in the course of the present

[1] The first two sentences of this item from *Eng R* XXVII (Mar 1796) 299. Cf C's subsequent sentences with ibid.

[2] "Within the last two years, the astonishing sum of 5,300,000l. has been subscribed in Great Britain, for the purpose of cutting *forty-three* additional canals; which have also actually begun!" *M Mag* I (Feb 1796) 71. The first sentence of this item is C's; the rest of the paragraph has been excerpted from "A Sketch of the History of Canals" in *Eng R* XXVII (Mar 1796) 286. The remainder of C's article on canals and wastelands is verbatim from ibid 289–92.

war, would have saved several millions, not only by quickening expeditions, but saving the convoys now employed between those two ports. It often happens that an expedition is detained for want of gunpowder; another for want of guns; a third for necessaries of the army, cables, anchors, &c. Add to all these, this capital consideration, that it requires a variety of winds to go from the river to Portsmouth; whereas the whole of any convoy, by means of a canal to Southampton, might be sent in two or three days. We are informed, that there is not above twenty miles to cut, in order to open the desired communication; a distance which, if government should go heartily to work, might be finished in the space of a twelve-month.

The Leeds and Liverpool canal yields to the proprietors, at this day, on their original shares, one hundred per cent. Although, in the cant language of the times, there be a rage for canals, yet this rage is not unreasonable, or carried to an excess. Internal canals form, perhaps, the most solid basis on which a monied capitalist can speculate. It is difficult to say to what pitch of convenience to the public, and advantage to the undertakers, they may not reach. When we reflect on the degree of stimulation that they must give to agriculture, mineralogy, manufactures, and commerce, we may be permitted to say, that, in all probability, the most sanguine among their promoters, in their calculations respecting their success, have fallen short of the truth. Let us cast our eyes around over the champaign lands of Great Britain, and consider how very small a portion thereof is cultivated to the utmost point of its improveability, and how large a portion is not cultivated at all. Let us also consider what are the spots and stripes on which the hand of industry has exerted all its power. They are the busy haunts, the frequented paths of men. The environs of towns and populous villages, the skirts of highways, and the borders of navigable rivers. Canals multiply roads and rivers, and, by multiplying these, multiply villages and towns. They bring the whole of the nation together as into one busy fair. And, as it has been said of science, that knowledge, which consists in comparison, is increased, not in proportion to the increase of individual ideas, but in a much higher proportion; so the wants and superfluities of different districts, produced by so great a fermentation, will be augmented in a ratio still higher than that of increased population. It is, indeed, scarcely possible that canals can be too thick. Holland is intersected with canals, like a dam-board or a piece of tartan; and yet who will say that they have canals in too great abundance?

In Holland, canals serve the purposes of commerce and manufactures, and of these almost only. In Britain they serve, also, or rather, they will serve the greater purpose of agriculture.

If we would behold a picture of canals, and the effects of canals, we must turn our eyes to China. China, perforated in every place by canals, and flourishing in internal commerce, is indifferent to that of the world; a reflection that naturally unites, in a native of this isle, at this time, ideas of apprehension, with sentiments of consolation. If the common destiny of nations shall bound, for a lapse of time, the Gallic empire, only by the Rhine, the Alps, the Pyrenees, and the Ocean, the trade of the world must, for a time, pass also into her hands. But even then, Britain, secure and exulting in her internal trade—her internal trade, nourishing with agriculture a hardy and virtuous race of men, may smile at all external pomp and power, and rejoice in exchange of a solid, safe, and secure, for an enervating and precarious commerce.

The formation of canals and roads, carried to a due extent, would render Britain to Europe what China is to Asia. The mass of varied industry to which these would give birth, the productions of nature and art, would bring the ships of foreign nations to our doors; and although we should recede from the rigour of the navigation act,[1] we should not lose, on the whole, in point either of security or comfort. Thousands, and even millions, of new hands, not pent up in corrupt, and corrupting towns, but every where scattered in villages and hamlets, and employed in the pursuits of agriculture, and the more necessary manufactures, would nourish up health and happiness with simplicity of manners. We should be abundantly able to defend our own country; we would have no need or temptation to invade or to migrate to any other. And if the Legislature, at the same time, should restrain the monopolisation of farms, by such means as are recommended by Captain Newte, in his instructive and truly patriotic, as well as amusing, Tour in England and Scotland,[2] or by any other means, and open an asylum to every one who might be inclined to cultivate the ground on his own account; or to provide,

[1] The various navigation acts had as their common purpose insuring that cargoes in the British dominions were carried in British vessels.

[2] Thomas Newte *Prospects and Observations on a Tour in England and Scotland, Natural, Oeconomical, and Literary* (1791) 380–92, esp 389, where he suggests that entails be abolished and that the legislature pass a law limiting the extent of farms or taxing large farms and barren or uncultivated lands in such a way that the proprietor either "cultivate[s] them himself, or resign[s] them to the community for general distribution". Newte is a pseudonym for William Thomson (1746–1817). See below, pp 242–3, 251–2, for excerpts from another of his travel-books.

at least, that every one might be readily furnished with as much ground, at a moderate rent, as might enable him to keep a cow, with some poultry and pigs—the charm of an independent and tranquil home—the holy influence of the *penates* and *lares familiares* would invite and allure the city slave to the salubrious air and free genius of the country. Instead of crouded cities full of diseases contagious to body and mind, we should have innumerable townships, as in America, in which the inhabitants, restored to the natural destination of man, would vary the monotonous and debasing uniformity of mere mechanism, by the alternate occupations of the fisher, the gardener, and the husbandman.

The formation of canals, by promoting the cultivation of the soil, and at the same time population, health, and virtue, not only tends directly to secure the empire of this fortunate island against foreign enemies, but also against domestic incendiaries.

By the present over-driven system of manufacturing, men are assembled in great numbers in towns and cities, for the interest and convenience of the master, but not those of the workman, who is of often subjected to great inconveniences, by failures in the demand for his manufacture, arising from war and other causes. Pressed by wants that he cannot supply, he listens with fond hope to any project of political change, whereby he may be tempted to imagine that his situation may be rendered more comfortable. From the centre of a few profligate persons, spending their last sixpence in an alehouse, doctrines are disseminated, which, in their progress, disturb the peace, and sometimes subvert the order of society. It is unnecessary to shew, that the contrary of all this is the case, and would be still more the case, if such arrangements as we have here recommended were established, in the country. In cities and towns the lower orders of men are often vicious, discontented and factious. Scattered in villages and hamlets, if there be not some egregious defect in the public œconomy, they are inoffensive, contented, and obedient to lawful authority.

It is with great satisfaction that we contemplate the measures pursued by the legislature for the improvement of waste lands and commons.[1] We hope they will adopt and pursue the principles so often

[1] Sir John Sinclair had introduced a bill in the Commons on 3 Feb to facilitate the division and use of waste-lands. How much the subject was on C's mind is shown in *Monody on the Death of Chatterton* (second version) line 62: "On many a waste he bids trim gardens rise". (*He* refers to the personified spirit of poetry.)

recommended, of using all prudent means for restoring each individual, willing to labour, to his share of the earth (unavoidably alienated by the involved relations and bearings of society); and raising the industrious day-labourer to the comfortable and dignified situation of an independent cultivator; to which design, the formation of canals is highly favourable and subservient.

PROVISIONS.[1]—The appearance of the next crops of Wheat in every part of the Kingdom is exceedingly promising. Oats are in great forwardness; the land is in excellent condition for Barley; and the Beans come remarkably strong. These excellent appearances added to a considerable foreign supply, have produced a proportionate reduction in the price of Wheat. In some places the markets have been glutted. But while Grain has thus lowered its price, Butcher's Meat and Potatoes have experienced an alarming advance.

PEACE or WAR.[2]—The state of things has at length, we are informed, made the proper impression on the minds of Ministers. They shrink from the consequences of their own system; and finding, we fear too late, the impossibility of going on, they are about to come to Parliament with an exposition of the terms they have offered to the French, and the answer they have received, and to submit to the wisdom of the Legislature the question of Peace or War.—This is the rumour. We of course speak from no other authority than report. The obvious remark of every impartial man upon such a reference would be—Are Ministers in earnest? Do they really demand the genuine Council of the Nation, and will they leave the Representatives of the People to their unbiassed opinion? Will Mr. PITT act on this great question as he did on the Slave Trade, strip himself of his Ministerial influence, and appear in his plain character as a man?—If so, the decision would be important. Their voice would be for Peace. But if not, it will be a mere showy manœuvre of mere quackery, by which they may cover their own wishes with the approbation of Parliament.

We shall endeavour to give an arranged account of our domestic Affairs similar to the preceding, every other Number.

BATAVIAN REPUBLIC

PETER PAULUS is dead. The Convention have decreed that he had not ceased to deserve well of his country. This Decree written on

[1] An abridged form of a "Report" in *M Mag* I (Mar 1796) 176. The scarcity, so strongly felt in 1795, was being eased and so consequently was the political pressure upon the ministry.

[2] From *M Chron* 4 Apr 1796.

vellum is to be presented to his widow; and at the same time the National Scarf with which he was decorated. Citizen PETER LEONARD Van De Kasteele[1] is chosen President in his place.

The Convention are about to pass vigorous means for the improvement of their Navy: The whole Nation have been solemnly invited by the Legislature, to engage able-bodied young Men for the Sea Service.

The accounts of an Insurrection in Sardinia, are confirmed.[2] The people of Caglians[3] began it: They put to death the General of the Troops, and the Intendent-General of the Finances and established [a] Provisionary Council of Government: They then dispatched Deputies to the King, claiming their Rights and Privileges; but not receiving a satisfactory answer, they determined on a Revolution, which they have accomplished, the whole Country having followed the example of Caglians. The Sardinians mean to throw themselves on the protection of the French.

DUBLIN, April 2.[4] The Public have been at a loss to know the meaning of the Pass-word *Eliphismatis*, which appeared in the Defender's Oath, as produced on the recent trials.[5] One of the diabolical and sanguinary confederacy, now in confinement, who was deeply concerned in their infernal plots, disclosed its origin, and is constituted of the first letter in every word in the following lines, in the acrostic stile, from which it certainly took its rise, and was used to disguise their horrid intentions.

E VERY
L OYAL
I RISH
P ROTESTANT
H ERETIC
I
S HALL
M URDER
A ND
T HIS
I
S WEAR

[1] Pieter Leonard van de Kasteele (1748–1810), Dutch lawyer, administrator, and poet. Item condensed from the *Sun* 5 Apr 1796.

[2] The *Gazetteer*, 25 Mar 1796, in a dispatch from Leghorn dated 1 Mar, printed the story of the insurrection in Cagliari; it was also reported by the *True Briton* 4 Apr, *Oracle* 7 Apr, etc.

[3] Cagliari.

[4] From the *Sun* 7 Apr 1796, including the "Letter from Longford" below (items also appeared in *The Times* 8 Apr, *True Briton* 8 Apr, and *Evening Mail* 6–8 Apr).

[5] E.g. the trial for treason of John

A Letter from Longford states, that 12 notorious robbers have been apprehended in that neighbourhood by the Limerick Militia. One fellow had a passage under ground from his own house into a field, the opening of which was through a ditch, covered occasionally with sods; a soldier who had been planted near this place, by chance perceived the sods fall in, and a man's head make its appearance, on which he presented his musquet, which caused the robber to attempt making his escape; but before he could do so, the soldier fired, and lodged a ball in his leg; he was consequently secured, and, with sixteen accomplices, sent to Cavan gaol, where they will be tried the ensuing Assizes.

We omitted to give the speech of the late President Paulus. They who have seen it elsewhere will not blame us, as it was indeed a *Dutch* Speech.[1]—The following proclamation however makes ample compensation.

PROCLAMATION[2]

Of the Dutch Convention, for manning the Navy, published at the Hague, March 16.

CITIZENS OF THE NETHERLANDS

DEAR COUNTRYMEN,

THE unjust and destructive War in which we have been involved by the British Ministry, cannot but attract our whole attention. It is the first object of our solicitude, that by our courage and prudence in the conduct of it, we may procure an honourable Peace, firmly establish our Freedom, and maintain the independence of our State, and the glory of our Ancestors. Our Navy, under Divine Providence, is the natural and only means to set bounds to the immeasurable insolence of the British Ministry, and to defend our Country against their treacherous conduct and cruel treatment. To this object the endeavours of the best Patriots have been uniformly directed since the time when our heavy chains were broken by the

Leary in Dublin, 3 Jan 1796. The Defenders were a secret Roman Catholic organisation banded together to oppose the actions of Protestant societies in Ireland. Later in 1796 the various bands of Defenders joined the United Irishmen. For other explanations of "eliphismatis", see below, pp 298–9.

[1] It was printed in full in the *Sun* 24 Mar 1796.

[2] From the *Sun* 7 Apr 1796.

assistance of our French brethren, since the day when the Stadtholder left the Batavian shores, the day when we began to breathe a freer air, and were at liberty to exert ourselves for the improvement of the great sources of our Prosperity, our Trade, our Fisheries, our Navigation, our Colonies, and our Manufactures. By their Navy, Fellow Citizens, did our Ancestors become great. The Batavian Flag was known, feared, and honoured in each of the four quarters of the world. Under our late Government it was insulted, and became the ridicule of nations. It is therefore our first duty to restore our Marine. The zeal of the Committee of Marine has done much, where nothing scarcely had before been done. Its exertions were incessant. But in the present state of our Navy, all hands seem to have lost their habits, and all hearts the inclination necessary for the service. The Batavian youth are no longer accustomed to the labours requisite on board the armed Fleets of their Country. Is our Nation then less brave,—less indignant against its enemies—or, do we less love our native land, than in the time of a RUYTER[1] or a TROMP ?[2] No, Fellow Citizens, no! Far from us be such a thought! We rely with confidence on your patriotism, and cannot doubt but you will act with vigour in the present critical situation of our Country; for why should we conceal that such is our situation, when to make it known must procure the remedy. Our ships, which are very numerous, and more than sufficient to secure us a superiority in our seas, and to cut off from the Enemy all supplies of Provisions and Stores from the North, and thus compel them to Peace—our ships are in want of men. The recruitings proceed with languor, and the measures hitherto taken have had little effect. Nor should this excite our wonder: they were of a partial nature, and not in consequence of the expression of the will of the Assembly, Representative of the whole Batavian Republic. This will is now made known: supported by you it shall deliver our Country. Let the people be called together in all the Towns and Villages of the Netherlands: Let the example of Haerlim be proposed to them; that Town so zealous for Liberty, that it has already raised two hundred young men for the Navy. Let all the Constitutional Authorities remind the

[1] Michel Adriaanszoon de Ruyter (1607–76), Dutch admiral. He defeated the English in a four-day battle off Dunkirk during the second Dutch-English war (1665–7) and commanded the navy against the combined English and French fleets during the third Dutch-English war (1672).

[2] Maarten Harpertszoon Tromp (1597–1653), Dutch admiral who defeated the British fleet in 1652 and was killed in an engagement against the British in 1653.

Batavian youth, that their Country looks up to them for her defence: they will not be deaf to her call. The time of oppression is past. The Fleet of the Republic is under the Command of true Patriots, who do not consider their Comrades as Slaves, but Fellow-Citizens. The attention of the Representatives of the people will be continually directed to provide for the wants of the Mariner, and they will consider the rewarding of heroism and faithful service as the most pleasing part of their great labours. Let therefore fathers exhort their sons, sisters their brothers, and the people in general the youth of the Country, to acts of heroism, and to engage in the Naval Service, to maintain the honour of the Batavian Flag, and defend their Native Land. When they shall thus nobly have fulfilled their duty, they will find their reward in our tender care for them and their relatives, in the approbation of every noble mind, and the congratulations and gratitude of all their Countrymen.

VAN DE CASTEELE.

Interesting Information respecting the conduct of the Bank in their late limitation of discounts.[1]

MR. BOYD, and the other Gentlemen of the Committee appointed to hold a conference with the Minister on the subject of the present alarming scarcity of money, had their interview with him on Tuesday last. All the causes of the present distress, as assigned by the Gentlemen who have the surest means of information, were fairly canvassed.—They were stated to be four in number:

1. The advance made by the Bank to Government, amounting in all to more than fourteen millions.

2. The drain of specie out of the kingdom, in consequence of the exchange being against us to every corner of the world.

3. The monopolies of almost every article of the first necessity, and particularly of grain.

4. The speculation in the funds, to an unexampled amount, which drew within its vortex all the floating money.

These were the causes assigned for the limited aid which the Bank had lately afforded to circulation, and for the consequent scarcity that was felt. It was impossible to deny their existence.

The first was within the knowledge of Government.—The Bank had advanced to the State near twelve millions, according to the

[1] From *M Chron* 7 Apr 1796. C has omitted the concluding paragraphs of this leading-article.

account laid upon the table of the House of Commons; and in their private dealings as a banking company, they had purchased, and taken out of the market, above two millions of Navy Bills. This sum was so much larger than, in usual circumstances, was ever employed in this way, that it occasioned a proportionate limitation of discounts. They had not the same power of ready money to bestow on trade.

The second was an evil which demanded all their vigilance as the guardians of public property. Two months ago they saw that the Exchange was at 31 to Hamburgh, and they found by the nature of the paper sent into them for discount, that men were taking advantage of the circumstance, and that bullion to a great and alarming amount was daily going out of the kingdom; which, added to the drain of our armies on the Continent, and in the Mediterranean, the subsidies to foreign powers, and the increased balance to the Northern nations from the demands of the war, made the sum actually exported in three years amount to sixteen millions sterling.

The third cause of scarcity had been too severely felt by all descriptions of men. No sooner had the Report of Parliament spread the alarm of a short crop, than schemes of monopoly had begun. Grain disappeared from the face of the earth, and wheat rose to 120s. per quarter. The whole of this was to be carried on by Bank paper.

But more than all the rest, perhaps, the fourth cause was the most seriously alarming, since the speculation in the funds was carried to an extent so unprecedented, that to enable them to make their bargains, twenty, thirty, nay forty per cent. was given for money, and of course the merchant, the tradesman, the manufacturer, who could only afford to give five per cent. for accommodation, could not be supplied,—and every guinea taken from the Bank was whelmed into this abyss. What made this the more alarming was, that every man of character and distinction in the country disowned the speculation. It was said to be done by foreigners, and yet every foreign house of eminence formally disclaimed it. And tho' avowedly the sink of all our ready money, it eluded the scrutinizing eye of alarm itself.

Such were the causes which it was acknowledged had influenced the Bank for the last two months to limit their discounts. The first was an imperious necessity. They had perhaps gone too far in their exertions for a cause in which true patriotism as well as enlarged wisdom would have been more sparing; but the advances were made. The three others were causes of prudence. They saw that men were acting upon their discounts. That they were looked to for fuel, which was to feed the flame, and if they had proceeded, it is impossible for conjecture to say to what an extent the exportation of our specie, the price of every necessary of life, and the bubble of speculation, would have been carried. They have checked the whole system.

The Exchange to Hamburgh is now 35 instead of 31, and it is in favour of England from every corner of the world.

The stores of the Monopolists are opened, and wheat which was 120, is now 80 shillings per quarter.

And the abandoned speculation is so blown, that it is doubtful whether prudent men will agree to a further continuation on any terms.

To the Bank of England, to its energy and wisdom—to its disregard of clamour and misinterpretation—to its intrepidity and steadiness in pursuing the good, old, and wholesome system of English caution, Great Britain is indebted, perhaps, for her salvation.

PROCEEDINGS IN THE BRITISH LEGISLATURE

HOUSE OF COMMONS

MONDAY, *April* 4

Nothing of importance transacted.

TUESDAY, *April* 5

The Legacy [Bill] was read a third time. On the motion for passing it ALDERMAN NEWNHAM renewed his former objections to it, and stated, in addition, that in case of epidemic disorders, persons might be liable to pay the tax five or six times in a year.—In short, the Bill was altogether so oppressive, that although this Country may be fit to live, it would hereafter be a Country no man would choose to die in. Mr. Fox moved, that the Debate be adjourned to that day fortnight. After a reply from Mr. Pitt, the House divided,—Ayes 16. Noes 64. The Bill was then passed. The debates on the Dog-Tax we are obliged to defer to our next Number.[1]

THOMAS GAGE[2]

The following reasons for further enquiry concerning the innocence or guilt of THOMAS GAGE, who now lies in Newgate under

[1] See below, pp 255–8.

[2] On 2 Apr 1796 William (not Thomas) Gage was sentenced to death in Bristol Guildhall for rioting and

sentence of Death, are submitted to the serious consideration of the inhabitants of BRISTOL.

ON the sixth day of June last, a number of persons illegally assembled together in the Market, and attacked the house of the Prosecutor with the stones, and took away his meat. The riot commenced about six o'clock, and continued till past nine, before which hour, the outrage for which Thomas Gage has been tried, and condemned, was sworn to have been committed.—The prisoner was apprehended between nine and ten o'clock. The principal and indeed the only material evidence for the prosecution, was Matthews, a Tyler, whose wife kept a Butcher's Shop in the Market, and who upon the conviction of William Gage is intitled to receive the sum of Forty Pounds by Act of Parliament.—Matthews positively swore that he saw the prisoner about Eight o'Clock in the mob, that he was very busy, and that he absolutely threw stones at six different times. Mr. Wilmott, Gage's master, swore that the prisoner was employed by him in his Brewery on the 6th day of June, 1795, in Redcliff-Street, and that he was actually in his service on the sixth day of June, that he saw the prisoner at his work at different periods of time,—to wit, on or about 6 o'clock, at about 7 o'clock, between the hours of 7 and 8 o'clock, and at 9 o'clock of the said 6th day of June, when he paid him his wages, and his other workmen, John Brice, Henry Osmond, and John Seal at the same time. That his men were much engaged in his work on the said 6th day of June, and that as usual he watched them, and after they had finished, about 9 o'clock he paid them their wages; and though he occasionally left the place when the prisoner was at work, yet he verily believes that the prisoner did not leave the Brewery from 5 o'clock on the 6th day of June until 9 o'clock of the same evening, as he must have noticed his absence. The counsel for the prisoner was so much satisfied with the evidence of the prisoner's master, that he declared that his life was safe.—But contrary to all expectation, and for want of other evidence which might have been produced, the prisoner was found guilty, and condemned to death. Since his conviction Wilmott's Affidavit has confirmed his testimony given at the Trial, and three of the prisoner's companions in work at the Brewery, viz. Brice, Osmond, and Seal have sworn before Dr. Small, that they were employed in the service of Mr. Wilmott at the

stealing meat. On 16 April he received a reprieve, but his subsequent fate has not transpired. In the remaining four issues of *The Watchman* C did not comment further on the case.

Brewery on the said 6th day of June, that they were all together at work with Gage the prisoner now under sentence of death, from 5 o'clock in the evening of the said 6th day of June until 9 o'clock of the same evening, and that Gage never quitted them, and that they were constantly at work together until 9 o'clock, when Mr. Wilmott paid them their wages, and that Gage could not have absented himself without their knowledge. John Seal further swears, that he accompanied Gage at 9 o'clock from the Brewery, after their wages were paid, to the Fox Inn in Redcliff-street, and there partook of a tankard of ale with the said prisoner in company with Thomas Stevens, that they parted company at *half past* 9 *o'clock* at the Fox, and the prisoner told this John Seal, that he should go into the market to buy a little meat for his family. They swear they did not hear concerning the Riots which happened in the market on the 6th of June until after 9 o'clock in the evening when they quitted the Brewery.

And they further swear, that they were not subpœna'd or had any notice to attend to give evidence, or they would have attended and given the evidence before stated. It is said, that the late Mayor, Mr. Smith, when Gage was first brought before him for examination, was particularly impressed with Matthews' evidence, as he felt the difficulty of identifying Gage in a mob, and of his ascertaining at the time he was himself in a place of danger of the number of times Gage threw stones.

These testimonies are printed to induce all persons, who have it in their power, to satisfy themselves as to the facts. They are more particularly addressed to those concerned in the prosecution: for upon them of all men living is it incumbent to examine into the real state of the case; and if they find the proofs of the alibi convincing, to exert themselves night and day to obtain a free pardon for the convict in the first place; and in the second to find him the best possible compensation for his bodily and mental sufferings.

This concise and unimpassioned statement seems most suitable to the present stage of this important transaction. Various rumours are in circulation; and if the author of the present paper should have reason on enquiry to believe some of them true, he shall think himself bound to call the attention of the whole people of Great-Britain to the circumstances of this trial. At no period since the Revolution have the lives of so many innocent men been attempted by perjury, at no period therefore ought the public eye to be more steadily fixed on courts of justice.

THE WATCHMAN

No. VII. TUESDAY, APRIL 19, 1796

Published by the Author, S. T. COLERIDGE, Bristol;
And by PARSONS, Paternoster-Row, London.

THAT ALL MAY KNOW THE TRUTH;
AND THAT THE TRUTH MAY MAKE US FREE!

WITH the deepest regret we present the following STATE PAPERS,[1] on the important Subject of PEACE, which have just been communicated by Lord Grenville to the Foreign Ministers at this Court.

NOTE

TRANSMITTED TO M. BARTHELEMI, BY MR. WICKHAM,[2]
MARCH 8, 1796.

The undersigned, his Britannick Majesty's Minister Plenipotentiary to the Swiss Cantons, is authorized to convey to Monsieur Barthelemi the desire of his Court to be made acquainted, through him, with the dispositions of France in regard to the object of a general pacification. He therefore requests Monsieur Barthelemi to transmit to him in writing (and after having made the necessary enquiries), his answer to the following questions:

1. Is there the disposition in France to open a negociation with his Majesty and his Allies for the re-establishment of a general peace, upon just and suitable terms, by sending, for that purpose, Ministers to a Congress, at such place as may hereafter be agreed upon?

2. Would there be the disposition to communicate to the undersigned the general grounds of a pacification, such as France would be willing to propose; in order that his Majesty and his Allies might

[1] Most of the London papers reprinted these three state papers from the *London Gazette*—e.g. the *Star* and *The Times* 11 Apr, *M Chron* and *Sun* 12 Apr 1796. For some reflections on this important correspondence, see below, pp 252–3, and for C's "Remonstrance to the French Legislators", see below, pp 269–73.

[2] François (later Marquis de) Barthélemy (1750–1830), French ambassador to Switzerland, and William Wickham (1761–1840), English minister to Switzerland.

thereupon examine in concert, whether they are such as might serve as the foundation of a negociation for peace?

3. Or would there be a desire to propose any other way whatever, for arriving at the same end, that of a general pacification?

The undersigned is authorized to receive from Monsieur Barthelemi the answer to these questions, and to transmit it to his Court: But he is not authorized to enter with him into negociation or discussion upon these subjects.

Berne, March 8, 1796.

(Signed) W. WICKHAM.

NOTE

TRANSMITTED TO MR. WICKHAM, BY M. BARTHELEMI, MARCH 26, 1796.

The undersigned, Ambassador of the French Republic to the Helvetic Body, has transmitted to the Executive Directory the note, which Mr. Wickham, His Britannic Majesty's Minister Plenipotentiary to the Swiss Cantons, was pleased to convey to him, dated the 8th of March. He has it in command to answer it by an exposition of the sentiments and dispositions of the Executive Directory.

The Directory ardently desires to procure for the French Republic a just, honourable and solid peace. The step taken by Mr. Wickham would have afforded to the Directory a real satisfaction, if the declaration itself, which that Minister makes, of his not having any order, any power to negociate, did not give room to doubt of the sincerity of the pacific intentions of his Court. In fact, if it was true, that England began to know her real interests; that she wished to open again for herself the sources of abundance and prosperity; if she sought for peace with good faith; would she propose a Congress, of which the necessary result must be, to render all negociation endless? Or would she confine herself to the asking, in a vague manner, that the French Government should point out any other way whatever, for attaining the same object, that of a general pacification?

Is it that this step has had no other object than to obtain for the British Government the favourable impression which always accompanies the first overtures for peace? May it not have been accompanied with the hope that they would produce no effect?

However that may be, the Executive Directory, whose policy has no other guide than openness and good faith, will follow, in its explanations, a conduct which shall be wholly conformable to them.

Yielding to the ardent desire by which it is animated, to procure peace for the French Republic, and for all Nations, it will not fear to declare itself openly. Charged by the Constitution with the execution of the laws, it cannot make, or listen to, any proposal that would be contrary to them. The Constitutional Act does not permit it to consent to any alienation of that, which, according to the existing laws, constitutes the territory of the Republic.

With respect to the Countries occupied by the French Armies, and which have not been united to France, they, as well as other interests Political and Commercial, may become the subject of a negociation, which will present to the Directory the means of proving how much it desires to attain speedily to an happy pacification.

The Directory is ready to receive, in this respect, any overtures that shall be just, reasonable, and compatible with the dignity of the Republic.

BASLE, the 6th of Germinal, the 4th year of the French Republic (26th of March, 1796).

(Signed) BARTHELEMI.

NOTE

The Court of London has received from its Minister in Switzerland, the Answer made to the Questions which he had been charged to address to Monsieur BARTHELEMI, in respect to the opening of a Negociation for the re-establishment of General Tranquillity.

This Court has seen, with regret, how far the tone and spirit of that Answer, the nature and extent of the demands which it contains, and the manner of announcing them, are remote from any disposition for Peace.

The inadmissible pretension is there avowed, of appropriating to France all that the Laws actually existing there may have comprized under the denomination of French Territory. To a demand such as this, is added an express declaration, that no proposal contrary to it will be made or even listened to: And this, under the pretence of an internal regulation, the provisions of which are wholly foreign to all other Nations.

While these dispositions shall be persisted in, nothing is left for the KING but to prosecute a War equally just and necessary.

Whenever his Enemies shall manifest more pacific sentiments, His Majesty will at all times be eager to concur in them, by lending himself, in concert with his Allies, to all such measures as shall be best calculated to re-establish General Tranquillity, on conditions just, honourable and permanent, either by the establishment of a Congress, which has been so often, and so happily, the means of restoring Peace to Europe; or by a preliminary discussion of the principles which may be proposed, on either side, as a foundation of a General Pacification; or, lastly, by an impartial examination of any other way which may be pointed out to him for arriving at the same salutary end.

Downing-Street, April 10, 1796.

The horrors of war must therefore be re-commenced.—Let those who sit by the fire-side, and hear of them at safe distance attentively peruse the following

Interesting Narration relative to the Campaign of 1794 *and* 1795.[1]

ABUSES unheard of in any former war existed in almost every department; and our helpless countrymen were given up to the mercy of Surgeon's Mates, furnished by a *cheap contract, and Deputy Commissaries*, whose interest it appeared to deprive them of every shadow of enjoyment. The enormous sum of forty thousand pounds sterling had been drawn for to supply the sick with wine; and such was the infamous behaviour of the MEDICAL STAFF, that the Surgeons and Mates are very much belied, if there were *not many of them* in the constant habits of robbing the sick, and of applying that necessary article to their own use, preferring the pleasure of carousing over flaggons of heady Port, to the *drudgery* of alleviating the pangs of the miserable and afflicted patients, whose hard fate placed them under the hands of such ignorant and inhuman Butchers.*

When we consider how many brave men were thus sacrificed, and that from fifteen to twenty guineas bounty money were at that time

* When a soldier fell sick and was ordered to the Hospital, his comrade would exclaim, "Ah poor fellow! we shall see thee no more, thou art under orders for the *shambles*."

[1] J. L. Lowes (*RX* 104–9 and 489 n 67) has indicated the connexion between this excerpt and C's lines on the horrors of war in *The Destiny of Nations*. Delving further, we find the source of the "Narration" in *An Accurate and Impartial Narrative of the War, by an Officer of the Guards . . . Containing . . . a Poetical Sketch of the Campaign of 1793 . . . also a Similar Sketch of the Campaign of 1794 . . . a Narrative of the Retreat of 1795 . . .* (2 vols 1795). C's first two paragraphs are from II 90–1 (var), including italics.

publickly offered for recruits, would it not have been more economical in Government, to have employed *Rush, Lind,*[1] and other respectable men, who offered their services at the commencement of the war, but whose demands were deemed exorbitant, than to have imported at so much per head, such numbers of inexperienced pretenders to a science above their comprehension, who scarcely knew in which hand to hold a lancet, or in what manner to place a tournequet.

The general orders[2] issued for the removal of the sick proved a death-warrant to numberless miserable objects. A description circumstantially detailed of their poignant sufferings during the retreat to Deventer, would form a tale "whose lightest word would harrow up the soul."[3] Constantly removed in open waggons, exposed to the intense severity of the weather, to drifting snow, and heavy falls of sleet and rain; frequently without any victuals till the army halted, and then but scantily provided; littered down in cold churches, upon a short allowance of dirty straw; and few of them enjoying the comforts of a single blanket, to repel the vigorous attacks of the night air; it is no wonder they expired, by hundreds, Martyrs to the most infamous and unpardonable neglect.

ON the morning[4] of the 17th Jan. 1795, I was sent upon a particular duty, to trace out a road over the common, by which the army and artillery might safely proceed to Looners. When the party marched, it was scarcely light, and as the day broke in upon us, the horrible scenes which it revealed, afforded a shocking proof of the miseries of a winter's campaign—On the common, about half a mile off the high road, we discovered a baggage cart, with a team of *five horses*, apparently in distress; I galloped towards the spot, and found the poor animals were stiff, but not dead; the hoar frost on their manes, plainly shewing they had been there the whole night. Not perceiving any driver with them, I struck my sword repeatedly on the canvass tilt, enquiring at the same time if there was any person in the cart; at

[1] The author of the *Narrative* was mistaken as to the availability of these famous physicians: Lind died in the summer of 1794, and Rush was an American—James Lind (1716–94), Benjamin Rush (1745–1813). It is possible, however, that the author referred not to the above Lind, who wrote a treatise on scurvy, but to the other James Lind (1736–1812), who had settled at Windsor, where he was physician to the royal household, and who befriended Shelley when the latter was at Eton.

[2] *An Accurate . . . Narrative* II 99–100.

[3] *Hamlet* I v 15–16 (var).

[4] *An Accurate . . . Narrative* II 101–4 (var), quoting an eye-witness account (italics as in the original).

length, a very feeble voice answered me, and someone underneath the canvass appeared to be making an effort to rise. A pair of naked *frost-nipt* legs were then advanced, and the most miserable object I ever beheld, sunk heavily upon the ground; the whole of his clothing so ragged and worn, that I can scarcely say he *was covered.* So stiff and frozen, was this miserable wretch, that he was by no means capable of moving: he informed me that his regiment, the Fifty-fourth, which he was following the preceding night, had lost its road, and in turning into another, he found his horses incapable of clearing the cart from the ruts, and that himself and his two comrades were left behind to proceed in the best manner they could; the two men he spoke of were then lying dead in the cart, having all three endeavoured to communicate to one another, a degree of warmth, by creeping close together. We placed the miserable survivor upon one of the horses of his team, and led him forwards till joined by the battalion; by that means his life was prolonged, yet, I fear, but for a season; for when placed in the hospital, his toes dropped off, frost-bitten, and his mass of blood appeared in a corrupted state. The whole of this day's march was marked by scenes of the most calamitous nature, similar to the one I have just recited. We could not proceed a hundred yards without perceiving the dead bodies of men, women, children, and horses, in every direction. One scene made an impression upon my memory, which time will never be able to efface. Near another cart, a little further on the common, we perceived a stout looking man, and a beautiful young woman with an infant, about seven months old, at the breast; all three frozen and dead.[1] The mother had most certainly expired in the act of suckling her child, as with one breast exposed, she lay upon the drifted snow, the milk to all appearance, in a stream, drawn from the nipple by the babe, and instantly congealed. The infant seemed as if its lips had but just then been disengaged, and it reposed its little head upon the mother's bosom, with an overflow of milk, *frozen* as it trickled from the mouth; their countenances were perfectly composed and fresh, resembling those of persons in a sound and tranquil slumber. About fifty yards advanced, was another dead man, with a bundle of linen clothes and a few biscuits, evidently belonging to the poor woman and child, and a little further, was [a horse][2] lying down, but not quite

[1] C used the mother, babe, and other details in *The Destiny of Nations* lines 195–252: *PW* (EHC) I 138–9. Southey quoted this passage in the notes to his poem *To Horror*, where he used the detail of the frozen breast of the mother: *Poems* (3rd ed Bristol 1799; vol I is dated Dec 1796) I 68–9.

[2] The omitted words came at the end of f 9 of PML MS MA 1916 and

dead, with a couple of panniers on his back, one of which contained, as we discovered, the body of another child, about two years of age, wrapped up in flannel and straw. This, as we afterwards heard, was the whole of one family: a serjeant's wife of the fifty-fifth, her brother and children; the man found with the horse and bundle, had remained behind his regiment to assist them, during a march, thus memorable for its miseries. He had just gained sight of a distant hamlet, where they might have obtained a shelter from the inclemency of the weather, when his strength failed him. The commanding Officer of the fifty-fifth, rode by at that critical moment, but too late to render them any service; and as the battalions passed the spot, the troops were witnesses in their turns of this melancholy scene.

ALL FOR THE BEST

WHAT at first we regret as misfortunes, the lapse of a few years generally proves to us to have been the means of blessings. In a Committee of Congress in June 1775, a declaration was drawn up containing an offer to Great Britain, that the colonies would not only continue to grant extraordinary aids in time of war, but also if permitted a free commerce, pay into the sinking fund such a sum annually for 100 years, as should be more than sufficient, if faithfully applied, to liquidate all the then debts of Great-Britain. The frustration of this scheme was deeply regretted by the patriots at that æra: yet had it happened, what would it have effected? In the present state of our administrations it would be ridiculous to suppose a faithful application. The sum would only have increased the powers of diffusing corruption. America would not have been a free and independent state, and her example would not have kindled France into liberty. There are however lessons which the American Revolution might have taught this country, but which it has not taught it. It has not taught English Ministers that a war against a nation of patriots must be as unsuccessful and calamitous, as it is iniquitous and abominable; that rebellion to tyrants is obedience to God;[1] and that

were lost as C turned to write on f 10. The error is therefore not chargeable to the printer.

[1] Attributed to Benjamin Franklin, from a supposititious epitaph on the regicide John Bradshaw (1602–59), president of the commission that tried Charles I. It was first published as a broadside and was later reprinted in Francis Blackburne *The Memoirs of Thomas Hollis* (1780). Thomas Jefferson used the slogan on his seal. See *The Papers of Thomas Jefferson* ed Julian P. Boyd (Princeton 1950–) I 677–9.

they therefore who struggle for freedom fight beneath the banners of omnipotence![1] It has not taught the English Ministers, that popular indignation must be removed by a removal of the causes, and cannot be *strait-waistcoated* by harsh and unconstitutional laws; that there is a crisis beyond which the overburthened people can endure no longer, and that obstinate refusals to reform confessed abuses lead in their consequences to coercive revolutions; those whirlwinds, by which God cleanseth pestilence! "The Lord standeth up to plead. O my people, they, who lead thee, cause thee to err. The Lord will enter into judgment with the princes—What mean ye, that ye beat my people to pieces, and grind the faces of the poor? I look for judgment and behold oppression, for the pleasant song of righteousness, and behold groaning."[2]

Accept these desultory reflections, Mr. Editor, from your constant reader.

POLITOPHYLACTOPHILUS.[3]

ANECDOTE OF PETER THE GREAT[4]

PETER THE GREAT, often punished with his own hands such delinquents as he did not wish to deliver up to the public executioner. The instances of this kind that are on record are almost innumerable. I select a single example. He had summoned a meeting of his council, I have forgot on what occasion, at seven in the morning. When he entered the senate-house, he was astonished to find not one of those arrived whom he had ordered to attend. By the time he had waited about ten minutes, and wrought himself up to a proper degree of rage, the president appears; who, seeing the storm that was about to fall on him, begins to make an apology; but in vain, Peter, whose passions never listened to excuses, instantly seizes and belabours him most severely. Every member shared the same fate

[1] Cf *Religious Musings* lines 62–3: "And marching onwards view high o'er their heads | His waving banners of Omnipotence". *PW* (EHC) I 111. Cf also *CN* I 22 and n: "Optimist—by having no will but the will of Heaven, we call in Omnipotence to fight our battles!"

[2] Isa 3.13, 3.12 (var), 3.14–15 (var), 5.7 (var).

[3] C loved such coinages, and if—at a rough guess—the name means "a lover of political guardianship", it could mean the editor of *The Watchman*.

[4] Peter I the Great (1672–1725), tsar of Russia. Reprinted from [William Thomson] *Letters from Scandinavia, on the Past and Present State of the Northern Nations of Europe* (2 vols 1796) I 21–2 (with an omission in the first sentence).

according to the order of his arrival, until General Gordon[1] appeared. The General was not a little alarmed at the appearance which the council-room presented. But the Emperor's rage was by this time pretty well exhausted, and he only told Gordon, that, as he had not been punctual to his time, he was very lucky in being *so far* behind it. "For," added he, "I am already sufficiently fatigued with beating these scoundrels; and I understand that a Scotch Constitution does not agree well with a drubbing."

THE Countries which, by the existing Laws in France, constitute the French Territory,[2] are;

1. France, as it stood at the commencement of the War.
2. The French Colonies in the West-Indies still occupied by France.
3. The Islands of France and Mauritius.
4. Martinico and Tobago.
5. The whole Island of St. Domingo.
6. Pondicherry, Chandenagore, Carical, Mahe, and the other French Establishments in India.
7. Avignon, and the County Venaissin.
8. Principality of Montbeliard, and Bishoprick of Porentrui.
9. Savoy, Nice, and Monaco.
10. Austrian Flanders and Brabant, and generally, whatever belongs to the EMPEROR on this side the Rhine.
11. Maestricht, Venlo, and Dutch Flanders.
12. The Bishoprick of Liege.

On the subject of all or any of these, the Directory refuses to make, or even to receive, any Proposal, and insists that the Negociation shall be preceded by an admission of this Claim on our part.

FRANCE[3]

AN event that occurred a few days ago at Rouen throws much light upon an eternal and indefatigable conspiracy: the Municipality of that Commune watched for a long time two persons whose measures were suspicious. The National Guard, commanded by

[1] Patrick Gordon (1635–99), a Scotsman in the Russian service, who helped Peter to the throne.

[2] The Directory, in answer to the British overture, had stated that negotiations for peace could not include any discussion of existing French territory. See above, p 237.

[3] From *M Chron* 11 Apr 1796 (quoting the French journal *Ami des lois*).

Citizen BEAUVAIS and LELIEVRE,[1] were sent in pursuit of them. The two suspected persons were seized; their names are MAURY and GERARD.—The former bears a name dear to the Counter-revolutionists, and which the famous Prince of the Church[2] has rendered illustrious in all Courts: the second shewed much zeal last year against the Terrorists; he defended himself with obstinacy, and he aimed several blows with his sabre at BEAUVAIS, who fortunately parried them. When they saw that resistance was vain, they attempted to make away with the papers of which they were the bearers, but they were not more successful; and the National Guards got possession of their correspondence, which informs us, that these Gentlemen were Inspectors-General of Royalism in the armies of the Republic which they had visited. Their notes upon the army of the Sambre and Meuse are not very advantageous to the Kings; they say, that it is composed of Terrorists, with whom nothing can be done; they speak their sentiments upon the other legions, and they represent their fears and hopes. But what in their correspondence is most alarming, is, that there are in Paris and its environs, 8000 bravoes, who are ready at the first signal to make a hecatomb of the men who have the audacity to inhabit the Luxembourg, and to concert and combine [to destroy] the happiness of the French people; they will destroy you also who give them laws; friends and foes of the 31st of May, the 10th of August forms your indictment.[3] You have usurped the power of the CAPETS, you have destroyed Feudality, Priesthood, and Nobility, you have thrown down Escutcheons, Crosses, and Sceptres; you will all be murdered in your curule chairs. LANJUINAS[4] will fall at the side of POULTIER,[5] and the blood of CHENIER[6] will flow with that of ISNARD.[7]

It appears by this intelligence, which is accurate, that there are

[1] Charles-Théodore Beauvais de Préau (1772–1825), later a general in the French armies. Adélaïde-Blaise-François Le Lièvre, Marquis de la Grange et de Fourilles (1766–1833), cavalry general.

[2] Jean-Siffrein Maury (1746–1817), a member of the Constituent Assembly (1789–91) who had left France in 1792, was made cardinal in 1794.

[3] The insurrection of 31 May 1793 spelled the end of the Girondists and the triumph of the Jacobins. On 10 Aug the government called for a mass conscription of the people—450,000 men were added to the armies to fight a total war.

[4] Jean-Denis (later Comte) Lanjuinais (1753–1827).

[5] François-Martin (later Comte) Poultier-Delmotte (1753–1826), French politician and editor, president of the Convention (1794).

[6] Marie-Joseph de Chénier (1764–1811), brother of the poet André, a member of the Council of 500 (1795).

[7] Maximin Isnard (1751–1825), French revolutionary, member of the Council of 500.

more dangerous conspiracies against the Government than those of the Terrorists, and that the latter, without leaders, money and allies, ought less to occupy our attention than men paid, cherished, and fostered by the Foreign Powers; by the fortunes of their relatives; by the elements of their past conspiracies; by the accomplices of Vendimiaire, who are not yet dispersed, and who correspond still with their chiefs; finally, by that crowd of writers who prostitute to them their criminal and venal pen. We cannot dissemble that the Terrorists have done much evil, but it was when they were the machines of Government, and existed only by the Government; left to their own strength, a single blast overthrows them. But the Royalists are connected with all the Kings of Europe, with all our vices, with all our proud egotists, whom the Republic conceals in her bosom, and whose number is alarming.—*From a French Journal.*

ANGERS, March 29.[1]—CHARETTE arrived here two days ago. I went to the prison in which he was confined to see his wounds dressed. I was beside him; he was in great pain; he had two contusions in his head, and his fingers were very much hurt. He said he had a strange feeling in his right hand, something like a scratch. When he was dressed, he said. "What do you want? This is done; I shall soon be well." He did not seem to expect that he would be put to death. Some persons drew him into a conversation with them, after giving him spirits. He delivered a warm eulogium upon CANCLAUX, HOCHE, and one General JACOB,[2] who are confined in the prisons of Nantes. He affirmed, that they had always fought well; and that it was wrong to keep them in confinement. He said he never believed that the French could fight so well, and with so much courage; particularly the Chasseurs of Cassel, and of the Mountain; and that if the French had not been divided in their opinions, the War in La Vendee would not have lasted two months. He was asked, why after the pacification he did not remain quiet? He replied, "Because they had not kept the promise which they made him."

They said to him, you have made us lose a great many men. "Ah! one cannot make pancakes without breaking the eggs." They asked him if he knew that STOFFLET had been shot? Yes; this was a scoundrel: as for me, I have been taken after my troops were defeated, but still I have been surprized. In fact, two Cavaliers in disguise went to the house of a peasant, telling him that they had wandered, that

[1] From the *Star* 11 Apr 1796.

[2] Jean-Baptiste-Camille (later Comte de) Canclaux (1740–1817), French cavalry general. Louis-Lazare Hoche (1768–97), French general who helped put down the Vendean revolt. Maximilien-Henri-Nicolas Jacob (1765–96), French general shot as a traitor.

the Republicans had pursued them, and that they did not know what rout General CHARETTE had taken. The peasant shewed them the wood where he was; they flew together to give notice to the detachment which invested the wood; they hunted him like a hare, and surprized CHARETTE, supported by two Cavaliers. What gave him most pain was, that he had not fallen in the field of battle. He wished to give his girdle full of Louis to TRAVOT,[1] who arrested him. He replied, that he had vanquished him, that he was satisfied, and that he might keep his Louis.—You are, said CHARETTE to him, a brave man; I have nothing more to offer you; I could wish that you had the sword sent me from England, but I cannot get it. I have sent to Paris to get a scabbard of silver for it; it is mounted in gold; but I cannot get it without betraying the possessor.

He has not been shot at Angers; his examination must be interesting. He was an impressive figure. He is lively, has a sweet voice, a brown complexion, most beautiful eyes, a chin rather long, and thick lips; he is well made. He asked for a pipe to smoke, which was given him. He had upon his arrival at Head-quarters, a private conversation with HEDOUVILLE,[2] TRAVOT, and VALENTINE, which was the reason why he was not examined at the prison, as they had examined all the others half an hour after their arrival. I waited till Ten o'Clock at night, which was two hours after he arrived.—They put him in a room; he asked for onions and cheese for supper, and lay down upon a bed, where he slept well till they came seeking him to go to Nantes. I am anxious to know the event of this journey. They say in our town, that the Patriots of Nantes wish to have him, because, being a native of Nantes, the people there will see that it is the same person who made his entry into that place after the pacification.

CHARETTE says, it is six months since he has quitted his boots. They said to him, your Nephew has been shot at Nantes. No, it was only my Cousin German, I know it. And by what means? By the orders which I sent him.

His dress consisted of a hussar vest, with *fleurs-de-lys*, stocking pantaloons of white wool, and boots, a scarlet girdle, and a white handkerchief marked with his name.

GENOA.[3]—The Government, true to its system of neutrality, have

[1] Jean-Pierre (later Baron) Travot (1767–1836).

[2] Gabriel-Théodore-Joseph (later Comte d') Hédouville (1755–1825), French general and diplomat.

[3] From the *Star* 11 Apr 1796 (C omitted the opening four paragraphs of a report dated 14 Mar).

in the mean time refused compliance with all the demands made by the Charge d'Affaires for the French Republic. They were reduced to one only, which was five millions in anticipation for the cession of Onielle and of Loano. The friends of the coalition, afraid without ground, lest the Republic of Genoa should depart from its system, have given information of the demands to the English Minister, who was at Milan, and who has arrived here within these three days, to obstruct their satisfaction by threats. In concert with the Imperial Minister, he has notified that all assistance, and all hope of any cession given to the French by the Genoese Government, will be considered by the Combined Powers as a declaration of War. The Combined Powers know that such a proceeding was unnecessary; but they have adopted it for the purpose of being able to say, that they have restrained the Genoese by terror, and for the purpose of having it in their power to treat them as enemies, if ever the coalition have the superiority.

Though the Genoese Government cannot lend any money to the French Republic, as well from want of the means, as from motives of policy, different individuals are disposed to treat with the French Agents. We are even afraid that many have already offered very considerable sums.

We are as yet ignorant what answer the Senate of Genoa has given to the English and Austrian Ministers; but it is probable, that the answer will be, that they will never depart from their Neutrality, and that they will support it against all the Belligerent Powers, to the utmost extent of the force that they can command.[1]

TO THE EDITOR

(TWO PORTRAITS IN ONE)

SIR,

YOU are doubtless acquainted with those ingenious designs, which, as one side or the other is held uppermost, present you with a bearded philosopher, or a blooming beauty. The following piece is in this style. As it stands before you, you have the father; if you change the affirmative periods into negative and v. v., you will have the son. It is by W. Seward, Esq.[2] When I tell you that the author is an alarmist, you may wonder that he should hold the

[1] Genoa was soon to be transformed, by the scheming of Bonaparte, into the Ligurian Republic—a prelude to annexation.

[2] William Seward (1747–99), man of letters, friend of Dr Johnson.

present admired minister so cheap. The peculiar turn of his studies will perhaps explain this deviation from a general law. He has long employed his leisure in contemplating "distinguished persons." The survey fixed in his mind a scale, by which when he came to measure Mr. Pitt, he found him a very dwarf in efficiency and (what properly makes up the other half of such a character), a giant in pretensions.

I do not gaze with the same rapture as Mr. S. "on the sack of nations." Lord Chatham in my estimation, was intent upon filling the world with admiration rather than with happiness, and I hold him much more fit for the minister of Gengis Khan than of Marcus Aurelius. In considering two men as war-ministers, it is, however, fair to contrast the nature and issue of their enterprizes. But luckily for the son, we are as content under the disgraces brought by his counsels on the British arms, as our predecessors were elated by the glorious victories of the father. B.[1]

LORD CHATHAM[2]

seems to have been one of those superior spirits, who, in mercy to mankind, are permitted occasionally to visit this lower world, to revive or create Nations, and to decide the fate of Empires.

The British Empire, sinking under the disability of his immediate predecessors, soon regained its pristine vigour under the influence of Lord Chatham. His great mind pervaded every part of it, and, like the torch of Prometheus, illuminated and animated the whole. Called into power at the middle time of life, and with some experience in the complicated business of politics, by the voice of the people, and against the inclination of his Sovereign, he never had the insolence to declare with what rank only of the executive department of Government he would do his country the honour and favour to be contented. In opposition to the Ministers of his Sovereign, he never, from spleen or from indignation, dared to attempt to innovate upon the established Constitution of his country, and, with a view to be a favourite with the people, cajole them with the hopes of an increase of their power and of their consequence, which he never in his heart intended they should possess. When Prime Minister, he never dealt

[1] "B" might be Beddoes or possibly George Burnett (c 1776–1811), friend of Southey and former Pantisocrat, but the giant-dwarf metaphor in the first paragraph suggests that C had a hand in its composition. Cf *CN* I 160 and n, I 30 and n.

[2] See Seward *Anecdotes of Some Distinguished Persons, Chiefly of the Present and Two Preceding Centuries* (2nd ed 4 vols 1795) II 361–3. The excerpt had appeared in the *European Magazine* XXVIII (Dec 1795) 388.

out the dignities and emoluments of office to persons merely because they were related to and connected with him, and whom he intended to direct, from the superiority of his understanding to theirs, and from his knowledge of their incapacity to fill the arduous and important stations which, at a very critical period of the State, he had assigned to them. In Council, when a baleful influence prevailed, which from jealousy of authority, and perhaps from meaner motives, by its improper interposition and dangerous interference, like the pernicious Remora, impeded and counteracted the motion of the great vessel of Government, he disdained to temporize, and, from views of interest or of fear, to keep the helm which he was not permitted to manage as he pleased. He nobly, and in the true spirit of the Constitution, declared, that he would be no longer responsible for measures which he was not permitted to guide. Of the manliness, of the wisdom, and of the virtue of this declaration, his fellow-citizens were so sensible, that when his Sovereign, the idol of his people, and himself met on an occasion of public festivity, he appeared to divide with the beloved Vicegerent of Heaven the applauses of the multitude!

Lord Chatham never degraded his mind with that attention to the patronage which his high situation afforded, nor divided and distracted his understanding by the minuteness of detail and the meaner operations of finance, which the most ordinary Clerk in his office could have managed as well as himself. The great powers of his mind were always directed to some magnificent object. He saw with the eye of intuition itself into the characters of mankind: he saw for what each man was fitted. His sagacity pervaded the secrets of the Cabinets of other countries; and the energy of his mind informed and inspirited that of his own. The annals of his glorious administration were not marked by the rise of stocks, or by the savings of a few thousand pounds, but by the importation of foreign millions, the spoil of cities, the sack of nations, by conquests in every part of the globe.

AN IRREGULAR ODE TO THE MOON[1]

I

NOW, when faint purpling o'er the western sky,
The Lord of day his faded lustre weaves,

[1] From the *Anthologia Hibernica* I (Jun 1793) 465, with many changes in the first stanza, the omission of the second stanza, and a change in line 2

And thro' yon wild wood's budding[1] leaves,
Shoots his last solitary ray.
O! let me woo thee from thy azure[2] shrine,
The mildness of thy snowy brow display![3]
The tranquil pause, the extacy divine,[4]
And all the witcheries of the Muse, are thine.

II

Lo from thy beamy quiver fall
Arrowy points, that pierce the ground,
And light the glow-worms twinkling lamp:
On the pale lake's margin damp
The fairy phantoms dance around,
'Till scar'd by frolic echo's cavern'd call
They quit their circle, shudd'ring flit away,
And meltingly in thy wan veil of humid light decay.

III

Oft, let me, by the dimpled stream
That kisses thy reflected beam,[5]
The solemn hour of midnight spend;
When no cares the bosom rend,
When Sorrow's piteous tale is done,
And Trouble sunk with the departed SUN.

IV

For Strife is HIS and grisly War,
And deaf'ning Tumult, never mute;
But, ON THY silent-moving car
Wait Peace, and dew-ey'd Pity's tender train,

of st III below. This is all that the *Anthologia* quotes; the last stanza is incomplete, and there are several more stanzas. PML MS MA 1916 ff 5–7 shows that C copied the first stanza as it appeared and then made his changes; these are indicated in the following notes.

[1] The *Anthologia Hibernica* reads "trembling".

[2] The *Anthologia* reads "saphire".

[3] The *Anthologia* reads "To my rapt eye thy snowey breast display, | Glowing thro' the gloom of night." In his ms C deletes the second line but leaves the first as it was originally.

[4] C omits the following line: "The vision'd scene serenely bright,".

[5] The *Anthologia* reads "Kissing thy reflected gleam". C's ms (f 6) reads "Kissing thy reflected beam".

And Love, sweet warbling to the soothing flute,
Whose dying note
Is wont to float
Seraphic, on the night gale's aery wing,
Tempting the planet-tribe their heav'nly hymns to sing.

V

Hear me! so may the bird of woe
Aye greet thee, from her bowry cell below;
And ocean's rapid surges stand
Check'd by thy silver hand.

THOMAS DERMODY.[1]

The following information is interesting, as it proves that *Gentlemanly* satisfaction might be given by Law, to the exclusion of that gothic compost of Suicide and Murder, called Duelling.

RUSSIA[2]

A YOUNG Irish Gentleman was lately at Moscow. One night he was present at a public masquerade. In walking through the rooms he inadvertently, in the crowd, pressed against a Russian Lady of high quality. The Princess complained of the rudeness; and the Gentleman, the moment he understood what had happened, went to the Lady, and made the most ample apology. The Princess expressed herself satisfied; and the Gentleman naturally supposed this affair settled.

A Russian Officer, probably some dependent of the Prince, the husband of the Lady, anxious to shew his attachment to the family, basely encouraged others of the company, no doubt by misrepresenting the matter, to insult this stranger, by crowding about him and shewing different signs of disapprobation. The Englishman, who kept the house, advised the Gentleman to leave the rooms, as it was idle to contend with hundreds.—He did so; but was followed unperceived by the Russian Officer, who in one of the entries leading

[1] Thomas Dermody (1775–1802). Dermody's appeal to C was compounded of his poverty, his belonging to a subject race (the Irish), his romantic sensibility, and his radical politics. His dissipation brought his career and his life to an early halt. In 1801 Southey wrote to C: "At Falmouth I bought Thomas Dermody's Poems for old acquaintance sake; alas! the boy wrote better than the man". *BE* I 242.

[2] [Thomson] *Letters from Scandinavia* II 91–4. See above, p 242 n 4.

out from the rooms came behind the Irish Gentleman, and pulled him down, assaulting him in the grossest manner. In this conduct, I am sorry to add, the Officer was not only abetted but assisted by the Prince his patron. Every country has some nobility to disgrace it.

The Landlord with difficulty rescued the stranger—the Prince and Officer ran away. The Gentleman, not being able to find the delinquents, applied to the Governor of Moscow for redress, who readily promised that exemplary punishment should be inflicted, and demanded to know what sort of satisfaction the Gentleman expected. The stranger replied, that although the Prince and his associate had behaved like scoundrels, he would be satisfied with the Prince's accepting a challenge to fight him in a duel. The Governor said, that such satisfaction was not permitted by the Laws of Russia, but that he would cheerfully grant any satisfaction which these did admit.

The stranger thanked the Governor for his politeness, and agreed to accept of an apology, which he wrote down, to be delivered by the Prince and the Officer in presence of the company assembled at the next masquerade. The masquerade was in consequence of this exhibition much crouded. The Governor himself attended; and the Prince and Officer, having mounted to the Orchestra, pronounced from it, in view of all the assembly, the apology dictated to them.

The Governor added,—"Thus will I punish any one who treats ill any stranger. Our city and country are not so full of foreigners, that we need drive them from us with rudeness and inhospitality. On the contrary, let us invite society so beneficial to us, with kindness and respect. I am ashamed for my country, that persons of such exalted rank should not shew a better example to their inferiors: but while I have authority, those who will not voluntarily shew a good example shall be held up an example at least of the justice of our laws."

Count ——, the Governor, deserves not merely the thanks of his country, but the esteem of mankind, for such a noble behaviour.

REFLECTIONS RELATIVE TO THE LATE STATE-PAPERS[1]

THE hopes of peace which have been so fondly entertained by many for some time past, have for the present completely vanished. Our Cabinet have published a declaration of their senti-

[1] For the Barthélemy–Wickham correspondence, see above, pp 235–7. Paragraph below from the *Star* 12 Apr 1796.

ments, and it now remains to be seen what line of conduct the French will follow in consequence. It would not surprize us to see them give up to the Emperor, almost without solicitation, the very territories concerning which the Executive Directory has declared the law precluded negociation; for we are still of opinion that the aim of the French is to have Peace, if possible, with all the world, except England, flattering themselves that then the united navies of France, Spain and Holland, will be able to drive the British from the ocean. Time will shew how far we are warranted in our opinion.

The following most striking passage we select from the Earl of Lauderdale's Letters to the Peers of Scotland,—Published in the year 1794.[1]

"IN his conscious incapacity to treat, we may anticipate with melancholy certainty the sure cause of protracted hostility: the habit of sacrificing principle to convenience may, indeed, induce the Minister to make a piece of miserable patch work of his character; but he, and those connected with him, must see *that every consideration of policy and wisdom precludes the possibility of his treating with success*. The instant he makes the attempt, by analysing his political character as a man, and his conduct as a Minister, the whole of our situation will stand unveiled to our enemy. They must know that necessity, not choice, dictates the measure. They must feel that want of ability to carry on the war, and not a wish to re-establish tranquillity, leads to the proposal. They must see that *fear of them, and not love of Peace*, actuates his conduct. In the very proposal they will best discern the extent of their victories: in the past language and conduct of Ministers they will alone be able to form a commensurate view of their present strength, and our humiliation. It would be laying the country at the feet of France, and stating in the plainest characters, that any terms must be accepted, because no resistance could any longer be made.

"But we cannot suppose the French so blind in their discernments, as not to have marked the political character of the man.—It requires not their ingenuity to discover that the depth of his necessitous submission, will be proportionate to the extent of his original arrogance and folly. Can we believe for a moment, that they are so lost

[1] James Maitland, Earl of Lauderdale (see above, p 17 n 4) *Letters to the Peers of Scotland* (1794) 239–43 (italics as in *M Chron*). These two quoted paragraphs and the following four are from *M Chron* 13 Apr 1796.

to the remembrance of even his recent policy, as not to observe, that in the conduct of the wary Empress of the North,[1] there is a rule and a guide laid down for their adoption? In treating with him, will they not imagine that it is but to refuse, and new concessions must be made? That it is only to deny, and fresh submission must ensue? The sacrifice of character, and of what he stated to be the interest of the nation, *to her*, will insure the concession of our dearest interests *to them*; and if in the year 1791, to preserve his place, the Minister made light of the honour of his country—when he attempts to treat, in the situation to which he has now reduced us, he will learn the consequence of such conduct, by the solid and calamitous sacrifices he will be obliged to make—sacrifices not made more to necessity than to his past and present impolicy and ambition. It will unfortunately, however, not be even necessary for them to look back to this memorable event: it is the nature of man to demand what he conceives would have been asked; and in the submissions that Mr. PITT would have forced upon France, we may form a competent judgment of the terms that he will have it in his power to make."

Such were the opinions of the noble Earl, whose zealous exertions as a Peer of Parliament are actuated by a firm conviction, that the junto who have the Administration of England in their hands, would sacrifice the best interests of the country to their love of office. It is a dreadful precipice upon which we stand, and surely it becomes the People of England to pause and demand whether England shall be sacrificed to the house of PITT. They are to weigh this Minister and his interests against Great-Britain; for we demand in fair argument, whether an opening is not made to a Negociation by the very answer, lofty as it is, which the Directory have given to our message? They reproach our Ministers with insincerity; they declare that they distrust their professions; but evidently shew that if they could have confidence in their wishes for Peace, they would meet the nation with frankness.

Let us then give to the French an unequivocal proof of our sincerity. Let us petition HIS MAJESTY to dismiss from his Councils men who have equally demonstrated their incapacity for war and peace. And with a new Administration, who have not sullied the character of England by abetting the Despots of Europe in their schemes of partition, nor disqualified themselves for Negociation by scolding the nation that they could not beat, let us with our own conquests in one hand, hold out to them with the other a fair and

[1] Catherine II of Russia.

equitable offer for the concessions which we think it important for the safety of Europe that we should demand from them.

They cannot believe that we shall surrender up the French and Dutch settlements we have taken, for nothing in return. They do not say so. Their answer will not admit of such an interpretation; but they say, in clear and intelligible words, that they do not see the features of sincerity in the Message of our present Ministers.

If it should be said, "What, shall we stoop to their insolence, even in return for our own? We will perish rather in the last ditch of our Island!" This is very spirited and very British; but it will not hold. The pressure is too heavy on the mass of the people already.—A very little more. A very few millions in addition to those we have already lavished, will bring us by necessity to that which ought now to be the choice of wisdom, and we shall at last be forced to call in those very men to rescue us from shipwreck, whose voices, if listened to, would have saved us from the storm.

PROCEEDINGS IN THE BRITISH LEGISLATURE

HOUSE OF COMMONS

TUESDAY, *April 5th.*

THE House resolved itself into a Committee to take into consideration the Leicester and Worcester petitions for a tax upon dogs. Mr Hobart[1] in the Chair.

Mr. DENT rose to state his own reasons and the opinions of other people concerning the motion of which he formerly had given notice for a tax upon dogs. He shewed that such a tax was not only desirable but necessary on account of their destruction of cattle and their great consumption of provisions. Allowing therefore one dog to every family, which he thought a moderate computation, there were two millions of dogs in this kingdom. By the proposed tax, this number would probably be reduced to one million; and the amount of the tax at half-a-crown annually on every dog without discrimination, except those which serve as guides to blind men, would be 125,000l. a year.

In the 2d part of the 4th volume of the Manchester Philosophical transactions,[2] 15,000 animals were reckoned to be annually destroyed,

[1] Henry Hobart (1738–99), MP for Norwich.

[2] The statistics are not to be found in the volume cited, though one author does deplore the increase of mad dogs, a subject that demands "the serious

and he believed he should not exaggerate if he reckoned them at 50,000. Fifty-one sheep, worth fifty guineas, have been worried and killed by a dog in Lancashire in one night. He had an account, transmitted to him from Devonshire, of a dog that had worried 400 sheep. It was stated in evidence upon a trial before Lord Chief Justice Hale,[1] that a dog had been watched, and seen to kill two sheep, and afterwards went into a pond and washed himself (*a loud laugh*). The fact being stated to the owner of the dog, was disbelieved because the dog was free from blood; but upon solicitation the dog was hung up by the heels, and he voided a considerable quantity, by which means he was found guilty of the accusation. However highly he valued his Right Hon. Friend, he was obliged to state that gentlemen's dogs were equally criminal with those of the poor, as a dog had been observed to do the same in the neighbourhood of Holwood,[2] and when some persons caught him and perused his collar, they found inscribed upon it a *Right Honourable* —— he left the Committee to fill up the blanks—(*a very loud laugh*). The dog however was pardoned out of respect to his master. (*another peal of laughter.*) As to the danger arising from the multiplicity of dogs, he had to inform the Committee that thirty-three people applied to the Manchester Infirmary in one week with the Hydrophobia. He informed them that allowing a penny per day for the food of one million of dogs, it amounted annually to 3,000,000l. which was 700,000l. more than all the rates of the aged poor of the country. So far he called upon the humanity of the house to adopt his motion. He had heard of a gentleman who contracted with his mealman at 800l. per annum for the supply of his kennel; another he knew to expend 400l. a year for the same purpose. A pack of fox hounds could not be kept for less than 1000l. 1500l. or 2000l. per year.

He then moved that a tax of half-a-crown a head upon each dog should be resolved on. He said if this resolution passed he should afterwards move for another tax upon unkennelled hounds.

Col. STANLEY[3] seconded the motion. The question being put,— "that it is the opinion of this Committee, that a duty of two shillings

---

and speedy attention of the Legislature". Samuel Argent Bardsley "Miscellaneous Observations on Canine and Spontaneous Hydrophobia" *Memoirs of the Literary and Philosophical Society of Manchester* IV pt 2 (1796) 486. This article contains the case of John Lindsay, which Dr Beddoes discusses in the next number of *The Watchman*; see below, pp 273–5.

[1] Sir Matthew Hale (1609–76), chief justice of the king's bench (1671).

[2] Pitt's country-house.

[3] Thomas Stanley (1749–1816), MP for Lancashire.

and six-pence per annum be imposed on dogs of every description."

Mr PITT approved of the laying of some tax on dogs: but thought that some distinction ought to be made between the poor and the opulent: between those who pay and those who do not pay any assessed taxes, that distinction he should propose thus: three shillings per annum for each dog that shall be kept by a person who pays any assessed taxes, and only one shilling for each dog kept by all those who do not pay assessed taxes. The shilling tax indeed might be applied entirely to parochial purposes; but the remaining two thirds of the duty he should propose to be brought forward for public purposes. He should therefore propose an amendment to the present resolution. That instead of a duty of 2s. 6d. there be a duty of 3s. on each dog, meaning afterwards to propose in a Committee on the Bill, that all persons who do not pay assessed taxes shall be charged only the duty of one shilling for each dog.

Mr. WILBERFORCE approved the tax.

Mr. LECHMERE supported the measure. He thought that gentleman who kept a pack of fox hounds should be compelled to pay high in proportion to their number. He thought also that all dogs whatever ought to be taxed, and though he should be execrated by some part of the fashionable world, he would not withstanding say, that of all the dogs in this country that he wished to be taxed highest, were ladies' lap-dogs. To see an athletic fellow six feet high in a janty livery with a couple of lap dogs under his arms, following a lady through Hyde or St James's Park for a whole morning, and following her home with such worthless animals to be fed upon the luxury of a table, was a disgrace to this country under its present circumstances.

Sir G. P. TURNER[1] mentioned several instances to shew, that dogs multiplied as they now are, were a great nuisance: they not only killed Sheep, but disturbed public worship: and there were many in the House who must recollect an instance of a dog's breaking in upon the gravity of that House, with a most indecorous yell, just at the moment that a late Noble Lord (North) was opening the Budget: one called out to know what member had interrupted the order of the House, when the Noble Lord, with his accustomed quickness and good humour, answered, it was the Member for *Bark*-shire.

The amendment, "that it is the opinion of this Committee, that

[1] Sir Gregory Page Turner, Bt (1748–1805), MP for Thirsk.

a duty not exceeding three shillings per annum shall be imposed on each dog, &c." was then put and carried.

WEDNESDAY, *April 6th.*

There being but 34 members in the House, they of course adjourned till to morrow.

THURSDAY, *April 7th.*

General SMITH rose to make his promised motion on the subject of the Barracks. He first animadverted on the enormous expence of their establishment, which had already amounted to 1,400,000l. The expence however was a small point in comparison of the principle. It did indeed demand serious consideration, when *every town was become a citadel, and every village a garrison.* When Barracks were provided capable of containing 34,000 troops, we ought to weigh well the purpose, they were meant to serve. Our peace establishment did not commonly exceed 1,500 men. Either therefore the undertaking was an unnecessary waste of the public treasury, or it betrayed an intention to raise our peace establishment to a force that would portend gloomy things to the liberties of the country, especially when combined with an expression of an honourable Gentleman, that Ministers were willing to employ a vigor beyond law. All this had been done without previous consent of Parliament: in direct opposition to the act for the regulation of the civil list, by which it was provided that no undertaking, the expence of which would exceed 500l. should be made without an estimate and the approbation of Parliament. He moved, "that it be referred to a Committee to investigate the expence of the establishment of Barracks, and the authority by which it had been undertaken."

The SECRETARY at WAR said, that although Barracks had been erected without any formal estimate having been presented, it had been done substantially with the knowledge and under the controul of the House. The general Question had not passed silently; a discussion had taken place on it in the year 1793, on the motion of Mr. M. A. Taylor.[1] He did allow the measure to be novel. There were previously Barracks in the country capable of containing 20,000 troops. New ones were added, because the old Barracks had been intended for the accommodation of the Infantry only, and many of them were inconveniently stationed. In answer to the ques-

[1] Michael Angelo Taylor (c 1757–1834), then MP for Poole, a Pittite who had gone over to the Whigs.

tion, what will be the use of these Barracks on the return of Peace, he observed, would there never again be a War? The running up of temporary Barracks was a considerable expence, and was it not better to have them raised once for all of durable and substantial kind, which although not always used, would be always ready for use. The evil of extending patronage he treated lightly—patronage must be placed somewhere. The salaries of the persons employed in the Barracks were by no means too great. The Officers under the Barrack-master, so far from meeting with sinecures, were obliged to attend constantly, were constantly employed, and had no perquisites: and considering how few temptations the office held out, he considered it very fortunate that they were filled by persons of such character and respectability. They were commonly half-pay officers, attached by long habit to the service, and he rejoiced that there was such a receptacle for the old and wounded officers who had grown grey in the service of their country. Mr. Wyndham allowed and justified the motive assigned by his opponents for the erection of these Barracks; he allowed, that they were meant to secure to the Government the attachment of the Troops. When Sedition and Treason were daily and nightly disseminated, he would say to the Soldiers in the words of a French Comedian,[1] "*If I cannot make them dumb*, I will make you *deaf*." That Ministers were willing to employ a vigor beyond law,[2] he would deliberately repeat; when it should again be deliberately repeated, that the duty of allegiance would cease on the enacting of a particular law, and that Resistance would be a question not of Morality, but of Prudence.

Mr. M. A. TAYLOR observed, that whenever Ministers were charged with a breach of the laws of their Country, they uniformly evaded it by asserting, that they had violated the forms only, not the substance. But did not the laws of the land *prescribe* those *forms*? Surely therefore there must be meaning in them: the legislature had established the *forms* as the means of preserving the *substance*. Mr. Taylor denied the sufficiency of barracks to the accomplishment of the end designed. For soldiers could not always be kept under lock and key; and if it were attempted, would not they feel that they themselves were made slaves in order to impose slavery on their countrymen? But if such discipline were practicable, so much the

[1] Sganarelle, in Molière *Le Médecin malgré lui* III vi.

[2] Windham is repeating his phrase of 23 Nov 1795 (see above, p 61 and n 1) and Fox's remark, in the same debate, that if the Two Bills passed, resistance would be "no longer a question of morality, but of prudence". *Parl Reg* XLIII 321.

worse. *They* only can be expected to fight with enthusiasm for their fellow-citizens, who having mingled with them had imbibed their notions and feelings. Mr. Wyndham had spoken with levity on the subject of patronage: the date was not far removed when he held very different sentiments. But time alters most things, and patriotism is too apt to melt away beneath the rays of court-favour. It became necessary therefore to inform the honourable Secretary, that the patronage of Government had increased to an alarming degree, and had been dangerously augmented by *his* coalition and that of his associates, by the number of places which it became necessary for the ministerial faction to provide for them, among which he reckoned the patronage of barracks. Advertisements of new offices daily stared him in the face. The burthens became daily more galling and oppressive to the people. And yet a system of barracks is justified on the principle that the people of England are *seditious!* The people of England *seditious?* Do they not bear tamely all the loads which a War commenced with barbarous wantonness, and conducted with shameful ignorance and unprincipled profusion, have heaped upon them? The people *seditious*? Have they not suffered their dearest privileges to be wrested from them, the liberty of the press and of speech? Have they not suffered two millions of money to be expended for *barracks* without the consent and recognition of parliament? Is it not ungrateful to reward such meek passiveness of spirit, such pious excess of resignation, by libelling the people of England as *seditious*? The Right Honourable Gentleman in a strain of high-flown sensibility rejoices, that an asylum has been procured for warriors, wounded and grown grey in the battles of their country, by appointing them barrack-masters! I (said Mr. Taylor) have made enquiries *respecting the barrack-master at Lincoln, and have discovered that he was a dancing-master and master of the ceremonies to the Lincoln Assembly! He was moreover a good electioneering man, and had formerly been a serviceable agent to a family of my acquaintance. That family had since fallen into decay, and as the dancing master shrewdly imagined, he should be better paid if he espoused the interests of the other party, he crossed hands, changed partners, and footed on the other side with Lord Hobart*[1] *and Colonel Cawthorne. And this he believed was the true cause of his appointment.* In fine, he regarded the barracks as having been erected for two grand purposes; first,

[1] Robert, Lord Hobart (1760–1816), later 4th Earl of Buckinghamshire; MP for Lincoln.

to overawe the people preparatory to the introduction of new burthens, and secondly, to extend ministerial patronage preparatory to a general election.

Mr. Fox observed, that a system of portentous danger had been made more dangerous by the sentiments, with which the authors of the system had justified it. Previously (said Mr. Fox) to my examination of the immediate subject, I must notice the Right Honourable Gentleman's allusion to a former declaration of mine. My sentiments with regard to the right of resistance are unchanged and unchangeable; and they are these. *In case of power used against the declared voice and for the oppression of the people, whether it be from a minister or a number of ministers, or appear in the shape of a majority in a senate, or from an union of Kings, Lords, and Commons,* RESISTANCE IS THE RIGHT OF THAT PEOPLE. *Under these principles I have been bred, under these principles I have lived, under these principles it is my duty to die!*—Reverting to the subject in debate, Mr. Fox observed that it was disgraceful in the extreme to our Army to suppose, that because there may be designing men in this country, that therefore the whole Military were easily to be corrupted: yet upon this supposition did the propriety of the Barrack system rest, as its only foundation. The Right Honourable Gentleman declares to our armies, "If I cannot make them dumb, I will make you deaf!" Alas! he cannot make them *partially* deaf. When he makes them *deaf* to sedition, he makes them deaf to all the sayings that nourish a sense of freedom in their minds. *Unconditional and indiscriminate obedience, is not the duty of a Soldier in a free state. He is to obey lawful commands; but so far from being bound to become a Liberticide, in case of illegal commands it is his duty at once to refuse obedience, and cease to be a Soldier, when by remaining a Soldier he would cease to be a Citizen!* The system of Barracks obtained in France before the Revolution. Did it secure the fidelity of the French Soldiers? Indeed it was extraordinary as well as unfortunate, that while his Majesty's Ministers were declaiming against the wickedness of the Rulers, and exhorting us to avoid the measures which led to the calamities of France, they themselves were daily imitating those very measures, and unless they were checked in their career, might bring on us the same calamities. *His Majesty's Ministers are the great Revolutionists of England, the powerful and effective Allies of Paine and Barlow. Paine asserts: and they furnish facts to prove the truth of Paine's assertions.* Paine said, "Your Constitution is a farce: do you not see that Parliament is nothing more than an arranged Majority, ready to register the edicts of the Minister? He proposes and Parliament is sure to comply."[1] What did the Ministers do? They heaped grievance on grievance, provoked discontent and called it Sedition—then under the pretext of danger, daily brought forward measures hostile to the very principles of the Constitution, and in contempt of the voice of the people, buoyed them up on the full tide of an obsequious majority. Could any one deny it? Have they not relied with such insolent confidence on the pliability of the House, as to disregard even the formality of asking its consent? Without the consent or knowledge of the House of Commons have they not spent two millions of money? And spent it in the erection of Barracks? *Barracks* which, they must know, have been always regarded with a jealous eye, and only partially permitted! And because our Ancestors reluctantly gave a partial permission, on this our Ministers justify their having universalized the system without permission: as if there were any resemblance between assenting on special application that a small part of a small army, should be kept in Barracks, and allowing Ministers to barrack the whole of a large army without our assent. This was to hunt for an exception, and then quote it as a rule. It had been said, that if the whole of the extent and expence of the present system of Barracks, had been laid before the House, they would not have agreed to it. He would not say so, for he scarcely could conceive a measure of Ministers, to which the House would not agree: but their conduct was certainly unconstitutional. Parliament had nothing left but either to bring Government into contempt by refusing to sanction what Government stood pledged for, or agree to measures, the principles of which tended to supersede the functions of the Legislature altogether. The Ministers professed a sanctified horror at the most distant prospect of innovation: yet they were themselves the greatest Innovators in this Country—they had altered the law of Treason, they had repealed an article in the Bill of Rights, and now they were about to justify a measure, which in its immediate consequences would be to vote the House of Commons useless.

The CHANCELLOR of the EXCHEQUER vindicated the sentiments of the SECRETARY at WAR. To affirm it an unconstitutional measure to separate the Soldier from the Citizen he thought unfounded, since by the uniform practice of Government, and the sub-

[1] A summation of, rather than a quotation from, Paine's remarks on the British Constitution in *Rights of Man*; see esp (1st ed 1791) 60–1, 153–4.

jection* to the Mutiny Law, a distinction between the Soldier, and the other parts of the Community was recognized and established.

Mr. WILLIAM SMITH supported the motion. One of the best excuses for the system of Barracks was the relief given to Inn-keepers; but allowing, as he did, the great burthen which they felt from quartering soldiers, might not compensation have been made to them? A part only of the enormous expence of Barracks would have afforded them essential relief. The Right Honourable Secretary had said, that our method of quartering soldiers hitherto was anomalous to the conduct of all other countries. He hoped in God, it would always be so! It had been the pride of Britons, that their Constitution was anomalous to that of other countries; and he trusted, that the constitutional mode of *quartering* soldiers, adopted by the wisdom of our ancestors, as best fitted to the preservation of a limited monarchy, would not be abandoned for the system of Barracks, a system fit only for the most absolute *despotism.*

Mr. COURTNEY in his happiest vein of irony complained of the unfairness and want of candour with which his Honourable Friend (the Secretary of War) had been treated. From an uncommon modesty his Honourable Friend had concealed from the House a most extraordinary and ample fund, to supply in great measure the enormous expence of erecting Barracks in every part of the kingdom. All the *dung* of the dragoon horses, which had till now remained the *douceur* and perquisite of the soldiers, was now to be sold by *open* contract, and the produce remitted to the War-Office to be applied to services of state. The Board of Agriculture had approved of this new regulation; and if with due decorum it could be extended to the Infantry, a standing army in Peace would be of the greatest utility, and our soldiers might *manure* the lands which they were prevented from cultivating.—Mr. Courtney asserted, likewise, that his Honourable Friend had been misunderstood in another part of his argument.

* These are *necessary* evils: necessary for the *purposes* of discipline without which an army could not be kept together. But because these *evils* are necessary *therefore* the soldier ought the more to mingle with his countrymen: that the sacred character of citizen,[1] which he might be apt to forget in the *ranks*, he might learn again in his *quarters.*

[1] The question of barracking troops became involved with another controversy arising out of the French Revolution: whether the soldier should enjoy the full rights of the citizen. Burke had protested against the French view, as Pitt does here. See *Reflections on the Revolution in France* (1790) 318–20. C naturally supports the position that Fox has just expressed. See above, pp 146–7; also *Declaration of . . . the Whig Club* (1796) 12, reprinted below, App B, p 389.

He had said, that the soldiers by being shut up in Barracks would be precluded from hearing detestable and seditious doctrines: he was too well acquainted with the generous sentiments of his Honourable Friend not to know that he alluded to the sentiments taught by Mr. Reeves and his associations, who were ramified in committees, sub-committees, and inferior clubs over the whole kingdom. Mr. Courtney said, he had sympathized with the Honourable Secretary in the pleasures which he had anticipated from the appointment of meritorious officers. Ministers had six-and-fifty new places to bestow: he was perfectly persuaded that fifty, at least, gallant and veteran officers had been provided for, without any regard to election-influence. He would therefore move for a new list of the Barrack-masters. After some conversation between Mr. Sheridan, Fox, and Grey, and Messrs. Pitt and Steel, on an apparent inconsistency in the accounts, the House divided on General Smith's motion—Noes 98. Ayes 24.

PORTSMOUTH,

April 8.

ADMIRAL CORNWALLIS[1]

THIS morning, about nine o'clock, the court assembled, and remained deliberating from that time until one, when the Court was opened, and strangers were admitted.

The JUDGE ADVOCATE then called over the names of the Members; and, after having noticed, in the usual forms, the occasion for which the Court had been assembled, the time it had sat, and read over the charges, he proceeded to deliver the SENTENCE:

That the court having heard the evidence in support of the charges exhibited against the Honourable WILLIAM CORNWALLIS, Vice-Admiral of the Red; and having heard his Defence, and the Evidence in his behalf; and having maturely weighed and considered the same, were of opinion,

That, with respect to the two first Charges, of his returning without leave, after having been ordered to proceed to Barbadoes, and of his disobeying the Orders he had received, MISCONDUCT WAS IMPUTABLE TO HIM, for not having shifted his Flag on board the MARS or MINOTAUR, and proceeding in either of them to the West-Indies—But in consideration of other circumstances, the Court

[1] From the *Star* or *Sun* 9 Apr 1796 or *M Chron* 11 Apr.

ACQUITTED HIM OF ANY DISOBEDIENCE in his conduct on that occasion.

"With respect to the Third Charge, of his having, after his return, disobeyed the orders of the Board of Admiralty, in not going out to the West-Indies in the ASTREA frigate, the Court were of opinion that the Charge was NOT PROVED; and therefore ACQUITTED Admiral CORNWALLIS upon that charge."

Admiral CORNWALLIS, who, during the trial conducted himself with great firmness and composure, heard the sentence read without any emotion; and then making a slight bow to the court, retired along with Mr. ERSKINE and some other friends.

Reports respecting the dissolution of Parliament have, within these few days, been many and various. Some have whispered about the report of an immediate dissolution: the most general opinion [is] that it will be dissolved in August.[1]

PLYMOUTH

April 9th.[2]

An express arrived at head-quarters, which states, that the Tinners had been very riotous; had struck the Under-Sheriff and a Corporal of the Worcester Militia, (the latter so severely that his life was despaired of); and had committed other acts of violence near Truro. Fortunately Major St. JOHN, and six companies of the Worcester Militia, with a six pounder, arrived on the spot. The Riot-Act was read, and the field-piece was elevated, and fired over their heads with cannister-shot. This at first had a good effect, and the Tinners retreated; but rallied again, when Major St. JOHN addressed them with great humanity, and told them, if they did not disperse, he must be compelled to point the field-piece, and fire amongst them. The tinners not regarding this humane advice, became more riotous, when the Worcester Militia advanced with great vivacity, and notwithstanding showers of brick-bats and stones hurled upon them, they made a brisk charge with fixed bayonets, and put the motley group to the rout.—They secured nine prisoners,

[1] The King dissolved Parliament on 19 May and called for a new election. Item from the *Star* 14 Apr (slightly altered).

[2] From the *Star* 12 Apr 1796; the report in *The Times* and *Gazetteer* 12 Apr includes an opening paragraph stating that about 3000 tinners had rioted against the high price of flour.

among whom were the fellows who so ill-treated the Under-Sheriff and the Corporal of the Worcester.—They are all committed to Bodmin gaol.

TO THE EDITOR OF THE WATCHMAN

SIR,

A CORRESPONDENT of yours who signs himself Phocion,[1] has been at an infinite deal of trouble in collecting the exaggerated reports of the proceedings against Jones and Binns; and in the relation has been pretty liberal with his invectives. I am well assured that the Birmingham Magistrates are too well employed to descend to a public dispute with him;—and nothing but a consciousness of the good qualities and eminent virtues of the Gentlemen so vilely traduced; and a sincere wish to avoid the charge of misprison, not of treason against Society, could have induced me to obtrude myself at all on the patience of your readers.

One would have thought that the services that the Magistrates, (whose cause I am attempting feebly to defend), have on many important occasions rendered to their country, would have entitled them to common decency and respect at least. Phocion seems to think that his fellow-citizens were hardly dealt by: but, I can assure you Sir, that the leniency, the kindness with which the Magistrates acted towards them, does honour to their feelings: and instead of exercising that rigour which the prisoners' offences might have warranted, they suffered the administration of their power to pass gently by them. Nay so desirous were they to remove the irksomeness of the necessary captivity of Jones and Binns, that they permitted the most unrestrained intercourse with them: and not only did they hold a levee on the Sunday, but were attended by a party of Ladies to tea on that afternoon.

If Phocion could bring himself to believe that Magistrates were actuated by a feeling sense of the unpleasant situation of Jones and Binns, and of the insults to which such a situation exposed them; rather than they were governed by a slavish fear of doing wrong, he would not treat the conveyance of those men to the public office in a coach, with that unmeaning sneer, that peevish expression of resentment that he has done. But the fact is, that Phocion seems so strongly governed by passion and prejudice, that with him it is a sort of

[1] For Phocion's (i.e. the Rev John Edwards's) contributions, see above, pp 127–30, 160–2, 199–201.

instinct, to permit no good sense to be attached to any thing that will possibly admit of a bad one. Even the wholesome admonition of the justice who said to Binns after he was admitted to bail, "take care how you come before us again, for when you do, we shall not behave to you so gently as we have done this time," could not but meet the forked censure of this disguised Phocion.

The "Skill" and "Presence" and "Ingenuity" of Mr. White on this occasion, was more necessary than the "narrow faculties" of Phocion can discover. He who in 1794 delivered back to their country a Hardy,[1] a Tooke,[2] and a Thelwal[3] from the strong grasp of the Law, could not suffer these, the meanest of his fellow creatures, to become its prey. As a wise and good Lawyer, he came to tender his advice on an unprecedented occasion, to the Magistrates; and to "administer Justice" to the captives; he came to loose the fetters that ignorance (not inhumanity) had rivetted on one of them. If in the seizure of the Gentleman's papers alluded to in No. 4; if in the "splitting the indictment;" if in the large bail demanded by the Magistrates; if in any part of their conduct they have acted any otherwise than as honest and humane officers, let them not be attacked from a masked battery, give them fair play.

Is there no regular proceedings pointed out in our law-books against Magistrates exercising an undue authority? Besides the Crown-office, have we not a Commons House of Parliament to appeal to, where our grievances however many, if real, will be sure to meet with redress? And though that honourable house refused an enquiry into the conduct of the Magistrates in the year that Birmingham was miraculously delivered from the machinations of artful, designing men, yet it cannot be supposed by any candid mind, that it proceeded from any connivance with them, but from a well grounded consciousness that the charges in circulation, were the effect of a peevish, vexatious, resentful disposition.

[1] Thomas Hardy (1752–1832), founder of the London Corresponding Society, was tried, along with Horne Tooke, Thelwall, and nine others, for high treason in the State Trials of 1794. He was brilliantly defended by Thomas Erskine and acquitted, as were the others.

[2] The Rev John Horne Tooke (1736–1812), notable wit and independent politician. See C's *Verses* addressed to him: *PW* (EHC) I 150–1, *CL* I 224–5.

[3] Thelwall, the principal orator of the London Corresponding Society, who, though a believer in peaceful change, so alarmed the government by his eloquence that he was partly responsible for the passing of the Two Acts. See above, p 98 and n 3. During the course of *The Watchman* he and C struck up a friendship after an amicable controversy. See *CL* I 204–5, 212–16, 220–2, 258–62, 276–87, and 293–5. In later years C's admiration cooled.

As Phocion has thought proper to conceal his name, I shall claim the same advantage, though I dare say from very different motives.

ANTI-PHOCION.[1]

BIRMINGHAM,
April, 15th 1796.

For the omission of the greater part of ANTI-PHOCION'S letter we offer no apology. Anti-Phocion will perceive that we have selected every thing that appears like fact or argument. The following is one, and not the most violent, of the passages omitted. "Come forward, thou MAGISTRATICIDE and tell the virtuous, injured Magistrates of Birmingham who advised thee to this assassin's trick; to what party thou hast been made the tool, once in thy life, and when injured innocence calls aloud for it, publickly correct your errors, or sullenly admit the shameless depravity of thy heart!" Having admitted an attack on the character of men in important situations, we should have deemed it criminal to have refused or delayed the publication of any communications in their defence. But we confess that we should have supposed the last paragraph of the printed copy of this letter *rank irony*, if other passages had not convinced us, that Anti-Phocion wrote in all the downright sincerity of violent anger.

The necessity (in a *moral* view) of inserting Anti-Phocion's letter, and the importance of the debate on the barracks, which we have therefore given to a length disproportionate to our limits, have united to make us defer the insertion of the Parliamentary Proceedings for the other days of the preceding week.[2] The debates will be given more or less abridged in proportion to their importance: and we earnestly recommend to our readers the attentive perusal of Mr. Taylor's and Mr. Fox's speeches; which we have employed our whole diligence to report in a manner worthy of them.

[1] That "Anti-Phocion" was a satiric mask for C or one of similar views is rendered probable by this ludicrous compliment to White, to whom the acquittal of Hardy and the others represented a setback, as it did also to the government; of a piece with this compliment are his praises of the House of Commons and the Birmingham magistrates. The italic phrase "*rank irony*" (paragraph below the letter) is an underlining of the joke.

[2] There were debates from Mon 11 Apr until Fri 15 Apr. These would occupy "the preceding week", since this issue of *The Watchman* was published on Tue 19 Apr; but the debates were not given, and instead C resumed with the debate of 18 Apr. See below, p 300.

THE WATCHMAN

No. VIII. WEDNESDAY, APRIL 27, 1796

Published by the Author, S. T. COLERIDGE, Bristol;
And by PARSONS, Paternoster-Row, London

THAT ALL MAY KNOW THE TRUTH;
AND THAT THE TRUTH MAY MAKE US FREE!

REMONSTRANCE TO THE FRENCH LEGISLATORS[1]

GUARDIANS of the LIBERTY of EUROPE! the Individual, who has devoted his Joys and his Sorrows to the Interests of the whole, partakes of the importance of the object which he has accustomed himself to contemplate. He addresses you therefore with that dignity with which his subject invests him: for he speaks in the name of HUMAN KIND. When America emancipated herself from the oppressive capriciousness of her old and doting Foster-Mother, we beheld an instructive speculation on the probable *Loss and Gain* of unprotected and untributary Independence; and considered the Congress as a respectable body of Tradesmen, deeply versed in the ledgers of Commerce, who well understood their own worldly concerns, and adventurously improved them. France presented a more interesting spectacle. Her great men with a profound philosophy investigated the interests common to all intellectual beings, and legislated for the WORLD. The lovers of Mankind were every where fired and exalted by their example: each heart proudly expatriated

[1] C's reactions to the Wickham–Barthélemy correspondence mark a crucial turn in his ideas about France. The correspondence first appeared in the London newspapers 11 Apr. C's initial response was to express grief over the continuation of the war by reprinting the "Interesting Narration" (above, pp 238–41). The *Star* and the *M Chron* editorially followed the standard Whig line of questioning the sincerity of the English offer, and in the same issue (pp 252–5) C reprinted excerpts from these editorials on the seeming intransigence or inability of Pitt and his party. But here, writing perhaps a fortnight after reading the correspondence, he subjects the French position to serious questioning and begins to turn toward the position expressed in *France: an Ode* (1798). Cf "Political Views", pp 209–10.

itself, and we heard with transport of the victories of Frenchmen, as the victories of Human Nature. But the effects of Despotism could not be instantly removed with the cause: and the Vices, and the Ignorance, and the Terrors of the multitude conspired to subject them to the tyranny of a bloody and fanatic faction. The fortune of France prevailed; and a Government has been established, which without counteracting the progressiveness, gratifies the more importunate frailties, of our present nature. To give stability to such a Constitution, it is needful only that its effects should be experienced. Peace therefore is necessary.

At this season, when all the creative powers of nature are in action, and all things animated and inanimate inspire the human heart with joy and kindliness, at this season, your executive Department have transmitted a paper, which, they knew would be the signal for recommencing the horrors of War. Legislators of France! if you had been nursed amid the insolent splendour of hereditary prosperity, ignorant of misery and unsympathizing with the miserable, I should not dare repeat to you the common-place pleadings of humanity.—But *you* are from among your countrymen.

> But *you* were nurs'd upon the self-same hills,
> Fed the same flocks by fountains, shades, or rills:[1]

You ought to tremble and weep beneath the stern necessity, that should command you to issue the mandate for the death even of *one* man—alas! what if for the death of perhaps half-a-MILLION? Permit me then to examine whether or no this necessity existed.—The Directory assign as their motives for rejecting his Britannic Majesty's overtures, first, their doubts respecting the sincerity of the English Court, and secondly, "the constitutional act, which does not permit it to consent to any alienation of that which according to the existing laws, constitutes the Territory of the Republic."—The Directory doubts the sincerity of the English Court, because Mr. Wickham who transmitted the overture, was not himself authorized to negociate.—If a disposition favourable to Peace had been discovered in the French Government, a man of greater name and dignity than the Minister to the Swiss Cantons, would have been appointed to treat with the August Legislature of France; but it ought not to have been expected, that the English Court should send a special messenger of high rank on an uncertain errand. To enquire concerning the intentions of the French Government, Mr. Wick-

[1] Milton *Lycidas* lines 23–4 (altered).

ham was well qualified by his being on the spot with the French Ambassador.

They doubt it likewise because a congress was proposed, "*of which the necessary result would be to render all negociation endless.*" The English Court on the other hand wished "*for the establishment of a congress, which has been so often and so happily the means of restoring Peace to Europe.*" A mere assertion opposed to a mere assertion, and therefore both without force. But the Directory *did* communicate the general grounds of a pacification: they inform the contending Powers, that France is determined to retain her most important conquests: That an act of the Constitution forbids their restoration. —How are other Nations dependent on your internal regulations? What if in a paroxysm of victory ye had passed an act for the junction of England to France? But the inhabitants of the Netherlands themselves wish this union:[1] and it would be unworthy a generous Republic to yield them up to their former Despotism. We should not use those arguments, of which our adversaries may equally avail themselves. To the same motives expressed in the same words the horrors of La Vendee are to be attributed. That no nation has the right of interfering with the affairs of another Country, is a general law: and general laws must not be dispensed with in compliment to the supposed justice of a particular case.

The detention of the Netherlands cannot therefore be defended on the ground of *Justice*: its *Policy* alone remains to be considered! O France! have thy Legislators already degenerated into such abject court-craft, as to know any distinction between Justice and Policy?— But wherein does this Policy consist? Your Commissioners have informed you that these Provinces, reserving an ample supply for themselves, produce Corn enough to supply a third of France. Surely the toil and the treasures, which must be wasted in another campaign, might enable France not to need this supply. Or even if this were impracticable (which it would be insolent unthankfulness to nature to affirm), yet how easily might the free Commerce between France and the Netherlands be made one of the articles of Peace! And is there such magic in the *name* of internal commerce, as to make it the fit object of another series of crimes and miseries? Again, some among you have asserted, that in order to your security against the future ambitious attempts of your cnemics, it is necessary that you should retain the Netherlands. Your enemies assert with at least equal plausibility, that in order to their security against your

[1] That is, with France.

ambition, it is necessary that you should not enlarge your territories. But, Legislators of France! if your system be true, a few years only of Peace would so increase your population and multiply your resources, as to place you beyond all danger of attack. The Tyrants of Europe will be ineffectually employed in preventing the irresistible influence of your example on their own subjects.—Let only your magnificent promises be performed, and we shall have no reason to doubt the Almightiness of Truth. That which in Theory has been ridiculed, must necessarily excite imitation, if realized: for why has it been ridiculed except that the despairing children of this world think it too excellent to be practicable? "Let us (says Condorcet)[1] be cautious not to despair of the human race. Let us dare to foresee in the ages that will succeed us, a knowledge and a happiness of which *we* can only form a vague and undetermined idea. Let us count on the *perfectibility* with which nature has endowed us; and on the strength of the human genius, from which long experience gives us a right to expect prodigies." These are the revolutionary measures which Wisdom prescribes—not the intrigues of your Emissaries, not the terror of your arms.

If however you persevere in your intentions, will your soldiers fight with the same enthusiasm for the Ambition as they have done for the Liberty of their Country? Will they not by degrees amid the stern discipline of arms and the horrors of War, forget the proud duties of *Citizens*, and become callous to the softer claims of domestic life? May not some future Dumourier find a more pliant Army? May not the distresses of the poor drive them to Anarchy? May not the rising generation, who have only *heard* of the evils of Despotism but have *felt* the horrors of a revolutionary Republic, imbibe sentiments favourable to Royalty? Will not the multitude of discontented men make *such* regulations necessary for the preservation of your Freedom, as in themselves destroy Freedom? Have not some of your supposed Patriots already deemed it expedient to limit the liberty of the Press? Legislators of France! in the name of Posterity

[1] C is adapting a passage from Condorcet *Outlines of an Historical View of the Progress of the Human Mind* (1795) 4 (Introduction). The *OED*'s first reference to "perfectibility" is 1794. It had already been used in Godwin's *Political Justice* (1793) I 43. Arthur O. Lovejoy writes: "The term 'perfectibility' to which—though it was apparently invented by Turgot in 1750—Rousseau probably did more than anyone else to give currency, became the catchword of Condorcet and other subsequent believers in the reality, necessity, and desirability of human progress through a fixed sequence of stages, in both past and future." *Essays in the History of Ideas* (Baltimore 1948) 25.

we adjure you to consider, that misused success is soon followed by adversity, and that the adversity of France may lead, in its train of consequences, [to] the slavery of all Europe!

TO THE EDITOR

SIR,

THE paper, from which the subjoined particulars are taken will obtain much attention from medical men. But to me the fact is most interesting in a moral and political view. I will not trouble you with all the ideas that crowded upon my mind on perusing the account; nor will I attempt a selection from the multitude. The extract cannot be read by any person with indifference; and those, who have most regard for their species, will be moved the most. Could the life and death of every individual be circumstantially recorded, the annals of the poor would exhibit a boundless variety of wretchedness. Yet this example would hardly be equalled. It was hard that strenuous resolution, prompted by kind affection, should lead to such a catastrophe, and that a human creature should have been distinguished in misery, merely because he was distinguished in merit, above an hundred thousand fellow-sufferers.

It may be proper to say a word of the cause or causes of the tremendous malady, to which the poor man fell a victim. No competent judge will I imagine, impute it *wholly* to the accident that happened twelve years before. Many will suppose that this accident had no share whatever in its production; and almost every one will set it down as probable that no such disorder would have taken place, if the patient had not been reduced to so deplorable a state of body and mind.

MEDICUS.[1]

John Lindsay, weaver, has been industrious, sober, and regular in his mode of living; but subject to low spirits from the difficulty he found, at times, of maintaining a wife and six young children. His exertions, however, were in general proportionate to his difficulties. But, from the depreciation of labour in 1794, he found, that the most rigid œconomy and indefatigable industry were not sufficient to

[1] In the margin of the annotated copy of *The Watchman* in the BM (p 233) C has noted: "Dr Beddoes". Beddoes drew his materials from Bardsley "Miscellaneous Observations on Canine and Spontaneous Hydrophobia: to Which is Prefixed, the History of a Case of Hydrophobia Occurring Twelve Years after the Bite of a Supposed Mad Dog" *Memoirs of the Literary and Philosophical Society of Manchester* IV pt 2 (1796) 431–88. (See above, pp 255–6 n 2.) The present extract is from pp 435–7, 441.

ward off, from himself and family, the calamities of hunger, debt, and the most abject poverty. The anxiety of his mind now became almost insupportable. As the last refuge for his distress, he applied, a few days previous to the attack of his complaint, to the Overseers of his Parish for their assistance to pay his rent, and thereby prevent the seizure of his goods; but obtained no relief. Overwhelmed with grief and disappointment, he yielded to despair, resigning himself and family to their wretched fate. He was soon roused from this state of fancied apathy, by the piercing cries of his children demanding bread. In a paroxysm of rage and tenderness, he sat down to his loom on the Monday morning, and worked night and day, seldom quitting his seat, till early on the ensuing Wednesday morning. During this period of bodily fatigue and mental anxiety, he was entirely supported by hasty draughts of cold butter-milk, sparingly taken. Nor did he quit the loom, until his strength was completely exhausted. He then threw himself upon his bed, and slept a few hours. On waking, he complained of giddiness and confusion in his head, and a general sense of weariness over his body. He walked five miles that morning, in order to receive his wages, for the completion of his work; and, on his return, felt much fatigued, and troubled with a pain in his head. During the night, his sleep was interrupted by involuntary and deep sighs—slight twitchings in the arms—and a sense of weight and constriction at the breast. He complained of much uneasiness at the light of a candle, that was burning in the room. On evacuating his urine, he was obliged to turn aside his head from the vessel, as he could not bear the sight of the fluid without great uneasiness. Being rather thirsty, he wished for balm tea to drink; but was unable to swallow it from a sense of pain and tightness, which he experienced about the throat, when the liquid was presented to him. He suddenly exclaimed, on perceiving this last symptom, "Good God! It is all over with me!" and immediately recalled to his Wife's recollection, the circumstance of his having been bitten,* twelve years ago, by a large dog apparently mad. The symp-

* Soon after this accident, he applied to a Surgeon at Ashton in this neighbourhood, who dressed the wound for a short time, and ordered the Ormskirk medicine[1] to be taken. The wound was speedily healed; and the Patient had never distrusted his being cured, till the moment he was unable to swallow liquids. I wrote to the Surgeon with a view of obtaining particular information relative to the state of the wound, &c.; but, the circumstance had altogether escaped his memory.

[1] Mr Hill's Ormskirk Medicine, which, according to an advertisement in the *London Chronicle* for 1796 (vol LXXIX p 3), was "prepared by the

ideal object; and then, with a ſudden and violent motion, buried his head underneath the bed-cloaths. The laſt time I ſaw him repeat this action, I was induced to enquire into the cauſe of his terror.—He eagerly aſked, if I had not heard howlings and ſcratchings? On being anſwered in the negative, he ſuddenly threw himſelf upon his knees, extending his arms in a defenſive poſture, and forcibly throwing back his head and body. The muſcles of the face were agitated by various ſpaſmodic contortions;—his eye balls glared, and ſeemed ready to ſtart from their ſockets;—and at that moment, when crying out in an agonizing tone:—"Do you not ſee that black dog?" his countenance and attitude exhibited the moſt dreadful picture of complicated horror, diſtreſs and rage, that words can deſcribe, or imagination paint!

WAR.

A new mode recommended.

WOULD it not be a better way of ſettling national diſputes, if, inſtead of employing men and blood-hounds in our armies, we were to employ either game cocks, or ſuch other animals as are known to poſſeſs courage and ferocity:—If this mode were adopted, at leaſt by Europeans, for whoſe benefit we chiefly write, wars, diſputes, and conteſts, whether for territory or commerce, for mountains or mole-hills, nay even for religion itſelf, might be carried on and decided without that effuſion of human blood, which, whatever ſome great folks may think, is of ſome little value. The method ſhould be this: one Prince declareth war againſt another, he challengeth him to ſend ſo many ſhake-bags or turn-outs, to a cockpit, ſuppoſe, for inſtance, in a neutral territory, where *fair play* may be ſhewn.

The feeders of each nation, the bench of biſhops, a delegation of the landed intereſt, and the monied men of both the contending nations, whether abſent or preſent, are to *bet* upon the cocks, and to continue to do ſo till one ſide or the other hath *loſt all their money*; the loſers to be deemed the vanquiſhed party, and to ſubmit to the terms preſcribed or dictated by the winners. This will appear no innovation, for

5. A page from *The Watchman* (1796) No VIII annotated by Coleridge. From a copy in the British Museum, Ashley 2842. See p 275.

toms of hydrophobia became gradually more severe till Saturday when he died. The physician who relates his case, particularized the following, among several other almost equally terrible, circumstances. I observed, he frequently fixed his eyes, with horror and affright, on some ideal object; and then, with a sudden and violent motion, buried his head underneath the bed-cloaths. The last time I saw him repeat this action, I was induced to enquire into the cause of his terror.—He eagerly asked, if I had not heard howlings and scratchings? On being answered in the negative, he suddenly threw himself upon his knees, extending his arms in a defensive posture, and forcibly throwing back his head and body. The muscles of the face were agitated by various spasmodic contortions;—his eye balls glared, and seemed ready to start from their sockets;—and at that moment, when crying out in an agonizing tone:—"Do you not see that black dog?" his countenance and attitude exhibited the most dreadful picture of complicated horror, distress and rage, that words can describe, or imagination paint![1]

WAR

A new mode recommended[2]

WOULD it not be a better way of settling national disputes, if, instead of employing men and blood-hounds in our armies, we were to employ either game-cocks, or such other animals as are

---

Messrs. Hill and Berry, for the Cure of the Bite of a Mad Dog", and was frequently but futilely prescribed, is said to have consisted of Armenian bole, alum, chalk, elecampane, and black pepper.

[1] In the BM annotated copy of *The Watchman*, C has written the following marginal comment at the end of this excerpt (pp 235–6): "In the year 1813 I reperuse this dreadful Case, communicated to me by Dr Beddoes—and my humble opinion is, that excessive Distress of Mind & in a less degree, but yet important, the abstraction of needful Stimulation, had, the first called into activity a lurking Poison, & the second deadened those vires naturæ medicatrices which under happier circumstances ‹would› have subdued & quieted it. It only confirms a fearful conjecture of mine, of 20 years standing, that no Disease was ever yet cured, but merely suspended—if of the nature of Poison. Ex. gr. I believe, no one who has had the Small Pox, Measles, &c, is as secure in Health, as they would have been, if that Poison had not been absorbed. Good Heavens! if this should be true, what an additional argument for the Vaccine Inoculation! as the means, like a Cathartic, of evacuating, first the Small Pox, & then itself.

"*S. T. Coleridge* 17 Feb[ry] 1813—
"71 Berners' Street
London—"

See the illustration opposite for the opening of C's annotation.

[2] From the *CI* 16 Apr 1796. At the end of the eighteenth and the beginning of the nineteenth century cock-fighting

known to possess courage and ferocity:—If this mode were adopted, at least by Europeans, for whose benefit we chiefly write, wars, disputes, and contests, whether for territory or commerce, for mountains or mole-hills, nay even for religion itself, might be carried on and decided without that effusion of human blood, which, whatever some great folks may think, is of some little value. The method should be this: one Prince declareth war against another, he challengeth him to send so many shake-bags or turn-outs, to a cockpit, suppose, for instance, in a neutral territory, where *fair play* may be shewn.

The feeders of each nation, the bench of bishops, a delegation of the landed interest, and the monied men of both the contending nations, whether absent or present, are to *bet* upon the cocks, and to continue to do so till one side or the other hath *lost all their money*; the losers to be deemed the vanquished party, and to submit to the terms prescribed or dictated by the winners. This will appear no innovation, for is it not practised very frequently in this country? Do we not sometimes read in our newspapers of a battle to be fought between the gentlemen of Lancashire and Cheshire; when all the world knows, that they fight only their cocks? Thus may a *just and necessary war* be carried on, and a *regular government* established, without the loss of an ounce of human blood; and thus may our happy constitution be protected, and *Christianity* promoted —not by the *sword* but by the *spur*—not by cutting the throats of men, but merely by cutting the throats of a few *chanticleers* in a *main* or a few *bye-battles!*

was as popular a sport as cricket later became, with thousands of pounds wagered on a "main"—a series of cock-fights with the winners progressively pitted against each other until all were killed but one. The cocks were often armed with artificial steel or silver spurs. Cock-fighting as a "new mode" of war may have been a novel suggestion, but it was a commonplace of the time to write of or to depict the "Cock Pitt"—Parliament—with gamecocks Pitt and Fox fighting a main.

TO A PRIMROSE[1]

[The first seen in the Season.]

————Nitens, et roboris expers,
Turget, et insolida est: et spe delectat.
OVID. METAM.[2]

THY smiles I note, sweet, early flower,
That peeping from thy rustic bower,
The festive news to earth dost bring,[3]
A fragrant messenger of spring.

But tender blossom, why so pale?
Dost hear stern winter in the gale?
And didst thou tempt th' ungentle sky
To catch one vernal glance and die?

Such the wan lustre sickness wears,
When health's first feeble beam appears;
So languid are the smiles that seek
To settle on the care-worn[4] cheek;

When timorous hope the head uprears,
Still drooping and still moist with tears;
If, thro' dispersing grief, be seen,
Of bliss the heavenly spark serene.

And sweeter far the early blow,
Fast following after storms of woe,
Than (comfort's riper season come,)
Are full blown joys, and pleasure's gaudy bloom.

[1] Though this poem has been attributed to him (*PW*—EHC—I 149), C borrowed it from the *Anthologia Hibernica* I (Jan 1793) 60 (var), where it is signed "S—" and dated 15 Feb 1791. In a note kindly sent me by the late A. E. Dobell I learn that in an annotated copy of *The Watchman* in his possession C wrote opposite this poem: "N.B. Not mine".

[2] *Metamorphoses* 15.202–3. Tr Frank Justus Miller (LCL 1958) II 379: "... is bright, swelling with life, but as yet without strength and solidity, and fills . . . with joyful expectation". The motto is also in the *Anthologia*.

[3] Cf the *Anthologia*: "To earth the festive tidings bring".

[4] In the *Anthologia* "care-drencht".

TO THE EDITOR[1]

SIR,

As a learned friend of mine was rummaging an old Trunk the other day, he discovered a false bottom, which, on examination, proved to be full of old parchments. But, what was his joy and surprise, when he discovered that the contents were neither more nor less than some of the lost Tragedies of Sophocles. As the writing is difficult, and the traces of the letters somewhat faded, he proceeds slowly in the task of decyphering. When he has finished, the entire Tragedies will be given to the Public. In the mean time I send you the following fragment, which my friend communicated to me, and which all real Critics will concur with me, I doubt not, in determining to be the genuine production of that ancient Dramatist. His characteristics are simplicity and sententiousness. These qualities, are conspicuous in the following Iambics, which contain a seasonable caution to parents against rashly trusting children out of their sight.— Though your Paper is chiefly occupied in plain English, you may sometimes gratify your learned readers with a little Greek: therefore give them this, if you think that it *will* gratify them. For the benefit of those whose Greek is rather rusty with disuse, I have added a Latin Version, which, I hope, is as pure and perspicuous as Latin Versions of Greek Tragedies commonly are.

I am, Sir, &c.

S. ENGLAND.

[1] From *M Chron* 13 Apr 1796, a parody of Ireland's Shakespeare forgeries (see above, pp 92–8). Professor Richard Porson (1759–1808) is the author, as C implies: note his "Aut professor aut diabolus", which did not appear in *M Chron*. For Porson's authorship see M. L. Clarke *Richard Porson, a Biographical Essay* (Cambridge 1937) 72, Porson *Tracts and Miscellaneous Criticisms* ed Thomas Kidd (1815) 154–7, and *The Correspondence of Richard Porson, M.A.* ed H. R. Luard (Cambridge 1867) 60–1, 70. I suspect Porson's hand in some earlier fooleries in a similar style in *M Chron*. A letter from "E Final" appeared on 7 Jan 1796, proving that Ben Jonson's genius was inspired by sack, and a love-letter from Guy, Earl of Warwick, to Princess Frizzegunnada appeared 10 Feb 1796. If these were indeed by Porson and C knew that he wrote for the *M Chron*, he would have been ready to attribute "S. England", a similar piece, to the same source, though he may have had direct knowledge. C knew James Perry, the editor of the *M Chron*, and had dined with him and Porson's friend Holcroft: see his letter to RS 17 Dec 1794: *CL* I 138–9. Porson married Perry's widowed sister in 1796.

A correspondent, obviously Porson himself, continued to make sport of Ireland in the *M Chron* of 14 Apr in a letter to the editor:

Sir,

As Mr. SAMUEL ENGLAND'S Greek and Latin Verses in your yesterday's Paper have puzzled some

Κρυσταλλοπήκτους τρίπτυχοι κόροι ροὰς
Ὥρᾳ θέρους ψαίροντες εὐτάρσοις ποσί,
Δινοῖς ἔπιπτον, οἷα δὴ πίπτειν φιλεῖ,
Ἅπαντες· εἶτ' ἔφευγον οἱ λελειμμένοι.
Ἀλλ' εἴπερ ἦσαν ἐγκεκλεισμένοι μοχλοῖς,
Ἢ ποσὶν ὀλισθανόντες ἐν ξηρῷ πέδῳ,
Χρυσῶν ἄν ἠθέλησα περιδόσθαι σταθμῶν,
Εἴ μη μέρος τι τῶν νέων ἐσώζετο.
Ἀλλ', ὦ τοκεῖς, ὅσοις μὲν ὄντα τυγχάνει,
Ὅσοις δὲ μή, βλαστήματ' ευτέκνου σποράς,
Ἢν εὐτυχεῖς εὔχησθε τάς θύραζ' ὁδοὺς
Τοῖς παισίν, εὖ σφὰς ἐν δόμοις φυλάσσετε.

Glacie-durata triplices pueri fluenta
Tempestate æstatis radentes pulchras-plantas habentibus pedibus,
In vortices ceciderunt, ut sane accidere solet,
Omnes; deinde effugerent reliqui.
Sin autem inclusi essent vectibus,
Aut pedibus labantes in arido campo,
Auri ponderis sponsione libenter contenderem,
Partem aliquam juvenum servari potuisse.
At, O parentes, tum vos, quibus esse contigit,

---

of your Fair Readers, I intended to have asked the favour of some of your Learned Correspondents to have given a translation; but, observing, in a Print, entitled *The Gold Mines of Ireland*, a reference to that admirable Work—*The renowned History of Giles Gingerbread*, I opened the book and found in it the following beautiful lines, ready cut and dry to my hands. If it is not contrary to the rules of your Paper to re-publish them for the benefit of the *unlearned*, here they are—

Three childrenne slydinge onne the ice,
Uponne a Summere's daye,
As it felle out, they alle felle inne,
The reste they ranne awaye.

Now hadde these childrenne been at home,
Or slydinge on dry grounde,
Ten thousande Pounds to one pennie,
They hadde not alle beene drownde.

You Parents that have childrenne deare,
And eke you that have none,
Iffe you would have them safe abroade,
Pray keepe them all at home.

To help with the joke, Porson fuses Ireland the country with Ireland the forger. *Giles Gingerbread* was a popular children's story (from John Newbery's Juvenile Library), in which one will search in vain for the nursery-rhyme above, the obvious purpose of which here is to illustrate Irish bulls. There was much excitement over the recent discovery of gold in Wicklow; W. H. Ireland's metal was fool's-gold.

Tum vos, quibus non contigit, germina pulchros-filios-procreantis
segetis,
Si felices optatis extra-domos itiones
Pueris vestris, bene eos intra domos servate.
Aut professor aut diabolus.

M. DE SOMBREUIL AND M. WINDHAM[1]

Mr. WINDHAM has at length published the Correspondence between him and M. de SOMBREUIL.—We have given Translations of the Letters.—The first Letter of M. de SOMBREUIL's shews, at least, that there was a very great want of concert and combination in the Quiberon Expedition.

LETTER FIRST

On board the John, Portsmouth Road, July 8, 1795.

SIR,

THE short stay which I made in London not having permitted me the honour of seeing you more than once, and my sudden departure having prevented me from conversing with you on several points of importance to me, in my present situation, I have sufficient confidence in your sagacity to be convinced, that I shall find such instructions as will serve me for a guide, and enable me to support the responsibility attached to my conduct, as well towards you as towards the Troops under my command.

A full conviction of the necessity of subordination joined to a zealous devotion to the cause in which I have embarked, induce me to fly with precipitation at the first signal I receive, and never allow me to urge the smallest objection. I say nothing of the discretion which a Government has a right to expect from those it employs; I have long since given sufficient proofs of mine; and I have reason to believe that they are such as will enable me to obtain, at least, those marks of confidence which are due to my situation.

[1] Charles Virot, Vicomte de Sombreuil (1769–95), French royalist executed 28 Jul 1795. Gen Tarleton had asked in the House of Commons for the production of these letters, but Windham had refused; then they were published in the *True Briton* 18 Apr. Sheridan had read them to the House in order to exculpate Sombreuil and to embarrass and discredit Windham, for the Quiberon expedition had been Windham's scheme. See *Parl Reg* XLIV (13–18 Apr 1796) 426, 432–4. The letters were reprinted in the other London papers—e.g. *The Times* and *M Chron* 19 Apr 1796—and the *M Mag* I (Apr 1796) 240–1 (which also printed the letter to Warren).

I have the honour to observe to you, Sir, that I am going with troops, of whose destination I know nothing but by public report, neither am I acquainted with their means of subsistence, nor, in the smallest degree, with the rules by which I am to regulate my conduct. What will be necessary with regard to ammunition, with which I am not, to my knowledge provided, and with regard to the support of those with whom I am to act; the means by which I am to carry on my correspondence with you, in a distant situation; and from whom I am, in all cases, to receive orders—these are points on which I request you to give me such instructions as will serve as a basis for my conduct.

I had the honour also to request that you would let me have an officer from the Department of Inspection. If you send me such a person, pray chuse a man who speaks both languages, that he may, on occasion, assist me in the translation of your letters; and that your orders may only be known to an officer chosen by Government.

I have the honour to be, with respect,
Your very humble servant,
Count CHARLES DE SOMBREUIL.

SECOND LETTER

SIR,

THE Letter which I have written to Sir JOHN WARREN[1] will give you every information in my power to afford, as well on my present situation, as on past events; I will not remind you of the letter which I wrote to you from Portsmouth, as you doubtless feel the force of the remarks which I there made; you must be sensible how much my heart suffers in these last moments; independently of the regret which I experience for the fate of my companions, you know what sacrifices an order so prompt obliged me to make.

I request you, Sir, to be so kind as to give to the bearer, a faithful man who has never abandoned me (and whom the losses I have sustained incapacitate me from rewarding) the sum of 500 Louis, to be shared with my other servants. This request will not appear indiscreet, as I have lost several Government Securities to a greater amount.

[1] For the letter, see below, pp 292–4.

I also recommend to you, Sir, the two persons about whom I spoke to you before I left London.

I have the honour to be,
Sir,
Your very humble servant,
Count CHARLES DE SOMBREUIL.

To Mr. WINDHAM, Secretary at War.

FARTHER PARTICULARS RELATING TO THE CAMPAIGN OF 1794 AND 1795[1]

AFTER the Troops had taken up their ground upon the heights, they were permitted to go in search of water, to the village of Famars, and under that pretext behaved most scandalously to the persecuted inhabitants, who were pillaged and deprived of the whole of their property; nay, their clothes were forcibly taken from off their backs, and they were seen almost naked at their cottage doors, wringing their hands in the greatest misery. The Officers of the different corps exerted themselves as much as possible, to discover and punish the offenders; and the Captain of a troop of Austrian hussars, upon being told that one of his men had torn the bed from under a woman and her infant, of which she had been but a short time delivered, cut down the hardened villain with his sabre, and left his body on a dunghill near the spot; this act of summary justice had the desired effect, by restraining in some degree, the unbridled licentiousness of the soldiery; the object of plunder was *fine cambric*, as great quantities were manufactured at the villages surrounding Valenciennes. Many of the British disgraced themselves by marauding, and a corporal of the First Regiment of Guards, who crossed a branch of the Rhonelle, to search a house on the opposite bank of the river, had encumbered his body with such a quantity of that article, which he had round his waist, that he was drowned in his endeavours to return.

From having been so long,[2] and so closely confined in casemates, which were at Valenciennes miserably bad, a dreadful fever raged amongst the inhabitants, and swept them off by hundreds. The fresh air had such an effect upon many of those sufferers, whose existence had been in misery prolonged till the surrender of the place,

[1] Another extract from *An Accurate . . . Narrative* I 42n (var). (See above, p 238.) Despite C's heading, this passage is about the campaign of 1793.

[2] Ibid I 62n.

that they were seen expiring in the street, the moment they were exposed to it.

Amongst the various details of miseries endured during the siege, the inhabitants told of a small convent, where the Nuns had taken refuge in one of the cellars; a thirteen-inch shell piercing through the roof, found its way to the very spot where they were assembled, and instantaneously destroyed, or miserably mangled the whole Sisterhood, to the number of fifteen.

Some British Officers, passing through the streets immediately after the town had been taken possession of in the name of his Imperial Majesty, observed a Bookseller's shop upon the *grand place*, appearing so neat, and so little damaged, that they entered it; and in the course of conversation congratulated the owner upon having escaped so well. Alas, Gentlemen, replied the poor fellow, with tears rising at the moment, the very first shell thrown into the town, deprived me in an instant, of my wife and two daughters.

On the 27th of October,[1] an advanced squadron of the 2d or Queen's Regiment of a dragoon guards, fell in at the village of *Sanghin*,[2] with a picquet of French Infantry, formed of 6 officers, and 150 men, on their retreat across the plains towards *Lezemes*.[3] They killed near 50 on the spot, and with their broad swords cut up the rest in such a manner (as they had formed a hollow square, and made a brave defence) that not above a dozen men escaped unhurt. In a most mangled state, nearly 100 miserable objects were brought as prisoners to the Duke's head-quarters; another squadron of the *Queen's* and some Austrian Hussars, having joined in the pursuit, the latter troops, keeping back till their enemies were thrown into confusion by the British charges, were then guilty of most unpardonable cruelties, for after cutting with their sabres till they had tired both hands, by way of *respite* from their labours, they drew their pistols from their holsters, and fired into the heaps of wounded. Every possible assistance was given to the suffering Frenchmen at Campaign,[4] all the surgeons in the camp were sent to dress their wounds, and his Royal Highness the Commander in Chief,[5] humanely

[1] 1793: Ibid I 110–11n.

[2] Sainghin.

[3] Lezernes.

[4] Camphain.

[5] Frederick Augustus, Duke of York and Albany (1763–1827), second son of George III. In 1793, at the insistence of his father, he took command of the contingent dispatched to Flanders to co-operate with the Austrian army under the Prince of Coburg. He was almost captured by the French in May 1794 and after several defeats returned to England in Dec, while his army was still retreating. His father rewarded his failures by promoting him to field-marshal.

ordered wine and food to be distributed amongst them, ere they were carried off to Tournay. Instances of ferocity and more than savage barbarity, in the Light Cavalry of his Imperial Majesty, were very frequent; the following is one amongst a number that occurred during the Campaign of 1793. They were generally entrusted with the conveyance of prisoners; and one of them having charge of a wounded Officer, reined in his horse as he was conducting him, and presenting a pistol and ball-cartridge, ordered the unfortunate Republican to load and then return it. His wishes were complied with, and the wretch in cold blood, blew out the unprotected Frenchman's brains with the contents.

Such was the wetness[1] of the season, while they were encamped near Campaign, that the soldiers every morning might be seen *lading* the water from their tents by *hat-fulls*; they were but scantily provided with *straw*, and consequently fell rapidly sick; two or three men of the guards were so affected, that they dropt down and died, when formed on the parade *for picquet!* one in particular was a Corporal of the 3d Regiment, who, the preceding day, appeared in perfect health. The general hospital at Tournay was filled with invalids, and the inattention to their comforts, which has since arisen to such a shameful height, was even at that early period of the war, conspicuous in the *medical* department. Two men were often placed in the same bed, the one complaining of a *dysentery*, the other of a *putrid fever*; death to both patients usually ensued from such *ignorance*, added to other instances of inhuman treatment and neglect, and the mortality was consequently *great. Sour Burgundy*, which was substituted for *port wine*, as it could be purchased at the rate of about ten-pence a bottle, was the only liquor served out to the sick, heightening *in general* their disorders: and a *regimental Surgeon* who had the *weakness* to feel for his suffering fellow-creatures, passing through the hospital one day, when absent from the camp, to visit the patients of his own battalion, was called on to procure them *water* to moisten their parched lips, as they had not, they declared, for many hours, been furnished with a drop of any kind of liquid!

[1] *An Accurate . . . Narrative* I 116n.

NANTES

April 1

CHARETTE[1]

CHARETTE, who was taken prisoner by TRAVOT, on the 2d of this month, was first taken to Angers and afterwards to Nantes, where he arrived on the 7th at midnight. On landing from the boat, he said, with a sigh, "It is here at length that the rascally English have conducted me."—This was the only instance in which he testified any emotion. He was conducted to the house of BOUSSAI, where he asked for a glass of water and a moment of repose. He retired and slept soundly.

The following morning at nine o'clock, he was taken before General DULITH,[2] and underwent an interrogatory. He refused to answer several questions. Being interrogated respecting DE LA ROBERIE,[3] he said, "that he did not know a greater scoundrel—that he fought, it was true, for a counter-revolution, but that he disavowed him as not being of his party." He was conducted under a strong guard to prison. The cries of "*Vive la Republique*," were heard from an immense crowd as he passed along; but whether it was from the military attendance, or from an amelioration of the manners of the people, nothing like insult proceeded from any quarter.

The countenance of CHARETTE was assured, his step was firm, and his deportment was calm. On the following day he was tried.

He answered every question without irritation, and even with coolness. Of the questions which were put to him, the following were amongst the most interesting:

He was asked, Whether, at the time of the pacification, the Representatives of the People had not promised him a King?

He answered in the negative. He said that no such thing had ever been mentioned, either in their public discourse or private conversation.

Why then had he violated the pacification?

[1] From the *Star* 15 Apr 1796 or *M Herald* 16 Apr (with slight changes).

[2] The name was "Dutilh" in the newspapers: Jean Duteil (1738–1820), French general.

[3] Armand Tafin, Marquis de la Rouarie (1756–93), French royalist who raised the first standard of revolt in western France (1792) with a plan for a royalist confederation of Brittany, Anjou, and Poitou. After his death the government seized his papers and tried to destroy his committees and commands.

Because he understood that the Representative GAUDIN[1] had put troops in motion for the purpose of seizing and carrying him off against the faith of the treaty.

Had he any correspondence with the Emigrants, or with foreign powers?

His reply was, that he had received but 15,000 livres from the English; that he had corresponded with them but for the short time that they were at the *Isle Dieu*; that he had received from them but little of arms or ammunition. He said that he had no continued correspondence with the Emigrants; that he had received only a cypher from the Counts d'ENTRAIGNES and d'ARTOIS,[2] with a brevet of Lieutenant General from LOUIS the XVIII. It was evinced to him that he had not been exact in his answer.

Had he any correspondence with the interior?

No! When he wanted arms or ammunition, he sent the peasants to seek them, and confided in their address.

When mention was made of the massacres at Machecoul and elsewhere, under his orders, he replied only by a sarcastic smile, intimating that he had merely done his duty.

He admitted that he had acted as Commander in Chief, and that he had fought for the establishment of Monarchy. But he said that, some days before he was surprized, a General, whom he did not name, had promised him protection, provided he would consent to quit the territory of the Republic. This letter, he said, was in the hands of the Cure of Montmaison, who he requested should be summoned. This letter, he said, would either confound his assertions, or prove the truth of what he had advanced.

The Jury, after hearing his official defender, retired to decide. In the mean time he chatted with those around him, and related the circumstances of his capture. Being asked, why he did not kill himself, he said, that it was contrary to his principles, and that he had always looked on suicide as an act of cowardice.

He heard the sentence read without the least emotion, and when he requested leave to speak, the deepest silence ensued. He then said, "he did not mean to retard, for a single instance,[3] the fate to which he was destined, but begged it as a favour, that the commission

[1] Martin-Michel-Charles Gaudin, later Duc de Gaëta (1756–1841), French financier and statesman.

[2] Emmanuel-Louis-Henri de Launay, later Comte d'Antraigues (c 1755–1812), French publicist and political adventurer. Charles Philippe, Comte d'Artois (1757–1836), younger brother of Louis XVI and Louis XVIII, later Charles X.

[3] An error for "instant".

would for his satisfaction send in search of the letter of which he had already spoken."

At five o'clock he was conducted to the *Place des Agricultures*. Five thousand men were drawn up in a square battalion, and the Clergyman GUIBERT assisted him in his last moments. He refused to go on his knees or have his eyes bandaged, but presenting his breast to the piquet, which was drawn up before him, he withdrew his left arm from the sling, and making a sign with his head that he was ready, the soldiers fired, and he dropt dead on the spot.

CHARETTE was no more than thirty-three years of age, and in height about five feet, four inches; his hair was dark, his eye-brows black and narrow, his eyes sunk, little and lively, his nose long and hooked, his mouth large, his chin long, much marked with the small-pox, a full breast, his thighs well made, his legs rather small, his voice feeble and effeminate, and his shape altogether handsome.

The courage of CHARETTE was proved in the difficulties of his situation. It was uniform and steady, but he was not susceptible of any lively passions. In the course of the last war when the Chevalier CHARETTE was Lieutenant of a man of war, and was walking upon the deck, an aukward sailor spilt a vessel of boiling pitch upon his feet. The Chevalier turned from him without any other observation, than "You rascal, you have scalded me." In talents and mental resources he was no more than an ordinary man. Like most chiefs of a party, he acquired an immense reputation; like them he has been enabled for a time to avail himself of that credit; and like them at last he perished as a malefactor.

FRANCE

MILITARY REGULATIONS.—The armies of the French are still on the Rhine.

> The Victor Gaul[1]
> Leans on his spear and breathes; yet still his eye
> Jealous and fierce.

The Austrian armies are on the other side. How can such large

[1] It is "Victor Pole" in the original: *The Celebrated Victory of the Poles over Osman the Turkish Emperor in the Dacian Battel. Translated from Casimire, B. IV. Od. 4, with Large Additions* lines 19–21 in Isaac Watts *Horae Lyricae* (5th ed 1727) 201–2.

masses be put in action in countries where subsistence cannot be provided? A very intelligent Austrian Officer said the other day to one of his countrymen, "That the Campaign could not be opened before the harvest, that the Austrian army distributed as it was through a vast extent of territory, might subsist; but that there were no means of procuring subsistence if the army were to be united in a mass: he supposed, that the French were much in the same situation as the Austrians."

INTERNAL REGULATIONS and FACTIONS.[1]—Those who have considered the appointment of General PICHEGRU to the embassy of Sweden as only an honourable exile, have not duly considered the importance of that mission, in the present moment, to the French People. If PICHEGRU is not to be at the head of their army, he could not be more honourably situated, than as Minister at Stockholm. The present state of the Swedish affairs is deeply interesting to France. The young King of Sweden is not inclined to the marriage with the PRINCESS OF MECKLENBURG, and has hitherto firmly opposed himself to the tyranny of the EMPRESS of all the RUSSIAS, in imposing upon him the *Shackles* of a Political Marriage. It is the most essential moment to France to preserve the independence of Sweden, as the views of Russia on the Porte are no longer disguised; and the SWEDE alone can, with pecuniary aid, check her ungovernable lust of empire.

Paris exhibits an alarming and tumultuous appearance.[2] The intrigues of the Jacobins and Royalists, their numbers and violence have provoked some severe decrees from the French Legislature. They have indeed veiled the face of Liberty. The Anarchists are indefatigable in seducing the minds of the multitude by preaching up doctrines, which will be true when they are practicable:—that is, when the majority of men are perfectly wise and virtuous. This happy period will not be accelerated by inculcating dispositions to rapine: and a system, which could not subsist a month except under the widely-diffused influence of Love and Knowledge, must be raised on a nobler basis than the rage and envy of the ignorant. The following paper, which has been profusely posted up by the Terrorists, will give some idea of these doctrines.

[1] The following paragraph from *M Chron* 21 Apr 1796 (altered and slightly condensed; for "her ungovernable lust of empire", *M Chron* reads "the ungovernable fury of her ambition").

[2] As reported in the London papers of 20–2 Apr, from French papers of 16–18 Apr.

"Analysis of the doctrine of Rœbeuf,[1] a tribune of the People proscribed by the Executive Directory, for having told truth.

"1. Nature has given to every man an equal right to the enjoyment of all properties.

"2. The aim of society is to defend this equality, often attacked by the strong and the wicked in the state of nature, and to augment, by the concurrence of all, every common enjoyment.

"3. Nature has imposed upon each the obligation of toiling: no one can shun labour without being criminal.

"4. Labours and enjoyments ought to be common to all.

"5. There is oppression when one man wears himself out by labour and wants every thing, while another has abundance and does nothing.

"6. No one can without being guilty of a crime, appropriate to himself, exclusively, the products of the earth or of industry.

"7. In a true society there should be neither rich nor poor.

"8. The rich who will not give up their superfluities to the indigent, are the enemies of the people.

"9. No one can by the accumulation of all the means, deprive another of the instruction necessary to his happiness. The instruction ought to be common.

"10. The aim of the revolution is to destroy inequality, and to establish the prosperity of all.

"11. The revolution is not terminated, because the rich absorb all property, and command exclusively, while the poor labour like real slaves, languish in misery, and are nothing in the State.

"12. The Constitution of 1793 is the true law of the French, because the people have solemnly accepted it; because the Convention had not the right to change it; because, to accomplish this aim, it butchered the people who called for the execution of that Constitution; and because it expelled and murdered the Deputies who considered it as their duty to defend it, &c. &c."

The most furious harangues are daily held in the Thuilleries, and cries of fury and death resound from the collected Auditors. We still more deeply regret the confusions and unsenatorial tumults which have manifested themselves in the council of five hundred. In the

[1] François-Noël Babeuf (c 1764–97), editor of the *Tribun du peuple*, wishing to transform the Revolution into a communist one, organised a conspiracy in the spring of 1796, was arrested on 10 May, and, the following year, was tried and sentenced to death. Babouvism was a forerunner of Marxism. This item was taken from the *Star* 21 Apr or *M Chron* 22 Apr 1796, including the corruption of Babeuf's name.

sitting of April 12th, on the motion of Thibaudean[1] to defer the report on the troubles to the South, there arose the most violent agitations, that too forcibly recalled the tempestuous consultations which preceded the deadly calm of Robespierre's dictatorship. ISNARD left the Tribune with his voice and gestures menacing those who opposed him. The President put on his hat. This signal of public danger calmed them for a moment; but the tumult was recommenced, when JOURDAN appeared in the Tribune. He implored to be heard; but in vain. Descending the Tribune with visible despair and agony he raised his hands to Heaven, and exclaimed,

YOU ARE STRIVING TO EXCITE A CIVIL WAR!

The dissention was at length appeased, and the motion of Treilkhand[2] adopted. "That a message should be sent to the Directory to demand the state of the South Departments, and the cause of the troubles which agitate them."

In the sittings of April 15th, the factious fury of the Royalist and Jacobin mobs alarmed the council into apparent unanimity; and they passed the following decrees, which, we trust, will be as transient as the melancholy necessity that demanded them.[3]

I. Those are criminal against the internal security of the Republic and the individual safety of citizens, and shall be punished with death, who, by speeches, writings, or publications, either distributed or posted, shall provoke the dissolution of the National Representation, or that of the Directory; or the murder of all or any of the members who compose them; the establishment of Royalty, or the Constitution of 1791, or of 1793, or of any other Government besides that of 1795; the invasion of public property, the plunder and division of private property, under the title of agrarian law, or in any other way. If the jury declare that there are mitigating circumstances belonging to the crime, the penalty of death may be converted into that of banishment.

II. The accused shall be prosecuted by the foreman of the Jury performing the functions of a police officer, and the trials shall be submitted to special Juries of Accusation and Sentence.

[1] Antoine-Claire (later Comte) Thibaudeau (1765–1854), French politician and historian, member of the Council of 500. This item was condensed from *M Chron* 22 Apr 1796.

[2] Jean-Baptiste Treilhard (1742–1810), French revolutionary and statesman, president of the Council of 500.

[3] The fifteen decrees below from *M Chron* 22 Apr 1796.

III. The foremen of the Juries of Accusation shall proceed on penalty of forfeiture, without delay, without intermission, and setting aside all other business.

IV. Every assemblage in which provocation shall be attempted of the nature of those provided for by the first article, assumes the character of a seditious mob: the good citizens shall apprehend the culpable, and, provided they are too weak, shall give information to the nearest armed force.

V. Those who shall be found in these assemblages, shall be bound to disperse at the first summons of the Magistrates or of the armed force. If they refuse to disperse, they shall be punished in the following manner: The foreigners, or those returned from banishment, with death: those who having had public employments have been accused, or outlawed and not acquitted, by banishment; and all others by five years imprisonment.

VI. If those thus assembled should resist the armed force charged to apprehend them, they shall be fired upon.

VII. Those who shall not obey the summons and who shall be seized on or apprehended, in consequence of their refusal, shall be prosecuted and punished as above.

VIII. All those who shall wear in public any other cockade than the national one, or any rallying sign, shall be punished with a year's imprisonment; but with banishment if seized in a mob.

And on April the 17th, the following:

I. No Journals, Gazettes or Periodical Works, shall be printed; nor Notices to the Public distributed; no Posting-bills printed or stuck up, without having the name of the author or authors, and the printer's name and place of abode.

II. All infraction of the preceding article, by omission of the name of the author or printer, or by inserting a false name, or false place of residence, shall be prosecuted by the Police Officer, and punished with six months imprisonment; and in case of a second offence, with two years imprisonment.

III. If the journals or periodical papers contain articles not signed, and extracts, or pretended extracts, from foreign papers; he who shall publish the aforesaid articles in his name shall be responsible for them.

IV. The distributors, venders, or posters up of papers contravening the first article, shall be punished according to the terms of the 2nd article.

V. The authors, printers, or posters of provocations declared criminal by the law of the 27th instant, shall be prosecuted in the mode then determined.

VI. The sellers and hawkers of periodical papers not signed, who cannot point out the authors of them, or who shall give false addresses, or the addresses of foreigners or persons having no fixed residence, shall be punished with two years imprisonment; and for a second offence with transportation.

VII. The printers, hawkers, or posters, who shall be apprehended, shall not be tried or set at liberty until after the trial of the author, or until the inutility of the searches for his discovery shall be manifest.

The executive Directory have addressed a proclamation to the Citizens of Paris detailing their own services and exposing the motives of the seditious assemblies. We were keenly disappointed in the perusal: it is the most tame and ill-written paper which has appeared since the commencement of the Revolution.

FINANCES. In consequence of these tumults, which threaten the stability of the new Constitution, the mandats have suffered a temporary depreciation.

POLITICAL VIEWS. See the Remonstrance in the beginning of this Number.[1]

(The following is the letter referred to in the second letter of Sombreuil to Mr. Wyndham.)[2]

To SIR JOHN WARREN, *Commander of the English Fleet, on board the Pomona, under Fort Quiberon.*

Aurai, June 22.

SIR,

I WAS far from expecting that it would have been my lot to send you such a detail of the events which took place on the fatal day that brought me hither, and to have a severe examination instituted on the conduct of the false and dastardly Traitor who has ruined our cause. M. De Puisaye,[3] having ordered me to take a position, in which I was to wait his orders, took the singular precaution of hastening to a ship, which he secured for his retreat, and thus

[1] Above, pp 269–73.

[2] See above, p 281.

[3] See above, p 181 n 4.

abandoned to their hard destiny a number of victims, whom he sacrificed.

The garrison of the fort having been forced, and the left wing of the division being already turned, the only resource that remained was precipitately to re-embark, which was rendered nearly impossible, by the proximity of the army. The regiments of D'Hervilly and Dresnay[1] abandoned or massacred their officers.

The greater part of the soldiers judging so bad a position desperate, dispersed into the country. I found myself hemmed in by the rock, at the extremity of the island, with 300 or 400 gentlemen, and a few of the men who still remained faithful to us, who were left unprovided with cartridges, none having been furnished but to the guards of the fort, notwithstanding repeated requests on my part. No doubt M. de Puisaye had his own reasons to justify this conduct, which we hope he will condescend to explain.

A number of vessels that still remained on the coast, might have afforded me the disgraceful retreat which M. De Puisaye so vigilantly seized, but the derelictions of my companions in arms would have been far more shocking to me than the lot which awaits me, I believe to morrow morning. I am bold to say, I deserve a better; and this you will acknowledge, together with all those who know me, if chance should ever permit any of the companions of my misfortune to reveal to the world the mysteries of this fatal, this unexampled day.

The consternation of an undisciplined and disorderly body of men, deserted by their commander, in whom implicit confidence had been placed, rendered it impossible for his studied security, to take those measures for the general safety, which he so providently secured for himself.

Thus bereft of every resource, I agreed to a capitulation, in order to save what could not escape; and the generality of the army, gave me to understand that every emigrant would be made prisoner and spared, like the others, but that I alone should be excepted.

Many will say, what could he do? Some will answer he ought to have died. Doubtless I shall die. But as I remained the only person to watch over the lot of those, who, the evening before, had twenty leaders, I could only exert what efforts were in my power, and these were ineffectual. Those, who left me no other to adopt, might rescue me from this responsibility.

[1] Louis-Charles, Comte d'Hervilly (1755–95), the French royalist general, wounded at Quiberon, died in London. Dresnay unidentified.

I make no doubt but that the dastard will attempt to give some colour to his flight; but I call on you, by the laws of honour, to communicate this letter to the public, *and no doubt* Mr. Windham *will have the goodness to add to it the letter I addressed to him from Portsmouth.* Farewell! I bid you farewell with that calmness which can alone result from purity of conscience, and the estimation of all the brave men who at present share my misfortune, and who prefer it to the escape of the coward; who, not having courage to fight with us, ought at least to have forewarned me; that esteem I value as a pledge of immortality. I fall a victim to his cowardice, and to the force of those arms that were for a length of time not unfortunate to me.

In this last moment I derive a source of enjoyment, if any can be tasted in a situation like mine, from the esteem of my companions in misfortune, and that of the enemy by whom we are conquered. Farewell! Farewell! all the world!

I am, Sir,

Your obedient servant,

(Signed) COMPTE CHARLES DE SOMBREUIL.

A French Officer,[1] on the 3d instant, going in a vessel from the Hague to Rotterdam, contracted an acquaintance with one of the passengers, a dealer in watches, who was going from the latter City to Brabant. The watchmaker was so well pleased with the patriotic effusions of his companion in the course of their passage, that, when the vessel arrived at its place of destination, both resolved to halt at the same inn, which is called the *Kleine Schippers Herberg*. They supped together, and afterwards amused themselves at cards until one in the morning; when they agreed to sleep in one room, and at length even in one bed. Unfortunately, however, the tradesman either by accident or carelesness, exhibited to his new acquaintance a purse richly stored with ducats. The officer, waiting until sleep had closed the unsuspicious traveller's eyes, stopped his mouth with a handkerchief, and almost instantly plunged a sword into his breast. The instrument missing the unfortunate man's heart, he awoke and struggled violently, but was unable to give any alarm. The officer chagrined at the disappointment, continued to hack the miserable victim until his intestines dropped out, and no signs of life appeared, when he dragged the body to a trunk which belonged to the murdered

[1] From the *Star* 22 Apr 1796 or the *London Packet* 22–5 Apr.

person, in order thus to conceal the main evidence of his dreadful deed, and, by cutting the joints of his thighs and arms, which were brought by that means to rest upon the body, he at length succeeded, and again locked up the trunk. Being unable, however, to wipe up all the blood which deluged the bed and the chamber, he stabbed himself in a part where no danger could result, and returned tranquilly to his pillow, where he actually slept so long the next morning, that the chamber-maid conceived it her duty to inform the gentlemen of the late hour. But [having] obtained no answer, she peeped through the key-hole, and seeing the floor covered with blood, gave an instant alarm. The police officers attended, broke open the door, and after a narrow search, discovered the horrible contents of the trunk. The Frenchman alledged, that what had happened was merely in his own defence, and shewed his wound as a demonstration of the intention of the deceased! He is, however, closely confined; but the friends of humanity suspect, that the monster will escape his merited punishment. The mangled body was taken to the Surgeon's Hall at Rotterdam, and exposed to public inspection for several days, in order to discover the unfortunate tradesman's name and family.

Extract of a Letter from a Gentleman of the first respectability in PHILADELPHIA, *to his Friend in* LONDON, *dated the first of March*, 1796.[1]

The Treaty with Spain is now before the Senate. It is very popular with them, and will, it is said, be unanimously adopted. Major B ——, a Member of the Senate, says, "the most sanguine American could not have composed one more for the honour and interest of the United States." It has added very much to the reputation of Mr. Pinckney,[2] as a patriot and a man of talents: his letters to the Prince Minister of Spain,[3] are, I have heard, masterly performances for sentiments and composition.

[1] From *M Chron* 22 Apr 1796.

[2] Thomas Pinckney (1750–1828), American diplomat, had in Oct 1795 negotiated the Treaty of San Lorenzo between Spain and the United States, which settled the boundary between the southern U. S. and Spain and allowed freedom of navigation on the Mississippi. It was unanimously ratified by the Senate.

[3] Manuel de Godoy (1767–1851), Prince of the Peace, prime minister.

WAR BETWEEN RUSSIA AND THE PORTE

PEST

March 30[1]

THE march of the Russian Troops to the Ottoman frontiers has long announced an approaching rupture between Russia and the Porte. It is expected that hostilities will soon break out. It is pretended that that which has determined the EMPRESS to hasten the opening of the Campaign, is her uneasiness at the preparation of the Turks both by sea and land, and information of France having sent officers and arms of all sorts to the Porte; in consequence, she has caused to be followed by three armies of fifty thousand men each, a Manifesto that she has published against the Divan, and she has determined to attack some parts of the Turkish Empire, before the French can have time to combine their plan of operations in the ensuing Campaign with that of the Mussulmen. Such are the motives that the Vienna Gazette assigns for the recent hostilities of which we are informed. We are assured the Russians have already taken the fortress of Choczim; and that an army under the command of General ROMANZOW has already reached the borders of the Dniester.

It is thought that this sudden invasion is an event concerted in execution of the Triple Alliance, and that its object is to oblige the GRAND SEIGNOR[2] to break all connection with the French.

It was while the South of Europe was exclusively attached to the war against France, that the Courts of Vienna, of Petersburgh, and London, concluded that famous Treaty of Alliance, of which the invasion of Poland was the prelude. This event, so important in itself, has not turned the attention of a single Power of Europe from the war they carry on against France.[3]

It has been demanded what part Great Britain has to take in the invasion of the Ottoman Empire by Russia. The writers clearly see, that no tender regard for the EMPRESS would lead that Power to engage in a business from which no particular good could result

[1] The following two paragraphs from *M Post* 19 Apr, *M Chron* 20 Apr, or *Evening Gazette* 18–20 Apr 1796, an extract from the *Vienna Gazette*.

[2] Selim III (1761–1808), Sultan of Turkey (1789–1807). The Triple Alliance for the maintenance of the European system had been concluded 28 Sept 1795.

[3] This paragraph and the following six paragraphs appeared in the *Oracle* 23 Apr 1796 (verbatim), dated Paris 18 Apr but not credited to *L'Eclair*.

to herself; they therefore concluded that the part she takes is positive and real. This conclusion, however, has been styled chimerical; but the chimera will become reality, if Europe do not recover from the delirium of its rage against the French Republic, and the Ottoman Empire will fall a prey to the ambition of Russia.

Austria will obtain an aggrandizement of territory near the centre of her hereditary states and in the neighbourhood of Hungary or Tyrol; Turkish Croatia, Dalmatia would bring her near to the Adriatic Sea, which she touches now only in the port of Trieste; and we know that any thing which conducts her nearer Italy, the eternal object of her ambition, pleases her infinitely.

It is highly worthy observation, that this ambitious House has never yet insisted strongly with Russia, that her share of Poland should be strictly defined. Perhaps this may be deferred by consent until the success of the invasion of the Ottoman empire be known; and we have read this year back, that by an eventual treaty of partition, the Court of Petersburgh would have for its share, the Turkish Provinces to the East as far as the western coasts of the Black Sea; and that the West should fall to that of Austria, as far as the eastern coasts of the Adriatic. It is easy to see thus how the Republic of Venice would run a risk of being inveloped in the mighty design of the Imperial Courts.

England, who probably cares little for the retaining Corsica,[1] and who notwithstanding keeps a fleet of 23 ships of the line in the Mediterranean, meditates, beyond a doubt, some important object in consequence of her new treaty with the Imperial Courts. With remarkable tenaciousness during a century, it must be observed, she has retained Gibraltar, which gives her the command of the Mediterranean. She has successively occupied Minorca and Corsica, to have in fact her hand always stretched out to the Commerce of the Levant. Now sole mistress of India and Bengal, she is more than ever induced to open the shortest course to her commerce with the Ganges and Indostan by the Red Sea and the Isthmus of Suez.

England has, therefore, calculated her advantage in being able to cover with her ships the seas of Constantinople and Greece, when the victorious Russians shall be received under the protection of her flag, no doubt some solid and imposing establishment, either in Candia, in Crete, or in the Morea.

Such an invasion would cause so immense an alteration in the

[1] Corsica, which England occupied in 1793, was evacuated after Spain declared war against her in Oct 1796. See also below, p 373.

political system, that one is amazed at the inaction of the Powers of Europe, and their little care to prevent the destruction of the Ottoman Empire not being as speedily effected as that of Poland. The present war must have annihilated all political foresight, that we permit an astonishing revolution to be accomplished without impediment, and of which all Europe is ready to become the theatre and the victim.—(*L' Eclair.*)

SIR SYDNEY SMITH[1]

A LETTER was received at the Admiralty last night from the First Lieutenant of the *Diamond* Frigate, off the Coast of France, containing an account of the Capture of that gallant Officer Sir SYDNEY SMITH.

Sir SYDNEY, in the night of Monday last, went in his Boat to cut out a French Luggar in the Port of *Havre*. This he accomplished, after some resistance, by which one Frenchman was killed; but deterred from immediately sailing by the rapidity of the current, he cast anchor. During the night, however, the Ship drove from her anchor; the cable, it is said, having been cut by one of the Prisoners, and was carried by the current above the Town.

In this situation, he was attacked on the morning of Tuesday, by all the Gun-boats and other Vessels which the Enemy could muster; and after a gallant, and even desperate resistance, against a Force so infinitely superior to his own, he found himself at length obliged to surrender. We are happy however to find, that he received no injury in the conflict.

IN the 6th Number we extracted from the Sun a plausible explanation of the mystical word ELIPHISMATIS.[2] We are now convinced of it's falsehood. The phrase *I shall murder*, is not only ungrammatical but the very reverse of the Irish Idiom, which uses *will* even where *shall* ought to have been used. But lest any doubt should remain in consequence of the correspondence between the words of the explanation and the letters of the Defender's pass-word, we shall subjoin that explanation and others that have occurred.

[1] From the *Sun* 22 Apr 1796. Sir William Sidney Smith (1764–1840), later the hero of Acre (1799), was harrying shipping off the north coast of France. He was kept a prisoner by the French for two years, when he escaped to England.

[2] See above, p 226.

E very
L oyal
I rish
P rotestant
H eretic
I
S hall
M urder
A nd
T his
I
S wear

E very
L unatic
I n
P atrick's
H ospital
I
S wear
M ay
A nswer;
T hat
I s
S illy

E very
L oyal
I rish
P rotestant
H ousekeeper
I
S hall
M aintain
A nd
T his
I
S wear

E very
L iberal
I rish
P atriot's
H onesty
I
S hall
M align
A nd
T his
I
S wear

E very
L ibeller
I ndustriously
P rostituting
H is
I nvention
S uch
M aliciously
A trocious
T ales
I mprudently
S uggests

E ssex-bridge[1]
L ibels
I nstigate
P rotestant
H atred
I nto
S avage
M alice
A gainst
T rue
I nnocent
S ubjects

E ccentric
L ies
I nfamously
P ropagated
H ave
I nduced
S everal
M istakenly
A larmed
T o
I rritate
S ociety

E very
L ord
I n
P ower
H ates
I ndustrious
S ilent
M erit
A nd
T akes
I ts
S ustenance

E very
L eech
I n
P lace
H opes
I reland
S hall
M aintain
A bsentees
T raitors
I nformers
S pies

[1] In Dublin, leading to the offices of government.

The intelligence received from Yarmouth confirms the report of another fleet having sailed from the Texel.

The Mayor of Yarmouth was last night informed by express that a Dutch fleet was in the North Seas.—The Hamburgh Packets will in consequence be detained at Cuxhaven.

GREAT-BRITAIN

We cannot give a clearer account of the state of the Country, than by abridging and methodizing the arguments used in the House of Commons by Mr. Pitt on the one side, and Mr. Fox and Mr. Grey on the other, on Monday, April 18; especially as the Premier's Speech on opening the budget is of too interesting a nature to be deferred.[1]

The CHANCELLOR of the EXCHEQUER for the additional duty on printed Calicoes which had been calculated at 135,000l. proposed to substitute the Tax on Dogs, (if his advice were pursued of applying a part of it to the necessities of the State; that part he calculated at 100,000l.) and a new regulation of the old duty on hats, which, when the tax was first proposed, was taken at 100,000l. and the first year it had produced 130,000l. but from the facility with which it was evaded, it had for the last year produced only 6000l. The new method, which he should propose, was to provide stamped linings, the revenue on which he estimated at 40,000l. certain. These would prove an ample substitute for the tax on Calicoes which he had abandoned. Mr. PITT then proceeded to state such services as had not been foreseen or included in the last statement which he made before Christmas, and the mode of defraying them.

And, first of the services, there had been incurred since the 31st of December last, and not provided for under the head of Army Extraordinaries, ——	535,000
Of Ordnance, —— ——	200,000
The additional sum required for Barracks he estimated at	267,000
The sum for Secret Service, above the sum included in the last estimate, and above the sum of 25,000l. allowed in time of peace, he took at ——	100,000
And the sum which in the last statement the Ways and Means were short of the Supply, ——	177,000

[1] The *Star* 19 Apr 1796 devoted almost its entire issue, including the front page (usually given to advertisements), to a report of this debate.

These services made together —— 1,279,000
To which he should add a sum which he felt would be necessary to make good the further Army Extraordinaries up to the end of the year 1796, —— 1,221,000

Making in all of new services above the statement opened in the month of December last for the service of the current year, the sum of —— 2,500,000

But there was another sum that must also be provided, for the increased Navy Debt which for the year 1796 would probably amount to 1,500,000l. which added to 2,500,000 the sum taken in his first estimate, would make the Navy Debt for 1796 four millions. Towards this however he was provided in cash to the amount of 1,200,000l. and he should also have resources to the amount of 800,000l. more. He proposed likewise to borrow a million in order to repay the Bank a sum which they had advanced on the credit of the Consolidated Fund on the supply of the year 1795.

He then observed, there was reason to believe that there would be no occasion for the greater part of the million voted for bounties for the importation of corn, and that, what might be wanted (300,000) would arise from the participation of the profits of the India company. He would therefore retract that million.

The Bank were in possession of 500,000 in Exchequer Bills. This sum it would be more convenient to them to receive in cash than in fund; but, upon the whole, there would be 7,000,000 of Exchequer and other bills to be provided for, and 500,000l. in cash; yet the whole interest need only to be raised for one sum, 1,600,000.; and 1½ per cent. of additional interest for the remainder.

Upon the whole, the annual sum necessary to be levied by taxes, for the interest of the sums to be raised by loan, would be 575,000*l.*

The connection of this part of his subject with that of the scarcity of money was sufficiently discernible. The cause, perhaps, was difficult to be ascertained. It might arise partly from the great remittances made to the Continent; and he must consider it as a symptom of the prosperity of the country, that these were not more felt. Mr. Pitt here entered into a discussion of the difference between funded and unfunded debt, as to its effect upon general credit, and then after giving notice of a Lottery, he proceeded to propose the means of providing for the interest of the sums to be newly funded. It was impossible to do this without laying some absolute burthens upon the country. The easiest which occurred to him was an additional tax upon wine; and as any tax less than such an one as might amount to a round sum, after the allowance of a reasonable profit, would be equally a burthen upon the consumer, without benefitting the public, he must propose, as last year, an additional duty of 20l. per ton, or 6d. per bottle. In estimating this at the same as the increase of last year, 600,000l. he was [obliged] to admit that [the] principle of supposing a new tax to produce no increase[1] of consumption was in some degree new; but the experience of last year justified him. In that period the duty had not only been paid upon 30,000 tons, but a greater quantity had been imported, so that the average exceeded that of former years. His intention was to extend this tax, like the former, to the stock in hand.

Mr. PITT now repeated the terms of the loan, of which the interest was to be paid by this tax. They were as follows:

£. 120	3 per cent. consols at 67	80 8 0
25	3 per cent. reduced at 66	16 10 0
0 5 6	Long Annuities at 18	5 1 9
		101 19 9

A discount of 4l. 14s. per annum, or 1l. 7s. for six months was to be added to this. After enlarging on our *flourishing situation*, he said, such was the state of this country in comparison with that of France, that, if we were true to ourselves, we might look for the happiest issue of a contest *undertaken for the end of rescuing this age and posterity from all the mischiefs attending a dissolution of civil society*. Mr. Pitt concluded by moving,

"That the sum of 7,500,000l. be raised by way of Loan."

Mr. GREY entered upon minute calculations upon the estimates made by the minister, and contended that he was not correct in some respects, and that in others he had not acted with sufficient justice towards the country, and declared that the minister, instead of coming forward with that lofty tone which he assumed that day, should have declared to the house that he had exceeded his estimates, and stated the several purposes for which money was wanted, *and then ask for a bill of indemnity*. Instead of this, the army was lately paid by Exchequer bills, to the great loss of the Colonels to whom they had been issued. He could prove that, though an immense debt had been contracted in the course of a year, the expences were not fairly provided for. As to the probable state of our peace establish-

[1] An error for "decrease".

ment, the minister said he had one million more than that sum was likely to be, and this calculation he seemed to have made from the estimates of Committees, which were never exact. In all probability the peace establishment would amount to upwards of twenty-two millions. The war added considerably to the amount of the taxes, and therefore in time of peace we might look for a considerable diminution of them, as was the case in the first years after the conclusion of the American war; and *during every year after the Hon. gentleman's coming into office, he was obliged to lay on a new tax.* He would recommend, as he had done before, an enquiry into the state of our finances, not for the purpose of depreciating them as had been improperly stated. He disapproved of the custom which had been followed, year after year, of depreciating the finances of our enemies, which, notwithstanding, turned out differently from the statements given of them. Ministers should rather look to the finances of their own country: *but a minister who was as incapable of making peace as of conducting a war, found it necessary to have recourse to such fallacious arguments, in order to excite the passions and expectations of that house, when, at the same time, he had not made a sufficient provision himself for the arrears of expences of the year.*

Mr. FOX said the Right Hon. Gentleman should have gone into an enquiry at the time his Honourable Friend moved for it. With respect to the depreciation of French mandats, he would admit that the finances of France were in a state of derangement, which would not admit of a comparison between them and those of our own country. But the same arguments had been used year after year with respect to the assignats; and, although the House was repeatedly deceived by such fallacious statements, the French got rid of all their assignats: therefore he desired that [the] House might not be deceived by a similar imposture with respect to the mandats, which they might equally get rid of; and *when the Minister could not tell within* SEVEN MILLIONS *what the expence of this year was to be*, the House should not listen to arguments by which they had been before deceived. He could never forget the emphatic words that had been used when the depreciation of assignats had been so much dwelt upon. It was then said that France was at her *last gasp*, in the expiring *agonies of existence*; and notwithstanding all her armies continued to be victorious: and she has been in such a state that the Ministers of England did think proper so far to change their former tone as to make some overtures for a negociation for peace with her. But the miseries of our own country could not be forgotten. And if the war was to be continued, the people had a right to demand what the object and grounds of it were, and what were the expences which they were incurring.

The Resolutions proposed by the Chancellor of the Exchequer were put, and carried without a division; and the report was ordered to be received to-morrow. Adjourned at one o'clock.

THE WATCHMAN

No. IX. THURSDAY, MAY 5, 1796

Published by the Author, S. T. COLERIDGE, Bristol;
And by PARSONS, Paternoster-Row, London.

THAT ALL MAY KNOW THE TRUTH;
AND THAT THE TRUTH MAY MAKE US FREE!

ANALYSIS
OF AN
"ESSAY ON THE PUBLIC MERITS OF Mr. PITT, By THOMAS BEDDOES, M.D."[1]

PERSONAL Attacks are culpable or vicious, when they are directed against the domestic, rather than the official, character of an individual; when without relation to public utility they are designed to stir up public indignation.—From this fault the Pamphlet before us is altogether free. The Author wages war with the *Minister*, and no where degrades his cause by stepping from the Senate or the Cabinet to Holwood House.

In an examination of the Minister's merits it is necessary that we should be informed, 1. What things ought to be done: 2. What it is in a Minister's power to do: 3. What of these the Minister has done: 4. What of these he has left undone: 5. What he has done instead of the things, which he could and ought to have done, but did not do. We shall endeavour to select whatever seems to convey such information, previously remarking, that the *arrangement* of the original work appears to us to be rather injudicious, and in a small degree perhaps to leave a confused effect on the recollection of the Reader, partly from the intermixture of miscellaneous matter (always indeed related to, but not always immediately connected with, the subject) and partly from the Author's having discussed the Minister's measures in chronological order.

1. What things ought to be done. The most essential of these

[1] London 1796.

desiderata are instanced in page 15,[1] and may be reduced to two heads, physical and moral. Physical—1. To prevent those circumstances, which do not depend on the individual's conduct, yet threaten deprivation of his comforts and necessaries. 2. To diffuse as large a share as possible of the blessings of nature to as large a number of people as possible. Moral—1. Faithfully to apply public contributions to the public service. 2. To prevent the fruits of industry from becoming the means of general corruption. 3. To diffuse as large a share as possible of the blessings of society to as large a number as is possible. Under the blessings of society we particularize protection, instruction, together with all the motives and restrictions, that tend to diminish or prevent intoxication, rioting, and the grosser vices. Secondly, what it is in a Minister's power to do? To this Quere we find no solution in the Doctor's essay: yet surely the Minister's powers ought to have been ascertained before his performances were appreciated. If we dared presume to supply the deficiency, we should answer without hesitation—Almost every thing evil, but scarcely any thing fundamentally right. The Empress of Russia at the nod of her caprice could tenant all the gibbets in her dominions, at the first impulse of ambition she can let loose all the furies of Death and Famine on her unoffending neighbours; but in every attempt which she has made, to diffuse knowledge and happiness among her subjects, to remove bad laws, or to substitute good ones, she has met from the Priests, the Landholders, and the People, obstacles that have almost in every instance frustrated her intentions, and sometimes with resistance that has shaken the foundations of her

[1] Beddoes sets forth his "political catechism" in *Public Merits* 15: "[1] How far am I secure against false alarms, fraud, and violence? [2] Do circumstances which I cannot controul threaten deprivation of the accommodations and necessaries of life? [3] Do unjust laws, encroachments on freedom by persons in power, or other public impediments prevent my hands from executing what my head has innocently devised? [4] Is the distinguishing bounty of nature to man frustrated by infringements on the privilege of speech? [5] Are the contributions of the people faithfully applied to the public service? [6] Do the fruits of my industry or possessions go to delude the weak, bribe the corrupt, and slaughter the innocent? [7] What share of the blessings of nature do my countrymen at large enjoy? [8] Are their sufferings on the increase or decline? [9] Are intoxication and the grosser vices on the wane? In charity of thought and action are they superior to their predecessors? [10] Do the less instructed begin to distinguish their preservers from their destroyers? or are they still ready, at the beck of a minister, to bawl for a war, and light bonfires for victories which will bring the rot of famine upon all the human creatures that have the misfortune to belong to them? [11] What are the causes of the growing happiness or misery, improvement or degeneracy of the community?"

authority. Despotism depraves those whom it injures;—but above all, the dispenser of an indirect despotism, resembles a Magician surrounded by spirits who obey him in all evil; because evil is their lucre and their delight: or the absolute leader of a banditti, who would be laughed at or murdered if he issued an order for the protection of travellers. Those who can answer the question *how* a Minister procures petitions, addresses, and majorities, should consider, whether a Minister could use those *means* to the destruction of themselves?[1] Whether *Pensioners* would vote for the abolition of pensions, sinecure placemen for the abolition of sinecure places, parliamentary contractors for the exclusion of contractors from Parliament: whether priests would bestir themselves to diffuse that knowledge, and that spirit of charity which would make priests useless or innoxious; or corporate electors sell their right of selling. Let only a bill for the abolition of our *foreign* slavery be brought into the House, and even Mr. Rose shall stand forwards an *independent* member. What if a Minister began the Herculean task of a thorough and home reform, would there be no *alarm* excited among the Lords of the bedchamber? No interior Cabinet whose secret workings would soon convince a premier, that a majority was not on all occasions at his command? These are not conjectures—the first years of the present reign exhibit *facts* in proof. The crime therefore of Mr. Pitt is, that knowing these things he did not imitate his Father, and relinquish an office, in which he is powerful only to do evil. Even the present war is in all human probability, not imputable to him, in chief. The Rights of Sovereigns had been atrociously insulted; and Mr. Pitt must have involved the country in a war, or have lost his place. Is this a mere assertion? Did not Lord North exert all his power in continuing a war which he himself condemned, and into which (he himself declared in the House of Commons that) the Court had precipitated the Country, contrary to *his* private advice and wishes?

The answer therefore to the IIId. point must necessarily be—Nothing. To the IVth. point—Every thing. The Vth. only remains to be considered, namely, what things the Minister has done instead. This has been treated fully and with the greatest fairness in the sixth chapter of the Doctor's Essay, under the article of the American Intercourse, the Commercial treaty with France, Irish propositions, commutation act, and sinking fund[2]—in every one of which he

[1] An echo of Berkeley's use of the query. See above, pp 102–3, 140.

[2] Briefly, Beddoes refers to (1) the resumption, after independence, of

discovers folly or imbecility, uselessness or danger. With great good sense he ridicules the absurdity of attributing to a Minister, all the prosperity of the Country during his administration, prosperity which in the bosom of peace and nursed by avarice, industry, and courage, even his mischievous interposition could not prevent the growth of.

"In the reign of queen Elizabeth, there lived at the end of a small village in South Wales, an old woman who gained her livelihood by going on errands to Brecknock. She stooped; her last remaining front-tooth projected into view; she was blind in one eye and blear of the other. Such a figure could not fail to set surmises afloat. One evening she was met by a furious blast on her return home. Next morning, her better eye was so much affected by a violent rheum, that she was forced to keep close in her cottage for some time. Meanwhile news arrives of the disaster of the Spanish fleet. In the ardour of speculation it occurs that the old woman has not been lately seen at her usual houses of call: and it is soon discovered that she had not appeared out of her own doors. 'Aye, aye,' said the politicians of Brecknock, 'we thought, sure enough, all along, there was something in it! Old Margery has not kept herself pent up all this while for nothing. These hurricanes were certainly of her raising.

" 'It is the cunning woman—the cunning woman of Llanbamlog, that has done for the *papishes*.' "[1]

Of the miscellaneous parts of the work, the account of the Minister's friends is so admirably given, that we are tempted to extract it.[2]

"I will not fatigue you with the roll-call of the several bands that compose this prime division. The most effective is doubtless that of which the members contrive to pass themselves on simplicity for advisers of the people. We have all heard it rumoured that the sum paid in 1760 to Smollett, Francis, Mallet,[3] and other authors hired

commercial relations with the United States, culminating in the Jay–Grenville Treaty of 1794; (2) the Commercial Treaty between England and France in 1786, resulting in an increase of trade between the two countries; (3) the eleven Irish Propositions were passed by the Irish Parliament in 1785 and laid before the House of Commons, their intent being to arrange Irish trade primarily for the benefit of the Irish; (4) the Commutation Act, which in order to reduce smuggling lowered certain import duties; (5) the Sinking Fund, Pitt's scheme to reduce the national debt by setting aside regular sums budgeted for the purpose.

[1] *Public Merits* 96–7.

[2] Ibid 40–4 (one paragraph omitted).

[3] Tobias Smollett (1721–71). Philip Francis was amanuensis to William Pitt, the elder, between Jan 1761 and May 1762. David Mallet (c 1705–65), poet and miscellaneous writer, editor of Bolingbroke, contributed to Smollett's *Critical Review*.

to write down Mr. Secretary Pitt exceeded forty thousand pounds, and the printing charges twice that sum.* This distribution of secret service money was accounted at that time a masterly (and it undoubtedly was an effective) stroke of policy. How then may the Minister applaud himself, if by at once enlisting the whole body of publishers of provincial newspapers into his first division, he have acquired the power of infusing into the commonalty of cities, and the commonalty of villages, just whatever inclinations his purposes may require? In this case, all that is required is to lie boldly, not skilfully; and four journalists will do more towards maddening the people than four hundred prudent persons, privately uttering their honest sentiments towards keeping them within the bounds of reason.

"This whole class of agents, whether engaged by the job or for all work, appears to receive regular pay—no matter whether in money or valuables—and often beforehand.

"The next is content with *what your honour pleases.* The composition of this second squadron, as much as I blush to disclose, you will be scandalized when you learn—but reproach be with the criminal and not the accuser. Our war-ministers, I am sure, will not be base enough to disown their obligation to the meek sons of the clergy. And if they should, forty-nine out of fifty fast sermons are at hand to convict them of ingratitude. We have, in fact, seen so many minds, catching military ardour from the voice of those that speak in the name of the Prince of Peace, that were Peter the hermit to re-appear among us, he need not despair of finding recruits for the Holy Land.

"The third is a mixed and motley class. Here we find the most mischievous of the votaries of folly. Dreaming of independence, they are susceptible of whatever impressions a minister chooses they should receive. The motives which it is necessary to play off on their minds are various. One becomes an accomplice in blood to extort a revenue which he is assured will lower the land-tax. A second is empowered to call his wife, *my lady.* A third has his relations quartered on the public; and *does it not stand to reason,* thinks he to himself, *that gentlemen-born should be maintained as gentlemen?* A fourth, were his lips to be touched with the wand of truth, would confess: *Mr. Manager, it is my humour to collect a little group of expectants round my board in the country. Enable me to act the patron*

* Anecdotes of Chatham, 1794, (p. 347.)[1]

[1] See [John Almon] *Anecdotes of the Life of the Rt. Hon. William Pitt, Earl of Chatham* (3rd ed 3 vols 1793) I 347. In the first edition the figure was £30,000.

over my circle. In this case, Sir, laying his hand on his heart and bowing, *you see your very humble servant to command.* A fifth is weak enough to suffer himself to be persuaded, that opinions are a fit mark for cannon balls. A sixth is told that war, the parent of national distress, will diminish national discontent; and straightway with complaisant stupidity, he sets to pile coals of fire on his own head.

"In the second rank of this division we should seek

Cits who prefer a guinea to mankind,[1]

anthropomorph animals furnished with scarce an idea of the relation between man and man, but such as the counting-house supplies, and fixing with the strong tenacious claw of ignorance upon the most fatal of political errors. Do you want their good-will? Place a commercial lure in prospect, whisper that our fleet wants but the word of command to pounce on the enemy's islands. They go home, dream that the city wharfs are paved with French-sugar-casks, and next day in full council pledge their lives to a cause in which they are well assured their little finger will never run the risque of a scratch.

"It would be easy to swell this catalogue. But my purpose is not to enumerate all the *instrumenta regni*—the new tools for which the statesman's craft is indebted to the mechanic genius of the present ministry.

"With good sort of folks, who are ever the staunch defenders of inveterate prejudices, when have the cabalistic state-phrases—*unnatural contest—disaffection—existing circumstances—just and necessary war*—been known to fail? and how easy is it to bring devout ladies to assist in conjuring up the civil storm, and to pipe round the tea-table to 'the dance of death'?"

But the most valuable chapter is the ninth, in which Dr. B. gives a minute, most accurate and affecting detail of the miseries of the poor in the country, and of the poor in towns. This detail amply verifies the Doctor's remark in his first chapter, that a Physician is peculiarly well-qualified for political research, since from the large portion of human misery which passes under his immediate inspection, he must unavoidably observe the distresses occasioned by the operation of unwise, or the neglect or abuse of useful laws. The Doctor makes several extracts from Dr. Ferriar's Medical Histories,[2] which, he acutely observes, would prove a striking counterpart to Mr. George Chalmer's Estimate of the comparative strength of

[1] Source untraced.

[2] John Ferriar *Medical Histories and Reflections* (2 vols 1792–5; vol III appeared 1798).

Great-Britain during the present and four preceding reigns.[1] One of these extracts presents a picture truly natural and affecting.[2]

"A young couple live very happily, till the woman is confined by her first lying-in. The cessation of her employment then produces a deficiency in their income at a time when expences unavoidably increase: she therefore wants many comforts, and even the indulgencies necessary to her situation. She becomes sickly, droops, and at last is laid up by a fever or pneumonic complaint: the child dwindles, and frequently dies. The husband, unable to hire a nurse, gives up most of his time to attendance on wife and child; his wages are reduced to a trifle; vexation and want render him at last diseased; and the whole family sometimes perishes, from the want of a small, timely supply, which their future industry would have amply repaid to the public. If such misery occurs, even when the master of a family is industrious and sober, it is easy to imagine the distress of some unfortunate creatures, who depend on a brutal debauchee. The injuries which defenceless women undergo in those situations are too horrible for description: I have met with instances of incurable diseases, occasioned by kicks or blows from the husband in his paroxisms of drunkenness."

To return to our Minister, for the honour of English sagacity we should be happy to discover other causes for his popularity and accession to power, than those assigned by Dr. Beddoes, but after serious recollection we must subscribe to the accuracy of the following catalogue.[3]

"*First, and principally*, the object was William Pitt, the son of William Pitt. The nation sagaciously discovered evidence of his merit in the sound of his name.

"2. He delivered himself in the most high-flying terms, on the

[1] George Chalmers *An Estimate of the Comparative Strength of Britain During the Present and Four Preceding Reigns; and of the Losses of Her Trade from Every War Since the Revolution* (new ed 1794). See *Public Merits* 162–7. In the absence of statistical data the trends in population were in great dispute. Humanitarians like Dr Richard Price and Dr James Currie, alarmed by governmental inattention to the general welfare, feared that the trend was downward (see also above, pp 109–10); tougher-minded persons like Chalmers, convinced of the beneficence of selfishness, maintained that population and wealth alike were increasing. He succinctly states his view: "Millions have become rich and happy, by considering the care of themselves, as the great object of life. Thousands have ruined themselves, and degraded their families, by troubling themselves about public affairs, more than their own." *Estimate* p lxxxv. Concerning the growth of population, Chalmers proved to be the better judge.

[2] *Public Merits* 165. From Ferriar II 207.

[3] *Public Merits* 58–9.

popular topics of influence and corruption. To make up for being the latest, he took care to be the loudest of those who clamoured for reform. This was his great merit or art.

"3. In virtue of his youth, he gained credit for incorruptible integrity.

"4. His manner was advantageous; he declared pompously; and when he reasoned, gave proofs of a quick, discerning, and cultivated mind. His speeches, in relation to his age, deserved distinguished approbation; they obtained blind admiration. An hundred young men at school and college would, in an essay, have turned the common places on liberty and patriotism, with equal dexterity, against the discomfited conductors of the American war. But not one could have been found so trained to the habit of uttering them promptly. Fluency of elocution however does not appear to be more closely connected with wisdom than facility or elegance of composition.

"5. By an act which, as it might equally proceed from patriotic disinterestedness, and the lowest cunning, his future conduct could alone render unequivocal, he confirmed the faith of a credulous people.*

"6. Certain candidates for power incurred our displeasure; and we, cool, dispassionate Englishmen! took their rival to our bosom in pure despite."

Of the political sagacity of Mr. Pitt, Dr. Beddoes observes,[2]—"The issue of our American contest was certain at his first appearance. With the assistance of his Majesty of Prussia, it was nothing hazardous to attempt to dragoon the Dutch into submission: and he may be content if his dear-bought Spanish laurels (supposing him to have gained any), are set against his Russian disgraces. One occasion only of difficulty has presented itself to him, and a few months perhaps will convince every unbribed spectator of his conduct, whether he possesses a larger share of penetration than Lord North."

On the whole we have risen from the perusal of this pamphlet with information variously increased. We were sorry to notice some

* This alludes to the Clerkship of the Pells, a place of considerable value, which Mr. Pitt gave to *Colonel Barré*[1] in lieu of his pension.

[1] Isaac Barré (1726–1802), British colonel and politician. In 1782, with the formation of the Rockingham ministry, he was appointed treasurer of the navy and granted a pension of £3200 a year on quitting that office. This unpopular grant was replaced by the clerkship of the Pells, which the younger Pitt conferred on him in 1784 and which Pitt could have taken for himself—a seemingly unselfish sacrifice, said by his enemies, however, to be fraught with political and personal calculations. The above footnote is C's, not Beddoes's.

[2] *Public Merits* 61.

degree of apparent illiberality in the eighth chapter, in which Archdeacon Supple[1] (the representative of our dignified clergy) is represented as deriving pleasure from his favourite son's scheme of tying a cannister to a dog's tail. The *esprit du corps* is bad indeed, but in their individual capacities as men and fathers of families, the clergy are generally blameless and often excellent. In our present imperfect natures, tendencies to religious persecution and strong feelings of humanity, inconsistent as they may appear, frequently exist together.[2] Besides, thanks to Mrs. Barbauld,[3] and to Berguin,[4] it has become universally *fashionable* to teach lessons of compassion towards animals. The style of the Essay is excellent. That is a perfect style in which we think always of the *matter*, and never of the *manner*. To this *praise* Dr. Beddoes would be entitled, did not his words too often send common readers to their dictionary. We instance—asperity of crimination, anthropomorph, and plenary acceptation. But the passion for *utility* is the prominent characteristic of this as of all other of the Doctor's Works. From his deepest scientific treatises, the most unscientific reader will not rise without having understood some part, without having learnt something of advantage in the ordinary occurrences of life. To this amiable passion our language is indebted for the tale of Isaac Jenkins;[5] a tale in every respect as superior to Sterne's Le Fevre,[6] as the vivid images of nature to the creatures of an eccentric imagination, as the feelings of active benevolence to the effusions of artificial sensibility.

Felix curarum, cui non Heliconia cordi
Serta.[7]

WHO has not sighed over the fates of Otway, Collins, and Chatterton,[8] and forgotten their imprudence in the contempla-

[1] Ibid 140.

[2] Cf "that deep feeling has a tendency to combine with obscure ideas" and leads to fanaticism. *Friend* (*CC*) I 106n. See also below, p 374.

[3] Anna Letitia Barbauld *Hymns in Prose for Children* (1781).

[4] Arnaud Berquin *L'Ami des Enfans* tr Rev M. A. Meilan *The Children's Friend* (24 vols 1786).

[5] Thomas Beddoes *The History of Isaac Jenkins, and of the Sickness of Sarah, His Wife, and Their Three Children with an Agreeable and Happy Sequel, Shewing the Good Effects of Their Worthy Friend Mr. Langford's Admonitions* (Madeley 1792).

[6] The pathetic story of Lieut Le Fever is told in *Tristram Shandy* vol VI chs 6–13.

[7] Statius *Silvae* 4.4.46–7. C had just used the passage as motto to *Poems* (1796); see *PW* (EHC) II 1135. Tr J. H. Mozley (LCL 1928) 233: "Happy thou in thy labours, who carest not for the chaplets of Helicon".

[8] Thomas Otway (1652–85), Williams Collins (1721–59), and Thomas

tion of their miseries?—But wretchedly as our men of genius have commonly lived and died, I have met with no instance so shocking as that of BOISSY, the *French* Poet.[1]

BOISSY, the author of several dramatic pieces, that were acted with applause, met with the usual fate of those men, whom the very genius, that fits them to be authors, incapacitates for successful authorship.—Their productions are too refined for the lower classes, and too sincere for the wealthier ranks of Society.[2] BOISSY in addition to great intellectual ability, possessed the virtues of Industry and Temperance; yet his works produced him fame only. He laboured incessantly for uncertain bread. Alas! I have yet mentioned but a small part of his miseries; the most heart-breaking calamity follows —*he had a Wife and Child.*[3] But melancholy as was his situation, he lost nothing of the poet's pride—he could not fawn at the table of a noble patron: and life became worse than death to the man, who depended for his casual morsel on the humour of an insolent bookseller.[4] He sunk into despondency. Death appeared to him as a friend, as a deliverer; and by sophistry and poetic declamation he justified and decorated the crime of Suicide.[5] His wife became his convert. She looked with stern and agonizing tenderness at her child, a beautiful boy of five years old; then snatching him to her bosom,[6] resolved that he should accompany his parents. They could not kill him—to swallow the poison themselves, or to plunge the knife into their bosoms, was an easy task; but nature revolted from the murder

Chatterton (1752–70) had in common, besides their "imprudence" and their "miseries", poverty and early death. See C's *Monody on the Death of Chatterton* and *To a Friend*: *PW* (EHC) I 125–31, 158–9.

[1] Louis de Boissy (1694–1758), writer of comedy. This introductory paragraph is C's; the anecdote, however, he found in [William Tooke] *Varieties of Literature from Foreign Literary Journals and Original MSS. Now First Published* (2 vols 1795) I 422–5, but he rewrote it, making it more personal and dramatic. Warren E. Gibbs first pointed out parallels between C's letters and the anecdote (without indicating C's source for the anecdote). See e.g. the letters to Cottle 22 Feb 1796 and to Poole 30 Mar: *CL* I 185–6, 194. *N&Q* CLX (Feb 1931) 99–100. The following footnotes indicate some but not all of C's alterations.

[2] This sentence is C's.

[3] Cf *Varieties* I 423: "He laboured and toiled unremittedly—his works procured him fame, but no bread. He languished, with a wife and child, under the pressures of the extremest poverty".

[4] C has added "and life . . . insolent bookseller".

[5] Cf *Varieties* I 423: " . . . he declaimed with all the warmth of poetic rapture of deliverance from this earthly prison . . .".

[6] For "looked . . . tenderness", *Varieties* I 423 reads "listened with participation"; and C has added "snatching him to her bosom".

of the child. What mode of death should they adopt? They made choice of the most horrible[1]—of starving: and they went to bed, resolving to rise from it no more. They had fasted part of the day; when their little son, who could not silence the calls of hunger by firmness of resolve, or recollection of past misery,[2] whimpering and crying asked for bread. The mother struggled against her agonies;[3] and they found means to keep him quiet, till from long abstinence they all sickened, and became unable to speak.

It occurred to one of BOISSY's friends, that it was extraordinary he should never find him at home. At first, he thought the family were removed; but on being assured of the contrary, he grew more uneasy. He called several times in one day: always nobody at home! At last he burst open the doors. Merciful Heaven! what a sight! BOISSY and his Wife in bed, pale, emaciated, unable to utter a sound. The little boy lay in the middle, his mother's arms thrown around him. The child began to cry, and made himself understood that he had nothing to eat.[4] The parents still lay in a perfect stupor. The friend took measures for their recovery, and imperfectly succeeded. But when they were restored to sense, they resisted his further efforts: and seemingly determined not to be snatched from death. But when the mother found that the child had left the middle of the bed, she turned her wasted eyes to seek him. She saw him eating, and his piteous moans moved a new love of life in her.[5] Nature did her office. Their friend procured them strengthening broths, which he put to their lips with the utmost caution—and they were saved.

The transaction made much noise in Paris, and at length reached the ears of the Marchioness de Pompadour. She immediately sent BOISSY a present of one hundred Louis d'ors and soon after procured him the profitable place of Comtrolleur du Mercure du France, with a pension for his wife and child, if they outlived him.

[1] Cf ibid I 423–4: "They were now firmly resolved to die. But what mode of death should they adopt? They made choice of the most horrible". C added "They could not kill . . . child".

[2] For "by firmness . . . misery", ibid I 424 reads "by artificial reasons".

[3] This clause added by C.

[4] Cf ibid I 424: "The child stretched out his little hands toward his deliverer and his first word was—bread!"

[5] In ibid I 425 the child held bread with one hand "and with the other alternately shook his father and mother; his piteous moans rouzed them at length from their deathlike slumber. It seemed at once to awaken a new love of life in their hearts".

EPITAPH, ON AN INFANT[1]

ERE Sin could blight, or Sorrow fade,
Death came with friendly care;
The opening Bud to Heaven conveyed,
And bade it Blossom there!

S. T. C.

THE Poetry, which we have yet seen, of savage nations, present us with descriptions of manners, totally dissimilar to our own, and those rude energies of mind which dignified the human animal,

When wild in woods the noble Savage ran.[2]

The following specimens of a Sclavonian nation are less elevated, but perhaps more interesting. They are the effusions of a people uncivilized themselves, yet groaning beneath the oppressions of civilized society. The Esthonians, a few of whose popular ballads we are about to give our readers, inhabit the upper regions of the Gulf of Finland: they are subject to the Germans, and never did human beings experience more cruel masters. The two latter ballads might be sung with feeling, and I fear, much truth by our own peasants.

I. SONG OF A FEMALE ORPHAN[3]

THE Sparrow-hawk has five beside herself: the Duck, always goes in pairs. I am quite alone: I have no Father, no Mother.[4] To whom shall I lament my woes? To whom shall I unbosom my distress? Behind whom shall I run, when people scold me?[5] Shall I complain

[1] *PW* (EHC) I 68. These lines had appeared already in *M Chron* 23 Sept 1794. Lamb asserted that their main merit in *Poems* (1796) was as a filler (to C 8–10 June 1796: *LL* I 18) and carried his irreverence further by applying the first two lines to the young porker in "A Dissertation upon Roast Pig". The poem is derivative; see *PW* (EHC) I 68n.

[2] Dryden *The Conquest of Granada* pt I I i.

[3] From [W. Tooke] *Varieties of Literature* I 30–1 (var). C's title. C omits lines and alters his selections from the "Popular Poetry of the Esthonians"; changes are given in the following notes.

[4] Cf ibid I 30: "I am alone, like the sparrow-hawk | And yet the sparrow-hawk has five besides herself. | I am alone, like the duck; | And yet the duck always goes in pairs. | I am alone, like the crane; | And yet the crane has six besides herself. | I am alone, like the pelican; | Yet she has two children. | I am quite alone, | Have no father, | No mother".

[5] Cf ibid: "On whom shall I lean when people scold me?"

to the crow-toe flowers? The crow-toe flowers fade.[1] Shall I complain to the meadow-grass? The meadow-grass will wither. Ah! that it could hear[2] my lamentation, the song of the wretched Orphan! Rise up, my loving father! Rise up, my loving Mother![3] "I cannot rise up, my daughter! I cannot rise up.[4] The green grass is grown over my head; the blades of grass grow thick on my grave; the blue mist of the forest is before my eyes; and on my feet the weeds and the bushes are grown."

II.[5] Note, the Summer is very short in Esthonia. So early as the middle of August heavy rains and bleet winds interrupt the haymaking. They are therefore obliged to work with redoubled force on the sun-shining days. A large plot of ground is assigned to each boor: the overseer stands by him with his stick in his hand, and is as much exercised by beating the workmen, as the workmen themselves by their toil. Even the little ones scarcely able to walk are forced to work, and often barbarously beaten before their parents. Each boor works separately. Thus all the comforts of society are denied him.

SONG OF THE HAYMAKERS[6]

So long as the haymaking lasts, till the grass is all mown down, so long must we ted the swathes![7] Ah! it is better to live in the bottomless pit, *more happy to be unhappy in hell*, than to belong to our farm! Before sun-rise we are already at work; after sun-set we must still be working; by moon-light the hay must be cocked.[8] The Oxen feed while under the yoke: the poor Geldings are always in the team. The Labourer stands on pointed sticks, his little ones totter about and cry because sharp thorns run into their tender feet.[9] Our Lord walks upon a white floor; our Lady wears a golden coronet;[10] our young

[1] Cf ibid I 31: "The flowers will fade", followed by the omitted lines: "Shall I complain to the flowers of parsley? | They will decay".

[2] Cf ibid: "And yet it hears".

[3] These two sentences are reversed in ibid, followed by the omitted lines: "Rise up, and shut my box; | Make fast the trunk that holds my bridal presents!"

[4] Cf ibid: "I cannot rise up, I am not awake!"

[5] From *Varities of Literature* I 33–4 (altered). "Bleet winds" is "bleak" in *Varieties*, and C has added the "barbarously beaten before their parents" and the subsequent sentences.

[6] *Varieties* I 34–5 (var). C's title.

[7] C had omitted "Till the weeds are all away, | Till the sabines are raked off, | While the stack is not yet made". The italics in the next sentence are C's.

[8] C reverses these clauses.

[9] For "his little ones . . . feet", I 35 reads "His little help-mates on the sharp thorns.—"

[10] Ibid reads "crown!"

Masters are drest very fine.[1] Let them but look on us poor Boors, how we are tormented and plagued—how our[2] little ones are tortured, if they run but a finger's length from their work. And we must be all kept dispersed.

III.[3] In the spring season there is frequently such a dearth, that the Peasants are obliged to fodder their cattle with the half-rotten straw of their thatched roofs. The German houses only have chimnies. "Ever since the chimnies came into the village," is the same as to say, "Ever since the Germans settled themselves in the country." The Lord may take as many people as he pleases, to be domestics in his house. The tributes paid to the Lord, are called righteousnesses, I suppose, ut lucus a non lucendo[4] from their iniquity.

SONG IN SPRING-TIDE[5]

THIS is the cause that the country is ruined, and the straw of the thatch is eaten away. The Gentry are come to live in the land. Chimnies between the village, and the proprietors on the white floors. The sheep brings forth a lamb with a white forehead—this is to be paid to my lord for a righteousness sheep: the sow farrows pigs—they go to the spit of the Lord: the hen lays eggs—they go into my lord's frying-pan: the cow drops a male calf—that goes into my lord's herd as a bull: the mare foals a horse foal—that must be for my lord's nag: the boor's wife has sons—they must go to look after my lord's poultry.

We add to these specimens of Esthonian poetry, a MADAGASCAR SONG[6]—translated from the Madagascar language by the Chevalier de Parny who resided a long time in that island.[7]

A Mother was dragging her only daughter to the beach, in order to sell her to the white men:

O Mother! thy bosom bore me; I was the first fruit of thy love; what

[1] The Masters (*Varieties* I 35) "wear silver rings! | They sit down in easy chairs, | Or walk up and down the hall".

[2] Ibid reads "the".

[3] *Varieties* I 35–6 (with an addition).

[4] "As 'a grove' from not being light"—proverbial for an absurd derivation. This last part of the sentence is C's addition.

[5] *Varieties* I 36 (var). C's title. Changes are minor: mainly "the lord" to "my lord".

[6] Ibid I 551–2 (var, with an omission).

[7] Évariste-Désiré de Forges, Vicomte de Parny (1753–1814), translated it into French; the English translator is unknown. The poem is No 9 of Parny's *Chansons madécasses*.

crime have I committed to deserve a life of slavery? I alleviate the sorrows of thy age. For thee I labour the ground: for thee I gather flowers: for thee I ensnare the fish of the flood. I have defended thee from the cold; I have borne thee when it was hot, into the shades of fragrant trees; I watched thee while thou slumberedst, and drove away from thy face the stings of Moskitoes. O Mother what will become of thee, when thou hast me no longer?[1] Thou wilt die in misery: I will think of thee when I am a slave, and cry bitterly because I am not with thee to assist thy wretchedness.[2] O mother! sell not thy only daughter.

It may be a pleasing task to some one of our poetical readers to versify the above—preserving their simplicity.

WHETHER EATING IN COMPANY BE CONDUCIVE TO HEALTH?[3]

DOCTOR Vasse[4] discussed this question seriously in the school of the Faculty of Medicine at Paris, and gravely determined it in the affirmative, that eating and drinking in company is really conducive to health. He published this medical question and his curious illustration of it. He divides entertainments into several classes; ordinary and extraordinary: the first consists of meats of a moderate price, in the other they are more expensive and splendid. At public entertainments, several families form one company; at private ones, there is only the daily preparation. He then enumerates many kinds of sociable meals; as the pascal lamb among the Jews, the love feasts among the primitive Christians, wedding dinners, merry-makings, twelfth day, Carnival and St. Martin's day.

Undertaking to shew the advantages of eating in company, he fixes three properties of the meals under consideration, viz. animal, moral, natural or physical. The first are such as do good to the body, the second benefit the mind, and the third are useful to both. Man, says the Doctor, is an animal formed for society, he is led by example, and

1 C omits "The money thou receivest will not give thee another daughter". *Varieties* I 552.

2 For "I will think . . . wretchedness" ibid reads "thou wilt die in misery, and my bitterest grief will be, that I cannot assist thee".

3 From the *Anthologia Hibernica* I (Apr 1793) 262–3; signed "H".

4 David Vasse, early eighteenth-century physician, professor of botany at the University of Paris. This *Quaestio medica* was discussed and published in 1733.

imitates what he sees done. If he observes another eat, he is desirous of doing the same, and his mouth immediately waters. This water is the saliva which dissolves the food, renders it more savoury and whets the appetite. That being sharpened, we eat with pleasure and grind our meat better. Where conversation and mirth preside at a table, we are obliged to keep the meat longer in our mouths, it is more penetrated with saliva, and digests better. The blood and spirits are in better order, the nutritive juice becomes sweeter, the circulation of the liquids is more completely executed, the heart, the seat of joy, is dilated and all the functions of the body conspire with a sort of emulation to promote health. The advantages accruing from eating in company are numerous: it always diverts chagrin and melancholy to dine with a number of people. The bare sight of many eating, drinking and singing, inspires good humour; the healths that pass around and agreeable conversation rouse the soul and make it shake off all dismal ideas. An union of persons either begins or is cemented, and misunderstandings are composed or removed.

In regard of the utility of entertainments to the whole man, we must know, that such is the intimate connection between the soul and body, that what is useful to one must infallibly be so to the other.

But our author goes one step further, as exercise is of no inconsiderable use, eating in company appears worthy of recommendation on that score. Here, says he, I shall be asked what exercise I mean, is it that of the teeth, which communicates electric motion to the frame? to which I answer, it is the motion of the hands and body in carving and helping, in accepting thanks and returning them, in the lively gestures before dinner and the no less sprightly ones after it.

But there is one material objection which should be removed, namely, that these entertainments are frequently productive of much disorder and irregularity, and therefore ought not to be indulged. To this our Doctor replies, that abuses will insinuate themselves every where, so that if all that is perverted should be prohibited, even eating and drinking and other innocent and useful human acts would incur the charge of criminality. Allowing evils sometimes to arise, are they not countervailed by the good arising from these entertainments? Such are the arguments used by Doctor Vasse to prove eating in company is conducive to health. They certainly evince the taste of the Doctor and the Faculty for good cheer. Besides doing his duty to the public as a physician in enforcing an interesting medical precept, the ideas as well as the reality of which gives rapture to the hungry and pleasure to the full epicure, we find he had another object in view; it seems there were some pragmatical, mortified and penurious licentiates in divinity, who, he justly remarks, had a zeal but not according to knowledge, who wished to put a stop to entertainments given to their fellow-students when they received the academic cap; but the Parliament of Paris by an arret continued the old laudable custom, and good cheer triumphed over the sour moroseness of these unenlightened Theologians.

ADDRESS[1]

THE EXECUTIVE DIRECTORY TO THE FRENCH ARMIES

DEFENDERS of the Country, the moment approaches, when you are again to take up your victorious arms; the moment approaches, when you are to quit a repose to which you consented in the hope alone that it would lead to an honourable peace: but the seas of blood which have flowed have not yet satiated the rage of your enemies. They unquestionably imagine that we are about to abandon the fruits of our victories, at the very moment when success is ready to crown them. They imagine that we are about to demand of them as cowards a peace which we have offered them as generous enemies. Let them conceive those unworthy expectations; we will not be surprised: they have never combated for liberty—but what they cannot be ignorant of, is, that the brave armies with which they wish again to try their strength, are the same by which they have been so often subdued. No; they have not forgotten the prodigies of French valour; they still recollect, with terror, both the redoubts of Gemappes, and the plains of Fleurns, and the frozen rivers of Holland: they recollect that the Alps and the Pyrenees have opposed to you but feeble barriers, and that the Peninsula of Quiberon became the tomb of all the parricidal slaves, which, in the hope of subjecting you to the yoke of a monster, dared to set their feet on the soil of the Republic. If they have forgotten all this, you will bring it to their recollection by blows still more terrible; you will learn them finally, that nothing can resist the efforts of a great nation which determines to be free.

[1] From the *Star* 27 Apr 1796, though it also was printed in most of the London papers—e.g. *M Chron*, *Sun*, and *The Times* 28 Mar. The *Star* misprinted Fleurus "Fleurns", as did C.

Brave Warriors, you have afforded the example of a disinterestedness which cannot exist unless among Republicans. Oftentimes, in the midst of the greatest scarcity of provisions, of an almost absolute want of the most indispensible objects, you have displayed that heroical patience, which, joined to your impetuous valour, so eminently distinguishes you, and which will signalize you to all nations, and to the eyes of posterity. Republican Soldiers, you will preserve this great character; and the moment when your situation has been meliorated, when, with an unanimous voice, the Representatives of the Nation have taken measures to provide efficaciously for your wants, you will redouble also your vigour and courage, to put an end to a war which can be terminated by new victories alone.

In vain has the French Government manifested to all the Powers which wage War against France, a sincere wish to restore at length the repose of exhausted Europe; it has in vain made to them the most just and moderate propositions; nothing has been capable of removing their deplorable blindness. Yes, brave Warriors, we must still have victories; and it is your energy alone that can put a stop to this devasting scourge. Prepare therefore for a last effort, and let it be decisive; let every thing yield to, let every thing be dissipated by, your phalanxes; let the new flags of your enemies, carried off by your triumphant hands, form, with the preceding ones, the trophy with which, in the name of France, always great in her misfortunes, always just in her prosperity, the equitable Peace you will give to the World will be proclaimed.

And you, generous Defenders, who shall have cemented that Peace with your blood, you will soon return to the bosom of your families, among your Fellow-Citizens, to enjoy your glory—terrible still, in your repose, to all the enemies of the Republic.

LETOURNEUR, President.[1]

[1] Charles-Louis-François-Honoré Letourneur de la Manche (1751–1817), one of the five members of the Directory.

FRANCE[1]

PARIS

April 25.

THE GENERAL IN CHIEF OF THE ARMY IN ITALY TO THE EXECUTIVE DIRECTORY.

"Head-Quarters at Carcare, 25th Germinal.[2]

"THE Campaign in Italy has commenced. I have to give you an account of the Battle of *Mentenotte*.[3]

"After three days movement to deceive us, General BEAULIEU[4] attacked, with a division of ten thousand Men, the right of the Army supported by VOLTRY.[5]

"The General CERVONI,[6] who commanded there, having under his orders the 70th and 99th Half Brigades, sustained the fire with the intrepidity which characterizes the Soldiers of Liberty. I was not deceived with respect to the true intentions of the Enemy. The instant I was informed of the circumstances of the Attack on the right, I ordered General CERVONI to wait the night, and to fall back, by a forced march, and concealing his movement from the Enemy, upon my centre, which was supported by the Heights of *Madona de Savona*.

"On the 24th, at four in the morning, BEAULIEU in person, with 15,000 men, attacked and beat in all the positions by which the centre of the army had been supported; at an hour after mid-day he attacked the Redoubt of *Monte-Lezino*,[7] which was behind the entrenchment. The Enemy returned several times to the charge, but this redoubt, guarded by 1500 men, was rendered impenetrable by the courage of those who defended it. The Chief of Brigade RAMPON,[8] who commanded there, by one of those strokes which characterize a soul great and formed for brilliant actions, made his

[1] From the *Sun* 27 Apr 1796, both letter and subsequent paragraphs. The *Star* 27 Apr and *M Chron* and *The Times* 28 Apr published a variant of the letter.

[2] This dispatch of 13 Apr marks the first appearance of Bonaparte as a major European figure. He forced the previously impregnable barrier of the Maritime Alps, defeated the coalition of Austria and the Piedmontese, and brought the kingdom of Sardinia to unconditional surrender on 17 May.

[3] The battle of Montenotte took place 11–12 Apr.

[4] Jean-Pierre, Baron de Beaulieu (1725–1819), commander-in-chief of the Austrian army in Italy and one of the emperor's Belgian subjects.

[5] Voltri, a town near Genoa.

[6] Jean-Baptiste Cervoni (1765–1809), French general born in Corsica.

[7] Monte Legino.

[8] Antoine-Guillaume (later Comte) Rampon (1759–1842), French general.

Troops, in the midst of the fire, take an oath to die to a man in the Redoubt. The Enemy passed the night within pistol-shot.

"During the night, General LAHARPE,[1] with all the troops of the right, took post behind the Redoubt of *Monte-Lezino.* At an hour after mid-night, I departed with the Generals BERTHIER and MESSENA,[2] the Commissioner SALICETTI,[3] with a part of the troops of the centre and the left. We moved by *Altare*, upon the flank and the rear of the Enemy.

"On the 22d at break of day, BEAULIEU, who had received a re-inforcement, and LAHARPE, attacked and fought with vigour and different success, when General MASSENA appeared, sowing death and terror on the flank and rear of the enemy, where M. ARGENTEAU[4] commanded: the rout of the Enemy was complete; two of their Generals, ROCCAVINA[5] and ARGENTEAU, were badly wounded. The loss of the Enemy was between three and four thousand men, of whom more than two thousand five hundred were made prisoners; a Colonel, eight or ten superior Officers, and several Colours were taken.

"When I shall have received all the reports, and shall be less engaged, I will send you a detailed account, which may make known to you those to whom their Country owes a particular acknowledgement.

"Generals, Officers and Soldiers, all supported, in this memorable affair, the glory of the French name.

(Signed) "BUONAPARTE."

The success of our Army in *Italy* has not stopped here. In the sitting of the Council of Five Hundred of yesterday,[6] the following message was read by the President from the Executive Directory:

"Citizen Representatives, the fortunate battle of *Montenotte*, which we informed you of by our message of the 2d of this month, was only, for the invincible Army of Italy, the prelude to successes still more brilliant—We have to-day to announce to you a Victory,

[1] Amédée-Emmanuel-François Laharpe (1754–96), Swiss general in the French service.

[2] Louis-Alexandre Berthier (1753–1815), later one of Napoleon's marshals and Prince de Wagram. André Masséna (1758–1817), later marshal of France and Duc de Rivoli.

[3] Antoine-Christophe Saliceti (1757–1809), of Corsica; French revolutionary and administrator in Italy.

[4] Eugen, Count Argenteau (1741–1819), Austrian field-marshal.

[5] Mathias, Freiherr Rukavina von Boynograd (1737–1817), Austrian field-marshal.

[6] The sitting of 5 Floréal, or 23 Apr.

decisive, and most memorable, gained by that Army at *Monte-Lezino*, over the united Piedmontese and Austrian Armies.

"The Enemy lost ten thousand five hundred Men, of whom eight thousand were made prisoners. They lost likewise 40 pieces of Cannon, with Horses, Mules, and Ammunition Waggons, 15 Stand of Colours, all their Equipage, and several Magazines.

"Our troops, Generals, Officers, Soldiers, are all covered with glory, and have shewn themselves worthy to defend the cause of Liberty.

"The General in Chief, BUONAPARTE, again directed this attack. The other Generals who seconded him in the most distinguished manner, are LAHARPE, ANGEREAU,[1] MASSENA, CERVONI, COSSE, MENARD, and GOUBERT.[2] This last was wounded in leaping into the Entrenchments of the Enemy. Two other Generals were killed at the head of their columns, performing prodigies of valour.

"The General PROVERA,[3] who commanded the Austro-Sardinian Army, was made Prisoner, after having evinced the most gallant resistance, with some Regiments which were taken with him.

"You will declare without doubt, that the Army of Italy has not ceased to deserve well of its Country."

GENOA[4] is the marine key of Italy, and is of such importance to the French, that we have no doubt but they will make themselves masters of it. However they may preserve its nominal independence, it will be their own to all useful purposes: and thus they secure a mine of wealth, an extensive granary, and the finest port in Italy. If the news of the defeat of the Austrians in Italy be true to the extent stated by the French, it may be considered as decisive, not only of the fate of Piedmont and the Milanese, but of Europe. For the EMPEROR can gain no success upon the Rhine to counter-balance the loss of Lombardy. It is the richest country in the world; and the revenue he draws from it has no drawback for its defence, as the Netherlands always had.

We shall find it difficult by any subsidy to induce the EMPEROR to continue the war, if this victory be real, or if it be not immediately repaired. He will sacrifice Belgium without further hesitation to save his Italian territories, and in this view the success of the French may

[1] Charles-Pierre-François Augereau (1757–1816), later marshal of France and Duc de Castiglione.

[2] Jean-Jacques Causse (1751–96), general of brigade. Jean-François-Xavier de Ménard (1756–1831), French general. Barthélemy-Catherine Joubert (1769–99), French general.

[3] Marquis de Provera (c 1740–1804) of Lombardy; Austrian field-marshal.

[4] This and the following paragraph from *M Chron* or *Star* 29 Apr 1796.

accelerate a general peace. But even if the victory be as complete as it is called, the overthrow of Turin and Milan must depend more on the dispositions of the country than on the force of the French. If the people are with them, as it is believed they are, their inroad will be dreadful, for the peasantry are almost in a state of nature, and may be instigated to any violence. Let it be recollected, however, that in their passage to Turin, they have the fortress of Coni on the left, which they must in prudence reduce, and in their road to Milan they have Alexandria to pass through.

STOCKHOLM[1]

April 8.

IN consequence of accounts from the Swedish Ambassador at Petersburgh, stating that the EMPRESS had collected an army on the borders of Finland, and given orders to fit out a fleet, his Majesty the King of Sweden finds himself under the necessity of giving similar orders, and placing his own territories in a state of defence; all the regiments in Sweden and the Grand Duchy of Finland are ordered to be ready to march, and a number of ships of war to be fitted for sea.

By a letter of the same date, we learn that the Courier who brought Baron STEDINGK,[2] our Ambassador at Petersburgh, the account of the preparations of war in Russia, left Petersburgh the 29th of March. Our Government have in consequence issued orders to the Commander in Chief, Lieutenant General Baron KLINGSFORT,[3] that the whole Finland army should march immediately to the borders, in order to defend them.

Another letter of the same date states the Finland army has received orders to collect at the fortress Lousia, on the frontiers, and that the garrison of this city have received orders to be ready to march.

The Russian army in Finland is said already to be 60,000 strong. The report that a declaration of war has been published by Russia against Sweden appears to be unfounded.

Great Britain possesses at present, the nerves of War, and the splendours of Peace: the whole of the trade to the East-Indies, and nearly the whole of that to the West; the whole of the American

[1] The following four paragraphs from *M Chron* or *Star* 25 Apr 1796.

[2] Count Curt Ludvig Christofer von Stedingk (1746–1836), Swedish ambassador to Russia.

[3] Count Wilhelm Mauritz Klingspor (1744–1814), Swedish general.

trade, and the greatest share in that of the Baltic and Mediterranean. Spain and Portugal are now obliged to come to Great Britain for all the articles of commerce with which they were formerly supplied from France. Nor was there ere any period in which there was a greater demand for our manufactories both woollen and cotton. So flourishing a commerce alleviates the burthens of old debts, by depreciating the value, while it enables us to contract new ones, by increasing the influx of money.[1]

In opposition to all this it may be said, that the resources of trade are at all times uncertain, and the more flourishing the trade, the more precarious: and the trade, which flourishes in consequence of the internal distresses of other nations, depends on a transient foundation.[2] FRANCE, though for the present isolated from commerce, possesses advantages more solid and durable in her various, extensive, and fertile lands, and in the numbers, genius, and spirit of her people.[3] The contest between FRANCE and GREAT-BRITAIN resembles a contest between a rich Merchant and an ancient Seigneur of a large landed property. The former has more ready money; but the fund, from which he draws it, is fluctuating and precarious: the latter has but little ready money; but he commands that of which money is only the symbol, property intrinsically valuable and liable to no accidents.[4]

SONNETS

BY THOMAS DERMODY

Written in the 15th year of his age.[5]

SONNET I

THRO' hazel copse oft studious let me roam,
When Love's last warblings melt the frozen year,
When the mute thrush broods o'er his little home,
And sobbing murmurs strike the musing ear;

[1] Above paragraph from *Eng R* XXVII (Apr 1796) 394 (var).

[2] Ibid (var). C omits three sentences.

[3] Ibid p 392 (the same sentence also appeared in the Mar issue p 299).

[4] Ibid p 352 (var), the end of a review of Vansittart's *Inquiry* (see above, p 220 and n 4).

[5] From the *Anthologia Hibernica* I (Mar 1793) 225 (var), the last eight lines of Sonnet II omitted (they continued at the top of the next column). For Dermody, see above, p 251 n 1. C included *Lonely I Sit upon the Silent Shore* in his Sheet of Sonnets in 1796; see *PW* (EHC) II 1141.

What time, when autumn sinks on winter grey,[1]
The dreary evening[2] falls in many a tear
Pallid and still with watery front severe,
Till, slow dissolved in radiant mist away
The dim horizon clears, and the soft moon
Floats thro' the blue expanse in silver pride;
Then 'tis most sweet from some tall mountain's side,[3]
To catch the melting shake of pastoral tune
Wild-warbled, or the simple bell, afar
Flinging faint pauses on the broken wind;
To mark the speckled cloud, the twinkling star,
Or the long waste of lonely night behind,
Fitting to solemn thought the pure, poetic mind.

SONNET II

LONELY I sit upon the silent shore,
Silent, save when the dashing surges break
'Gainst some steep cliff, in low, and sullen roar,
Or the hoarse gulls on night's still slumber shriek.
Soft streams in tremulous vibration o'er
Ocean's broad, frownless front, the lunar ray,
Borne in full many a dimpling wave away,
Or strew'd in glittering points, and seen no more.
Tranquillity has spread her raven plume
Streak'd with faint grey, and shadowy blue, around;
While *Silence* (catching the dull, frequent sound
Of yon dim sail whitening the distant gloom)
Lies in her cell abrupt, where howling SPRITE
Starting terrific from his floating bier
Ne'er enters, nor the swart hags of the night
Who drink the sob of death with ruthless ear.

PORTSMOUTH, APRIL 28.[4] In consequence of the rise of flour, a very large mob assembled in St. George's Square, Portsea, mostly consisting of persons belonging to the Dock-Yard and the Victualling Office: About a thousand of them came very quietly into Portsmouth to state their grievance to Sir John Carter, one of the Magistrates,

[1] Cf the *Anthologia* I 225: "When golden autumn . . ."
[2] Cf ibid: "Meanwhile the evening".
[3] Cf ibid: "How sweet, from some tall mountain's shadowy side".
[4] From the *Star* 29 Apr 1796.

who promised to do every thing in his power to reduce the price, and requested they would go home peaceably; instead of which, they returned to Portsea, joined the others, and destroyed several bakers' houses, among which were those of Mr. Stigant, Mr. Pratt, Mr. Snook, Mr. Boyes, and many more. They assembled again last night in greater numbers, at least five thousand; three of the ringleaders were taken into custody by the peace officers and put into the cage; but they were very soon liberated by the mob, who broke the cage open, and entirely demolished them.[1] The Magistrates then called upon the Buckinghamshire Militia and Yeomen Cavalry—read the riot act, and then ordered them to disperse the mob. Several of them were under the necessity of firing before they would disperse; two persons, who were observed to have been particular busy in destroying the cage, were taken into custody, and sent into Portsmouth gaol under a strong guard of the Militia. The greatest praise is due to the officers and men on this occasion, who conducted themselves in a cool and determined manner: they are now under arms, and are just marched to Portsea, where it is reported the mob intend assembling again this evening.

The Yeomen Cavalry were also ordered to attend, but an express is just arrived from their commanding officer at Fareham, ordering their attendance there immediately.

MR. ALEXANDER LAMETH[2]

THE public have heard that Mr. ALEXANDER LAMETH, after having been for 39 months a prisoner in the Prussian dominions, for 23 months of which he was in a subterraneous dungeon, was recommended by his physicians to take the waters of Bath, as a means of recovering his constitution from the shock it had sustained by this cruel confinement.

It was natural for a person who had sacrificed his popularity in France, to his desire of saving the King and the Royal Family, who had struggled only for a limited Monarchy, and had been the determined enemy of all the horrors which have taken place, to find in England a warm and hospitable reception.

[1] An error for "it".

[2] From *M Chron* 30 Apr 1796, with omissions. As with Lafayette (above, p 183) C wishes to expose the inconsistency and inhumanity of the Coalition. Alexandre-Théodore-Victor, Comte de Lameth (1760–1829), had served under Rochambeau in the American Revolution and under Lafayette in the war with Austria. He returned to France 1799 and served under Napoleon.

But no such thing, he received a letter from Mr. CARTER, the Private Secretary of the Duke of PORTLAND, to come to Burlington-house, and there he was informed that he must immediately quit the kingdom. Mr. Lameth represented the state of his health, and trusted that the humanity of the English Government, if not the hospitality, would procure for him a short stay in the only place of Europe where he could hope for the recovery of his health; and at any rate he expected that they would inform him of the motives why he was to be subjected to such an order. Mr. CARTER told him that the Duke of PORTLAND did not think it necessary to assign the motives of his conduct; and as to the representation of his health, he was instructed to say, that it was not judged proper that he should *sleep more than one night in London.*

Mr. Lameth then only desired that he might be permitted to embark for Altona on board a neutral vessel, as it was contrary to his principles to sail in any vessel *armed* against his country. This was granted—and a King's Messenger conducted him on Wednesday last to Gravesend, to put him on board a neutral vessel in the river.

Mr. Lameth was ten days in London, eight of which he spent in his bed; and we understand that in all that time he was visited by two or three persons, his countrymen and friends.

A CURIOUS ADVERTISEMENT IN THE LEYDEN GAZETTE[1]

IT has pleased the Sovereign Dispenser of all Things, to take unto himself, last night, my Wife, Lady Anne, Countess of Welderen, born at Whitwell; she died at a very advanced age, after a lingering decay, and an illness of three months and a half. I notify this loss, so sensible and painful to me, to my relations and friends, intreating them to spare me all letters of condolence.

(Signed) J. W. DE WELDEREN.

Hague, April 3.

DITTO, IN THE AMSTERDAM GAZETTE

THIS morning, about ten o'clock, my dear Wife, Catharine Elizabeth Uhlenbrock, was happily delivered of a girl; I advise my relations and friends of this circumstance by this present.

JOHN HARBRINKE.

Amsterdam, 10*th April*, 1796.

[1] From *M Chron* 29 Apr 1796 or *Sun* 30 Apr.

BRISTOL, April 27.[1] Last night between the hours of nine and ten, several of the French Prisoners, escaped from the prison at Stapleton, near this city; but we have since learnt many of them have been taken.

EXETER, April 27.[2] On Thursday evening last, a bundle containing a quantity of brimstone, gunpowder, and other combustible matter, was discovered to have been laid on the corner of the stairs belonging to the house of Miss Lovatt, closely adjoining the dwelling-house, &c. of Mr. Pim, fuller, in Westgate-Street; in which it appeared that there had been lighted coals placed, for the purpose of setting fire to the whole premises; but owing to the hurry in which it was laid on the spot, it is supposed the fire was smothered. And on Saturday night another attempt was discovered to have been made on the house of Mr. Thomas Underhill, in the same street, by lighted brimstone and other combustibles having been thrust under the window-shutters, and which had communicated to the dwelling-house; but being immediately discovered, was fortunately got under [control] without any material injury. The shocking consequences which must have followed, had these villanous designs taken effect, are easy to be conceived. It certainly appears to have been done with the intention of plunder. We hope, however, those notorious villains will be discovered, to receive the punishment due to their crime.

A pocket-book[3] was found a few days ago by a gentleman of the name of Sykes, in which was contained, among other writings, an agreement between several monopolizers of corn, to form an association for the purpose of keeping up and increasing the price of wheat. The gentleman immediately delivered it to the Secretary of State, and proper measures will no doubt, be taken to bring the persons concerned in this unlawful combination to justice. The pocket-book proves to be the same which has been for some days advertized, and a reward of 500l. offered for it.

The Court of Kings Bench[4] lately decided a question of great importance to the coasting trade of this kingdom. They held, that common carriers by water were subject to the same rules as common carriers by land; that is, that they shall make good the loss of all property committed to their care, unless occasioned by the act of God, or the king's enemies.

[1] From the *Sun* 30 Apr 1796.

[2] From ibid.

[3] This item from *The Times*, *Star*, or *True Briton*, 23 Apr 1796 or *E. Johnson's British Gazette, and Sunday Monitor* 24 Apr.

[4] From the *Star* 14 Apr 1796.

About 70 men of the 20th regiment landed at Plymouth on Tuesday last from on board a transport lately arrived from the West-Indies. Many of them are in an unhealthy state. They are the remains of 700 fine fellows, who have been thus reduced by the ravages of the yellow fever.[1]

In consequence of the reiterated solicitations of the French Government,[2] the Senate of Venice has at last ordered LOUIS XVIII. instantly to quit Verona, as well as the whole territory of Venice. The fate of this unfortunate Prince is truly distressing. At first obliged to quit the Court of his Father-in-law, the King of SARDINIA, he is now also expelled from his last retreat. The Cabinet of Vienna has prohibited him in the most positive terms to enter the Austrian territory, and has also threatened to disband the army of the Prince of CONDE, should he attempt to do so. Thus banished from his own dominions; driven out of those which belong to the Princes of his family; and prevented from seeking shelter in the provinces of the petty Princes of Italy, by the fear of exposing them to the resentment of the French Republic, where is he now to find an asylum?[3]

Lately died at Aberdeen in the 77th year of his age, George Campbell, D.D. F. R. S. Edinburgh, late principal and professor of Divinity in the Marischal College and University of Aberdeen, and one of the Ministers of Aberdeen, well known and esteemed for his excellent writings in defence of revelation, and for his admirable translation of the four Gospels, with dissertations prefixed.[4]

A second squadron of Dutch men of war,[5] comprising 7 ships from 60 to 74 guns, with 9 frigates and smaller vessels, sailed from the Texel on Sunday or Monday last. The Admiralty, on Wednesday, were apprized of the circumstance, and immediately dispatched messengers to Hull, Lynn, Bridlington, Whitby, Sunderland, Newcastle, and the other places along the coast, prohibiting the sailing of vessels bound for Northern ports.

[1] Above item from the *Star* 21 Apr 1796 (slightly altered). By 1796, yellow fever and Maroon uprisings had accounted for 40,000 dead and 40,000 unfit for service in the British troops in the West Indies. J. Steven Watson *The Reign of George III* (Oxford 1960) 370.

[2] This item from the *Star* 30 Apr 1796 or *E. Johnson's British Gazette* 1 May. *The Times* 30 Apr concludes with a sentence on "the pride the English nation feels" in giving asylum to the royalist exiles.

[3] Louis XVIII (1755–1824) found temporary exile with the Duke of Brunswick at Blankenburg (until 1797).

[4] Campbell (1719–96) attacked Hume in his *Dissertation on Miracles* (1762), having sent the ms to his friendly opponent before publication; his translation of the Gospels appeared in 1789. The *M Mag* printed an obituary (promised the month before) in May: I 343–4.

[5] Item from the *Star* 25 Apr 1796.

The anxiety of the public[1] to learn the further effects of the victories of the French in Italy, is naturally great. The general opinion seems to be, that they will force either the Emperor or the King of Sardinia, or both, to an immediate Peace. It is not so much the number of men that they have killed and taken, as the impression that it will make on a disaffected country. The Piedmontese peasantry are to a man ripe for a revolt, and all subordination is likely to be destroyed by a blow so terrible. The first feeling of the KING of SARDINIA therefore, will be to save himself by negociation, and it will not be inconsistent with the hereditary politics of Turin, to listen to propositions of an alliance with the French, for the reduction of Austrian Lombardy. At least it is likely for the EMPEROR to dread such a compact, and after such a footing gained by the French, we suspect it will be a race of cunning, who shall be the first to make their peace with this conquering enemy.

Extract of a Letter from Calcutta, 24th Dec. 1795.[2]

"OF the many strange events that have lately happened, that of *our* supplying *you* with bread, is not the least remarkable. To keep in unison with it, *we* have only to apply to Carolina to supply Bengal with rice, and then the system will be complete; a victory of possibilities over all human calculation.

"The only intelligence that has transpired by the last over-land packet, is that *you* are starving; and in return you may expect to hear (probably by this conveyance), that *we* are in a hopeful way in India. This army is not to be amused by speeches. They have no better opinion of the integrity of a House of Commons, than the House have of theirs; and it requires something more than the eloquence of Mr. Dundas to lull the Officers into security. Tho' I am not in the secret, I own I am not without apprehensions that, before this reaches you, you will hear of the army having taken upon itself the redress of its grievances. On this you may rely. They are fully prepared, and do not want resolution, inclination, or unanimity.

"In consequence of an advertisement from the Governor, Sir John Shore,[3] prohibiting for the future certain meetings of Military Officers, a deputation from that corps was appointed to wait on him; and

[1] From *M Chron* 30 Apr 1796.

[2] From *M Chron* 29 Apr 1796. Following the item above, the *M Chron* 30 Apr stated that its reason for publishing the letter from Calcutta in its issue of the day before was to "give our readers some faint idea of the critical state of our possessions in the East".

[3] John Shore (1751–1834), governor-general of India 1793–8; created Baron

by them he was told, in very plain English, that to his prohibition they neither would nor could ——; and that as to their object, they both could and would, &c. Upon which Sir John Shore thought it advisable to retract his order, and pacify them with promises as well as he could."

FROM THE
LONDON GAZETTE
April 26.[1]

Admiralty Office, April 26.

DISPATCHES, of which the following are copies and extracts, have been received at this Office from Sir Edward Pellew, Bart.[2]

(The first is an extract of a letter from Sir Edward Pellew, mentioning the capture of a French Frigate, the particulars of which are contained in the following letter from Captain Cole:)[3]

La Revolutionaire at Sea, April 13, 1796.

SIR,

IT being so dark, when I came alongside the French Frigate L'Unite, that you could not observe the conduct of the two ships, I beg leave to report to you, that not being able to prevail upon her Commander, Citizen Durand,[4] to surrender, after some minutes conversation, I opened a close and well directed fire upon him. After we had sustained the fire of her stern chases some time, and upon firing the second broadside, he called out that he had struck. I had at the same moment directed the helm to be put to port, in order to board him, as the ships were going under a press of sail, at the rate of ten knots, and drawing near the shore.

Allow me, Sir, to express to you how much I feel myself obliged to my First Lieutenant, Edward Ellicott, for his very particular attention in keeping sight of the chase, and for his steady and manly courage when close engaged. The cheerfulness with which he put himself at the head of the Boarders, promised me the happiest suc-

Teignmouth 1798; a pious but ineffectual administrator. It was Shore's surrender to the demands of the mutinous officers that eventually caused his recall.

[1] Reprinted by the London papers —e.g. *M Chron, Star*, and *The Times* 27 Apr 1796.

[2] Sir Edward Pellew (1757–1833), 1st Bt (1796) and 1st Viscount Exmouth (1816), admiral in 1814, at this time commanded a squadron of five frigates off Brest.

[3] Capt Francis Cole, of the *Révolutionnaire* (captured from the French in 1794).

[4] Charles-Alexandre-Léon Durand, Comte de Linois (1761–1848), then captain, later vice-admiral.

cess, if that event had been necessary, and which was only stopped by the Enemy's calling to surrender.

In this short contest the highest praise is due to my officers and ship's company, and the effect of their steady conduct is striking in the number of killed and wounded, of which a list is annexed.

I cannot sufficiently express my own good fortune in not having lost an officer or man, which is to be attributed to the enemy's firing at the masts and rigging.

I am, &c.
FRA. COLE.

L'Unite, Citizen Durand, Commander. Killed 9,—Wounded desperately, 11.
Sir Edward Pellew, Bart, &c. &c.

Indefatigable, Falmouth, April 23, 1796.

SIR,

I HAVE most sensible pleasure in desiring you to inform my Lords Commissioners of the Admiralty of my arrival at this Port, accompanied by the French National Frigate La Verginie, of 44 guns, eighteen and nine pounders, and 340 men, commanded by Citizen Bargaret,[1] Capitaine de Vaisseau, who sailed from Brest singly, four days ago, to cruise off the Lizard in this favourite Frigate, which is considered the finest and fastest sailer in the French Navy, and of the largest dimensions, being 158 feet long, and 43 broad.

On Wednesday morning the 20th instant, after I had sealed my dispatches for their Lordships, laying to under the Lizard, with the squadron, waiting for the French Frigate L'Unite our prize, to weather that point, I observed a ship coming in from the sea, which in my mind looked rather suspicious; and, on her not answering the private signal, when she tacked from us, I immediately gave chace to her, accompanied by the Amazon and La Concorde (having by signal directed La Revolutionaire to attend her prize into port, and the Argo to proceed to Plymouth.) The superior sailing of the Indefatigable gave me the satisfaction of coming up with her, after a chace of fifteen hours, and running one hundred and sixty eight miles. Fortunately the wind prevented her from steering for Ushant, or she must have escaped.

A little past midnight, I commenced action with the enemy, which was closely continued under a crowded sail, for one hour and forty-five minutes. The enemy, who fought gallantly, was by this time

[1] Capt Bergeret.

much crippled, her mizzen-mast and main-top-mast being shot away. The Indefatigable was not much less disabled, having lost her gaff and mizzen-top-mast, the main-top-sail was rendered useless by an unlucky shot cutting both leech-ropes. In this situation we passed the enemy without power of avoiding it, having no after-sail to back, and I had long discovered we had not only to combat a ship of large force, but that her commander was completely master of his profession, in whose presence I could not commit myself with impunity, by throwing my ship in the wind, without submitting to be raked by him.

She had not at this time struck, and we kept close a-head of her, receiving new braces to enable us to bring the ship to, to renew the attack.

At this period La Concorde appeared in sight, close under her stern; and, upon the enemy seeing her, she fired a gun to leeward, and struck her light, as a signal of surrender.

Although a very few minutes would have placed the Indefatigable again along side of her, I am confident she would not have surrendered without further resistance, had not the Concorde so timely come up.

I am extremely indebted to Captain Hunt and Reynolds,[1] for their very particular attention in keeping after us during the night on so many courses, which nothing but the most delicate observance of my signals would have enabled them to do, their distance astern being so great.

Their Lordships are well aware how difficult it is in a night action with a flying Enemy, whose rate of sailing is little inferior to her antagonist, to choose her situation; and, when it is remembered how often this ship changed her's in the action, I need scarcely say what great attention was paid to my orders by every officer under my command.

To Lieutenants Pellowe, Thomson, and Norway, my thanks are above expression. Lieutenant Williams, of the Marines, and Mr. Bell, the Master, who were immediately about my person, rendered me the most essential services. The ship's company, who have been my faithful companions during the war, and are indeared to me by their uniform exertions, manifested on this occasion nothing but ardour and zeal.

But above all other pleasures I feel is that of informing their Lord-

[1] Capt Anthony Hunt, of the *Concorde*; Capt Robert Carthew Reynolds, of the *Amazon*, later rear-admiral.

ships, that I have lost neither officer nor man in the contest. The enemy suffered considerably, having 14 or 15 killed, 17 badly wounded and 10 slightly; the ship much shattered in her hull, and four feet water in her hold, from shot holes.

I have sent La Concorde to Plymouth with La Virginie, and shall proceed with the Amazon, who has lost her head, for the same place, to morrow, in order to repair the damages we have sustained in the action.

I am, &c.

EDW. PELLEW.

(An Extract of a Letter from Admiral Murray, on the American Coast, merely mentions the capture of L' Aurore (French Corvett), prize to his Majesty's ship Cleopatra. She had only fifty men on board when taken.)[1]

DUKE OF NORFOLK AND LORD MALDEN[2]

IN consequence of a Publication addressed by Lord MALDEN to the Inhabitants of the Borough of Leominster,[3] the Duke of NORFOLK, accompanied by Capt. WOMBWELL, of the First West York Regiment of Militia, and Lord MALDEN, accompanied by Capt. TAYLOR,[4] Aid-de-Camp to His Royal Highness the Duke of YORK, met on Saturday evening in a field beyond Paddington. The parties having taken their ground, and the word being given by one of the Seconds, they fired without effect. The Seconds then thought proper to offer their interference; and, in consequence of a conversation which passed while the parties were on the ground, Capt. TAYLOR was authorized by Lord MALDEN to say, that his Lordship believes that the Duke of NORFOLK had not violated any engagement he had made, and that his Grace did not consider his Agent as

[1] The *Aurore* was captured the same day as the *Virginie* (22 Apr), by Capt Charles Rowley, of the *Cleopatra*, under the command of Rear-Admiral George Murray.

[2] From the *Sun* or *M Herald* 2 May; most of the London papers—e.g. *M Chron* and *The Times*—printed only the first communication, not giving the electioneering correspondence. The *Oracle* printed the first letter 2 May, the electioneering correspondence 4 May.

[3] C's interest in this story is due to his detestation of duels and to the fact that his friend Pollen was standing for Parliament under the sponsorship of Lord Essex. See also above, p 115. According to *The Times* 4 May, Malden and Norfolk used weapons that "neither had the art of knowing how to manage . . . Lord Malden fired first, and had nigh shot himself; and when the Duke of Norfolk presented his pistol, it was locked. After the first fire, the seconds interfered".

[4] Herbert Taylor (1775–1839), secretary to the Duke of York 1794; later Sir Herbert and a lieut-gen.

having done so. Mr. WOMBWELL at the same time assured Lord MALDEN, from the Duke of NORFOLK, that it was not his Grace's intention to deviate from any thing he had before asserted, with respect to his or Mr BIDDULPH's intention of not indemnifying for the money expended in treats. Lord MALDEN replied, that if his Grace considered it in that light, his Lordship was confident his Grace would not have countenanced his Agent.

(Signed) J. WOMBWELL.
H. TAYLOR.

The following is the Electioneering Correspondence between the two Noble Lords, about the Borough of Leominster, which led to the Duel.

COPY

"Liverpool, April 9, 1796.

"MY LORD,

"BEING on a journey into the North, on business, your Lordship's letter of the 4th overtook me on the road, after I had left Leominster, from which place I had wrote.

"Had I been there on the 28th, I should probably have used my endeavours, with all I could influence, to have hindered the treat, from a wish that treating might not go on; but do not consider the presence of Mr. Morris, after it was over, or even had he been present as a guest, under the circumstances, as a violation of the Agreement. This is my opinion, and leaving your Lordship to retain your own, I shall not farther discuss any thing that relates to the treat of Easter-Monday.—When I wrote that I was told unfair use had been made of my letters by persons to whom you had communicated them, I certainly could not mean your Lordship.

I have the Honour to be,
My Lord,
Your Lordship's obedient humble Servant,
"NORFOLK.

"Right Hon. Lord Viscount MALDEN."

COPY

"MY LORD, *London, April* 12, 1796.

"YOUR Grace would have received a more early answer to your letter of the 5th inst. dated from Leominster, had I known where to direct to you. From the general tenor of your conduct in the whole of this business, I am not surprized that the result of your inquiries respecting Mr. Morris's behaviour should have terminated as they have done. Your Grace and your agents have examined the evidence; the witness in favour of Mr. Morris, I imagine, was Mr. Morris himself, or some person of that description, and consequently he has been honourably acquitted. I wish, my Lord, I could say the same of your Grace in this transaction. Had you, my Lord, thought fit to make exact inquiries for the true purpose of gaining real information of all that had passed, with a view of doing justice to the inhabitants of the Borough, who were injured by the breach of the engagement, as well as to myself and my friends, who were more particularly concerned in it, you would have discovered that Mr. Morris was directly and positively the person who had violated that agreement, proposed at first, and entered into, on the part of Mr. Hunter's agent, and Mr. Pollen, at the request of your own friends. Mr. Edwards and Mr. Elrington informed Mr. Morris, that the treat on Easter Monday was about to take place, and requested him to say if he knew for whom it was intended. Mr. Morris replied, he was not obliged to answer questions. Mr. Edwards assured him it was designed for Mr. Biddulph's friends, and that he (Mr. Edwards) had discharged his duty by giving Mr. Morris that information.

"It is also an undeniable fact, my Lord, that Mr. Morris was in the Grange before dinner; and particularly invited one of Mr. Pollen's friends to dine there, and opened a hurdle in the field for the purpose of admitting him, which he declined; and, during the time of dinner, Mr. Morris, with his wife, and others of his friends, were present; and a person whom Mr. Edwards had requested to attend, purposely to know how far your Grace's agent might think proper (after the agreement that had been entered into) to countenance this proceeding, is ready to make oath, that he saw Mr. Morris shake one man by the hand at the table, and said, that 'he hoped he would enjoy himself, and be made comfortable;' and yet your Grace justifies Mr. Morris, and acquits him of being a party concerned in this business.—Allow me to say, that your Grace would have given Mr. Morris, and your other agents, a fairer opportunity of defending their conduct, had you confronted them with Mr. Edwards, and others, who were ready to support their charges by substantial evidence. This, my Lord, would have been open, manly, and proper investigation, carrying with it at least the appearance of a wish to know the truth, instead of establishing that kind of mock trial, which could only be looked upon as an insult to common sense, candour, and justice.

"The facts which I have stated, my Lord, cannot be controverted or denied, and, as such, they completely establish an infraction of the Agreement entered into by your avowed Agents; and as your Grace, so far from disavowing their conduct, appears eager in its justification, and decided in the approval of all those unequivocal violations of our Engagement, your Grace obliges me to consider you personally as having had an equal share in all these transactions, which I have already censured in terms so strong; and I shall feel myself justified in continuing to do so in the most public manner possible, that no doubt may remain in the minds of the inhabitants of the Borough of Leominster, who were the persons first induced to violate so solemn an Engagement.

"I have the Honour to be,
"My Lord,
"Your Lordship's most obedient humble Servant,
"MALDEN.

"To His Grace the Duke of Norfolk.

"P.S. Your Grace declines further to discuss the subject. My Lord, I never asked discussion as a favour, but offered it as a kindness, in order to afford your Grace an opportunity of justifying yourself from an imputation in which you was evidently implicated, until you cleared yourself by a disavowal of the conduct of your several Agents.

"The allowance with which your Grace wishes to end this business, of each party retaining their own opinions, however liberal to me, is not quite extensive enough. The Borough of Leominster, and the Country at large, will form its opinion upon the obligation of a solemn Engagement between Gentlemen; the propriety and liberal confidence in which I originally addressed your Grace, upon the first supposition of its being violated; the clearness of your Grace's explanation; and the justness of those sentiments in which I am at last forced to speak so publickly on the whole transaction."[1]

[1] Here followed a list of errata in No 9; the corrections have been incorporated into the text.

THE WATCHMAN

No X. FRIDAY, MAY 13, 1796

Published by the Author, S. T. COLERIDGE, Bristol;
And by PARSONS, Paternoster-Row, London

THAT ALL MAY KNOW THE TRUTH;
AND THAT THE TRUTH MAY MAKE US FREE!

IN 1660 the people of Denmark made a voluntary surrender of their liberties to the crown: and it is said, they have found it a wise and beneficial measure. I am not acquainted with the Danish Constitution prior to this, nor have I seen the form of their petition; I will draw out what I suppose it might have been: and let me be pardoned, if the notions are too much *anglicized.*

To our sovereign Lord, the King, a Petition from the oppressed People of DENMARK.[1]

SIRE!

WE have been dreaming that we were a free nation: and when the voice of truth has half-awakened us, we have scared her away with the angry impatience of slumber, and again resigned ourselves to the pleasing delusion. But, sire! we are now awake! we perceive

[1] The surrender of their liberties by the people of Denmark served many times in the eighteenth century as a cautionary tale. Fox referred to it in debate on 10 Nov 1795, Thomas Percival spoke of the "rash surrender" in 1790 ("An Appendix to the Inquiry Concerning the Principles of Taxation" *Memoirs of the Literary and Philosophical Society of Manchester* III 622), and Paley in his *Principles of Moral and Political Philosophy* in 1785 (bk 6 ch 6, II 198), James Burgh in his *Political Disquisitions* in 1775 (II 370, III 274, 410–12), and Priestley in his *Essay on the First Principles of Government* in 1771 (2nd ed, p 63), all mention it. J. T. Rutt, in his edition of Priestley's *Theological and Miscellaneous Works* (25 vols 1817–31) XXII 35n, gives what may be the original English source, Robert, Viscount Molesworth *Account of Denmark* (4th ed 1738) 30 (this edition was in the Bristol Library); my reference is to Molesworth *An Account of Denmark, as It Was in the Year 1692* (3rd ed 1694) 49–74 (ch 7, "The Manner how the Kingdom of Denmark became Hereditary and Absolute"). The actualities of the case were of no moment to C, for he used it as a framework for a satire on the supineness of the public in allowing Pitt to master it. The piece is a self-borrowing from *PD* (1795) 48–52.

that we are not free, and we are conscious likewise, that from our ignorance or depravity we are incapable of true freedom. The sole objects of the present petition are, that you would make our chains less heavy, and prevent our manners from becoming more depraved: and in order to this, that you would be graciously pleased to assume to yourself the *forms* of that absolute power, the realities of which you have long possessed. Even in that house, which in our old laws is supposed to be the organ of the people, a large majority of the members hold their seats by their own right, or by the nomination of private patrons. The remainder are elected indeed; but the electors are so few, that they must be considered a burdensome privileged order, and in no wise the PEOPLE. Their votes are notoriously bought; and so ignorant and corrupt are they, that the right of election is not merely useless; it is fatal to our prosperity and morals. It is a right given them to sell their consciences: a right to bring down the curse of Heaven upon the nation by the frequency and daringness of their perjuries: a right by the contagion of their gluttony, drunkenness, and party-feuds to render us less and less susceptible of that liberty, with the forms of which it would mock us. And with regard to the legislature, we are conscious, sire! that the plans, which your royal wisdom and the wisdom of your honourable counsellors prepare in your cabinet, are always adopted by the house of nobles, and by that body, misnamed, the house of the people. By dismissing them from a participation of the sovereignty, we should therefore *lose nothing:* and we should gain much. To them we do owe in great measure the weight and multitude of our taxes, the frequency of wars, and the decay of virtue and piety among us. For although they constantly adopt all your royal plans, yet they expect to be rewarded for their promptness: in order to which an infinity of pensions and places is necessary, to the great impoverishment of the honest and the laborious part of your Majesty's subjects. And we suspect, sire! that your servants, to whom is intrusted the management of this market, feel less aversion from the horrors of war from the knowledge, that a war may afford a specious pretext for multiplying such pensions, and doth necessarily increase their patronage to an extent which may be truly styled enormous.

We observe, sire! a second source of war in the noisy and incessant abuse of your Majesty's measures; which it has become a fashion of state for a few men to pour forth in the legislature, and by which they make known their desires to be admitted to a share of your royal bounties. This abuse, springing altogether from their angry disappointment, or their eager hopes, or their impatient necessities, is mixed up with the noblest sentiments borrowed from the works of the enlightened and unluxurious ancients, and falsely and dangerously applied to these times and this nation. For we are convinced, sire! that our vast commerce has made general among us that dependence and selfishness and unmanly love of splendour and pleasure, which necessarily preclude all public spirit. Freedom is the RIGHT and natural CONSEQUENCE of VIRTUE; but for the vicious to claim it is SEDITION. Self-love however prevents men from perceiving or remembering this truth: and the harangues of an ambitious faction daily dispersed through your Majesty's realms by means of printed reports, spread far and wide principles of innovation and discontent, which sometimes assume so threatening an aspect, that the evils of a foreign war are resorted to in order to prevent their diffusion. And from the same source it arises, that Government which ought to employ itself for the benefit of the people, is engrossed by the anxieties of self-preservation, and that legislative power, which might have been successfully exerted to the cure and prevention of national immorality, is wasted in degrading hostilities against libels and treason. Hence arises an appearance of a diversity of interest in the crown and the nation; and hence too it becomes possible, that even in your Majesty's bosom the feelings of paternal anger may occasionally displace the emotions of parental love.

We therefore your people of Denmark, are willing, O beloved King! to concenter in you all the forms and powers of national sovereignty. We acknowledge with heart-felt joy, that piety, temperance, and humanity are the distinguishing marks of your Majesty's character; and we believe, that by this solemn and public manifestation of our love and filial confidence, we shall incline you yet more to wish above all things the virtue and comfort of us, your assembled children; and by removing the obstacles (arising from the present necessity of corruption and terror in order to carry on the business of Government) we shall enable you to realize such wishes. Henceforward we expect, that the treasures which are yearly scrambled for by the sons of clamour, will either remain with the people and increase their domestic comforts, or be drawn out for the reward of genius and virtue, and the promotion of arts, sciences, and true religion. Countless millions will no longer be expended to shed blood and bring famine and pestilence. The barracks so thickly scattered over your Majesty's realms, we have full confidence that you will convert into national schools: the instruments of slaughter, will be beat into ploughshares and pruning-hooks: and the immense magazines, in which they were piled up, will burst with grain reapt by rejoicing industry from the drained swamp, and the cultivated waste-lands! And your petitioners shall ever pray, &c.

Extract from Dr. Beddoes's POSTSCRIPT *to his Defence of the* BILL *of* RIGHTS *against* GAGGING BILLS.[1]

"IT has ever been my opinion, *that the salvation of every State depends on the reasonableness of the great body of the people.* This quality is necessary to security against two great evils: *first,* the strong propensity which all ministers have to plunge nations into war. This in a country, where freedom of discussion is permitted, they can effect only by inflaming the passions, except where a war is strictly defensive. Now there is a pretty certain sign by which you may know whether war be just and inevitable. We are not to conclude that it is certainly so, when rich men send mere addresses to offer life and fortune in its support, believing at the same moment, that their little finger will never receive a scratch. It is when the opulent are in earnest ready to take the field and share the common danger. Accordingly, when a country is actually invaded, we see all men flying to arms with one accord: for all feel the justice of the war. At the beginning of the present war our passions were raised to a dreadful height. Abhorrence of the various cruelties perpetrated in France made us venture the hazardous step with a kind of phrenzy. That abhorrence was in itself just, but it misled us. The Almighty has not commissioned the people of one country to try, and punish those of another for crimes committed within themselves. You, the labouring part of the people, have been generally brought to reason

[1] *A Word in Defence of the Bill of Rights, Against Gagging Bills* (Bristol 1795). C's quotation occurs in a Postscript added a few days after the original edition (new pagination) pp 2–3 (Beddoes's italics). The Bristol Central Library and the London Library have the only copies of this reprint of the pamphlet known to me. When first published, "Gagging Bills" was in black-letter on the title-page to emphasise the emergency, and an advertisement in the *Bristol Gazette* 19 Nov 1795 announced the publication with: "This Day is published, And to be on Sale while the Liberty of the Press continues . . .". Beddoes was the first to call such repressive legislation "gagging bills", although C, reminiscing years later, declared that it had "then [been] the fashion to call them" that: *BL* ch 10 (1907) I 120. Joseph Jekyll (for whom see above, p 60) said on 16 Nov 1795 in the House of Commons: ". . . two bills, one of which assassinated the best privileges of the Constitution; the other gags the mouth of every British subject." *Parl Reg* XLIII 169–70.

on this subject. And no wonder! for you most severely feel the discipline of the great instructress, *Adversity!* The rich like you wish the war over. Like you, they have in a great measure withdrawn their confidence from MR. PITT. The warmest of his admirers cannot now believe him a tenth part of the man he promised he would be at his outset. But that strange infatuation, which led them to imagine that measures which must necessarily increase general misery, could produce more general content, and that opinions are a fit mark for cannon-balls, seems still to hold possession of their minds. A little more time will, however, I trust, dislodge it. Then will a minister, whose history will white-wash Lord North, be obliged to resign the station of which he has proved himself so unworthy. Then will all your magistrates and opulent citizens join heart and hand with the less opulent, in a respectful but firm petition to the legislature for that which will secure property and order, plenty and content—need I add, for PEACE!—But we must take care to express no *disaffection* to the administration of MR. PITT. With former ministers we could make free to find fault. But when we speak of him, we must be cautious to take off the hat and bow the head.

"I come now to the second danger of a State, against which the *rationality* of the people is its sole security. A rational people cannot be the dupes of wicked demagogues; who have in fact no other means of mischief than wicked ministers; nor any other end. They too seek power and profit by damping the reason, and firing the passions, of the uninstructed. Both set out by cajoling the multitude; both employ fraud to pilfer popularity. At first they talk alike of reform, of correcting abuses, of diminishing the influence of the Crown, of abolishing useless sinecures, and reducing extravagant salaries.—This *may* be an honest man's language. But we can easily see, whether the thoughts travel the same road with the words. If during years of profound peace, the poor man (whether he dwell in garret, cellar, or cottage) feel not more comfortable by his fire-side, be assured, the minister is a double-tongued impostor; however his meteor-patriotism may for an instant have

Flamed in the forehead of the morning sky![1]

"As to the Demagogue, there is a mark by which one who can neither write or read may distinguish him at once. If after a fine flowing speech, the hearers feel black revengeful thoughts boiling in their bosom; if at what he says, they be ready to start away in order to

[1] Milton *Lycidas* line 171 (altered).

tear, burn, and destroy, be assured the speaker only wants to set neighbour to worry neighbour, as if they were so many tygers, instead of Christians. Now whenever men turn tygers, they may devour for a while, but at last they will surely be destroyed themselves. What Falstaff says of *honour*[1] is true also of *vengeance*. Vengeance cures no sores, sets no bones, replaces no limbs, brings no dead man back to life."

TO THE EDITOR OF THE WATCHMAN

SIR,

The tendency of the following extracts being to diminish the sum of human misery, I hope they will find a place in your excellent paper.

H. F. I.[2]

WE feel happy on every occasion of testifying our Gratitude to those friends of humanity, whose exertions are directed to the abridgement of moral evil. We feel particularly so in noticing an excellent "Essay on the abuse of spiritous liquors," by Dr. Fothergill;[3] which we sincerely hope will produce the effects desired by its benevolent author; whose energy of mind, joined with a love of virtue and abhorrence of vice, is strongly charactered in this little work. We shall best explain the author's motives in his own words[4] —"this little essay though composed with a fervent desire of rendering it useful to all whom it may concern of whatever station, yet it is chiefly designed for the benefit of the inferior ranks, among whom this vice (of dram-drinking) is most predominant: would we could add, and to them wholly confined! for then it would soon become as unfashionable as it is contemptible. My aim has been to render the language sufficiently intelligible to ordinary capacities, without disgusting the more enlightened readers by vulgarity of style.

"Among the lower class of dram drinkers," he states,[5] "it matters not whether the liquor be genuine or adulterated, provided it be cheap and possess the power of procuring speedy intoxication. Thus in the room of French Brandy, they are commonly presented with a fiery malt spirit. This as we are informed, is sometimes corrected or rather disguised by the addition of another noxious ingredient, viz. Aquafortis." Gin, he informs us,[6] that cheap and favourite liquor among the common people, is nothing else than a distillation from coarse turpentine, such as is used by farriers. This disgusting com-

[1] *1 Henry IV* v i 133.

[2] Not identified.

[3] Anthony Fothergill *An Essay on the Abuse of Spirituous Liquors* (Bath 1796).

[4] Ibid v–vi (slightly altered).

[5] Ibid 9 (slightly altered).

[6] Ibid 9–10.

position is daily swallowed by thousands of poor with insatiable avidity. It is to prevent the disease, poverty and wretchedness, necessarily attendant on this vice that he points out, by a method by which the abuse might be regulated by government, and in the end overpowered. He affectingly describes the consequences of this practice.[1]—"None but those who have witnessed such scenes, can conceive the unspeakable misery into which this vice has plunged innumerable poor families. It totally disqualifies men for activity and habits of industry, and when it has reduced them to abject poverty, they soon lose that spirit of independence, which ought to be their pride as Englishmen. The time misspent in riot and debauch not only occasions an immense loss of labour, but disposes to incessant dissipation and aversion from all mental and corporeal improvement. Drunkenness is the secret bane of society; it ruins the peace of families, destroys conjugal endearments, and strikes at the very root of population."

The regulations he recommends are these:[2]

1.—To give all possible encouragement to the useful arts, particularly to agriculture, and to expedite the cultivation of the waste lands and commons.

2.—To establish houses of industry similar to those in Holland.

3.—To establish friendly societies throughout the kingdom.

4.—To restrict distilleries and increase the duty on spiritous liquors.

5.—To reduce the number of public-houses and reform their various abuses.

6.—To establish honorary premiums for the encouragement of merit among the members of the aforesaid institutions.

" Were this plan once effectually carried into execution,[3] (and it certainly is not impracticable) it would strike at the root of one of the greatest of our national evils and afford ample provision for the poor. For by thus removing the principal cause, might poverty itself, in a great measure be prevented, the poor rates reduced, and at length finally abolished. And many millions would be annually saved to the landed interest. Then might the health of the common people be preserved—their morals improved—their independence secured —their industry encouraged—and their virtue rewarded."

He proceeds to prove the necessity of some such regulation, by stating the injury received by the country[4] "In the year 1751, the number of dram-drinkers in Great Britain, according to a very able

[1] Ibid 10 (var).
[2] Ibid 13–14.
[3] Ibid 14 (var).
[4] Ibid 11–12 (var, with omissions).

Politician,* amounted to at least 400,000. On balancing the accounts between the profit arising to Government and the damage accruing to the nation at large; he endeavours to prove that a loss little less than 4,000,000l. must yearly fall on the trading and landed interests, and the revenue of Great Britain. If to this we add the damage the nation sustains by the premature and untimely deaths of so many British subjects, how shall we estimate the loss! Can we longer wonder why our parishes are over-burthened with poor? why our prisons overflow with insolvent debtors and desperate felons;—or why our poor rates amounting to a sum little short of 3,000,000l. a year, should be rapidly increasing?"—Of its effects on the human frame, he says,[2] "The Chemists who first discovered the art of obtaining from innocent ingredients a noxious intoxicating spirit, perhaps little dreamt that the disclosure of that fatal secret, like the opening of Pandora's box, would instantly let loose upon mankind such a formidable train of evils;—Exclusive of war, pestilence and famine, those dreadful scourges of nations, it is perhaps the most deadly and insidious foe that ever infested this country. For this evil spirit, like a destroying angel, stalks through the land with a steady though silent step, every where spreading its baleful influence over our cities and villages.

"In tracing[3] the effects of ardent spirit on the human body, we find that it exerts its pernicious influence, first, on the stomach, the inner coat of which is exposed to its full action. On the liver it seems to exert a specific power, and by endurating and enlarging its substance, vitiates the bile, interrupts its course and renders it incapable of performing its functions. From its action on these two important organs, its effects are propagated far and wide to other parts of the system. But to enumerate the manifold sufferings which conspire to embitter the lives of dram-drinkers, would require a whole volume. Suffice it to observe in general, the liver being diseased and the constitution enfeebled, the jaundice ensues: this gradually slides into an incurable dropsy which closes the fatal scene! Some who escape jaundice or dropsy, contract gout or stone, palsy or insanity, while others are suddenly taken off by apoplexy. For this poison, whether slow or quick in its operation, is always *sure* at last." On the mind

* The Dean of Gloucester.[1]

[1] Josiah Tucker (1712–99), the noted economist, in his *An Impartial Inquiry into the Benefits and Dangers Arising to the Nation from the Present Very Great Use of Low-priced Spirituous Liquors* (1751).

[2] Fothergill *Essay* 15 (var, with an omission).

[3] Ibid 17–18 (var, with omissions).

and morals, its effects are not less to be dreaded.[1] "It overthrows memory, judgment, and all the intellectual powers, introducing in their place a temporary pleasure; converting at once a rational inoffensive being into a furious animal, and prompting him to commit acts of mischief and extravagance, which, in his cooler hours, he would contemplate with abhorrence. If sobriety the main guardian of virtue, being once banished, a direct avenue is opened for the admission of every vice; I had almost said, of every crime." The author concludes with laying down, "Rules and admonitions for the prevention and cure of this vice." He says:[2]

"1.—Let no strong liquors be lightly ventured upon as a remedy against bodily pain or uneasiness of mind.

"2.—Let those who have been enticed frequently to taste spiritous liquors or rich cordials, till at length they begin to have a fondness for them, reflect a moment on the danger of their situation, and resolve to make a speedy and honourable retreat.

"3.—I now proceed to the more difficult part of my task, the bold the arduous attempt to reclaim the thorough-paced dram-drinkers, whose habit has been contracted in youth, strengthened by indulgence, and rivetted by time.

"1. Let it be a rule never to drink but from a particular decanter marked for the purpose; and whenever a glass of liquor is poured out, replace it immediately with an equal quantity of water, and pursue this steadily till the effects are reduced to mere water—or

"2. Drink constantly out of one glass, and the moment it is emptied drop into it a single drop of melted sealing-wax, and continue this daily until there be no longer room for a drop of spirits.

"These methods have been recommended and practised by some, and we are assured the inveterate habit has been entirely subdued. But relinquishing this pernicious habit suddenly does not appear to be such a dangerous undertaking as you have been taught to imagine. Otherwise how comes it that those drunkards who have been all at once debarred the use of spirits in a well regulated prison, have not only been cured of their former propensity, but their health has been improved, and their life prolonged? Instead therefore of the slow and uncertain expedients recommended by others, let me advise you, by a bold stroke, to break the enchantment at once. Not a drop of spirits of any kind must be tasted on any pretence whatsoever. Frequent cravings after the delusive liquor, with certain unpleasant feelings,

[1] Ibid 21–2 (var, with omissions).

[2] Ibid 26–30 (altered, with omissions).

must and will sometimes obtrude themselves. These for a while, though not dangerous, will be found irksome: they may however be banished by an occasional cup of ginger or ginseng tea, or rather by brisk exercise and firm resolution. But were these sensations a thousand times more troublesome, not an inch of ground must be yielded till you have gained a complete victory. The conflict, remember, is not for the fading laurel, a tinselled wreath, but for those more blooming, more substantial honours, which *Health*, the *Daughter* of *Temperance* only can bestow. For it is thine *O Health, and thine alone* to diffuse through the human frame, that genial warmth, that serene sunshine, which glows in the cheek—which sparkles in the eye—and which animates the whole!"

FRAGMENT

BY A WEST-INDIAN[1]

NEAR where with Tropic heats bright CANCER glows,
And Sun-beams glitter with perennial force;
Girt by[2] the azure wave an Island lies,
Called by the Spaniards, *ANTIENT.[3]
The balmy East here holds perpetual sway,[4]
And blows[5] salubrious to the toil-worn Slave.
The Eastern Shore receives the welcome Gale,
And leads to Caverns, or the brow of rocks;
To gravel banks with glitt'ring Shell-fish strew'd,
To deep-green Mangrove, or the shadowing branch
Of lofty Cedar,† dropping blossoms white,
That tremble as they fall, and meet the wave
Progressive to their root. Here, oft at Eve,[6]

* Antigua.

† The *white* Cedar.

[1] William Gilbert, who was born in Antigua (see above, p 168 n 1). The fragment comes from *The Hurricane* canto I lines 1–4, 189–202, 204–7, which was published later in the year; see ibid (Bristol 1796) [viii]: "A friend is the occasion of this Advertisement; who, having printed some lines of this Poem in a Miscellany that could not fail to introduce it respectably, in the best sense of the word, has thereby acquired a right to have his feelings attended to, in things that may affect the credit of the Poem. He once passed to me a very strong opinion against the Metre of some verses. . . ." Undoubtedly C. The following notes therefore indicate changes in the lines: *The Hurricane* (1796) 9, 20–1.

[2] Cf ibid canto I line 3: "Girt with".

[3] Ibid line 4 continues: "Its breadth is". However, the fragment jumps from line 4 to line 189.

[4] Cf ibid line 189: "The balmy trade-wind breathed refreshing airs".

[5] Cf ibid line 190: "And blew".

[6] Cf ibid line 197: ". . . at even".

When length'ning shadows to the calmy wave
Shot dubious twilight and alluring gloom,
I've sat[1] contemplative—and viewed the breeze
Checquer the water, with far-streaming light
That glistened as with gems: I've sat and thought[2]
That all the hopes attending various man,
Were robbers of his rest; I've thought that Love
Was all the sum indulgent Heaven e'er meant[3]
To form our[4] Bliss. I thought so and was blest.

GILBERT.

TRIBUTE
TO THE MEMORY OF A DECEASED FRIEND

(By Mr. ROSCOE, of LIVERPOOL, *Author of the life of Lorenzo de Medici.*)[5]

To enjoy the Rewards of a happier State,
And to live in the Memory of his surviving Friends,
On the Fifth Day of December, 1795, departed this Life,

EDWARD ROGERS,

Of EVERTON, *Merchant, aged* 45 *years,*

MORTAL, from yon lower sphere,
Ere eternal joys thou share,
Are thy earthly duties done,
Husband, father, friend, and son?

1 Cf ibid line 200: "I sat"; also line 202.

2 Ibid line 203 (omitted here) continues: "Ambition was a folly; glory madness;".

3 Cf ibid line 206: ". . . e'er made".

4 Cf ibid line 207: "To constitute his . . .".

5 From *M Mag* I (Apr 1796) 226, or possibly sent by the Rev J. Edwards to C, for it had been published as a broadsheet at the end of 1795, where the last line reads as it does below (*M Mag* has a typographical error: ". . . reap'd it joy"). See the reproduction of the broadsheet in George Chandler *William Roscoe of Liverpool* (1953) 85. William Roscoe (1753–1831), historian and leading figure in the liberal Liverpool group, had recently (Feb 1796) published his celebrated *Life of Lorenzo de' Medici*. Roscoe wrote to Edwards 20 Jul 1796: ". . . It was with much concern I found [Coleridge] had adopted the resolution of discontinuing his periodical paper of the 'Watchman.' . . . I have no doubt but that the paper in question would, if continued, have been of very extensive utility . . .". Henry Roscoe *The Life of William Roscoe* (2 vols 1833) I 232. Edwards showed the letter to C; see C's letter to Wade [22 Aug] 1796: *CL* I 230.

Hast thou o'er a parent's head
Drops of filial fondness shed?
What the pleasure—hast thou prov'd
'Tis to love and to be lov'd?

Hast thou, with delighted eyes,
Seen thy num'rous offspring rise?
Hast thou in the paths of truth
Led their inexperienc'd youth?

Didst thou e'er in sadness bend
O'er the sorrows of a friend?
Didst thou hasten, unappall'd
When thy sinking country call'd?

Husband, father, friend, and son,
Well thy journey hast thou run;
Life has known its best employ,
Sown in virtue, reap'd in joy.

AMERICA[1]

It will be recollected, that much opposition was made in America to the Treaty concluded between Lord GRENVILLE and Mr. JAY.[2] On the 24th of March, the House of Representatives passed a Resolution, which had for its object to procure a copy of the instructions granted to Mr. JAY relative to that Treaty. In reply to this request, General WASHINGTON returned the following Answer, which was received in London on Monday. It unites firmness with temperance, and wisdom with decision.

"*To the House of Representatives. Wednesday, the 30th March.*

"*Gentlemen of the House of Representatives,*

"WITH the utmost attention I have considered your Resolution of the 24th inst. requesting me to lay before your House a Copy of the instructions to the Minister of the United States, who

[1] From the *Sun* or *True Briton* 4 May 1796. The letter alone appeared in most of the London papers—e.g. *The Times* 3 May and the *Star* 5 May.

[2] For the heavy concessions he made to Britain John Jay (1745–1829), American statesman and jurist, was burned in effigy at public meetings.

negociated the treaty with the King of Great Britain, together with the correspondence and other documents, relative to that treaty, excepting such of the said papers as any existing Negociation may render improper to be disclosed.

"In deliberating on this subject, it was impossible for me to lose sight of the principle which some have avowed in its discussion, or to avoid extending my views to the consequences which must flow from the admission of that principle.

"I trust, that no part of my conduct has ever indicated a disposition to withhold any information which the Constitution has enjoined upon the President as a duty to give, or which could be required of him by either House of Congress, as a right; and, with truth, I affirm, that it has been, as it will continue to be, while I have the honour to preside in the Government, my constant endeavour to harmonize with the other branches thereof, so far as the trust delegated to me by the People of the United States, and my sense of the obligation it imposes to 'preserve, protect, and defend the Constitution,' will permit.

"The nature of Foreign Negociations requires caution; and their success must often depend on secresy; and even when brought to a conclusion, a full disclosure of all the measures, demands, or eventual concessions, which may have been proposed or contemplated, would be extremely impolitic; for this might have a pernicious influence on future Negociations, or produce immediate inconveniences; perhaps danger and mischief, in relation to other Powers. The necessity of such caution and secresy was one cogent reason for vesting the power of making Treaties in the President, with the advice and consent of the Senate; the principle on which that body was formed, confining it to a small number of Members. To admit then a right in the House of Representatives to demand, and to have as a matter of course, all the papers respecting a Negociation with a Foreign Power, would be to establish a dangerous precedent.

"It does not occur that the inspection of the papers asked for, can be relative to any purpose under the cognizance of the House of Representatives, except that of an Impeachment, which the Resolution has not expressed. I repeat, that I have no disposition to withhold any information which the duty of my station will permit, or

The Senate ratified the treaty 22 Jun 1795 by a bare two-thirds majority. The Jeffersonian or Republican party, which wished to preserve a close connexion with France, tried to block the treaty in the House of Representatives by refusing to appropriate monies for the commissions set up by the treaty.

the public good shall require to be disclosed; and in fact, all the papers affecting the Negociation with Great Britain, were laid before the Senate, when the Treaty itself was communicated for their consideration and advice.

"The course which the debate has taken on the Resolution of the House, leads to some observation on the mode of making Treaties under the Constitution of the United States.

"Having been a Member of the General Convention, and knowing the principles on which the Constitution was formed, I have never entertained but one opinion on this subject; and from the first establishment of the Government to this moment, my conduct has exemplified that opinion, that the power of making Treaties is exclusively vested in the President, by and with the advice of the Senate, provided two-thirds of the Senators present concur; and that every Treaty so made and promulgated, thenceforward became the law of the land. It is thus that the Treaty-making power has been understood by Foreign Nations; and in all Treaties made with them, we have declared, and they have believed, that when ratified by the President, with the advice and consent of the Senate, they became obligatory. In this construction of the Constitution, every House of Representatives has heretofore acquiesced; and until the present time, not a doubt or suspicion has appeared to my knowledge, that this construction was not the true one. Nay, they have more than acquiesced; for until now, without controverting the obligation of such Treaties, they have made all the requisite provisions for carrying them into effect.

"There is also reason to believe that this construction agrees with the opinions entertained by the State Conventions, when they were deliberating on the Constitutution, especially by those who objected to it, because there was not required in *Commercial Treaties* the consent of two-thirds of the whole Senate, instead of two-thirds of the Senators present; and because in Treaties respecting territorial and certain other rights and claims, the concurrence of three-fourths of the whole number of the Members of both Houses respectively was not made necessary.

"It is a fact declared by the General Convention, and universally understood, that the Constitution of the United States was the result of a spirit of amity and mutual concession. And it is well known, that under this influence the smaller States were admitted to an equal representation in the Senate with the larger States; and that this branch of the Government was invested with great powers; for on the equal participation of those powers, the sovereignty and political safety of the smaller States were deemed essentially to depend.

"If other proofs than these, and the plain letter of the Constitution itself, be necessary to ascertain the points under consideration, they may be found in the Journals of the General Convention, which I have deposited in the Office of the Department of State. In those Journals it will appear that a proposition was made, 'that no Treaty should be binding on the United States, which was not ratified by a law,' and that the proposition was explicitly rejected.

"As, therefore, it is perfectly clear to my understanding, that the assent of the House of Representatives is not necessary to the validity of a Treaty; as the Treaty with Great Britain exhibits in itself all the objects requiring legislative provision, and on which these papers called for can throw no light; and as it is essential to the due administration of the Government, that the boundaries fixed by the Constitution between the different Departments, should be preserved—a just regard to the Constitution, and to the duty of my office, under all the circumstances of this case, forbid a compliance with your request.

GEO. WASHINGTON.

"*United States, March* 30, 1796."

This Message has been committed to a Committee of the whole House.

ANECDOTES

OF PERSONS CONNECTED WITH THE FRENCH REVOLUTION[1]

DUMOURIER

DUMOURIER possesses singular acquirements: he is a good orator, an able politician, an excellent writer, and one of the best generals of his age. His father also, was a man of talents, and by insisting that he should never learn any thing by heart, prevented him, according to his own account, from ever forgetting any thing!

It has been generally supposed that he acquired an immense sum of money during the revolution; but he solemnly declares this to be a cruel and unjust aspersion; and boasts that he is now indebted to his *pen*, as he was formerly to his *sword*, for his support.

He has an uncommon facility at composition, writes with elegance upon all subjects, and is intimately acquainted with every thing

[1] From *M Mag* I (Apr 1796) 219–21 (with omissions).

relating either to the politics or the wars of Europe. He received a sum equal to 500l. of our money, for his life, from a bookseller at Hamburgh, in the neighbourhood of which city, and within its territory, he now resides, with

MAD. GENLIS—SILLERY—BRULART.[1]

who occupies part of the same house, and like himself, is employed in writing.

MIRABEAU, MIRANDA, WILKES.[2]

These three very celebrated men met one day by invitation at the house of a respectable gentleman in Chesterfield-street, May-fair. Mr. H. after dinner expected great entertainment from his guests; but, unfortunately for him, the orator and the general had a violent dispute relative to some trifling subject, which rendered the early part of the evening uncomfortable. To complete the mortification, they both soon after attacked John Wilkes on the barbarity and inhumanity of the English nation, an instance of which they gave, in *the execution of several young men for trifling offences, in the course of that very morning!* The hoary patriot retorted the charge, and turning towards Mirabeau (it was before the revolution) sarcastically asked him, what he thought of the very *humane* mode of breaking on the wheel, as practised at the *Greve*, when the *Noblesse* were accustomed to bespeak seats at particular windows, as if they had been going to a comedy!!!

BRISSOT

This very celebrated man, while in England, lodged in Brompton-row, in the second or third house on the right hand side. On his

[1] Stéphanie-Félicité du Crest de Saint-Aubin (1746–1830), married to Charles Brûlart de Genlis, later Marquis de Sillery (he was guillotined), had been mistress to the Duc d'Orléans and governess to his children. Her *Adèle et Théodore; ou Lettres sur l'éducation* had been translated into English in 1783; other translations followed, then *The Beauties of Genlis* (1787). She had visited England in 1791 and, according to the hostile *Times* 9 May 1796, had asked permission to establish a school for democracy at London, whereupon the government asked her "to be at liberty in all the rest of the world".

[2] Honoré-Gabriel-Victor Riqueti, Comte de Mirabeau (1749–91), French orator and revolutionary leader, President of the National Assembly 1791. Francisco Miranda (c 1750–1816), Venezuelan general and adventurer, who joined the French revolutionary army and later helped to liberate South America. He had tried to get Pitt's help in his plans for liberating South America from Spain. For Wilkes, see above, p 205 and n 5.

publishing a very able dissertation on *Criminal Law*, he sent a copy to Mrs. Macauley Graham,[1] who invited him to her house, had him often at her table, and entertained a great esteem for him. From that respectable lady, he received a letter of introduction to general Washington, by whom he was well received, and so fond was he of the Atlantic continent, that to the day of his unjust execution, he always wished that he had been born the son of an American peasant. While in England, he wrote many articles in the *Courier de Londres*. M. Brissot retained his antient simplicity of manners. He was never intoxicated with power, nor did he ever suffer his mind to be debased by avarice. Robespierre and his associates knowing what effect such a charge would have upon the people, accused him of wallowing in riches:—when his wife was arrested, she was employed in mending his linen, and nursing their offspring.

AGRICULTURE

Monthly Report for April

(This Report was faithfully made up for the MONTHLY MAGAZINE, from an actual Correspondence in nearly 29 Districts of Great Britain; and is transplanted from the last Number of that valuable Work.)[2]

THE present, on account of the mildness of the weather, has proved an uncommonly favourable season for every operation in husbandry. Little rain having fallen since the month of February, the fields ploughed since that time have benefited much by the dry weather, which, with the seasonable frosts in March, have reduced the soil to a powder, with small labour to the harrow.

The WHEATS throughout the kingdom exhibit a degree of strength and forwardness very unusual so early in the season, and should the ensuing month (generally the most trying) prove mild, with moderate showers, there can be little doubt of a most abundant crop. In Scotland particularly, so great an extent of wheat was never before seen, which in general, looks well, and far superior to the crop of last year.

The spring seed time has been remarkably good. Great part of the grain is beginning to appear, and it looks very regular and promising.

[1] Catharine Macaulay Graham (1731–91), British historian.

[2] *M Mag* I (Apr 1796) 264. In *M Mag* the report was based on "20" districts.

In the Northern counties, the fields intended for BARLEY are in forward preparation; what has been sown begins to peep through the soil. In stiff soils in the Western districts, the Barley sowing goes on with difficulty, through the want of spring showers.

The RYE-GRASS and CLOVER are generally good, and very early, a circumstance much in favour of the fine LAMBING season, as they afford plentiful food to the ewes, instead of Turnips, which have this season gone off so early. In the North of the island the appearance of the Clover and Rye-Grass is, however, not so flattering, the plants of Clover being very thin in most places.

The fields intended for TURNIPS are far advanced in culture, many have been twice plowed, and are in fine tilth.

There is a fine prospect of APPLES in the western CYDER counties.

The dry spring has been highly favourable to SHEEP in general, and particularly productive in LAMBS.

It is at length ascertained, and the fact is confirmed by some of the best informed of our correspondents, that no real scarcity has ever existed in this country, and that the late High Prices of Wheat have been the sole work of monopolists. The CORN MARKETS have never been more plentifully supplied than during the last month, and the prospect of large importations, added to the alarm that has taken place among the speculators, will, no doubt, keep the prices moderate till after the ensuing harvest.

CATTLE and SHEEP are higher than was ever remembered; and from the great demand, it is to be feared will continue so. Every thing is picked up; LEAN STOCK was never known to fetch such prices, and FAT STOCK is nearly as much above the usual rates as the lean.

From the great stock of last year's HAY on hand, and the promising appearance of the Spring, the price of that article has fallen considerably.

WOOL, in the western counties, sells in the fleece at 30s. per weight of 30½ lb.

POTATOES have fallen 1s. per sack. GRASS SEEDS have sunk in value more than one-fourth. The market continues very heavy for HOPS, bags sell from 50 to 90s, pockets from 60 to 100s.

FRANCE[1]
OFFICIAL BULLETIN
OF THE OPERATIONS OF THE FRENCH ARMY IN ITALY

The General in Chief of the Army in Italy, to the Executive Directory.
Head-quarters, Carcare, 25 Germinal,[2] April 15.

"I HAVE given you an account of the opening of the campaign, on the 20th of this month, and I have informed you of the signal victory gained by the army of Italy, on the fields of Montenotte; I have now to give you an account of the battle of Millesimo.

"After the battle of Montenotte, I removed my headquarters to Carcare; I ordered General Laharpe to remove his to Sosello,[3] to menace the eight battalions that the enemy had in that city, and to march the next day by a rapid and secret course to the city of Cairo.

"General Massena marched with his division to the heights of Dego; the General of Division, Angereau,[4] who had been on the march two days, was in the plains of Carcare; the General of Brigade occupied the heights of Biestro; General of Brigade Joubert, with the first brigade of infantry, occupied the interesting position of Sainte Marguerite.

"On the 21st, at break [of] day, the General Angereau forced the passes of Millesimo, at the same time that Generals Menard and Joubert drove the enemy from all the neighbouring positions, surrounding by a bold and prompt manœuvre, a corps of 1500 Austrian grenadiers, at the head of whom was Lieutenant-General Proveyra, who far from laying down his arms, and surrendering prisoner of war, retired to the summit of the mountains of Cossaria,[5] and entrenched himself in the ruins of an old castle, extremely strong by its position. General Angereau advanced his artillery, and cannonaded him during several hours. At eleven o'clock, vexed to have my march stopped by a few men, I summoned General Proveyra to surrender. He solicited to speak to me, but a strong cannonade on my right, prevented me from then going to him.—He treated with General Angereau during several hours; but the conditions he required being unreasonable, and the night approaching, General

[1] All the following documents (to p 367) reprinted verbatim from the front page of the *M Chron* 7 May 1796 (the importance of the French victories took precedence over the advertisements that almost invariably filled its front page).

[2] 26 Germinal, or 14 Apr.

[3] Sassello.

[4] Augereau.

[5] Cosseria.

Angereau formed four columns, and marched to the Castle of Cossaria. Already the intrepid General Joubert, a good General for his knowledge and military talents, had entered the enemy's trenches with seven men, but he was struck on the head and thrown to the ground, and his soldiers thinking him dead, the movements of his column relaxed. His wounds are not dangerous.

"The second column, commanded by General Banel,[1] marched in great silence, with arms on the shoulder, when that brave General was killed at the foot of the enemy's entrenchment.

"The third column, commanded by the Adjutant General Quenin,[2] was equally disconcerted in its march, a ball having killed that officer. The whole army greatly regrets the loss of those two brave officers. In the mean time the night coming on, gave me reason to suppose the enemy would defend themselves sword in hand, for which I made preparations.

"On the 25th, at break of day, the Austrian and Sardinian army, and the French army, found themselves within sight of each other; my left commanded by General Angereau, blockaded Proveyra; several of the enemies regiments among whom was that of Begliose,[3] attempted to penetrate my centre. General Menard vigorously repulsed them; I soon after ordered him to fall back on my right; and before one o'clock at noon, General Massena attacked the left of the enemy, which occupied with strong entrenchments and batteries the village of Dego. We pushed on our troops to the road from Dego to Spino.[4]

"General Laharpe marched with his division in three columns close in a mass; that of the left commanded by General Causse, passed the Bermida,[5] under the eye of the enemy, and attacked their left wing. General Cervoni, at the head of the second column, also traversed the Bermida, under protection of one of our batteries, and marched immediately on the enemy. The third column, commanded by General Boyer,[6] turned a ravin, and cut off the retreat of the enemy.

"All these movements, seconded by the intrepidity of the troops, and the talents of the Generals, accomplished the purpose expected. Coolness is the result of courage, and courage is possessed by all Frenchmen.

[1] Pierre Banel (1766–96).
[2] Quesnin.
[3] Belgioioso.
[4] Spigno.
[5] Bormida.
[6] Pierre-François-Joseph, Baron Boyer (1772–1851), who fought in all the campaigns of the Revolution and with Napoleon in Italy and Egypt.

"The enemy surrounded on all sides, had not time to capitulate; our columns spread death among them, and put them to flight. While our right made the necessary dispositions for attacking the left of the enemy, General Proveyra, with his troops in Cossaria, surrendered prisoners of war.

"Our soldiers attacked the enemy on all sides and pursued them. General Laharpe put himself at the head of four squadrons of cavalry, and briskly followed them.

"We have by this victory, taken between seven and nine thousand prisoners, among whom are a Lieutenant-General, and about twenty or thirty Colonels, and almost the whole of the following regiments: three companies of Croats, a battalion of Pelegrini, Stein, Vilhem, Schroeder,[1] Tentack,[2] four companies of artillery, several superior officers of engineers, in the service of the Emperor, and the regiments of Montserrat, of the Marine, of Suze, and four companies of the grenadiers in the service of the King of Sardinia; twenty-two pieces of cannon, with caissons, &c. and 15 stand of colours.

"The enemy has between 2000, and 2500 men killed, among whom is a colonel, an aid-du-camp to the King of Sardinia.

"I will send you further particulars, as soon as I shall have received the details of this glorious affair.

(Signed) "BUONAPARTE."

The Commander in Chief of the Army of Italy to the Executive Directory.

Head-quarters, Carcare, 26 Germinal,[3] April 16.

"I HAVE given you an account, Citizen Directors, of the two victories which our Army has obtained over the Combined Armies of Austria and Sardinia. I have now to inform you of the operations of the army on this day, the 26th Germinal, that is to say, of the battle of Dego, of that of St. Jean,[4] of the possession of Montezemo,[5] and of my junction with the division of General Seurrurier,[6] which I had left to guard the Tenardo[7] and the valley of Oneglia.

"The right of the army, fatigued with the action of the evening before, which was not over till a very late hour, entirely abandoned to the security of victory, suffered itself to be driven at day-break

1 Wilhelm Schroeder.
2 Teutsch.
3 27 Germinal, or 15 Apr.
4 San Giovanni.
5 Montezemolo.
6 Jean-Mathieu-Philibert Sérurier (1742–1819), later Comte Sérurier and marshal of France.
7 Tanaro.

from the village of Dego by 7000 Austrians, who attacked them with the greatest boldness. Beaulieu hoping to repair his checks, assembled these 7000 men, the chosen troops of his army, to make this effort of despair.

"In the right wing the *generale* was soon beat, and immediately after at the Head-quarters.

"General Massena, the moment he had rallied a part of his troops, began the attack. Our troops were repulsed three different times.

"When I came up, I found General Causse rallying the 99th half brigade, charging the enemy and ready to push them with the bayonet, when he fell mortally wounded. The manner in which he had conducted himself on the preceding evening, and his intrepid conduct at the moment of his death, have caused him to be greatly regretted by the soldiery.

"The first thing he asked me when he saw me, was, 'Is Dego retaken?'—It was two o'clock in the afternoon, and nothing was as yet decided. I was now forming into a column the 39th half brigade, commanded by the General of Brigade Victor,[1] when the Adjutant-General Lances[2] rallied the 8th half brigade of light infantry, and put himself at its head on the left of the attack. For an instant his troops hesitated, but he determined their conduct by his intrepidity. This brave officer, during the action, had an epaulet carried away by a ball. During the war, he has distinguished himself by his activity, his courage, and his talents. I demand of you for this officer the appointment of General of Brigade, vacant by the death of General Causse.

"The cavalry completed the enemy's rout, and took a great number of prisoners.

"The loss of the enemy is estimated at 2000 men, of whom 1400 are prisoners. Among these are several officers of distinction.

"We have lost the chief of Brigade Rondeau, stiled *the brave*, and the Chief of Brigade Dupuis.

"The Adjutant General Vignolle,[3] Sub-Chief of the Staff, and Citizen Marat,[4] my Aid-de-Camp, and a Chief of Brigade, contributed much to the success of this day.

"On another side, General Rusca[5] made himself master of the

[1] Claude-Victor Perrin, called Victor (1764–1841), later Victor, Duc de Bellune and marshal of France.

[2] François Lanusse (1772–1801).

[3] Martin (later Comte de) Vignolle (1763–1824), French general and army administrator.

[4] Joachim Murat (1767–1815), later marshal of France and King of Naples in 1808.

[5] Jean-Baptiste-Dominique (later Baron) Rusca (1759–1814).

important post of St. Jean, which commands the valley of Bermida. He took two guns, and made 100 prisoners.

"The General of Division, Serrurier, possessed himself of the heights of Balizolo, of Bagnascoe, and of Ponte-Nocetro.[1] He made sixty-one prisoners, among whom is a Lieutenant-Colonel.

"General Angereau has taken possession of the redoubts of Montezemo, which the enemy evacuated on his approach. He has thus opened our communications with the valley of Tenaro, and with the division of General Serrurier.

"It is impossible for me to describe to you all the traits of courage which have been displayed, and to give you the names of those who have particularly distinguished themselves. As soon as our movements are a little relaxed and the relations of the different Generals sent to the Staff, I shall hasten to communicate them to you.

(Signed) "BUONOPARTE."

Extract of a Letter from the Commissioner of the Executive Directory, stationed with the Army of Italy, to Citizen Carnot.

"Millesimo, 27 Germinal, April 17.[2]

"I WRITE you these two lines to inform you, that the Piedmontese army has evacuated the entrenched camp of Ceva as well as that place, in which our troops are now stationed. They have merely left five or six hundred men in the fort, who will not make a long resistance."

SUMMONS SENT TO GENERAL PROVEYRA

"You are surrounded, Sir, on all sides; your resistance will only occasion a fruitless effusion of blood. If in a quarter of an hour you do not surrender, I will not spare one of you."

GENERAL PROVEYRA'S ANSWER

"My intention is to defend myself to the last extremity."

CAPITULATION

GENERAL PROVEYRA, and the corps which he commands, shall defile towards Carcare, the head-quarters of the French army, with

[1] Battifollo, Bagnasco, Ponte Nucetto. [2] 15 Apr.

the honours of war; they shall lay down their arms after having defiled.

A. Accepted, with the restriction, that the Officers shall be allowed to proceed on their parole, and till they have been exchanged, to their homes.—Conformable to the original.

The Aid-de-Camp of the Commander in Chief.

(Signed) JUNOT.[1]

THIRD VICTORY

The Commander in Chief of the Army of Italy to the Executive Directory

Head-Quarters at Lezino,[2] 3 Floreal, April 21.

"I HAVE to give you an account of the taking of Ceva, of the battle of Mondovi and of our entry into this place.

"The 27th, General Angereau went to Montelezo,[3] and attacked the redoubts which defend the entrenched camp at Ceva, which were defended by eight thousand Piedmontese. The columns commanded by Generals Beyraud[4] and Joubert, fought all the day and took the greatest number of them. The loss of the enemy amounted to about 300 men; we have lost the Chief of the 39th half brigade.

"The enemy fearing to be turned in the night by Castelino,[5] evacuated the entrenched camp in the night. At break of day, General Serrurier entered the town of Ceva, and invested the citadel. We have found in the town some resources for provisions.

"The Piedmontese army driven from Ceva, took a position at the confluence of the Cursaglia[6] and Tanaro, having its right supported by Notre Dame de Vico, and its centre by the Bicoque.[7] The 1st instant, General Serrurier attacked the right of the enemy, by the village of St. Michel.[8] He passed the bridge under their fire, and after three hours combat, obliged them to evacuate the village; but the Tenaro not being fordable, the division which attacked the left could not cross, and the enemy reinforced in its right, obliged General Serrurier to retreat, which he did in the best order. The same night he returned to his former position. The enemy lost about 150 men.

[1] Jean-Androche Junot (1771–1813), later Duc d'Abrantès and governor of Venice.

[2] Lesegno.

[3] Montezemolo.

[4] Martial Beyrand (1768–96), French general who was killed in battle several months later.

[5] Castellino.

[6] Corsaglia.

[7] Vicoforte . . . Bicocca.

[8] San Michele.

"The situation of the enemy was formidable, surrounded by two deep and rapid rivers. They had cut down all the bridges, and planted batteries on the banks. We passed the whole of the second in making dispositions, seeking by false manœuvres, to conceal our intentions.

"At two o'clock, after midnight, General Massena passed the Tanaro, near Ceva, and entered the village of Lezengo.[1] Generals Gieux and Florella[2] stopped at the Bridge of Torre. My design was to march to Mondovi, and oblige the enemy to change the field of battle; but General Colli[3] fearing the issue of a combat at two o'clock after midnight retreated, leaving behind all his artillery, and took the road for Mondovi. At break of day the two armies were within sight of each other. The battle began in the village of Vico; General Gieux marched to the left of Mondovi; Generals Florella and Domartin[4] attacked and took the redoubt which covered the centre of the enemy, and the Sardinian army abandoned the field of battle: the same night we entered Mondovi.

"The enemy has lost 1800 men, of whom 1300 are made prisoners. A Piedmontese General has been killed, and three are made prisoners. Eleven stand of colours, and eight pieces of cannon, have also fallen into our hands.

"Our whole army regret the fate of General Stengel,[5] who was mortally wounded charging at the head of one of the regiments of cavalry.

(Signed) "BUONOPARTE."

P. S. To-morrow I will send you twenty-one stand of colours, four of which belong to the Body-Guards of the King of Sardinia.

Letter from the Executive Directory to General Buonoparte, Commander in Chief of the Army of Italy

Paris, 6 Floreal, April 25,[6] 4th Year of the Republic, one and indivisible.

"CITIZEN GENERAL—the Executive Directory has received with the liveliest satisfaction, the news of the victory obtained in Italy

[1] Lesegno.

[2] Jean-Joseph Guieu (1758–1817). Pascal-Antoine Fiorella (1752–1813), a Corsican.

[3] Louis-Léonard-Gaspard Venance, Marquis de Colli-Ricci (1760–1809), Piedmontese general in the French service.

[4] Elzéar-Auguste Cousin de Dommartin (1768–99).

[5] Henri-Christian-Michel, Baron de Stengel (1744–96), a German in the French service since 1760.

[6] 24 Apr.

over the Austrians. In appreciating such signal advantages at the entry of a campaign, which a dislike for peace on the part of the enemies of the Republic has forced us to engage in, it is satisfactory to the nation to see justified in you by the laurels you have just reaped, the choice it has made of you to lead the army of Italy to victory. Receive then, General, the tribute of national gratitude: merit it still more and more, and prove to Europe, that Beaulieu in having changed the field of battle, has not changed his enemy; that defeated in the North, he will be constantly and equally defeated by the brave army of Italy; and that with such defenders, liberty will triumph over the feeble efforts of the enemies of the Republic."

To General Laharpe

"YOU have for a long time accustomed the friends of the Republic to hear your name mentioned whenever the army of Italy has obtained any successes. Your patriotism and your talents warrant to the Directory and to all France, that you will still share the glory and the victories which are reserved for the brave division you command during the course of the present campaign.

To General Massena

"THE Directory has seen by the report of the Commander in Chief that you contributed not a little to the successes of the glorious days on the 20th and 21st Germinal. It did not expect less from your courage and your talents, which are, to the Directory, a sure guarantee of the victories the army of Italy is about to obtain.

To General Cervoni

"THE labours of the last campaign had rendered your courage too conspicuous to the Directory not to enable it to anticipate that in making their earliest attack on you the Austrians would afford you the first advantage.

To the Chief of Brigade Rampon

"INTREPID soldier! the lover of liberty—continue to serve her cause. Let the oath you administered to the brave soldiers you commanded in the redoubt of Montelesimo,[1] be occasionally repeated by all Republicans who are worthy to take it; and let it serve to fortify in them, if there be such a need, the hatred of slavery, and

[1] Monte Legino.

the desire of subduing the enemies who have not renounced the mad project of imposing chains upon us. French valour will, without doubt, soon force them to demand that peace for which they now manifest so great an aversion. You will have concurred towards this aim by your example, and by the heroical trait which does you so much honour. Can there be a sweeter recompence for a friend of his country and of the Republic?"

Sketches of the LIFE *of* KOSCIUSKO, *from an History of Poland, lately published.*[1]

THADEE KOSCIUSKO[2] is about forty years of age, of middling stature, and of a fierce and penetrating aspect. He was born a gentleman; but his family not being in affluent circumstances, he was sent to the school of cadets, to be educated for the army. From this school it has been usual for the kings of Poland to send annually four of its youths into foreign countries, to perfect themselves in military tactics, and the art of war. Kosciusko had the good fortune to be one of these selected youths. He was patronized by the king, and sent into France with the best recommendations, where he studied upwards of four years in the military academy of Versailles, and returned to Poland with the reputation of being a very skilful engineer. Soon after this he was appointed to the command of a company of artillery in the regiment of the crown, and was looked up to as a man of courage and eminence in his profession.

About this time it was that he captivated the affections of a young lady of the first family and fortune in Poland. The lovers had contrived many private interviews before the parents of the lady had an opportunity of discovering their connection; in all of which Kosciusko conducted himself by the rigid rules of honour and virtue. He therefore conceived himself warranted in making an open declaration of their mutual regard, and in soliciting the consent of the lady's friends for an immediate celebration of their nuptials. But being a leading family among the nobles, an alliance with Kosciusko was deemed inconsistent and degrading; hence a peremptory refusal was experienced, and an insuperable bar put to the fond hopes of the anxious lovers. Kosciusko, however, after finding it impossible to gain the

[1] [Stephen Jones] *The History of Poland* (1795) 467–9. C may have taken this extract from *B Critic* VII (Apr 1796) 400–2, where it appeared in a review of the work.

[2] Thaddeus Kosciusko (1746–1817). C had contributed to *M Chron* (16 Dec 1794) a sonnet based upon the false assumption that Kosciusko had been killed in battle. *PW* (EHC) I 82–3.

consent of her parents, had the address to carry off the lady, and was rapidly pursuing his route to France, when the unfortunate circumstance of their carriage breaking down, and no possibility of having it replaced or repaired with requisite speed, gave the enraged father, and a strong party of relatives, an opportunity of coming up with them. Here a very fierce rencounter ensued, in which Kosciusko was eventually reduced to the unpleasant dilemma of being obliged either to kill the father, or give up the daughter. Humanity prevailed even over the force of affection. He returned his sword peaceably to the scabbard, and nobly restored the fair prize to his pursuers, rather than spill the blood of him who gave her being.

The public conversation, in all the upper circles, turning on this event, and the feelings of Kosciusko being considerably hurt, he obtained leave of absence from his sovereign, and went to America. At that period the late unfortunate war with England was carrying on with full vigour. Kosciusko offered himself a volunteer to Washington, and was honoured with an important command in his army. After the peace, he returned with the Marquis de la Fayette to France, where the French officers who had served in that campaign, and Dr. Franklin, always spoke of him as a man of equal magnanimity, fortitude, and courage, and to whom America was greatly indebted for his services.

Kosciusko having thus acquired reputation abroad, returned, with the laurels, to his native country, where he afterwards distinguished himself in three battles which Prince Poniatowski[1] fought with the Russians, at the time of the diet of Targowicz;[2] and it is said, that if the councils of Kosciusko had been followed in that short war, affairs would have taken a better turn. When, therefore, Stanislaus found himself obliged to cease hostilities, Kosciusko, despising an inactive life, again procured leave to enter into foreign service. He went to Pisa in the month of December 1793, where he professed himself going to Geneva; but, in fact, he went to Paris. He was there introduced to many of the leading members of the convention, whose policy induced them to present him with ten millions of livres to stir up an insurrection in Poland, in order to draw off the Prussian army from acting with the allies, and to con-

[1] Prince Józef Anton Poniatowski (1763–1813), later minister of war in the grand duchy of Warsaw and marshal of France.

[2] The Confederation of Targowica, held on 14 May 1792 and formed by the opposition party in Poland, who were led by rich Poles resident in St Petersburg, was an instrument by which Catherine II further encroached on Polish independence.

fine the attention of Frederick-William to a different part of the continent.

LAW REPORT[1]

COURT OF KING'S BENCH

SATURDAY, *May* 7

INSULT TO HIS MAJESTY

KYD WAKE,[2] who was convicted at the Sittings after last Hilary Term, of having, on the first day of the present Sessions of Parliament, insulted HIS MAJESTY in his passage to and from Parliament, by hissing, and using several indecent expressions, such as, "No George, no War," &c. was brought up to receive the Judgment of the Court.

Mr. JUSTICE ASHHURST[3] pronounced Sentence as follows:

"KYD WAKE, You have been tried and found guilty upon an indictment that has been preferred against you, which states, that on the 29th of October, in the 36th year of His present Majesty's reign, His Majesty was going to the House of Peers to meet his Parliament; and that you, being a person of an evil disposition, and also a great number of others, being persons of violent and seditious minds, and disaffected to His Majesty, and intending to break and disturb the peace, and to insult and villify our Lord the King, and to move and incite his Majesty's Subjects to hatred and contempt of His Majesty, did, for the purposes aforesaid, unlawfully and riotously meet together to disturb the peace of our Lord the King, and assembled round His coach, and made a very great riot, tumult, and disturbance, by hissing, hooting, and groaning, and used divers indecent, contemptuous, and disorderly gestures; and did riotously, tumultuously, and seditiously use and proclaim aloud the following scandalous words—No War—Down with George—No George: and did for a long time continue thus riotously assembled, and committing the same outrages.

1 From the *Sun* 9 May 1796 (one short paragraph omitted).

2 The attack on the king's coach, for which Wake received sentence, occurred on 29 Oct 1795 and precipitated the introduction of the Two Bills.

3 William Henry Ashurst or Ashhurst (1725–1807), judge of the king's bench, 1770–99. Erskine later wrote a couplet on him:

> Judge Ashurst, with his *lantern jaws*,
> Throws *light* upon the English laws.

John, Lord Campbell *The Lives of the Lord Chancellors* (8 vols 1845–69) VI 686.

"Upon this Indictment you have been found guilty on very full and clear evidence. This insult which you have offered to your Sovereign, is of a very flagitious and atrocious nature, and shews a very bad and malignant heart. Indeed, if there had been any wish to stretch the Laws to their utmost rigour, it may be doubtful, whether the crime of which you have been found guilty, might not have amounted to a crime of a much deeper die; for it has a manifest tendency to withdraw the affections of His Majesty's Subjects from their lawful Sovereign, and to excite the mob to disaffection and rebellion. This is the return you have made for the protection you have enjoyed under the auspicious Government of the best of Kings, and under the mildest and most excellent system of Laws. I would have you remember, that there is perhaps no other Kingdom in the World, where for such an offence, the offender's life would not have paid the forfeit. In the Affidavit which you read in mitigation of punishment, when you were last brought into Court, you endeavoured to shew that the contemptuous gestures and behaviour imputed to you towards His Majesty, were owing to your short-sightedness, and that your eagerness to gratify your curiosity in seeing His Majesty, occasioned those involuntary distortions of countenance, which might be construed into contemptuous gestures. This does not seem to be very natural. But supposing it were the fact, your zeal and eagerness to see the King did not necessarily occasion your uttering the words imputed to you, namely, *Down with George—No George—No War*. And yet these words are sworn by two witnesses to have been spoken by you, and often repeated. And even you yourself do dare not upon oath to deny the speaking of them. You have not dared to swear that you never did utter these words; but you say it can never be thought that you should speak them. This is a very singular way of denying them.

"You have said further, that none of these words have been proved to be spoken by you. What your idea of proof is, I do not pretend to know, but this I know, that two persons have concurred in positively swearing that you did speak these words; and the Court and Jury are equally satisfied that you did.

"You next urge as a matter of compassion, that you are a married man, and that you and your wife depend on your daily labour for support. It would have been well, if that thought had influenced your mind before you committed that flagitious act proved upon you. One is sorry that it is the lot of the innocent to suffer with the guilty. That, however, will sometimes necessarily happen in the course of human events; but the claims of your Country have a much louder call than those of any individual whatever; and I hope when you think hereafter on the misery you have brought on your innocent family, by your own misconduct, that it will operate as a check to restrain you from future mischief, and will likewise be a warning to the rest of the World.

"It now becomes my duty to pronounce the sentence of the Court; which is, that you be committed to the custody of the Keeper of the Penitentiary House in and for the County of Gloucester, and be kept to hard labour for the space of five years; and within the first three months of that time, that you stand in and upon the Pillory for one hour, between the hours of eleven and two o'clock in the afternoon, in some public street in Gloucester, on a market day; and that you give sureties in 1000l. for your good behaviour for the term of ten years, to be computed from the expiration of the said five years; and that you be further imprisoned till you find the said sureties."

SONNET[1]

(On Lord Lansdowne's late Motion in the House of Lords.)

SHELBURNE! on Truth's strong wing that warning call
Rose o'er the sphere. The peers of Sydney's fame
Heard, in their halls of bliss, thy voice appal
Yon recreant crew, that plot their country's shame.

Attesting echoes, through the conscious mind
To thy accusing tones that inly thrill,
Of those great martyrs strike the sense refined
And each quick pang a parent feels instil.

And eager see they bend, with rescuing arm
To rouse their Britain, lost in sleep profound,
That if again thou pour the loud alarm
Responsive crouds may swell the patriot sound,
Shake with awakening shout the fields of air,
And from their impious feast, Corruption's vampires scare.

T. B.

[1] The poem later appeared in *M Mag* I (May 1796) 314 (var), where it is signed "*Clifton* T. B.". Dr Thomas Beddoes lived in Clifton. (Among other changes, lines 7–8 read: ". . . martyrs on the sense refined | Strike the dread watch-note of o'erhanging ill.") The Marquis of Lansdowne

In an early Number of THE WATCHMAN we presented our Readers with the admirable Speech of PRESIDENT WASHINGTON on receiving the French Banners;[1]—we have been since favoured, by an American Correspondent, with the Speech of the French Minister, which we cannot praise more highly than by saying, It was worthy of the occasion.[2]

CITIZENS REPRESENTATIVES,

THE connections which nature,—reciprocal wants, and a happy concurrence of circumstances, have formed between two free nations, cannot but be indissoluble. You have strengthened those sacred ties, by the declarations, which the minister plenipotentiary of the United States, has made in your name, to the National Convention, and to the French People. They have been received with rapture by a nation, who know how to appreciate every testimony which the United States have given to them of their affection. The colours of both nations, united in the centre of the National Convention, will be an everlasting evidence of the part which the United States have taken in the success of the French Republic.

You were the first defenders of the rights of man, in another hemisphere. Strengthened by your example, and endowed with an invincible energy, the French people have vanquished that tyranny, which, during so many centuries of ignorance, superstition, and baseness, had enchained a generous nation.

Soon did the people of the United States perceive, that every victory of ours, strengthened their independence and happiness. They were deeply affected at our momentary misfortunes, occasioned by treasons, purchased by English gold. They have celebrated with rapture the successes of our brave armies.

None of these sympathetic emotions have escaped the sensibility of the French nation. They have all served to cement the most intimate and solid union that has ever existed between two nations.

The Citizen Adet,[3] who will reside near your government, in quality of minister plenipotentiary of the French Republic, is

(formerly the Earl of Shelburne), with a view to revealing the supposed illegalities of Chancellor Pitt, made a motion in the House of Lords on 2 May for certain reforms in public offices.

[1] See above, pp 42–3.

[2] The *Oracle* 25 Feb, the *St. James's Chronicle* 25–7 Feb, and the *M Post* 26 Feb 1796 had printed it together with Washington's speech.

[3] Pierre-Auguste Adet (1763–1832), French chemist and statesman; minister plenipotentiary to the United States in 1795.

specially instructed to tighten these bands of fraternity and mutual benevolence. We hope that he may fulfil this principal object of his mission, by a conduct worthy of the confidence of both nations, and of the reputation which his patriotism and virtues have acquired him.

An analogy of political principles,—the natural relations of commerce and industry;—the efforts and immense sacrifices of both nations in the defence of liberty and equality; the blood which they have spilled together; their avowed hatred for despots;—the moderation of their political views; the disinterestedness of their councils; —and especially the success of the vows which they have made in presence of the Supreme Being, to be free or die; all combine to render indestructible the connections which they have formed.

Doubt it not, Citizens;—we shall finally destroy the combination of tyrants;—you, by the picture of prosperity, which in your vast countries, has succeeded to a bloody struggle of eight years: we, by that enthusiasm which glows in the breast of every Frenchman. Astonished nations, too long the dupes of perfidious kings, nobles, and priests, will eventually recover their rights, and the human race will owe to the American and French nations, their regeneration and a lasting peace.

PARIS, 30th Vendemiaire, 3d year of the French Republic, one and indivisible.

The members of the Committee of Public Safety,

J. S. DELMAS,[1] MERLIN (of Douai), &c. &c.

SOME gloomy accounts were received on Tuesday last from Corsica.[2] Nothing official has been suffered to transpire. On Tuesday night it was stated both above and below the bar of the House of Lords, that a Revolt had taken place at Bastia; that the Corsicans, by a stratagem, had obtained possession of the Arms of the British Troops; and that THE REVOLTERS HAD MADE SIR GILBERT ELLIOT A PRISONER.[3]

IN the Analysis of the "ESSAY on the Merits of Mr. PITT by Dr. BEDDOES," in our last Number, we noticed a degree of apparent

[1] Jean-François-Bertrand Delmas (1754–c 98), French politician; president of the Council of 500.

[2] This paragraph from the *Star* 11 May 1796.

[3] When England assumed the protectorate of Corsica in 1794 Elliot was made viceroy. The revolt in Corsica was settled when Elliot met the demands of the leaders by dissolving the Corsican parliament and other acts of appeasement. He evacuated the island

illiberality in the introduction of the eighth Chapter, in which the Archdeacon is represented as an accomplice in his Son's scheme of tying a cannister to the tail of a Dog.[1] On a re-perusal of the passage, we perceive that this scheme was conveyed by the Boy in a *whisper* to his Brother, and is not supposed to have been heard by the Father: and such, we are assured, was the Author's intention. Our Readers therefore will consider the reprehension as unfounded.

ADDRESS

TO THE READERS OF THE WATCHMAN

THIS is the last Number of the WATCHMAN.—Henceforward I shall cease to cry the State of the political Atmosphere. While I express my gratitude to those friends, who exerted themselves so liberally in the establishment of this Miscellany, I may reasonably be expected to assign some reason for relinquishing it thus abruptly. The reason is short and satisfactory—the Work does not pay its expences. Part of my Subscribers have relinquished it because it did not contain sufficient original composition, and a still larger number, because it contained too much. Those, who took it in as a mere Journal of weekly events, must have been unacquainted with FLOWER'S Cambridge Intelligencer;[2] a Newspaper, the style and composition of which would claim distinguished praise, even among the productions of *literary leisure*; while it breathes every where the severest morality, fighting fearlessly the good fight against Tyranny, yet never unfaithful to that Religion, "whose service is perfect Freedom." [3] Those on the other hand, who expected from it much and varied original composition, have naturally relinquished it in favour of the New MONTHLY MAGAZINE;[4] a Work, which has almost monopolized the talents of the Country, and with which I should have continued a course of literary rivalship with as much success, as might be supposed to attend a *young Recruit* who should oppose himself to a Phalanx of disciplined Warriors. Long may it continue

in Oct 1796, and the French reconquered it. The *M Chron* printed a similar report of the revolt 12 May 1796.

[1] See above, p 313.

[2] With *CI* and its editor, Benjamin Flower, C had had for several years a close connexion; see *CL* I 98n, 116, and 196–7; *PW* (EHC) I 16n, 19n, 29n, and 57n; also Introduction, above, p xxvii.

[3] Book of Common Prayer: Morning Prayer, A Collect for Peace.

[4] See above, p 92 n 3. C entered into an engagement with the *M Mag* in the autumn of 1796 (see *CL* I 259, 263, and 270), although he deplored its irreligious tone (*CL* I 268).

to deserve the support of the Patriot and the Philanthropist, and while it teaches RATIONAL LIBERTY, prepare it's readers for the enjoyment of it, strengthening the intellect by SCIENCE, and softening our affections by the GRACES! To return to myself,—I have endeavoured to do well. And it must be attributed to defect of ability, not of inclination or effort, if the words of the Prophet be altogether applicable to me, "*O Watchman! thou hast watched in vain!*"[1]

S. T. COLERIDGE.

FINIS

[1] C said the lines were spoken by Ezekiel "when, I suppose, he was taking a prophetic glimpse of my sorrow-sallowed Cheeks" (to Poole 5 May 1796: *CL* I 208), associating Ezek 3.17 and 33.7 perhaps with the closer passage in Ps 127.1: "the watchman waketh but in vain". Perhaps he was also thinking of his favourite Isaiah, "I have laboured in vain": Isa 49.4.

APPENDIX A

PROSPECTUS AND ADVERTISEMENTS

PROSPECTUS AND ADVERTISEMENTS

COTTLE first published what was long thought to be, as he claimed it was, the Prospectus of *The Watchman*.[1] It was really a copy of the handbill advertising the appearance of No 1, with a few omissions and changes—e.g. "On Tuesday the 1st Day of March, 1796, was published" became "On Tuesday, the 1st of March, 1796, will be published". A copy of the true Prospectus came into the possession of H. Buxton Forman and was first reprinted in the *Athenaeum* No 3450 (9 Dec 1893) 808–9. That is the text given in this edition, above, pp 3–6.

C had asked Josiah Wade to go to London to obtain subscribers, make arrangements for a London publisher, and "to procure folio Bill Posters and to insert advertisements in the London Papers".[2] Advertisements appeared in at least two London newspapers, the *Star* (20 Feb 1796) and the *M Chron* (25 and 29 Feb 1796), and in *Aris's Birmingham Gazette* as well.[3] The zealous Wade, so C says, announced *The Watchman* with long bills "in letters larger than had ever been seen before", which "eclipsed the glories even of the lottery puffs".[4] One of Wade's main objectives being to secure a London publisher, C directed him to George Robinson the bookseller for aid and advice. At that time C thought that James Ridgway might do,[5] but finally the choice was John Parsons of Paternoster Row. Parsons's affiliation was announced in large broadsides measuring 12⅝ inches by 7¾.[6] An approximate facsimile is printed overleaf.

[1] Cottle *E Rec* I 151–2.

[2] EHC *Studies* 17.

[3] John Colmer *Coleridge: Critic of Society* (Oxford 1959) 32n.

[4] *BL* ch 10 (1907) I 119.

[5] Letter to Wade [2 Feb 1796]: *CL* I 181.

[6] See George P. Winship *TLS* No 1209 (19 Mar 1925) 199, the principal authority on the Prospectus of *The Watchman*. See also *C Bibl* (Wise *TLP*) 60.

TO SUPPLY AT ONCE THE PLACES OF A REVIEW, NEWSPAPER, AND ANNUAL REGISTER!!!

On Tuesday the 1st Day of March, 1796, was published,

NUMBER 1

(Price Fourpence)

OF A

Miscellany,

TO BE CONTINUED EVERY EIGHTH DAY,

UNDER THE NAME OF

THE WATCHMAN

BY

S. T. COLERIDGE,

Author of the ADDRESSES TO THE PEOPLE, A PLOT DISCOVERED, &c. &c.

This Miscellany will be comprised in Two Sheets, or *Thirty-Two Pages*, closely printed; the Size, Octavo—the Type, Long Primer.

ITS CONTENTS

I.—An History of the Domestic and Foreign Occurrences of the preceding Days.

II.—The Speeches in both Houses of Parliament: and, during the Recess, select Parliamentary Speeches, from the Commencement of the Reign of Charles the First to the present Æra, with Notes historical and biographical.

III.—Original Essays and Poetry.

IV.—Review of interesting and important Publications.

ITS ADVANTAGES

I.—There being no Advertisement, a greater Quantity of original Matter must be given, and the Speeches in Parliament will be less abridged.

II.—From its Form, it may be bound up at the End of the Year, and become an Annual Register.

III.—This last Circumstance may induce Men of Letters to prefer this Miscellany to more perishable Publications, as the Vehicle of their Effusions.

IV.—Whenever the Opposition and Ministerial Prints differ in their Accounts of Occurrences, &c. such Difference will be always faithfully stated.

☛ *Orders from the Country Booksellers regularly executed by PARSONS, Bookseller, Paternoster-Row, London.*

The known forms of advertisement for *The Watchman* are as follows: (1) The original quarto Prospectus. The three copies known to me are in the British Museum (Ashley Library), the Harvard University Library, and the collection of Professor C. B. Tinker, now in the Yale University Library. (2) Newspaper advertisements. Handbills of these may also have been printed. (3) The Parsons folio broadsheet. The two known copies, now in the Harvard University Library, were once Cottle's and, presumably, were used by him in *E Rec*.

APPENDIX B

DECLARATION OF THE WHIG CLUB

DECLARATION OF THE WHIG CLUB

[The following is a reprint of the pamphlet published early in 1796, *Declaration of, and Form of Association Recommended by the Whig Club.*[1]]

WHEN a Society of private men feel themselves bound to propose a great national measure to the people, justice to their own character and respect for the public judgment require that they should make known the reasons which have moved them to such a proceeding. We confess that it is, and ought to be unusual, because it can be justified by no ordinary circumstances: but we think that the situation of the country no longer permits us to confide the support of our principles to the individual exertions of our members. The WHIG CLUB, invariably adhering to the principles of the British Constitution as established at the Revolution, cannot be unconcerned spectators of the destruction of the most important securities of Public Liberty which were provided at that glorious æra.[2]—The Constitution can, in our judgment, now only be restored by the exercise of that just authority which the National Opinion must ever possess over the proceedings of the Legislature. We, therefore, deem it our duty, by every means which yet are legal, to appeal to the judgment of the People, and to procure a Declaration of their opinion.[3]

[1] For the background of this pamphlet see above, Introduction, p xxxvii. Lucyle Werkmeister informs me that a contemporary newspaper credited James Macintosh with the authorship.

[2] The title-page to the club-book (1792) reads *Whig Club, Instituted in May 1784, by John Bellamy. To be Composed of Gentlemen who solemnly pledge themselves to support the Constitution of This Country, according to the Principles Established at the Glorious Revolution.* Standard Whig toasts included "The Rights of the People", "The Friends of Freedom", "The Cause for which Hampden bled in the Field and Sidney on the Scaffold", "The House of Brunswick, and may they never forget the Principles which placed their Family upon the Throne of Great Britain", and "May the Example of one Revolution prevent the Necessity of Another". From time to time others were added, such as toasts to Whig heroes like Washington or Franklin or some current parliamentary leader. The Whig Club, as a party organisation, seems to have been exempt from the penalties of the Two Acts.

[3] The propriety of political associations was a much debated subject. Lord George Gordon's Protestant associations in 1780 had produced serious disorders in London, and after the French Revolution the Jacobin Clubs had added terror to the idea of political associations. See Sir Thomas Erskine May *The Constitutional History of England since the Accession of George the Third* ed Francis Holland (3 vols 1912) II 23–36.

With this view, we have invited our fellow-subjects to associate for obtaining the Repeal of the two Statutes passed in the present session of Parliament.

In one of these Statutes[1] we see public Assemblies of British Subjects, though their proceedings shall be the most orderly and peaceable, and their object unquestionably legal, fettered by restrictions hitherto unknown to the law and practice of this kingdom. Those meetings which shall not submit to these new and disgraceful conditions are subjected to dispersion, under pain of death; and those which shall be held in compliance with them are made liable to such perpetual and vexatious interruption, at the discretion of Magistrates, that there never can be wanting an opportunity for disturbing their deliberations and defeating their objects. Such a law we cannot but regard as repugnant to the genius and character of this free nation. The Constitution of Great Britain is established on the consent and affection of the People, and can only rest, with dignity or safety, on those genuine foundations of all social authority. When purely administered it will ever make itself respected by its own beneficence and justice. It has for ages instructed the world by the example of a Government which builds its strength only on its justice, and secures the obedience of its subjects by their love of Liberty. It can neither require the aid of a system of constraint and terror, nor even receive it without danger of destruction. Its ruling principle is the Right of the People to manifest their opinion on their public concerns; a right of which the frequent, unrestrained and fearless exertion can alone create and preserve in a people that free spirit and conscious independence, without which the forms of a free Constitution are worthless and unavailing. This right alone guards and protects the secure enjoyment of every other privilege. The House of Commons is our security against the encroachments of the Crown. The King's Prerogatives and the Privileges of the House of Peers are our securities against our own Representatives. But no human wisdom can provide any safeguard against a possible combination of all the branches of the Legislature to oppress or betray the community, but by enabling the great body of the nation freely to pronounce their opinion on the acts and measures of Government by Petition and Remonstrance to the King or either House of Parliament, and by Speech and Publication to their Fellow-Subjects; unfettered by any previous restraint, and subject only to the animadversion of the Law on those overt-acts of Treason, Tumult, Disorder or Sedition, which may be committed by individuals under pretence of exercising those invaluable rights.—This unrestrained communication of opinion is at once the only check to which it is possible to subject supreme power, and the wisest means for averting popular violences. To watch the exercise of these Rights with suspicion, to clog it with jealous and ignominious conditions, and, above all, to subject it to the arbitrary discretion of Magistrates appointed by the Crown, is to break that spirit from which such privileges derive their whole use and

[1] Pitt's Bill for the more effectually preventing Seditious Meetings and Assemblies was introduced on 10 Nov 1795, was passed into law, and was signed by the King on 18 Dec.

value. To impose on them any previous restraint is substantially to take them away. They cannot be so restrained without being reduced to a dependence on the pleasure of that very authority upon which they are to operate as a controul, and against which they are reserved as a security. To restrain is therefore to destroy them.

But the provident wisdom of our ancestors did not leave these sacred privileges to rest on the mere foundation of their own justice and necessity. They were solemnly asserted at the Revolution in the instance of Petition, where they had been recently violated. The great Statesmen and Lawyers who framed the DECLARATION OF RIGHTS,[1] when they asserted the Right of the People to Petition, did, by necessary implication, also assert their Right of Assembling to consider such matters as might legally be the subject of Petition.—The assertion of a right comprehends that of the means which are necessary for its exercise. The restraints of the present Statute, therefore, in our opinion, amount to an abrogation of the most important article in that solemn compact between the British nation and the new race of Princes whom it raised to the throne.

Though the other Statute of which we complain be speciously entitled "An Act for the safety and preservation of his Majesty's Person and Government,"[2] we are confident that by our opposition to it we shall not incur the imputation of disloyalty among honourable and reasonable men. We have formed our principles of loyalty upon those of a Parliament which had recent and ample experience of the effect of sanguinary Laws, and we shall deliver the Declaration in the memorable language of their record—"The state of every King, Ruler, and Governor of every Realm, Dominion or Commonalty, standeth and consisteth more assured by the love and favour of the subjects towards the Sovereign, Ruler or Governor, than in the dread and fear of Laws made with rigorous pains and extreme punishment." (I Mar. C. i.)[3]

Guided by this principle of our ancestors, which appears to us as to be as full of truth and wisdom as of humanity, we cannot view without alarm an attempt to remove those boundaries of Treason which were ascertained and established by the Act of King Edward the Third:[4] a Law which has been endeared to Englishmen, by the experience of four Centuries; by a

[1] The Declaration of Right, a document drawn up by a committee of the House of Commons, was enacted into law as the so-called Bill of Rights (1689), the fifth article of which proclaimed that "it is the right of the subjects to petition the king, and all commitments and prosecutions for such petitioning are illegal".

[2] Introduced by Lord Grenville in the House of Lords on 6 Nov 1795 and entitled "An Act for the Safety and Preservation of His Majesty's Person and Government against Treasonable and Seditious Practices and Attempts", it was signed by the King on 18 Dec.

[3] The year 1625.

[4] The act of 1351 (25 Edw III c 2) defined high treason as compassing and imagining (i.e. attempting or contriving) the death of the king, queen, or their eldest son and heir; violating the king's companion (i.e. the queen), his eldest daughter unmarried, or the wife of the king's eldest son and heir; levying war against the king in his realm; giving aid and comfort to the king's enemy; slapping the chancellor, treasurer, or the king's justices while administering justice.

recollection of the peace and happiness which have ever prevailed in those fortunate periods when it was observed; by a review of that oppression of innocence and insecurity of Government which have almost universally accompanied or followed every departure from its strict letter; and by the zeal and ardour with which so many successive Parliaments, after experience of the mischiefs of such deviations, have recurred, as a refuge from those miseries to the simplicity, precision, and humane forbearance of that venerable Statute.

Another clause of the same Act which authorizes the punishment of transportation on the second conviction, even for words spoken, appears to us equally repugnant to the merciful spirit of the Law of England. By applying the punishment of felony to a misdemeanor frequently of no very aggravated guilt, it converts what was designed as the chastisement of profligate and dangerous offenders into an engine, by which a Minister may crush his political opponents.

The infliction of cruel and unusual punishment is prohibited by the tenth clause of the Bill of Rights; and although that clause was, undoubtedly, pointed at the then recent abuse of judicial discretion in the cases of State offenders, yet it is founded on a principle which condemns the Legislative introduction of a punishment still more cruel and unusual than any which is recorded even in the detestable annals of the Star Chamber.

It is indeed a punishment which, in the feelings and apprehensions of those who are likely to be the objects of the vengeance of power, is scarce inferior to death. Had it in former times been sanctioned by the Legislature, it might have subjected the most illustrious asserters of our Liberties, a Locke or a Somers,[1] to the combined miseries of banishment, imprisonment and slavery in a barbarous country with a gang of outcasts and felons. Removed from the view of their fellow subjects, their sufferings in a remote region are forgotten or unknown, and their spirit is no longer supported by that consolation which they might otherwise have found in general sympathy for an unjust conviction or a cruel punishment, while distance and oblivion deliver the agents of power from that dread of public observation and resentment, which is so wholesome and necessary a check on the tyrannical exercise of authority. The same rigour, which, if practised at home, would spread the alarm of tyranny throughout the Nation, may be inflicted on a distant exile without odium or danger. It is the nature of this punishment to be, at once the most safe for those who inflict, and the most cruel to those who suffer it, to deprive the oppressed of consolation, and to deliver the oppressor from restraint.

The authors of these Statutes do, indeed, expressly admit that they materially restrain the liberty of the subject, but they contend that such restraints are necessary, and that if necessary they are just.[2]

We do not affirm that general principles are never in any degree to give way to the exigency of circumstances. But we assert, that the

[1] John, 1st Baron Somers (1651–1716), who presided over the committee that drew up the Declaration of Right and took a leading part in the settlement of the monarchy in 1689, was with Locke revered as a patron of the Whig party.

[2] See above, p 48 and n 1.

right of discussion and remonstrance is so essential to the Constitution, that it cannot be controuled or restrained without a surrender of the Constitution itself. When pleas of necessity are urged, let it never be forgotten that pleas of necessity are the ready instruments and common justifications of power without right, and that the means by which nations are enslaved, have ever been pretended to be necessary to their security. We never can admit that the delinquency of individuals ought to work a forfeiture of the Liberties of a Nation. A necessity for new restraints and penalties could only have arisen in the present instance, from the inadequacy of the law, which we on our parts utterly deny, which neither has been, nor can be proved, and which the preambles of these Acts, themselves do not even venture to assert. Laws, such as these, we should have felt it our duty, at all times, most strenuously to have opposed. But there are many circumstances peculiar to the present time, which appear to us greatly to aggravate their malignity and danger. We cannot forget the system of measures of which they are a part, the disposition from which they appear to flow, the reasons by which they are supported, and the consequences to which they seem intended to lead.

They originate with Ministers, who are making daily encroachments on the constitution, who patronize the dissemination of opinions which tend to its subversion, and who have never spared any rigour of political persecution, to crush that freedom of discussion which endangered their own power. They are attempted to be justified on principles fruitful in future encroachments on Liberty, and by reasons, which, if they were valid, would compel us to conclude, that the Free Constitution of Great Britain is no longer compatible with its quiet, and that our only refuge from Anarchy is in the establishment of Despotism. They are introduced in the midst of a calamitous War, when the solicitude of many good men for Liberty has been weakened, by an artfully excited dread of confusion, and when the overgrown influence of the Crown receives continual accessions of strength from the burdens and distresses of the People. They are the measures of men who by an unexampled waste of public money, have acquired unbounded means of corruption. They have been passed into laws when a standing army, great beyond example, is kept up in the heart of the kingdom; when an attempt is systematically, though, we trust, vainly pursued to divide the soldiery from their fellow-subjects; at a time when every effort has been employed to subdue the spirit of the people, to pervert their opinions, and to render their most virtuous feelings subservient to the designs of their Oppressors. Thus possessed of the combined influence of delusion, corruption and terror, the framers of these acts seem to have thought the favourable moment at length arrived for securing impunity to their own offences, and permanence to the corruptions and abuses of government, by imposing silence on the people. This project has hitherto been successful. By the extension of the Law of Treason, and by the combination of vague description with cruel punishment in other State Offences, Ministers have gained the most formidable engine of political persecution that can be possessed by a Government. By restraints, amounting almost to prohibition, on the Right of the People to assemble, to deliberate, and to petition, they have shaken the security of every other Civil and Political Privilege.

In this awful conjuncture it appears to us to be the duty of every man who wishes to see his country neither submitted to the yoke of slavery nor exposed to the dreadful necessity of appealing to force, for the recovery of its Liberties, to unite in a respectful but firm application to the Legislature, for the destruction of these alarming innovations, and the restoration of the ancient Free Constitution of Great Britain. We cannot think that such an effort will be unsuccessful. The usurpations of our Rights are yet recent and immature. The spirit of this nation is not, as Ministers have too hastily supposed, extinct; and prudence itself will not suffer the Legislature to despise the collective opinion of the People.

They will rather, we trust, imitate the conduct of that wise Parliament, whose language we have already quoted, and, like them, declare, that "trusting his Majesty's loving subjects will, for his clemency to them shewed, love, serve, and obey him the more heartily and faithfully, than for dread and fear of pains of body; his Majesty is contented and pleased that the severity of such like extreme, dangerous and painful laws shall be abolished, annulled and made frustrate and void." (I Mar. C. 1.)

To obtain this happy result, and to prepare the way for such an application to Parliament, by Petition, as may carry with it the weight and authority of the National Opinion, we have invited our Fellow-Subjects to unite in the employment of every lawful means for procuring a repeal of these Acts.

The measure which we propose is unquestionably legal and constitutional; and it appears to us to be not only justified, but called for, by the exigency of the times. WHEN BAD MEN CONSPIRE GOOD MEN MUST ASSOCIATE.[1]

Resolved, That the following be the

FORM OF ASSOCIATION.

We whose Names are hereunto subscribed, calling to mind the virtuous and memorable exertions of our ancestors in all past ages for the public happiness and freedom of this Nation, do solemnly engage and pledge ourselves to each other and to our country, to employ every legal and constitutional effort to obtain the repeal of two statutes, the one entitled, "An Act for the more effectual preventing Seditious Meetings and Assemblies," *the other*, "An Act for the Safety and Preservation of his Majesty's Person and Government, against Treasonable and Seditious Practices and Attempts," *Statutes which we hold to be subversive of the ancient and undoubted Liberties of Englishmen, as claimed, demanded, and insisted upon at the Glorious Revolution in* 1688, *and finally declared, asserted and confirmed by the Bill of Rights.*

[1] "When bad men combine, the good must associate; else they will fall, one by one, an unpitied sacrifice in a contemptible struggle". Edmund Burke *Thoughts on the Causes of the Present Discontent* (1770) 55. Burke is thus being quoted against himself.

INDEX

INDEX

* = Coleridge's footnotes q = quoted
n = editorial footnotes tr = translated

Textual misspellings—sometimes Coleridge's, but more often eighteenth-century newspaper idiosyncrasies and errors—are indicated within parentheses and quoted, following the correct or preferred spelling; e.g. Althorp ("Althorpe").

All works appear under the author's name; anonymous works, newspapers, periodicals, etc are listed under titles.

Subentries are arranged alphabetically, sometimes in two parts, the first containing general references, the second particular places or works. For example, under London, "newspapers", "riots", etc precede British Museum, Cavendish Square, etc; under Burke, "argues in metaphors", "swinish multitude", etc precede *A Letter to a Noble Lord*, *Reflections on the French Revolution*, etc.

Birth dates of persons now living are not given.

Watchman, The

I GENERAL REFERENCES II CONTRIBUTIONS, DEPARTMENTS, EXCERPTS III TEXTUAL

I GENERAL REFERENCES

II CONTRIBUTIONS, DEPARTMENTS, EXCERPTS